"The Fairman Rogers' Four-in-Hand" by Thomas Eakins

THE ANNALS
OF
AMERICA

THE ANNALS OF AMERICA

Volume 11

1884 - 1894

Agrarianism and Urbanization

William Benton, *Publisher*

ENCYCLOPÆDIA BRITANNICA, INC.

Chicago London Toronto Geneva Sydney Tokyo Manila

The editors wish to express their gratitude for permission to reprint
material from the following sources:

Ginn and Company for Selection 42, from *The Great
Plains,* by Walter Prescott Webb.

Harvard University Press for Selection 38, from *The
Letters of Theodore Roosevelt,* ed. by Elting E. Morison,
Vol. I, Cambridge, Mass.: Harvard University Press,
Copyright 1951 by the President and Fellows of Harvard College.

Charles Scribner's Sons for Selection 36, from *Selections from the Correspondence of Theodore Roosevelt and
Henry Cabot Lodge 1884-1918,* Vol. I.

The University of Minnesota Press for Selection 75,
from *The Welsh in America: Letters from the Immigrants,* ed. by Alan Conway, Minneapolis: The University of Minnesota Press, © Copyright 1961 by the
University of Minnesota.

CODED SOURCES IN THIS VOLUME

54 Fed. 994

The Federal Reporter. Cases Argued and Determined in the Circuit Courts of Appeals and Circuit and District Courts of the United States. St. Paul, 1893. Vol. 54, pp. 994ff.

Richardson

A Compilation of the Messages and Papers of the Presidents 1789-1897. Edited by James D. Richardson. In 10 vols. Washington, 1896-1899. Vol. 8, 9 reprinted 1900.

Statutes

The Public Statutes at Large of the United States of America from the Organization of the Government in 1789, etc., etc. In 79 vols. as of August 1966. 1848 *et seq.* Vol. 24, Washington, 1887; Vol. 26, Washington, 1891.

Contents

AGRARIANISM AND URBANIZATION
In Pictures

Technology and the City 51-64

Though rural America was still dominant over the cities in terms of
sheer numbers, the cities were clearly the centers and sources of
American life. Technology and the American city have long enjoyed
a symbiotic relationship: An advancing technology gave tremendous
impetus to the continued growth and internal development of
cities; cities provided in turn the necessity, the material, the money,
and the environment for rapid technological progress.

Politics: 1884-1894 137-146

The period was marked by a growing rift between government
and popular opinion. In striking contrast to the continuing
Republican conservatism in Washington, the growing liberalism
that had spawned the farmers' organizations and the early labor
unions attempted full national status with the formation of the
Populist Party in 1892. Dogged by single-issue and sectional
factions, Populism produced few tangible results.

End of the Frontier 253-266

By 1890 there was no more frontier; with a few small exceptions
the country was permanently settled. What remained to be
done was the difficult and sometimes dangerous task of holding
and developing what had been gained. The obstacles to this
development were many, and the Indian had the misfortune to
be counted among them; he succumbed more quickly than did
the land to the white man's progress.

The heavy investment in industrialization that had followed the
Civil War began to return undreamed-of dividends. Aided by the
astounding advance of technology, industry was creating vast wealth
for the country. Under the laissez faire system inherited from
a simpler age, the wealth tended strongly to concentrate in a
relatively few, and often inexperienced, hands. Thus was created
a class of nouveau riche and a new style of life for America,
that of conspicuous consumption.

The nouveau riche of the new industrial society eagerly
appropriated the traditional trappings of wealth, among them
the patronage of the arts. Their wealth, however, often exceeded
their sensitivity; the result was an ostentatious display of
bad taste common enough to give the period the title of the
"Gilded Age." Behind the glitter, however, a rich native
tradition in art was being continued and polished and would
soon gain the recognition it deserved.

The city of Chicago epitomized in a great many ways the moods
and changes of the period. Never a cosmopolis like New York,
Chicago was nonetheless the paradigmatic American city; its central
location and its role as a transportation hub guaranteed that all
the currents of American life would find expression in this city.

Introduction

Despite the recurring scandals of the Grant administration, and despite the feeling that President Grant himself, though not personally implicated, was a weak and vacillating executive, a group of Republicans advocated his nomination for a third term in the White House in 1880 (Rutherford B. Hayes, President from 1876 to 1880, refused a second term). When James A. Garfield of Ohio was nominated, it was thought advisable to placate the pro-Grant New York delegation with the offer of second place on the ticket. Levi P. Morton declined, but the nomination was accepted by Chester A. Arthur, a New York lawyer whose political career had been marked by controversy. Garfield and Arthur were elected. The public had been unenthusiastic about Arthur from the first, and there was wide displeasure when he actively opposed the President in a contest over political patronage in New York that had been going on for some years, and in which Arthur had previously played a suspect part. Thus when Garfield was assassinated, on September 19, 1881 (see Volume 10, Selection 113), and Arthur became President, there was dismay among his foes, and apprehension among his friends.

They had not reckoned with the peculiar alchemy of the office. Arthur's first addresses were clear, judicious, and reassuring, and he soon gained the confidence of the nation and won the approval of some of his severest critics. He supported the Pendleton Law, passed in 1883, for the reform of the civil service, vetoed a bill prohibiting Chinese immigration for 20 years (in contravention of the Treaty of 1880), and kept a close watch on the federal Treasury. Despite his inauspicious beginnings, he turned out well. (See Selections 7 and 14.)

He never became really popular, however, and the Republicans discarded him in 1884 and nominated James G. Blaine. The Democrats thought they had a good chance and nominated the fiercely independent governor of New York, Grover Cleveland. The ensuing campaign was probably the bitterest in U.S. history. Cleveland was hurt by the charge that as a young bachelor in Buffalo he had fathered an illegitimate child. Thousands of Republicans marched in torchlit processions to the jingle:

> Ma! Ma! Where's my Pa?
> Gone to the White House. Ha! Ha! Ha!

But Blaine, too, was vulnerable. He was apostrophized as "James G. Blaine, Continental Liar from the State of Maine," and, when it was revealed by the so-called Mulligan Letters that in securing a land grant for a railroad line he had been given a franchise to sell its bonds at a high commission, Democrats seized on a damning phrase in one of the letters to compose their own marching verse:

Burn this letter! Burn this letter!
Burn, burn, oh, burn this letter!

Appropriately, perhaps, in such a campaign, the decisive factor was contributed by a maladroit supporter with a penchant for alliteration. Blaine came to New York a week before the election and was visited by a group of Protestant ministers. Their spokesman, the Reverend Samuel Burchard, announced to the press their opposition to the party of "Rum, Romanism, and Rebellion," a phrase the tired candidate allowed to go unchallenged. Blaine's strongest pocket of support in New York City was the Irish, who appreciated his anti-British record as secretary of state under Garfield. Enough of them objected to this description of the Democratic Party to lose for Blaine the city, the state, and therefore the election.

Most historians consider Cleveland the best U.S. President between Lincoln and Theodore Roosevelt, but this says as much about his competition as about the accomplishments of his two (separated) administrations. In fact, his four years in office between 1885 and 1889 were marked by more defeats than victories — he soon learned that almost everything he did offended somebody — and he had little to do with the most notable action of his first term. This was the passage of the Interstate Commerce Act, in 1887. People and firms that depended upon railroads for their livelihood had long complained about such practices as discriminatory rates, long and short haul differentials, rebates, and so on, and as early as 1874 a Senate Committee had proposed that the government build competing lines to force the offenders to mend their ways, but the recommendation was ignored. The states took matters into their own hands with the passage of the so-called Granger Laws; these worked well enough until the Supreme Court ruled in 1886 that they did not apply in interstate commerce. Spurred by this decision, and by extensive evidence of railroad shenanigans, a strong majority in both houses gave its support to the Interstate Commerce Act. Besides requiring the railroads to toe the mark, the bill established an Interstate Commerce Commission of five to administer the law, investigate complaints, and secure redress of abuses through the courts.

The last provision was the law's practical undoing: the courts would not cooperate. By 1900 the I.C.C. had been reduced to little more than a fact-finding agency — so much so that in 1902, an adviser could recommend to the president of the Chicago, Burlington and Quincy Railroad that it would be against his own best interest to work for the law's repeal. "The Commission," wrote Richard Olney, attorney general during Cleveland's second administration, "as its functions have now been limited by the courts, is, or can be made, of great use to the railroads. . . . The part of wisdom is not to destroy the Commission, but to utilize it." (For discussion of the background of the Interstate Commerce Act see Volume 10, Selections 66 and 67, and, in this volume, Selections 28 and 72.)

Of greater import to Cleveland personally were the pension and tariff controversies that raged throughout this decade. As for the first, it had become common practice to pass private pension bills for Civil War veterans without investigation. Cleveland provoked ill will when he began to scrutinize the bills that he was asked to sign, and soon made an enemy of the Grand Army of the Republic (the Civil War veterans' organization). The controversy came to a head in 1887, when Cleveland, moved by deep conviction, vetoed an omnibus Dependent Pensions bill, urging that the pension list be kept as a "roll of honor." The opposition of the G.A.R. helped defeat him in 1888.

As for the controversy about tariff reform, Cleveland devoted his entire 1887 congressional message to the subject. Tariffs had been raised in 1875 to the 40 percent level. This high level doubtless helped to protect infant domestic industries, but it offended the South and West, and what was perhaps worse in those frugal times before high defense and welfare budgets, it produced a large surplus. This was a serious problem, for Cleveland could not think of anything to do with the money that would not have a severe deflationary effect. The obvious solution was to decrease the surplus by lowering the tariff.

This was easier said than done. Congress failed to act in accordance with Cleveland's recommendation, and in fact went just the other way in 1890, when Benjamin Harrison occupied the presidency, by raising the tariff so high that trade fell off. This "solution" of the problem outraged the South and West so deeply that the Republicans were swept out in 1892, and Cleveland was returned to the White House.

One way to reduce the surplus, of course, was to increase pensions. And Harrison tried resolutely to undo everything that Cleveland had accomplished in this realm. He appointed James "Corporal" Tanner, a past national commander of the G.A.R., as Commissioner of Pensions, and watched complacently as the party paid its debt to the old soldier vote. "God help the surplus!" exclaimed Tanner on taking office. And Congress enacted in 1890, and Harrison signed, a Dependent Pensions bill almost identical to the one that Cleveland had vetoed. (For discussion of these matters, see Selections 17 and 34.)

Harrison's administration saw the passage of two laws that carried the hopes of those who would reform American society, but that in both cases proved to be ineffective. One was the Sherman Antitrust Act of 1890 (see Selection 63), the other the Sherman Silver Purchase Act of the same year (see Selections 70 and 102). Discussion of both, however, is better reserved to the Introduction to the next volume.

Of greater import were two events that had long and complex backgrounds in American history, as well as profound effects on the country's future. The first, strictly speaking not one event but rather a series of them, was the long-feared clash between the labor unions and the new industrial capitalists. (See, for example, in Volume 10, Selection 117.) There had been strikes before, and some of them had resulted in bloodshed; indeed, labor's desperation showed itself from the Civil War on. Since the 1860s, for example, a secret miner's organization known as the "Molly Maguires" had spread terror and death throughout the Pennsylvania coal fields (see Volume 10, Selection 74). In 1876, the so-called Tompkins Square Riot erupted in New York when police tried to break up a rally that was to be addressed by radicals; and in the ensuing years even worse riots shook Baltimore, Chicago, St. Louis, and Martinsburg, West Virginia, where in 1879 nine people died, and Pittsburgh, where in the same year twenty-six people lost their lives and there was $10 million of damage.

Worse was to come. On May 4, 1886, a cordon of police moved into Haymarket Square in Chicago to disperse a meeting of Anarchists and Communists that, until then, had been peaceful. Someone threw a bomb, and seven policemen were killed and many wounded. The so-called Haymarket Massacre sent tremors of shock through the American people. At last, it seemed, the class hatred and warfare that had long characterized European society had been transported to the New World. Among the casualties of the affair was the first national labor organization, the Knights of Labor (founded in 1869 — see Volume 10, Selection 88, and in this volume, Selection 29), which, although it had nothing to do with the meeting or with the bomb, was blamed for having helped to arouse the passions that allowed such violence. Thus disgraced, however irrationally, the Knights of Labor sank into oblivion, to be replaced two years later by the American Federation of Labor, which carefully avoided any radical taint in its formative years.

Others suffered, too. The state of Illinois moved against the Anarchists in a spirit of revenge. Eight prominent leaders were put on trial, and seven were sentenced to death and the eighth to fifteen years in prison. The charge was not that they had thrown the bomb or known anything about it, or even in every case that they had even attended the meeting, but simply that by preaching anarchism they had conspired in the crime. (See Selection 25.) A public campaign was waged to save their lives, but the state showed no mercy. Four were hanged in 1887, one committed suicide, and only in 1893 — in an act of great political courage — did Governor John Peter Altgeld pardon the three survivors still in prison, condemning their trial as a mockery of justice. (See Selections 84 and 85.)

There were other serious labor troubles of these years. The Homestead Strike of July 1892 saw Carnegie Steel Company guards (Pinkertons) hired by Henry C. Frick fight a pitched battle with the strikers who occupied the town. The militia was called out to quell the disturbance, and although the strikers' defeat helped elect Cleveland in the fall, it also retarded the unionization of steelworkers for forty years. Martial law was declared in Idaho mines on July 14, 1892, to put down a strike of miners there. And one of the most famous strikes of all occurred during May, June, and July of 1894, when Pullman Company workers led by Eugene V. Debs struck against the institution of the "company town" (see Selections 97-100). Sympathy walkouts by railroad workers occurred throughout the West and Midwest, and for a while trains did not run beyond Chicago. The company refused to negotiate, federal troops were called out to deliver the mails, and the courts forbade any interference with the trains. Debs was imprisoned for violating the latter injunction, which, however, instead of silencing him made him a national figure: starting in 1900, he ran five times for President on the Socialist ticket. (For other important pro- and anti-labor statements in this volume, see Selections 2-3, 22-24, 26-27, 32, 73-75, 83, and 86-87.)

The other great event of the period covered by this volume was perhaps more symbolic than real. The Census of 1890 reported that the settled areas of the United States were, as of that year, so widely distributed that a "frontier" no longer existed. No one paid much attention except the historian Frederick Jackson Turner, who in 1893 published a paper, called "The Significance of the Frontier in American History," in which he pointed to the passing of the frontier, discussed its characteristic effects on American character and institutions, and predicted some future results of what he conceived to be a radical change in the country's life. The essay, which is probably the most famous single work by an American historian, is reprinted in full here as Selection 88. (For other discussions of the Western frontier and of life on the Great Plains, see Volume 10, Selections 94 and 102, and, in this volume, Selections 4, 42-45, 66-69, 77, and 90.)

One other selection in the volume requires special mention. It is usually said that Tocqueville's *Democracy in America* is the best book by a foreigner about our country. If Tocqueville has any serious competition, it is from James Bryce, who made the first of his numerous visits to the United States in 1870, began his great work on the structure and workings of the American Constitution in 1883, and published it in 1888 as *The American Commonwealth*. Portions of this long book are reprinted here, as Selection 37. At any rate, Bryce's is probably the second best book about America ever written by a visitor.

The 1870s and '80s have been called "The Gilded Age," after the title of a book by Mark Twain and Charles Dudley Warner, published in 1873. The phrase was never intended as a compliment. In the view of many observers, both then and now, the gilt that covered the metal of the times was pretty thin, and even worn off in places. The age, as the poet John Donne said of another end-of-century decade in another country, may have been iron — and rusty, too.

Nevertheless, the latter part of the nineteenth century was marked by notable intellectual and artistic achievements. In painting, there were Thomas Eakins and Winslow Homer; in architecture, Henry H. Richardson, Louis Sullivan, and Frank Lloyd Wright; in sociology, Lester Frank Ward and William Graham Sumner; in philosophy and psychology, Charles Sanders Peirce and William James; in law, Oliver Wendell Holmes, Jr.; in literature, Mark Twain himself and Henry James; in history, Francis Parkman and Henry Adams. These brilliant minds shine with a peculiar and perhaps ironic luster in the general darkness of the time. (For writings by and about these figures, see, beside those already mentioned in other contexts, in Volume 10, Selections 45, 52, 78, 93, 105, and 111; and in this volume, Selections 8, 10, 33, 40, 71, 87, 91, and 103.)

Chronology:1884-1894

1884

May 17. Organic Act is passed; it applies the laws of Oregon to the "civil and judicial district" of Alaska, which has been governed in turn by the War and Treasury departments up to this time.

May 28. National Greenback-Labor Party meets and nominates Benjamin F. Butler of Massachusetts for President. Butler has also received (May 14) presidential nomination of Anti-Monopoly Party, with which the Greenback Party has joined to form the People's Party. **June 6.** Republicans at Chicago nominate James G. Blaine of Maine for President, with John A. Logan of Illinois as his running mate. Independent Republicans bolt convention, feeling Blaine is corrupt, and later back Democratic choice; group is sarcastically nicknamed "Mugwumps," Indian word meaning "chiefs." **July 11.** Democrats nominate Grover Cleveland, governor of New York, for President and Thomas A. Hendricks of Indiana for Vice-President. **July 23.** Prohibition Party nominates John P. St. John of Kansas.

Oct. 1-Nov. 1. World conference, meeting in Washington, D.C., recommends that meridian of Greenwich, England, be basis for counting mean time and longitude.

Oct. 6. Naval War College established at Newport, Rhode Island, to give naval officers postgraduate training.

Nov. 4. After campaign in which Democrats publicize Mulligan Letters, which expose Blaine's corrupt dealings as speaker of the House, and Republicans accuse Cleveland of having fathered an illegitimate child (he admits it immediately), Cleveland wins election. Blaine loses key state of New York by 1,100 votes when he fails to disavow statement of delegation of his supporters calling Democrats the party of "Rum, Romanism, and Rebellion"; silence loses him the Catholic vote. Popular vote is Cleveland, 4,880,000; Blaine, 4,850,000; Butler (partially supported by Republicans in hope he will reduce Cleveland vote), 175,000; St. John, 150,000. Electoral vote is Cleveland, 219; Blaine, 182. Although Republicans in the House gain 18 seats, it is not enough to alter Democratic control.

Dec. 6. Last part, the capstone, placed on Washington Monument in Washington, D.C. Monument is dedicated in February 1885 and opened in October 1888.

In Ku Klux Klan cases, Southern Negroes, kept from voting by the Klan, appeal to U.S. Supreme Court; Court holds that interference by private persons with a citizen's right to vote in federal elections is a federal crime, since this right does not depend only on state law but also on the Constitution and U.S. laws.

Ottmar Mergenthaler patents his mechanical typesetter, which casts and sets type for printing. Called the Linotype machine, it revolutionizes mass-circulation newspaper production.

Lewis E. Waterman produces first practical fountain pens; unsuccessful attempts have been made since the seventeenth century.

Samuel Clemens ("Mark Twain") publishes *The Adventures of Huckleberry Finn,* epic novel of Mississippi River frontier, a criticism of social ills, such as slavery and feuding, as well as an entertainment. Joel Chandler Harris writes realistically of Georgia poor whites in *Mingoy, and Other Sketches in Black and White,* and later (1887) of Negroes under Reconstruction in *Free Joe and Other Georgian Sketches.*

1884 - 1885

Nov. 15-Feb. 26. International Berlin Conference on African Affairs, called by Germany and France, meets in Berlin. U.S. attends and agrees to work for the abolition of slavery and of the still-flourishing slave trade in Africa but does not ratify final agreements, which also involves acquisition of African territory.

1884 - 1889

Improved techniques in anesthesia include injection of cocaine into nerves to anesthetize surrounding areas, use of cocaine as a spinal anesthetic, and also as a local anesthetic. In surgery, technique for examining the stomach by means of endoscope inserted through the mouth is improved; appen-

dicitis is identified as a specific infection, and first appendectomy after correct diagnosis is performed; first brain tumor operation in U.S. is performed; operations for hernia and breast removal are perfected. Emphasis on diagnosis, as well as technical excellence in surgery, begins with opening of St. Marys Hospital (later known as Mayo Clinic) in Rochester, Minnesota, by brothers William J. and Charles H. Mayo.

1884 - 1895

Edward L. Trudeau, pioneer in tuberculosis therapy, founds the Adirondack Cottage Sanatorium at Saranac Lake, New York, in 1884; in 1894 he establishes first research laboratory in the U.S. for study of tuberculosis. Early diagnosis of the disease is helped greatly by discovery of X rays by Wilhelm C. Röntgen in 1895.

1884 - 1899

Naturalist painter Winslow Homer, having settled permanently in Maine, where he remains in seclusion except for occasional painting trips, paints some of his finest oils and watercolors, such as "The Life Line," "Eight Bells," "The Gulf Stream," and "Rum Cay." His fresh style has at first been unpopular, but critics begin to appreciate him at about this time.

1885

Feb. 26. Congress passes Contract Labor Act. Immigration of laborers under contract to work for cost of passage is forbidden; exceptions are allowed for skilled, professional, and domestic workers.

April 3. Land Commissioner William A. J. Sparks suspends entries of all land titles suspected of being fraudulent; move makes available to actual settlers 2,750,000 acres of land hitherto controlled by speculators and big business. In following two years Sparks advises many reforms of land laws, but in 1887 he resigns after dispute about a land-grant railroad case, and many of his reforms are revoked.

Nov. 25. Vice-President Thomas A. Hendricks dies at Indianapolis, Indiana, after less than a year in office.

Beginning of large immigration from eastern and southern Europe, known as "New Immigration." Many immigrants in following years are Jews from Russia, escaping persecution.

Largest lead source in the world, the Bunker Hill and Sullivan mines, discovered in Kellogg, Idaho. This, and Sunshine Silver Mine, in Shoshone County, found at the same time, eventually yield $250 million in silver and lead.

William Dean Howells, novelist and critic, publishes *The Rise of Silas Lapham,* landmark in realistic, sympathetic treatment of new industrial classes. Mark Twain publishes first volume of Ulysses S. Grant's *Personal Memoirs.* Grant, almost penniless, does not live to see great success of the two-volume work, written during his final illness, but his family receives about $500,000 from its sale.

First true skyscraper completed; Chicago's Home Life Insurance Building is made possible by the new use of all-iron frame construction.

Privately endowed Leland Stanford, Jr. University established near Palo Alto, California.

1885 - 1887

Overstocking of ranges during cattle boom of previous years causes beef price crash. Drought and severe cold follow during next two years.

1885 - 1900

Most architecture of the period is derived from classic sources; Charles F. McKim, Stanford White, Cass Gilbert, and George B. Post design such buildings as the Low Memorial Library at Columbia University, New York; Boston Public Library; Minnesota State Capitol; Supreme Court Building, Washington, D.C. During same period Louis H. Sullivan and Frank Lloyd Wright turn to functional design, as in the Chicago Auditorium and Chicago Stock Exchange Building; Wright also begins development of his "prairie style" homes.

1886

Jan. 19. Presidential Succession Act of 1792 is replaced by new law providing that if both President and Vice-President are unable to serve, they will be succeeded by Cabinet officers in order of creation of their departments.

Oct. 28. President Cleveland dedicates Statue of Liberty, erected on Bedloe's (present-day Liberty) Island in New York Harbor. A gift to the U.S. from the French people, it has been under construction since 1874 in France; 151 feet high and weighing 225 tons, it has been shipped in 214 packing cases in previous year. Raising of funds in the U.S. to build the pedestal has delayed its erection, but money is finally raised by Joseph Pulitzer, owner of *New York World.*

Dec. 8. American Federation of Labor founded at Columbus, Ohio, on nonpolitical craft union principles. Twenty-five trade unions participate, but unskilled workers are not represented. Samuel Gompers is elected president and, except for year 1895, continues in office until 1924. Gompers has been instrumental in founding predecessor organization, Federation of Organized Trades and Labor Unions of U.S.A. and Canada, in 1881.

In *Wabash, St. Louis & Pacific Railroad Company* v. *Illinois,* Supreme Court invalidates a state railroad-regulating law, holding that only Congress can control interstate commerce; decision is in some aspects contrary to that in Granger cases of 1877, resulting in area where neither federal government nor states have control. In *Santa Clara County* v. *Southern Pacific Railroad,* Court establishes that the word "persons" in the Fourteenth Amendment applies not only to individuals but also to legal "persons," such as corporations.

Elihu Thomson patents electric welding machine, which is used in construction work to replace riveting, especially later in automobile industry.

Frances Hodgson Burnett's book about a model little gentleman, *Little Lord Fauntleroy,* becomes immediately popular and in next 20 years makes a generation of boys uncomfortable.

Painter and anatomy teacher Thomas Eakins, one of half dozen greatest American painters, is dismissed from Pennsylvania Academy of Fine Arts for employing undraped models in mixed life class; a master of anatomy, he earlier has painted a medical group, "The Gross Clinic," and later executes "The Agnew Clinic." He also paints portraits and sports subjects, notably "Max Schmitt in a Single Scull"; some of his portraits are so penetrating as to be offensive to their subjects.

Roman Catholic Archbishop James Gibbons of Baltimore, Maryland, becomes second U.S. Cardinal.

1886 - 1887

May 4, 1886. Bomb explodes in Haymarket Square, Chicago, after police break up anarchist meeting protesting treatment of strikers at McCormick Harvesting Machine Company on previous day; 7 policemen and 4 workmen die, and 70 policemen are wounded. **Aug. 20.** Eight agitators are convicted; 7 are sentenced to death, 1 to imprisonment. **Nov. 11, 1887.** Following commutations of sentences of 2 agitators and suicide of 1, remaining 4 are hanged. Identity of bomb thrower is never established. Public alarm at supposed radical control of labor movement, as well as failure in previous year of several strikes, is instrumental in lessening effectiveness of labor movements, especially the Knights of Labor, which expires within a few years.

1887

Jan. 20. Renewal of U.S.-Hawaii Treaty for reciprocal commerce is ratified by Congress after it is altered to include exclusive right of U.S. to build an armed naval base at Pearl Harbor, near Honolulu.

Feb. 3. Congress passes Electoral Count Act to avoid such disputes as that in 1876 election; law makes each state responsible for its electoral returns, which must be affirmed according to law of that state. Congress has no power over vote unless state cannot decide or fraud is committed.

Feb. 4. Congress passes Interstate Commerce Act. Granger laws principle of public regulation of railroads is embodied in powers of first federal regulatory agency, the Interstate Commerce Commission. Commission's rulings are rarely supported by the U.S. Supreme Court, and it is, therefore, not very effective, but passage of Act indicates public realization that changing economy requires changed methods of control.

Feb. 11. In move that antagonizes organized war veterans, President Cleveland vetoes Dependent Pension Bill, which provides pensions unrelated to war injuries. Pensions of Civil War veterans have by this time become a major drain on the U.S. Treasury in spite of policy of careful investigation of claims.

March 2. Hatch Act grants federal subsidies for agricultural experiment and education programs by states; legislation is an extension of Morrill Act of 1862.

March 5. Tenure of Office Act of 1867 is repealed. Independent presidential power to remove officials from office is restored after President Cleveland's insistence on constitutional right.

June 7. President Cleveland signs routine War Department order authorizing return to the South of captured Confederate battle flags. **June 15.** Protest from Union veterans and Republican politicians is so great that Cleveland cancels order. Flags are not finally returned for 18 years.

Dec. 6. Convinced that high protective tariffs have kept prices high and encouraged formation of trusts, President Cleveland, without consulting members of his party, concentrates his annual message on a plea for tariff reductions; Democratic high-tariff advocates are angered by move.

Physicists Albert A. Michelson and Edward W. Morley perform experiment that establishes that the velocity of the earth has no effect on the velocity of light; result is inspiration for Albert Einstein's Special Theory of Relativity.

Melvil Dewey founds State Library School in Albany, New York. He has earlier, in 1876, proposed his decimal system of library cataloging and is largely responsible for efficiency in library methods throughout the U.S.

1887 - 1888

June 25-July 26, 1887. Representatives of Britain, Germany, and the U.S. meet in Washington to discuss control of Samoa. British (having come to an agreement before meeting) support German claim to right of mandate over islands; meeting closes without decision. Germany then deports Samoan ruler and installs German-influenced government, which in following year discriminates against British and U.S. commerce. By end of 1888, tension has increased to point of all three countries' stationing warships in Samoa's Apia Harbor.

1888

Feb. 15. British and U.S. representatives in Washington work out Bayard-Chamberlain Treaty and practical arrangements to carry it out in effort to put an end to U.S.-Canadian conflict over Atlantic fisheries. **Aug. 21.** Republican Congress rejects treaty, partly because of reciprocal tariff clause, but practical arrangements remain basis for U.S.-Canadian fishing operations until 1923, when Canada rejects them.

March 12. Blizzard lasting 36 hours paralyzes New York City, 400 people die, and property damage is enormous, as transportation stoppage and cutoff of communications isolate city from the world. Messages from New York to Boston are sent by way of England.

May 16. Union Labor Party nominates Alson J. Streeter of Illinois for President. **May 17.** United Labor Party nominates Robert H. Cowdrey of Illinois for President. **May 31.** Prohibition Party nominates Clinton B. Fisk of New Jersey. **June 5.** Democrats, meeting in St. Louis, renominate President Cleveland, with Allen G. Thurman of Ohio as his running mate. **June 25.** Republicans at Chicago nominate Benjamin Harrison of Indiana for President and Levi P. Morton of New York for Vice-President. Democratic platform stresses revision of high protective tariff. Republican platform calls for continuation of tariff and high pensions for war veterans. Enormous campaign fund raised by Republicans makes possible widely publicized criticism of President Cleveland's low tariff policy, vetoes of pension bills, and consent to Confederate flag return. **Oct. 21.** Republicans publish falsified letter ostensibly from an uncertain naturalized citizen (but actually written by a Republican) asking British minister to U.S. how to vote in election and answer of minister that he should vote for Cleveland. Indignation over foreign interference in election loses many votes for Democrats.

June 13. U.S. Department of Labor is established by Congress; it is not given Cabinet rank until 1913.

Nov. 6. Benjamin Harrison carries all states except Solid South, Connecticut, and New Jersey. Popular vote is Harrison 5,447,000; Cleveland, 5,540,000; although Cleveland's popular plurality is almost 100,000, he receives only 168 electoral votes to Harrison's 233.

George Eastman perfects Kodak hand camera, making possible first amateur photography. Camera is preloaded with enough roll film for 100 two-inch diameter round photographs. When film has been exposed, camera with film is returned to factory. Prints and reloaded camera are then returned to owner.

Edward Bellamy publishes his utopian *Looking Backward, 2000-1887,* describing a society that provides for social and economic human needs. It eventually sells 1 million

copies. Bellamy's later advocacy of nationalization of public services, especially in his magazine, the *Nationalist,* helps form platform of Populist Party in 1892 James Bryce, for six years British ambassador to the U.S., publishes *The American Commonwealth,* dealing with the structure and functions of the Constitution; the work, whose author is a friend and admirer of the U.S., is read throughout the country.

Composer Edward A. MacDowell settles in Boston after study and teaching in Europe; among compositions written there by first serious composer to be nationally recognized are *Woodland Sketches, Sonata Tragica,* and First and Second *(Indian)* Suites. After MacDowell's death in 1908, his widow establishes (1910) the MacDowell Colony for composers, writers, and artists at farm in Peterborough, New Hampshire.

By this year, trusts have grown so numerous that many important and minor U.S. industries are organized as combinations; among them are reaping, mowing, and threshing machines, plows, petroleum, copper, steel rails, steel and iron beams, wrought iron pipe, stoves, rubber, coal, beef, sugar, whiskey, glass, and even castor oil.

1889

March 2. Kansas passes first antitrust law, followed by North Carolina, Tennessee, and Michigan in the same year and 11 other Western and Southern states in following two years. But since state laws are unable to deal with interstate monopolies, demand develops for federal antitrust legislation. New Jersey establishes itself as home of giant corporations by authorizing incorporation of holding companies within the state.

March 16. Poised warships of Britain,

Germany, and the U.S. in Apia Harbor, Samoa, are wrecked by hurricane, thus averting naval battle. President Harrison in the meantime, on March 14, has sent three representatives to Berlin conference on Samoa. **June 14.** Samoan treaty (Treaty of Berlin), signed by three nations, provides for Samoan independence under protectorate of all three nations.

May 31. Dam above Johnstown, Pennsylvania, breaks when Conemaugh River is swelled by heavy rains; four towns are destroyed before river drowns Johnstown in 30 feet of water; about 2,300 people are killed.

June. Andrew Carnegie sets forth his theory of philanthropy in "The Gospel of Wealth" (originally titled "Wealth"), article that defends capitalism but urges businessmen to adjust its inequalities by donating their wealth to deserving causes.

Sept. 9. Producer Charles Frohman opens Bronson Howard's most popular play, *Shenandoah,* in New York City; theme is conflict between loyalty to the U.S. and the Confederacy caused by the Civil War.

Nov. 2. Dakota Territory is divided into states of North and South Dakota. President Harrison shuffles proclamations before signing to avoid conflict about order; thus, either is thirty-ninth or fortieth state. Two widely separated centers of population have led to division. Population of North Dakota is about 180,000, most settlers having arrived in last 20 years. South Dakota's population is about 350,000, having increased greatly since discovery of gold in Black Hills in 1874.

Nov. 8. Montana becomes forty-first state of the Union. It has previously been part of Oregon country, then part of Idaho Territory, and later Territory of Montana. First population boom in 1860s has been result

of gold discovery; 1889 population is about 143,000.

Nov. 11. Washington becomes forty-second state. Until 1863 Washington Territory has included Idaho. Puget Sound area has developed earliest, but gold discoveries and railroads have brought settlers to interior. In 1878 Congress has refused statehood request because of small population, but by 1889 population has reached 357,000.

Nov. 14. Nellie Bly, reporter for *New York World,* starts on round-the-world trip. Attempt to better record of Jules Verne's fictional journey *Around the World in Eighty Days* is successful when she reaches home in 72 days, 6 hours, 11 minutes, and 14 seconds.

Dec. 6. Jefferson Davis, former President of the Confederate States of America, dies in New Orleans at age 81.

Mark Twain publishes his satire on literary treatment of the Age of Chivalry, *A Connecticut Yankee in King Arthur's Court.* Theodore Roosevelt publishes two volumes of his *The Winning of the West,* a history of early settlements west of the Alleghenies; final work is four volumes.

First classes begin at Barnard College for women, founded as part of New York City's Columbia University.

First safety bicycles are produced in quantity; result is greatly increased popularity of bicycling and severe traffic problems. Bicycle having two equal-sized wheels, with saddle between them, quickly replaces those with one large and one very small wheel. By 1893 more than a million bicycles are in use in the U.S.

1889 - 1890

Oct. 2-April 19. First International Conference of American States meets at Washington, D.C., with U.S. and 17 Latin-American countries (all except the Dominican Republic) attending. The U.S., which has called Conference, attempts to establish customs union, but other countries are unwilling. By adjournment on April 19, Conference has set up inter-American organization that is later called Pan American Union and has established basis for reciprocal tariffs as authorized by McKinley Tariff Act of following year.

1889 - 1893

April 22, 1889. Having yielded to pressure of boomers (homesteaders) to buy Indian lands and open Oklahoma (Indian Territory) to white settlement, U.S. declares land open. Wild rush into area starts at pistol shot, and within 24 hours claims covering about 2 million acres have been staked by 50,000 settlers; in one day Guthrie is organized with nearly 15,000 inhabitants and Oklahoma City with 10,000. **May 2, 1890.** Congress forms Oklahoma Territory of lands not allotted to Indians. **1891 and 1892.** U.S. buys 4 million more acres of Indian land and opens them to settlement. **Sept. 16, 1893.** Second large rush to 6-million-acre Cherokee Outlet results in settlement of 100,000 people.

1890

June 27. Dependent Pension Act provides liberal pensions for needy or disabled Union Civil War veterans, whether war injured or not, and their families; within a few years number of pensioners has increased by one-third, and amount paid has jumped from about $90 million to $150 million.

July 2. Growing demand for federal control of monopolies results in passage of Sherman Antitrust Act, which empowers government and federal courts to prevent restraint of interstate and foreign commerce. Wording of Act fails to make clear what is considered a trust as well as what is considered restraint of trade, and whether railroads and labor unions are included in combinations. Thus, Act is ineffective and weakly enforced, and monopolies and combinations continue to grow.

July 3. Idaho becomes forty-third state of the Union, with a population of 88,500, largely gold seekers. Admission to Union follows long controversy over plan to divide Idaho Territory between Washington and Nevada, which has been rejected by Congress.

July 10. Wyoming is admitted to Union as forty-fourth state. Territory has been organized in 1869 to protect and govern settlements along railroads. Bunchgrass and buffalo grass of plains have attracted cattlemen, but winter of 1886-1887 has been so severe that one-sixth of cattle have died.

July 14. Congress passes Sherman Silver Purchase Act, a compromise between Western agrarian and silver states and pro-tariff interests of the East. U.S. Treasury is required to purchase monthly an amount of silver about equal to U.S. silver production (4,500,000 ounces), paying for it with notes redeemable in gold or silver. Measure tends to reduce U.S. gold reserve and weaken confidence in U.S. currency; it is repealed in 1893.

Oct. 1. McKinley Tariff raises duties to new highs, averaging about 50 percent, largely for protection of industry rather than revenue. Executive agreements for reciprocal raising of tariffs to equal duties of other countries are authorized for first time.

Oct. 1. Congress creates Weather Bureau as part of Department of Agriculture.

Nov. 1. Mississippi becomes first state to

restrict Negro civil rights by writing "understanding" clause into new constitution; clause requires voters to be able to read and understand state constitution.

Nov. 4. Democratic victories in congressional elections of 39 states result in shift to Democratic control of House of Representatives; reaction against McKinley Tariff is largely responsible.

Dec. 15. Sioux Chief Sitting Bull is killed by soldiers in South Dakota during U.S. Army effort to curb religious Ghost Dance, a rite dedicated to restoration of Indian lands taken by whites that is thought to be dangerous to white population of area. **Dec. 29.** Two hundred Sioux are massacred by cavalry at Battle of Wounded Knee Creek. Ghost Dance war ends in following month when sympathetic Indian agency government is set up.

1890 census shows population of 62,948,000; immigration since last census has been 5,247,000, largely from northern and western Europe, although substantial numbers have come from southern and eastern Europe during period. Settled areas are so widely distributed that census reports frontier no longer exists. Illiteracy is estimated at about 13 percent of population, about 4 percent less than in 1880.

How the Other Half Lives by Jacob A. Riis shocks many into awareness of city slum conditions and results in beginning of reforms. At this time, fortunes of about 1 percent of U.S. population total more than possessions of remaining 99 percent.

William Dean Howells publishes his novel *A Hazard of New Fortunes,* with background of New York City streetcar strike. William James publishes his *The Principles of Psychology,* the first important American treatment of experimental psychology.

Poems by Emily Dickinson, 114 selections from hundreds of poems, is issued reluctantly by publisher who fears that her original style will not be acceptable to the public; he, therefore, alters many poems. Writings have been found by her sister after her death four yours earlier. Though critics are hostile, public enthusiasm leads eventually to publication of all poems found.

Anna Sewell's *Black Beauty,* published years earlier in England, is first published in the U.S. by American Humane Education Society. Five Rudyard Kipling books are published in widely sold cheap editions made possible by pirating books just before International Copyright Agreement; among them are *Soldiers Three* and *Mine Own People.*

U.S. Post Office Department prohibits mailing of *The Kreutzer Sonata* by Leo Tolstoi; New York Governor Theodore Roosevelt calls Tolstoi a "sexual and moral pervert."

1891

March 3. Congress establishes Circuit Courts of Appeals to ease burden of U.S. Supreme Court.

March 3. Congress repeals Timber Culture Act of 1873 and passes Forest Reserve Act, by which the President is permitted to close public forest land to settlement for establishment of national parks. In following two years 13 million acres are closed.

March 4. International Copyright Act is passed; Act protects works of British, French, Belgian, and Swiss authors in U.S. Extensive pirating of foreign books by American publishers has resulted in loss of sales to U.S. authors and loss of royalties to foreign authors. Copyright protection is eventually extended to almost all nations.

May 5. Carnegie Hall, endowed and built by Andrew Carnegie, opens in New York City.

July 31. Thomas A. Edison patents his kinetoscopic camera, which takes moving pictures on a strip of film; film, called a peep show, is seen by one person at a time when he looks into a lighted box and turns a crank. Later, pictures are projected onto a screen.

Nov. 9. Charles H. Hoyt's play *A Trip to Chinatown*, a farce about San Francisco, closes after 650 performances, longest consecutive run to this date.

Three federal prisons are authorized by Congress; they are to be built at McNeil's Island, off coast of Washington; Leavenworth, Kansas; and Atlanta, Georgia; they are first nonmilitary federal prisons.

George E. Hale, founder of Kenwood Observatory in Chicago, takes first successful sun photograph with spectroheliograph of his own invention. He later establishes Mount Wilson (California) Observatory as part of the Carnegie Institution of Washington (D.C.).

Hamlin Garland, advocate of literary realism, publishes his collection of stories of the hardships of farm life, *Main-Travelled Roads*.

Whitcomb L. Judson takes out patent on a slide fastener (zipper).

Endowed by John D. Rockefeller, University of Chicago is established, first classes begin in following year. Throop Polytechnic Institute is founded in Pasadena, California; classes begin in same year; name is changed in 1920 to California Institute of Technology. First correspondence school (now called International Correspondence School, Scranton, Pennsylvania) is opened; purpose is to teach miners working methods that will add to safety of coal mines.

James A. Naismith, of Springfield, Massachusetts, invents basketball as an indoor substitute for baseball and football in YMCA Training College.

Sculptor Augustus Saint-Gaudens unveils Washington, D.C. memorial, commonly known as "Grief," a memorial to Mrs. Henry Adams; memorial to Colonel Robert Shaw in Boston, Massachusetts, is also by this artist. Other important sculptors of the period are Daniel Chester French, whose "Lincoln" for the Lincoln Memorial in Washington is not dedicated until 1922, and George Grey Barnard, whose work includes "The Struggle of the Two Natures in Man" and "The Prodigal Son."

1891 - 1892

March 14, 1891. Mob storms New Orleans jail and lynches 11 Italian immigrants, 3 of whom are Italian nationals, after freeing of Sicilians who have been accused and acquitted of murder of New Orleans sheriff. **March 31.** After Secretary of State Blaine refuses to take action on ground that crime is a state matter, Italy recalls its minister to the U.S., and the U.S. recalls its Italian minister. **April 12, 1892.** U.S. offers Italy $25,000 indemnity, and matter is settled when Italy accepts.

Oct. 16. Mob in Valparaiso, Chile, attacks U.S. sailors on shore leave, killing 2 and injuring 17, after U.S. Navy has seized Chilean ship transporting arms from San Diego, California, for rebels in Chilean civil war. Chile's assertion that no reparations or apology are due results in request for declaration of war by President Harrison in January 1892. Chile finally apologizes and pays $75,000 to injured sailors and relatives of dead.

1892

Jan. 11. The U.S. approves international agreement against African slave trade.

Feb. 22. Preliminary convention of the Populist Party is held at St. Louis, Missouri; Western and Southern farm organizations, labor, Granger, and Greenbackers have, since 1889, worked to form a third party believed necessary to end agricultural depression.

Feb. 29. England and the U.S. agree to international arbitration of disputes over ocean seal hunting in the Bering Sea. U.S. has leased sealing rights to a private company within the three-mile limit, and Canadians have hunted seals in waters beyond the limit. The U.S. has seized some Canadian vessels and called hunting in the area "piracy." In following year, international tribunal, with representatives of France, Italy, and Sweden, decides against the U.S., prohibits sealing for part of the year as a conservation measure, and eventually fixes an indemnity of $473,000, which the U.S. pays to Britain five years later.

May 5. Geary Chinese Exclusion Act extends exclusion for 10 years; it requires Chinese laborers to register and provides for deportation of those not specifically allowed to stay in the U.S.

June 10. Republican convention at Minneapolis, Minnesota, renominates President Benjamin Harrison, with Whitelaw Reid of New York as his running mate; platform supports McKinley high protective tariff and is ambiguous on currency. **June 21.** Democrats at Chicago nominate former President Grover Cleveland, with Adlai E. Stevenson of Illinois for Vice-President; platform stresses tariff for revenue only and attacks Silver Purchase Act of 1890. **June 29.** Prohibition Party meets at Cincinnati

and nominates John Bidwell of California. **July 2.** Populist convention opens in Omaha, Nebraska, but few Southerners are represented because of fear of Negro control. Convention nominates General James B. Weaver, former Greenbacker of Iowa, for President and James G. Field of Virginia for Vice-President. Platform: free coinage of silver in ratio of 16 to 1 to gold; government ownership of railroads, telephone, and telegraph; graduated income tax; restrictions on immigration; eight-hour day; popular election of U.S. senators; and secret ballot. **Aug. 28.** Socialist Labor Party nominates Simon Wing of Massachusetts.

July 6. Strikers at Carnegie steel mill in Homestead, Pennsylvania, protesting wage cuts and demanding recognition of their union, fire on Pinkerton detectives hired by management to break strike; 10 are killed and many wounded in pitched battle. **July 9.** Governor of Pennsylvania sends state troops to restore and keep order; they remain at mill for three months until strike is declared over, and most workers return as nonunion men. Strike damages steel unions to such an extent that there is no important union for 40 years.

July 14. Federal troops are sent to Coeur d'Alene, Idaho, silver mines and martial law is declared when strikers clash with strikebreakers. Strikes also occur in Wyoming and Tennessee; Tennessee strike is in protest against use of convict labor. President Harrison resorts to use of federal troops to enforce court injunctions in several cases.

Oct. 15. President Harrison proclaims 1,800,000-acre Crow Indian reservation in Montana open to settlement.

Nov. 8. Grover Cleveland, who has firmly supported the gold standard and avoided taking a strong stand on the tariff, wins election by popular vote of 5,555,000 to

Harrison's 5,183,000; Weaver receives 1,030,000 votes. Electoral vote is Cleveland, 277; Harrison, 145; and Weaver, 22. Public opposition to McKinley Tariff and alarm over year's labor disputes have contributed to Republican defeat. Democrats gain control of both Senate and House.

Dec. 27. Cathedral of St. John the Divine is begun in New York City; planned as largest church in the U.S., it is built on three-block site in Romanesque and, later, Gothic style; to present day, it is not completed.

The Adventures of Sherlock Holmes by Sir Arthur Conan Doyle is first Sherlock Holmes publication to be widely read in America. Eventually, books, theater, radio, movies, and television build popularity until detective becomes perhaps most popular fictional character in present-day U.S.

1892 - 1893

Sept. 1892. Tool and bicycle makers Frank and Charles Duryea of Massachusetts make first gasoline automobile in U.S., testing it indoors for fear of ridicule; motor is not powerful enough to make it successful, but they build one with more power in the following year. William Morrison of Iowa builds first successful electric automobile also in 1892. Curious crowds hamper its movement in Chicago streets so much that police have to clear the way. **1893.** Henry Ford road tests his first successful automobile.

Oct. 20, 1892. World's Columbian Exposition is dedicated at Chicago to celebrate anniversary of discovery of America. Vice-President Levi Morton delivers address, and John Philip Sousa's band provides music. Opening officially in May 1893, and running until November, fair and exposition cover 686 acres, cost about $28 million, and

are visited by 21 million persons. Orderly grouping of buildings, lakes, and gardens, planned under leadership of Daniel Burnham, Richard Morris Hunt, and others, stimulates city planning movement throughout U.S. Classical style of most buildings ignores current original American trends, revives taste for Roman style, and hastens decline of taste for Gothic and Romanesque.

1892 - 1894

"Daisy Bell" ("A Bicycle Built for Two"), published in 1892, and "The Sidewalks of New York," published in 1894, are immediately popular and to present day are on list of all-time song hits.

1893

Jan. 4. President Harrison offers amnesty to all violators of federal antipolygamy laws, passed in 1862 and 1882, on condition that laws be observed from this time onward; laws have been aimed at Mormon multiple marriage practice. In 1890 Mormon Church has withdrawn its sanction of polygamy, but some elders who have acquired several wives before that time have had problem of what to do with them.

March 1. Congress passes Diplomatic Appropriations Act, creating post of ambassador to countries that send ambassadors to the U.S. Hitherto, highest rank has been minister. **April 3.** Thomas F. Bayard is appointed U.S. ambassador to Great Britain, first American in that office to hold that rank.

April 21. Financial Panic of 1893 begins when U.S. gold reserve falls below $100 million mark, considered safe minimum. U.S. Treasury has been drained of gold by sales of securities by foreign investors; in addition, revenues have decreased because of McKinley Tariff, and increased veterans'

The Westward Expansion

Soon after the Revolutionary War Americans began to assure themselves that it was their destiny to occupy all the territory west to the Pacific Ocean between Canada and Mexico. The immense land cession of the Louisiana Purchase in 1803 fortified this belief, and the Mexican War cessions in 1848 confirmed it. But westward expansion was compounded of other factors besides the mere addition of territory. Also involved were land speculation, the Indian barrier, the search for new resources and more farmland, government land policies, and the ever present quest for the opportunity to make a better life than had been found in the East.

The land west of the Alleghenies became part of the national domain by land cession from the original thirteen states after 1780. These states retained only some specified areas for "military reserves" to satisfy promises made to the militia who fought in the Revolution (Map 3). In the 1780s the national government began formulating the policies by which the western lands would be settled, governed, and eventually broken up into new states.

The westward expansion was not strictly a contiguous movement, as Map 5 shows. The large area beyond the Mississippi Valley, consisting of the Great Plains and mountainous regions, was at first bypassed in favor of the West Coast. The great attractions in the Far West were, of course, silver and gold, while the "Great American Desert" was looked upon as inhospitable country where a good living could not be made. It was not until the decades after the Civil War that agriculture and permanent settlements came to the arid lands beyond the Mississippi Valley farm belt.

Maps prepared by Uni-Map Inc., Palatine, Ill.
for Encyclopaedia Britannica, Inc.

WESTERN LANDS
1780-1805

CANADA
Buffalo
N.Y.
LAKE MICHIGAN
Ft. Detroit
LAKE ERIE
Erie
Ft. Miami
Cleveland
PENN.
Ft. Dearborn
OHIO
1803
Pennsylvania
Donation Lands,
1783
Pittsburgh
Ft. Wayne
U.S. Military
District,
1787 & 1796
Wheeling
Ft. Defiance
Zanesville
Maryland
Mil. Res.
1781
INDIANA TERR.
1803-1805
Virginia
Military
Reserve,
1784
Chillicothe
Cincinnati
Marietta
St. Louis
Vincennes
VIRGINIA
Louisville
Staunton
Kaskaskia
Frankfort
Lexington
KENTUCKY
1792
Virginia Military Reserve, 1781
North Carolina
Military Reserve,
1783
Nashville
North Carolina
Mil. Res.
1780
NORTH
CAROLINA
Raleigh
Knoxville
Fayetteville
TENNESSEE
1796
Chattanooga
South Carolina
Military Reserve,
1778
SOUTH
CAROLINA
Ft. San
Fernando
Columbia
Georgia
Mil. Res.
1784
Augusta
MISSISSIPPI TERR.
1804-1812
Charleston
GEORGIA
Savannah
Washington
Natchez
ATLANTIC OCEAN
Mobile
Pensacola
St. Marks
New Orleans
FLORIDA
(Spanish)
St. Augustine
GULF OF MEXICO

LOUISIANA TERRITORY
(Under Government of Indiana Territory)
1804-1805

APPALACHIAN MTS.

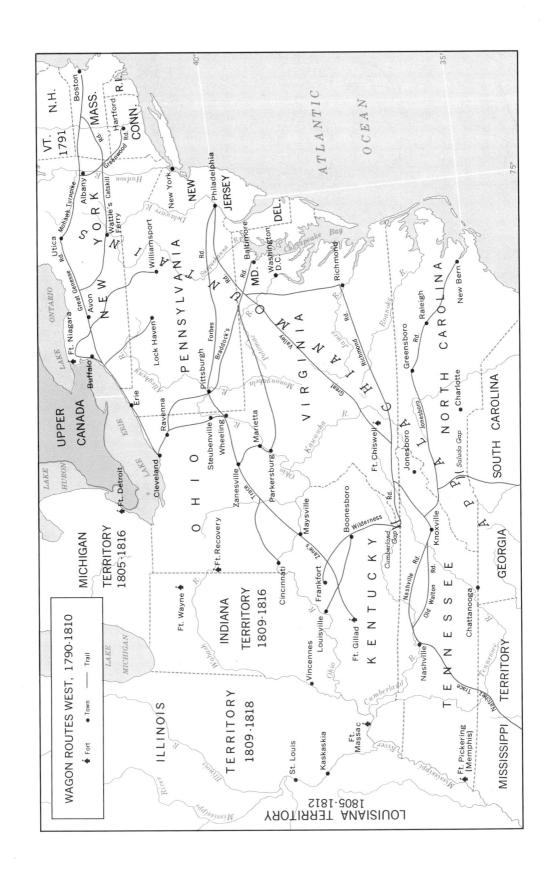

WAGON ROUTES WEST, 1790-1810

† Fort   • Town   — Trail

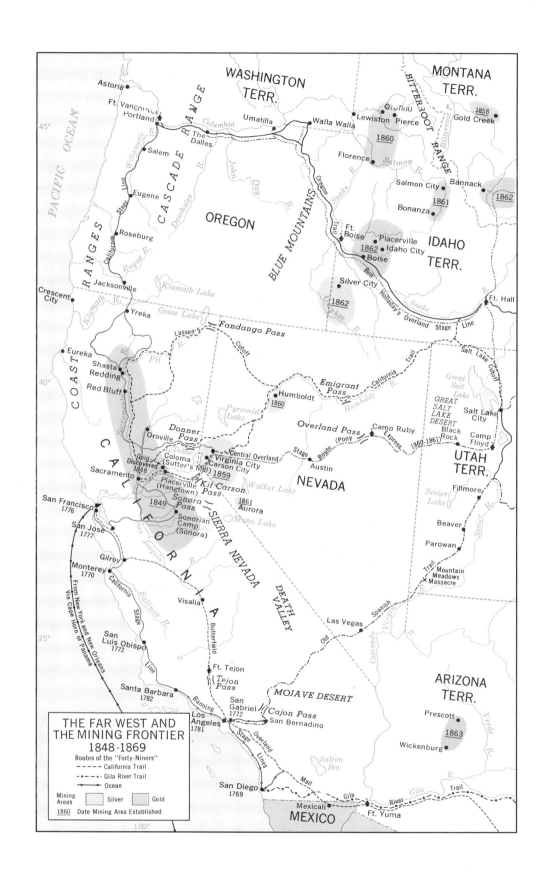

THE FAR WEST AND
THE MINING FRONTIER
1848-1869

Routes of the "Forty-Niners"
- - - - California Trail
-·-·- Gila River Trail
●——● Ocean

Mining
Areas   [Silver] [Gold]
1860   Date Mining Area Established

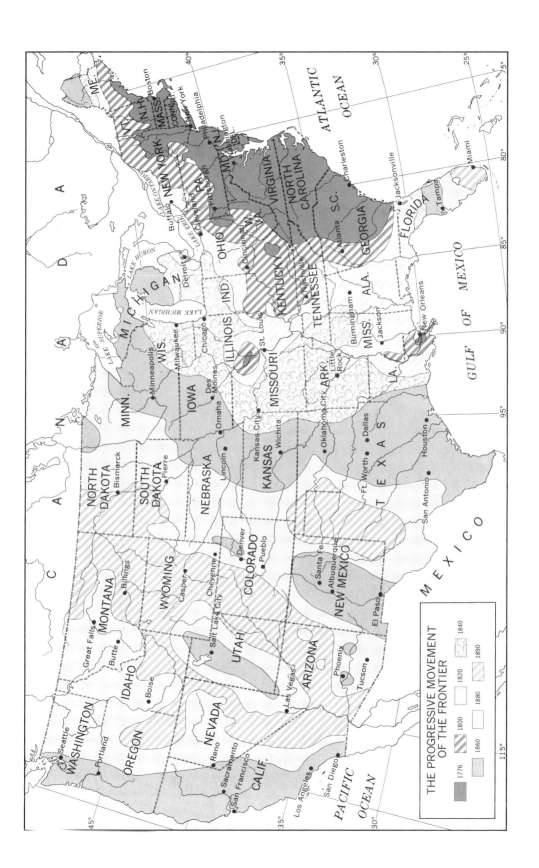

THE PROGRESSIVE MOVEMENT
OF THE FRONTIER

1776	1840
1800	1890
1860	1880

1884

1.

Laurence Gronlund: Collective Control of the Instruments of Production

Before the Civil War, reform movements with a socialist orientation had been semi-utopian in outlook, hoping by their communal experiments to create ideal conditions for the development of a new order. After the war, the older theories of social reform no longer seemed adequate to the new industrial society, which was marked by problems of monopoly, labor strife, and prevailing social discontent. Social and economic thinkers such as Karl Marx wrote of the total transformation of society. Laurence Gronlund was an avowed Marxist who adapted Marx's ideas to American society. His Coöperative Commonwealth *predicted the inevitable triumph of socialism in highly industrial societies, but the triumph, for Gronlund, was to come about without Marx's class struggle. The fifth chapter of Gronlund's book, from which the following selection is taken, described the new commonwealth.*

Source: *The Coöperative Commonwealth,* Boston, 1884, pp. 100-131.

EXTEND IN YOUR MIND division of labor and all the other factors that increase the productivity of labor; apply them to *all* human pursuits as far as can be; imagine manufactures, transportation, and commerce conducted on the grandest possible scale, and in the most effective manner; then add to division of labor its *complement:* CONCERT; introduce *adjustment* everywhere where now there is anarchy; add that *central regulative system* which Spencer says distinguishes all highly organized structures, and which supplies "each organ with blood in proportion to the work it does" and — behold the COOPERATIVE COMMONWEALTH!

The Cooperative Commonwealth, then, is that future social order — the natural heir of the present one — in which all important instruments of production have been taken under collective control; in which the citizens are consciously public functionaries; and in which their labors are rewarded according to results.

A definition is an argument. It shows that our critics, when they style Socialism a Utopia, do not know about what they are talking. We can imagine a caterpillar, more knowing than its fellows, predicting to another that some day they both will be butterflies, and the other sneeringly replying: "What utopian nonsense you are talking there!" Our censors are just as ignorant of the groundwork of Socialism. For our definition makes it evident that the Cooperative

Commonwealth is not to be regarded as a product of personal conceit but as *an historical product,* as a product in which our whole people are unconscious partakers. When the times are ripe for social cooperation, it will be just as expedient as feudalism was or as private enterprise was, when each, respectively, made its appearance. It will prove its right to control by virtue of its own superior fitness.

Or is there anything utopian in predicting that division of labor will go on increasing? Has not wholesale production already vindicated its right to be the ruling system, and is it utopian to assert that private ownership of capital, so far from being necessary to production in wholesale, will prove a greater and greater obstruction to its inevitable development? Is it utopian to expect that all enterprises will become more and more centralized, until in the fullness of time they all end in *one* monopoly, that of society? Are not, indeed, *anti*monopolists — as far as they believe that they can crush the big establishments or even prevent their growth — the real Utopists?

But that is by no means all. We have not yet sufficiently emphasized the *central* fact of society of *today.* Not alone is the necessity which we claim will drive the nations into Socialism steadily growing, *but all civilized societies are being driven into Socialism under our very eyes* — if we may apply the word "driven" to an inward impulse. Not alone are the conditions for the establishment of the New Order fast ripening but the New Order is among us and asserting itself vigorously. Not only is the social organism growing from the circumference by society multiplying and subdividing its activities and again concentrating them but the central regulative system *has* silently put in an appearance and *is* irresistibly organizing one social activity after another.

This is a *fact,* of *transcendent significance;* and yet our politicians, the gentlemen of our "editorial staffs," our would-be-wise leaders and statesmen, all, indeed, except

Socialists, seem not to have the smallest inkling of it.. They all look upon the factory legislation across the ocean and here and the agitation for nationalization of the land and national control of the telegraphs as isolated, rash expedients; and those who have adopted the accepted theories forthwith condemn this legislation and agitation and loudly proclaim that society — is going astray!

But the fact is that our modern civilization mainly consists in this that the state — that is, society in its organized form — has of late been constantly expanding its jurisdiction and has more and more contracted the sphere of individual ownership and control. Why, nearly everything the state now manages for us was once entrusted to private individuals. . . .

This fact of "the centralization of power in the national government," as it is called, is the central fact of society everywhere *now.* You may deny everything else, but you cannot deny that. You cannot look at a Democratic paper without seeing a lament over the fact. The Democrats, though, are giving undue credit to the Republicans in charging it to their account, for they were but humble instruments in the hands of the laws of the universe; if the Democrats should come into power, they would have to be "centralizers" to the same extent. The social organism has once for all got the impetus in that direction, and the movement is gathering greater momentum. That is why it is now everywhere in the air. That is why this fact is *the true rationale of Socialism.*

The cry: "Beware, it is *socialistic!*" will have absolutely no effect. The state will go on expanding its jurisdiction, hurry on to its destiny, without asking or caring if it is "Socialistic." The workingmen and grangers will continue to importune the state to come to their relief, without knowing anything about Socialism. Henry George has written a book that has enticed very many persons very far out on the road to Socialism, protesting all the time that he is not a

Socialist. Frederic Harrison abominates Socialism, and yet preaches "Look to the state! From *that* you can expect the highest experience and skill, publicity, concentration of power, real and efficient control, a national aim and spirit and far more true responsibility."

But it is evident that the process of placing all industries and all instruments of labor under collective control will be carried on with far more energy and directness when once the true leaders learn that the state is not some power outside of the people, but that it is the social organism itself and that, as an organism, it is destined to grow until it embraces all social activities. Hitherto the state has acted from impulse, in opposition to accepted theories. But a logical foundation of some sort is necessary to all great movements. Rousseau's theory of a "Social Contract," though false, did in that way a great service to humanity. . . .

If now social cooperation is that to which we are certainly drifting, it is undeniably the wiser course, instead of calling it names, to inquire if not that which is "socialistic" may also be good, and to try to find out the character of that New Regime. We shall therefore here suggest the most notable respects in which its *economic* features are likely to promote the social welfare.

It must be evident to every fair-minded man that this New Order — where every worker will be remunerated according to *results* — is in no sense *communistic*. Socialism and Communism are, in fact, two radically different systems; and yet they are constantly confounded, even by well-informed people. We wish we could in a serious work like this entirely ignore the vulgar conception of Communism: that it proposes "to divide all property into equal parts," but when a man like Professor Fawcett of England gives currency to this vulgarism in these very words and then proceeds to lecture us, saying: "If the state divided all lands among the inhabitants, there

would gradually arise the same inequality of wealth which exists now," we must notice it sufficiently to say that nowadays no one outside of a lunatic asylum proposes any such thing, and that Professor Fawcett ought to know it.

The Communism we refer to is that practised by the Shakers and similar bodies, bound together by some form of religious belief or unbelief. Their peculiar method of giving practical effect to their doctrines is different from ours; we believe that to retire from the world, as they do, is a poor way of reforming the world; we believe it is with reformers as with yeast — it must be mixed with the dough to act upon it; if kept to itself, it spoils. But their *principles* — in which they agree with political Communists — are diametrically opposed to ours. Communists make *all* property common property, while our Commonwealth will place only the *instruments of production* — land, machinery, raw materials, etc. — under collective control. They require everyone to do his share of labor and allow him to consume as he needs. Our Commonwealth leaves everybody at perfect liberty to work as much or as little as he pleases, or not at all, but makes his consumption exactly commensurate with his performances. Adam Smith observed that "the produce of labor is the natural recompense of labor" and St. Paul laid it down: "whoever does not work, neither shall he eat" and the New System — as our definition points out — will put these doctrines into practice.

In short, the motto of Socialism is: "Everybody according to his *deeds*"; that of Communism is: "Everybody according to his *needs.*" The Communist motto is undoubtedly a very generous one, more generous than ours; but our motto is more just, taking human nature as it is; and the fact that Socialists take human nature as it is, is just their merit. Indeed, if we define capitalism as the fleecing of the weak by the strong, Communism might be said to be a fleecing of the strong by the weak, an observation already made by Proudhon; though the "strong" under our system simply means those buoyed up to the top, while under the latter system they would mean the truly, physically or intellectually, strong.

Communism must therefore plead guilty to the charges: first, that it means to abolish the institution of property and, next, that it must result in crushing out all individuality. Socialism not only will do neither of these things but the *very reverse*. Instead of taking property away from everybody, *it will enable everybody to acquire property*. It will truly sanctify the institution of individual ownership by placing property on an unimpeachable basis — that of being *the result of one's individual exertions*. Thereby it will afford the very mightiest stimulus for individuality to unfold itself. Property will belong to its possessor by the strongest of all titles, to be enjoyed as he thinks proper, *but not to be used as an instrument of fleecing his fellow citizens*.

Next let us pass in review one of the chief industries after another and note the most obvious advantages that will flow from social cooperation. But especially here will our motto apply: that "our purpose is not to make people read but to make them think." For the experience of our readers will naturally supply them with innumerable other cases in point. . . .

The advantages of the Commonwealth being *the sole merchant* are evident: they will be all that our grangers and voluntary cooperationists are in the habit of expecting from their schemes. . . . Under our Commonwealth the small shopkeepers, peddlers, commission merchants, and all of that sort will disappear. No more need for bribing newspapers for puffs; no longer any temptation to use lying labels or sell adulterated goods. A bale of cotton will not as now have to be sold ten times over to get from the producer into the hands of the consumer; nor will the people of Philadelphia be

bled to the extent of $6.50 for a ton of coal which only costs, all expenses and outlays included, $1.50 at the mouth of the mine. Nevermore shall we find twenty drugstores in a little town that only needs one.

No, indeed! In place of that we shall have great permanent bazaars, embracing all possible articles of consumption, of which stores like that of Jordan Marsh & Co., in Boston, or, still better, the one . . . in Philadelphia, are only insignificant miniature models — but thanks to their chiefs for furnishing us those models!

The salesmen and saleswomen in those bazaars will be quite different beings from those of the present day, who are very often slaves from morning till late at night. They will, like all other citizens, be independent human beings, with plenty of leisure at their command.

The greatest gain to society, however, in taking control of commerce will perhaps be found in the suppression of that talent, so peculiar to our plutocrats and seemingly acquired by them with their mother's milk — the faculty of speculation, a talent which contributes nothing to production, but whose only end and aim is the transfer of wealth from one pocket into another. Nearly all workers are devoid of that talent. The New Regime will, like the Man of the New Testament, lash the howling lunatics, the brokers and cornerers, out of our stock and other exchanges, which will be devoted to nobler uses; for cooperation and speculation are strangers.

"Trade" — as far as it means the buying and selling of goods for the sake of *profit* — will at home be changed into distribution of the produce of labor among the workers, and as to foreign countries into genuine *commerce, i.e.,* the exchange of such home products we do not need for such foreign products we may need.

These changes in manufactures and commerce will naturally affect transportation in a remarkable degree. While now our mails, railroads, ships, and wagons do business for innumerable private concerns; in the New Commonwealth they will do business for *one*, only. What a colossal concentration and simplification of transportation does that, in itself, imply! Bear in mind simply the mass of drays and wagons of every sort which now in every one of our populous cities choke up our streets and distract most people's nerves! Think of the amount of human and animal labor now absolutely wasted in this way! It might, indeed, be difficult for those now living to recognize the aspect of our cities to be brought about by this simplification, alone, under the new order of things. Even New York may thereby become a clean city.

Transportation itself, of course, will be taken under collective control, and thus the radical wrong undone of granting public concessions to individuals for the express purpose of making our highways subservient to private interests. For what are now our railway corporations but a clique of persons empowered by law to use these highways, in the *first place,* for their *own benefit,* and only incidentally for the public convenience?

It is just as easy to demonstrate the vast superiority of *social-cooperative farming* over the present style.

The prevailing isolated mode of agriculture wastes an immense amount of human and animal labor, of time and of materials. What an economy would there not be in having one large stable, one large yard, one large barn in the place of one hundred stables, yards, and barns? Anyone can estimate for himself what an enormous sum of money could be saved in one single item when he learns that the fences of Indiana alone, if extended in a single line, would go around the globe nearly fourteen times and cost no less than $200 million. How many wagons and horses will not be rendered superfluous when the Cooperative Commonwealth takes charge of agriculture? How many persons will not be made available for manufacturing and other productive pur-

suits? And as to time, these words of Professor Fawcett are suggestive: "It has been calculated that a steam cultivator would plow a square field of ten acres in half the time occupied in plowing two fields of five acres each, and with two-thirds the expense."

But why waste any words in abstract demonstration? Do not our "bonanza farms" teach us practically the lesson? And will not the hundreds of "bonanza farms" of the near future eventually knock the lesson even into the heads of our country cousins? Do they not already practically demonstrate that there are a hundred things requisite for thorough farming that only can be had by cultivation on a grand scale? Do not the "creameries" that everywhere are springing up show that butter and cheese can be made much better and more cheaply in one dairy than on a hundred farms? Our farmers cannot help finding out by and by, that social-cooperative farming will prove to them an immense benefit, simply in a *financial* point of view. . . .

The desire for — that is, the power of — consumption in the body of the citizens is thus boundless. And they will have the means to pay for all there is to consume. Under the New Order all will be productive workers; they will be paid an equivalent for what they produce — not merely one-half of it as now under the wage system — in some form. Consequently their *purchasing power* will in all cases balance the total production.

There *is* a demand for the labor of every man under any well-ordered social system. If there is a waste of men now, it is the fault of the wage system. A slave was actually worth what he would fetch, and there were very few slaves who would fetch nothing. Why, in a free Commonwealth, should men be of less account? Cattle are valuable; why not men? Carlyle remarks: "A white European man, standing on his two legs, with his two five-fingered hands at his shackle bones and miraculous head on his shoulders, is worth, I should say, from 50 to 100 horses."

By giving all the idle employment; by putting all our parasites and superfluous workers where they can work productively, the Commonwealth will create the needed effective demand, and more than that: The stock of the good things of this life *will thereby be very much enlarged,* perhaps doubled.

But do not believe that when we say that the state will furnish all profitable employment that we mean that everyone will have to do manual labor. Labor undoubtedly will then come to honor; work will then be a beneficent law and not an oppressive rule as now, but brainwork will have its due weight: the New Commonwealth will not be a state of mechanics. In all states that at present pretend to give its citizens educational facilities, it seems to be entirely overlooked that education and aspiration go hand in hand. Our country, in particular, which gives such of our young men and women who can afford to improve themselves free access to high schools, colleges, and universities, afterwards leaves them to scramble for a precarious existence, for which their very education has unfitted them; yet an educated pauper is the most pitiable subject of all.

Our Commonwealth, on the other hand, will nourish the aspirations it has awakened; it will use for its own good the talents it has matured and enable every man and woman to develop his or her peculiar aptitudes, whether it be in brainwork or handwork. This fact, that every citizen will be able to follow his or her peculiar bent, will also itself vastly increase the productive result of all social activities, for it is well known that a person accomplishes most when he works in the line of his greatest inclination.

We may note here that the enlargement of the purchasing power of the masses will also contribute considerably to increase the wealth of society by materially changing the

character of the demand from what it is at present. That is to say, articles of use and beauty will more and more crowd out the costly goods, which at present are principally in demand because, and only because, they are costly and by that quality enable our money-aristocracy to display their wealth.

It has been computed that if everybody now worked at some useful calling, everybody could live in comfort on four hours' daily labor. There is some good reason for believing that this computation is not so very far from being correct. But who can doubt that in the Coming Commonwealth, with all objects of desire thus increased, the hours of labor could be very much reduced, and yet everybody, willing to work, have everything that heart could wish?

Why should anybody then object to being restrained from working more than six or four hours a day? That very many workingmen should object to such a check on their liberty *now,* when they often are reduced to absolute want by seasons of enforced idleness, is natural enough and may be noted as the immovable stumbling block in the way of those who agitate for a compulsory eight-hour law under the present system.

In our Commonwealth all men and women can be endowed with that supreme good — leisure, the mother of culture. Observe, there is the greatest difference in the world between leisure and idleness. The idler, whether poor or rich, has no leisure, for it means the delightful hours reserved from some regular employment, of not too long duration, and which secures the satisfaction of all material wants.

Under the New Regime "charity" and "charitable institutions" will be things of the past. By the way, is it not a pity that the noble word "charity" has in this hypocritical era come to mean — almsgiving? In our Commonwealth no alms will be given; indeed, *nothing will be had gratis.* Everybody will get the full produce of his labor in direct revenues or in public benefit. Every citizen will be *entitled* to the use of all public institutions, be it of libraries, of schools for his children, of hospitals, asylums, or assistance in his old age, on the same principle as the insured is entitled to the amount named in his policy on the happening of a certain event. This makes it clear how our Commonwealth is to be the general insurer; and our various companies that insure against so many forms of risk point out the right road to pursue. They, indeed, embody whatever of corporate responsibility there is left in this chaotic age.

We should therefore say that the Cooperative Commonwealth will be highly promotive of social welfare by securing to all its citizens abundance; by furnishing them leisure; and by enabling them to follow their natural bent. Work will no longer be a tribute to physical necessity but a glad performance of social office. It will for the first time in human history establish harmony between personal egoism and the public welfare by simply distributing the forces of the social organism in accordance with its real needs.

2.

HENRY DEMAREST LLOYD: Monopoly and Social Control

Henry Demarest Lloyd, the earliest of the social reformers who were later to be called "muckrakers," became familiar with the problem of trusts and monopolies while financial editor of the Chicago Tribune. *His "Story of a Great Monopoly" (1881) exposed the methods of the Standard Oil and railroad trusts and established him as a champion of the consumer, independent competitor, and the laborer. Lloyd's conviction that "liberty and monopoly cannot live together" and that goods "cooperatively produced [must be] cooperatively enjoyed" led him to attack all forms of monopoly in "Lords of Industry," portions of which follow.*

Source: *North American Review*, June 1884.

WHEN PRESIDENT GOWEN of the Reading Railroad was defending that company, in 1875, before a committee of the Pennsylvania legislature, for having taken part in the combination of the coal companies to cure the evil of "too much coal" by putting up the price and cutting down the amount for sale, he pleaded that there were fifty trades in which the same thing was done. He had a list of them to show the committee. He said:

Every pound of rope we buy for our vessels or for our mines is bought at a price fixed by a committee of the rope manufacturers of the United States. Every keg of nails, every paper of tacks, all our screws and wrenches and hinges, the boiler flues for our locomotives are never bought except at the price fixed by the representatives of the mills that manufacture them. Iron beams for your houses or your bridges can be had only at the prices agreed upon by a combination of those who produce them. Fire brick, gas pipe, terra-cotta pipe for drainage, every keg of powder we buy to blast coal are purchased under the same arrangement. Every pane of window glass in this house was bought at a scale of prices established exactly in the same manner. White lead, galvanized sheet iron, hose and belting and files are bought and sold at a rate determined in the same way.

When my friend Mr. Lane was called upon to begin his speech the other day and wanted to delay because the stenographer had not arrived, I asked Mr. Collins, the stenographer of your committee, if he would not act. He said, no, it was against the rules of the committee of stenographers. I said, "Well, Mr. Collins, I will pay you anything you ask. I want to get off." "Oh," said he, "prices are established by our combination, and I cannot change them." And when we come to the cost of labor, which enters more than anything else in the cost of coal, we are met by a combination there and are often obliged to pay the price fixed by it.

Adam Smith said in 1776: "People of the same trade hardly meet together even for merriment and diversion but the conversation ends in a conspiracy against the public or in some contrivance to raise prices." The expansive ferment of the new industry, coming with the new science, the new land, and the new liberties of our era, broke up these "conspiracies," and for a century we have heard nothing of them; but the race to overrun is being succeeded by the struggle to divide, and combinations are reappearing on all sides. This anyone may see from the reports of the proceedings of the conventions and meetings of innumerable associations of manufacturers and dealers and even producers which are being held almost constantly. They all do something to raise prices or hold them up, and they wind up with banquets for which we pay.

Four years ago the Chicago Lumbermen's Exchange adopted a resolution declaring it to be "dishonorable" for any dealer to make lower prices than those published by it for the control of prices in one of the greatest lumber markets of the world. Monthly reports are required by this exchange from dealers so that accurate accounts may be kept of stock on hand in order to regulate prices. The price lists of the exchange are revised and made "honest" at monthly banquets. In February 1883, it was found that members who ostensibly adhered to the price lists dipped into the dishonorable practice of competition on the sly by giving buyers greater than the usual discounts. This was then forbidden, and another pathway of competition closed. . . .

The mills of Puget Sound, which supply a large proportion of the lumber consumed in the Pacific states, formed a combination last year to regulate the production and sustain prices. It is said by the local newspapers that the mills which do not belong to the association are hired to stand idle, as there are too many mills, and the association finds it profitable to sustain prices at the cost of thousands of dollars paid out in this way. The lumber market of the Pacific Coast is ruled by the California Lumber Exchange, and that is controlled by a few powerful firms. The prices of redwood are fixed by the Redwood Manufacturers' Association, and those of pine by the Pine Manufacturers' Association. During the past year the retail dealers of San Francisco have had to sign contracts with these associations, binding themselves to buy only from members of the associations, to buy and sell only at prices fixed by them, to give time and discount only according to rule, and to keep accounts so that every item will be clear to the inspectors hired by the associations to look after the retailers. Finally, the retailer binds himself, if he is "found guilty" of committing any of the forbidden sins, to pay a fine which may amount to $1,000, to be divided among the faithful. The literature of business can show no more remarkable productions than the printed forms of these contracts. This system is in imitation of the "special contracts" with shippers which have been put in force by the Central Pacific Railroad.

Western ranchmen complain that the competition of buyers is disappearing. They declare that there exist at the Chicago stockyards combinations of buyers who, by their ability to make large purchases and their agreement to offer but one price, get cattle at their own figures. One member of the "ring" does the buying today; another tomorrow; and so on. The cattle kings have combinations to defend themselves from cattle thieves, state legislatures, and other enemies, and propose to extend this category so as to include the middlemen at the stockyards. The Stockgrowers' Association of Wyoming have $100 million in cattle. At the recent convention held by this body in Cheyenne, it was unanimously declared that its business had been "seriously injured by the pooling arrangements prevailing among buyers at the Chicago stockyards," and the executive committee were instructed to obtain the fullest possible information as to the means by which cattle might be shipped direct to the European consumer.

Last July, Messrs. Vanderbilt, Sloan, and one or two others out of several hundred owners of coal lands and coal railroads, met in the pleasant shadows of Saratoga to make "a binding arrangement for the control of the coal trade." "Binding arrangement" the sensitive coal presidents say they prefer to the word "combination." The gratuitous warmth of summer suggested to these men the need the public would have of artificial heat, at artificial prices, the coming winter. It was agreed to fix prices and to prevent the production of too much of the raw material of warmth by suspensions of mining. In anticipation of the arrival of the cold wave from Manitoba, a cold wave was sent out all over the United States, from their parlors in New York, in an order for half-time work by the miners during the first three months of this year, and for an increase of prices. These are the means this combination uses to keep down wages — the price of men, and keep up the price of coal — the wages of capital. . . .

The coal combination was again investigated by the New York legislature in 1878, after the combination had raised the prices of coal in New York to double what they had been. The legislature found that private mine operators who were not burdened like the great companies with extravagant and often corrupt purchases of coal lands, heavily watered stock, and disadvantageous contracts forced on them by interested directors, and who have only to pay the actual cost of producing the coal, "can afford to sell at a much less price than the railroad coal-producing companies, and would do so if they could get transportation from the mines to the market." This is denied them by the great companies.

"The private operators," says the report, "either find themselves entirely excluded from the benefits of transportation by reason of the high freights, or find it for their interest to make contracts with the railroads by which they will not sell to others, and so the railroads have and will keep the control of the supply of the private operators." To those who will not make such contracts, rates are fixed excluding them from the market, with the result, usually, of forcing them to sell their property to the lords of the pool. "The combination," the committee declared, "can limit the supply and thereby create such a demand and price as they may deem advisable." . . .

One of the sights which this coal side of our civilization has to show is the presence of herds of little children of all ages, from six years upward, at work in the coal breakers, toiling in dirt and air thick with carbon dust, from dawn to dark, of every day in the week except Sunday. These coal breakers are the only schools they know. A letter from the coal regions in the Philadelphia *Press* declares that "there are no schools in the world where more evil is learned or more innocence destroyed than in the breakers. It is shocking to watch the vile practices indulged in by these children, to hear the frightful oaths they use, to see their total disregard for religion and humanity." In the upper part of Luzerne County, out of 22,000 inhabitants, 3,000 are children between six and fifteen years of age, at work in this way.

"There is always a restlessness among the

miners," an officer of one of the New York companies said, "when we are working them on half time." The latest news from the region of the coal combination is that the miners are so dissatisfied with the condition in which they are kept, by the suspension of work and the importation of competing Hungarian laborers in droves, that they are forming a combination of their own, a revival of the old Miners and Laborers' Association, which was broken up by the labor troubles of 1874 and 1875.

Combination is busy in those soft-coal districts, whose production is so large that it must be sent to competitive markets. A pool has just been formed covering the annual product of 6 million tons of the mines of Ohio. Indiana and Illinois are to be brought in, and it is planned to extend it to all the bituminous-coal districts that compete with each other. The appearance of Mr. Vanderbilt, last December, in the Clearfield district of Pennsylvania, at the head of a company capitalized for $5 million, was the first entry of a metropolitan mind into this field. Mr. Vanderbilt's role is to be that of producer, carrier, dealer, and consumer, all in one.

Until he came, the district was occupied by a number of small companies and small operators, as used to be the case in the anthracite field in the old days. But the man who works himself, with his sons, in a small mine, cutting perhaps from twenty to forty tons a day, cannot expect to survive the approach of the Manhattan capitalist. The small Clearfield producers, looking at the fate of their kind in the anthracite country, greeted Mr. Vanderbilt's arrival with the question, "What is to become of us?" "If the small operator," said one of the great man's lieutenants, "goes to the wall, that is his misfortune, not our fault." In March last the prominent Clearfield companies gave notice that wages must be reduced on the 1st of April, and immediately thereafter a union of their employees resolved that if the reduction, which they de-

clared to be "without reason," was made they would strike. . . .

On the theory of "too much of everything," our industries, from railroads to workingmen, are being organized to prevent milk, nails, lumber, freights, labor, soothing syrup, and all these other things from becoming too cheap. The majority have never yet been able to buy enough of anything. The minority have too much of everything to sell. Seeds of social trouble germinate fast in such conditions. Society is letting these combinations become institutions without compelling them to adjust their charges to the cost of production, which used to be the universal rule of price. Our laws and commissions to regulate the railroads are but toddling steps in a path in which we need to walk like men. The change from competition to combination is nothing less than one of those revolutions which march through history with giant strides. It is not likely that this revolution will go backward. Nothing goes backward in this country except reform. When Stephenson said of railroads that where combination was possible competition was impossible, he was unconsciously declaring the law of all industry.

Man, the only animal which forgets, has already in a century or two forgotten that the freedom, the independence of his group, of the state, and even of the family, which he has enjoyed for a brief interval, have been unknown in most of the history of our race and in all the history of most races. The livery companies of London, with their gloomy guildhalls, their wealth, their gluttony and wine-bibbing, their wretched Irish estates, exist today, vain reminders to us of a time when the entire industry of Europe was regimented into organizations, voluntary at first, afterward adopted by the law, which did what our pools of railroads, laborers, manufacturers, and others are trying to do. Not only prices but manners were pooled. "The notion," says Cliffe Leslie, "that every man had a right to settle where he liked, to carry on any occupation he thought fit, and in whatever manner he chose, to demand the highest price he could get, or, on the contrary, to offer lower terms than anyone else, to make the largest profit possible, and to compete with other traders without restraint was absolutely contrary to the spirit of the ages that preceded ours." This system existed for centuries. It is so unlike our own that the contemplation of it may well shake us out of our conceit that the transitions, displacements, changes, upheavals, struggles, exterminations — from Indians to sewing women — of the last 250 years were the normal condition of the race.

Those were not exceptional times. Our day of free competition and free contract has been the exceptional era in history. Explorer, pioneer, protestant, reformer, captain of industry could not move in the harness of the guild brother, the vassal, the monk, and were allowed to throw away medieval uniforms. But now "the individual withers; the world is more and more." Society, having let the individual overrun the new worlds to be conquered, is reestablishing its lines of communication with him. Literary theorists still repeat the cant of individualism in law, politics, and morals; but the world of affairs is gladly accepting, in lieu of the liberty of each to do as he will with his own, all it can get of the liberty given by laws that let no one do as he might with his own. The dream of the French Revolution, that man was good enough to be emancipated from the bonds of association and government by the simple proclamation of "Liberty, Fraternity and Equality," was but the frenzied expression of what was called freedom of self-interest in a quieter but not less bloody revolution, if the mortality of the factories, the mines, and the tenements be charged to its account. A rope cannot be made of sand; a society cannot be made of competitive units.

We have given competition its own way and have found that we are not good

Library of Congress

Henry Demarest Lloyd

enough or wise enough to be trusted with this power of ruining ourselves in the attempt to ruin others. Free competition could be let run only in a community where everyone had learned to say and act, "I am the state." We have had an era of material inventions. We now need a renaissance of moral inventions, contrivances to tap the vast currents of moral magnetism flowing uncaught over the face of society. Morals and values rise and fall together. If our combinations have no morals, they can have no values. If the tendency to combination is irresistible, control of it is imperative.

Monopoly and antimonopoly, odious as these words have become to the literary ear, represent the two great tendencies of our time: monopoly, the tendency to combination; antimonopoly, the demand for social control of it. As the man is bent toward business or patriotism, he will negotiate combinations or agitate for laws to regulate them. The first is capitalistic; the second is social. The first, industrial; the second, moral. The first promotes wealth; the second, citizenship. These combinations are not to be waved away as fresh pictures of folly or total depravity. There is something in them deeper than that.

The Aryan has proved by the experience of thousands of years that he can travel. "But travel," Emerson says, "is the fool's paradise." We must now prove that we can stay at home and stand it as well as the Chinese have done. Future Puritans cannot emigrate from Southampton to Plymouth Rock. They can only sail from righteousness to righteousness. Our young men can no longer go west; they must go up or down. Not new land but new virtue must be the outlet for the future. Our halt at the shores of the Pacific is a much more serious affair than that which brought our ancestors to a pause before the barriers of the Atlantic and compelled them to practise living together for a few hundred years. We cannot hereafter, as in the past, recover freedom by going to the prairies; we must find it in the society of the good.

In the presence of great combinations, in all departments of life, the moralist and patriot have work to do of a significance never before approached during the itinerant phases of our civilization. It may be that the coming age of combination will issue in a nobler and fuller liberty for the individual than has yet been seen; but that consummation will be possible, not in a day of competitive trade but in one of competitive morals.

3.

T. Thomas Fortune: The Common Cause of Negro and White Labor

In 1877 federal troops were withdrawn from the South and Reconstruction collapsed. From that time on the Southern Negro was largely at the mercy of his state or local governments. Educational, political, and job opportunities diminished and the Republican Party left the Negro to fight his own battles. The Civil Rights Cases of 1883, along with numerous state decisions, relegated the free Negro to second-class citizenship. In the South he could work the land as a hired laborer, tenant farmer, or perhaps get his own land if he were fortunate. Or he could go North or West, which many did, only to encounter a rising wave of racism. In 1884 T. Thomas Fortune, editor of the New York Age *and a former slave, analyzed the problems facing the Negro in a book entitled* Black and White: Land, Labor, and Politics in the South. *The concluding chapter of this work is reprinted here.*

Source: *Black and White,* New York, 1884, pp. 234-242.

I KNOW IT IS NOT FASHIONABLE for writers on economic questions to tell the truth, but the truth should be told, though it kill. When the wail of distress encircles the world, the man who is linked by "the one touch of nature" which "makes the whole world kin" to the common destiny of the race universal; who hates injustice wherever it lifts up its head; who sympathizes with the distressed, the weak, and the friendless in every corner of the globe, such a man is morally bound to tell the truth as he conceives it to be the truth.

In these times, when the lawmaking and

enforcing authority is leagued against the people; when great periodicals — monthly, weekly, and daily — echo the mandates or anticipate the wishes of the powerful men who produce our social demoralization, it becomes necessary for the few men who do not agree to the arguments advanced or the interests sought to be bolstered up to "cry aloud and spare not." The man who with the truth in his possession flatters with lies, that "thrift may follow fawning," is too vile to merit the contempt of honest men.

The government of the United States confiscated as "contraband of war" the slave population of the South, but it left to the portion of the unrepentant Rebel a far more valuable species of property. The slave, the perishable wealth, was confiscated to the government and then manumitted; but property in land, the wealth which perishes not nor can fly away, and which had made the institution of slavery possible, was left as the heritage of the robber who had not hesitated to lift his iconoclastic hand against the liberties of his country. The baron of feudal Europe would have been paralyzed with astonishment at the leniency of the conquering invader who should take from him his slave, subject to mutation, and leave him his landed possessions which are as fixed as the universe of nature. He would ask no more advantageous concession.

But the United States took the slave and left the thing which gave birth to *chattel slavery* and which is now fast giving birth to *industrial slavery;* a slavery more excruciating in its exactions, more irresponsible in its machinations than that other slavery, which I once endured. The chattel slaveholder must, to preserve the value of his property, feed, clothe, and house his property, and give it proper medical attention when disease or accident threatened its life. But industrial slavery requires no such care. The new slaveholder is only solicitous of obtaining the maximum of labor for the minimum of cost. He does not regard the man as of any consequence when he can no longer produce. Having worked him to death, or ruined his constitution and robbed him of his labor, he turns him out upon the world to live upon the charity of mankind or to die of inattention and starvation. He knows that it profits him nothing to waste time and money upon a disabled industrial slave. The multitude of laborers from which he can recruit his necessary laboring force is so enormous that solicitude on his part for one that falls by the wayside would be a gratuitous expenditure of humanity and charity which the world is too intensely selfish and materialistic to expect of him.

Here he forges wealth and death at one and the same time. He could not do this if our social system did not confer upon him a monopoly of the soil from which subsistence must be derived, because the industrial slave, given an equal opportunity to produce for himself, would not produce for another. On the other hand, the large industrial operations, with the multitude of laborers from which Adam Smith declares employers grow rich, as far as this applies to the soil, would not be possible, since the vast volume of increased production brought about by the industry of the multitude of coequal small farmers would so reduce the cost price of food products as to destroy the incentive to speculation in them and at the same time utterly destroy the necessity or the possibility of famines, such as those which have from time to time come upon the Irish people.

There could be no famine, in the natural course of things, where all had an opportunity to cultivate as much land as they could wherever they found any not already under cultivation by some one else. It needs no stretch of the imagination to see what a startling tendency the announcement that all vacant land was free to settlement upon condition of cultivation would have to the depopulation of overcrowded cities like New York, Baltimore, and Savannah, where the so-called pressure of population upon subsistence has produced a hand-to-hand fight for existence by the wage workers in every avenue of industry.

This is no fancy picture. It is a plain, logical deduction of what would result from the restoration to the people of that equal chance in the race of life which every man has a right to expect, to demand, and to exact as a condition of his membership of organized society.

The wag who started the "forty acres and a mule" idea among the black people of the South was a wise fool; wise in that he enunciated a principle which every argument of sound policy should have dictated, upon the condition that the forty acres could in no wise be alienated, and that it could be regarded only as property as long as it was cultivated; and a fool because he designed simply to impose upon the credulity and ignorance of his victims. But the justness of the "forty acre" donation cannot be controverted. In the first place, the slave had earned this miserable stipend from the government by 200 years of unrequited toil; and, second, as a freeman, he was inherently entitled to so much of the soil of his country as would suffice to maintain him in the freedom thrust upon him. To tell him he was a freeman and at the same time shut him off from free access to the soil upon which he had been reared, without a penny in his pocket and with an army of children at his coattail — some of his reputed wife's children being the illegitimate offspring of a former inhuman master — was to add insult to injury, to mix syrup and hyssop, to aggravate into curses the pretended conference of blessings.

When I think of the absolutely destitute condition of the colored people of the South at the close of the Rebellion; when I remember the moral and intellectual enervation which slavery had produced in them; when I remember that not only were they thus bankrupt but that they were absolutely and unconditionally cut off from the soil, with absolutely no right or title in it, I am surprised — not that they have already got a respectable slice of landed interests; not that they have taken hold eagerly of the advantages of moral and intellectual opportunities of development placed in their reach by the charitable philanthropy of good men and women; not that they have bought homes and supplied them with articles of convenience and comfort, often of luxury — but I am surprised that the race did not turn robbers and highwaymen, and, in turn, terrorize and rob society as society had for so long terrorized and robbed them. The thing is strange, marvelous, phenomenal in the extreme.

Instead of becoming outlaws, as the critical condition would seem to have indicated, the black men of the South *went manfully to work* to better their own condition and the crippled condition of the country which had been produced by the ravages of internecine rebellion; *while the white men of the South, the capitalists, the land sharks, the poor white trash, and the nondescripts, with a thousand years of Christian civilization and culture behind them, with "the boast of chivalry, the pomp of power," these white scamps, who had imposed upon the world the idea that they were paragons of virtue and the heaven-sent vicegerents of civil power, organized themselves into a band of outlaws, whose concatenative chain of auxiliaries ran through the entire South, and deliberately proceeded to murder innocent men and women for* POLITICAL REASONS *and to systematically rob them of their honest labor because they were too accursedly lazy to labor themselves.*

But this highly abnormal, unnatural condition of things is fast passing away. The white man, having asserted his superiority in the matters of assassination and robbery, has settled down upon a barrel of dynamite, as he did in the days of slavery, and will await the explosion with the same fatuity and self-satisfaction true of him in other days. But as convulsions from within are more violent and destructive than convulsions from without, being more deep-seated and therefore more difficult to reach, the next explosion will be more disastrous, more far-reaching in its havoc than the one which metamorphosed social conditions in the South, and from the dreadful reactions of which we are just now recovering.

As I have said elsewhere, the future struggle in the South will be, not between white men and black men but between capital and labor, landlord and tenant. Already the cohorts are marshaling to the fray; already the forces are mustering to the field at the sound of the slogan.

The same battle will be fought upon Southern soil that is in preparation in other states where the conditions are older in development but no more deep-seated, no more pernicious, no more blighting upon the industries of the country and the growth of the people.

It is not my purpose here to enter into an extended analysis of the foundations upon which our land system rests, nor to give my views as to how matters might be remedied. I may take up the question at some future time. It is sufficient for my purpose

to have indicated that the social problems in the South, as they exfoliate more and more as resultant upon the war, will be found to be the same as those found in every other section of our country; and to have pointed out that the questions of "race," "condition," "politics," etc., will all properly adjust themselves with the advancement of the people in wealth, education, and forgetfulness of the unhappy past.

The hour is approaching when the laboring classes of our country, North, East, West, and South, will recognize that they have a *common cause,* a *common humanity,* and a *common enemy;* and that, therefore, if they would triumph over wrong and place the laurel wreath upon triumphant justice, without distinction of race or of previous condition, *they must unite!* And unite they will, for "a fellow feeling makes us wond'rous kind." When the issue is properly joined, the rich, be they black or be they white, will be found upon the same side; and the poor, be they black or be they white, will be found on the same side.

Necessity knows no law and discriminates in favor of no man or race.

We are Republicans, and don't propose to leave our party and identify ourselves with the party whose antecedents have been Rum, Romanism, and Rebellion.

> SAMUEL DICKINSON BURCHARD, speaking for a group of clergymen calling on Republican presidential candidate James G. Blaine, New York, Oct. 29, 1884

A mugwump is a fellow with his mug on one side of the fence and his wump on the other.

> ANON., campaign slogan, 1884; the liberal Independents who split from the Republican Party to support Cleveland instead of Blaine were called mugwumps

If nominated, I will not accept. If elected, I will not serve.

> WILLIAM TECUMSEH SHERMAN, answer to telegram from the Republican Convention asking him to be the presidential candidate in 1884

4.

Thomas T. Crittenden: Trade and Commerce for the Southwestern States

Immigrants had never favored the South as a region for settlement. They preferred the North and West, where, because of economic diversification, the opportunities seemed greater. Following the Civil War the South remained predominantly agricultural and very poor. The industry that did develop was brought in and owned by Northerners. To improve its economic status, the South made many efforts to attract European immigrants, hoping to replace the Negro labor force and to become economically independent of the North. To accomplish these goals organizations like the Southern Immigration Association were formed. The following selection is the address of Governor Crittenden of Missouri at the convention of the association, held in March 1884 at Nashville, Tennessee.

Source: *Proceedings of the First Annual Session of the Southern Immigration Association of America*, Nashville, 1884, pp. 6-10.

I CAME HERE IN OBEDIENCE to an invitation to attend a meeting of the Southern Immigration Association, not so much with a disposition to participate in it as a delegate as by my presence to give it the endorsement of the state of Missouri. The intimate relations existing between Missouri and the South are very strong. They are bound together by business, social, family ties, similarity in laws and customs, so that anything that tends to the advancement of the South in some degree tends to the advancement of Missouri's interests, and vice versa.

Properly speaking, Missouri is not a Southern state, belonging as she does by her geographical position to the West, but there is nothing that goes to build up the commercial and financial greatness of the South that does not, more or less, affect the interest of Missouri. I felt, therefore, that it was my duty as governor of the state of Missouri to appear in this convention with a view to cultivating these social and business relations with this section to a greater extent than have heretofore attained, and beg to represent among others the large number of Tennesseeans who are now residents in the state of Missouri, and who feel and always have felt a deep interest in everything that tends to the advancement of the interests of their native state.

This convention is one of the most important happenings in the history of the South. Not so much from the number of delegates and the sections represented but because it is the germ, the organization of a scheme which must inevitably redound to the greatness of the South. The Western states have in the past adopted such means as have secured a large immigration from both the Eastern states and foreign countries, and that immigration, in addition to our own energy and thrift, has developed those states into a strong and controlling power in the government. The South has only to pursue the same course to reap the same rewards. And when the South and West are joined together in a great commercial power they will have a controlling and decided voice in the Congress of the United States. This will give us the means necessary to build up our arteries of commerce — our rivers — so long rendered useless for the want of sufficient appropriation.

The leading men of these two sections can no longer neglect these great interests. We hear the tread of coming generations and their voices demanding that we shall pursue such a course as will furnish room, means, facilities, and commerce for their employment and accommodation.

Nature has bestowed upon the South all the elements of a great country, and we must use our best endeavors to develop these great resources. I believe in the infinite power of God, and bow my head in thanks for the great good He has bestowed upon this common country of ours, the South and the West, and acknowledge the possibilities of a great country being developed out of these natural gifts; but at the same time I believe in that Napoleonic idea that God gives the results of victories as much to long guns and many guns as He does to the discipline and energy of the soldiers. We must do our part now in this great work, and if we do not we will hereafter be held to a responsibility fearful to contemplate.

The war desolated the South, it is true; but at the same time it developed in its people wonderful ingenuity, applicability, and enterprise, and gave impetus to the development of those marvelously rich resources of which her people are so justly proud.

I was on the other side, fighting in the ranks over which waves the flag that now designates our common country, and it is useless for me to give my reasons for so doing, for the day for consideration of matters like that has long passed, and the lessons learned from the war show that it is not entirely to be regretted, and the new

Library of Congress

Thomas T. Crittenden, Democrat of Missouri

South will be more prosperous than it ever was in its palmiest days. If this day has not already come, when it does arrive the people will not look so much with feelings of regret upon the past as they will look with intensified interest upon the happenings of the present, and the hopes that are continually being realized, and the bright prospects for the future.

In the South are those great national waterways which, if properly controlled and improved, will contribute to it a wealth far greater and a position far more prominent in the sisterhood of states than it has ever enjoyed in the past. A few years ago we had an open river from St. Paul to New Orleans, the natural highway of the commerce of the West and the South, but its mouth was blocked so that, for the want of some capital, commerce at this great outlet was in a manner paralyzed. Congress, however, made a sufficient appropriation, and a genius — Captain Eads — was found, who, in the face of the unfavorable prediction of nearly all of his brother engineers, made the outlet of the Mississippi into the Gulf of

Mexico, as I was told by the captain of an English vessel a short time ago, navigable for the largest-sized ships that carry on the commerce between the nations over the high seas. This has opened up commerce to the markets of the world and makes our land so much the more valuable. I predict that, with the proper amount appropriated, Galveston, Texas, and Brunswick, Georgia, will become great ports, and so will many other Southern harbors.

There is no reason why the South should not have these harbors and other means of access by which they can send their most valuable staples to the markets of the world.

There is no reason why she should not possess that great prestige that her natural wealth, mineral and agricultural, should give her.

Why should articles from her iron and cotton be manufactured beyond her borders, and the articles made of them be reshipped and resold to her with all the intervening profits? I see no reason.

No, with the proper economy which has already been taught in this section, the resources can be made to prove of the great advantage to her that they have to other sections of this country, and even foreign nations.

5.

Preston M. Sutton: The Liberal Arts in an Agricultural College

The Morrill Act of 1862, by providing federal land grants and funds for agricultural and mechanical colleges, contributed to the growth of such great universities as Cornell, Wisconsin, and Missouri; but it also stimulated the establishment of many small, narrowly vocational schools. The legislatures of the respective states were given the option of deciding how the federal grants could best be used. In 1873 the Iowa legislature had passed a bill in which provision for liberal studies in the agricultural college at Ames was omitted. In 1884 state Senator Preston Sutton of Marshalltown offered a bill to repeal the act of 1873 and substitute a law calling for "a broad, liberal and practical course of study." Portions of Senator Sutton's speech in support of the bill are reprinted below.

Source: *The Aurora*, March 1884.

This bill provides that there shall be adopted and taught at the Iowa State Agricultural College a broad, liberal, and practical course of study in which the leading branches of learning shall relate to agriculture and the mechanic arts, but which shall also include such other branches of learning as will most liberally and practically educate the agricultural and industrial classes in the several pursuits and professions in life, including military tactics. It proposes to enact this in lieu of Section 1621, which it repeals and which specifies as a course of study geology, mineralogy, meteorology, entomology, zoology, animal and vegetable anatomy, veterinary surgery, and bookkeeping, and permits no other studies except such as are directly connected with agriculture. It will thus be seen that this bill proposes to change the law so as to provide a general and liberal course of study in which agriculture and the mechanics' arts shall have a leading place, and to repeal the exclusive course that is now provided by the statute.

When this change is proposed in regard to perhaps the most important educational institution in our state, I am aware that the bill proposing it should be based upon valid considerations, and considerations that look only to the permanent welfare of the institution. For this reason I desire to be heard somewhat fully that I may have a fair opportunity to lay before the Senate, with reasonable clearness, the reasons which have led me to offer this bill. It has received the careful consideration of the present faculty of the college, and has the approval, as I believe, of all the more particularly informed friends of the school of whatever faction (if there be different factions), and comes to the Senate with the unanimous approval of the committee on the Agricultural College. . . .

The Agricultural College is demanding especial attention of this legislature. It is the best-endowed educational institution in this state. In fact it is the only educational institution in the state having a permanent endowment of any considerable amount. The endowment fund of this college is very close to three-quarters of a million of dollars. This fund and other property belonging to the college reaches beyond a million dollars. This endowment, when properly applied to the purpose for which it was made, will give us one of the grandest colleges this country has ever known. . . .

I desire to call your attention to the fact that this endowment of three-quarters of a million is not ours; that we hold it in trust only. . . . I then desire to call your atten-

tion to the purpose of the trust as defined by Congress, also as interpreted by the author of the act of Congress [Morrill Act]. . . .

As the Grecians prescribed an education and a training for their youth in order that they might become the greatest heroes of the world, so would it seem that the author of this act of Congress undertook to provide an education for the toiling sons of America that will enable them to attain to the highest possible citizenship; not soulless bodies nor bodiless souls but men who are strong, physically, mentally, and morally; men who by labor are allied to the laboring masses and whose learning enables them to grapple with all the questions of business, of science, and of state. All the great men of this country have come from the industrial classes, and this act undertakes to place learning within the ready reach of that class upon which a free country must depend, not only for its producers but also its statesmen and its soldiers as well. Hence this act provides that the purpose of the act shall be the liberal and practical education of the industrial classes in the several pursuits and professions of life, thus educating the sons of toil to the performance of duty that a citizen of a free country may be called upon to discharge.

It provides that the college shall teach those branches of learning that relate to agriculture and the mechanic arts but not to the exclusion of the classics and such other sciences as are necessary to a liberal and practical education. It wisely leaves it to the legislatures of the several states to say how these branches of learning shall be taught, but specifies that it shall be in such manner as will best promote the liberal and practical education of the industrial classes in the several pursuits and professions of life. . . .

The Congress of 1862 evidently thought that agriculture and the mechanic arts could not be better benefited than by so educating the agricultural and industrial classes that they might be qualified to discharge any and all of the duties of life; and it was to this purpose that the lands were dedicated, and from that purpose we have no right to divert them. . . . For this act of Congress provided that those lands should be given to such states only as provided colleges for this liberal education, and should be used for that purpose alone and no other. The board wanted the lands, but it was hard for it to give up its pet ideas of special and technical education.

The honorable gentlemen who composed that board had planned a purely agricultural college devoted wholly to agriculture, which they no doubt had good reason to believe would best benefit agriculture and stand as a lasting monument of what they had done for the greatest of all great industries. The college was their pride, and justly so. They had made it, and they had built their hopes upon it, and they wanted to see it stand just as they had planned it. But they wanted these lands.

Now there came a struggle, and I have no doubt it was an honest one, but I must contend it was not a successful one. They desired to be the trustees of this great trust from the government but wanted to avoid the plain, expressed purpose of the trust, which was a liberal and practical education in the several pursuits in life, and misappropriate it to special and technical education in the sole pursuits of agriculture and such mechanic arts as are directly connected with agriculture. The legislature undertook to help the board out of their dilemma by getting up an act which would seem to turn the Agricultural College over to the purpose required by the act of Congress and yet retain to the old college its original character. . . .

Now, I have no quarrel to make with the honorable and philanthropic gentlemen who started out to give to Iowa an exclusively agricultural school. I have my own opinion

whether any school can be made useful which is devoted technically to a single pursuit. These gentlemen had their opinions also, and they had a right to their opinions, and they had a right to insist that the one single purpose of the college should be strictly adhered to until they themselves turned it over to another and more liberal purpose. They turned the college to another and broader purpose in order to secure to it a great endowment. This endowment, however, was accepted upon the express condition that every dollar of it should be inviolably appropriated (that is the language of the law) to the promotion of the liberal and practical education in the several pursuits and professions; and our Agricultural College today has no other fund whatever except the fund we agreed to so appropriate. The whole plan of the congressional agricultural college was liberal and practical education. The plan of the old state agricultural college was technical and exclusive education. The two plans were entirely different, and when the legislature interposed the plan of the state college and applied this fund to its exclusive use, the legislature misappropriated these funds.

The one plan was for an exclusive and special education in a single pursuit and the other for a liberal education in the several pursuits. One was to teach exclusively agriculture and the other to teach such branches of learning as related to agriculture and the mechanic arts, together with such other studies as would give to the industrial classes a broad and liberal education. I say it was unwise to attempt a compromise between two plans, so absolutely different, and it has proved to have been very unwise.

By thus attempting to unite two plans so adverse in their character we have a plan partly of one and partly of the other, and still not wholly either the one plan or the other. It leaves it so that the friends of each plan can contend for conflicting measures. And for this very reason there has been an irrepressible conflict in this school. The energies of the school have been divided and much of its strength exhausted in unfriendly and fruitless contention. Were it not too serious it would be almost amusing to witness the struggle that has gone on in this college between the old plan and the new. We would see one set of men reciting the act of Congress and construing it for broad and liberal education, and then another set reading the act of the legislature and clinging with all the fondness of a father to the old farm.

One side would read from the act of Congress: The branches of learning relating to agriculture and the mechanic arts, without "excluding" anything, not even the classics, necessary to promote the liberal and practical education of the industrial classes in the several pursuits and professions of life, and then insist that the funds devoted by the act of Congress should be used for the purposes as herein set forth, and would beg that history and literature might be made regular studies in the school so that the students could be taught the history of agriculture, the history of liberty, the history of their country, the history of all great causes, and the history of the world's great men. The other side would read from the act of the legislature the course of study provided for the old Legislative College of 1858, as follows: mineralogy, meteorology, entomology, zoology, geology, etc., and such other studies only as will directly connect the college with the agricultural interests of the state, and that side would insist that history was a dangerous study that led the youths to long for other than agricultural pursuits, and thus would they contend for absolute technical agricultural education. . . .

History is not only absolutely essential to learning but history may be said to be learning itself. Learning without history is Hamlet with Hamlet left out. The only learning that the artists of this capitol have

personified is history. They have given us the beautiful picture of America relating her history. There is nothing that America is so proud of as of her history. Nothing so inspires the American heart to high ambition as the study of American history, and yet we have a college pretending to give a liberal education with her doors locked against history.

Now is this liberal education? I ask you is it even practical education? What is practical education? It certainly is not a bare technical knowledge of physical science. A man may read the rocks and all of the lessons they teach, and study the flowers till he can call them all by name, and be able to analyze all the minerals and measure their component parts, and be able to give the name and character of every specimen of animal or insect life, and still not be able practically to apply his learning to the solution of a single problem in life. . . .

The German schools have been technical. The German education has ever been of the most technical character. It has made profound scholars in the technical sciences, but it has failed to develop great men in the affairs of life or of state. It spent itself in the solution of abstract questions until Germany retrograded into absolute and iron monarchy. The framers of this great educational law were not in favor of that kind of education. The framers of this bill intended to educate the American sons of toil in all the affairs of life and state; to make them strong and trustworthy freemen, learned and capable freemen, free to choose the pursuit or the profession in life that God made them, and each of them, to fill, freemen possessed of a practical and liberal knowledge of the great industries of our country and a knowledge that should reach beyond these industries to the country itself. . . .

When I visited our Agricultural College last fall and saw its beautiful fields and herds of cattle, its lawns and its woods, and its commodious buildings, and its laboratories and libraries, and contemplated its magnificent endowment fast nearing a million, I thought I could see the possibility of one of the grandest institutions of learning that the world has ever known — a grand temple of learning where learning shall lead labor by the hand and confer upon him all her manifold blessings. A college that may carry the broadest of learning into every toiler's home, and that may prepare the sons of toil for the broadest possible usefulness to all mankind.

The providing of such a college I believe it to be the true purpose of the act of Congress that gave us these lands. I believe by the acceptance of these lands we have pledged the honor of the state to the maintenance of that purpose alone. To that end I have in good faith offered the bill to which I have called your attention, and perhaps at too great length. I believe it truly and wisely settles the purpose of this college, which, for the good of the college, should have been settled long ago, and which cannot be settled too finally nor too soon. To the provisions of this bill I invite the conscientious and careful consideration of this honorable Senate.

6.

George Ticknor Curtis: Presidential Elections and the Spoils System

George Ticknor Curtis and other reformers of the Gilded Age criticized American politics for adopting the credo of big businessmen like the Southern Pacific's Collis P. Huntington. "If you have to pay money to have the right thing done," Huntington said of his bribery in behalf of his railroad, "it is only just and fair to do it." Curtis attacked political parties for paying party workers "to have the right thing done" — payment usually being in government jobs and favors rather than cash. In an article entitled "How Shall We Elect Our Presidents?" Curtis urged changes in the electoral laws to eliminate the corruption fostered by the spoils system.

Source: *Century Illustrated Monthly Magazine,* November 1884.

An American writer of some local repute in his day, addressing his countrymen soon after the Constitution of the United States went into operation, said: "You have nothing to fear from your Constitution; your Constitution has everything to fear from you." This antithesis contained some truth when it was uttered; it contains some now. Our Constitution is, in its theory, the most nearly perfect system of free government that was ever devised. It has but few defects; and although, when it had been completed and was first promulgated, it seemed to that generation very hazardous to commit such powers of government to a central authority acting for the whole people of the United States, so that the Constitution as originally framed had to be amended, the true way in which the system should be regarded, in judging of its merits, is to consider the first ten amendments just as if they had been incorporated into the text of the instrument as it came from the hands of its framers. Thus complemented by the addition of certain restrictive and explanatory clauses, there was as little danger to liberty from the Constitution as there was danger of anarchy, notwithstanding the anxiety felt by our grandfathers when they gave their assent to the new government. But while the people have had nothing to fear from the Constitution, the Constitution has often had a good deal to fear from the people and their public servants. False constructions, loose official interpretations, departures from the intent and spirit of many of its provisions, the strifes of parties, the antagonisms of sections, the conflicts of local interests, the ambitions of individuals — these and many other causes for which the Constitution itself is not responsible have at different times powerfully contributed to bring this nearly perfect system of government into much peril.

I do not now propose to treat of the great schism which, nearly a quarter of a century ago, seemed likely to end in a permanent disruption of the Union and, by consequence, in the loss of the Constitution. I now seek to direct public attention to an evil that has been growing in magnitude for a period of about fifty years, and which is today one of the most serious and menacing of all the causes that may finally lead to an overthrow of this form of government. I allude to the abuses of the electoral system — abuses of the machinery which the Constitution established for constituting the executive head of the government.

There can be very little question about the intent of the plan by which the framers of the Constitution proposed to have the office of President of the United States filled at stated intervals of four years. Whether this period was or was not too short, there can be no doubt that the method of election was well-devised. It inter-

posed between the people of each state and the ultimate choice a body of electors, measured in numbers by the aggregate representation of the state in the two houses of Congress. The design of this intermediate body was twofold: first, to avoid the tumults that might attend a direct vote of the people for a chief executive officer to whom such great powers were to be committed; and, second, to enable the functionaries called electors to exercise a deliberate and independent choice from among the public men of the country for an office of so much dignity and authority. The fact that the first President was chosen under circumstances which operated as a distinct moral instruction to the electors to cast the votes of their states for Washington does not detract from the obvious design of the electoral system.

While the men who made that system anticipated that to insure the success of the experiment of their new government Washington must be and would be the first President, they so framed the electoral machinery that in subsequent elections the choice would, as they believed, take place without any moral or any other kind of instruction to compel the selection of the individual to fall upon a previously designated person. In like manner, although at the time when the Constitution went into operation there were, properly speaking, no parties or party divisions — for the differences between the friends of the Constitution and its opponents certainly did not amount to organized parties such as we have since known — yet it was foreseen that questions of administration and public policy would necessarily lead to the formation of parties; and it is quite certain that one of the chief reasons for interposing a body of electors by whom the office of President was to be filled was to avoid in some degree the dictation and control of parties, and to allow some scope for the voice of minorities in the electoral colleges.

So, too, when we interpret the text of the

electoral system by known historical facts and contemporary documents and discussions, there can be no doubt that one of the chief purposes of this system was to have the President appointed by public functionaries who should act without the control of positive instruction respecting the individual for whom they were to cast the votes of their states. This view of the original design of the electoral bodies leaves to political parties all the scope that they ought to have in the choice of a President; for it leaves the dominant majority of the people of every state to appoint as electors men of their own political faith and opinions, and at the same time it avoids the dictation of the individual to whom the electoral votes of the states are to be given.

The members of an electoral college, appointed by the votes of a majority of the people of a state, may properly, and will naturally, cast their electoral votes for some public man who is of the same party; but it is simply an abuse of the electoral system, as it was originally designed to operate, to have the electors put under a moral, an honorary, or any other obligation not in any case to vote for any person but the individual who is designated, or, as it is called, "nominated," by a party convention.

Let us now see what has come about in the past forty or fifty years. Before the advent of the so-called national conventions, nominations for the presidency were made by bodies called caucuses composed of the members of Congress who were adherents of the respective parties of the time. This was a method that was open to some of the objections which belong to the convention system of nominations; that is to say, all nominations which operate finally as positive instructions to the state electors, however they may be made, are bad because they lead to intrigue, to the exclusion of the best men, to more or less of corruption, and, therefore, to a violation of the original design of the electoral system. But the

nominating caucuses that were held at the seat of government by the political parties, and were composed of such members of Congress as chose to take part in them, bad as they were on some accounts, did not lead to a tithe of the evils of the convention system. It is to the consequences of this system of national party conventions, as it has operated ever since it was resorted to, that I wish to draw the attention of reflecting men, and then to consider whether anything can be done to put an end to it, and at the same time to leave to political parties all the vigor and activity that they ought to have in a popular government like ours.

The operation of the convention system is this. An irresponsible body, unknown to the Constitution or the laws, the creature of a usage only, and organized by the action in primary assemblies of probably not a tenth part of the American people, assembles in some great city. Some of the delegations come with positive instructions from the political cabals which appointed them to secure the nomination of a particular individual, who may or may not be a person of national reputation. Other delegations are not so positively fettered, but perhaps they are under the operation of a device called the "unit rule," whereby the whole vote of the delegation is thrown by a majority of its members, an ingenious plan for suppressing the voices of a minority of the delegation in the final count of the votes of the whole convention. In addition to the regular delegates from the different states, come organized bands of noisy partisans to "work" for their respective candidates. Here and there may be seen eminent citizens, who have traveled great distances from their homes with the patriotic purpose of bringing about a good nomination. The influence, however, of this class of men is often lost in the tumultuary excitements of the scene.

The assembly is usually convened in some very large building which admits of enormous crowds in its galleries; and these crowds, composed of the most heterogeneous materials, often partake of some of the characteristics of a mob. It has not seldom happened that wise deliberation and conscientious action have been impossible under such circumstances; and it has sometimes happened that the presiding officer has been unable to distinguish between the decisions of the body itself and the decisions of the surrounding vociferating and excited galleries.

In the discussions, conferences, bargains, and combinations that take place out of the sittings of the convention, if money is not used, and used in large sums, to buy votes, these bodies have been belied for many years. The probability is that for at least twenty years, in the nominating conventions of both of the great political parties, money has been a factor. But these transactions are so conducted that they are unknown to any but the vendors and purchasers of the votes. The staple of the argument that is openly pressed for this or that candidate for the nomination is his ability to "carry" this or that state which is supposed likely to be "the battleground" or one of the battlegrounds of the election. The "pivotal states," as they are denominated in the political jargon of these occasions, sometimes make the nomination turn upon considerations of the lowest kind.

Something in the past history of a public man is supposed to give him the best chance to capture the "soldier" vote, or the "Irish" vote, or the "German" vote, or the "Negro" vote, or the liquor or the antiliquor interest, or the workingman's interest, and so on through all the catalogue of diversified prejudices and passions which sway, or are supposed to sway, the popular impulses of different localities or classes at these times of the quadrennial ballot for a President. Very little is heard of the solid grounds on which the public character of a statesman ought to be able to challenge

public confidence; very little of the qualities which should fit a man for the office. Nearly the whole effective force of a great party is expended in calculation of the elements of what is called the "strength" of the different prominent men of the party.

An accurate definition of this curious quality of political strength excludes the personal fitness of a man to be President of the United States and includes his supposed "availability," which means some adventitious capacity to win more votes in the election than any one else. Undoubtedly, so long as the convention system of nominations, with all their binding force, is continued, the quality that is universally understood as "strength," low as it is in the scale of calculations, is an element of some importance. But let any one follow out the whole process of these nominations and the working of the whole machinery and then compare it with the obvious design of the electoral system, and he will be convinced that if the framers of the Constitution could have foreseen in what their system was to result, they never would have established it. . . .

We have wandered so far from the principles of the Constitution — they are so little understood at the present day by the great body of citizens — that perhaps the statement that the Constitution does not contemplate or intend that the President shall be conclusively designated by a popular vote will cause some surprise. Yet there is no proposition concerning the Constitution that can be made more indisputable than this. In the discussions which attended its formation and adoption, we can trace the effort to frame a system by which the President could be appointed without being absolutely elected by the votes of the people. Project after project was brought forward in the Federal Convention, all of them of a different character, but all designed as substitutes for a direct appointment by the people. At one time it was proposed that the national executive should be appointed by the national legislature; at another, by the legislatures of the states; and still another plan was that electors should be chosen by the state legislatures or appointed by the state executives. At length, after the most laborious and careful consideration, the plan was adopted of electors to be appointed by the different states according to the ratio of their representation in Congress.

These officers were interposed between the popular vote and the actual choice, with the intent that they should make the choice upon high public motives without positive instruction, pledge, or obligation binding them to vote for a specified person. It was intended to secure a body of electors whose calm and sound judgment might be relied upon to prevent the executive office from falling into the hands of men of great personal popularity, or influence, or distinction, not accompanied by high qualifications for its duties. It was doubtless not intended to exclude the sense of the people from the consideration of the electors. But it was certainly intended that the electors should exercise a real choice; that they should weigh the sense of the people but not be controlled by it if a sound judgment of the public good required them to disregard it. They were to be the agents of the people in choosing *a* President, but not to be their agents for the inevitable selection of a particular individual. No other function in the government was assigned to them. Having discharged their trust, they were to return into the body of their fellow citizens.

But this wise and careful institution has lost its purpose. The electors exercise no choice, no judgment, no volition. They come into official existence pledged to vote for a particular candidate, and they are assumed to be dishonorable men and traitors to their party if they do not obey its behests. In some states they are appointed by a majority of the voters; in some a plurality only determines the person for whom they are to vote, while a majority of votes have perhaps been cast against him.

It has fared no better with the people. The candidate for whom the electors are expected and required to vote is not only designated before they have assembled but he is designated by a body that is unknown to the law, that derives its existence and authority from those who choose to get together and institute it, and who are, too, a numerical minority of the political party in whose name they claim to act. But notwithstanding the total want of all proper authority, notwithstanding the fact that the primary assemblies which appoint the delegates to the nominating conventions notoriously embrace but a small part of the voters of a party, the power of these conventions is immense. To break away from their dictation requires an effort that few men who feel party obligations like to make.

The people have not only accepted the control of the conventions over the electors but they have lost all proper freedom of choice in casting their own votes. The election is supposed to be popular. It is not a popular election, if by that is meant that the people, or a majority of them, express their preferences by their votes. They have no opportunity for such an expression. They are just as much debarred from all proper freedom of choice as if a foreign army, able to overrun and overawe the country, were to land on our coast and say: "Choose for your executive one of two men whom we present to you." The people do not choose the President; they determine which of two "candidates" shall be President, and this is all. . . .

The emancipation of the country from the evils of the spoils system may do something to break up the convention system of making nominations. But it needs to be supplemented by an emancipation of the people and the presidential electors from the thralldom which confines the choice of a President to designated candidates. I conceive that the following plan, if it can receive the support of disinterested men of all parties, would go far to accomplish the object. . . .

No more important or dignified function exists in this government of ours than that which is assigned by the Constitution to the presidential electors. In the aggregate they constitute a very numerous body; as numerous as the whole number of the two houses of Congress. Chosen for a temporary but most sacred function, and dissolved as soon as they have performed it, they would be, if assembled in one body, less likely to be swayed by improper or factious motives than bodies which are to continue in existence, and are closely connected with the parties and factions of the time. If they can be emancipated from the thralldom which now binds them, we might expect to see men of the highest order of character willing to assume and exercise a function of such transcendent importance, instead of seeing, as we now see, these appointments distributed as empty honors among the politicians, or as party compliments to men to whom there is at present nothing else to give, and who will make as good machines as anybody.

Why not, then, assemble the whole body of the electors at the seat of government, making them an electoral chamber, and constituting the body itself the judge of the elections, qualifications, and returns of its own members? We should thus obviate the necessity for returning the certificates of their appointments to any public officer who was not an officer of the electoral chamber itself, and should vest in the body itself every question that could arise on any of the certificates. Every certificate would be filed with some designated officer of the chamber, and the chamber would proceed to organize itself as other public bodies do in whom the same power is lodged. Of course the different members of the chamber would come with their party affinities and predilections; but, acting in public, and with a sense of their responsibility to the nation as well as to their constituents, they would be compelled to decide with decency every preliminary question that could arise. If we are willing to trust this power to every legislative body in the land, why not trust it to the presidential electors? They will be or might be removed from many of the improper and unfair motives that sometimes sway the action of legislative bodies on questions of contested seats.

Still it may be frankly admitted that this plan could not work well unless the force of the obligation which now compels every elector to vote for a designated candidate, and not to vote for any other, can be broken. Where, by the law of the state, its electors are chosen on one ticket by a plurality vote of the people, the entire electoral vote of that state is now cast for a candidate who may not be the choice of a majority of all the voters. It is true that where the law of a state admits of the appointment of electors by districts, the elector of any district can make his vote and the wishes of his constituents felt in the final count. But assemble the whole body of the electors in one chamber, and let them vote for a president per capita, without regard to the fact whether they were elected on general state tickets or elected in districts, and minorities and sometimes even majorities would be better represented in the final result than they are now. It seems to be a reasonable calculation that this method of voting in the electoral chamber, after it had become appreciated by the people of all the states, would strongly stimulate them to select men worthy of the electoral trust, who would not, under all imaginable circumstances, surrender their judgments to the dictate of a nominating convention, which has perhaps been packed in the interest of some one man.

I am by no means disposed to forget the

potency of political parties, nor the force of their machinery. But I am not arguing with the common run of politicians. I put it to the sober sense of the people — if anything that I can think or say can reach them — whether parties are of any value to *them* excepting as a means of carrying out some public policy; and whether our present mode of nominating and electing our presidents is either necessary or useful to the legitimate objects of a party. I grant that so long as the spoils remain the grand objective point of party exertion and activity, or so long as the control of the public patronage is coupled as a means to the accomplishment of a public policy as an end, so long we must have nominating conventions and the consequent degradation of the electoral system. But destroy the spoils system, eliminate entirely the cohesive power of the public plunder from the means which hold parties together, and we shall break up this mode of choosing presidents and still leave to political parties all their legitimate functions.

If we can choose a President in the mode which I have ventured to sketch, he will still be the representative of a party in every sense in which he ought to be; for the electors who appointed him would represent the public policy of a party; but he would not be a President bound to reward with office the partisans who had procured his nomination by a national party convention. We should thus destroy the vice of these conventions, and should still leave to them all the virtue that they can have, for they could still meet and resolve and announce their policies by platforms or otherwise. The vice of the system is the absolute dictation to the electors, which makes it impossible for them to think of but one candidate for the office. . . .

But I have been told in answer to this plan that the parties will still make their nominations, and that the force of these nominations will not be lessened by having the electors assemble and act as one chamber. There will be, it is said, just the same dictation, just the same honorary and imperative obligation to vote for the one man only. This may fairly be doubted, if we can once have what civil service reform aims to accomplish. When that is effected, the national party conventions, if they continue to be held, will be attended chiefly by men who will seek to make them exclusively organs for declaring some public policy.

It is not at all necessary that some one presidential candidate should be presented to the people as the sole representative of a party policy. The electors of each state will come to the proposed chamber as representatives of the policy preferred by the voters who have appointed them to exercise the electoral trust. Unrestricted in their choice in all but one respect, they will be at liberty to select from among the public men of the same party the man whom they deem the most eligible for the office. They can therefore give, as they do not now give, due weight to all those considerations of character and capacity which ought to govern their votes. As no bargains have been made by them or for them, or by or for anyone else, they will have no stipulations to fulfill by their votes; and the sole restriction that they will be under will be the public expediency of choosing some qualified statesman who concurs in the public policy of the party which made them electors. The President, when thus chosen, will be free to give his attention to the legitimate objects of the party association, and will not be obliged to consider how he is to pay his political debts, for he will have none to discharge.

7.

"The Dodger"

"The Dodger" grew out of the farmers' efforts for agrarian reform in the period following the Civil War. Later, it was used to satirize James G. Blaine in his presidential campaign against Grover Cleveland — a campaign in which Blaine Republicans charged Cleveland with personal immorality and evading military service in the Civil War, while Cleveland supporters stirred old suspicions of corruption in Blaine's record. The version of "The Dodger" presented here was transcribed from memory for the Library of Congress records by Mrs. Emma Dusenberry of Mena, Arkansas, who learned it in the 1880s.

✬ THE DODGER

Oh, the candidate's a dodger, yes, a well-known dodger,
Oh, the candidate's a dodger, yes, and I'm a dodger, too.
He'll meet you and treat you and ask you for your vote,
But look out, boys, he's a-dodging for a note!

Chorus:
Oh, we're all dodging, a-dodging, dodging, dodging,
Oh, we're all dodging our way through the world.

Oh, the lawyer he's a dodger, yes, a well-known dodger,
Oh, the lawyer he's a dodger, yes, and I'm a dodger, too.
He'll plead your case and claim you for a friend,
But look out boys, he's easy for to bend!

Oh, the preacher he's a dodger, yes, a well-known dodger,
Oh, the preacher he's a dodger, yes, and I'm a dodger, too.
He'll preach you the gospel and tell you of your crimes,
But look out, boys, he's a-dodging for your dimes!

Oh, the merchant he's a dodger, yes, a well-known dodger,
Oh, the merchant he's a dodger, yes, and I'm a dodger, too.
He'll sell you goods at double the price
And when you go to pay him, you'll have to pay him twice!

Oh, the farmer he's a dodger, yes, a well-known dodger,
Oh, the farmer he's a dodger, yes, and I'm a dodger, too.
He'll plow his cotton, he'll hoe his corn,
And he'll make a living just as sure as you're born!

Oh, the lover he's a dodger, yes, a well-known dodger,
Oh, the lover he's a dodger, yes, and I'm a dodger, too.
He'll hug you and kiss you and call you his bride,
But look out, girls, he's a-telling you a lie!

8.

Lester F. Ward: Mind as a Social Factor

Lester Ward, an early American exponent of modern "evolutionary" sociology, presented his theories on the relation between man and his environment in such works as The Psychic Factors of Civilization *(1893) and other texts on sociology. Ward's writings encouraged many social reformers in their efforts to eliminate poverty and to provide adequate education for all. In the following article of 1884, Ward attacked the laissez faire theory of politics and its apologists among the Social Darwinists.*

Source: *Mind: A Quarterly Review of Psychology and Philosophy,* October 1884.

AFTER MANY CENTURIES of exclusive study of the soul, the thinkers of the world turned their attention for some centuries more to the study of the intellect. During all this time, the true influence of mind as a social factor was left quite out of view. At last there rose up the scientific philosophy which essayed to explain the nature of mind. Its dependence upon organization in general and upon brain in particular was proved by scientific experimentation, and the domain of metaphysics became that of psychology. Mind was shown to be a function of body and psychology became a department of biology.

Man has now taken his true position in the animal world as a product of development. Brain, which alone raises him above other animals, has been developed in the same manner as the other anatomical characters. The brain is the organ of the mind, its physical seat and cause. Mind is therefore a natural product of evolution, and its achievements are to be classed and studied along with all other natural phenomena. Such is the scientific conception of mind.

The modern scientist places all objects in the midst of an infinite series of antecedents and consequents. Organic forms as well as inorganic must take their places in this series — the animal no less than the plant, the man no less than the beast. Mind itself is a link of this endless chain. Its activities consist in the transmission of the properties of its antecedents to its consequents. The quantity of force in the universe is constant. No power can increase or diminish it. All attempts on the part of the creatures of this constant and unchangeable force to modify its normal effects are not less vain because such creatures happen to have acquired the faculty of observing the changes going on in nature.

The protracted study of nature's processes leads to admiration of them, and the belief has become prevalent that they are not only unalterable but also in some way necessarily beneficent. Nature has made great progress in developing organized beings and is assumed to be still working in this direction. The natural method is always the true method, and to find it out is the aim of all scientific investigation. Out of this earnest and laudable strife to discover the true method of nature has grown, logically enough, the assumption that when found it must be something of great worth.

It is commonly supposed that the highest wisdom of man is to learn and then to follow the ways of nature. Those dissatisfied people who would improve upon the natural course of events are rebuked as meddlers with the unalterable. Their systems are declared utopian, their laws *bruta fulmina* [vain threats]. All efforts in this direction are held to be trifling and are stigmatized as so many ignorant attempts to nullify the immutable laws of nature. This general mode of reasoning is carried into all departments of human life.

In government, every attempt to improve the condition of the state is condemned and denounced. Curiously enough, here the claim is illogically made that such measures are harmful. In fact, unfortunately for the whole theory, they have often been proved to be so. But this, of course, proves their efficacy. This glaring inconsistency is, however, overlooked, and government is implored not to adopt wise and successful measures but to refrain from adopting any, to let society alone, and thus allow the laws of nature to work out their beneficent results.

In commerce and trade, absolute freedom is insisted upon. Free trade is the watch-word of this entire school. The laws of trade, they maintain, are natural laws. As such they must be better than any human rules. And here again we find them insisting that regulation is injurious to trade, although it is at the same time declared to be nugatory.

In social affairs, these doctrines are carried to their extreme logical outcome. The laws of nature as they manifest themselves in society must be left wholly untouched. The passions of men will neutralize and regulate themselves. Competition can be depended upon to correct abuses. The seller must be allowed to exaggerate and misstate the nature of his wares. This has the effect to sharpen the wits of the buyer, and this develops the brain. To dilute, adulterate, or even poison food and medicine for personal gain is not objectionable, since the destruction thereby of a few unwary consumers only proves their unfitness to survive in society. As in general commerce, so in private business, competition must be free. If a dealer, by selling at a loss, can hold out until all his competitors have been driven from the field, in order then to recover more than his losses by the monopoly he will enjoy, his right to do this must not be questioned. It is under such conditions and by the aid of such discipline that man and society have developed.

Education must be that of experience. Knowledge must be gained by efforts to avoid the consequences of ignorance already felt. The intellectual development of the child must be an epitome of that of the race. It is thus only that nature operates, and surely nature is greater and wiser than man.

All schemes of social reform are unscientific. Public charities tend to bolster up unworthy elements in society that nature has declared unfit to survive. Temperance reforms tend only to abridge individual liberty, for even the liberty to destroy oneself should be respected. Philanthropy is zeal without knowledge, while humanitarianism is fanaticism.

This general class of views antedated by many years the publication by Spencer and Darwin of their formulated doctrines of the "survival of the fittest" and "natural selection." But it cannot be denied that these doctrines, supported as they were by facts fresh from nature, have greatly strengthened this habit of thought. Nature's method is now much better known than formerly, and it is now well understood that an utterly soulless competition constitutes its fundamental characteristic.

Surely man cannot go astray in following in the footsteps of nature. Let him learn from the animal world. He has descended from some of the humble stocks which he is now studying. Nature's plan has raised him from the condition of a beast to that of a rational being. It has created and developed society and civilization. Unless tampered with by "reformers," all the operations of society would be competitive. Competition is the law of nature out of which progress results. Sociology, as its founder insisted, must be based on biology, and the true sociologist must understand this biologic law. Those who propose to apply methods to society which are opposed to the methods of nature are supposed to be ignorant of these fundamental truths and are called empiricists, "meddlers," and "tinkers."

Such, I say, is the tenor and tendency of modern scientific thought. I do not say that all scientific men hold these views. I merely maintain that leading ones have formulated and inculcated them as natural deductions from the established facts of science, and that the public mind is rapidly assimilating them. . . .

Is there any way of answering these arguments? Can the laissez-faire doctrine be successfully met? That all attempts to do this have been timidly made cannot be denied. That these have been few and feeble is

equally certain. While there has existed in the minds of many rational persons a vague sense of some hidden fallacy in all this reasoning, none have felt competent to formulate their objections with sufficient clearness and force to warrant pitting them against the resistless stream of concurrent science and philosophy of the nineteenth century. There has, however, been developing of late a more or less marked apprehension with regard to the possible consequences of this mode of thought. The feeling is distinct in the best minds, and to a large extent in the public mind, that the tendency of modern ideas is nihilistic. It is clear that if they become universally accepted they must work stagnation in society. The laissez-faire doctrine is a gospel of inaction, the scientific creed is struck with sterility, the policy of resigning all into the hands of nature is a surrender.

But this recognition is by no means proof that the prevalent opinions are false. At best it can only suggest this on the ground that true doctrines should be progressive. But this would be a *petitio principii* [begging the question]. Nature is not optimistic, still less anthropocentric. For aught we know, the laws of nature are such as make a recognition of strict scientific truth a positive barrier to social advancement. The argument we have been considering must be refuted, if at all, by legitimate counter-argument. . . .

The laissez-faire doctrine fails to recognize that, in the development of mind, a virtually *new power* was introduced into the world. To say that this has been done is no startling announcement. It is no more than has taken place many times in the course of the evolution of living and feeling beings out of the tenuous nebulae of space. For, while it is true that nature makes no leaps, while, so long as we consider their beginning, all the great steps in evolution are due to minute increments repeated through vast periods; still, when we survey the whole field, as we must do to comprehend the scheme, and contrast the extremes, we find that nature has been making a series of enormous strides and reaching from one plane of development to another. It is these independent achievements of evolution that the true philosopher must study.

Not to mention the great steps in the cosmical history of the solar system and of the earth, we must regard the evolution of protoplasm, the "physical basis of life," as one of those gigantic strides which thenceforth completely revolutionized the surface of our planet. The development of the cell as the unit of organization was another such stride. The origin of vertebrate life introduced a new element, and the birth of man wrought still another transformation. These are only a few of nature's revolutions. Many more will suggest themselves.

And, although in no single one of these cases can it be said at what exact point the new essence commenced to exist, although the development of all these several expressions of nature's method of concentrating her hitherto diffused forces was accomplished through an unbroken series of minute transitional increments continued through eons of time; still it is not a whit less true that each of these grand products of evolution, when at length fully formed, constituted a new cosmic energy, and proceeded to stamp all future products and processes with a character hitherto wholly unknown upon the globe.

It is in this sense, and in this only, that I claim the development of mind — of the thinking, reasoning, inventing faculty of the human brain — as another, and one of the best marked, of the great cosmic strides that have characterized the course of evolution and belong to the legitimate methods of nature.

It is, for example, only to a limited extent and in the most general way that we can apply the same canons to the organic as to the inorganic world. It is usually, but falsely, supposed that the student of biology need know nothing of physics, the assumption being that they have nothing in common. While this error is fatal to all fundamental acquaintance with the laws of life, it well illustrates the immensity of the advance from one realm to the other. The same could be said, in varying degrees of obviousness, of every one of the ascending steps to which reference has been made. I freely admit that the theologians and metaphysicians commit the most fatal error in treating the soul, or mind, as independent of the body, but this enormous fallacy is scarcely greater than that of the modern evolutionist, who, finding out their dependence, ignores the *magnitude* of the step by which mind was made a property of body and proceeds as though no new factor had entered into the world.

But all this may be regarded as mere generality. Let us come to something more specific.

It has always been a marvel to my comprehension that wise men and philosophers, when smitten with the specious logic of the laissez-faire school, can close their eyes to the most obtrusive fact that civilization presents. In spite of the influence of philosophy, all forms of which have thus far been negative and nihilistic, the human animal, with his growing intellect, has still ever realized the power that is vouchsafed through mind, and has ever exercised that power. Philosophy would have long since robbed him of it and caused his early extermination from the earth but for the persistence, through heredity, of the impulse to exercise in self-preservation every power in his possession; by which practice alone he first gained his ascendancy ages before philosophy began.

The great fact, then, to which I allude is that, in spite of all philosophy, whether mythologic, metaphysical, or naturalistic, declaring that man must and can do nothing, he *has,* from the very dawn of his intelligence, been transforming the entire surface of the planet he inhabits. No other animal performs anything comparable to what man performs. This is solely because no other possesses the developed psychic faculty.

If we analyze mind into its two departments, sense and intellect, we shall see that it is through this latter faculty that these results are accomplished. If we inquire more closely into the mode by which intellect operates, we shall find that it serves as a guiding power to those natural forces with which it is acquainted (and no others), directing them into channels of human advantage. If we seek for a single term by which to characterize with precision the nature of this process, we find this in *invention*. The essential characteristic of all intellectual action is invention.

Glancing now at the ensemble of human achievement, which may be collectively called civilization, we readily see that it is all the result of this inventive process. All practical art is merely the product of successful invention, and it requires no undue expansion of the term, nor extraordinary power of generalization, to see in all human institutions only modified forms of arts and true products of the intellectual, or inventive, faculty.

But what is the general result of all this? An entirely new dispensation has been given to the world. All the materials and forces of nature have been thus placed completely under the control of one of the otherwise least powerful of the creatures inhabiting the earth. He has only to know them in order to become their master. Nature has thus been made the servant of man. Thus only has man succeeded in peopling the entire globe while all other animals are restricted to narrow faunal areas. He has also peopled certain portions far more densely than any other species could have done, and he seems destined to continue multiplying his numbers for a long time yet in the future. But this quantitative proof is even less telling than the qualitative. When we con-

fine our attention to the elite of mankind, we do not need to have the ways specified in detail by which the powers of mind have exalted the intellectual being above all other products of creation.

At the present moment, the most dense and the most enlightened populations of the globe occupy what are termed temperate latitudes, which means latitudes in which for from three to five months each year vegetation ceases entirely, the waters are locked in ice, and the temperature frequently sinks far below the zero of the Fahrenheit thermometer. Imagine the thin-skinned, furless animal man subsisting in such a climate. Extinguish his fires, banish his clothing, blot out the habitations that deck the civilized landscape. How long would the puny race survive? But these are not products of nature, they are products of *art*, the wages of thought — fruits of the intellect.

When a well-clothed philosopher on a bitter winter's night sits in a warm room well lighted for his purpose and writes on paper with pen and ink, in the arbitrary characters of a highly developed language, the statement that civilization is the result of natural laws and that man's duty is to let nature alone so that untrammeled it may work out a higher civilization, he simply ignores every circumstance of his existence and deliberately closes his eyes to every fact within the range of his faculties. If man had acted upon his theory, there would have been no civilization and our philosopher would have remained a troglodyte.

But how shall we distinguish this human, or anthropic, method from the method of nature? Simply by reversing all the definitions. Art is the antithesis of nature. If we call one the natural method, we must call the other the artificial method. If nature's process is rightly named natural selection, man's process is artificial selection. The survival of the fittest is simply the survival of the strong, which implies, and might as well be called, the destruction of the weak. And if nature progresses through the destruction of the weak, man progresses through the *protection* of the weak. This is the essential distinction.

In human society the psychic power has operated to secure the protection of the weak in two distinct ways: first, by increasing the supply of the necessities of life, and, second, by preventing the destruction of life through the enemies of man. The immediate instrumentality through which the first of these processes is carried on is art, the product of invention. The second process takes place through the establishment of positive institutions. . . .

The truth thus comes forth from a rational study of nature and human society that social progress has been due only in very slight degree to natural evolution as accomplished through the survival of the fittest, and its chief success has resulted from the reduction of competition in the struggle for existence and the protection of the weaker members. Such competition, insofar as it has been permitted to operate, has tended to lower the standard of the fittest and to check advancement. It is not, of course, claimed that the natural method has ever been fully overcome. It has always operated, and still operates, powerfully in many ways. It has been chiefly in the simpler departments of physical and mechanical phenomena that the psychic, or anthropic, method has superseded it. The inventive arts have been the result. Vital forces have yielded to some extent to the influence of mind in bringing about improved stocks of animals and vegetables, and even certain social laws have come under rational control through the establishment of institutions.

Still, every step in this progress has been contested. It was not enough that the intellect was feeble and ill-fitted to grapple with such problems. It was not enough that ignorance of nature's laws should cause unnumbered failures. A still stronger barrier was presented by the intellect itself in the form of positive error embodied in philosophy. . . . Philosophy has always been negative and nihilistic, and has steadily antagonized the common sense of mankind. It is only quite recently that there has come into existence anything like a truly *positive* philosophy, *i.e.,* a philosophy of *action.* The intellectual power of enlightened man has at length become sufficient to grasp the problems of social life. A large body of truth has been accumulated by which to be guided in their solution.

Positive error in the drawing of false conclusions from established facts is now the chief obstacle. Rational interpretation has come to prevail in all the lower departments of phenomena. It is chiefly in the complex departments of psychic and social action that error still holds sway. Nothing remains to be done but to apply the established canons of science to these higher fields of activity. Here there is still competition. Here the weaker still go to the wall. Here the strong are still the fittest to survive. Here nature still practises her costly selection which always involves the destruction of the defenseless. The demand is for still further reduction of competition, still greater interference with the operations of natural forces, still more complete control of the laws of nature, and still more absolute supremacy of the psychic over the natural method of evolution.

These ends will be secured in proportion as the true nature of mind is understood. When nature comes to be regarded as passive and man as active, instead of the reverse as now, when human action is recognized as the most important of all forms of action, and when the power of the human intellect over vital, psychic and social phenomena is practically conceded, then, and then only, can man justly claim to have risen out of the animal and fully to have entered the human stage of development.

1885

9.

Mariana Griswold Van Rensselaer: Church Architecture in America

Mrs. Schuyler Van Rensselaer, who had been educated by private tutors and through foreign travel, turned her attention to literature and the study of art upon the death of her husband in 1884. Mrs. Van Rensselaer produced a long series of articles and books on art and architecture, both American and European, her Book of American Figure Painters *appearing in 1886. Her works, expressive of a new American interest in art in the 1880s and 1890s, encouraged the development of purely American art forms. In the following article Mrs. Van Rensselaer decried the vogue of imitating medieval styles that was still apparent in the design of American churches.*

Source: *Century Magazine,* January 1885.

It is still too general an idea that his ecclesiastical work must be the easiest part of a modern architect's activity. It is still too commonly supposed that the medieval styles offer him a multitude of models which, exactly copied or but slightly modified, will answer all his purposes, that he must be able to imitate discreetly and skillfully, but need give no thought to the fundamental problems of his art, since these were fully worked out in ages past and settled once for all. Such belief in the present adequacy of medieval precedents — a belief which awhile ago was almost superstitious in its protests against the use of any other style or the desirability of modern innovation — is, I need hardly say, of but recent origin.

Gothic art died with the dying supremacy of the Catholic Church, and till our own day no one wished for its reanimation. As the various classic fashions succeeded one another, each in its turn was used for all ecclesiastical as well as for all secular constructions. In the seventeenth century the genius of Wren brought practical fitness, and often structural though not decorative beauty, out of the elements then in favor. Later on, when the pseudo-Greek temple was in vogue, no good end was attained. And then came the "Gothic Revival," bringing change where change was sorely needed. Its results, however, were not of unmixed good, for reason and common sense were ostracized from its early counsels. The newly recognized beauty of medieval work so intoxicated a generation that had been fed on the dry pabulum of classic nullities that its eyes were blinded to the change which had come over practical requirements, or else persuaded that this change was a misfortune to be deplored and disregarded.

Nor, in its new-found desire for the "ecclesiastical feeling" so evident in Gothic art, did it reflect upon the necessity of truth in architectural expression — a necessity which robs "ecclesiastical feeling" of all but a dilettante, archaeologic, superficially aesthetic value, unless it is the unforced voice of the actual devotional mood of those who build. Many of Wren's churches were far more appropriate to current needs than those of earlier days; but his inventions were despised and a distinct backward step was taken, the pernicious doctrine being taught that architectural "art" need not concern itself with matters of fitness and veracity.

For a while we in America accepted this view of church building almost as implicitly as did our English brethren, and with less excuse than they; for where the Anglican church is preeminent, far less change has come in practical or expressional necessities than where, as is the case with us, a majority of the people belong to the extremer Protestant communions. For a while we believed in the entire adequacy of an imitated medieval art to meet needs which in truth are modern in the full sense of the word. But of late this belief, though still, as I have said, both widespread and strong, is neither so universal nor so implicit as it was; and we may rejoice to note the fact. Not that Gothic art is of necessity to be abandoned for some other; and not that we need wish for that "new style" for which the lovers of mere novelty are longing. "Style" is not the question at all — only the rational or irra-

tional use of whatever style may be selected.

The thing that is most important and that will best justify a hopeful looking toward the future is — here, no less than in any other branch of architecture — that we should reason about our work, should accept nothing on the mere authority of ancient precedent or for the mere sake of artistic charm. If we do thus accept a style, we shall never work with it in a really vigorous way. We shall be copyists only, and, to judge by the average of modern work, not such successful copyists that even superficial beauty will result. But if our art is founded on reason and intelligent common sense, we shall learn to do good work at least. Whether it will eventually grow to be very beautiful work or not will depend upon the gifts with which nature sees fit to endow us. But neither fundamental excellence nor satisfying, vital beauty can grow from any other basis.

But perhaps I should stop a moment now to prove that our needs are indeed quite different from those of Gothic-building generations.

It will hardly be questioned that the medieval architect was inspired not by the *fond*, the basis, the essentials of Christianity, not by those things which the simplest of Protestant sects may claim to hold in common with the church of Hildebrand, but by the specialized demands of this church. If we know the plan and features of a medieval structure, we know how accurately they were fitted to the performance of the Catholic ritual. If we follow the course of architectural history, we know how they grew up and grouped themselves as that ritual expanded and crystallized into shape, absorbing a thousand beliefs, traditions, rites, and ceremonies with which fundamental Christianity had little enough to do and which Protestantism has cast aside.

It is true that such a church may be used for Protestant forms of worship. But we can say as much of any spacious interior;

and the plea of partial appropriateness, which is valid with regard to existent and venerable structures, strikes below the mark when new creations are in question.

With those sects — dominant, as I have said, with us — that have abandoned ritual altogether, the whole character and whole intention of the service have been changed. It is no longer a sacrifice offered for the people by its priests, no longer a gorgeous ceremonial to be but vaguely seen, no longer an elaborate musical rite in a stranger tongue, but a common act in which the laity take a far more direct and personal share, and of which every word must be caught by all. It needs no chapels for a populous pantheon of saints; no spacious chancel for a numerous clergy; no broad aisles for processional pomp and show; and even the altar must change in place as well as purport when it is called a communion table. Moreover — and this is no unimportant point — that love of physical comfort which is a peculiarly modern characteristic asks for stationary cushioned seats, for unobstructed sight and sound, for warmth and ventilation, and for thorough lighting both by day and night. Do such needs get rational satisfaction from the old cathedral type, or even from that of the English parish church of other days?

And it is the same with regard to our expressional necessities. The medieval architect expressed not some fundamental sentiment common to Christianity as a whole but the special sentiments of its medieval phase, the peculiar mental mood and social state to which those sentiments owed their birth. The church was then the one great social fact and influence that ruled mankind with undisputed sway. It inspired, demanded, and absorbed all the activity of man's more peaceful moods; took the entire tribute not only of his heart but of his mind and hand and purse. And it absorbed nothing more wholly than art. In its cathedrals was expressed all that we now express in our public buildings, our charitable institutions, our civic adornments, and our sumptuous private homes. Into its treasuries went all those minor works which are now dispersed to a myriad secular ends. Hence the size and richness, the pomp and splendor, the magnificence in effect and the lavish care in detail of a medieval sanctuary.

But today we have no "church" in the same sense of the word. We have a number of different communions, banded together for the simple purposes of common worship and moral teaching, which are without direct secular influence or importance, and absorb but a part of our mental activity, our artistic energy, or our superabundant wealth. Consider, too, the devotional temper of medieval men. Consider their blind unreasoning faith in a thousand things we have long since questioned and denied; consider their mysticism, their love of symbolism and allegory, their passion for the gloomy, the obscure, the terrible, the grotesque, the vague, intangible, vast, and supersensual. Is this the devotional attitude of our time? Can their huge interiors, their vanishing perspectives, their soaring vaults, their dim religious light, their wealth of symbolic detail, their throngs of forgotten saints, their expression of the insignificance of the individual and the supremacy of the priesthood, their testimony that man should approach his Maker through the medium of a sumptuous allegoric ceremonial — can these things be in harmony with the mood a Protestant brings to the house of God today?

I do not forget the profound emotion that an ancient church must still excite in any susceptible breast. We need not try to analyze it at the moment; but when our future building is in question, then we must. Then we must ask ourselves how much of this emotion is really religious, how much artistic or historic in its promptings; and further, how much of its really religious portion is genuine and personal, how much sympathetic and imaginative. We must ask whether such a structure would be the natural result if our own needs and minds and hearts were given full and true expression.

We are gradually groping our way, I think, to a perception of these facts and a belief that we should respect them in our practice. Already we have acknowledged that in practical ways the ancient ecclesiastical type is not so entirely adequate as we once supposed. And if we do not so definitely question its expressional fitness, at least we no longer strictly limit the architect thereto in his search for "ecclesiastical feeling." Very rightly we demand that such feeling should exist, and neither unnaturally nor irrationally we believe that it may be wrought through the adaptation of some medieval mode more easily than in any other way. Perhaps it would be too much to expect that as free an adaptation as is necessary should as yet be within the power of our artists to accomplish or of our public to desire.

Perhaps we should be unduly impatient did we feel surprise at the illogical attempts which are so often made by the architect, so often prescribed and not merely tolerated by those from whom he holds commission, attempts to secure a quite new type of interior, and at the same time to preserve the general exterior effect and all the decorative detail of the ancient type. Perhaps only re-peated unsuccessful efforts will suffice to prove how illogical they are, how illogical it is to disassociate the practical from the expressional, artistic side of any art; how foolish to forget that the charm of Gothic was not abstract and superficial but resulted naturally from convenient structural dispositions and the true expressional impulse of its own day and land.

The problem our architects here have before them is as novel as it is difficult and important. Nothing just like it was ever proposed before, since other generations built naively, and we must build self-consciously, and distracted by the very richness of the legacy they have left us. It would be idle to hope that any one man or any one generation of men could fully master such a task. But it will be treacherous if any shirks his quota of the work. Each must do his little part, for it is only thus that architecture ever grows. Each must study his problem from the center outward and not from the outside in, settling first the bones and sinews of his structure and then trying to fit them with a true integument of beauty. This may well draw its inspiration from medieval precedents; but, even so, it will be something very different from what we most often find today, a mere patchwork of attractive but mendacious shreds stripped from the trunk and limbs of an ancient body quite unlike the new.

———————◆———————

Form follows function.
Louis Henry Sullivan

10.

Louis Sullivan: Characteristics and Tendencies of American Architecture

Louis Sullivan early developed a dislike for the prevalent Gothic style of architecture, which he dubbed "Gothic in its pantalettes." His work with Richard Hunt and with Major William Le Baron Jenney (originator of skeletal construction), as well as study at the prestigious École des Beaux-Arts in Paris, convinced Sullivan that he must find for architecture a rule of universal applicability. When Sullivan, at the age of twenty-nine and a partner of famed Chicago architect Dankmar Adler, delivered the following address to the Western Association of Architects in St. Louis, he had already worked out a solution to the problem of forming national style. The speech was given two years before the design of Chicago's famous Auditorium Theater (1887, renovated 1967) that first brought him national attention.

Source: *The Inland Architect and Builder,* November 1885, pp. 58-59.

Many who have commented upon the practice of architecture in this country have regarded the absence of a style, distinctively American, as both strange and deplorable; and with a view to betterment they have advanced theories as to the nature, and immediate realization, of such a style that evidence a lack of insight equally strange and deplorable. These theories have been for the greater part suggested by the feelings awakened in contemplating the matured beauty of Old World art, and imply a grafting or transplanting process. They have been proved empirical by the sufficient logic of time; their advocates having ignored the complex fact that, like a new species of any class, a national style must be a growth, that slow and gradual assimilation of nutriment and a struggle against obstacles are necessary adjuncts to the purblind processes of growth, and that the resultant structure can bear only a chemical or metaphysical resemblance to the materials on which it has been nurtured.

We will, therefore, for the purposes of this paper, disregard these dreams of a Minerva-like architectural splendor springing full-formed into being, and look rather for the early signs of a spontaneous architectural feeling arising in sympathy with the emotions latent or conspicuous in our people.

It is reasonable to believe than an unconquered country, peopled by colonization and natural increase, may bear in its younger and its coming generations a race whose birthright, implying freedom to receive and assimilate impressions, shall nurture emotions of rare quality and of a fruitfulness commensurate with the energy in an unexhausted soil.

It would be erroneous to assume that there will be no evidence of the activity of such emotions until, as a large accumulation, they break all bonds asunder. The individual is from day to day seeking expedients by means of which to shape his immediate surroundings into a realization of his desires, and we may assume it to be quite probable that the initial impelling force, operating through the individual, has already in many cases produced significant and valuable results. These results, if not thoroughly typical, must have in them much that is eminently characteristic, and that bear the stamp of internal origin.

To test this hypothesis we have therefore but to look into the daily life of our architecture, and, in the complexion of its many fleeting phases, seek here and there for instances, some perhaps almost trivial, in which the existence of spontaneous and characteristic emotional feeling may be detected. Sometimes we shall find this impulse appearing as an element of warmth, tingeing scholastic formalism; sometimes as a seemingly paradoxical inspiration in the works of the uncultivated. We may certainly expect to meet with it in the efforts of those upon whose imagination the chromatic eloquence of words and of music have taken strong holds. And above all, we are to look for it in the creations of the gifted ones whose souls are finely attuned to the touching beauty of nature and of humanity.

To an apprehension of this subtle element, we may be happily guided by the suggestions of analogy. Our recent American literature comes aptly to this use. Glancing through its focusing substance as through the lens of a camera, we may perceive an image of the abstraction we seek, and by an extension of the process, we may fix an impression of its form and texture, to be developed at will.

Our literature is the only phase of our national art that has been accorded serious recognition, at home and abroad. The noticeable qualities of its present phases seem to be: excessive regard for minute detail; painful self-consciousness of finish; timidity and embarrassment in the delineation of all but the well-behaved and docile emotions; and a tacit fiction as to the passions — all beautifully executed with much patient, earnest labor, and diplomatically tempered to the understanding.

Exquisite, but not virile, our latter-day literature illustrates quite emphatically the quality of our tentative and provisional culture, which must ere long throw off these seedling leaves, when a higher temperature shall infuse glowing vitality into root and stem, and exuberant foliation give more certain assurance of the coming flower of our soil. Our literature, and in fact all that which we Americans complacently call our art, is too much a matter of heart and fingers, and too little an offspring of brain and soul. One must indeed have faith in the processes of nature to prophesy order eventuating upon so strange a chaos of luxuries. But to this end, transmitted knowledge must gradually be supplemented by the fresh impressions of the senses and the sensibilities, the fund so accumulated yielding richly of its own increase. This supplemental acquisition must of necessity be of slow growth, for we have all been educated to a dependence upon our artistic inheritance.

Our art is for the day, is suited to the day, and will also change as the day changes. The law of variation is an ever present force, and coordination is its goal. The first step toward a new order of things is accomplished when there appear minds receiving and assimilating fresh impressions, reaching new conclusions, and acting upon them. By this sign, we may know that such a movement is already upon us, and by the aid of the indicated literary analogy we may follow its erratic tendencies, and note its increase in strength and individuality; we may see the germ of poetry which each man has within him slowly awakening into life, and may feel the presence of an American romanticism.

This romanticism is, in the main, also exquisite but not virile. It seeks to touch all things with softened hand. Under the influence of its warmth of feeling, hard lines flow into graceful curves, angularities disappear in a mystical blending of surfaces.

One by one the completed styles of foreign climes are passing under this hand, each in turn being quietly divested of its local charm, and clothed in a sentiment and mannerism unmistakably our own. Power laments, meanwhile, at the feet of a modern Omphale, his voice attuned to the domestic hum of the times.

Appreciation of the beauties of this romanticism is to some extent dependent upon the verbal explanation and comment of its exponents. A knowledge of their vocabulary is often of assistance in disclosing softness and refinement in many primitive expedients and revealing beauty in barren places. Familiarity with the current phraseology of the allied arts is also useful in assisting the student to a comprehension of many things apparently incomprehensible. Metaphor and simile are rampant in this connection, a well-chosen word often serving to justify an architectural absurdity.

But overloaded as is this fabric of impulse with florid and complicated intertwinings of affection, when we examine the material thereof, we find it excellent and valuable.

Searching critically among the works executed in this feeling, we note in the varying examples, and indeed in parts of the same structure, a curious *mélange* of super-sentimentalisms. Conspicuous at first glance, in some an offensive simplicity, in others a highly wrought charlatanism; further, we perceive ingenuity in device, or superb flow of spirits, all more or less leavened with stubborn common sense. After such an investigation, we may gladly become convinced that behind a somewhat uncertain vision resides a marvelous instinct.

National sensitiveness and pride, conjoined with fertility of resource, will aid as active stimuli in the development of this instinct toward a more rational and organic mode of expression, leading through many reactions to a higher sphere of artistic development.

We are now in the primary department, vaguely endeavoring to form a plastic alphabet by means of which to identify our beliefs. Progress in this respect has been very slow and results meager; for our beliefs have still within them too much of uncertainty and diffidence to take rank as convictions. Without these latter a sufficient creating power is lacking. The formation of an alphabet and the simplest combinations of its terms are matters of much importance; and easy progress in this respect is seriously impeded by complications of thought. To look at things simply and clearly is quite easy, until counterinfluences are set at work; then comes a struggle for survival, which now and then is successful, the result being an addition, however small, to our stock of elementary forms.

The ability to develop elementary ideas organically is not conspicuous in our profession. In this respect, the architect is inferior to the businessman and financier, whose capacity to expand a simple congenial idea, once fixed, into subtle, manifold, and consistent ramifications is admirable, and a shining example which we have often ignored, creating thereby an undesirable impression.

This view leads us on to a consideration of the element of power. Until this element is widely introduced into our work, giving it the impress of brilliancy, intuition, and great depth of feeling, that work, exhaustively considered, will remain but little more than a temporary expedient.

The presence of power, as a mental characteristic in one class of our people, augurs well for the belief that it may pervade our ranks. The beginnings of power are usually so crude and harsh as to be revolting to a refined taste, and hence it is instinctively shunned; but once subtilized, flushed with emotion and guided by clear insight, it is a worker of miracles. Responsive to its ardent wooings, nature yields up her poetic secrets.

We surely have in us the germ of artistic greatness, no people on earth possessing more of innate poetic feeling, more of ideality, greater capacity to adore the beautiful than our own people; but architects as a professional class have held it more expedient to maintain the traditions of their culture than to promulgate vitalizing thought. Here then we are weak; and should sentiment gain a pronounced ascendency, we may remain weak.

On us rests partially the responsibility, and partially on the public. We have at times individually sought to lead the public, when we more wisely should have followed it; and have, as a body, often followed, when, with beneficent results we could have led. While we may compromise for a time, through a process of local adaptation, no architectural style can become a finality that runs counter to popular feeling. The desire at once to follow and to lead the public should be the initial attitude of our profession toward the formation of a national style; for while we conduct the technical operations, the shaping and controlling process is mainly in the hands of the public who are constantly keeping us within bounds. We cannot wholly escape this control while we are without a national architecture fully representing the wishes of the public, and ministering to its conceptions of the beautiful and the useful. This can evidently not come to pass forthwith, for the public itself can only partially and imperfectly state its wants.

Responding readily, however, to the intuition of those who anticipate its desires, it accepts provisionally year by year all the satisfaction it can get; so that while one recognized style after another shall pass through our hands to be tried and finally rejected in the search for permanent satisfaction, a modified residuum from each will doubtless be added to a fund representing our growth in emotional and spiritual wealth. The progress of this growth toward consummation in a national style involves the lives of many generations, and need be of but little practical concern to us of today. We work at short range and for immediate results. Perhaps, however, there would be infused into our profession an abiding *esprit de corps,* should consideration of this subject and its associated themes lead to a substantial agreement upon our status, our tendencies, and our policy.

If the conclusions set forth in this paper be accepted as correct, it becomes clearly evident, however, that the formative beginnings of this national style, now in progress, are of the utmost immediate interest to us, in part through feelings of patriotism, in part because of a surmise that those who approach most nearly in the substance of their work and administration to the qualities inherent to our race and potential to a national style, will come nearest to the hearts of our people.

Harassed though the architect may be by the cares and responsibilities of his daily life, there exists nevertheless within him, in the midst of this turmoil, an insuppressible yearning toward ideals. These delicate promptings should be both protected and nourished, that, like the flowering plants springing by the sun's gentle persuasion from little seeds buried in the coarser elements of the soil, they also, because of the warmth of human feeling, may bloom at times by the wayside, yielding refreshing odors and the joy of color to the plodding wayfarer.

The soft beams of the full-orbed moon fall with pathetic caress upon the slumbering life of the world; paling with the dawn, her tender vigil ended, she melts into the infinite depths when the ruddy herald of day proudly summons the workers. So does the soul watch over its greater ideals until the thrilling radiance of power shall awaken them to action.

Ideal thought and effective action should so compose the vital substance of our works that they may live, with us and after us, as a record of our fitness, and a memorial of the good we may have done. Then, in the affluence of time, when a rich burden of aspiring verdure may flourish in the undulating fields of thought, wrought into fertility through the bounty of nature and the energy of the race, the mellowed spontaneity of a national style reaching its full and perfect fruition shall have come from out the very treasury of nature.

11.

George Washington Cable: The Negro Freedman in American Society

After serving in the Confederate Army during the Civil War, George Washington Cable wrote several romantic novels about the South, of which Old Creole Days *is the most famous. His knowledge of Southern life led him to adopt positions on social and political questions that made his fellow Southerners resent him. One nonfiction work that was especially unpopular in the South was a collection of papers published under the title* The Silent South *(1885). Its publication aroused such hostility that Cable moved his family to Massachusetts. The first chapter in the book, "The Freedman's Case in Equity," was a plea for just treatment of the Negro. A portion of it is reprinted below.*

Source: *The Silent South,* New York, 1885, pp. 1-38.

THE GREATEST SOCIAL PROBLEM before the American people today is, as it has been for a hundred years, the presence among us of the Negro.

No comparable entanglement was ever drawn round itself by any other modern nation with so serene a disregard of its ultimate issue, or with a more distinct national responsibility. The African slave was brought here by cruel force and with everybody's consent except his own. Everywhere the practice was favored as a measure of common aggrandizement. When a few men and women protested, they were mobbed in the public interest, with the public consent. There rests, therefore, a moral responsibility on the whole nation never to lose sight of the results of African-American slavery until they cease to work mischief and injustice.

It is true these responsibilities may not fall everywhere with the same weight; but they are nowhere entirely removed. The original seed of trouble was sown with the full knowledge and consent of the nation. The nation was to blame; and so long as evils spring from it, their correction must be the nation's duty.

The late Southern slave has within two decades risen from slavery to freedom, from freedom to citizenship, passed on into political ascendancy, and fallen again from that eminence. The amended Constitution holds him up in his new political rights as well as a mere constitution can. On the other hand, certain enactments of Congress, trying to reach further, have lately been made void by the highest court of the nation. And another thing has happened. The popular mind in the old free states, weary of strife at arm's length, bewildered by its complications, vexed by many a blunder, eager to turn to the cure of other evils, and even tinctured by that race feeling whose grosser excesses it would so gladly see suppressed, has retreated from its uncomfortable dictational attitude and thrown the whole matter over to the states of the South. Here it rests, no longer a main party issue but a group of questions which are to be settled by each of these states separately in the light of simple equity and morals, and which the genius of American government does not admit of being forced upon them from beyond their borders. Thus the whole question, become secondary in party contest, has yet reached a period of supreme importance. . . .

We need to go back to the roots of things and study closely, analytically, the origin, the present foundation, the rationality, the rightness of those sentiments surviving in us which prompt an attitude qualifying in any way peculiarly the black man's liberty among us. Such a treatment will be less abundant in incident, less picturesque; but it will be more thorough.

First, then, what are these sentiments? Foremost among them stands the idea that he is of necessity an alien. He was brought to our shores a naked, brutish, unclean, captive, pagan savage, to be and remain a kind of connecting link between man and the beasts of burden. The great changes to result from his contact with a superb race of masters were not taken into account. As a social factor he was intended to be as purely zero as the brute at the other end of his plowline. The occasional mingling of his blood with that of the white man worked

no change in the sentiment: one, two, four, eight, multiplied upon or divided into zero, still gave zero for the result.

Generations of American nativity made no difference; his children and children's children were born in sight of our door, yet the old notion held fast. He increased to vast numbers, but it never wavered. He accepted our dress, language, religion, all the fundamentals of our civilization, and became forever expatriated from his own land; still he remained, to us, an alien. Our sentiment went blind. It did not see that gradually, here by force and there by choice, he was fulfilling a host of conditions that earned at least a solemn moral right to that naturalization which no one at first had dreamed of giving him. Frequently he even bought back the freedom of which he had been robbed, became a taxpayer, and at times an educator of his children at his own expense; but the old idea of alienism passed laws to banish him, his wife, and children by thousands from the state, and threw him into loathsome jails as a common felon for returning to this native land.

It will be wise to remember that these were the acts of an enlightened, God-fearing people, the great mass of whom have passed beyond all earthly accountability. They were our fathers. I am the son and grandson of slaveholders. These were their faults; posterity will discover ours; but these things must be frankly, fearlessly taken into account if we are ever to understand the true interests of our peculiar state of society.

Why, then, did this notion, that the man of color must always remain an alien, stand so unshaken? We may readily recall how, under ancient systems, he rose, not only to high privileges but often to public station and power. Singularly, with us the trouble lay in a modern principle of liberty. The whole idea of American government rested on all men's equal, inalienable right to secure their life, liberty, and the pursuit of happiness by governments founded in their own consent. Hence, our Southern forefathers, shedding their blood, or ready to shed it, for this principle, yet proposing in equal good conscience to continue holding the American black man and mulatto and quadroon in slavery, had to anchor that conscience, their conduct, and their laws in the conviction that the man of African tincture was, not by his master's arbitrary assertion merely, but by nature and unalterably an alien. . . .

Thus we stood at the close of the Civil War. There were always a few Southerners who did not justify slavery and many who cared nothing whether it was just or not. But what we have described was the general sentiment of good Southern people. There was one modifying sentiment. It related to the slave's spiritual interests. Thousands of pious masters and mistresses flatly broke the shameful laws that stood between their slaves and the Bible. Slavery was right; but religion, they held, was for the alien and menial as well as for the citizen and master. They could be alien and citizen, menial and master, in church as well as out; and they were.

Yet over against this lay another root of today's difficulties. This perpetuation of the alien, menial relation tended to perpetuate the vices that naturally cling to servility, dense ignorance and a hopeless separation from true liberty; and as we could not find it in our minds to blame slavery with this perpetuation, we could only assume as a further axiom that there was, by nature, a disqualifying moral taint in every drop of Negro blood. The testimony of an Irish, German, Italian, French, or Spanish beggar in a court of justice was taken on its merits; but the colored man's was excluded by law wherever it weighed against a white man. The colored man was a prejudged culprit. . . .

All at once the tempest of war snapped off at the ground every one of these arbitrary relations without removing a single one of the sentiments in which they stood rooted. Then, to fortify the freedman in the tenure of his new rights, he was given the ballot. Before this grim fact the notion of alienism, had it been standing alone, might have given way. The idea that slavery was right did begin to crumble almost at once. . . . With like readiness might the old alien relation have given way if we could only, while letting that pass, have held fast by the other old ideas. But they were all bound together.

See our embarrassment. For more than a hundred years we had made these sentiments the absolute essentials to our self-respect. And yet if we clung to them, how could we meet the freedman on equal terms in the political field? Even to lead would not compensate us; for the fundamental profession of American politics is that the leader is servant to his followers. It was too much. The ex-master and ex-slave — the quarterdeck and the forecastle, as it were — could not come together. But neither could the American mind tolerate a continuance of martial law. The agonies of Reconstruction followed.

The vote, after all, was a secondary point, and the robbery and bribery on one side, and whipping and killing on the other, were but huge accidents of the situation. The two main questions were really these: on the freedman's side, how to establish republican state government under the same recognition of his rights that the rest of Christendom accorded him; and on the former master's side, how to get back to the old semblance of republican state government, and — allowing that the freedman was *de facto* a voter — still to maintain a purely arbitrary superiority of all whites over all blacks and a purely arbitrary equality of all blacks among themselves as an alien, menial, and dangerous class.

Exceptionally here and there someone in the master caste did throw off the old and accept the new ideas, and, if he would allow it, was instantly claimed as a leader by the newly liberated thousands around him. But just as promptly the old master race branded him also an alien reprobate, and in ninety-nine cases out of a hundred, if he had not already done so, he soon began to confirm by his actions the brand on his cheek. However, we need give no history here of the dreadful episode of Reconstruction. Under an experimental truce its issues rest today upon the pledge of the wiser leaders of the master class: Let us but remove the hireling demagogue, and we will see to it that the freedman is accorded a practical, complete, and cordial recognition of his equality with the white man before the law. As far as there has been any understanding at all, it is not that the originally desired ends of Reconstruction have been abandoned but that the men of North and South have agreed upon a new, gentle, and peaceable method for reaching them; that, without change as to the ends in view, compulsory reconstruction has been set aside and a voluntary reconstruction is on trial.

It is the fashion to say we paused to let the "feelings engendered by the war" pass away, and that they are passing. But let not these truths lead us into error. The sentiments we have been analyzing, and upon which we saw the old compulsory reconstruction go hard aground — these are not the "feelings engendered by the war." We must disentangle them from the "feelings engendered by the war," and by Reconstruction. They are older than either. But for them slavery would have perished of itself, and emancipation and reconstruction been peaceful revolutions.

Indeed, as between master and slave, the "feelings engendered by the war," are too trivial, or at least were too short-lived, to demand our present notice. One relation and feeling the war destroyed — the patriarchal tie and its often really tender and benevolent sentiment of dependence and pro-

tection. When the slave became a freedman, the sentiment of alienism became for the first time complete. The abandonment of this relation was not one-sided; the slave, even before the master, renounced it. Countless times, since Reconstruction began, the master has tried, in what he believed to be everybody's interest, to play on that old sentiment. But he found it a harp without strings. The freedman could not formulate but he could see all our old ideas of autocracy and subserviency, of master and menial, of an arbitrarily fixed class to guide and rule, and another to be guided and ruled. He rejected the overture.

The old master, his well-meant condescensions slighted, turned away estranged, and justified himself in passively withholding that simpler protection without patronage which any one American citizen, however exalted, owes to any other, however humble. Could the freedman in the bitterest of those days have consented to throw himself upon just that one old relation, he could have found a physical security for himself and his house such as could not, after years of effort, be given him by constitutional amendments, Congress, United States marshals, regiments of regulars, and ships of war. But he could not; the very nobility of the civilization that had held him in slavery had made him too much a man to go back to that shelter; and by his manly neglect to do so he has proved to us who once ruled over him that, be his relative standing among the races of men what it may, he is worthy to be free.

To be a free man is his still distant goal. Twice he has been a freedman. In the days of compulsory reconstruction he was freed in the presence of his master by that master's victorious foe. In these days of voluntary reconstruction he is virtually freed by the consent of his master, but the master retaining the exclusive right to define the bounds of his freedom. Many everywhere have taken up the idea that this state of affairs is the end to be desired and the end actually sought in Reconstruction as handed over to the states. I do not charge such folly to the best intelligence of any American community; but I cannot ignore my own knowledge that the average thought of some regions rises to no better idea of the issue.

The belief is all too common that the nation, having aimed at a wrong result and missed, has left us of the Southern states to get now such other result as we think best. I say this belief is not universal. There are those among us who see that America has no room for a state of society which makes its lower classes harmless by abridging their liberties, or, as one of the favored class lately said to me, has "got 'em so they don't give no trouble." There is a growing number who see that the one thing we cannot afford to tolerate at large is a class of people less than citizens; and that every interest in the land demands that the freedman be free to become in all things, as far as his own personal gifts will lift and sustain him, the same sort of American citizen he would be if, with the same intellectual and moral caliber, he were white.

Thus we reach the ultimate question of fact. Are the freedman's liberties suffering any real abridgment? The answer is easy. The letter of the laws, with a few exceptions, recognizes him as entitled to every right of an American citizen; and to some it may seem unimportant that there is scarcely one public relation of life in the South where he is not arbitrarily and unlawfully compelled to hold toward the white man the attitude of an alien, a menial, and a probable reprobate, by reason of his race and color. One of the marvels of future history will be that it was counted a small matter, by a majority of our nation, for 6 million people within it, made by its own decree a component part of it, to be subjected to a system of oppression so rank that nothing could make it seem small except the fact that they had already been ground under it for a century and a half.

Examine it. It proffers to the freedman a certain security of life and property, and then holds the respect of the community, that dearest of earthly boons, beyond his attainment. It gives him certain guarantees against thieves and robbers, and then holds him under the unearned contumely of the mass of good men and women. It acknowledges in constitutions and statutes his title to an American's freedom and aspirations, and then in daily practice heaps upon him in every public place the most odious distinctions, without giving ear to the humblest plea concerning mental or moral character. It spurns his ambition, tramples upon his languishing self-respect, and indignantly refuses to let him either buy with money, or earn by any excellence of inner life or outward behavior, the most momentary immunity from these public indignities even for his wife and daughters. Need we cram these pages with facts in evidence, as if these were charges denied and requiring to be proven? They are simply the present avowed and defended state of affairs peeled of its exteriors.

Nothing but the habit, generations old, of enduring it could make it endurable by men not in actual slavery. Were we whites of the South to remain every way as we are, and our 6 million blacks to give place to any sort of whites exactly their equals, man for man, in mind, morals, and wealth, provided only that they had tasted two years of American freedom, and were this same system of tyrannies attempted upon them, there would be as bloody an uprising as this continent has ever seen. We can say this quietly. There is not a scruple's weight of present danger. These 6 million freedmen are dominated by 9 million whites, immeasurably stronger than they, backed by the virtual consent of 30-odd million more. Indeed, nothing but the habit of oppression could make such oppression possible to a people of the intelligence and virtue of our Southern whites, and the invitation to practise it on millions of any other than the children of their former slaves would be spurned with a noble indignation.

Suppose, for a moment, the tables turned. Suppose the courts of our Southern states, while changing no laws requiring the impaneling of jurymen without distinction to race, etc., should suddenly begin to draw their thousands of jurymen all black, and well-nigh every one of them counting not only himself but all his race better than any white man. Assuming that their average of intelligence and morals should be not below that of jurymen as now drawn, would a white man, for all that, choose to be tried in one of those courts? Would he suspect nothing? Could one persuade him that his chances of even justice were all they should be or all they would be were the court not evading the law in order to sustain an outrageous distinction against him because of the accidents of his birth? Yet only read white man for black man, and black man for white man, and that — I speak as an eyewitness — has been the practice for years, and is still so today — an actual emasculation, in the case of 6 million people both as plaintiff and defendant, of the right of trial by jury.

In this and other practices the outrage falls upon the freedman. Does it stop there? Far from it. It is the first premise of American principles that whatever elevates the lower stratum of the people lifts all the rest and whatever holds it down holds all down. For twenty years, therefore, the nation has been working to elevate the freedman. It counts this one of the great necessities of the hour. It has poured out its wealth publicly and privately for this purpose. It is confidently hoped that it will soon bestow a royal gift of millions for the reduction of the illiteracy so largely shared by the blacks. Our Southern states are, and for twenty years have been, taxing themselves for the

same end. The private charities alone of the other states have given $20 million in the same good cause. Their colored seminaries, colleges, and normal schools dot our whole Southern country, and furnish our public colored schools with a large part of their teachers.

All this and much more has been or is being done in order that, for the good of himself and everybody else in the land, the colored man may be elevated as quickly as possible from all the debasements of slavery and semi-slavery to the full stature and integrity of citizenship. And it is in the face of all this that the adherent of the old regime stands in the way to every public privilege and place — steamer landing, railway platform, theater, concert hall, art display, public library, public school, courthouse, church, everything — flourishing the hot branding iron of ignominious distinctions. He forbids the freedman to go into the water until *he* is satisfied that he knows how to swim, and, for fear he should learn, hangs millstones about his neck. This is what we are told is a small matter that will settle itself. Yes, like a roosting curse, until the outraged intelligence of the South lifts its indignant protest against this stupid firing into our own ranks.

I say the outraged intelligence of the South, for there are thousands of Southern-born white men and women in the minority in all these places — in churches, courts, schools, libraries, theaters, concert halls, and on steamers and railway carriages — who see the wrong and folly of these things, silently blush for them and withhold their open protests only because their belief is unfortunately stronger in the futility of their counsel than in the power of a just cause. I do not justify their silence; but I affirm their sincerity and their goodly numbers. Of late years, when condemning these evils from the platform in Southern towns, I have repeatedly found that those who I had earlier been told were the men and women in whom the community placed most confidence and pride — they were the ones who, when I had spoken, came forward with warmest hand grasps and expressions of thanks, and pointedly and cordially justified my every utterance. And were they the young South? Not by half. The graybeards of the old times have always been among them, saying in effect, not by any means as converts, but as fellow discoverers, "Whereas we were blind, now we see." . . .

Is the freedman a free man? No. We have considered his position in a land whence nothing can, and no man has a shadow of right to drive him, and where he is being multiplied as only oppression can multiply a people. We have carefully analyzed his relations to the finer and prouder race with which he shares the ownership and citizenship of a region large enough for ten times the number of both. Without accepting one word of his testimony, we have shown that the laws made for his protection against the habits of suspicion and oppression in his late master are being constantly set aside, not for their defects but for such merit as they possess. We have shown that the very natural source of these oppressions is the surviving sentiments of an extinct and now universally execrated institution; sentiments which no intelligent or moral people should harbor a moment after the admission that slavery was a moral mistake. We have shown the outrageousness of these tyrannies in some of their workings,

and how distinctly they antagonize every state and national interest involved in the elevation of the colored race.

Is it not well to have done so? For, I say again, the question has reached a moment of special importance. The South stands on her honor before the clean equities of the issue. It is no longer whether constitutional amendments but whether the eternal principles of justice are violated. And the answer must — it shall — come from the South. And it shall be practical. It will not cost much. We have had a strange experience; the withholding of simple rights has cost much blood; such concessions of them as we have made have never yet cost a drop. The answer is coming.

Is politics in the way? Then let it clear the track or get run over, just as it prefers. But, as I have said over and over to my brethren in the South, I take upon me to say again here, that there is a moral and intellectual intelligence there which is not going to be much longer beguiled out of its moral right of way by questions of political punctilio, but will seek that plane of universal justice and equity which it is every people's duty before God to seek, not along the line of politics — God forbid! — but across it and across it and across it as many times as it may lie across the path, until the whole people of every once slaveholding state can stand up as one man, saying, "Is the freedman a freeman?" and the whole world shall answer, "Yes."

———————————◆———————————

. . . . I hadn't done nothing. But that's always the way; it don't make no difference whether you do right or wrong, a person's conscience ain't got no sense, and just goes for him anyway. If I had a yaller dog that didn't know no more than a person's conscience does I would pison him. It takes up more room than all the rest of a person's insides, and yet ain't no good, nohow. Tom Sawyer he says the same.

SAMUEL L. CLEMENS ("MARK TWAIN"), *Huckleberry Finn*

Elevated railway at Burling Slip, New York; from a stereograph by Charles Bierstadt

TECHNOLOGY AND THE CITY

In 1865, Fitzhugh Ludlow noted, "The property on the northwest corner of Broadway and Chamber Street, now occupied in part by one of Delmonico's restaurants, was purchased by a New York citizen, but lately deceased, for the sum of $1,000: its present value is $125,000." Industry and commerce, technology and architecture combined to make New York the city it is. The rapid transit system began with the 3-mile-long Ninth Avenue El in 1871. By 1885 there were four such lines in Manhattan and the Lexington Avenue line opened in Brooklyn.

The first modern apartment buildings with elevators began to appear in the early 1870s, and the introduction of the electric elevator in 1891 allowed the construction of buildings up to 150 ft. high. The Brooklyn Bridge, which has been taken by many artists — notably Hart Crane in "The Bridge" — as symbolic of the dynamism of America, was opened in 1883. It was the first bridge over the East River, connecting Manhattan and Brooklyn, and was for twenty years the longest suspension bridge in the world.

(Above) Cable cars on Broadway in New York City during the late 1880s; (below) South Street, New York, 1892. Large sailing ships were still used, carrying bulk cargoes along the coast

(Above) View of the old post office in New York during the early 1880s when horse cars were still a primary means of transportation; (below) horse-drawn fire engine

(Above) Brooklyn Bridge over the East River in New York, 1890; (below) the elaborate gate of the Greenwood Cemetery in New York. Its extensive landscaping was widely copied

(Above) Bandit's Roost, 59½ Mulberry St., New York; photograph by Jacob Riis; (below) Hart's Island with unknown dead persons from New York City being shipped to potter's field, 1888

Wanamaker's Department Store in Philadelphia in the early 1880s

Parallel to the development of the city, patterns of life began to take on modern features. Commuting to the city from suburban Brooklyn began to be common in the 1860s, at the same time that the city was growing at an unprecedented rate. The concentration of population in the city created the mass market; the problem of distribution was met as the department store evolved out of the small general or dry-goods store. Public utilities and facilities of various sorts were also made possible by large populations.

(Right) Early Kodak snapshot of a street scene in Washington, 1888; (below) view from the Stotesbury home in the Philadelphia suburbs, 1885

(Above) Public gardens in Boston in the 1880s; (below left) ''I am to be Queen of the May''; from a stereograph by B. W. Kilburn; (below right) ''The Merry Bootblacks''; from a Kilburn stereo taken in Washington during inauguration activities, 1889

Steamboats at the levee in Vicksburg, Miss., 1885

The South needed more than recovery, for it had been economically inferior to the North even before the war. The first requirement for development was money that had to come primarily from the East. Industrialization did not operate in the South as it did elsewhere — there was the resistance of traditional agrarianism; a high proportion of outside capital drew off profit; and the Negroes supplied a class of labor, too dispossessed to be exploited, which automatically filled the lowest stratum and effectively nullified any thought of reform.

Picking cotton in Georgia

Shooting craps on the lower deck of the steamer, "City of St. Louis"

(Above left) Loading ocean vessels on the docks of Savannah, Ga., the largest resin market in the world; (above right) weaving room of a cotton mill in Augusta, Ga.; (below) women working in a cigarette factory in Richmond, Va.; from an engraving for "Harper's Weekly" in 1887

(Top) View of a small resort hotel in Virginia, the "Forest Inn," 1890; (above) servant carrying food from the cookhouse to the main mansion, Tuckahoe Plantation, Virginia, about 1890; (below) convict labor being employed along the levee in Mississippi, about 1890

(Above) Street vendors selling oysters and fish in Charleston, South Carolina; (above right) view of the Tennessee State Capitol, Nashville, Tennessee. The building was designed by William Strickland, and completed after the Civil War; (below) New Orleans

View in an unidentified village in eastern Pennsylvania, 1881

Baking bread in an outdoor oven in the Pennsylvania German country, 1882; (above right) members of the Shaker community at New Lebanon, New York; (below) cutting wheat in Pennsylvania

View down the main street in Concord, Massachusetts;

The same technology which accelerated industrialization in the cities made it possible for fewer and fewer farmers to produce more and more food. Thus a shift in population from rural to urban areas was inevitable; such a shift was continual from 1800, and the proportion of rural population dropped sharply from 80 to 60 percent between 1860 and 1900. But an urban population did not necessarily mean an urban civilization; the culture of rural and small town America, which flourished during this period, persisted as a strong influence on American thought and as an endemic form of nostalgia in later, less simple times.

(Left) Drugstore in Vermont; (below) Great Barrington, Massachusetts, both about 1880

Launching the last clipper at McKay's shipyard, Boston, 1869

(Above) New Bedford after the passing of the whaling era; vacationers watch the nets come in

12.

John Fiske: American Federalism and World Federation

Though his contemporaries considered him an important philosopher and historian, John Fiske is remembered primarily as an ardent defender and popularizer of the theory of evolution over which a bitter fight was waged in intellectual circles in the last years of the nineteenth century. Fiske's enthusiasm for evolutionary theory, which he transformed into a historical theory of inevitable human progress, is evident in the following portion of his article "Manifest Destiny," published in 1885.

Source: *Harper's New Monthly,* March 1885.

WE HAVE SEEN how desirable it is that self-governing groups of men should be enabled to work together in permanent harmony and on a great scale. In this kind of political integration the work of civilization very largely consists. We have seen how in its most primitive form political society is made up of small self-governing groups that are perpetually at war with one another. Now the process of change which we call civilization means quite a number of things, but there is no doubt that it means primarily the gradual substitution of a state of peace for a state of war. This change is the condition precedent for all the other kinds of improvement that are connoted by such a term as "civilization."

Manifestly the development of industry is largely dependent upon the cessation or restriction of warfare; and furthermore, as the industrial phase of civilization slowly supplants the military phase, men's characters undergo, though very slowly, a corresponding change. Men become less inclined to destroy life or to inflict pain; or, to use the popular terminology, which happens to coincide precisely with that of the doctrine of evolution, they become less *brutal* and more *humane.* Obviously, then, the primary phase of the process called civilization is the gen-eral diminution of warfare. But we have seen that a general diminution of warfare is rendered possible only by the union of small political groups into larger groups that are kept together by community of interests, and that can adjust their mutual relations by legal discussion, without coming to blows. . . .

Let us consider . . . to what conclusions the rapidity and unabated steadiness of the increase of the English race in America must lead us as we go on to forecast the future. Carlyle somewhere speaks slightingly of the fact that the Americans double their numbers every twenty years, as if to have 40 million dollar-hunters in the world were any better than to have 20 million dollar-hunters. The implication that Americans are nothing but dollar-hunters, and are thereby distinguishable from the rest of mankind, would not perhaps bear too elaborate scrutiny. But . . . we have been considering the gradual transfer of the preponderance of physical strength from the hands of the war-loving portion of the human race into the hands of the peace-loving portion — into the hands of the dollar-hunters, if you please, but out of the hands of the scalp-hunters. Obviously to double the numbers of a preeminently industrious, peaceful, orderly, and free-thinking community is somewhat to increase the weight in the world of the tendencies that go toward making communities free and orderly and peaceful and industrious. So that, from this point of view, the fact we are speaking of is well worth considering, even for its physical dimensions.

I do not know whether the United States could support a population everywhere as dense as that of Belgium, so I will suppose that, with ordinary improvement in cultivation and in the industrial arts, we might support a population half as dense as that of Belgium, and this is no doubt an extremely moderate supposition. Now a very simple operation in arithmetic will show that this means a population of 1.5 billion, or more than the population of the whole world at the present date. Another very simple operation in arithmetic will show that if we were to go on doubling our numbers even once in every twenty-five years, we should reach that stupendous figure at about the close of the twentieth century, that is, in the days of our great-great-grandchildren. I do not predict any such result, for there are discernible economic reasons for believing that there will be a diminution in the rate of increase. The rate must nevertheless continue to be very great in the absence of such causes as formerly retarded the growth of population in Europe.

Our modern wars are hideous enough, no doubt, but they are short. They are settled with a few heavy blows, and the loss of life and property occasioned by them is but trifling when compared with the awful ruin and desolation wrought by the perpetual and protracted contests of antiquity and of the Middle Ages. Chronic warfare, both private and public, periodic famines, and sweeping pestilences like the Black Death — these were the things which formerly shortened human life and kept down population. In the absence of such causes, and with the abundant capacity of our country

for feeding its people, I think it an extremely moderate statement if we say that by the end of the next century the English race in the United States will number at least 600 or 700 million.

It used to be said that so huge a people as this could not be kept together as a single national aggregate, or, if kept together at all, could only be so by means of a powerful centralized government, like that of ancient Rome under the emperors. I think we are now prepared to see that this is a great mistake. If the Roman Empire could have possessed that political vitality in all its parts which is secured to the United States by the principles of equal representation and of limited state sovereignty, it might well have defied all the shocks which tribally organized barbarism could ever have directed against it. As it was, its strong centralized government did not save it from political disintegration. One of its weakest political features was precisely this, that its strong centralized government was a kind of close corporation, governing a score of provinces in its own interest rather than in the interest of the provincials.

In contrast with such a system as that of the Roman Empire, the skillfully elaborated American system of federalism appears as one of the most important contributions that the English race has made to the general work of civilization. The working out of this feature in our national Constitution by Hamilton and Madison and their associates was the finest specimen of constructive statesmanship that the world has ever seen. Not that these statesmen originated the principle, but they gave form and expression to the principle which was latent in the circumstances under which the group of American colonies had grown up, and which suggested itself so forcibly that the clear vision of these thinkers did not fail to seize upon it as the fundamental principle upon which alone could the affairs of a great people, spreading over a vast continent, be kept in a condition approaching to something like permanent peace.

Stated broadly, so as to acquire somewhat the force of a universal proposition, the principle of federalism is just this: that the people of a state shall have full and entire control of their own domestic affairs, which directly concern them only, and which they will naturally manage with more intelligence and with more zeal than any distant governing body could possibly exercise; but that, as regards matters of common concern between a group of states, a decision shall in every case be reached, not by brutal warfare or by weary diplomacy but by the systematic legislation of a central government which represents both states and people, and whose decisions can always be enforced, if necessary, by the combined physical power of all the states. This principle, in various practical applications, is so familiar to Americans today that we seldom pause to admire it, any more than we stop to admire the air which we breathe or the sun which gives us light and life. Yet I believe that if no other political result than this could today be pointed out as coming from the colonization of America by Englishmen, we should still be justified in regarding that event as one of the most important in the history of mankind. For obviously the principle of federalism, as thus broadly stated, contains within itself the seeds of permanent peace between nations, and to this glorious end I believe it will come in the fullness of time.

And now we may begin to see distinctly what it was that the American government fought for in the late Civil War — a point which at the time was by no means clearly apprehended outside the United States. We used to hear it often said, while that war was going on, that we were fighting not so much for the emancipation of the Negro as for the maintenance of our Federal Union; and I doubt not that to many who were burning to see our country purged of the

folly and iniquity of Negro slavery this may have seemed like taking a low and materialistic view of the case. From the standpoint of universal history it was nevertheless the correct and proper view. The emancipation of the Negro, as an incidental result of the struggle, was no doubt a priceless gain, which was greeted warmly by all right-minded people.

But deeper down than this question, far more subtly interwoven with the innermost fibers of our national well-being, far heavier laden, too, with weighty consequences for the future weal of all mankind, was the question whether this great pacific principle of union, joined with independence, should be overthrown by the first deep-seated social difficulty it had to encounter, or should stand as an example of priceless value to other ages and to other lands. The solution was well worth the effort it cost. There have been many useless wars, but this was not one of them, for, more than most wars that have been, it was fought in the direct interest of peace, and the victory so dearly purchased and so humanely used was an earnest of future peace and happiness for the world.

The object, therefore, for which the American government fought was the perpetual maintenance of that peculiar state of things which the Federal Union had created — a state of things in which, throughout the whole vast territory over which the Union holds sway, questions between states, like questions between individuals, must be settled by legal argument and judicial decisions, and not by wager of battle. Far better to demonstrate this point once for all, at whatever cost, than to be burdened hereafter, like the states of Europe, with frontier fortresses and standing armies and all the barbaric apparatus of mutual suspicion! For so great an end did this most pacific people engage in an obstinate war, and never did any war so thoroughly illustrate how military power may be wielded by a people that has passed entirely from the military into the industrial stage of civilization.

The events falsified all the predictions that were drawn from the contemplation of societies less advanced politically. It was thought that so peaceful a people could not raise a great army on demand; yet within a twelvemonth the government had raised 500,000 men by voluntary enlistment. It was thought that a territory involving military operations at points as far apart as Paris and Moscow could never be thoroughly conquered; yet, in April 1865, the Federal armies might have marched from end to end of the Gulf states without meeting any force to oppose them. It was thought that the maintenance of a great army would beget a military temper in the Americans, and lead to manifestations of Bonapartism — domestic usurpation and foreign aggression; yet the moment the work was done the great army vanished, and a force of 25,000 men was found sufficient for the military needs of the whole country.

It was thought that eleven states which had struggled so hard to escape from the federal tie could not be readmitted to voluntary cooperation in the general government, but must henceforth be held as conquered territory — a most dangerous experiment for any free people to try; yet within a dozen years we find the old federal relations resumed in all their completeness, and the disunion party powerless and discredited in the very states where once it had wrought such mischief.

Such has been the result of the first great attempt to break up the federal Union in America. It is not probable that another attempt can ever be made with anything like an equal chance of success. Here were eleven states, geographically contiguous, governed by groups of men who for half a century had pursued a well-defined policy in common, united among themselves, and marked off from most of the other states by a difference far more deeply rooted in the groundwork of society than any mere economic difference — the difference between slave labor and free labor. These eleven states, moreover, held such an economic relationship with England that they counted upon compelling the naval power of England to be used in their behalf. And, finally, it had not yet been demonstrated that the maintenance of the federal Union was something for which the great mass of the people would cheerfully fight.

Never could the experiment of secession be tried, apparently, under fairer auspices; yet how tremendous the defeat! It was a defeat that wrought conviction — the conviction that no matter how grave the political questions that may arise hereafter, they must be settled in accordance with the legal methods the Constitution has provided, and that no state can be allowed to break the peace. It is the thoroughness of this conviction that has so greatly facilitated the reinstatement of the revolted states in their old federal relations; and the good sense and good faith with which the Southern people, in spite of the chagrin of defeat, have accepted the situation and acted upon it, is something unprecedented in history, and calls for the warmest sympathy and admiration on the part of their brethren of the North.

The federal principle in America has passed through this fearful ordeal and come out stronger than ever, and we trust it will not again be put to so severe a test. But with this principle unimpaired, there is no reason why any further increase of population or of territory should overtask the resources of our government. In the United States of America a century hence we shall therefore doubtless have a political aggregation immeasurably surpassing in power and in dimensions any empire that has as yet existed. . . .

When in America we wish to illustrate in one word the wonderful growth of our so-called Northwestern states, we refer to Chicago, a city of half a million inhabitants standing on a spot which fifty years ago was an uninhabited marsh. In Australia the city of Melbourne was founded in 1837, the year when the present queen of England began to reign, and the state of which it is the capital was hence called Victoria. This city, now just forty-eight years old, has a population half that of Chicago, has a public library of 200,000 volumes, and has a university with at least one professor of worldwide renown.

When we see, by the way, within a period of five years, and at such remote points upon the earth's surface, such erudite and ponderous works in the English language issuing from the press as those of Professor Hearn of Melbourne, of Bishop Colenso of Natal, and of Mr. Hubert Bancroft of San Francisco, even such a little commonplace fact as this is fraught with wonderful significance when we think of all that it implies. Then there is New Zealand, with its climate of perpetual spring, where the English race is now multiplying faster than anywhere else in the world, unless it be in Texas and Minnesota. And there are in the Pacific Ocean many rich and fertile spots where we shall very soon see the same things going on.

It is not necessary to dwell upon such considerations as these. It is enough to point to the general conclusion that the work which the English race began when it colonized North America is destined to go on until every land on the earth's surface that is not already the seat of an old civilization shall become English in its language, in its religion, in its political habits and traditions, and to a predominant extent in the blood of its people. The day is at hand when four-fifths of the human race will trace its pedigree to English forefathers, as four-fifths of the white people in the United States trace their pedigree today. The race thus spread over both hemispheres, and from the rising to the setting sun, will not fail to keep that sovereignty of the sea and that commercial supremacy which it began to acquire when England

first stretched its arm across the Atlantic to the shores of Virginia and Massachusetts.

The language spoken by these great communities will not be sundered into dialects like the language of the ancient Romans, but perpetual intercommunication and the universal habit of reading and writing will preserve its integrity, and the world's business will be transacted by English-speaking people to so great an extent that whatever language any man may have learned in his infancy, he will find it necessary sooner or later to learn to express his thoughts in English. And in this way it is by no means improbable that, as Jacob Grimm long since predicted, the language of Shakespeare will ultimately become the language of mankind.

In view of these considerations as to the stupendous future of the English race, does it not seem very probable that in due course of time Europe, which has learned some valuable lessons from America already, will find it worthwhile to adopt the lesson of federalism in order to do away with the chances of useless warfare which remain so long as its different states own no allegiance to any common authority? War, as we have seen, is with barbarous races both a necessity and a favorite occupation; as long as civilization comes in contact with barbarism it remains a too frequent necessity; but as between civilized and Christian nations it is an absurdity.

For example, we sympathize keenly with wars such as that which Russia has lately concluded for setting free a kindred race and humbling the worthless barbarian who during four centuries has wrought such incalculable damage to the European world. But a sanguinary struggle for the Rhine frontier, between two civilized Christian nations who have each enough work to do in the world without engaging in such a strife as this, will, I am sure, be by and by condemned by the general opinion of mankind. Such questions will have to be settled by discussion in some sort of federal council or parliament if Europe would keep pace with

America in the advance toward universal law and order. All will admit that such a state of things is a great desideratum.

Let us see if it is really quite as utopian as it may seem at the first glance. No doubt the lord who dwelt in Haddon Hall in the fifteenth century would have thought it very absurd if you had told him that within 400 years it would not be necessary for country gentlemen to live in great stone dungeons with little cross-barred windows and loopholes from which to shoot at people going by. Yet today a country gentleman in Massachusetts may sleep securely without locking his front door.

We have not quite done away with robbery and murder, but we have at least made private warfare illegal; we have arrayed public opinion against it to such an extent that the Police Court usually makes short shrift for the misguided man who tries to wreak vengeance on his enemy. Is it too much to hope that by and by we may similarly put public warfare under the ban? I think not. Already in America, as we have seen, it has become customary to deal with questions between states just as we would deal with questions between individuals. This we have seen to be the real purport of American federalism. To have established such a system over one great continent is to have made a very good beginning toward establishing it over the world.

To establish such a system in Europe will no doubt be difficult, for here we have to deal with an immense complication of prejudices, intensified by linguistic and ethnological differences. Nevertheless the pacific pressure exerted upon Europe by America is becoming so great that it will doubtless before long overcome all these obstacles. I refer to the industrial competition between the Old and the New World, which has become so conspicuous within the last ten years. Agriculturally, Minnesota, Nebraska, and Kansas are already formidable competitors with England, France, and Germany;

but this is but the beginning. It is but the first spray from the tremendous wave of economic competition that is gathering in the Mississippi Valley. Presently, as with increase of population, labor grows cheaper in America, the competition in manufactures also will become as keen as it is now beginning to be in agriculture, as the recent industrial history of New England abundantly proves.

Now this economic pressure exerted upon Europe by the United States will very soon become so great that it will be simply impossible for the states of Europe to keep up such military armaments as they are now maintaining. The disparity between the United States, with a standing army of only 25,000 men, and the states of Europe, with their standing armies amounting to 2 or 3 million men, is something that cannot be kept up. The economic competition will become so keen that European armies will have to be disbanded, the swords will have to be turned into plowshares, and thus the victory of the industrial over the military type of civilization will at last become complete.

But to disband the great armies of Europe will necessarily involve the forcing of the great states of Europe into some sort of federal relation, in which congresses will become more frequent, in which the principles of international law will acquire a more definite sanction, and in which the combined physical power of all the states will constitute (as it now does in America) a permanent threat against any state that dares for selfish reasons to break the peace. In some such way as this, I believe, the industrial development of the English race outside of Europe will by and by enforce federalism upon Europe. I do not ignore the difficulties that grow out of differences in language, race, and creed; but we have seen how Switzerland has long since triumphantly surmounted such difficulties on a small scale. To surmount them on a great scale will soon be the political problem of Europe, and it is America which has set the example and indicated the method.

Thus we may foresee in general how, by the gradual concentration of physical power into the hands of the most pacific communities, we may finally succeed in rendering warfare illegal all over the globe. As this process goes on, it may, after many more ages of political experience, become apparent that there is really no reason, in the nature of things, why the whole of mankind should not constitute politically one huge federation, each little group managing its local affairs in entire independence, but relegating all questions of international interest to the decision of one central tribunal supported by the public opinion of the entire human race. I believe that the time will come when such a state of things will exist upon the earth, when it will be possible (with our friends of the Paris dinner party) to speak of the United States as stretching from pole to pole, or with Tennyson to celebrate the "parliament of man and the federation of the world."

Indeed, only when such a state of things has begun to be realized can civilization, as sharply demarcated from barbarism, be said to have fairly begun. Only then can the world be said to have become truly Christian. Many ages of toil and doubt and perplexity will no doubt pass by before such a desideratum is reached. Meanwhile it is pleasant to feel that the dispassionate contemplation of great masses of historical facts goes far toward confirming our faith in this ultimate triumph of good over evil. Our survey began with pictures of horrid slaughter and desolation; it ends with the picture of a world covered with cheerful homesteads, blessed with a Sabbath of perpetual peace.

13.

JOSIAH STRONG: The Superiority of the Anglo-Saxon Race

When Josiah Strong became secretary of the Congregational Home Missionary Society in 1881, he undertook to revise a small manual published by the society. Our Country: Its Possible Future and Its Present Crisis, *published in 1885, contained a forceful statement of his personal philosophy and bore strong evidence of the influence of the Social Darwinist thought that was being popularized in America by William Graham Sumner and John Fiske. The chapter from which the following selection is taken is notable as one of the early projections of the doctrine of American Manifest Destiny onto a worldwide scale.*

Source: *Our Country*, New York, 1885: "The Anglo-Saxon and the World's Future."

EVERY RACE which has deeply impressed itself on the human family has been the representative of some great idea — one or more — which has given direction to the nation's life and form to its civilization. Among the Egyptians this seminal idea was life, among the Persians it was light, among the Hebrews it was purity, among the Greeks it was beauty, among the Romans it was law. The Anglo-Saxon is the representative of two great ideas, which are closely related. One of them is that of civil liberty.

Nearly all of the civil liberty in the world is enjoyed by Anglo-Saxons: the English, the British colonists, and the people of the United States. To some, like the Swiss, it is permitted by the sufferance of their neighbors, others, like the French, have experimented with it; but, in modern times, the peoples whose love of liberty has won it, and whose genius for self-government has preserved it, have been Anglo-Saxons. The noblest races have always been lovers of liberty. That love ran strong in early German blood and has profoundly influenced the institutions of all the branches of the great German family; but it was left for the Anglo-Saxon branch fully to recognize the right of the individual to himself, and formally to declare it the foundation stone of government.

The other great idea of which the Anglo-Saxon is the exponent is that of a pure *spiritual* Christianity. It was no accident that the great Reformation of the sixteenth century originated among a Teutonic rather than a Latin people. It was the fire of liberty burning in the Saxon heart that flamed up against the absolutism of the pope. Speaking roughly, the peoples of Europe which are Celtic are Catholic, and those which are Teutonic are Protestant; and where the Teutonic race was purest, there Protestantism spread with the greatest rapidity. But, with rare and beautiful exceptions, Protestantism on the continent has degenerated into mere formalism. . . . Evidently it is chiefly to the English and the American peoples that we must look for the evangelization of the world.

It is not necessary to argue to those for whom I write that the two great needs of mankind that all men may be lifted up into the light of the highest Christian civilization are, first, a pure, spiritual Christianity and, second, civil liberty. Without controversy, these are the forces which, in the past, have contributed most to the elevation of the human race, and they must continue to be, in the future, the most efficient ministers to its progress. It follows, then, that the Anglo-Saxon, as the great representative of these two ideas, the depositary of these two greatest blessings, sustains peculiar relations to the world's future, is divinely commissioned to be, in a peculiar sense, his brother's keeper. Add to this the fact of his rapidly increasing strength in modern times, and we have well-nigh a demonstration of his destiny. . . .

This race is multiplying not only more rapidly than any other European race but far more rapidly than *all* the races of continental Europe. . . . It is not unlikely that, before the close of the next century, this race will outnumber all the other civilized races of the world. Does it not look as if God were not only preparing in our Anglo-Saxon civilization the die with which to stamp the peoples of the earth, but as if He were also massing behind that die the mighty power with which to press it? My confidence that this race is eventually to give its civilization to mankind is not based on mere numbers — China forbid! I look forward to what the world has never yet seen united in the same race; viz., the greatest numbers *and* the highest civilization.

There can be no reasonable doubt that North America is to be the great home of the Anglo-Saxon, the principal seat of his power, the center of his life and influence. Not only does it constitute seven-elevenths of his possessions but his empire is unsevered, while the remaining four-elevenths are fragmentary and scattered over the earth. Australia will have a great population; but its disadvantages, as compared with North America, are too manifest to need mention. Our continent has room and resources and climate; it lies in the pathway of the nations; it belongs to the zone of power; and, already, among Anglo-Saxons, do we lead in population and wealth. Of England, Franklin once wrote: "That pretty island which, compared to America, is but a stepping-stone in a brook, scarce enough of it above water to keep one's shoes dry." England can hardly hope to maintain her relative importance among Anglo-Saxon peoples when her "pretty island" is the home of only one-twentieth part of that race.

With the wider distribution of wealth and increasing facilities of intercourse, intelligence and influence are less centralized and peoples become more homogeneous; and the more nearly homogeneous peoples are, the more do *numbers tell.* America is to have the great preponderance of numbers and of wealth, and, by the logic of events, will follow the scepter of controlling influence. This will be but the consummation of a movement as old as civilization — a result to which men have looked forward for centuries.

John Adams records that nothing was "more ancient in his memory than the observation that arts, sciences, and empire had traveled westward; and in conversation it was always added that their next leap would be over the Atlantic into America." He recalled a couplet that had been "inscribed, or rather drilled, into a rock on the shore of Monument Bay in our old colony of Plymouth:

The Eastern nations sink, their glory ends,
And empire rises where the sun descends." . . .

It surely needs no prophet's eye to see that the civilization of the *United States* is to be the civilization of America and that the future of the continent is ours. In 1880, the United States was the home of more than one-half of the Anglo-Saxon race; and, if the computations already given are correct, a much larger proportion will be here a hundred years hence. It has been shown that we have room for at least a thousand million. . . .

But we are to have not only the larger portion of the Anglo-Saxon race for generations to come, we may reasonably expect to develop the highest type of Anglo-Saxon civilization. If human progress follows a law of development, if "Time's noblest offspring is the last," our civilization should be the noblest; for we are "The heirs of all the ages in the foremost files of time," and not only do we occupy the latitude of power but *our land is the last to be occupied in that latitude.* There is no other virgin soil in the North Temperate Zone. If the consummation of human progress is not to be looked for here, if there is yet to flower a higher civilization, where is the soil that is to produce it? Whipple says: "There has never been a great migration that did not result in a new form of national genius." Our national genius is Anglo-Saxon, but not English; its distinctive type is the result of a finer nervous organization, which is certainly being developed in this country. . . .

There is abundant reason to believe that the Anglo-Saxon race is to be, is, indeed, already becoming, more effective here than in the mother country. The marked superiority of this race is due, in large measure, to its highly mixed origin. Says Rawlinson: "It is a general rule, now almost universally admitted by ethnologists, that the mixed races of mankind are superior to the pure ones"; and adds: "Even the Jews, who are so often cited as an example of a race at once pure and strong, may, with more reason, be adduced on the opposite side of the argument." . . .

There is here a new commingling of races; and, while the largest injections of foreign blood are substantially the same elements that constituted the original Anglo-Saxon admixture, so that we may infer the general type will be preserved, there are strains of other bloods being added, which, if Mr. Emerson's remark is true, that "the best nations are those most widely related," may be expected to improve the stock and aid it to a higher destiny. If the dangers of immigration . . . can be successfully met for the next few years, until it has passed its climax, it may be expected to add value to the amalgam which will constitute the new Anglo-Saxon race of the New World.

Concerning our future, Herbert Spencer says:

> One great result is, I think, tolerably clear. From biological truths it is to be inferred that the eventual mixture of the allied varieties of the Aryan race, forming the population, will produce a more powerful type of man than has hitherto existed, and a type of man more plastic, more adaptable, more capable of undergoing the modifications needful for complete social life. I think whatever difficulties they may have to surmount and whatever tribulations they may have to pass through, the Americans may reasonably look forward to a time when they will have produced a civilization grander than any the world has known.

It may be easily shown, and is of no small significance, that the two great ideas of which the Anglo-Saxon is the exponent are having a fuller development in the United States than in Great Britain. There the union of church and state tends strongly to paralyze some of the members of the body of Christ. Here there is no such influence to destroy spiritual life and power. Here, also, has been evolved the form of government consistent with the largest possible civil liberty. Furthermore, it is significant that the marked characteristics of this race are being here emphasized most. Among the most striking features of the Anglo-Saxon is his moneymaking power — a power of increasing importance in the widening commerce of the world's future. We have seen . . . that, although England is by far the richest nation of Europe, we have already outstripped her in the race after wealth, and we have only begun the development of our vast resources.

Again, another marked characteristic of the Anglo-Saxon is what may be called an instinct or genius for colonizing. His un-equaled energy, his indomitable perseverance, and his personal independence made him a pioneer. He excels all others in pushing his way into new countries. It was those in whom this tendency was strongest that came to America, and this inherited tendency has been further developed by the westward sweep of successive generations across the continent. So noticeable has this characteristic become that English visitors remark it. Charles Dickens once said that the typical American would hesitate to enter heaven unless assured that he could go farther west.

Again, nothing more manifestly distinguishes the Anglo-Saxon than his intense and persistent energy; and he is developing in the United States an energy which, in eager activity and effectiveness, is peculiarly American. This is due partly to the fact that Americans are much better fed than Europeans and partly to the undeveloped resources of a new country, but more largely to our climate, which acts as a constant stimulus. . . .

What is the significance of such facts? These tendencies enfold the future; they are the mighty alphabet with which God writes His prophecies. May we not, by a careful laying together of the letters, spell out something of His meaning? It seems to me that God, with infinite wisdom and skill, is training the Anglo-Saxon race for an hour sure to come in the world's future. Heretofore there has always been in the history of the world a comparatively unoccupied land westward, into which the crowded countries of the East have poured their surplus populations. But the widening waves of migration, which millenniums ago rolled east and west from the valley of the Euphrates, meet today on our Pacific Coast. There are no more new worlds. The unoccupied arable lands of the earth are limited and will soon be taken. The time is coming when the pressure of population on the means of subsistence will be felt here as it is now felt in

Europe and Asia. Then will the world enter upon a new stage of its history — *the final competition of races, for which the Anglo-Saxon is being schooled.*

Long before the thousand millions are here, the mighty *centrifugal* tendency inherent in this stock and strengthened in the United States will assert itself. Then this race of unequaled energy, with all the majesty of numbers and the might of wealth behind it — the representative, let us hope, of the largest liberty, the purest Christianity, the highest civilization — having developed peculiarly aggressive traits calculated to impress its institutions upon mankind, will spread itself over the earth. If I read not amiss, this powerful race will move down upon Mexico, down upon Central and South America, out upon the islands of the sea, over upon Africa and beyond. And can anyone doubt that the result of this competition of races will be the "survival of the fittest"? . . .

Every civilization has its destructive and preservative elements. The Anglo-Saxon race would speedily decay but for the salt of Christianity. Bring savages into contact with our civilization and its destructive forces become operative at once, while years are necessary to render effective the saving influence of Christian instruction. Moreover, the pioneer wave of our civilization carries with it more scum than salt. Where there is one missionary, there are hundreds of miners or traders or adventurers ready to debauch the native. Whether the extinction of inferior races before the advancing Anglo-Saxon seems to the reader sad or otherwise, it certainly appears probable. I know of nothing except climatic conditions to prevent this race from populating Africa as it has peopled North America. . . .

Some of the stronger races, doubtless, may be able to preserve their integrity; but, in order to compete with the Anglo-Saxon, they will probably be forced to adopt his methods and instruments, his civilization

and his religion. Significant movements are now in progress among them. While the Christian religion was never more vital, or its hold upon the Anglo-Saxon mind stronger, there is taking place among the nations a widespread intellectual revolt against traditional beliefs. "In every corner of the world," said Mr. Froude, "there is the same phenomenon of the decay of established religions. . . . Among Mohammedans, Jews, Buddhists, Brahmins, traditionary creeds are losing their hold. An intellectual revolution is sweeping over the world, breaking down established opinions, dissolving foundations on which historical faiths have been built up."

The contact of Christian with heathen nations is awaking the latter to new life. Old superstitions are loosening their grasp. The dead crust of fossil faiths is being shattered by the movements of life underneath. In Catholic countries, Catholicism is losing its influence over educated minds, and in some cases the masses have already lost all faith in it. Thus, while on this continent God is training the Anglo-Saxon race for its mission, a complemental work has been in progress in the great world beyond. God has two hands. Not only is He preparing in our civilization the die with which to stamp the nations, but, by what Southey called the "timing of Providence," He is preparing mankind to receive our impress. . . .

In my own mind there is no doubt that the Anglo-Saxon is to exercise the commanding influence in the world's future; but the exact nature of that influence is, as yet, undetermined. How far his civilization will be materialistic and atheistic, and how long it will take thoroughly to Christianize and sweeten it, how rapidly he will hasten the coming of the kingdom wherein dwells righteousness, or how many ages he may retard it, is still uncertain; but *it is now being swiftly determined.* Let us weld together in a chain the various links of our logic which we have endeavored to forge.

Is it manifest that the Anglo-Saxon holds in his hands the destinies of mankind for ages to come? Is it evident that the United States is to be the home of this race, the principal seat of his power, the great center of his influence? Is it true . . . that the great West is to dominate the nation's future? Has it been shown . . . that this generation is to determine the character, and hence the destiny, of the West? Then may God open the eyes of this generation!

When Napoleon drew up his troops before the Mamelukes under the shadow of the Pyramids, pointing to the latter he said to his soldiers: "Remember that from yonder heights forty centuries look down on you." Men of this generation, from the pyramid top of opportunity on which God has set us, *we look down on forty centuries!* We stretch our hand into the future with power to mold the destinies of unborn millions.

> We are living, we are dwelling,
> In a grand and awful time,
> In an age on ages telling —
> To be living is sublime!

Notwithstanding the great perils which threaten it, I cannot think our civilization will perish; but I believe it is fully in the hands of the Christians of the United States, during the next fifteen or twenty years, to hasten or retard the coming of Christ's kingdom in the world by hundreds, and perhaps thousands, of years. We of this generation and nation occupy the Gibraltar of the ages which commands the world's future.

14.

THEODORE ROOSEVELT: Public Office and Private Gain

Theodore Roosevelt began his public career almost by chance. World travel and a Harvard education had prepared him for several careers among which he declined to choose, turning instead to the study of history. Then in 1882 the New York Republican Party drafted him as a candidate for the state legislature, largely because of his respectable, upper-class background. Roosevelt, only twenty-four years old, quickly became a leader and during his three terms often irritated his peers by his independent attitude and accessibility to newspaper reporters. In the legislature he worked for practical reforms, among them better laws for the relief of workingmen. Always critical of misbehavior in public office, Roosevelt wrote the following account of his experiences in the New York legislature in 1885.

Source: *American Ideals*, Homeward Bound Edition, New York, 1910, pp. 78-101.

IN THE THREE LEGISLATURES of which I have been a member, I have sat with bankers and bricklayers, with merchants and mechanics, with lawyers, farmers, day laborers, saloon keepers, clergymen, and prizefighters. Among my colleagues there were many very good men; there was a still more numerous class of men who were neither very good nor very bad, but went one way or the other, according to the strength of the various conflicting influences acting around, behind, and upon them; and, finally, there were many very bad men. Still, the New York legislature, taken as a whole, is by no means as bad a body as we would be led to believe if our judgment was based purely on what we read in the great metropolitan papers; for the custom of the latter is to portray things as either very much better or very much worse than they are. . . .

The representatives from different sections of the state differ widely in character. Those from the country districts are generally very good men. They are usually well-to-do farmers, small lawyers, or prosperous storekeepers, and are shrewd, quiet, and honest. They are often narrow-minded and slow to receive an idea; but, on the other hand, when they get a good one, they cling to it with the utmost tenacity. They form very much the most valuable class of legislators. For the most part they are native Americans, and those who are not are men who have become completely americanized in all their ways and habits of thought. One of the most useful members of the last legislature was a German from a western county, and the extent of his Americanization can be judged from the fact that he was actually an ardent Prohibitionist. Certainly no one who knows Teutonic human nature will require further proof.

Again, I sat for an entire session beside a very intelligent member from northern New York before I discovered that he was an Irishman. All his views of legislation, even upon such subjects as free schools and the impropriety of making appropriations from the treasury for the support of sectarian institutions, were precisely similar to those of his Protestant-American neighbors, though he was himself a Catholic. Now, a German or an Irishman from one of the great cities would probably have retained many of his national peculiarities.

It is from these same great cities that the worst legislators come. It is true that there are always among them a few cultivated and scholarly men who are well educated, and who stand on a higher and broader intellectual and moral plane than the country members, but the bulk are very low indeed.

They are usually foreigners of little or no education, with exceedingly misty ideas as to morality, and possessed of an ignorance so profound that it could only be called comic, were it not for the fact that it has at times such serious effects upon our laws. It is their ignorance, quite as much as actual viciousness, which makes it so difficult to procure the passage of good laws or prevent the passage of bad ones; and it is the most irritating of the many elements with which we have to contend in the fight for good government. . . .

Bribe taking . . . undoubtedly at times occurs in the New York legislature. This is what is commonly called "a delicate subject" with which to deal, and, therefore, according to our usual methods of handling delicate subjects, it is either never discussed at all, or else discussed with the grossest exaggeration; but most certainly there is nothing about which it is more important to know the truth.

In each of the last three legislatures there were a number of us who were interested in getting through certain measures which we deemed to be for the public good, but which were certain to be strongly opposed, some for political and some for pecuniary reasons. Now, to get through any such measure requires genuine hard work, a certain amount of parliamentary skill, a good deal of tact and courage, and above all, a thorough knowledge of the men with whom one has to deal, and of the motives which actuate them. In other words, before taking any active steps, we had to "size up" our fellow legislators, to find out their past history and present character and associates, to find out whether they were their own masters or were acting under the directions of somebody else, whether they were bright or stupid, etc., etc. As a result, and after very careful study, conducted purely with the object of learning the truth, so that we might work more effectually, we came to the conclusion that about a third of the members were open to corrupt influences in some form or other; in certain sessions the proportion was greater, and in some less. Now it would, of course, be impossible for me or for anyone else to prove in a court of law that these men were guilty, except perhaps in two or three cases; yet we felt absolutely confident that there was hardly a case in which our judgment as to the honesty of any given member was not correct. . . .

From the causes indicated, it is almost impossible to actually convict a legislator of bribe-taking; but at the same time, the character of a legislator, if bad, soon becomes a matter of common notoriety, and no dishonest legislator can long keep his reputation good with honest men. If the constituents wish to know the character of their member, they can easily find it out. And no member will be dishonest if he thinks his constituents are looking at him; he presumes upon their ignorance or indifference. I do not see how bribe-taking among legislators can be stopped until the public conscience becomes awake to the matter. Then it will stop fast enough; for just as soon as politicians realize that the people are in earnest in wanting a thing done, they make haste to do it. The trouble is always in rousing the people sufficiently to make them take an *effective* interest — that is, in making them sufficiently in earnest to be willing to give a little of their time to the accomplishment of the object they have in view. . . .

A member from a large city can often count upon the educated and intelligent men of his district showing the most gross ignorance and stupidity in political affairs. The much-lauded intelligent voter — the man of cultured mind, liberal education, and excellent intentions — at times performs exceedingly queer antics.

The great public meetings to advance certain political movements irrespective of party, which have been held so frequently during the past few years, have undoubtedly done a vast amount of good; but the very men who attend these public meetings and inveigh against the folly and wickedness of the politicians will sometimes on election day do things which have quite as evil effects as any of the acts of the men whom they very properly condemn. . . .

It is this kind of ignorance of the simplest political matters among really good citizens, combined with their timidity, which is so apt to characterize a wealthy *bourgeoisie,* and, with their shortsighted selfishness, in being unwilling to take the smallest portion of time away from their business or pleasure to devote to public affairs, which renders it so easy for corrupt men from the city to keep their places in the legislature. In the country, the case is different. Here the constituencies, who are usually composed of honest though narrow-minded and bigoted individuals, generally keep a pretty sharp lookout on their members, and, as already said, the latter are apt to be fairly honest men. Even when they are not honest, they take good care to act perfectly well as regards all district matters, for most of the measures about which corrupt influences are at work relate to city affairs.

The constituents of a country member know well how to judge him for those of his acts which immediately affect themselves; but as regards others they often have no means of forming an opinion, except through the newspapers — more especially through the great metropolitan newspapers — and they have gradually come to look upon all statements made by the latter with reference to the honesty or dishonesty of public men with extreme distrust. This is because our newspapers, including those who professedly stand as representatives of the highest culture of the community, have been in the habit of making such constant and reckless assaults upon the characters of even very good public men as to greatly detract from their influence when they attack one who is really bad. . . .

Many men go to the legislature with the set purpose of making money; but many others, who afterward become bad, go there intending to do good work. These latter may be well-meaning, weak young fellows of some shallow brightness, who expect to make names for themselves; perhaps they are young lawyers, or real-estate brokers, or small shopkeepers. They achieve but little success; they gradually become conscious that their business is broken up, and that they have not enough ability to warrant any expectation of their continuing in public life; some great temptation comes in their way (a corporation which expects to be relieved of perhaps $1 million taxes by the passage of a bill can afford to pay high for voters); they fall, and that is the end of them. Indeed, legislative life has temptations enough to make it unadvisable for any weak man, whether young or old, to enter it.

The array of vicious legislators is swelled by a number of men who really at bottom are not bad. Foremost among these are those most hopeless of beings who are handicapped by having some measure which they consider it absolutely necessary for the sake of their own future to "get through." One of these men will have a bill, for instance, appropriating a sum of money from the state treasury to clear out a river, dam the outlet of a lake, or drain a marsh. It may be, although not usually so, proper enough in itself, but it is drawn up primarily in the interest of a certain set of his constituents who have given him clearly to understand that his continuance in their good graces depends upon his success in passing the bill; he feels that he must get it through at all hazards. The bad men find this out, and tell him he must count on their opposition unless he consents also to help their measures; he resists at first but sooner or later yields; and from that moment his fate is sealed, so far as his ability to do any work of general good is concerned.

A still larger number of men are good enough in themselves, but are "owned" by third parties. Usually the latter are politicians who have absolute control of the dis-

trict machines, or who are, at least, of very great importance in the political affairs of their district. A curious fact is that they are not invariably, though usually, of the same party as the member; for in some places, especially in the lower portions of the great cities, politics become purely a business; and, in the squabbles for offices of emolument, it becomes important for a local leader to have supporters among all the factions. When one of these supporters is sent to a legislative body, he is allowed to act with the rest of his party on what his chief regards as the unimportant questions of party or public interest, but he has to come in to heel at once when any matter arises touching the said chief's power, pocket, or influence.

Other members will be controlled by some wealthy private citizen who is not in politics, but who has business interests likely to be affected by legislation, and who is, therefore, willing to subscribe heavily to the campaign expenses of an individual or of an association so as to ensure the presence in Albany of someone who will give him information and assistance. . . .

There are two classes of cases in which corrupt members get money. One is when a wealthy corporation buys through some measure which will be of great benefit to itself, although, perhaps an injury to the public at large; the other is when a member introduces a bill hostile to some moneyed interest, with the expectation of being paid to let the matter drop. The latter, technically called a "strike," is much the most common; for, in spite of the outcry against them in legislative matters, corporations are more often sinned against than sinning. It is difficult . . . in either case to convict the offending member, though we have very good laws against bribery. The reform has got to come from the people at large. It will be hard to make any very great improvement in the character of the legislators until respectable people become more fully awake to their duties, and until the newspapers become more truthful and less reckless in their statements. . . .

The people of means in all great cities have in times past shamefully neglected their political duties, and have been contemptuously disregarded by the professional politicians in consequence. A number of them will get together in a large hall, will vociferously demand "reform," as if it were some concrete substance which could be handed out to them in slices, and will then disband with a feeling of the most serene self-satisfaction, and the belief that they have done their entire duty as citizens and members of the community. It is an actual fact that four out of five of our wealthy and educated men, of those who occupy what is called good social position, are really ignorant of the nature of a caucus or a primary meeting, and never attend either. Now, under our form of government, no man can accomplish anything by himself; he must work in combination with others; and the men of whom we are speaking will never carry their proper weight in the political affairs of the country until they have formed themselves into some organization, or else, which would be better, have joined some of the organizations already existing.

But there seems often to be a certain lack of the robuster virtues in our educated men, which makes them shrink from the struggle and the inevitable contact with rough politicians (who must often be rudely handled before they can be forced to behave); while their lack of familiarity with their surroundings causes them to lack discrimination between the politicians who are decent, and those who are not; for in their eyes the two classes, both equally unfamiliar, are indistinguishable. Another reason why this class is not of more consequence in politics, is that it is often really out of sympathy — or, at least, its more conspicuous members are — with the feelings and interests of the great mass of the American people; and it is a discreditable fact that it is in this class that what has been most aptly termed the "colonial" spirit still survives. Until this survival of the spirit of colonial dependence is dead, those in whom it exists will serve chiefly as laughing stocks to the shrewd, humorous, and prejudiced people who form nine-tenths of our body politic, and whose chief characteristics are their intensely American habits of thought, and their surly intolerance of anything like subservience to outside and foreign influences.

From different causes, the laboring classes, even when thoroughly honest at heart, often fail to appreciate honesty in their representatives. They are frequently not well-informed in regard to the character of the latter, and they are apt to be led aside by the loud professions of the so-called labor reformers, who are always promising to procure by legislation the advantages which can only come to working men, or to any other men, by their individual or united energy, intelligence, and forethought. Very much has been accomplished by legislation for laboring men by procuring mechanics' lien laws, factory laws, etc.; and hence it often comes that they think legislation can accomplish all things for them. And it is only natural, for instance, that a certain proportion of their number should adhere to the demagogue who votes for a law to double the rate of wages, rather than to the honest man who opposes it. When people are struggling for the necessaries of existence, and vaguely feel, no matter how wrongly, that they are also struggling against an unjustly ordered system of life, it is hard to convince them of the truth that an ounce of performance on their own part is worth a ton of legislative promises to change in some mysterious manner that life system.

In the country districts, justice to a member is somewhat more apt to be done. When, as is so often the case, it is not done, the cause is usually to be sought for in the numerous petty jealousies and local rivalries which are certain to exist in any small community whose interests are narrow and most of whose members are acquainted with each other. And, besides this, our country vote is essentially a Bourbon or Tory vote, being very slow to receive new ideas, very tenacious of old ones, and hence inclined to look with suspicion upon anyone who tries to shape his course according to some standard differing from that which is already in existence.

The actual work of procuring the passage of a bill through the legislature is in itself far from slight. The hostility of the actively bad has to be discounted in advance, and the indifference of the passive majority, who are neither very good nor very bad, has to be overcome. This can usually be accomplished only by stirring up their constituencies; and so, besides the constant watchfulness over the course of the measure through both houses and the continual debating and parliamentary fencing which is necessary, it is also indispensable to get the people of districts not directly affected by the bill alive to its importance so as to induce their representatives to vote for it.

Thus, when the bill to establish a state park at Niagara was on its passage, it was found that the great majority of the country members were opposed to it, fearing that it might conceal some land-jobbing scheme, and also fearing that their constituents, whose vice is not extravagance, would not countenance so great an expenditure of public money. It was of no use arguing with the members, and instead the country newspapers were flooded with letters, pamphlets were circulated, visits and personal appeals were made, until a sufficient number of these members changed front to enable us to get the lacking votes.

15.

A Practical Program for Economists

The American Economic Association was formed at Saratoga, New York, in September 1885. The aim of the association was a scientific approach to economics in an era of increasingly complex industrial and social problems. To members of the association the "old orthodoxy" of laissez faire was obsolete and unworkable. The following selection comprises the Objects and Platform of the association, followed by a statement by Richard T. Ely of Johns Hopkins University, who was acting secretary.

Source: *Publications of the American Economic Association:* Richard T. Ely, *Report of the Organization of the American Economic Association,* Baltimore, 1886.

THE NEED OF AN ASSOCIATION designed to promote independent economic inquiry and to disseminate economic knowledge was keenly felt long before any determined effort was made to establish the desired organization. Suggestions looking to the formation of a society of economists were heard from time to time, but no active steps in this direction appear to have been taken before the spring of 1885, when it was agreed that the time was ripe for action, and it was determined to test the feelings in this matter of those who would be likely to prove helpful in associated scientific work in economics.

The class of men required for this purpose was, it was believed, a large and constantly growing one. Men were wanted who were investigators — men, consequently, who did not believe that the entire range of economic knowledge had been compassed. It follows from this that it was not proposed to form a society of advocates of any political opinion or set of political opinions, as for example, free trade or protection. It was not meant to deny that a free-trade club or a protectionist club might have its legitimate sphere, but it was held that this sphere lay outside the realm of science. Likewise it was not aimed to form a society to champion any class interests, either of rich or of poor, either of employer or of employee.

What was desired was a society which, free from all trammels, should seek truth from all sources, should be ready to give a respectful hearing to every new idea, and should shun no revelation of facts, but, on the contrary, should make the collection, classification, and interpretation of facts its chief task. The ideal of this new society, as it presented itself to the minds of its projectors, was to seek light, to bear light, to diffuse light — ever the highest aim of all true science.

A statement of the objects of the proposed association and a platform were drawn up, which, while intended to be merely provisional, would be calculated to attract those who believed in economic research, who thought that there was a great work to be done in economics, and who for other reasons might be able to work together profitably. This platform, it must be distinctly asserted, was never meant as a hard and fast creed which should be imposed on all members, and least of all was it intended to restrict the freest investigation.

The statement of objects and the proposed platform read as follows:

OBJECTS OF THIS ASSOCIATION

1. The encouragement of economic research.
2. The publication of economic monographs.
3. The encouragement of perfect freedom in all economic discussion.
4. The establishment of a bureau of information designed to aid all members with friendly counsels in their economic studies.

PLATFORM

1. We regard the state as an educational and ethical agency whose positive aid is an indispensable condition of human progress. While we recognize the necessity of individual initiative in industrial life, we hold that the doctrine of laissez faire is unsafe in politics and unsound in morals; and that it suggests an inadequate explanation of the relations between the state and the citizens.

2. We do not accept the final statements which characterized the political economy of a past generation; for we believe that political economy is still in the first stages of its scientific development, and we look not so much to speculation as to an impartial study of actual conditions of economic life for the satisfactory accomplishment of that development. We seek the aid of statistics in the present and of history in the past.

3. We hold that the conflict of labor and capital has brought to the front a vast number of social problems whose solution is impossible without the united efforts of church, state, and science.

4. In the study of the policy of government, especially with respect to restrictions on trade and to protection of domestic manufactures, we take no partisan attitude. We are convinced that one of the chief reasons why greater harmony has not been attained is because economists have been too ready to assert themselves as advocates. We believe in a progressive development of economic conditions which must be met by corresponding changes of policy.

A prospectus containing this statement and platform was sent to a majority of those interested in political economy in our colleges and met with a hearty response in nearly every quarter. While there were not wanting criticisms of some of the phrases, there was general approval of the aims of the projected American Economic Association. . . .

STATEMENT OF DR. RICHARD T. ELY

ONE CONCLUSION is undoubtedly warranted. The time is ripe for such an association.

Passing over to the prospectus, it is scarcely necessary to say much about the first three "objects" of the association. We want to encourage research by the employment of all means at our command, and to publish monographs. This seems better than the publication of a journal of political and economic science, for the reason that it promises nothing which cannot be fulfilled. It is important to avoid anything which can prove a fiasco, always discouraging and likely to subject one to ridicule.

It seems to me — and all consulted have been of the same opinion — that we ought by no means to attempt anything which will not in all probability prove a success. If we take one step at a time, we shall make satisfactory progress and I think in the end, rapid progress. The idea, then, is to publish matter worthy of publication as fast as we may be able to do so. If the series of monographs should in course of time grow naturally into a magazine, we could rejoice in a substantial success.

The fourth "object" contemplated in my opinion, and I think in the opinion of others who assisted in formulating the "objects," was merely advice to those throughout the country who should join the association and desire to pursue economic studies systematically. This advice might be by means of printed lists of books to be read, accompanied by useful suggestions about profitable methods of study and research.

But in the editorial about our movement in the *Philadelphia Times* of August 20, I find an idea which may prove valuable. The writer of this editorial in question evidently supposed the intention was to establish a bureau for the collection of statistical, social, and economic material — "Quellen-Material" — digests of which were to be published. The final paragraph of the article reads as follows: "The scope of this enterprise is greater than that of any official Bureau of Labor Statistics can well be, because its operations will be less liable to interruption through a change of party supremacy or a failure of appropriations."

This is ambitious but may it not prove practicable? Might we not gather together at some central point a mass of valuable material? The work indicated is, I think, somewhat similar to that of the London Statistical Society, which has its own library, and it is such work that Professor Henry C. Adams suggests that we undertake.

One aim of our association should be the education of public opinion in regard to economic questions and economic literature. In no other science is there so much quackery, and it must be our province to expose it and bring it into merited contempt. A review at each of our meetings of the economic works of the past year, if published in our proceedings, might help in the formation of enlightened judgment.

Coming to the platform, a position is first of all taken in regard to the state, because it is thought necessary precisely at this time to emphasize its proper province. No one invited to join this association, certainly no one who has been active in calling this meeting, contemplates a form of pure socialism. "We recognize the necessity of individual initiative." We would do nothing to weaken individual activity, but we hold that there are certain spheres of activity which do not belong to the individual, certain functions which the great cooperative society — called the state — must perform to keep the avenues open for those who would gain a livelihood by their own exertions. The avenues to wealth and preferment are continually blocked by the greed of combinations of men and by monopolists, and individual effort and initiative are thus discouraged. Two examples will suffice.

You know that in the Western grazing regions water is often scarce, and those who control the streams virtually own the country. Now it is a notorious fact that unlawful combinations seize upon these streams and, keeping others from them, retain exclusive privileges which shut off effectually individual exertions on the part of those not in the ring. A second example is found in unjust discriminations in freight charges which have built up the fortunes of the favored and ruined competitors. In looking over the field of economic life, it is evident that there is a wide feeling of discouragement, repressing the activities of the individual, because the avenues to material well-being are so often blocked. Then there are things which individuals ought not to perform because the functions concerned are public; and in certain places the wastes of private competition are too enormous. There are, likewise, important things which individual effort is powerless to effect, *e.g.*, the education of the masses.

We hold that the doctrine of laissez faire is unsafe in politics and unsound in morals, and that it suggests an inadequate explanation of the relations between the state and the citizens. In other words, we believe in the existence of a system of social ethics; we do not believe that any man lives for himself alone, nor yet do we believe social classes are devoid of mutual obligations corresponding to their infinitely varied interrelations. All have duties as well as rights, and, as Emerson said several years ago, it is time we heard more about duties and less about rights. We who have resolved to form an American Economic Association

hope to do something toward the development of a system of social ethics.

It is asked: What is meant by laissez faire? It is difficult to define laissez faire categorically, because it is so absurd that its defenders can never be induced to say precisely what they mean. Yet it stands for a well-known, though rather vague, set of ideas, to which appeal is made every day in the year by the bench, the bar, the newspapers, and our legislative bodies. It means that government, the state, the people in their collective capacity, ought not to interfere in industrial life; that, on the contrary, free contract should regulate all the economic relations of life and public authority should simply enforce this, punish crime, and preserve peace. It means that the laws of economic life are natural laws like those of physics and chemistry, and that this life must be left to the free play of natural forces. One adherent uses these words: "This industrial world is governed by natural laws. . . . These laws are superior to man. Respect this providential order — let alone the work of God."

The platform then emphasizes the mission of the state and the mission of the individual in that state. *To distinguish between the proper functions of the two must be one of the purposes of our association.*

The mission of the church is likewise emphasized, and for this there is good reason which cannot, perhaps, be better stated than in the words of Professor Macy of Iowa College. I quote from a letter recently received from him:

> The preacher, in an important sense, is to be the originator of true social science; his work is to render possible such a science.
> The physical scientist needs no preacher. There is an external material thing which compels belief. For the most part, men have no selfish interest in believing other than the truth in regard to the material world. Those who devote themselves to the study of matter are led nat-

urally into a truth-loving and truth-telling spirit, and they can laugh at the preacher. But those who devote themselves to the study of the conflicting interests of men have on their hands altogether a different task. There is no external material thing to solve their doubts, and men prefer to believe that which is not true; and when they believe the truth, they often think it best to pretend to believe the false. Falsehood, deception, lying, and above all an honest and dogged belief in error — these are athwart the path which might lead to a real social science. And who can tackle these better than the preacher?

In addition to these words of Professor Macy, it may be said that we wish to accomplish certain practical results in the social and financial world, and believing that our work lies in the direction of practical Christianity, we appeal to the church, the chief of the social forces in this country, to help us, to support us, and to make our work a complete success, which it can by no possibility be without her assistance.

The religious press of the country can aid us greatly in our task, and it will not, I believe, refuse its cooperation. Its influence is enormous, and notwithstanding all that has been said against it to the contrary, I believe that today it is the fairest, purest, and most liberal press in the country.

The fourth paragraph in the platform seems to me to be imperatively necessary. We want to proclaim to the world that political economy is something much broader than partisan controversies about free trade and protection, that we are in fact neither free traders nor protectionists in the partisan sense of those words.

It may be asked: Why have any platform at all? Why not simply invite all interested in political economy to come together and aid in economic research?

The reply is not a difficult one. This association intends to combine two ends. It proposes to influence public opinion; also to investigate and study. Now, if there has ever been found in any place an economic society without the advocacy, either open or concealed, of certain tendencies, at least, it has not come to my knowledge. I do not believe it would be wise to attempt such a thing. The fundamental differences between economists are so radical that they cannot all work profitably together.

Our platform is very broad and will include nearly all those who can cooperate advantageously with us. It advocates simply certain methods of study and the accomplishment of reforms by certain means which alone seem to us to promise valuable results. We believe in historical and statistical inquiries and examinations into actual conditions, and should we include those who do not, there would be division at the start. If two people are journeying together to a certain goal and come to a fork in the road, it is evident that they must part company if each insists on believing that their common destination lies in a different direction. That is our case. We have little faith that the methods advocated by certain economists will ever lead to any valuable results. They may take their own way, and far be it from us to hinder them, but we must part company.

Again, it is not easy to arouse interest in an association which professes nothing. This proposed economic association has been greeted with enthusiasm precisely because it is not colorless, precisely because it stands for something.

Finally, it is of the utmost importance to us to emphasize certain fundamental views in order to bring them prominently before the public. It is essential that intelligent men and women should distinguish between us and certain economists in whom there is little faith. The respect for political economy as it has been hitherto taught is very slight. I think it has been kept alive largely by ignorance, on the one hand; on the other, by the cloak it affords to wrongdoing and the balm it offers to still the voice of outraged conscience.

On every side we find intelligent people dissatisfied with it, throwing all political economy to the winds, while John Stuart Mill repudiated his own economic system, and one of the most careful students of economic facts, Thorold Rogers, finds its conclusions so at variance with the results of his investigations that he rejects it with scorn and believes it necessary to build up a new political economy by a long and careful process, piecemeal, as he himself expresses it. We of this association must come before the public with the unequivocal asser-

tion that we, also, refuse to accept as final "the statements which characterize the political economy of a past generation, and that we believe our science is in the first stages of its scientific development."

Our attitude is a modest one and must, I think, appeal to the best intelligence of the country. We acknowledge our ignorance, and if we claim superiority to others, it is largely on the very humble ground that we know better what we do not know. We confess our ignorance but are determined to do our best to remedy it, and we call upon those who are willing to go to work in this spirit to come forward and help us.

16.

Woodrow Wilson: The Declining Prestige of the Presidential Office

A series of weak Presidents in the ten years or so before the Civil War opened the way for the U.S. Senate to assume a dominant position in the federal government. The towering figure of Lincoln reversed the trend, but the postwar controversies between the Executive and the Legislative branches over Reconstruction resulted in the reassertion of congressional dominance. Woodrow Wilson analyzed this rift between the Executive and Legislative branches of government in his first book, Congressional Government. *The book, which was his doctoral thesis at Johns Hopkins University, was published in 1885. The following selection is from the introduction.*

Source: *Congressional Government: A Study in American Politics,* Boston, 1885, pp. 1-57.

We are the first Americans to hear our own countrymen ask whether the Constitution is still adapted to serve the purposes for which it was intended; the first to entertain any serious doubts about the superiority of our own institutions as compared with the systems of Europe; the first to think of remodeling the administrative machinery of the federal government and of forcing new forms of responsibility upon Congress.

The evident explanation of this change of attitude toward the Constitution is that we have been made conscious, by the rude shock of the war and by subsequent developments of policy, that there has been a vast alteration in the conditions of government; that the checks and balances which once obtained are no longer effective; and that we are really living under a Constitution essentially different from that which we have been so long worshiping as our own peculiar and incomparable possession. In short, this model government is no longer conformable with its own original pattern. While we have been shielding it from criticism it has slipped away from us.

The noble charter of fundamental law given us by the convention of 1787 is still our Constitution; but it is now our *form of government* rather in name than in reality, the form of the Constitution being one of nicely adjusted, ideal balances, while the actual form of our present government is simply a scheme of congressional supremacy. National legislation, of course, takes force now as at first from the authority of the Constitution; but it would be easy to reckon by the score acts of Congress which can by no means be squared with that great instrument's evident theory. We continue to think, indeed, according to long-accepted constitutional formulas, and it is still politically unorthodox to depart from old-time phraseology in grave discussions of affairs; but it is plain to those who look about them that most of the commonly received opinions concerning federal constitutional balances and administrative arrangements are many years behind the actual practices of the government at Washington, and that we are farther than most of us realize from the times and the policy of the framers of the Constitution.

It is a commonplace observation of historians that, in the development of constitutions, names are much more persistent than the functions upon which they were originally bestowed; that institutions constantly undergo essential alterations of character while retaining the names conferred upon them in their first estate; and the history of our own Constitution is but another illustration of this universal principle of institutional change. There has been a constant growth of legislative and administrative practice, and a steady accretion of precedent in the management of federal affairs, which have broadened the sphere and altered the

functions of the government without perceptibly affecting the vocabulary of our constitutional language. . . .

It is said that there is no single or central force in our federal scheme; and so there is not in the federal *scheme*, but only a balance of powers and a nice adjustment of interactive checks, as all the books say. How is it, however, in the practical conduct of the federal government? In that, unquestionably, the predominant and controlling force, the center and source of all motive and of all regulative power, is Congress. All niceties of constitutional restriction and even many broad principles of constitutional limitation have been overridden and a thoroughly organized system of congressional control set up, which gives a very rude negative to some theories of balance and some schemes for distributed powers, but which suits well with convenience and does violence to none of the principles of self-government contained in the Constitution. . . .

Besides, in ordinary times it is not from the executive that the most dangerous encroachments are to be apprehended. The legislature is the aggressive spirit. It is the motive power of the government, and unless the judiciary can check it, the courts are of comparatively little worth as balance wheels in the system. It is the subtile, stealthy, almost imperceptible encroachments of policy, of political action, which constitute the precedents upon which additional prerogatives are generally reared; and yet these are the very encroachments with which it is hardest for the courts to deal and concerning which, accordingly, the federal courts have declared themselves unauthorized to hold any opinions. They have naught to say upon questions of policy. Congress must itself judge what measures may legitimately be used to supplement or make effectual its acknowledged jurisdiction, what are the laws "necessary and proper for carrying into execution" its own peculiar powers, "and all other powers vested by" the "Constitution in the government of the United States, or in any department or officer thereof."

The courts are very quick and keen-eyed, too, to discern prerogatives of political discretion in legislative acts, and exceedingly slow to undertake to discriminate between what is and what is not a violation of the spirit of the Constitution. Congress must wantonly go very far outside of the plain and unquestionable meaning of the Constitution, must bump its head directly against all right and precedent, must kick against the very pricks of all well-established rulings and interpretations, before the Supreme Court will offer it any distinct rebuke. . . .

But, besides and above all this, the national courts are for the most part in the power of Congress. Even the Supreme Court is not beyond its control; for it is the legislative privilege to increase, whenever the legislative will so pleases, the number of the judges upon the supreme bench — to "dilute the Constitution," as Webster once put it, "by creating a court which shall construe away its provisions"; and this on one memorable occasion it did choose to do. . . .

It is noteworthy that Mr. Adams, possibly because he had himself been President, describes the executive as constituting only *"in some degree"* a check upon Congress, though he puts no such limitation upon the other balances of the system. Independently of experience, however, it might reasonably have been expected that the prerogatives of the President would have been one of the most effectual restraints upon the power of Congress. He was constituted one of the three great coordinate branches of the government; his functions were made of the highest dignity; his privileges many and substantial — so great, indeed, that it has pleased the fancy of some writers to parade them as exceeding those of the British Crown. And there can be little doubt that had the presidential chair always been filled by men of commanding character, of ac-

knowledged ability, and of thorough political training, it would have continued to be a seat of the highest authority and consideration, the true center of the federal structure, the real throne of administration, and the frequent source of policies. Washington and his cabinet commanded the ear of Congress and gave shape to its deliberations; Adams, though often crossed and thwarted, gave character to the government; and Jefferson, as President no less than as secretary of state, was the real leader of his party. But the prestige of the presidential office has declined with the character of the Presidents. And the character of the Presidents has declined as the perfection of selfish party tactics has advanced. . . .

I am disposed to think, however, that the decline in the character of the Presidents is not the cause but only the accompanying manifestation of the declining prestige of the presidential office. That high office has fallen from its first estate of dignity because its power has waned; and its power has waned because the power of Congress has become predominant. The early Presidents were . . . men of such a stamp that they would under any circumstances have made their influence felt; but their opportunities were exceptional. What with quarreling and fighting with England, buying Louisiana and Florida, building dikes to keep out the flood of the French Revolution, and extricating the country from ceaseless broils with the South American republics, the government was . . . constantly busy, during the first quarter century of its existence, with the adjustment of foreign relations; and with foreign relations, of course, the Presidents had everything to do, since theirs was the office of negotiation.

Moreover, as regards home policy, also, those times were not like ours. Congress was somewhat awkward in exercising its untried powers, and its machinery was new and without that fine adjustment which has since made it perfect of its kind. Not having as yet learned the art of governing itself to the best advantage, and being without that facility of legislation which it afterward acquired, the legislature was glad to get guidance and suggestions of policy from the executive.

But this state of things did not last long. Congress was very quick and apt in learning what it could do and in getting into thoroughly good trim to do it. It very early divided itself into standing committees which it equipped with very comprehensive and thoroughgoing privileges of legislative initiative and control, and set itself through these to administer the government. . . .

The executive was losing and Congress gaining weight; and the station to which cabinets finally attained was a station of diminished and diminishing power. There is no distincter tendency in congressional history than the tendency to subject even the details of administration to the constant supervision, and all policy to the watchful intervention, of the standing committees.

I am inclined to think, therefore, that the enlarged powers of Congress are the fruits rather of an immensely increased efficiency of organization, and of the redoubled activity consequent upon the facility of action secured by such organization, than of any definite and persistent scheme of conscious usurpation. It is safe to say that Congress always had the desire to have a hand in every affair of federal government; but it was only by degrees that it found means and opportunity to gratify that desire; and its activity, extending its bounds wherever perfected processes of congressional work offered favoring prospects, has been enlarged so naturally and so silently that it has almost always seemed of normal extent, and has never, except perhaps during one or two brief periods of extraordinary political disturbance, appeared to reach much beyond its acknowledged constitutional sphere. . . .

What makes it the more important to understand the present mechanism of national government, and to study the methods of congressional rule in a light unclouded by theory, is that there is plain evidence that the expansion of federal power is to continue, and that there exists, consequently, an evident necessity that it should be known just what to do and how to do it when the time comes for public opinion to take control of the forces which are changing the character of our Constitution. . . .

Unquestionably, the pressing problems of the present moment regard the regulation of our vast systems of commerce and manufacture, the control of giant corporations, the restraint of monopolies, the perfection of fiscal arrangements, the facilitating of economic exchanges, and many other like national concerns, among which may possibly be numbered the question of marriage and divorce; and the greatest of these problems do not fall within even the enlarged sphere of the federal government. Some of them can be embraced within its jurisdiction by no possible stretch of construction, and the majority of them only by wresting the Constitution to strange and as yet unimagined uses. Still there is a distinct movement in favor of national control of all questions of policy which manifestly demand uniformity of treatment and power of administration such as cannot be realized by the separate, unconcerted action of the states; and it seems probable to many that, whether by constitutional amendment or by still further flights of construction, yet broader territory will at no very distant day be assigned to the federal government.

It becomes a matter of the utmost importance, therefore, both for those who would arrest this tendency and for those who, because they look upon it with allowance if not with positive favor, would let it run its course, to examine critically the government upon which this new weight of responsibility and power seems likely to be cast, in order that its capacity both for the work it now does and for that which it may be called upon to do may be definitely estimated.

1886

17.

GROVER CLEVELAND: A Skeptical View of Pension Legislation

No President before Franklin D. Roosevelt exercised the veto power more freely or more often than Grover Cleveland, who in his first administration vetoed more than 400 bills. Most of them were special-interest legislation conferring pensions on Civil War veterans, the plethora of which was prompted by a Treasury surplus and by the political influence of the Grand Army of the Republic, the Civil War veterans' organization. The G.A.R. tended to support Republicans, and Cleveland, as a Democrat, had few if any political debts to pay to veterans; but he probably would have vetoed most of the bills in any case, for as he once remarked in connection with one such bill, "though the people support the government, the government should not support the people." One such veto, of June 21, 1886, is reprinted below.

Source: Richardson, VIII, pp. 436-438.

MY OBJECTION TO THIS BILL is that it is of no possible advantage to the beneficiary therein mentioned. It directs that her name be placed upon the pension roll, subject to the provisions and limitations of the pension laws. The effect of such legislation would be to permit Mrs. De Krafft to draw a pension at the rate of $30 each month from the date of the approval of the bill. On the 26th day of February, 1886, under the provisions of the general pension law, she was allowed a pension of this exact sum, but the payments were to date from November 10, 1885.

I am so thoroughly tired of disapproving gifts of public money to individuals who in my view have no right or claim to the same, notwithstanding apparent congressional sanction, that I interpose with a feeling of relief a veto in a case where I find it unnecessary to determine the merits of the application. In speaking of the promiscuous and ill-advised grants of pensions which have lately been presented to me for approval, I have spoken of their "apparent congressional sanction" in recognition of the fact that a large proportion of these bills have never been submitted to a majority of either branch of Congress, but are the result of nominal sessions held for the express purpose of their consideration and attended by a small minority of the members of the respective houses of the legislative branch of government.

Thus in considering these bills I have not felt that I was aided by the deliberate judgment of the Congress; and when I have deemed it my duty to disapprove many of the bills presented, I have hardly regarded my action as a dissent from the conclusions of the people's representatives.

I have not been insensible to the suggestions which should influence every citizen, either in private station or official place, to exhibit not only a just but a generous appreciation of the services of our country's defenders. In reviewing the pension legislation presented to me, many bills have been approved upon the theory that every doubt should be resolved in favor of the proposed beneficiary. I have not, however, been able to entirely divest myself of the idea that the public money appropriated for pensions is the soldiers' fund, which should be devoted to the indemnification of those who in the defense of the Union and in the nation's service have worthily suffered, and who in the day of their dependence resulting from such suffering are entitled to the benefactions of their government. This reflection lends to the bestowal of pensions a kind of sacredness which invites the adoption of such principles and regulations as will exclude perversion as well as insure a liberal and generous application of grateful and benevolent designs.

Heedlessness and a disregard of the principle which underlies the granting of pensions is unfair to the wounded, crippled soldier who is honored in the just recognition of his government. Such a man should never find himself side by side on the pension roll with those who have been tempted to attribute the natural ills to which humanity is heir to service in the Army. Every relaxation of principle in the granting of pensions invites applications without merit and encourages those who for gain urge honest men to become dishonest. Thus is the demoralizing lesson taught the people that as against the public Treasury the most questionable expedients are allowable.

During the present session of Congress, 493 special pension bills have been submitted to me, and I am advised that 111 more have received the favorable action of both houses of Congress and will be presented within a day or two, making over 600 of these bills which have been passed up to this time during the present session, nearly three times the number passed at any entire session since the year 1861. With the Pension Bureau, fully equipped and regulated by the most liberal rules, in active operation, supplemented in its work by constant special legislation, it certainly is not unreasonable to suppose that in all the years that have elapsed since the close of the war a majority of the meritorious claims for pensions have been presented and determined.

I have now more than 130 of these bills before me awaiting executive action. It will be impossible to bestow upon them the examination they deserve, and many will probably become operative which should be rejected. In the meantime, I venture to suggest the significance of the startling increase in this kind of legislation and the consequences involved in its continuance.

———◆———

I stand today to voice the sentiment of the young men of my state when I speak for Grover Cleveland. His name is upon their lips. His name is in their hearts. They love him, gentlemen, and respect him, and they love him and respect him not only for himself, for his character, for his integrity, for his iron will, but they love him most for the enemies he has made.

E. S. Bragg, speech at Democratic National Convention, 1884

18.

Andrew Carnegie: The Picture Lover and the Picture Buyer

Although steel manufacturer Andrew Carnegie managed to make money at a nearly unprecedented rate, he always maintained that his real interests and goals in life were other than monetary — were instead learning, writing, the arts, and public benevolence. He frequently contributed articles on a variety of subjects to journals such as the North American Review, *and in 1886 he published a book,* Triumphant Democracy, *in which he set out to demonstrate the superiority of American institutions to those of the Old World, especially Britain. The following selection from that work is taken from the chapter entitled "Art — Painting and Sculpture."*

Source: *Triumphant Democracy,* Revised edition, New York, 1893, Ch. 11.

Art, in fact, is the effort of man to express the ideas which nature suggests to him of a power above nature, whether that power be within the recesses of his own being, or in the Great First Cause of which nature, like himself, is but the effect. — Bulwer.

If side by side with progress in material things there was not found corresponding progress in the higher things of the spirit, there would be but little cause for congratulation among the citizens of the republic. If there was not spreading among the masses of the people along with their material blessings a love of the beautiful; if with their comforts there did not come the love of music; if, in short, "art," using the term in its broadest sense, did not shed everywhere around its elevating influence, we should have little reason to be proud or hopeful of our country, much less to extol it. To reach her proper position and play her part among the nations, she must not only be the wealthiest country in the world but richest in the diffusion of refinement and culture among the people.

It is not enough that the American workman should be in receipt of the highest wages and enjoy the best living. He should also be most appreciative of all the refinements of life, and his habits should be better than those of his fellows in other lands. His home must be more artistic, its interior in better taste, its furniture finer, its sanitary arrangements more perfect, and especially must it be to a greater degree than that of any corresponding class the home of music. There must be more and better books, engravings, and pictures, even in the humblest dwelling, compared with the workman's home in other lands. We must see there, if nothing else, at least the picture from the illustrated newspaper, or the chromo neatly framed, the flowerpot on the windowsill, the melodeon, or even the piano, and at every point the cheering evidence of a budding taste for better, finer, more artistic surroundings. The chromo on the wall, the flowerpot on the windowsill of the toiler's home mean much more for the republic than the picture gallery or the conservatory of the city home of the millionaire.

The world has long considered political rights and government the province of the few. So also has it considered art as beyond the multitude. In the political field the republic has proclaimed a new gospel, the right of every citizen to an equal share in the government. It is her mission also, we fully believe, to teach the nations that art should likewise be universal; not the luxury of the few but the heritage of the whole people. There are many proofs that good progress is now being made in this direction. The more general diffusion of art in every department is a marked and gratifying movement of our time. Art in the new land had naturally a feeble beginning.

In 1826 the National Academy of Design was organized in New York, under the presidency of Samuel F. B. Morse, as the successor of the American Academy of Fine Arts, which died after the fire of the same year had destroyed its art collection. Similar institutions had been founded early in Philadelphia and in Boston, but the National Academy has always exercised a paramount influence in the development of American art. It remains today the principal art society, although much in need of enlarged and better galleries situated farther uptown.

About ten years later the American Art Union, an incorporated institution for the distribution, by lot, of works of art, came into existence, and during more than a decade aided much in educating the people and in bringing into notice many artists who might otherwise have found it difficult to win recognition. But this gain was loss; the influence of the lottery system must have transcended a hundredfold any possible advantage gained through it by art. Happily, the day for such gambling is over, but we meet with the evil still where one would least expect it. . . .

Several small public galleries, like those of the Athenaeum in Boston, and of the Historical Society in New York, and a few private collections were found in different parts of the country which exercised a considerable influence in raising the standard of popular taste. People began to buy pictures and, as was natural, began by buying very poor pictures. European dealers, taking advantage of the comparative ignorance of the country in art matters, flooded the principal cities with alleged examples of the old masters, which found a ready sale forty or fifty years ago, but which gradually disappeared as their worthlessness was understood; and now it would be difficult to find one of these early art treasures of America in any respectable house, unless it may have been preserved among the rubbish of the garret. The experience thus gained was of the utmost value.

The American, with his quick perception, soon learned to distinguish between the good and the bad, and though his taste may in some cases seem a little "loud" to the European connoisseur, he seldom buys anything which is absolutely worthless. He is recognized now in the European markets as one of the shrewdest as well as one of the most liberal buyers. Throughout the world, whenever art treasures come under the hammer, the American is found in competition with nobles, and even with crowned heads, and he is no mean competitor; for he is not afraid to spend his dollars where he is sure of getting his money's worth. Thus, during the past few decades, there has been a constant flow of works of art to the United States. There is no city of importance in the country which has not its public gallery of painting and sculpture, as well as many private collections in the houses of its citizens. These latter are often exhibited as loan collections and exert a most beneficial influence in creating a taste for art.

The movement of modern French paintings to this country began early in the seventies and was mainly due to the influence of William M. Hunt, of Boston, who had studied under Couture and Millet, and had become deeply impressed with the work that these artists and their great contemporaries were doing. He saw that these were landscapes and figures that were sure to live and to acquire more and more value as their superior qualities became better known. He returned to Boston full of enthusiasm over the Barbizon School, as it came to be called, taking its name from the little village on the edge of the Fontainebleau Forest where these artists — Millet, Rousseau, Diaz, Dupré, and others — had their studios. He imparted some of his enthusiasm to wealthy Boston amateurs, who began to import their paintings. New York was quick to appreciate their beauty, and soon the collectors of the two cities vied with each other in the attempt to secure choice examples of the work of these great painters and those associated with them, such as Corot, Daubigny, and Troyon.

From that time until now the New World has been steadily transferring to the galleries of its collectors the greatest paintings produced by this, the most famous school of artists of the century. The artists, the dealers, and the wealthy amateurs well knew the extent to which the best modern works of the French school were being imported to the private galleries of the United States. But the great public was hardly aware of the number and the value of these paintings until the Morgan and the Seney collections were thrown upon the market a few years ago. New York's private galleries, it was suddenly discovered, were filled with them, and the further fact was made manifest that the Shaw, Brimmer, Wigglesworth, and other Boston galleries contained some of the finest examples of the Barbizon School.

It is estimated by a good judge, who is thoroughly conversant with the private galleries, not only on the seaboard but in Detroit, Milwaukee, Cincinnati, Chicago, and other cities, that modern French art is better represented in the United States than it is in any country but France today. There are more than fifty examples of Meissonier alone in this country. And the eagerness of collectors to possess these great works, and

their willingness to pay high prices for them, were well illustrated when Judge Hilton bought Meissonier's "1807" at the Stewart sale for $66,000. There is no doubt but that a loan collection of a hundred modern French paintings could be made in this country which could not be matched for quality or for commercial value anywhere else in the world, France alone excepted.

The lesson, my readers, of all this is not far to seek. It shows how the New is absorbing the art treasures of the Old World. When wealth and taste go hand in hand, such a movement, once begun, is bound to continue. Twenty-five years hence Frenchmen may have to visit the galleries of Boston, New York, Philadelphia, Pittsburgh, Baltimore, Cincinnati, Detroit, Chicago, and St. Paul in order to study the work of their own Fontainebleau School. None of these paintings return to France. When once here they are here for all time. . . .

The foreign reader must not infer from what is said of the American fondness for the French school of art that the Americans have no painters of their own. They have hundreds of wonderfully clever painters who have mastered the technique, many having acquired their proficiency in the studios of the French masters. Sargent and Whistler are men whose genius is recognized in Paris and London as well as in America. Other names equally, or almost equally, famous, who, in the present generation, have won a high and enviable place, will occur to the reader. While we have not yet produced a Rousseau or a Daubigny, our group of landscape painters are doing admirable work — work that will live. In figure pictures and *genre* our painters are rapidly approaching the French. The average of our portrait painting is reputed to be as high as the English standard. If there is a branch in which American painters are weak, it is in the historical, allegorical, and imaginative. This was a field in which West and Allston excelled. The note of their time, however, was romantic, and they felt its influence and echoed it. The watchword of art at the present day is "truth to nature." By and by a reaction will set in, and the imagination will be given freer play.

Meanwhile much is being done to encourage American artists. The National Academy exhibitions have improved greatly in the last few years; the Society of American Artists exerts a stimulative influence; throughout the West, art is gaining the attention of the men who since the war have been bringing the continent into subjection; traveling scholarships and prizes have been generously established by which promising young men are sent abroad for a year's study; public galleries are becoming richer each year in works well worthy of attention; and in many other ways native art is being fostered. Several collections of paintings already prove what fine examples in every branch of art can be gathered among the works of native painters, if patience and taste and a patriotic pride in the achievements of one's fellow countrymen govern the selection. The gift of $1 million, netting $50,000 per annum, made to the Pittsburgh Art Gallery, is conditioned upon at least six pictures by American artists being purchased each successive year, to be displayed in chronological order. If the wishes of the donor be properly carried out by the Art Committee, we shall in time have a collection of great historical value as showing the development of the national school of painting.

The Fine Arts Society of New York deserves notice. In the whole history of artistic progress in the republic, we know of nothing to compare with this in several of its features. The Society is formed by a consolidation of the Architectural League, the Society of American Artists, and the Art Students' League. Each of these had a small fund and was able to contribute its third to a capital of $50,000. Upon this slender financial basis, but strong in faith and ability, the newly elected officers began their work, which in less than a year has culminated in the recent opening of the Fine Arts Building in Fifty-seventh Street, in which there have already been held three notable exhibitions, each among the best of its kind. The society is teaching 640 students. The total spent upon the property is less than $500,000, which causes every experienced visitor to inquire how so much could have been done with so little.

The secret is that it has been a labor of love throughout. The organizers and all the officers have labored without salary, the architect designed the building without compensation, and such a building as reflects credit upon Mr. Hardenbergh; the contractors worked without profit; and at the head of the whole matter was an irrepressible man whose name deserves to be recorded in the history of art progress in America. Knowing how greatly we shall incur his displeasure, we nevertheless venture to write it down in full — Howard Russell Butler. We know of no undertaking that shows the character of the American more thoroughly than this — such effort, enthusiasm, organizing power, general ability, and self-devotion. No wonder that such qualities attracted and held the attention and drew forth the support of our most important patrons of art. The new gallery, connected with the rear of the main building, is called the George W. Vanderbilt Gallery, and justly so, for he it was who surprised the society by conferring upon it this invaluable gift.

Would that my conscience would permit me to leave the subject of American painting without an expression of heartfelt regret that this new art society is far too much French — Frenchy. The recent exhibition, in the words of a true patron of art, "was almost as bad as the Salon — the subjects as a rule unworthy, the landscapes blurred and sketchy, and the nude vulgar." One consolation remains. These young Frenchy Americans are to be taught another needed lesson. The picture lover and the picture buyer, offended at such a display, will evince his displeasure by showing the value, or rather the no-value, he places upon works which attempt thus to prostitute art to vulgar and unholy ends. If art is to devote itself to the perpetuation of aught but what is noble and pure, may we never be cursed by possessing it. Thank the fates, American literature so far is pure.

America has developed within the past half-century a school of sculpture which has won recognition both at home and abroad, though a visit to the national capital and to the public squares of some of the larger cit-ies would scarcely induce such an opinion. Many of her sculptors have been educated under Italian influences but have drawn their inspiration rather from the antique than the modern Italian school. Some who stand foremost at home today have not enjoyed the benefit, or disadvantage perhaps, of foreign instruction, and their works, consequently, possess more of the flavor of the soil, so to speak, than do those which have been executed in strict accordance with the academic rules transmitted from antiquity. It is possible that these may develop in time into a purely American school of sculpture, which shall be recognized and take its place as such in the art history of the world.

19.

JOHN H. VINCENT: The Chautauqua Movement

The Chautauqua movement began in 1874 at Fair Point, New York, when Methodist clergyman John Vincent (later bishop) organized a summer community devoted to secular as well as religious education. The original eight-week program in the arts, sciences, and humanities led to other groups and lecturers who traveled the country promoting adult education. The formal Chautauqua organization revolved about the Literary and Scientific Circle, which provided guided reading courses and formal examinations to groups and individuals across the nation. Bishop Vincent outlined his plans and hopes for the organization in a book, the first chapter of which is reprinted here.

Source: *The Chautauqua Movement*, Boston, 1886, pp. 1-15.

THE TASK I HAVE TAKEN upon myself is to tell, in a simple way, the story of Chautauqua — a story of today; without romantic, heroic, or tragic element; a story of the people; a story in which the scholars will be interested, because the scholars are a part of the people; a story in which the rich and the refined will be interested — the rich who are truly refined and the refined whether rich or poor — because they be-lieve in the brotherhood of the race and in its high destiny and are proud to account themselves a part of it.

I shall make no effort to excite the pity of the wealthy and the learned for the poor and the illiterate — class for class, upper for lower. Chautauqua is not one of the "associated charities," nor is it a department of "home missions." It comes alike to the door of want and of wealth, with proffered blessings for both, and is as likely to gain entrance at one door as at the other. It deals with matters which, by the order of an impartial Providence, belong to "all classes and conditions of men." The full-orbed "Chautauqua idea" must awaken in all genuine souls a fresh enthusiasm in true living and bring rich and poor, learned and unlearned, into neighborship and comradeship, helpful and honorable to both.

Education, once the peculiar privilege of the few, must in our best earthly estate become the valued possession of the many. It is a natural and inalienable right of human souls. The gift of imagination, of memory, of reason, of invention, of constructive and executive power, carries with it both prerogative and obligation. No man dare with impunity surrender, as to himself, this endowment, nor deny to his neighbor the right and obligation which it involves. Given, intellectual potentiality; required, intellectual discipline and power. The law holds among leaders of thought, teachers and lawmakers; among nobles and the favorites of fortune. It holds no less among the lowly — the plebeians and the peasants of society.

Diversity in the direction of talent and difference in degree, together with inequalities of social condition, may modify the demand upon the individual for culture and service; but the utter neglect of intellectual capacity is criminal, whether it be by menial or millionaire. It involves a wrong to self, to the family, to the state — to self, since it leaves him blind whom God created to enjoy the light; to the family, since it turns him into a physical or commercial machine whom God appointed to be companion and comforter; to the state, since it makes him a mere figurehead — whether of clay or gold — whom God intended to be a counselor and helper and to "have dominion" according to the measure of his power.

No man has a right to neglect his personal education, whether he be prince or plowboy, broker or hod carrier. He needs knowledge and the wisdom which makes knowledge available. Where the power lies, there rests responsibility for its use. Circumstances seem to favor the prince and to be against the plowboy; but, after all, the latter, overcoming adverse conditions, may acquire an education worth a great deal more to the world than that of the prince with his opportunities.

Struggle against what men call fate brings power. One hour of study every day, with heroic purpose, may prove more valuable to the student than five hours a day of easy memorizing and reciting. The prince may complete his course in a few years and, having "finished," graduate. The plowboy, moving slowly, may require four times the number of years to cover the same ground; but that length of time may be an advantage to the humble student. It may require greater concentration when he does study; and the long hours of manual labor may be enriched by thought, and thus may knowledge gain a firmer hold and its vitalizing power be increased.

Chautauqua has a work to do for college graduates. It enters protest against the suspension of intellectual effort when the compulsory regime of the recitation room has been remitted — a fault so common and so pernicious that college men themselves frequently bring into disrepute the college system. Intellectual activity must be continuous in order to promote intellectual health and efficiency. College life is the vestibule to a great temple. He who crosses its pavement and reads the inscriptions on its doors, but goes no farther, might as well never have entered the campus at all. Too many suspend literary pursuit when the diploma is won and the world of business opens before them.

Chautauqua provides, for such as these, incentives to a personal review of the entire college curriculum in a series of English readings. It urges them to prosecute advanced courses of study and suggests a plan by which college prestige and power may be used in helping less favored neighbors who desire education. This last class is large. It is made up of eager minds who need direction and encouragement. They would ask questions and gratefully accept assistance if college graduates would simply place themselves within reach.

Chautauqua has therefore a message and a mission for the times. It exalts education — the mental, social, moral, and religious cultures of all who have mental, social, moral, and religious faculties; of all, everywhere, without exception. It aims to promote a combination of the old domestic, religious, educational, and industrial agencies; to take people on all sides of their natures and cultivate them symmetrically, making men, women, and children everywhere more affectionate and sympathetic as members of a family; more conscientious and reverent, as worshipers together of the true God; more intelligent and thoughtful as students in a universe of ideas; and more industrious, economical, just, and generous, as members of society in a workaday world.

The theory of Chautauqua is that life is one and that religion belongs everywhere. Our people, young and old, should consider educational advantages as so many religious opportunities. Every day should be sacred. The schoolhouse should be God's house. There should be no break between Sabbaths. The cable of divine motive should stretch through seven days, touching with its sanctifying power every hour of every day.

Kitchen work, farm work, shop work, as well as school work, are divine. They hide rare pearls in their rough shells. They are means of discipline in the highest qualities of character, and through them come some of the greatest and mightiest energies from the heavens. People should be guarded against the baleful heresy that, when they leave the hour of song, prayer, and revival power and go to homely service in shop or field, they are imperiling spiritual life, as

though only so-called sacred services could conserve it.

We need an alliance and a hearty cooperation of home, pulpit, school, and shop — an alliance consecrated to universal culture for young and old; for all the days and weeks of all the years; for all the varied faculties of the soul, and in all the possible relations of life.

Chautauqua teaches that each of these institutions embodies and represents an idea, and that every man needs in his own life these representative ideas — the home idea of mutual love and tenderness; the church idea of reverence and conscientiousness; the school idea of personal culture; and the shop idea of diligence, economy, and mutual help. The young and the old need these things. The rich and the poor need them. Capital and labor need them. The educated and the illiterate need them.

Chautauqua says therefore: Give them to the people. Hold up high standards of attainment. Show the learned their limitations and the illiterate their possibilities. Chautauqua pleads for a universal education; for plans of reading and study; for all legitimate enticements and incitements to ambition; for all necessary adaptations as to time and topics; for ideal associations which shall at once excite the imagination and set the heart aglow. Chautauqua stretches over the land a magnificent temple, broad as the continent, lofty as the heavens, into which homes, churches, schools, and shops may build themselves as parts of a splendid university in which people of all ages and conditions may be enrolled as students. It says: Unify such eager and various multitudes. Let them read the same books, think along the same lines, sing the same songs, observe the same sacred days — days consecrated to the delights of a lofty intellectual and spiritual life. Let the course of prescribed reading be broad and comprehensive; limited in its first general survey of the wide world of knowledge; opening out into special courses, according to the reader's development, taste, and opportunity. Show people out of school what wonders people out of school may accomplish. Show people no longer young that the mind reaches its maturity long after the school days end, and that some of the best intellectual and literary labor is performed in and beyond middle life.

College halls are not the only places for prosecuting courses of study. College facilities are not the only opportunities for securing an education. A college is possible in everyday life if one choose to use it; a college in house, shop, street, farm, market, for rich and poor, the curriculum of which runs through the whole of life; a college that trains men and women everywhere to read and think and talk and do; and to read, think, talk, and do with a purpose; and that purpose, that they may *be:* a college that trains indolent people to work with their own hands; that trains people who work with their hands to work also with their brains — to think in their work, to think for their work, and to make other people work and think. ·

A plan of this kind, simple in its provisions, limited in its requirements, accepted by adults, prosecuted with firm purpose, appealing to the imagination and to the conscience must work miracles, intellectual, social, and religious, in household, neighborhood, and nation. And this is the "Chautauqua Idea"; and the idea in active operation is the *Chautauqua* of which I write.

Its benefits are manifold and obvious. It brings parents into fuller sympathy with their children at the time when sympathy is most needed — sympathy with them in their educational aims, sympathy with them in lines of reading and study.

It helps parents to help the teachers of their children, preparing infants under school age to make a good beginning; inciting and assisting the children who have entered school to do good work in preparation and recitation; protecting them against the peculiar temptations of playground and classroom; holding them to the end of the high-school course; inspiring them to seek the higher education of the college or to pursue after-school courses of reading and study at home.

So general a scheme of education must increase the refining and ennobling influence of home life, promoting self-control and dignity of deportment, mutual respect and affection, a laudable family pride, and true social ambition; giving the whole house an air of refinement; touching, with artistic skill, floors, walls, and windows; finding the right place and the right light for the right picture; putting the right book on shelf and table; furnishing a wider ·range of topics for home conversation; crowding out frivolity and gossip; removing sources of unrest and discontent at home; making evenings there more agreeable than life on the street; creating a real independence of the outside world, and making one's own house the center of the whole world of science, literature, art, and society.

Windows open out through every wall; and beyond vines, trees, and garden, the inmates see the old world of history, the new world of science, the rich world of literature, the royal world of art. And through skylights they look up and see the world of God — His love and holiness and the boundless life to which He invites us. And thus they all in that household learn that, seen aright, all realms of knowledge, both past and present, are flooded with the light of God.

Popular education through the Chautauqua scheme increases the value of the pulpit by putting more knowledge, thoughtfulness, and appreciation into the pew and encouraging the preacher to give his best thought in his best way.

It must put more good sense into popular religious utterances, so that the talk of the prayer meeting will be sobered by wisdom and directed by tact, thus gaining in its influence over cultivated people, and especially over the young people of high school and lecture hall. It must enable everybody more accurately to measure the worth and the limitations of science and must cause them to fear far less the dogmatism of pseudoscientists concerning religious facts and doctrines.

Such popular education must increase the power of the people in politics, augmenting the independent vote which makes party leaders cautious where lack of conscience would make them careless concerning truth and honesty.

It must tend to a better understanding between the classes of society, causing the poor to honor wealth won by honest ways of work, by skill and economy; to despise wealth and winners of wealth when greed and trickery gather the gold; to honor knowledge and a taste for knowledge, whether it be found clad in fine linen or in linsey-woolsey; to hate with resolute and righteous hatred all sham and shoddy, all arrogance and pretentiousness; to avoid struggles between capital and labor, and to promote, in all possible ways, the glorious brotherhood of honesty, sympathy, and culture — a culture that addresses itself to all sides of a man's nature.

Under the auspices of this great Chautauqua "everyday college," you may imagine the soliloquy of a woman more than forty-five years of age. She says:

"I am busy with many duties — household cares or shop work. I have something to do all the time. There seems no end to calls, toils, worry, and weariness. In kitchen, parlor, farm, or factory, something is to be done.

"I am old — that is, older than I once was. Don't let us talk about that. Gray hairs? No, you cannot find any gray hairs in my head — or can you? Never mind. The heart's young, and it's nobody's business how old the bones are.

"I am going to college! Never mind about thirty years or fifty or seventy: I am going to college. Harvard? No, nor Yale, nor Boston, nor Middletown, nor Evanston,

nor Wellesley. I don't want to mix with a lot of reckless boys or ambitious girls just now. I have enough of them at home or in the neighborhood. I am going to college, my own college, in my own house, taking my own time; turning the years into a college term; turning my kitchen, sitting room, and parlor into college halls, recitation rooms, and laboratory. What a *campus* I have! green fields and forests, streams and mountain ranges, stretching out to the sunset. What a dome surmounts my college! vast space, blue background, billowy clouds, resplendent stars! What professors I have, in books! immortal books of history and science and art, books of poetry, fiction, and fact.

"In my college are enrolled the names of glorious men and women who never enjoyed any other college — Shakespeare, Benjamin Franklin, Washington Irving, John G. Whittier, Horace Greeley, Abraham Lincoln, and hosts of others who went to their own college and wrought out their own education, as I will do in 'my college.' I can never be what they were; but I can be something and can make the world better and children happier and life nobler because of the feeble efforts I put forth to get a better education.

"I am going to college! I want to improve all my talents. I have intellect. I intend to develop and enrich it. I must know more. I must love to know. I must know more for the sake of larger influence over others for their good — children, servants, neighbors, church associates. God has given me at least one talent. I ought to improve it. I will improve it.

"I am going to college! I am a 'child of a King,' and have a right to my inheritance. 'All things are yours.' Well, I want to take up my property in stars and flowers and in the knowledge men have gathered about my royal Father's kingdom. Astronomers, bring me what you have discovered in the outlying domains of my Father's universe!

Geologists, tell me the story you have learned from the rocky pages of the earth concerning the beginnings and the development of the planet I live on. Thus I intend to lay hold of all the treasure seekers and teachers and high priests of nature and literature and art and bid them bring the truth they hold, my Father's truth, *my* truth, and place the goodly inheritance at my feet. 'Whatsoever things are true . . . think on these things.' I am going to college!

" 'Where am I going?' I shall stay at home and construct a college there. My house — small, poorly furnished (never mind) — is my college center. My neighbors, the richest of them and the poorest, the most humble and ignorant and the most scholarly shall be my professors. I will ask questions about everything and of everybody, till I find out what I want to know. Some of the stupidest people can tell me something, and when I draw them out I do them good. Getting, I can give.

"And don't talk to me about age. Let the poet answer your raven cry:

But why, you ask me, shall this tale be
    told
To men grown old or who are growing
    old?
It is too late! Ah! nothing is too late
Till the tired heart shall cease to
    palpitate.
Cato learned Greek at eighty; Sophocles
Wrote his grand *Oedipus,* and Simonides
Bore off the prize of verse from his
    compeers,
When each had numbered more than
    fourscore years;
And Theophrastus at fourscore and ten
Had but begun his *Characters of Men;*
Chaucer, at Woodstock with the
    nightingales,
At sixty wrote the *Canterbury Tales;*
Goethe at Weimar, toiling to the last,
Completed *Faust* when eighty years were
    past.

These are, indeed, exceptions; but they
    show
How far the gulf stream of our youth
    may flow
Into the arctic regions of our lives,
When little else than life itself survives.
Shall we, then, idly sit us down and say:
The night hath come: it is no longer day?
The night hath not yet come: we are not
    quite
Cut off from labor by the failing light.
Something remains for us to do or dare;
Even the oldest tree some fruit may bear;
For age is opportunity no less
Than youth, though in another dress;
And as the evening twilight fades away,
The sky is filled with stars invisible by
    day."

THE ENTIRE CHAUTAUQUA MOVEMENT is based upon the following propositions:

1. The whole of life is a school, with educating agencies and influences all the while at work, from the earliest moment to the day of death. These agencies and influences should be wisely and continuously applied by and in behalf of each individual, through life, according to circumstances, capacities, and conditions.

2. The true basis of education is religious. The fear of the Lord is the beginning of wisdom — the recognition of the Divine existence and of His claims upon us as moral beings; the unity and brotherhood of the race, with all that brotherhood involves; harmony with the Divine character as the ideal of life for time and eternity; and the pursuit and use of all science in personal culture, the increase of reverent love for God, and of affectionate self-sacrifice and labor for the well-being of man.

3. All knowledge, religious or secular, is sacred to him who reverently surrenders himself to God, that he may become like God according to the divinely appointed processes for building character. And he has a right to all attainments and enjoyments in

the realm of knowledge for the possession of which he has capacity and opportunity. Science, travel, literature, the works of art, the glories of nature — all things are his who is one with God. This law applies to the poor and lowly, as well as to the rich and so-called "favored classes" of society. It gives lofty ideals to lowly life and transforms humble homes into places of aspiration and blessedness.

4. In mature life, beyond the limits of the usual school period, the intellect is at its best for purposes of reading, reflection, and production. While the training of the schools may discipline the juvenile mind and thus give it an advantage as its powers mature, the discipline of everyday life in solving problems of existence, support, and business gives a certain advantage to the so-called uneducated mind during the middle period of life. Between the ages of twenty and eighty lie a person's best intellectual and educational opportunities; and he needs direction, encouragement, and assistance in order to use them most effectively.

5. Early lack of culture, felt by full-grown people, begets a certain exaltation of its value and desirability and a craving for its possession. This craving creates intellectual susceptibility and receptivity and renders the more easy the acquisition of knowledge. Mere verbal memory may be less efficient in these adult years; but the power of reasoning and of utilizing knowledge for practical results is much greater than in the early years.

6. The necessity for wise direction, assistance, and encouragement of this mature intellectual power and desire is as great as in the period of youth and of school life. Therefore, grown people need courses of study outlined, books for reading indicated, questions answered, associations formed, and all the conditions guaranteed which tend to promote hope, confidence, ambition, and strong purpose.

7. Where a mature mind desires to use its energies and opportunities to the maximum of its possibility and to do thorough intellectual work of the most exacting sort, the influence of the best teachers may be brought to bear upon him by frequent correspondence, including questions, answers, praxes, theses, and final written examinations of the most exhaustive and crucial character. To such persistent purpose and faithful effort, after rigid testing, there should come the testimonials and honors in diploma and degree to which any student, anywhere else or at any other period of his life, would be entitled.

8. The advantage of mental attrition by personal recitation and conversation is a large factor in the schools. This advantage may be enjoyed by voluntary associations, local circles, contact with resident scholars, occasional attendance upon special lectures, and class recitations in local high schools, seminaries, and colleges, and at summer schools and assemblies.

These are some of the fundamental thoughts on which the Chautauqua movement is based. It is a school for people out of school who can no longer attend school — a college for one's own home; and leads to the dedication of everyday life to educational purposes.

The Chautauqua movement embraces:

1. Work done at Chautauqua and similar assemblies, in lectures and by class instruction, for a few weeks every summer.

2. Work done away from Chautauqua, in voluntary *reading* through the year, which reading is under direction and is reported to headquarters at Plainfield, N.J.

3. Work done away from Chautauqua during the entire year, in *study*, under faithful teachers, by correspondence; such work being tested by final examinations of a rigid character, and rewarded by certificates, diplomas, and the usual scholastic degrees.

20.

Charles Taze Russell: What Jehovah's Witnesses Stand For

The religious sect known as the Jehovah's Witnesses or International Bible Students was founded by Charles Taze Russell sometime in the 1870s. The sect is popular today among the underprivileged in urban areas and has a large following among Negroes; its publication, The Watchtower, *first issued by Russell in 1879, is widely distributed. Russell's most important work was* Food for Thinking Christians, *which appeared in 1881 and was reissued as* Millennial Dawn, *Vol. I, in 1886. He had attracted attention with an earlier booklet,* The Object and Manner of Our Lord's Return, *in which he had predicted the second coming of Christ in the fall of 1874. The millennial doctrine remained central in his later writings and was opposed by him to the traditional doctrine of eternal punishment for the wicked. Politically, as the following passage from* Millennial Dawn *illustrates, Russell taught a philosophy of total noninvolvement in the affairs of the world, which, in his view, had long since become the province of the Antichrist. The withdrawal from political life, including refusal of active military service, has resulted in frequent persecution of the sect.*

Source: *The Divine Plan of the Ages,* Brooklyn, 1922, pp. 263-272.

As we compare the condition of the world today with its condition at any former period, we find a marked difference in the sentiments of the masses. The spirit of independence is now abroad, and men are not so easily blindfolded, deceived, and led by rulers and politicians, and therefore they will not submit to the yokes of former days. This change of public sentiment has not been a gradual one, from the very beginning of man's effort to govern himself, but clearly marked only as far back as the sixteenth century; and its progress has been most rapid within the last fifty years. This change, therefore, is not the result of the experience of past ages but is the natural result of the recent increase and general diffusion of knowledge among the masses of mankind.

The preparation for this general diffusion of knowledge began with the invention of printing, about A.D. 1440, and the consequent multiplication of books and news periodicals. The influence of this invention in the general public enlightenment began to be felt about the sixteenth century; and the progressive steps since that time all are acquainted with. The general education of the masses has become popular, and inventions and discoveries are becoming everyday occurrences. This increase of knowledge among men, which is of God's appointment and comes to pass in His own due time, is one of the mighty influences which are now at work binding Satan — curtailing his influence and circumscribing his power in this "Day of *Preparation*" for the setting up of God's kingdom in the earth.

The increase of knowledge in every direction awakens a feeling of self-respect among men and a realization of their natural and inalienable rights, which they will not long permit to be ignored or despised; rather, they will go to an opposite extreme. Glance back along the centuries and see how the nations have written the history of their discontent in blood. And the prophets declare that because of the increase of knowledge a still more general and widespread dissatisfaction will finally express itself in a worldwide revolution, in the overthrow of all law and order; that anarchy and distress upon all classes will be the result; but that in the midst of this confusion the God of heaven will *set up* His kingdom, which will satisfy the desires of all nations. Wearied and disheartened with their own failures, and finding their last and greatest efforts resulting in anarchy, men will gladly welcome and bow before the heavenly authority and recognize its strong and just government. Thus man's extremity will become God's opportunity, and "the desire of all nations shall come" — the kingdom of God, in power and great glory (Hag. 2:7).

Knowing this to be the purpose of God, neither Jesus nor the apostles interfered with earthly rulers in any way. On the contrary, they taught the church to submit to these powers, even though they often suffered under their abuse of power. They taught the church to obey the laws and to respect those in authority because of their office, even if they were not personally worthy of esteem; to pay their appointed taxes, and, except where they conflicted with God's laws (Acts 4:19; 5:29), to offer no resistance to any established law (Rom. 13:1-7; Matt. 22:21). The Lord Jesus and the apostles and the early church were all law-abiding, though they were separate from and took no share in the governments of this world.

Though the powers that be, the governments of this world, were ordained or arranged for by God, that mankind might gain a needed experience under them, yet the church, the consecrated ones who aspire to office in the coming Kingdom of God, should neither covet the honors and the emoluments of office in the kingdoms of this world, nor should they oppose these powers. They are fellow citizens and heirs of the heavenly kingdom (Eph. 2:19), and as such should claim only such rights and privileges under the kingdoms of this world as are accorded to *aliens*. Their mission is not to help the world to improve its present condition, nor to have anything to do with its affairs at present. To attempt to do so would be but a waste of effort; for the world's course and its termination are both clearly defined in the Scriptures and are fully under the control of Him who in His own time will *give us* the kingdom.

The influence of the *true* church is now and always has been small — so small as to count practically nothing politically; but however great it might appear, we should follow the example and teaching of our Lord and the apostles. Knowing that the purpose of God is to let the world fully test its own ability to govern itself, the true church should not, while in it, be *of* the world. The saints may influence the world only by their separateness from it, by letting *their light* shine; and thus through their lives the spirit of truth *reproves* the world.

Thus — as peaceable, orderly obeyers and commenders of every righteous law, reprovers of lawlessness and sin, and pointers forward to the promised Kingdom of God and the blessings to be expected under it, and not by the method commonly adopted of mingling in politics and scheming with the world for power, and thus being drawn into wars and sins and the general degradation — in glorious chastity should the prospective Bride of the Prince of Peace be a power for good, as her Lord's representative in the world.

The Church of God should give its *entire*

attention and effort to preaching the Kingdom of God and to the advancement of the interests of that Kingdom according to the plan laid down in the Scriptures. If this is faithfully done, there will be no time nor disposition to dabble in the politics of present governments. The Lord had no time for it; the apostles had no time for it; nor have any of the saints who are following their example.

The early church, shortly after the death of the apostles, fell a prey to this very temptation. The preaching of the coming Kingdom of God, which would displace all earthly kingdoms, and of the crucified Christ as the heir of that Kingdom, was unpopular, and brought with it persecution, scorn, and contempt. But some thought to improve on God's plan, and, instead of suffering, to get the church into a position of favor with the world. By a combination with earthly powers they succeeded. As a result, papacy was developed, and in time became the mistress and queen of nations. (Rev. 17:3-5; 18:7).

By this policy everything was changed; instead of suffering, came honor; instead of humility, came pride; instead of truth, came error; and instead of being persecuted, she became the persecutor of all who condemned her new and illegal honors. Soon she began to invent new theories and sophistries to justify her course, first deceiving herself, and then the nations, into the belief that the promised millennial reign of Christ *had come*, and that Christ the King was represented by her popes, who reigned over the kings of the earth as His vicegerents. Her claims were successful in deceiving the whole world. "She made all nations drunk" with her erroneous doctrines (Rev. 17:2), intimidating them by teaching that eternal torment awaited all who resisted her claims. Soon the kings of Europe were crowned or deposed by her edict and under her supposed authority.

Thus it comes that the kingdoms of Europe today claim to be Christian kingdoms and announce that their sovereigns reign "by the grace of God," *i.e.,* through appointment of either papacy or some of the Protestant sects. For though the Reformers abandoned many of papacy's claims to ecclesiastical jurisdiction, etc., they held to this honor which the kings of earth had come to attach to Christianity. And thus the Reformers fell into the same error, and exercised the authority of monarchs in appointing and sanctioning governments and kings, and denominating such "Christian kingdoms," or kingdoms of Christ. So we hear much today of that strange enigma, "The Christian World" — an enigma, indeed, when viewed in the light of the true principles of the gospel. Our Lord said of His disciples, "They are not of the world, even as I am not of the world." And Paul exhorts us, saying, "Be not conformed to this world" (John 17:16; Rom. 12:2).

God never approved of calling these kingdoms by the name of Christ. Deceived by the church nominal, these nations are sailing under false colors, claiming to be what they are not. Their only title, aside from the vote of the people, is in God's *limited* grant, spoken to Nebuchadnezzar — until He come whose right the dominion is.

The claim that these imperfect kingdoms, with their imperfect laws and often selfish and vicious rulers, are the "kingdoms of our Lord and His Anointed" is a gross libel upon the true Kingdom of Christ, before which they must shortly fall, and upon its "Prince of Peace" and righteous rulers (Isa. 32:1).

Another serious injury resulting from that error is that the attention of the children of God has thereby been attracted away from the promised heavenly kingdom; and they have been led to an improper recognition of and intimacy with earthly kingdoms and to almost fruitless attempts to engraft upon these wild, worldly stocks the graces and morals of Christianity, to the neglect of the gospel concerning the true Kingdom and the hopes centering in it. Under this deception, some are at present very solicitous that the name of God should be incorporated into the Constitution of the United States, that *thereby* this may become a Christian nation.

The Reformed Presbyterians have for years refused to vote or hold office under this government *because* it is not Christ's Kingdom. Thus they recognize the impropriety of Christians sharing in any other. We have great sympathy with this sentiment, but not with the conclusion that if God's *name* were mentioned in the Constitution, that fact would transform this government from a kingdom of this world to a kingdom of Christ, and give them liberty to vote and to hold office under it. O, how foolish! How great the deception by which the "Mother of harlots" has made all nations drunk (Rev. 17:2); for in a similar manner it is claimed that the kingdoms of Europe were transferred from Satan to Christ and became "Christian nations." . . .

The world is fast coming to realize that the "kingdoms of this world" are not Christ-like, and that their claim to be of Christ's appointment is not unquestionable.

Men are beginning to use their reasoning powers on this and similar questions; and they will act out their convictions so much more violently as they come to realize that a deception has been practised upon them in the name of the God of Justice and the Prince of Peace. In fact, the tendency with many is to conclude that Christianity itself is an imposition without foundation, and that, leagued with civil rulers, its aim is merely to hold in check the liberties of the masses.

O that men were wise, that they would apply their hearts to understand the work and plan of the Lord! Then would the present kingdoms melt down gradually — reform would swiftly follow reform, and liberty follow liberty, and justice and truth would prevail until righteousness would be established in the earth. But they will not do this, nor can they in their present fallen state; and so, armed with selfishness, each will strive for mastery, and the kingdoms of this world will pass away with a great time of trouble, such as was not since there was a nation. Of those who will be vainly trying to hold to a dominion which has passed away, when the dominion is given to Him whose right it is, the Lord speaks, urging that they are fighting against Him — a conflict in which they are sure to fail.

21.

Emma Lazarus: "The New Colossus"

Emma Lazarus' precocity as a poet brought her works public attention when she was a girl of eighteen, but her interest in her Jewish heritage was slower to develop, and lay dormant until she learned of the 1879-1883 Russian pogroms against the Jews. When Jewish refugees began arriving in the United States in 1881, Miss Lazarus organized relief programs and published a bitter attack on the pogroms in Century Magazine. *The last five lines of her sonnet, "The New Colossus," were selected for inscription on the pedestal of the Statue of Liberty, dedicated October 28, 1886.*

Source: *Poems*, Boston, 1889, Vol. II.

THE NEW COLOSSUS

Not like the brazen giant of Greek fame,
With conquering limbs astride from land to land;
Here at our sea-washed, sunset gates shall stand
A mighty woman with a torch, whose flame
Is the imprisoned lightning, and her name
Mother of Exiles. From her beacon-hand
Glows world-wide welcome; her mild eyes command
The air-bridged harbor that twin cities frame.
"Keep, ancient lands, your storied pomp!" cries she
With silent lips. "Give me your tired, your poor,
Your huddled masses yearning to breathe free,
The wretched refuse of your teeming shore.
Send these, the homeless, tempest-tossed to me:
I lift my lamp beside the golden door!"

22.

Henry Clews: The Folly of Organized Labor

Henry Clews, who began his career as a clerk in an import house, had by the time of the Civil War opened and successfully established his own investment house on Wall Street and acquired a reputation as a financier in America and abroad. By the end of the war, Livermore, Clews & Mason ranked second in volume of government bond transactions, and Clews could afford to turn his attention to questions of public policy. As a businessman and advisor to President Grant, Clews had advocated conservative economic policies and, as the following document indicates, was especially concerned with the danger he felt the growth of unionism posed to maintenance of an orderly industrial business system.

Source: *North American Review,* June 1886.

The Knights of Labor have undertaken to test, upon a large scale, the application of compulsion as a means of enforcing their demands. The point to be determined is whether capital or labor shall, in future, determine the terms upon which the invested resources of the nation are to be employed.

To the employer, it is a question whether his individual rights as to the control of his property shall be so far overborne as to not only deprive him of his freedom but also expose him to interferences seriously impairing the value of his capital. To the employees, it is a question whether, by the force of coercion, they can wrest, to their own profit, powers and control which, in every civilized community, are secured as the most sacred and inalienable rights of the employer.

This issue is so absolutely revolutionary of the normal relations between labor and capital, that it has naturally produced a partial paralysis of business, especially among industries whose operations involve contracts extending into the future. There has been at no time any serious apprehension that such an utterly anarchical movement could succeed so long as American citizens have a clear perception of their rights and their true interests; but it has been distinctly perceived that this war could not fail to create a divided if not hostile feeling between the two great classes of society; that it must hold in check not only a large extent of ordinary business operations but also the undertaking of those new enterprises which contribute to our national progress, and that the commercial markets must be subjected to serious embarrassments.

From the nature of the case, however, this labor disease must soon end one way or another; and there is not much difficulty in foreseeing what its termination will be. The demands of the Knights and their sympathizers, whether openly expressed or temporarily concealed, are so utterly revolutionary of the inalienable rights of the citizen and so completely subversive of social order that the whole community has come to a firm conclusion that these pretensions must be resisted to the last extremity of endurance and authority; and that the present is the best opportunity for meeting the issue firmly and upon its merits.

The organizations have sacrificed the sympathy which lately was entertained for them on account of inequities existing in certain employments; they stand discredited and distrusted before the community at large as impracticable, unjust, and reckless; and, occupying this attitude before the public, their cause is gone and their organization doomed to failure. They have opened the floodgates to the immigration of foreign labor, which is already pouring in by the thousands; and they have set a premium on nonunion labor, which will be more sought for than ever, and will not be slow to secure superior earnings by making arrangements with employers upon such terms and for such hours as may best suit their interests. Thus, one great advantage will incidentally come out of this crisis beneficial to the workingman, who, by standing aloof from the dead-level system of the unions, will be enabled to earn according to his capacity and thereby maintain his chances for rising from the rank of the employee to that of the employer.

This result cannot be long delayed; because not only is loss and suffering following close upon the heels of the strikers, but the imprudences of their leaders are breeding dissatisfaction among the rank and file of the organizations, which, if much further protracted, will gravely threaten their cohesion. It is by no means certain that we may not see a yet further spread of strikes, and possibly with even worse forms of violence than we have yet witnessed; but, so long as a way to the end is seen, with a chance of that end demonstrating to the organizations that their aspirations to control capital are impossible dreams, the temporary evils will be borne with equanimity. The coolness with which the past phases of the strikes

Library of Congress

Henry Clews

have been endured shows that the steady judgment of our people may be trusted to keep them calm under any further disturbance that may arise.

It is quite evident that the backbone of the strike is broken and that the worst is past, and that a general recovery of trade will assert itself, more or less, in spite of whatever obstacles may be raised by the labor organizations.

The labor movement inaugurated as a stupendous undertaking and announced to come off on the 1st of May, now past, has been a signal failure. The cause of justice and peace has achieved for itself new prestige sufficient to give it longevity, for the reason that the strike movement has been deprived of justification and right of existence.

Before the strike at the Missouri Pacific, Jay Gould was one of the most hated men in the country. He was anxious to have public respect and sympathy. He had made all the money he wanted and was willing to spend part of it in gaining the respect and honor of the country. What his money could not do for him this strike on the Missouri Pacific has done. The sympathy and goodwill which previously was with the strikers has been shifted from them to him. There is no doubt that the strikers selected the Missouri Pacific because it was a property with which Gould was known to be most largely identified and because they thought that general execration would be poured out on him in any event. But instead of injuring Mr. Gould they have done him an inestimable service.

The timely and forcible action of Mayor Harrison, of Chicago, will put dynamiters and rioters where they belong, and thus divide the sheep from the goats in a very short time. If officials would sink political bias, the country would soon be rid of lawbreakers and disturbers of the peace. As this plan has now been adopted, it will be far-reaching in its effect, and stop mob gatherings, riotous speechmaking, and other such bad incentives which recently have been so conspicuous in Chicago, Milwaukee, St. Louis, and elsewhere. The laboring classes, who are parties to the strike, will now have an opportunity to retire to their homes, where there will be more safety than in the streets — which will bring to them reflection; they will then soon become satisfied that they are the aggrieved parties; and the not-unlikely result will be their turning upon the leaders who have deceived them.

There have been numerous vacancies created by the strikers voluntarily resigning. There has been no difficulty in filling these vacancies by those that are equally capable, if not more so, from other countries flocking to our shores. The steam ferry which connects this country and Europe has demonstrated this by the steamer that arrived in six days and ten hours' time from European shores to our own. As the interval between the downtrodden and oppressed operatives of the Old World and America is thus reduced to hours, Europe will quickly send to us all the labor we need to meet the emergency. Mrs. Gray, the Third Avenue Railroad Company, and the Missouri Pacific are the generals that have won the victory. Strikes may have been justifiable in other nations but they are not justifiable in our country, and there is where the mistake was in organizing such a movement. The Almighty has made this country for the oppressed of other nations, and therefore this is the land of refuge for the oppressed, and the hand of the laboring man should not be raised against it.

The laboring man in this bounteous and hospitable country has no ground for complaint. His vote is potential and he is elevated thereby to the position of man. Elsewhere he is a creature of circumstance, which is that of abject depression. Under the government of this nation, the effort is to elevate the standard of the human race and not to degrade it. In all other nations it is the reverse. What, therefore, has the laborer to complain of in America? By inciting strikes and encouraging discontent, he stands in the way of the elevation of his race and of mankind.

The tide of emigration to this country, now so large, makes peaceful strikes perfectly harmless in themselves, because the places of those who vacate good situations are easily filled by the newcomers. When disturbances occur under the cloak of strikes, it is a different matter, as law and order are then set at defiance. The recent disturbances in Chicago, which resulted in the assassination of a number of valiant policemen through some cowardly Polish nihilist firing a bomb of dynamite in their midst, was the worst thing that could have been done for the cause of the present labor agitation, as it alienates all sympathy from them. It is much to the credit, however, of Americans and Irishmen that, during the recent uprising of the labor classes, none of them have taken part in any violent measures whatsoever, nor have they shown any sympathy with such a policy.

If the labor troubles are to be regarded as only a transient interruption of the course of events, it is next to be asked: What may be anticipated when those obstructions disappear? We have still our magnificent country, with all the resources that have made it so prosperous and so progressive beyond the record of all nations. There is no abatement of our past ratio of increase of population; no limitation of the new sources of wealth awaiting development; no diminution of the means necessary to the utilization of the unbounded riches of the soil, the mine, and the forest. Our inventive genius has suffered no eclipse. In the practical application of what may be called the commercial sciences, we retain our lead of the world. As pioneers of new sources of wealth, we are producing greater results than all the combined new colonizing efforts which have recently excited the ambitions of European governments. To the overcrowded populations of the Old World, the United States still presents attractions superior to those of any other country; as is evidenced by the recent sudden revival of emigration from Great Britain and the Continent to our shores.

23.

ALEXANDER CLARK: Socialism and the American Negro

Among the myriad schemes developed in the later years of the nineteenth century for securing civil rights and advancing prosperity, Socialism was hailed by some as holding out hope of a better life not only for Negroes but for all the underprivileged. Negro authors such as T. Thomas Fortune, in Black and White: Land, Labor, and Politics in the South, *advocated that all workingmen, black and white, unite in the common cause of progress. The Negro press reacted to these ideas with editorials and articles such as the following by Alexander Clark, a Negro attorney in Chicago and an outspoken critic of the Socialist philosophy.*

Source: *The A.M.E. Church Review,* July 1886: "Socialism."

THE DEMAND OF THE SOCIALISTS that the state shall assume control of enterprise and industry is already being anxiously considered by the English Ministry in respect of furnishing employment to the starving workingmen of London and other cities, just as it had to be practically accepted all through the dynasty of Napoleon III, in the regal improvement carried on over France to give occupation to the French *ouvriers.* Is this the first fatal crevasse in the embankments so long building against the proletariat? Must the order of the day confess itself a failure? Happily, these apprehensions do not confront us to any alarming extent in this country. The spirit of industrial capital is . . . auspiciously beginning to accord with the fraternal claims of labor.

Along with the recognition of the mutuality of interest in industrial circles, must come a popular and legislative inquisition into the relations of monopolies and the republic; the disproportionate accumulation of private wealth; the plutocratic absorption of landed estates; the inequalities of taxation; the question of the best currency for the people; the crimes against the ballot box, North and South; the proscription of race and sex; class legislation; railroad discriminations and oppression; extortions of telegraphy and the crime against the public morals and the people of watered stock; promotion of savings banks; industrial education in the public schools; the eight-hour system; government insurance; and other matters affecting the general welfare. I believe that the vital interests involved in these many and complex problems may be safely confided to the care of a vigilant, intelligent, right-asserting, and liberty-loving people.

To no portion of the American public does the subject of Socialism address itself with the interest it possesses for 7 million Africo-American citizens. They have cause, transcending the grievances of the vaunted Commune, for revenging themselves upon the cruelties of old systems. They might be excused for listening to the siren voices of the Socialists. But under stress of burning wrongs and the opportunity of retributive justice, they demonstrate their ability to "stand still and see the salvation of God." To the alluring spirit of the Commune they will not the less maintain their souls against temptation.

In grand harmony with the beneficent spirit to whose hands I so confidently commit the future, this century has been glorified with the magistracy of Abraham Lincoln and the Emancipation Proclamation. What brighter augury can the Africo-American desire of a future to which he looks for his emancipation from ignorance, from poverty, and from the lingering inequalities of race?

That we may not be confounded and misled by the ambiguity of terms and possibly become involved in the plots of anarchists and other evil designing men, is it not well that, as Africo-Americans, we remain standing face to face, and in faith with Providence who is the great counsel and help of nations as well as individuals, and continue our trust in that genius of American liberty which struck the shackles from 4 million of our people and lifted legislation to the summit of Sumner's Magna Charta of our civil rights?

We want nothing of Socialism or the Commune, the strike or the boycott, the mob or the riot. For us be it sufficient that we emulate the spirit and faith of Lincoln, Grant, Sumner, and their noble compeers, men devoted to liberty and justice, but equally the friends and champions of law and order as the benign agencies of man's highest good. Let us be beguiled into following no flag of murky hues or strange device, but stand, unbound by any complications, with free consciences, in the simple dignity and loyalty of American citizens, and giving our heart's whole allegiance to God and country.

24.

A. S. WHEELER: The Product of Labor

The "Lords of Industry," as Henry Demarest Lloyd called the oligarchs of the Gilded Age, were characteristically blind to the abject poverty that went hand in hand with their great wealth. If poverty was recognized at all, it was blamed not on the economic system of the time but on the indolence and improvidence of the poor, who, as Joseph Medill of the Chicago Tribune *once declared, squandered "their earnings on intoxicating drinks, cigars and amusements." The rich man's view of "the labor question" is revealed in the following speech by A. S. Wheeler, delivered to the Commercial Club of Boston on October 16, 1886.*

Source: *Andover Review,* November 1886: "The Labor Question."

IN THE CONDITIONS now existing in this country, the sober and industrious man who labors with his hands, the wage earner, is, as a rule, able to procure a comfortable livelihood for himself and family, and in addition, if prudent, to lay up something for sickness and age. There are, of course, exceptions; but it is the rule, and not the exception, that is to be considered in propositions that affect the whole mass.

Why is it that some, and a few, get a larger share of the product than the great majority? It is because they possess superior judgment, skill, and sagacity; because they have greater mental force. I have three cords of wood to be sawed; one man saws two cords, another man one cord. Shall I not pay him who saws two cords twice as much as I pay him who saws one cord? Everybody will say yes. But suppose, by some ingenious device of his, he saws the two cords in half the time the other saws the one cord, is he not entitled to the double pay all the same? Two men engage in fishing in the same boat; they have the same tackle and the same bait. One, by his superior skill, catches twice as many fish as the other; is not each entitled to the fish he

has caught? The one goes home with fish enough to supply his own family with food, and has a surplus to sell and procure other articles of necessity or comfort, and the other has barely enough for food for his own family and no surplus.

And so in every department and kind of human activity. A few have the capacity to obtain more of the product, and they use that capacity and realize its fruits. The inequality in distribution results from the inequality in the individuals. The strongest mentally or physically always get the largest share, and where the mental and physical are united there will be the largest share of all. But the reformer says this is precisely the evil of which we complain. It is not right that one should receive more than another. The man who toils all day and goes home at night wearied should receive as much as he who directs and who does not bear the heat and burden of the day. He whose hands are hard should receive as much as he whose hands are soft.

It is contrary to natural justice and equity that a small part of the community should live in luxury while the mass have barely what suffices for the necessities of life, and that obtained by grinding toil. The answer is twofold. But it must be restated that it is only the actual product that is or can be divided. That product arises from two kinds of labor, mental and physical; because capital is simply the unconsumed product of past labor. The man who has mental capacity actually does more toward making up the total of the product than he who has only physical force, who can only labor with his hands. All will agree that of two men working with their hands, if one is stronger, works harder and more hours, and consequently gets more for his labor than the other, he is entitled to what he gets; and if thereby his family has more comforts, there is no injustice or wrong.

For the same reason, if a man, by reason of superior mental capacity, is able to produce more than another, he is entitled to that larger quantity. He does more work and simply receives the product of that extra work. It is work that may not be visible to the eye, but it is nonetheless work, and it is the kind of work that tells, that increases the sum total of the entire product. The steam that gives motion to the engine is not visible to the eye. But what would avail the steel, the iron, the brass which present so imposing an appearance in the huge machine and whose movements so impress the mind of the spectator were it not for that invisible power which gives force to what would otherwise be an inert mass, utterly valueless so far as accomplishment is concerned?

So it is with capital. Capital of itself can do nothing. It is only as it is made use of, as it is directed by force, that any further product can be obtained through its instrumentality. And here a word as to capital and the capitalist. Two men at twenty-one commence work, with nothing but their hands and their brains. They work a year in the same shop and for the same wages; the one spends all he earns, the other saves something. At the beginning of the second year, one has some capital, the other none.

The first year, both were simply wage earners. The second year, one continues simply a wage earner, the other is a capitalist — no matter how small, still a capitalist.

He keeps on saving, the other continues spending all. Presently the one who saves, if he has the requisite mental ability, becomes an employer. He avails himself of his past savings and of the labor of those who do not save, and who, from whatever cause, continue all their lives wage earners and nothing more; and finally, by his judgment, energy, and skill, saving every year more of the product that he acquires than he consumes, he becomes rich — a large capitalist — and secures for himself and family all that is requisite for the necessities, comforts, conveniences, and pleasures of life.

This is simply the effect of cause. There is no wrong or injustice. Each gets the product of his labor. One gets more than the other because he does more work. He works with his hands and his brains, the other only with his hands. But again, the total product is increased by the mental labor or force of those who have the higher degree of capacity. Were it not for that, we should still be living in caves and clothed with skins. It is the labor of the few that has raised man from barbarism to civilization.

Suppose two men cast upon an uninhabited island, destitute of any means of subsistence but their hands and what they may procure from the natural resources of the place. Beginning in this way, they are able at first to obtain only the bare necessities of life. One has an inventive brain: he devises implements with which to increase the product of their labor. By the aid of these they obtain comforts and conveniences. The product is increased. The man of mind will obtain the largest share, and is he not entitled to it? Has he not earned it? But the man who labors only with his hands will also be benefited. He will obtain more than he would have done had both continued to labor only with their hands and such rude appliances as they could find; so that his condition would be improved by the work of the other. So far, then, from finding fault or complaining of the other's greater prosperity, he should be grateful for it, as he is himself so much better off than he otherwise would have been.

This is precisely what has happened in this country. The increase of production during the last half century has been enormous, and the consequent increase of the means of comfort. Why this increase? If the mechanism and processes had remained the same, if no enterprises — the devices of large and active brains — had been entered upon, there would have been no such increase. The increase has been due to the judgment, skill, and sagacity of the few, and the few have obtained the larger share of the total which is the fruit of their labor. But all this while, the mass, the wage earners, have been getting more and more. They receive greater wages, and the purchasing power of those wages is greater than fifty years ago. The condition of the laboring class has improved relatively as much as the condition of what is called the capitalist class. This, of course, is a question of fact, not of opinion. But it is incontestable that such is the fact.

No doubt those who employ labor will seek to obtain that labor as cheaply as possible. Such is human nature, that the strong are inclined to take advantage of the weak. But somehow it is that when the condition of one class of the community is improved, the condition of every class is also improved, the vicious and criminal only excepted. . . .

Sometimes, but rarely, by means of strikes laborers succeeded in obtaining higher wages. If the laborers are not receiving their proportion of the product, that is, not receiving the wages to which they are entitled, I see no reason why they should not leave their work *en masse*. I see no reason why they should not form combinations to improve their condition.

This, however, by no means justifies the laborers who strike from preventing or endeavoring to prevent other men from working for wages that are not satisfactory to themselves. Such action is a violation of every principle of liberty and common sense. In case of a strike the employer must either comply with the demands of the strikers, employ other laborers, or discontinue the business, unless, as more usually happens, the strikers return to work. Most strikes have been unsuccessful because the demands of the laborers have been unreasonable.

Neither sentimental nor moral considerations can settle the rate of wages any more than they can regulate the rate of interest for money or the price of wheat or cloth. . . . The wages of those employed in the labor which enters into the production of those commodities, therefore, must be governed by this law of demand and supply. This is no matter of theory or speculation. Law rules here as in nature, a law not enacted by any legislature and depending for its execution on governmental officials, but law arising from the nature of things and which is self-executing.

Fortunate it is that such is the case. Communistic, socialistic, and all sorts of theories have been tried, often by well-meaning persons, who have been sincerely desirous of doing good to their fellowmen, but they have been failures. Those which have apparently succeeded have been those where the parties engaged have, consciously or unconsciously, obeyed the general law, and where the respective forces, mental and physical, employed have received their proportionate share of the fruits of the combined labor. There have been and are cases where one party has voluntarily given to the other of his share. Indeed this is constantly done. But this is charity, and however beautiful this grace of charity, however much we admire and praise it, however much we ought to practise it ourselves, it is not the principle which can be relied on to govern human action in the universal working of that action. In that field it is law and not grace that rules.

The objection is made to the practical bearing of the views above stated as to the effect of the law of demand and supply on the rate of wages, that at the present time, owing to the "manipulations" of the cunning and unscrupulous, the law does not have its normal and wholesome operation; that a few obtain not what they are legitimately entitled to from the larger product obtained through the application of mental force but, by their manipulations, acquire an undue share. And the colossal fortunes made by a few men in the last ten or twenty years are referred to as evidence of this.

But those fortunes, where they have not been fairly the result of increased production, resulting from new enterprises or new processes, have been made by capitalists preying on capitalists, and they have not been taken out of the earnings of the wage earners. Those fortunes are the results of manipulations of existing capital in the way of speculation and have nothing to do with current production or the division of that product. So, too, with the great corporations, objects of peculiar suspicion just now. The aggregation of capital by means of association in corporations has been of actual benefit to the laborers in the increase of production, the cheapening the cost of commodities in common use, and the advance of wages. . . .

Again, it has been said that a large part of modern commercial skill lies in watching the operation of demand and accommodating the supply to it, and that a considerable factor, as things are today, is in watching the demand and so "manipulating" the supply, sometimes even "throttling" it, as to create artificial values and concentrate in very few hands the profits that should flow naturally and proportionately to all. True, it is of almost supreme importance that the demand be so watched that the supply should be accommodated to it. In the vast complexity of the operations growing out of

the interchange of commodities, unless the supply of each be regulated according to the demand for each, there will be difficulty, and the impossibility of always forming a correct judgment in this respect by the managers of production occasions loss whenever mistakes are made. And at times the mistakes have been such as to create very serious disturbances in the whole industrial system. With man's limited knowledge and faculties such mistakes will from time to time be made.

If there was never a mistake in the construction of the machinery or the operation of a railroad, there would be no accidents; but no one proposes to abandon railroads because of the occasional loss of life and injuries to persons and property from those mistakes, but rather to impress upon the managers the importance of using all possible care to avoid the mistakes. The answer to the suggestion of "manipulating" and "throttling" the supply is that it cannot be done to an extent sufficient to affect in an appreciable degree the general operation of the law. It has done and may do so in rare and strictly exceptional cases. But as matter of fact, those who have attempted operations of this character have generally failed to accomplish their object and have been themselves involved in ruin.

The result of business experience in this matter is that the manager of capital, the employer of labor, who carefully examines the field, ascertains the normal demand, and regulates his contribution of supply to that demand, succeeds, and in his success the laborers he employs share. He may (and it will be in proportion to his judgment and sagacity) obtain a large share of profit — or, in other words, grow rich — but the men and women he employs will participate in his prosperity and obtain more than they otherwise would.

One of the errors which now possess the minds of the honest portion of the laboring classes is, to use the words of another, "that capacity guided by cunning is not so much increasing production as manipulating its results and profits in its own interests." I concede that there are plenty of men willing and desirous, nay, even striving, to do this, but they cannot succeed. The laws which govern are stronger than they are, and in striving to evade or violate those laws they will, as they always have done, with rare exceptions, fail.

There always has been, and probably will be, discontent in the world. And a certain kind of discontent is essential to human progress. If everybody was satisfied with everything as it is, there would be no improvement. That discontent which leads to action in the way of progress, in the way of really bettering man's condition and in making man himself better, is a noble element of character, and the nations who have had the most of it have made the greatest advances in civilization. But the discontent which is now agitating the laboring class in this country arises from ignorance, and the efforts they have made in the way of strikes, boycotting, and the like, while they have done harm to the employers, have done more harm to the laborers themselves. They and their families have been the greatest sufferers.

25.

AUGUST SPIES: Address at the Haymarket Trial

Chicago, which was known as a center of discontent and also of radical and anarchist sentiments, was the scene of frequent labor agitation for an eight-hour day between 1884 and 1886. On May 3, 1886, a clash took place between strikers and scab laborers brought in to break a strike at the McCormick Harvesting Machine Company. The police were summoned and in the confusion six men were killed. A protest meeting was called by anarchists for the next evening at Haymarket Square on the Near West side of the city. Mayor Carter Harrison attended for a while and found the meeting peaceable except for the impassioned addresses of some anarchist leaders. He ordered the police reserves home and left the scene. Sometime later, however, a subordinate police officer, angered by the speeches, marched upon the meeting with a large force and ordered it to disperse. Thereupon a bomb was thrown, killing seven policemen and injuring many others. Under an excited public opinion the anarchist leaders were indicted, tried, and found guilty, although the actual bomb thrower was never brought forward. The death penalty was imposed on seven and life imprisonment on an eighth. The following selection is taken from a statement made to the Court on October 7, by August Spies, one of four who were eventually hanged.

Source: *The Chicago Martyrs*, San Francisco, 1899, pp. 1-16.

IN ADDRESSING THIS COURT I speak as the representative of one class to the representative of another. I will begin with the words uttered 500 years ago, on a similar occasion, by the Venetian Doge Faberi, who, addressing the court, said: "*My defense is your accusation; the causes of my alleged crime your history!*"

I have been indicted on a charge of murder, as an accomplice or accessory. Upon this indictment I have been convicted. There was no evidence produced by the state to show or even indicate that I had any knowledge of the man who threw the bomb, or that I myself had anything to do with the throwing of the missile, unless, of course, you weigh the testimony of the accomplices of the state's attorney and Bonfield, the testimony of Thompson and Gilmer, by the price they were paid for it. If there was no evidence to show that I was legally responsible for the deed, then my conviction and the execution of the sentence is nothing less than willful, malicious, and deliberate murder, as foul a murder as may be found in the annals of religious, political, or any other sort of persecution.

There have been many judicial murders committed where the representatives of the state were acting in good faith, believing their victims to be guilty of the charge accused of. In this case the representatives of the state cannot shield themselves with a similar excuse; for they themselves have fabricated most of the testimony which was used as a pretense to convict us; to convict us by a jury picked out to convict! Before this court and before the public, which is supposed to be the state, I charge the state's attorney and Bonfield with the heinous conspiracy to commit murder.

I will state a little incident which may throw light upon this charge. On the evening on which the Praetorian guards of the Citizens' Association, the Bankers' Association, the Association of the Board of Trade men, and the railroad princes attacked the meeting of workingmen on the Haymarket — with murderous intent — on that evening, about 8 o'clock, I met a young man, Legner by name, who is a member of the Aurora Turnverein. He accompanied me and never left me on that evening until I jumped from the wagon, a few seconds before the explosion occurred. He knew that I had not seen Schwab that evening. He knew that I had no such conversation with anybody as Mr. Marshall Field's protégé,

Thompson, testified to. He knew that I did not jump from the wagon to strike the match and hand it to the man who threw the bomb.

He is not a Socialist. Why did we not bring him on the stand? Because the honorable representatives of the state, Grinnell and Bonfield, spirited him away. These honorable gentlemen knew everything about Legner. They knew that his testimony would prove the perjury of Thompson and Gilmer beyond any reasonable doubt. Legner's name was on the list of witnesses for the state. He was not called, however, for obvious reasons. Aye, he stated to a number of friends that he had been offered $500 if he would leave the city, and threatened with direful things if he remained here and appeared as a witness for the defense. He replied that he could neither be bought nor bulldozed to serve such a damnable and dastardly plot.

When we wanted Legner, he could not be found; Mr. Grinnell said — and Mr. Grinnell is an honorable man! — that he had himself been searching for the young man, but had not been able to find him. About three weeks later I learned that the very same young man had been kidnaped and taken to Buffalo, N.Y., by two of the illustrious guardians of "law and order," two Chicago detectives. Let Mr. Grinnell, let the Citizens' Association, his employer, let them answer for this! And let the public sit in judgment upon the would-be assassins!

No, I repeat, the prosecution has not established our legal guilt, notwithstanding the purchased and perjured testimony of some, and notwithstanding the originality of the proceedings of this trial. And as long as this has not been done, and you pronounce upon us the sentence of an appointed vigilance committee acting as a jury, I say, you, the alleged representatives and high priests of "law and order," are the real and only lawbreakers, and in this case to the extent of murder. It is well that the people know this. And when I speak of the people I don't mean the few coconspirators of Grinnell — the noble politicians who thrive upon the misery of the multitudes. These drones may constitute the state, they may control the state, they may have their Grinnells, their Bonfields, and other hirelings! No, when I speak of the people I speak of the great mass of human bees, the working people, who unfortunately are not yet conscious of the rascalities that are perpetrated in the "name of the people" — in their name.

The contemplated murder of eight men, whose only crime is that they have dared to speak the truth, may open the eyes of these suffering millions; may wake them up. Indeed, I have noticed that our conviction has worked miracles in this direction already. The class that clamors for our lives, the good, devout Christians, have attempted in every way, through their newspapers and otherwise, to conceal the true and only issue in this case. By simply designating the defendants as anarchists and picturing them as a newly discovered tribe or species of cannibals, and by inventing shocking and horrifying stories of dark conspiracies said to be planned by them, these good Christians zealously sought to keep the naked fact from the working people and other righteous parties, namely: that on the evening of May 4, 200 armed men, under the command of a notorious ruffian, attacked a meeting of peaceable citizens! With what intention? With the intention of murdering them, or as many of them as they could.

I refer to the testimony given by two of our witnesses. The wage workers of this city began to object to being fleeced too much; they began to say some very true things, but they were highly disagreeable to our patrician class; they put forth — well, some very modest demands. They thought eight hours' hard toil a day for scarcely two hours' pay was enough. This "lawless rabble" had to be silenced! The only way to silence them was to frighten them and mur-

August Spies, convicted of murder after Haymarket Riot

der those whom they looked up to as their leaders. Yes, these "foreign dogs" had to be taught a lesson so that they might never again interfere with the high-handed exploitation of their benevolent and Christian masters. Bonfield, the man who would bring a blush of shame to the managers of the St. Bartholomew night — Bonfield, the illustrious gentleman with a visage that would have done excellent service to Doré in portraying Dante's fiends of hell — Bonfield was the man best fitted to consummate the conspiracy of the Citizens' Association, of our patricians.

If I had thrown that bomb, or had caused it to be thrown, or had known of it, I would not hesitate a moment to say so. It is true that a number of lives were lost — many were wounded. But hundreds of lives were thereby saved! But for that bomb, there would have been a hundred widows and hundreds of orphans where now there are a few. These facts have been carefully suppressed, and we were accused and convicted of conspiracy by the real conspirators and their agents. This, your honor, is one reason why sentence should not be passed by a court of justice — if that name has any significance at all.

"But," says the state, "you have published articles on the manufacture of dynamite and bombs." Show me a daily paper in this city that has not published similar articles! I remember very distinctly a long article in the *Chicago Tribune* of February 23, 1885. The paper contained a description and drawings of different kinds of infernal machines and bombs. I remember this one especially, because I bought the paper on a railroad train, and had ample time to read it. But since that time the *Times* has often published similar articles on the subject, and some of the dynamite articles found in the *Arbeiter-Zeitung* were translated articles from the *Times,* written by Generals Molineux and Fitz John Porter, in which the use of dynamite bombs against striking workingmen is advocated as the most effective weapon against them.

May I learn why the editors of these papers have not been indicted and convicted for murder? Is it because they have advocated the use of this destructive agent only against the "common rabble"? I seek information. Why was Mr. Stone of the *News* not made a defendant in this case? In his possession was found a bomb. Besides that, Mr. Stone published an article in January which gave full information regarding the manufacture of bombs. Upon this information any man could prepare a bomb ready for use at the expense of not more than ten cents. The *News* probably has ten times the circulation of the *Arbeiter-Zeitung.* Is it not likely that the bomb used on May 4 was one made after the *News'* pattern? As long as these men are not charged with murder and convicted, I insist, your honor, that such discrimination in favor of capital is incompatible with justice, and sentence should therefore not be passed.

Grinnell's main argument against the defendants was — "They were foreigners; they were not citizens." I cannot speak for the others. I will only speak for myself. I have been a resident of this state fully as long as Grinnell, and probably have been as good a citizen — at least, I should not wish to be compared with him. Grinnell has incessantly appealed to the patriotism of the jury. To that I reply in the language of Johnson, the English litterateur, "an appeal to patriotism is the last resort of a scoundrel." . . .

Grinnell has intimated to us that anarchism was on trial. The theory of anarchism belongs to the realm of speculative philosophy. There was not a syllable said about anarchism at the Haymarket meeting. At that meeting the very popular theme of reducing the hours of toil was discussed. But, "Anarchism is on trial!" foams Mr. Grinnell. If that is the case, your honor, very well; you may sentence me, for I am an anarchist. I believe with Buckle, with Paine, Jefferson, Emerson, and Spencer, and many other great thinkers of this century, that the state of castes and classes — the state where one class dominates over and lives upon the labor of another class, and calls this order — yes, I believe that this barbaric form of social organization, with its legalized plunder and murder, is doomed to die and make room for a free society, voluntary association, or universal brotherhood, if you like. You may pronounce the sentence upon me, honorable judge, but let the world know that in A.D. 1886, in the state of Illinois, eight men were sentenced to death because they believed in a better future; because they had not lost their faith in the ultimate victory of liberty and justice! . . .

You, gentlemen, are the revolutionists! You rebel against the effects of social conditions which have tossed you, by the fair hand of fortune, into a magnificent paradise. Without inquiring, you imagine that no one else has a right in that place. You insist that you are the chosen ones, the sole proprietors. The forces that tossed you into the paradise, the industrial forces, are still at work. They are growing more active and intense from day to day. Their tendency is to elevate all mankind to the same level, to have all humanity share in the paradise you now monopolize. You, in your blindness, think you can stop the tidal wave of civilization and human emancipation by placing a few policemen, a few Gatling guns, and some regiments of militia on the shore; you think you can frighten the rising waves back into the unfathomable depths whence they have arisen by erecting a few gallows in the perspective. You who oppose the natural course of things, you are the real revolutionists. You and you alone are the conspirators and destructionists!

Said the court yesterday, in referring to the Board of Trade demonstration: "These men started out with the express purpose of sacking the Board of Trade building." While I can't see what sense there would have been in such an undertaking, and while I know that the said demonstration was arranged simply as a means of propaganda against the system that legalizes the respectable business carried on there, I will assume that the 3,000 workingmen who marched in that procession really intended to sack the building. In this case they would have differed from the respectable Board of Trade men only in this — that they sought to recover property in an unlawful way, while the others sack the entire country lawfully and unlawfully — this being their highly respectable profession.

This court of "justice and equity" proclaims the principle that when two persons do the same thing, it is not the same thing. I thank the court for this confession. It contains all that we have taught and for which we are to be hanged in a nutshell! Theft is a respectable profession when practised by the privileged class. It is a felony when resorted to in self-preservation by the other class. Rapine and pillage are the order of a certain class of gentlemen who find this mode of earning a livelihood easier and preferable to honest labor — this is the kind of order we have attempted, and are now trying, and will try as long as we live to do away with.

Look upon the economic battlefields! Behold the carnage and plunder of the Christian patricians! Accompany me to the quarters of the wealth creators in this city. Go with me to the half-starved miners of the Hocking Valley. Look at the pariahs in the Monongahela Valley, and many other mining districts in this country, or pass along the railroads of that great and most orderly and law-abiding citizen Jay Gould. And then tell me whether this order has in it any moral principle for which it should be preserved. I say that the preservation of such an order is criminal — is murderous.

It means the preservation of the systematic destruction of children and women in factories. It means the preservation of enforced idleness of large armies of men, and their degradation. It means the preservation of intemperance, and sexual as well as intellectual prostitution. It means the preservation of misery, want, and servility on the one hand, and the dangerous accumulation of spoils, idleness, voluptuousness, and tyranny on the other. It means the preservation of vice in every form. And last, but not least, it means the preservation of the class struggle, of strikes, riots, and bloodshed. That is your "order," gentlemen. Yes, and it is worthy of you to be the champions of such an order. You are eminently fitted for that role. You have my compliments!

26.

"Eight Hour Day"

The struggle of labor organizations to reduce the workingman's day from ten to eight hours reached its peak in the 1880s. In Chicago the movement culminated in the McCormick Company and Haymarket riots of 1886, which led to its decline because it became associated in the popular mind with anarchists and extremist groups. "Eight Hour Day" was a rallying song of the crusade.

🎵 EIGHT HOUR DAY

We mean to make things over, we are tired of toil for naught,
With but bare enough to live upon, and ne'er an hour for thought;
We want to feel the sunshine, and we want to smell the flowers,
We are sure that God has willed it, and we mean to have eight hours.
We're summoning our forces from the shipyard, shop, and mill.

Chorus:
Eight hours for work, eight hours for rest, eight hours for what we will.
Eight hours for work, eight hours for rest, eight hours for what we will.

The beasts that graze the hillside, and the birds that wander free,
In the life that God has meted, have a better lot than we.
Oh hands and hearts are weary, and homes are heavy with dole.
If our life's to be filled with drudgery, what need of a human soul?
Shout, shout the lusty rally, from shipyard, shop, and mill.

Ye deem they're feeble voices that are raised in labor's cause?
But bethink ye of the torrent, and the wild tornado's laws.
We say not toil's uprising in terror's shape will come,
Yet the world were wise to listen to the monetary hum.
Soon, soon the deep-toned rally shall all the nations thrill.

From factories and workshops in long and weary lines,
From all the sweltering forges, and from out the sunless mines,
Wherever toil is wasting the force of life to live,
There the bent and battered armies come to claim what God doth give,
And the blazon on the banner doth with hope the nation fill.

Hurrah, hurrah for labor, for it shall arise in might;
It has filled the world with plenty, it shall fill the world with light.
Hurrah, hurrah for labor, it is mustering all its powers
And shall march along to victory with the banner of Eight Hours.
Shout, shout the echoing rally till all the welkin thrill.

1886 - 1887

27.

RUTHERFORD B. HAYES: Wealth in the Hands of the Few

President Rutherford B. Hayes's unsympathetic attitude toward the trusts, which most of his fellow Republicans tended to approve, lost him the support of his party early in his administration. Having left the White House in 1881 after only one term, Hayes retired to his Ohio home and occupied himself with enlarging his library, fulfilling numerous speaking engagements, and working for humanitarian causes. His concern over the power of concentrated wealth is illustrated by the following passages from his diary; they were written in 1886 and 1887.

Source: *Diary and Letters of Rutherford Birchard Hayes,* Charles R. Williams, ed., Vol. IV, Columbus, O., 1924, pp. 261-262, 277-278, 286, 312, 354-355.

January 22, 1886. Friday. How to distribute more equally the property of our country is a question we (Theodore Clapp and I) considered yesterday. We ought not to allow a permanent aristocracy of inherited wealth to grow up in our country. How would it answer to limit the amount that could be left to any one person by will or otherwise? What should be the limit? Let no one receive from another more than the law gives to the chief justice, to the general of the Army, or to the president of the Senate. Let the income of the property transmitted equal this, say $10,000 to $20,000. If after distributing on this principle there remains undistributed part of the estate, let it go to the public. The object is to secure a distribution of great estates to prevent accumulation.

January 24. Sunday. The question for the country now is how to secure a more equal distribution of property among the people. There can be no republican institutions with vast masses of property permanently in a few hands, and large masses of voters without property. To begin the work, as a first step, prevent large estates from passing, by wills or by inheritance or by corporations, into the hands of a single man. Let no man get by inheritance or by will more than will produce at 4 percent interest an income equal to the salary paid to the chief justice, to the general of the Army, or to the highest officer of the Navy — say an income of $15,000 per year or an estate of $500,000. . . .

March 17. Wednesday. I go to Toledo to attend the celebration of St. Patrick's Day by Father Hannan's people. I shall talk to the text, "America, the Land of the Free and the Home of the Brave," with special reference to Father Hannan's motto "Religion, Education, Temperance, Industry"; and this again in behalf of such measures and laws as will give to every workingman a reasonable hope that by industry, temperance, and frugality he can secure a home for himself and his family, education for his children, and a comfortable support for old age.

March 18. Thursday. At Toledo yesterday and until 1 P.M. today. At Father Hannan's St. Patrick's Institute last evening. I spoke of the danger from riches *in* a few hands, and the poverty of the masses. The capital and labor question. General Comly regards the speech as important. My point is that free government cannot long endure if property is largely in a few hands and large masses of the people are unable to earn homes, education, and a support in old age. . . .

March 19. Friday. No man, however benevolent, liberal, and wise, can use a large fortune so that it will do half as much good in the world as it would if it were divided into moderate sums and in the hands of workmen who had earned it by industry and frugality. The piling up of estates often does great and conspicuous good. Such men as Benjamin Franklin and Peter Cooper knew how to use wealth. But no man does with accumulated wealth so much good as the same amount would do in many hands.

March 20. Saturday. The funeral of General Devereux (at Cleveland today) was largely attended. With General Leggett, General Barnett, and General Elwell, and many others of the Loyal Legion — those named as honorary pallbearers — saw and heard all that belonged to the impressive fu-

Library of Congress

Rutherford B. Hayes

neral. The leading traits of General Devereux were unusual tact in dealing with all sorts of men and all sorts of difficult questions, courage, and integrity. The president of the New York Central, Mr. (Chauncey M.) Depew, introduced me to Cornelius Vanderbilt. I could not help regarding him with sympathy. One of our Republican kings — one of our railroad kings. Think of the inconsistency of allowing such vast and irresponsible power as he possesses to be vested by law in the hands of one man!

March 26. Friday. Am I mistaken in thinking that we are drawing near the time when we must decide to limit and control great wealth, corporations, and the like, or resort to a strong military government? Is this the urgent question? I read in the (Cleveland) *Leader* of this morning that Rev. Dr. Washington Gladden lectured in Cleveland last night on "Capital and Labor." Many good things were said. The general drift and spirit were good. But he leaves out our railroad system. Shall the railroads govern the country, or shall the people govern the railroads? Shall the interest of railroad kings be chiefly regarded, or shall the interest of the people be paramount?

May 12. On the labor question, my position is: 1. The previous question always must be in any popular excitement *the supremacy of law.* All lawless violence must be suppressed *instantly, with overwhelming force and at all hazards.* To hesitate or tamper with it is a fatal mistake. *Justice, humanity, and safety* all require this. 2. I agree that labor does not get its fair share of the wealth it creates. The Sermon on the Mount, the Golden Rule, the Declaration of Independence, all require extensive reforms to the end that labor may be so rewarded that the workingman can, with temperance, industry, and thrift, *own a home, educate his children, and lay up a support for old age.* 3. The United States must begin to deal with the whole subject. I approve heartily of President Cleveland's message and so said at the great soldiers' meeting at Cleveland.

February 25, 1887. Friday. As to pensions I would say our Union soldiers fought in the divinest war that was ever waged. Our war did more for our country than any other war ever achieved for any other country. It did more for the world, more for mankind, than any other war in all history. It gave to those who remained at home and to those who come after it in our country opportunities, prosperity, wealth, a future, such as no war ever before conferred on any part of the human race.

No soldier who fought in that war on the right side nor his widow nor his orphans ought ever to be forced to choose between starvation and the poorhouse. Lincoln in his last inaugural address — just before the war closed, when the last enlistments were going on — pledged the nation "to care for him who hath borne the battle and for his widow and his orphans." Let that sacred pledge be sacredly kept.

December 4. Sunday. In church it occurred to me that it is time for the public to hear that the giant evil and danger in this country, the danger which transcends all others, is the vast wealth owned or controlled by a few persons. Money is power. In Congress, in state legislatures, in city councils, in the courts, in the political conventions, in the press, in the pulpit, in the circles of the educated and the talented its influence is growing greater and greater. Excessive wealth in the hands of the few means extreme poverty, ignorance, vice, and wretchedness as the lot of the many. It is not yet time to debate about the remedy.

The previous question is as to the danger — the evil. Let the people be fully informed and convinced as to the evil. Let them earnestly seek the remedy and it will be found. Fully to know the evil is the first step toward reaching its eradication. Henry George is strong when he portrays the rottenness of the present system. We are, to say the least, not yet ready for his remedy. We may reach and remove the difficulty by changes in the laws regulating corporations, descents of property, wills, trusts, taxation, and a host of other important interests, not omitting lands and other property.

◆

The man who dies rich dies disgraced.
ANDREW CARNEGIE

A man who has a million dollars is as well off as if he were rich.
JOHN JACOB ASTOR

1887

28.

The Interstate Commerce Act

The Interstate Commerce Act of 1887 inaugurated the federal policy of regulation and control of business enterprises. Public indignation over railroad policies was in part responsible for the Act, but equally necessary for the passage of such a bill by the Senate was the acquiescence of railroad owners and other businessmen, who saw federal regulation as the only way to stop ruinous competition between the roads. The Act created a five-man commission empowered to resolve problems of transport rate discrimination, rate rebates, use of terminal facilities, and shortage of freight cars. Weaknesses of the Act, coupled with debilitating rulings by the Supreme Court, made subsequent legislation necessary to strengthen the commission and enlarge its scope of activities.

Source: *Statutes*, XXIV, pp. 379-387.

An act to regulate commerce

Be it enacted by the Senate and House of Representatives of the United States of America in Congress assembled, that the provisions of this act shall apply to any common carrier or carriers engaged in the transportation of passengers or property wholly by railroad, or partly by railroad and partly by water when both are used, under a common control, management, or arrangement, for a continuous carriage or shipment, from one state or territory of the United States, or the District of Columbia, to any other state or territory of the United States, or the District of Columbia, or from any place in the United States to an adjacent foreign country, or from any place in the United States through a foreign country to any other place in the United States, and also to the transportation in like manner of property shipped from any place in the United States to a foreign country and carried from such place to a port of transshipment, or shipped from a foreign country to any place in the United States and carried to such place from a port of entry either in the United States or an adjacent foreign country: *Provided, however*, that the provisions of this act shall not apply to the transportation of passengers or property, or to the receiving, delivering, storage, or handling of property, wholly within one state, and not shipped to or from a foreign country from or to any state or territory as aforesaid.

The term "railroad" as used in this act shall include all bridges and ferries used or operated in connection with any railroad, and also all the road in use by any corporation operating a railroad, whether owned or operated under a contract, agreement, or lease; and the term "transportation" shall include all instrumentalities of shipment or carriage.

All charges made for any service rendered or to be rendered in the transportation of passengers or property as aforesaid, or in connection therewith, or for the receiving, delivering, storage, or handling of such property, shall be reasonable and just; and every unjust and unreasonable charge for such service is prohibited and declared to be unlawful.

Section 2. That if any common carrier subject to the provisions of this act shall, directly or indirectly, by any special rate, rebate, drawback, or other device, charge, demand, collect, or receive from any person or persons a greater or less compensation for any service rendered, or to be rendered, in the transportation of passengers or property, subject to the provisions of this act, than it charges, demands, collects, or receives from any other person or persons for doing for him or them a like and contemporaneous service in the transportation of a like kind of traffic under substantially similar circumstances and conditions, such common carrier shall be deemed guilty of unjust discrimination, which is hereby prohibited and declared to be unlawful.

Section 3. That it shall be unlawful for any common carrier subject to the provisions of this act to make or give any undue or unreasonable preference or advantage to any particular person, company, firm, corporation, or locality, or any particular description of traffic, in any respect whatsoever, or to subject any particular person, company, firm, corporation, or locality, or any particular description of traffic, to any undue or unreasonable prejudice or disadvantage in any respect whatsoever.

Every common carrier, subject to the provisions of this act shall, according to their respective powers, afford all reasonable, proper, and equal facilities for the interchange of traffic between their respective lines, and for the receiving, forwarding, and delivering of passengers and property to and from their several lines and those connecting therewith, and shall not discriminate in their rates and charges between such connecting lines; but this shall not be construed as requiring any such common carrier to give the use of its tracks or terminal facilities to another carrier engaged in like business.

Section 4. That it shall be unlawful for any common carrier subject to the provisions of this act to charge or receive any greater compensation in the aggregate for the transportation of passengers or of like kind of property, under substantially similar circumstances and conditions, for a shorter than for a longer distance over the same line, in the same direction, the shorter being included within the longer distance; but this shall not be construed as authorizing any common carrier within the terms of this act to charge and receive as great compensation for a shorter as for a longer distance: *Provided, however,* that upon application to the Commission appointed under the provisions of this act, such common carrier may, in special cases, after investigation by the Commission, be authorized to charge less for longer than for shorter distances for the transportation of passengers or property; and the Commission may from time to time prescribe the extent to which such designated common carrier may be relieved from the operation of this section of this act.

Section 5. That it shall be unlawful for any common carrier subject to the provisions of this act to enter into any contract, agreement, or combination with any other common carrier or carriers for the pooling of freights of different and competing railroads, or to divide between them the aggregate or net proceeds of the earnings of such railroads, or any portion thereof; and in any case of an agreement for the pooling of freights as aforesaid, each day of its continuance shall be deemed a separate offense.

Section 6. That every common carrier subject to the provisions of this act shall print and keep for public inspection schedules showing the rates and fares and charges for the transportation of passengers and property which any such common carrier has established and which are in force at the time upon its railroad, as defined by the 1st Section of this act. The schedules printed as aforesaid by any such common carrier shall plainly state the places upon its railroad between which property and passengers will be carried, and shall contain the classification of freight in force upon such railroad, and shall also state separately the terminal charges and any rules or regulations which in anywise change, affect, or determine any part or the aggregate of such aforesaid rates and fares and charges. Such schedules shall be plainly printed in large type, of at least the size of ordinary pica, and copies for the use of the public shall be kept in every depot or station upon any such railroad, in such places and in such form that they can be conveniently inspected.

Any common carrier subject to the provisions of this act receiving freight in the United States to be carried through a foreign country to any place in the United States shall also in like manner print and keep for public inspection, at every depot where such freight is received for shipment, schedules showing the through rates established and charged by such common carrier to all points in the United States beyond the foreign country to which it accepts freight for shipment; and any freight shipped from the United States through a foreign country into the United States, the through rate on which shall not have been made public as required by this act, shall, before it is admitted into the United States from said foreign country, be subject to customs duties as if said freight were of foreign production; and any law in conflict with this section is hereby repealed.

No advance shall be made in the rates, fares, and charges which have been established and published as aforesaid by any common carrier in compliance with the requirements of this section, except after ten days' public notice, which shall plainly state the changes proposed to be made in the schedule then in force and the time when the increased rates, fares, or charges will go into effect; and the proposed changes shall be shown by printing new schedules, or shall be plainly indicated upon the schedules in force at the time and kept for public inspection. Reductions in such published rates, fares, or charges may be made without previous public notice; but whenever any such reduction is made, notice of the same shall immediately be publicly posted and the changes made shall immediately be made public by printing new schedules, or shall immediately be plainly indicated upon the schedules at the time in force and kept for public inspection.

And when any such common carrier shall have established and published its rates, fares, and charges in compliance with the provisions of this section, it shall be unlawful for such common carrier to charge, demand, collect, or receive from any person or persons a greater or less compensation for the transportation of passengers or property, or for any services in connection therewith, than is specified in such published schedule of rates, fares, and charges as may at the time be in force.

Every common carrier subject to the provisions of this act shall file with the Commission, hereinafter provided for, copies of its schedules of rates, fares, and charges which have been established and published in compliance with the requirements of this section, and shall promptly notify said Commission of all changes made in the same. Every such common carrier shall also file with said Commission copies of all contracts, agreements, or arrangements with other common carriers in relation to any traffic affected by the provisions of this act to which it may be a party. And in cases where passengers and freight pass over continuous lines or routes operated by more than one common carrier, and the several common carriers operating such lines or routes establish joint tariffs of rates or fares or charges for such continuous lines or routes, copies of such joint tariffs shall also, in like manner, be filed with said Commission.

Such joint rates, fares, and charges on such continuous lines so filed as aforesaid shall be made public by such common carriers when directed by said Commission, insofar as may, in the judgment of the Commission, be deemed practicable; and said Commission shall from time to time prescribe the measure of publicity which shall be given to such rates, fares, and charges, or to such part of them as it may deem it practicable for such common carriers to publish, and the places in which they shall be published; but no common carrier party to any such joint tariff shall be liable for the failure of any other common carrier party thereto to observe and adhere to the rates, fares, or charges thus made and published.

If any such common carrier shall neglect or refuse to file or publish its schedules or tariffs of rates, fares, and charges as provided in this section, or any part of the same, such common carrier shall, in addition to other penalties herein prescribed, be subject to a writ of mandamus, to be issued by any Circuit Court of the United States in the judicial district wherein the principal office of said common carrier is situated or wherein such offense may be committed, and if such common carrier be a foreign corporation, in the judicial circuit wherein such common carrier accepts traffic and has an agent to perform such service, to compel compliance with the aforesaid provisions of this section.

And such writ shall issue in the name of

the people of the United States, at the relation of the Commissioners appointed under the provisions of this act; and failure to comply with its requirements shall be punishable as and for a contempt; and the said Commissioners, as complainants, may also apply, in any such Circuit Court of the United States, for a writ of injunction against such common carrier, to restrain such common carrier from receiving or transporting property among the several states and territories of the United States, or between the United States and adjacent foreign countries, or between ports of transshipment and of entry and the several states and territories of the United States, as mentioned in the 1st Section of this act, until such common carrier shall have complied with the aforesaid provisions of this section of this act.

Section 7. That it shall be unlawful for any common carrier subject to the provisions of this act to enter into any combination, contract, or agreement, expressed or implied, to prevent, by change of time schedule, carriage in different cars, or by other means or devices, the carriage of freights from being continuous from the place of shipment to the place of destination; and no break of bulk, stoppage, or interruption made by such common carrier shall prevent the carriage of freights from being and being treated as one continuous carriage from the place of shipment to the place of destination, unless such break, stoppage, or interruption was made in good faith for some necessary purpose, and without any intent to avoid or unnecessarily interrupt such continuous carriage or to evade any of the provisions of this act. . . .

Section 11. That a commission is hereby created and established to be known as the Interstate Commerce Commission, which shall be composed of five commissioners, who shall be appointed by the President, by and with the advice and consent of the Senate. . . .

Not more than three of the commissioners shall be appointed from the same political party. No person in the employ of or holding any official relation to any common carrier subject to the provisions of this act, or owning stock or bonds thereof, or who is in any manner pecuniarily interested therein, shall enter upon the duties of or hold such office. Said commissioners shall not engage in any other business, vocation, or employment. No vacancy in the Commission shall impair the right of the remaining commissioners to exercise all the powers of the Commission.

Section 12. That the Commission hereby created shall have authority to inquire into the management of the business of all common carriers subject to the provisions of this act, and shall keep itself informed as to the manner and method in which the same is conducted, and shall have the right to obtain from such common carriers full and complete information necessary to enable the Commission to perform the duties and carry out the objects for which it was created; and for the purposes of this act the Commission shall have power to require the attendance and testimony of witnesses and the production of all books, papers, tariffs, contracts, agreements, and documents relating to any matter under investigation, and to that end may invoke the aid of any court of the United States in requiring the attendance and testimony of witnesses and the production of books, papers, and documents under the provisions of this section. . . .

Section 13. That any person, firm, corporation, or association, or any mercantile, agricultural, or manufacturing society, or any body politic or municipal organization complaining of anything done or omitted to be done by any common carrier subject to the provisions of this act in contravention of the provisions thereof, may apply to said Commission by petition, which shall briefly state the facts; whereupon a statement of the charges thus made shall be forwarded by the Commission to such common carrier, who shall be called upon to satisfy the com-

plaint or to answer the same in writing within a reasonable time, to be specified by the Commission. If such common carrier, within the time specified, shall make reparation for the injury alleged to have been done, said carrier shall be relieved of liability to the complainant only for the particular violation of law thus complained of. If such carrier shall not satisfy the complaint within the time specified, or there shall appear to be any reasonable ground for investigating said complaint, it shall be the duty of the Commission to investigate the matters complained of in such manner and by such means as it shall deem proper.

Said Commission shall in like manner investigate any complaint forwarded by the railroad commissioner or railroad commission of any state or territory, at the request of such commissioner or commission, and may institute any inquiry on its own motion in the same manner and to the same effect as though complaint had been made. No complaint shall at any time be dismissed because of the absence of direct damage to the complainant. . . .

Section 20. That the Commission is hereby authorized to require annual reports from all common carriers subject to the provisions of this act, to fix the time and prescribe the manner in which such reports shall be made, and to require from such carriers specific answers to all questions upon which the Commission may need information. Such annual reports shall show in detail the amount of capital stock issued, the amounts paid therefor, and the manner of payment for the same; the dividends paid, the surplus fund, if any, and the number of stockholders; the funded and floating debts and the interest paid thereon; the cost and value of the carrier's property, franchises, and equipment; the number of employees and the salaries paid each class; the amounts expended for improvements each year, how expended, and the character of such improvements; the earnings and receipts from each branch of business and from all sources; the operating and other expenses; the balances of profit and loss; and a complete exhibit of the financial operations of the carrier each year, including an annual balance sheet.

Such reports shall also contain such information in relation to rates or regulations concerning fares or freights, or agreements, arrangements, or contracts with other common carriers, as the Commission may require; and the said Commission may, within its discretion, for the purpose of enabling it the better to carry out the purposes of this act, prescribe (if in the opinion of the Commission it is practicable to prescribe such uniformity and methods of keeping accounts) a period of time within which all common carriers subject to the provisions of this act shall have, as near as may be, a uniform system of accounts, and the manner in which such accounts shall be kept.

Section 21. That the Commission shall, on or before the 1st day of December in each year, make a report to the secretary of the interior, which shall be by him transmitted to Congress, and copies of which shall be distributed as are the other reports issued from the Interior Department. This report shall contain such information and data collected by the Commission as may be considered of value in the determination of questions connected with the regulation of commerce, together with such recommendations as to additional legislation relating thereto as the Commission may deem necessary.

29.

James Cardinal Gibbons: A Defense of the Knights of Labor

The Knights of Labor, by its use of secret rituals — many of them adapted from the Masonic Order — incurred the displeasure of the Catholic archbishop of Canada and through his influence was condemned by the Vatican as a society unfit for Catholics to join. James Cardinal Gibbons of Baltimore called the Catholic bishops of America and the leaders of the Knights to a meeting during the course of which he was shown copies of the Knights' constitution, with the result that he became convinced that the group posed no danger to the tenets or practices of the Church. When Gibbons was in Rome he presented the following memorial of February 20, 1887, in behalf of the Knights, to church authorities. Gibbons won his case: the organization was recognized, and the ban on it in Canada was lifted.

Source: Allen S. Will, *Life of James Cardinal Gibbons,* Baltimore, 1911, pp. 151-161.

IN SUBMITTING TO THE HOLY SEE the conclusions which, after several months of attentive observation and reflection, seem to me to sum up the truth concerning the association of the Knights of Labor, I feel profoundly convinced of the vast importance of the consequences attaching to this question, which is but a link in the great chain of the social problems of our day, and especially of our country.

In treating this question I have been very careful to follow as my constant guide the spirit of the encyclical letters in which our Holy Father Leo XIII has so admirably set forth the dangers of our times and their remedies, as well as the principles by which we are to recognize associations condemned by the Holy See. Such was also the guide of the Third Plenary Council of Baltimore in its teachings concerning the principles to be followed and the dangers to be shunned by the faithful, either in the choice or in the establishment of those various forms of association toward which the spirit of our popular institutions so strongly impels them.

And, considering the evil consequences that might result from a mistake in the treatment of organizations which often count their members by thousands and hundreds of thousands, the Council wisely ordained . . . that, when an association is spread over several dioceses, not even the bishop of one of these dioceses shall condemn it, but shall refer the case to a standing committee consisting of all the archbishops of the United States; and even these are not authorized to condemn, unless their sentence be unanimous. And in case they fail to agree unanimously, then only the supreme tribunal of the Holy See can impose a condemnation; all this in order to avoid error and confusion of discipline.

This committee of archbishops held a meeting toward the end of last October at which the association of the Knights of Labor was specially considered. To this we were not impelled by the request of any of our bishops, for none of them had asked it; and I must add that among all the bishops we know of but two or three who desire the condemnation. But our reason was the importance attached to the question by the Holy See itself, and this led us to examine it with all possible care. After our deliberations, the result of which has already been communicated to the Sacred Congregation of the Propaganda, only two out of the twelve archbishops voted for condemnation; and their reasons were powerless to convince the others of either the justice or the prudence of such a condemnation.

In the following considerations I wish to state in detail the reasons which determined the vote of the great majority of the committee — reasons whose truth and force seem to me all the more evident after this lapse of time; nor will I fail to do justice to the arguments advanced on the other side:

1. In the first place, though there may be found in the constitution, laws, and official declarations of the Knights of Labor things that we would not approve, still, we have failed to find in them those elements so clearly pointed out by the Holy See, which would class them among condemned associations:

a. In their form of initiation there is no oath.

b. The obligation to secrecy by which they keep the knowledge of their business from enemies or strangers is not such as to hinder Catholics from manifesting everything to competent ecclesiastical authority, even outside of confession. This has been positively declared to us by their chief officers.

c. They make no promise of blind obedience. The object and laws of the association are distinctly declared, and the obligation of obedience does not go beyond them.

d. They not only profess no hostility against religion or the Church but their declarations are quite to the contrary. The Third Plenary Council commands . . . that condemnation shall not be passed on any association without the previous hearing of its officers or representatives. Now, their president, when sending me a copy of their constitution, declared that he is a devoted Catholic; that he practises his religion faithfully and receives the sacraments regularly; that he belongs to no Masonic society or other association condemned by the Church; that he knows nothing in the organization of the Knights of Labor contrary to the laws of the Church; that, with filial submission, he begs the pastors of the Church to examine their constitution and laws, and to point out anything they may find objectionable, promising to see to its correction.

Assuredly, there is in all this no hostility to the authority of the Church, but, on the contrary, a disposition in every way praiseworthy. After their convention, held last year in Richmond, he and several of the principal members, devout Catholics, made similar declarations concerning the action of that convention, the documents of which we expect to receive shortly.

e. Nor do we find in this organization any hostility to the authority and laws of our country. Not only does nothing of the kind appear in their constitution and laws but the heads of our civil government treat with respect the cause which such associations represent. The President of the United States told me personally, a few weeks ago, that he then had under consideration a proposed law for the amelioration of certain social grievances, and that he had had a long conversation on these topics with Mr. Powderly, the president of the Knights of Labor.

The Congress of the United States, in compliance with the views presented by President Cleveland in his annual message, is at present engaged in framing measures for the improvement of the condition of the laboring classes, in whose complaints they acknowledge that there is a great deal of truth. And our political parties, far from considering them the enemies of the country, vie with each other in championing the evident rights of the workingmen, who seek not to resist or overthrow the laws but only to obtain just legislation by constitutional and legitimate means.

These considerations, which show that in these associations those elements are not to be found which the Holy See has condemned, lead us to study, in the second place, the evils which the association contends against and the nature of the conflict.

2. That there exist among us, as in all other countries of the world, grave and threatening social evils, public injustices which call for strong resistance and legal

remedy, is a fact which no one dares to deny — a fact already acknowledged by the Congress and the President of the United States. Without entering into the sad details of these evils, whose full discussion is not necessary, I will only mention that monopolies, on the part of both individuals and of corporations, have everywhere called forth, not only the complaints of our working classes but also the opposition of our public men and legislators; that the efforts of monopolists, not always without success, to control legislation to their own profit cause serious apprehensions among the disinterested friends of liberty; that the heartless avarice, which, through greed of gain, pitilessly grinds not only the men but even the women and children in various employments, makes it clear to all who love humanity and justice that it is not only the right of the laboring classes to protect themselves but the duty of the whole people to aid them in finding a remedy against the dangers with which both civilization and social order are menaced by avarice, oppression, and corruption.

It would be vain to dispute either the existence of the evils or the right of legitimate resistance or the necessity of a remedy. At most, a doubt might be raised about the legitimacy of the form of resistance and of the remedy employed by the Knights of Labor. This, then, is the next point to be examined.

3. It can hardly be doubted that, for the attainment of any public end, association — the organization of all interested — is the most efficacious means — a means altogether natural and just. This is so evident and, besides, so conformable to the genius of our country, of our essentially popular social conditions, that it is unnecessary to insist upon it. It is almost the only means to public attention to give force to the most legitimate resistance, to add weight to the most just demands.

Now, there already exists an organization which presents innumerable attractions and

James Cardinal Gibbons, head of the Baltimore archdiocese and second American cardinal

advantages, but with which our Catholic workingmen, filially obedient to the Holy See, refuse to unite themselves; this is the Masonic Order, which exists everywhere in our country and which, as Mr. Powderly has expressly pointed out to us, unites employers and employed in a brotherhood very advantageous to the latter, but which numbers in its ranks hardly a single Catholic. Nobly renouncing advantages which the Church and conscience forbid, our workingmen join associations in no way in conflict with religion, seeking nothing but mutual protection and help, and the legitimate assertion of their rights. Must they here also find themselves threatened with condemnation, hindered from their only means of self-defense? . . .

Among all the glorious titles which the Church's history has deserved for her, there is not one which at present gives her so great influence as that of "Friend of the People." Assuredly, in our democratic country, it is this title which wins for the Catholic Church not only the enthusiastic devotedness of the millions of her children but

also the respect and admiration of all our citizens, whatever be their religious belief. It is the power of this title which renders persecution almost an impossibility and which draws toward our Holy Church the great heart of the American people.

And since it is acknowledged by all that the great questions of the future are not those of war, of commerce, or of finance but the social questions — the questions which concern the improvement of the condition of the great popular masses, and especially of the working people — it is evidently of supreme importance that the Church should always be found on the side of humanity — of justice toward the multitudes who compose the body of the human family. . . .

In our country, above all, this social amelioration is the inevitable program of the future, and the position which the Church should hold toward it is surely obvious. She can certainly not favor the extremes to which the poor multitudes are naturally inclined; but, I repeat, she must withhold them from these extremes by the bonds of affection, by the maternal desire which she will manifest for the concession of all that is just and reasonable in their demands, and by the maternal blessing which she will bestow upon every legitimate means for improving the condition of the people.

6. Now let us consider for a moment the consequences which would inevitably follow from a contrary course — from a course of want of sympathy for the working class, of suspicion for their aims, of ready condemnation for their methods.

a. First, there would be the evident danger of the Church's losing, in popular estimation, her right to be considered the friend of the people. The logic of the popular heart goes swiftly to its conclusions, and this conclusion would be most pernicious, both for the people and for the Church. To lose the heart of the people would be a misfortune for which the friendship of the

few rich and powerful would be no compensation.

b. There would be a great danger of rendering hostile to the Church the political power of our country, which has openly taken sides with the millions who are demanding justice and the improvement of their condition. The accusation of being un-American — that is to say, alien to our national spirit — is the most powerful weapon which the enemies of the Church can employ against her. It was this cry which aroused the Know-Nothing persecution thirty years ago, and the same would be used again if the opportunity offered. To appreciate the gravity of this danger it is well to remark that not only are the rights of the working classes loudly proclaimed by each of our two great political parties but it is not improbable that, in our approaching national elections, there will be a candidate for the office of President of the United States as the special representative of the popular complaints and demands.

Now, to seek to crush by an ecclesiastical condemnation an organization which represents more than 500,000 votes, and which has already so respectable and so universally recognized a place in the political arena, would, to speak frankly, be considered by the American people as not less ridiculous than rash. To alienate from ourselves the friendship of the people would be to run great risk of losing the respect which the Church has won in the estimation of the American nation and of forfeiting the peace and prosperity which form so admirable a contrast with her condition in some so-called Catholic countries. Angry utterances have not been wanting of late, and it is well that we should act prudently.

c. A third danger — and the one which most keenly touches our hearts — is the risk of losing the love of the children of the Church and of pushing them into an attitude of resistance against their Mother. The world presents no more beautiful spectacle

than that of their filial devotion and obedience; but it is well to recognize that, in our age and in our country, obedience cannot be blind. We would greatly deceive ourselves if we expected it. Our Catholic workingmen sincerely believe that they are only seeking justice, and seeking it by legitimate means. A condemnation would be considered both false and unjust and, therefore, not binding. We might preach to them submission and confidence in the Church's judgment; but these good dispositions could hardly go so far. They love the Church, and they wish to save their souls; but they must also earn their living, and labor is now so organized that without belonging to the organization it is almost impossible to earn one's living.

Behold, then, the consequences to be feared. Thousands of the Church's most devoted children, whose affection is her greatest comfort and whose free offerings are her chief support, would consider themselves repulsed by their Mother and would live without practising their religion. Catholics who have hitherto shunned the secret societies would be sorely tempted to join their ranks. The Holy See, which has constantly received from the Catholics of America proofs of almost unparalleled devotedness, would be considered, not as a paternal authority but as a harsh and unjust power. Surely these are consequences which wisdom and prudence counsel us to avoid.

7. But, besides the dangers that would result from such a condemnation and the impracticability of putting it into effect, it is also very important that we should carefully consider another reason against condemnation, arising from the unstable and transient character of the organization in question. It is frequently remarked by the press and by attentive observers that this special form of association has in it so little permanence that, in its present shape, it is not likely to last many years. Whence it follows that it is not necessary, even if it were just and pru-

dent, to level the sole condemnations of the Church against so evanescent an object. The social agitation itself will, indeed, last as long as there are social evils to be remedied; but the forms of organization meant for the attainment of this end are naturally provisional and short-lived. They are also very numerous, for I have already remarked that the Knights of Labor is only one among many labor organizations.

To strike, then, at one of these forms would be to commence a war without system and without end; it would be to exhaust the forces of the Church in chasing a crowd of changing and uncertain specters. The American people behold with perfect composure and confidence the progress of our social contest and have not the least fear of not being able to protect themselves against any excesses or dangers that may occasionally arise. Hence, to speak with the most profound respect, but also with the frankness which duty requires of me, it seems to me that prudence suggests, and that even the dignity of the Church demands, that we should not offer to America an ecclesiastical protection for which she does not ask and of which she believes she has no need. . . .

Now, as I have already indicated, out of the seventy-five archbishops and bishops of the United States, there are about five who desire the condemnation of the Knights of Labor, such as they are in our own country; so that our hierarchy are almost unanimous in protesting against such a condemnation. Such a fact ought to have great weight in deciding the question. If there are difficulties in the case, it seems to me that the prudence and experience of our bishops and the wise rules of the Third Plenary Council ought to suffice for their solution.

Finally, to sum up all, it seems to me

that the Holy See could not decide to condemn an association under the following circumstances:

1. When the condemnation does not seem to be *justified,* either by the letter or the spirit of its constitution, its law, and the declaration of its chiefs.

2. When the condemnation does not seem *necessary* in view of the transient form of the organization and the social condition of the United States.

3. When it does not seem to be *prudent* because of the reality of the grievances complained of by the working classes and their acknowledgment by the American people.

4. When it would be *dangerous* for the reputation of the Church in our democratic country, and might even lead to persecution.

5. When it would probably be *inefficacious* owing to the general conviction that it would be unjust.

6. When it would be *destructive* instead of beneficial in its effects, impelling the children of the Church to disobey their Mother and even to enter condemned societies, which they have thus far shunned.

7. When it would turn into suspicion and hostility the singular devotedness of our Catholic people toward the Holy See.

8. When it would be regarded as a cruel blow to the authority of bishops in the United States, who, it is well known, protest against such a condemnation.

Now, I hope that the considerations here presented have sufficiently shown that such would be the effect of condemnation of the Knights of Labor in the United States.

Therefore, I leave the decision of the case, with fullest confidence, to the wisdom and prudence of Your Eminence and the Holy See.

"Liberty Enlightening the World"; military salute at the dedication of the Statue of Liberty

POLITICS: 1884-1894

The politics of the period 1884-1894 were balanced between a constant governmental conservatism with a mild interest in reform and a rising popular liberalism. Though the Republican domination of the presidency was broken twice by Cleveland, official policy changed little throughout the period; the limitation of silver coinage, maintenance of the tariff, and general "soundness" in governmental finance were paramount. The rather disorganized popular movement began with farmers' organizations against railroads, moved through single-issue splinter groups such as the Greenback and Anti-monopoly parties, and eventually developed into the Populist Party in 1892. A genuine attempt at a farmer-worker alliance, in all sections, the party produced a national platform in 1892 which was a broad program of reform and regulation in agriculture, industry, and government. The alliance and broad-front aspects of the movement, however, were never sufficiently accepted by the body of members to keep the party together. The tendency to concentrate on single and regional issues remained strong, and extraneous and damaging concerns often defeated the party's main purposes; such was the effect of the linking of Populism with racism in the South, and particularly with the fundamentalist religious views of Bryan in 1896.

(Above left) Ben Butler, supporter of the inflationary Greenback movement and candidate for President in 1884 for the People's Party; (above right) Chester Arthur, photo by Bell, 1882

Sensitivity to corruption and injustice seems to have increased in the decades following the scandals of Grant's administration. Economic reform, directed primarily at the trusts and monopolies, dominated the field; programs for state or federal regulation led eventually to the Interstate Commerce Act of 1887, while fiscal reformers turned the free silver and Greenback issues into the Populist Party of the 1890s. Chester A. Arthur, supposed to be the puppet of party bosses, surprised everyone by reviving the long-delayed issue of civil service reform.

(Left) Thomas Nast, cartoonist for "Harper's Weekly" whose caricatures broke the Tweed Ring in New York City. Later he championed civil service reforms. (Below) Grant reading on the porch of his home, 1885. Corruption in his administration was a major stimulus for removing the spoils system

Cartoons depicting some of the issues of the last decades of the 19th century: (Above) "Church and State — No Union Upon any Terms"; cartoon by Thomas Nast

(Above left) "Return of the Boy with Currency" from "Inflation at the Crossroads" by Petroleum V. Nasby; (above right) "What We Must Do about It. Citizen Hercules, make a clean sweep of the dirt and the cause." (Below) "The Bosses of the Senate" by Keppler in "Puck," 1889

THE GRANGER

IN TRAINING FOR CONGRESS

GIFT FOR THE GRANGERS

(Above and left) Two views of the Grange movement in lithographs published in 1873

Founded in 1867 to promote progressive agricultural methods, the Patrons of Husbandry — the Grange — was the organized movement needed to prompt governmental regulation of the railroads. Originally enacted at the state level, the "Granger laws" led to federal regulation under the Interstate Commerce Commission. Monopoly capital evoked further opposition in the form of labor organizations. The National Labor Union in 1866 and the Knights of Labor in 1869 were early attempts to construct a countervailing power to capital, but both, for various reasons, failed. In spite of massive anti-union sentiment roused by the Haymarket Riot in 1886, the American Federation of Labor, founded that year, was to be highly successful.

Leading officers of the Grange: (front row, left to right) William Saunders, first national master; D. W. Adams, national master in 1873; O. H. Kelley, national secretary and founder of the Grange. Others shown are local chapter leaders

"An Optical Delusion"; cartoon opposing the economic theories of Henry George that became popular with the laboring classes in the 1880s

(Above) State militia entering Homestead, Pa., to put down strike in 1892; (left) 1885 cover for "Frank Leslie's Illustrated" depicting an anarchist; (below) "Puck" cartoon attacking Cardinal Gibbons' support of the Knights of Labor

(Above) Wade Hampton, governor of South Carolina, was one of the last of the planter class to be elected. His defeat by "Pitchfork Ben" Tillmann in 1890 signalled the rise of Populist as well as racist traditions in Southern politics

Segregation was unnecessary in the pre-war South. When the institution of slavery was removed and the Northern interference of Reconstruction ended, however, legal and paralegal safeguards were required to maintain the social status quo. Yet segregation as a system, though long common in the North, was rather slow in developing. Segregation in education grew naturally with the spread of Negro education, but separate public accommodations and institutions were not the rule through the South until 1907. By that time the Supreme Court had decided Plessy v. Ferguson, validating Jim Crow laws for half a century to come.

(Top) Booker T. Washington, president of Tuskegee Institute and advocate of Negro self-help; Negro school in South Carolina; (below) comment on exclusion of Negro veterans from encampment

(Above) "Anti-Chinese Wall; the American wall goes up as the Chinese original goes down";
(below) Chinese fire hose team in Deadwood, S.D.

From the 1870s on, an increasing percentage of immigrants came from the Orient and southern and eastern Europe. Their willingness to work for low wages angered the American working class, which feared for its jobs. Anti-Chinese riots occurred in many western cities, finally resulting in the Chinese Exclusion Act of 1882. As native sentiments heightened, taxes and restrictions were placed on all immigrants. (Below left) examining immigrants' eyes on Ellis Island; (below right) immigrant family in New York, 1889

THE CURIOUS EFFECT OF CLEAN LINEN UPON THE DEMOCRATIC PARTY.

(Right) Grover Cleveland; (above) Thomas Nast pictures an uncomfortable Tammany Tiger hampered by Cleveland's uncompromising honesty and independence from the bosses

Largely due to the questionable reputation of James Blaine, Republican candidate for President in 1884, and to the renegade Mugwumps, Grover Cleveland became the first Democratic President since the war. Though his election was considered a catastrophe by Republicans, his policies actually differed little from those of his predecessors: civil service reform, ending of silver coinage, rehabilitation of the Navy, protection of public lands. Cleveland's greatest opposition centered on his advocacy of tariff reduction; this became the first real partisan issue in years and lost Cleveland the election of 1888 to Republican Benjamin Harrison.

(Left) Anti-tariff cartoon argues that the ''inevitable result'' of industry protected from outside competition is over-production and in the end, a recession and unemployment; (below) Midwestern wheat for export arriving in New York

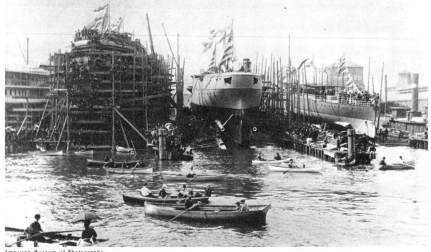

Launching of the cruiser "Vesuvius," 1888, in Philadelphia

A FRIENDLY ADMONITION.

JOHN BULL—"Don't poke him up, Bizzy—He's a very patient bird, but is almighty nasty when he's roused—I speak from experience!"

(Left) With a growing Navy and greater interest in world power, the U.S. came in conflict with Germany over naval rights in Samoa. The German vessel (above) was wrecked before a compromise was found. (Below) pro-tariff cartoon: "Declaration of Dependence"

DECLARATION OF INDEPENDENCE, JULY 4th, 1776.

(Right) Benjamin Harrison; (above) Harrison appointed Theodore Roosevelt to the post of Civil Service commissioner in 1889. Roosevelt used the post to expound the need for reform but the powers of the office were limited

Benjamin Harrison was a thoroughly unimpressive President whose administration was best known for its incredibly open veterans' pensions policy. Except for Secretary of State Blaine's imaginative foreign policy, Harrison's term was little more than an interlude in the battle over fiscal policy; though he was elected as a high-tariff advocate, the passage of the prohibitive McKinley Tariff in 1890 effectively ended his presidency. The election of 1890 returned a heavy Democratic majority to the House.

(Right) Harrison and his incompetent commissioner of pensions were criticized for handing out government surplus funds to Civil War pensioners too liberally; (below) a cartoonist comments on the immigration debate by suggesting that they draw the line to exclude first "ruined marquis looking for an heiress, played out actors, beggered German Baron, English Dude, German opera singer"

30.

WALT WHITMAN: On the Sources of His Style

In an 1887 letter to W. S. Kennedy, Walt Whitman, contradicting his own earlier statements, denied that the works of Ralph Waldo Emerson had exerted any influence on Leaves of Grass. *Certainly Emerson had been enthusiastically responsive to the work's first edition (which appeared in 1855), writing to Whitman: "I greet you at the beginning of a great career, which yet must have had a long foreground somewhere, for such a start." Most critics agree that some part of Emerson's writings — perhaps his essay "The Poet" — influenced Whitman, and that Whitman probably denied the influence because, as he grew older, he believed ever more ardently that* Leaves of Grass *was his wholly original creation, completely unrelated to all poetry that had gone before.*

Source: William Sloane Kennedy, *Reminiscences of Walt Whitman*, London, 1896, pp. 76-77.

Dear W. S. K.

It is of no importance whether I had read Emerson before starting *L. of G.* or not. The fact happens to be positively that I had *not*. The basis and body and genesis of the *Leaves*, differing I suppose from Emerson and many grandest poets and artists, was and is that I found and find everything in the *common concrete*, the broadcast materials, the flesh, the common passions, the tangible and visible, etc., and in *the average*, and that I radiate, work from, these outward — or rather hardly wish to leave here but to remain and celebrate it all. Whatever the amount of this may be or not be, it is certainly *not Emersonian*, not Shakespeare, not Tennyson — indeed, the antipodes of E. and the others in essential respects. But I have not suggested or expressed myself well in my book unless I have in a sort included them and their sides and expressions too — as this orb the world means and includes all climes, all sorts, *L. of G.*'s word is *the body,*

including all, including the intellect and soul; E.'s word is mind (or intellect or soul).

If I were to unbosom to you in the matter, I should say that I never cared so very much for E.'s writings, prose or poems, but from his first personal visit and two hours with me (in Brooklyn in 1866 or '65?) [The query mark his; he means '55 or '56] I had a strange attachment and love for *him* and his contact, talk, company, magnetism. I welcomed *him* deepest and always — yet it began and continued *on his part*, quite entirely; HE always sought ME. We probably had a dozen (possibly twenty) of these meetings, talks, walks, etc. — some five or six times (sometimes New York, sometimes Boston) had good long dinners together. I was very happy — I don't think I was at my best with him — he always did most of the talking — I am sure he was happy too.

That visit to me at Sanborn's, by E. and family (see pp. 189-90 *Specimen Days),* and the splendid formal-informal family dinner *to me*, next day, Sunday, Sept. 18, '81, by E., Mrs. E., and all, I consider not only a victor event in my life, but it is an after explanation of so much and offered as an apology, peace offering, justification, of much that the world knows not of. My dear friend, I think I know R.W.E. better than anybody else knows him — and loved him in proportion, but quietly. Much was revealed to me.

WALT WHITMAN

31.

JAMES CARDINAL GIBBONS: The Progress of the Catholic Church in America

James Gibbons, archbishop of Baltimore and a highly respected figure in Catholic and secular circles, shared with Pope Leo XIII a firm conviction that the real future of the Catholic Church lay in the democratic societies. Pope Leo appointed Gibbons apostolic delegate to the 1884 Third Plenary Council of Baltimore, which under Gibbons' strong influence pledged itself to support American civil institutions. Gibbons soon set an example of that support in his memorial in defense of the Knights of Labor, presented to Church authorities on February 20, 1887. Elevated to the rank of cardinal in 1886, Gibbons delivered the following address at his installation as titular head of the Church of Santa Maria in Trastevere, Italy, on March 25, 1887.

Source: *Catholic Mirror*, April 2, 1887.

IT IS TO ME EXCEEDINGLY GRATIFYING that the Holy Father has assigned as my titular church this beautiful and historic basilica, the first church ever erected in honor of the Virgin Mother of God; and I regard it as an auspicious circumstance that my own Cathedral Church of Baltimore, the oldest cathedral in the United States, is also dedicated to our Blessed Lady. The venerable temple in which we are assembled leads us back to the days of the catacombs. It was founded by Pope St. Calixtus in the year 224. It was reconstructed by Pope Julius in the fourth century and renovated by another supreme pontiff in the twelfth.

That ceaseless solicitude which the Roman pontiffs have exhibited in erecting the material temples which adorn this city, they have also manifested on a larger scale in building up the spiritual walls of Sion in every age.

Every student of history must be deeply impressed with the overruling action of the papacy in the evangelization and civilization of the Christian world. I place these words together, for a nation is civilized in proportion as it receives the light of the Gospel. It was the vigilant zeal of the Holy See that sent Augustine to England, and Patrick to Ireland, and Pelagius to Scotland, and that sent Francis Xavier to evangelize the Indies; and all those other heroes of Christ's Church who bore, amid suffering and trials, the bright light of truth into the regions of pagan darkness. And coming down to a later period, scarcely were the United States formed into an independent government when Pius VII, of happy memory, established there the Catholic hierarchy and appointed the illustrious John Carroll first bishop of Baltimore.

This event, so important to us, occurred less than a hundred years ago — a long period, indeed, in our history, but how brief in that of Rome eternal! Our Catholic community in those days numbered only a few thousand souls, scattered chiefly through the states of New York, Pennsylvania, and Maryland, and were served by the merest handful of priests. Thanks to the fructifying grace of God, the grain of mustard seed then planted has grown to be a large tree, spreading its branches over the length and the width of our fair land. Where only one bishop was found in the beginning of this century, there are now seventy-five serving as many dioceses and vicariates. For their great progress under God and the fostering care of the Holy See, we are indebted in no small degree to the civil liberty we enjoy in our enlightened republic.

Our Holy Father, Leo XIII, in his luminous encyclical on the constitution of Christian states, declares that the Church is not committed to any particular form of civil government. She adapts herself to all; she leavens all with the sacred leaven of the Gospel. She has lived under absolute empires; she thrives under constitutional monarchies; she grows and expands under the free republic. She has often, indeed, been hampered in her divine mission and has had to struggle for a footing wherever despotism has cast its dark shadow like the plant excluded from the sunlight of heaven, but in the genial air of liberty she blossoms like the rose!

For myself, as a citizen of the United States, without closing my eyes to our defects as a nation, I proclaim, with a deep sense of pride and gratitude, and in this great capital of Christendom, that I belong to a country where the civil government holds over us the aegis of its protection without interfering in the legitimate exercise of our sublime mission as ministers of the Gospel of Jesus Christ.

Our country has liberty without license, authority without despotism. Hers is no spirit of exclusiveness. She has no frowning fortifications to repel the invader, for we are at peace with all the world! In the consciousness of her strength and of her goodwill to all nations, she rests secure. Her harbors are open in the Atlantic and Pacific to welcome the honest immigrant who comes to advance his temporal interest and to find a peaceful home.

But, while we are acknowledged to have a free government, we do not, perhaps, receive due credit for possessing also a strong government. Yes, our nation is strong and her strength lies, under Providence, in the majesty and supremacy of the law, in the loyalty of her citizens to that law, and in the affection of our people for their free institutions.

There are, indeed, grave social problems which are now engaging the earnest attention of the citizens of the United States. But I have no doubt that, with God's blessings, these problems will be solved by the calm judgment and sound sense of the American people without violence or revolution or injury to individual right.

As an evidence of his benevolence and goodwill to the great republic of the West, as evidence of his appreciation of the venerable hierarchy of the United States, and as an expression of his kind condescension for the ancient See of Baltimore, our Holy Father, Leo XIII, has been graciously pleased to elevate its present incumbent in my humble person to the dignity of the purple.

For this mark of exalted favor I offer the Holy Father my profound thanks in my own name and in the name of the clergy and people under my charge. I venture also to thank him in the name of my venerable colleagues the bishops, the clergy, as well as the Catholic laity of the United States. I presume to thank him also in the name of our separated brethren of America, who, though not sharing our faith, have shown that they are not insensible to the honor conferred on our common country, and have again and again expressed their warm admiration of the enlightened statesmanship, the apostolic virtues, and benevolent charities of the illustrious pontiff who now sits in the Chair of Peter.

32.

Colorado Child Labor Law

Throughout the nineteenth century, efforts to put a curb on the use of child labor were halting and sporadic. A few states passed child labor laws, but they were usually worded so as to be easily evaded both by employers and by parents who needed the income. Business leaders denounced attempts to restrict child labor as socialistic, communistic, and injurious to the rights of parents. By late in the century, child labor was a problem of national proportions over which enough public sentiment could occasionally be aroused for a state to pass a law such as the following Colorado statute of March 7, 1887.

Source: *Laws Passed at the Sixth Session of the General Assembly of the State of Colorado, Convened at Denver, on the fifth day of January, 1887,* Denver, 1887, pp. 76-77.

An act to prohibit the employment of children under fourteen years of age for certain work.

Be it enacted by the General Assembly of the State of Colorado:

Section 1. That any person who shall take, receive, hire, or employ any children under fourteen years of age in any underground works, or mine, or in any smelter, mill, or factory shall be guilty of a misdemeanor; and upon conviction thereof before any justice of the peace or court of record shall be fined not less than $10 nor more than $50 for each offense: *Provided,* that a jury on the trial of any such case before a justice of the peace, shall be called and impaneled as in the case of assault and battery, and that the jury in such cases shall designate the amount of the fine in their verdict.

Section 2. That whenever any person shall before a justice of the peace make oath or affirm that the affiant believes that this act has been or is being violated, naming the person charged with such violation, such justice shall forthwith issue a warrant to a constable, or other authorized officer, and such officer shall arrest the person or persons so charged, and bring him or them before the justice issuing such warrant for a hearing. And it shall be the duty of all constables and policemen to aid in the enforcement of this act.

Section 3. That in default of the payment of the fine or penalty imposed under any of the provisions of this act, it shall be lawful for any justice of the peace, or court of record before whom any person may be convicted of a violation of any of the provisions of this act, to commit such person to the county jail, there to remain for not less than twenty days nor more than ninety days.

33.

Henry James: The Inequities of the American Copyright Law

As early as 1783 copyright legislation was enacted in several states. A national copyright act was passed in 1790, and refinements of it became law in 1831 and in 1870, but none of these statutes extended copyright protection to books not published in America. On November 15, 1887, the noted author Henry James addressed the following letter to a meeting of the American Publishers' Copyright League, urging it to promote an international copyright agreement that would extend to foreign authors the same protection James received from the British government as an American publishing in Great Britain.

Source: *The Critic*, December 10, 1887: "International Copyright."

THERE HAVE BEEN FEW ACCIDENTS in my life that I regret more deeply than that of my being separated by so wide a distance from the privilege of taking part in your meetings of the 28th and 29th of this month. I enter with such cordial sympathy into the aims and efforts of the American Copyright League and entertain such earnest hopes for its success, that it would, besides the great personal pleasure, have been an extreme satisfaction to me to feel that I might, in my small measure, testify directly to the excellent cause and help, in however insignificant a degree, to establish the reform we all so eagerly wait for and remove the wrong we all so deeply deplore. Where justice is so closely in question and the profession of letters so intimately concerned. I am almost ashamed to be away. I am to some extent consoled, however, by this reflection, that the very fact of my being in London and not in New York only serves to fortify the conviction which I share with you, and of which I wish I could give you the benefit in some better eloquence — some communication more immediately operative.

For it is through my observation of the case here, while you are observing it at home, that it is impressed upon me that Americans enjoy in another country a cour-

Henry James; portrait by John Singer Sargent, 1913

tesy and an advantage which, among ourselves, we have so long and so ungenerously denied to the stranger, even when the stranger has given us some of the most precious enjoyment we know — has delighted and fortified and enriched us. I have all the material benefit of publishing my productions in England. I have only to put them forth shortly before their appearance in the United States to secure an effective copyright. The circumstance that the profit in question would be much more important if my writings were more so does not alter my sense of its being sadly out of keeping with the genius of our people to withhold reciprocity in a matter in which my own case is simply a small illustration.

It is out of keeping with the genius of our people to have to take lessons in liberality — in fair dealing — from other lands and to keep its citizens, in relation to those more hospitable countries, in a false, indefensible, intolerable position. To feel this strongly, indeed, to know our unenviable eminence in this respect, I do not mean to imply that the American must cross the Atlantic; for your organized existence is in itself a proof of our active conscience, of the manner in which all informed, all intelligent feeling seeks expression. But I speak as one who happens to have had for a good while this particular light and this particular humiliation of seeing the right thing done and not being able to feel that it is *we* who do it; being condemned to feel, on the contrary, that it is we who have refused to do it — erratically, perversely, and so incongruously that it would be grotesque if it were not lamentable.

This consciousness is in general so unfamiliar and so odious to our liberal national spirit that I should not venture to allude to it even at a family party like the present occasion if it did not seem that of the two forms of indiscretion the greater would be to blink the fact of an anomaly so gross. What, indeed, could be a grosser one than that on a point of public policy so closely connected with our national honor, the American should have to give up his case? What could be in greater contradiction with the way he feels in general about his country than that he should have to admit that, in this especial and conspicuous instance — covering so vast a ground — her practice is lamentably at fault, her sagacity densely clouded, her behavior unenlightened and uncivilized? That her sense of honesty has really failed her is an admission he will not make, for he *knows*, in all his instincts, that it has only to feel the monitory touch through other preoccupations to place itself immediately at the service of a better wisdom.

The attention of the American people has only to be effectually called to the cause you advocate to exert a considerable retrospective resentment upon those who have endeavored to perpetuate their mistake and to introduce those who have suffered by it to the enjoyment of a full equality. To see vividly that we cannot hold up the American head about the world when the subject of copyright is broached is to number the days of a system which carries such detestable incidents in its bosom.

You all know how the truth shines on this subject, but one is tempted to lengthen a letter which helps one to reach across the Atlantic. Having been witness of the fact that whatever other discomforts they may suffer the English people have not been disastrously affected by allowing copyrights to be within reach of that branch of the Anglo-Saxon stock which uses, on the whole, the same tongue as themselves and cultivates, on the whole, the same ideals — having satisfied myself of that, I must give the assurance of my belief that our own adoption of the straight course would be equally free from calamity.

Let it not be said — for then we may as well quit the field altogether — that we cannot *afford* the straight course. If the English can afford it in the manner in which I have touched — in regard to the American when the American lives among them — they can afford it also when the American does not; and I absolutely decline to believe (let no one attempt to persuade you) that we are not a whit less equipped for the strain — if strain there would in any degree be.

I know of no honorable thing that we cannot afford to do, least of all a thing that concerns our being as clever as other people. We are so clever that there is only one more thing we want, to be in complete possession of our birthright, and that is the rupture of the last loose knot that ties us to a dead tradition. Our denial of copyright to the stranger has been, it is said, in the interest of universal reading. But our universal reading has done us little good if it has not taught us that it is better to be strong than to be coddled — and coddled in the least invigorating of all ways, at other people's expense. We know not how strong we are until we try, and we cannot try till we are

in the erect attitude. Then it will be found, I think, that we do not want easier terms than our fellows.

Seeing English people ready to pay for their American books and enjoying them the more from feeling that, having paid, they have a right to criticize (substantial privilege and delightful freedom!), I perceive no shadow of ground why we should plead incapacity; for our power to pay is certainly as great as our power to understand; and our power to understand is certainly as great as theirs. It is precisely because we *are* a universally reading public that it is of the greatest importance there should be no impediment to our freedom. There is a fatal impediment so long as there is this odious awkwardness in our confessing how we came by our pleasure. The real impediment is not in the burden of paying for the English books we think good enough to read but not good enough to thank the authors for . . . the real impediment is that this irresponsibility of ours is tainted with a vice which passes into our intelligence itself.

The taint pervades our whole attitude, and it prevents us from being free; it prevents us from being frank; it prevents us from being as validly and comfortably founded in our intellectual culture as we are in other matters. It condemns us to be tongue-tied; for, if you may not look a gift horse in the mouth, in what queer relation do you stand to a book which is not only a gift but a gift whether the giver has willed or no? So long as we withhold copyright from the stranger whom we make a stranger only by our passing strange process of domesticating him, so long as we go in for bargains of which the profit are all for ourselves and the burden all for the other party, so long must we relinquish the precious prerogative of free appreciation and of criticism. . . .

The bright American mind does not want exceptional terms, or humiliating bargains, or baby-treatment, or pilfered pleasures of any kind; and it has a total disbelief in any privileges of which the source is not pure. It owes too much to books — which are the blessings of life — not to open its heart to the whole body of our English utterance, not to feel that we have all inherited together the magnificent library of our race, not to detest the idea of refusing the tax which will keep up the institution. The institution is essentially ours, and its honor and health, its competition with other institutions of the same order depend on its not being mutilated — chopped into two.

Let us not introduce small differences into great harmonies. Let us work for each other and with each other and not condemn any of those who work for us to work without us. I am with you in sympathy, in spirit, and am completely of your opinion that we will read better and write better and think better and *feel* better, as we say, when the air is clearer, and that the air will be clearer only when justice is done.

34.

GROVER CLEVELAND: Surplus Revenues and the Tariff

Grover Cleveland's third annual message to Congress, on December 6, 1887, called for tariff reductions. Since the federal surplus was annually over $100 million, and prices on commodities were kept artificially high by import taxes, the President felt the time was right for Congress to reduce the tariff on many items. His message, a portion of which appears below, did not have the desired effect. Instead, it made the tariff an issue in the 1888 presidential campaign, in which Cleveland was defeated, and in 1890 the McKinley Tariff Act raised duties to unprecedented levels.

Source: Richardson, VIII, pp. 580-591.

YOU ARE CONFRONTED at the threshold of your legislative duties with a condition of the national finances which imperatively demands immediate and careful consideration.

The amount of money annually exacted, through the operation of present laws, from the industries and necessities of the people largely exceeds the sum necessary to meet the expenses of the government. When we consider that the theory of our institutions guarantees to every citizen the full enjoyment of all the fruits of his industry and enterprise, with only such deduction as may be his share toward the careful and economical maintenance of the government which protects him, it is plain that the exaction of more than this is indefensible extortion and a culpable betrayal of American fairness and justice. This wrong inflicted upon those who bear the burden of national taxation, like other wrongs, multiplies a brood of evil consequences.

The public Treasury, which should only exist as a conduit conveying the people's tribute to its legitimate objects of expenditure, becomes a hoarding place for money needlessly withdrawn from trade and the people's use, thus crippling our national energies, suspending our country's development, preventing investment in productive enterprise, threatening financial disturbance, and inviting schemes of public plunder. This condition of our Treasury is not altogether new, and it has more than once of late been submitted to the people's representatives in the Congress, who alone can apply a remedy. And yet the situation still continues; with aggravated incidents, more than ever presaging financial convulsion and widespread disaster.

It will not do to neglect this situation because its dangers are not now palpably imminent and apparent. They exist nonetheless certainly, and await the unforeseen and unexpected occasion when suddenly they will be precipitated upon us. . . .

While the functions of our National Treasury should be few and simple, and while its best condition would be reached, I believe, by its entire disconnection with private business interests, yet when, by a perversion of its purposes, it idly holds money uselessly subtracted from the channels of trade, there seems to be reason for the claim that some legitimate means should be devised by the government to restore in an emergency, without waste or extravagance, such money to its place among the people.

If such an emergency arises, there now exists no clear and undoubted executive power of relief. Heretofore the redemption of 3 percent bonds, which were payable at the option of the government, has afforded a means for the disbursement of the excess of our revenues; but these bonds have all been retired, and there are no bonds outstanding, the payment of which we have a right to insist upon. The contribution to the sinking fund which furnishes the occasion for expenditure in the purchase of bonds has been already made for the current year, so that there is no outlet in that direction.

In the present state of legislation, the only pretense of any existing executive power to restore at this time any part of our surplus revenues to the people by its expenditure consists in the supposition that the secretary of the Treasury may enter the

market and purchase the bonds of the government not yet due, at a rate of premium to be agreed upon. The only provision of law from which such a power could be derived is found in an appropriation bill passed a number of years ago, and it is subject to the suspicion that it was intended as temporary and limited in its application, instead of conferring a continuing discretion and authority.

No condition ought to exist which would justify the grant of power to a single official, upon his judgment of its necessity, to withhold from or release to the business of the people, in an unusual manner, money held in the Treasury, and thus affect at his will the financial situation of the country; and if it is deemed wise to lodge in the secretary of the Treasury the authority in the present juncture to purchase bonds, it should be plainly vested and provided, as far as possible, with such checks and limitations as will define this official's right and discretion and at the same time relieve him from undue responsibility.

In considering the question of purchasing bonds as a means of restoring to circulation the surplus money accumulating in the Treasury, it should be borne in mind that premiums must of course be paid upon such purchase, that there may be a large part of these bonds held as investments which cannot be purchased at any price, and that combinations among holders who are willing to sell may unreasonably enhance the cost of such bonds to the government.

It has been suggested that the present bonded debt might be refunded at a less rate of interest and the difference between the old and new security paid in cash, thus finding use for the surplus in the Treasury. The success of this plan, it is apparent, must depend upon the volition of the holders of the present bonds; and it is not entirely certain that the inducement which must be offered them would result in more financial benefit to the government than the purchase of bonds, while the latter proposition would reduce the principal of the debt by actual payment instead of extending it.

The proposition to deposit the money held by the government in banks throughout the country for use by the people is, it seems to me, exceedingly objectionable in principle, as establishing too close a relationship between the operations of the government Treasury and the business of the country and too extensive a commingling of their money, thus fostering an unnatural reliance in private business upon public funds. If this scheme should be adopted, it should only be done as a temporary expedient to meet an urgent necessity. Legislative and executive effort should generally be in the opposite direction and should have a tendency to divorce, as much and as fast as can be safely done, the Treasury Department from private enterprise.

Of course it is not expected that unnecessary and extravagant appropriations will be made for the purpose of avoiding the accumulation of an excess of revenue. Such expenditure, besides the demoralization of all just conceptions of public duty which it entails, stimulates a habit of reckless improvidence not in the least consistent with the mission of our people or the high and beneficent purposes of our government.

I have deemed it my duty to thus bring to the knowledge of my countrymen, as well as to the attention of their representatives charged with the responsibility of legislative relief, the gravity of our financial situation. The failure of the Congress heretofore to provide against the dangers which it was quite evident the very nature of the difficulty must necessarily produce caused a condition of financial distress and apprehension since your last adjournment, which taxed to the utmost all the authority and expedients within executive control; and these appear now to be exhausted. If disaster results from the continued inaction of Congress, the responsibility must rest where it belongs. . . .

Our scheme of taxation, by means of which this needless surplus is taken from the people and put into the public Treasury, consists of a tariff or duty levied upon importations from abroad and internal revenue taxes levied upon the consumption of tobacco and spirituous and malt liquors. It must be conceded that none of the things subjected to internal revenue taxation are, strictly speaking, necessaries. There appears to be no just complaint of this taxation by the consumers of these articles, and there seems to be nothing so well able to bear the burden without hardship to any portion of the people.

But our present tariff laws, the vicious, inequitable, and illogical source of unnecessary taxation, ought to be at once revised and amended. These laws, as their primary and plain effect, raise the price to consumers of all articles imported and subject to duty by precisely the sum paid for such duties. Thus the amount of the duty measures the tax paid by those who purchase for use these imported articles. Many of these things, however, are raised or manufactured in our own country, and the duties now levied upon foreign goods and products are called protection to these home manufactures, because they render it possible for those of our people who are manufacturers to make these taxed articles and sell them for a price equal to that demanded for the imported goods that have paid customs duty.

So it happens that while comparatively a few use the imported articles, millions of our people, who never used and never saw any of the foreign products, purchase and use things of the same kind made in this country, and pay therefor nearly or quite the same enhanced price which the duty adds to the imported articles. Those who buy imports pay the duty charged thereon into the public Treasury, but the great majority of our citizens, who buy domestic articles of the same class, pay a sum at least approximately equal to this duty to the home manufacturer. This reference to the operation of our tariff laws is not made by way of instruction but in order that we may be constantly reminded of the manner in which they impose a burden upon those who consume domestic products as well as those who consume imported articles, and thus create a tax upon all our people.

It is not proposed to entirely relieve the country of this taxation. It must be extensively continued as the source of the government's income; and in a readjustment of our tariff the interests of American labor engaged in manufacture should be carefully considered, as well as the preservation of our manufacturers. It may be called protection or by any other name, but relief from the hardships and dangers of our present tariff laws should be devised with especial precaution against imperilling the existence of our manufacturing interests. But this existence should not mean a condition which, without regard to the public welfare or a national exigency, must always insure the realization of immense profits instead of moderately profitable returns. As the volume and diversity of our national activities increase, new recruits are added to those who desire a continuation of the advantages which they conceive the present system of tariff taxation directly affords them. So stubbornly have all efforts to reform the present condition been resisted by those of our fellow citizens thus engaged that they can hardly complain of the suspicion, entertained to a certain extent, that there exists an organized combination all along the line to maintain their advantage.

We are in the midst of centennial celebrations, and with becoming pride we rejoice in American skill and ingenuity, in American energy and enterprise, and in the wonderful natural advantages and resources developed by a century's national growth. Yet when an attempt is made to justify a scheme which permits a tax to be laid upon every consumer in the land for the benefit of our manufacturers, quite beyond a reasonable demand for governmental regard, it suits the purposes of advocacy to call our manufactures infant industries still needing the highest and greatest degree of favor and fostering care that can be wrung from federal legislation.

It is also said that the increase in the price of domestic manufactures resulting from the present tariff is necessary in order that higher wages may be paid to our workingmen employed in manufactories than are paid for what is called the pauper labor of Europe. All will acknowledge the force of an argument which involves the welfare and liberal compensation of our laboring people. Our labor is honorable in the eyes of every American citizen; and as it lies at the foundation of our development and progress, it is entitled, without affectation or hypocrisy, to the utmost regard. The standard of our laborers' life should not be measured by that of any other country less favored, and they are entitled to their full share of all our advantages.

By the last census it is made to appear that of the 17,392,099 of our population engaged in all kinds of industries, 7,670,493 are employed in agriculture, 4,074,238 in professional and personal service (2,934,876 of whom are domestic servants and laborers), while 1,810,256 are employed in trade and transportation, and 3,837,112 are classed as employed in manufacturing and mining. . . .

The farmer and the agriculturist, who manufacture nothing, but who pay the increased price which the tariff imposes upon every agricultural implement, upon all he wears, and upon all he uses and owns, except the increase of his flocks and herds and such things as his husbandry produces from the soil, is invited to aid in maintaining the present situation; and he is told that a high duty on imported wool is necessary for the benefit of those who have sheep to shear in order that the price of their wool may be increased. They, of course, are not reminded that the farmer who has no sheep is by this scheme obliged, in his purchases of clothing and woolen goods, to pay a tribute to his fellow farmer as well as to the manufacturer and merchant, nor is any mention made of the fact that the sheep owners themselves and their households must wear clothing and use other articles manufactured from the wool they sell at tariff prices, and thus as consumers must return their share of this increased price to the tradesman. . . .

In speaking of the increased cost to the consumer of our home manufactures resulting from a duty laid upon imported articles of the same description, the fact is not overlooked that competition among our domestic producers sometimes has the effect of keeping the price of their products below the highest limit allowed by such duty. But it is notorious that this competition is too often strangled by combinations quite prevalent at this time, and frequently called trusts, which have for their object the regulation of the supply and price of commodities made and sold by members of the combination. The people can hardly hope for any consideration in the operation of these selfish schemes.

If, however, in the absence of such combination, a healthy and free competition reduces the price of any particular dutiable article of home production below the limit which it might otherwise reach under our tariff laws, and if with such reduced price its manufacture continues to thrive, it is entirely evident that one thing has been discovered which should be carefully scrutinized in an effort to reduce taxation.

The necessity of combination to maintain the price of any commodity to the tariff point furnishes proof that someone is willing to accept lower prices for such commodity and that such prices are remunerative; and lower prices produced by competition prove the same thing. Thus where either of these conditions exists a case would seem to be presented for an easy reduction of taxation.

The considerations which have been presented touching our tariff laws are intended only to enforce an earnest recommendation that the surplus revenues of the government be prevented by the reduction of our customs duties, and at the same time to emphasize a suggestion that in accomplishing this purpose we may discharge a double duty to our people by granting to them a measure of relief from tariff taxation in quarters where it is most needed and from sources where it can be most fairly and justly accorded.

Nor can the presentation made of such considerations be with any degree of fairness regarded as evidence of unfriendliness toward our manufacturing interests or of any lack of appreciation of their value and importance. These interests constitute a leading and most substantial element of our national greatness and furnish the proud proof of our country's progress. But, if in the emergency that presses upon us, our manufacturers are asked to surrender something for the public good and to avert disaster, their patriotism, as well as a grateful recognition of advantages already afforded, should lead them to willing cooperation.

No demand is made that they shall forego all the benefits of governmental regard; but they cannot fail to be admonished of their duty, as well as their enlightened self-interest and safety, when they are reminded of the fact that financial panic and collapse, to which the present condition tends, afford no greater shelter or protection to our manufactures than to other important enterprises. Opportunity for safe, careful, and deliberate reform is now offered; and none of us should be unmindful of a time when an abused and irritated people, heedless of those who have resisted timely and reasonable relief, may insist upon a radical and sweeping rectification of their wrongs.

The difficulty attending a wise and fair revision of our tariff laws is not underestimated. It will require on the part of the Congress great labor and care, and especially a broad and national contemplation of the subject and a patriotic disregard of such local and selfish claims as are unreasonable and reckless of the welfare of the entire country.

Under our present laws more than 4,000 articles are subject to duty. Many of these do not in any way compete with our own manufactures, and many are hardly worth attention as subjects of revenue. A considerable reduction can be made in the aggregate by adding them to the free list. The taxation of luxuries presents no features of hardship; but the necessaries of life used and consumed by all the people, the duty upon which adds to the cost of living in every home, should be greatly cheapened.

The radical reduction of the duties imposed upon raw material used in manufactures, or its free importation, is of course an important factor in any effort to reduce the price of these necessaries. It would not only relieve them from the increased cost caused by the tariff on such material but the manufactured product, being thus cheapened, that part of the tariff now laid upon such product, as a compensation to our manufacturers for the present price of raw material could be accordingly modified. Such reduction or free importation would serve besides to largely reduce the revenue.

It is not apparent how such a change can have any injurious effect upon our manufacturers. On the contrary, it would appear to give them a better chance in foreign markets with the manufacturers of other countries, who cheapen their wares by free material. Thus our people might have the opportunity of extending their sales beyond the limits of home consumption, saving them from the depression, interruption in business, and loss caused by a glutted domestic market and affording their employees more certain and steady labor, with its resulting quiet and contentment.

The question thus imperatively presented for solution should be approached in a spirit higher than partisanship and considered in the light of that regard for patriotic duty

which should characterize the action of those entrusted with the weal of a confiding people. But the obligation to declared party policy and principle is not wanting to urge prompt and effective action. Both of the great political parties now represented in the government have by repeated and authoritative declarations condemned the condition of our laws which permit the collection from the people of unnecessary revenue, and have in the most solemn manner promised its correction; and neither as citizens nor partisans are our countrymen in a mood to condone the deliberate violation of these pledges.

Our progress toward a wise conclusion will not be improved by dwelling upon the theories of protection and free trade. This savors too much of bandying epithets. It is a *condition* which confronts us, not a theory. Relief from this condition may involve a slight reduction of the advantages which we award our home productions, but the entire withdrawal of such advantages should not be contemplated. The question of free trade is absolutely irrelevant, and the persistent claim made in certain quarters that all the efforts to relieve the people from unjust and unnecessary taxation are schemes of so-called free traders is mischievous and far removed from any consideration for the public good.

The simple and plain duty which we owe the people is to reduce taxation to the necessary expenses of an economical operation of the government and to restore to the business of the country the money which we hold in the Treasury through the perversion of governmental powers. These things can and should be done with safety to all our industries, without danger to the opportunity for remunerative labor which our workingmen need, and with benefit to them and all our people by cheapening their means of subsistence and increasing the measure of their comforts.

35.

Edward Bellamy: A Utopian Social Economy

Though both utopian and socialist literature had been popular in America for a generation, Edward Bellamy's novel Looking Backward *was an unprecedented and influential success, selling well over a quarter of a million copies in two years. Unlike social critics who dealt with the various faults and failures of capitalistic society, Bellamy rejected such a society entirely and depicted a national utopian socialist system in which everyone shared on an equal basis in the products of the economy. The plot of the story takes the protagonist, Julian West, from 1887 to the year 2000 by means of a hypnotic trance. Upon being awakened, he is introduced by his host, Dr. Leete, to an entirely new social and economic order. The following selections from the book comprise the conversations between West and Dr. Leete in which the former is apprised of his new surroundings.*

Source: *Looking Backward: 2000-1887*, Boston, 1888.

My host . . . resumed. . . . "The Bostonians of your day had the reputation of being great askers of questions, and I am going to show my descent by asking you one to begin with. What should you name as the most prominent feature of the labor troubles of your day?"

"Why, the strikes, of course," I replied.

"Exactly; but what made the strikes so formidable?"

"The great labor organizations."

"And what was the motive of these great organizations?"

"The workmen claimed they had to organize to get their rights from the big corporations," I replied.

"That is just it," said Dr. Leete; "the organization of labor and the strikes were an effect, merely, of the concentration of capital in greater masses than had ever been known before. Before this concentration began, while as yet commerce and industry were conducted by innumerable petty concerns with small capital, instead of a small number of great concerns with vast capital, the individual workman was relatively important and independent in his relations to the employer. Moreover, when a little capital or a new idea was enough to start a man in business for himself, workingmen were constantly becoming employers and there was no hard and fast line between the two classes.

"Labor unions were needless then, and general strikes out of the question. But when the era of small concerns with small capital was succeeded by that of the great aggregations of capital, all this was changed. The individual laborer, who had been relatively important to the small employer, was reduced to insignificance and powerlessness over against the great corporation, while at the same time the way upward to the grade of employer was closed to him. Self-defense drove him to union with his fellows.

"The records of the period show that the

outcry against the concentration of capital was furious. Men believed that it threatened society with a form of tyranny more abhorrent than it had ever endured. They believed that the great corporations were preparing for them the yoke of a baser servitude than had ever been imposed on the race, servitude not to men but to soulless machines, incapable of any motive but insatiable greed. Looking back, we cannot wonder at their desperation, for certainly humanity was never confronted with a fate more sordid and hideous than would have been the era of corporate tyranny which they anticipated.

"Meanwhile, without being in the smallest degree checked by the clamor against it, the absorption of business by ever larger monopolies continued. In the United States there was not, after the beginning of the last quarter of the century, any opportunity whatever for individual enterprise in any important field of industry, unless backed by a great capital. During the last decade of the century, such small businesses as still remained were fast-failing survivals of a past epoch, or mere parasites on the great corporations, or else existed in fields too small to attract the great capitalists. Small businesses, as far as they still remained, were reduced to the condition of rats and mice, living in holes and corners, and counting on evading notice for the enjoyment of existence.

"The railroads had gone on combining, till a few great syndicates controlled every rail in the land. In manufactories, every important staple was controlled by a syndicate. These syndicates, pools, trusts, or whatever their name fixed prices and crushed all competition except when combinations as vast as themselves arose. Then a struggle, resulting in a still greater consolidation, ensued. The great city bazaar crushed its country rivals with branch stores, and in the city itself absorbed its smaller rivals, till the business of a whole quarter was concentrated under one roof, with a hundred former proprietors of shops serving as clerks. Having no business of his own to put his money in, the small capitalist, at the same time that he took service under the corporation, found no other investment for his money but its stocks and bonds, thus becoming doubly dependent upon it.

"The fact that the desperate popular opposition to the consolidation of business in a few powerful hands had no effect to check it proves that there must have been a strong economical reason for it. The small capitalists, with their innumerable petty concerns, had in fact yielded the field to the great aggregations of capital, because they belonged to a day of small things and were totally incompetent to the demands of an age of steam and telegraphs and the gigantic scale of its enterprises. To restore the former order of things, even if possible, would have involved returning to the day of stagecoaches. Oppressive and intolerable as was the regime of the great consolidations of capital, even its victims, while they cursed it, were forced to admit the prodigious increase of efficiency which had been imparted to the national industries, the vast economies effected by concentration of management and unity of organization, and to confess that since the new system had taken the place of the old, the wealth of the world had increased at a rate before undreamed of. To be sure, this vast increase had gone chiefly to make the rich richer, increasing the gap between them and the poor; but the fact remained that, as a means merely of producing wealth, capital had been proved efficient in proportion to its consolidation. The restoration of the old system with the subdivision of capital, if it were possible, might indeed bring back a greater quality of conditions, with more individual dignity and freedom, but it would be at the price of general poverty and the arrest of material progress.

"Was there, then, no way of commanding the services of the mighty wealth-producing principle of consolidated capital without bowing down to a plutocracy like that of Carthage? As soon as men began to ask themselves these questions, they found the answer ready for them. The movement toward the conduct of business by larger and larger aggregations of capital, the tendency toward monopolies, which had been so desperately and vainly resisted, was recognized at last, in its true significance, as a process which only needed to complete its logical evolution to open a golden future to humanity.

"Early in the last century the evolution was completed by the final consolidation of the entire capital of the nation. The industry and commerce of the country, ceasing to be conducted by a set of irresponsible corporations and syndicates of private persons at their caprice and for their profit, were entrusted to a single syndicate representing the people, to be conducted in the common interest for the common profit. The nation, that is to say, organized as the one great business corporation in which all other corporations were absorbed; it became the one capitalist in the place of all other capitalists, the sole employer, the final monopoly in which all previous and lesser monopolies were swallowed up, a monopoly in the profits and economies of which all citizens shared. The epoch of trusts had ended in the great trust. In a word, the people of the United States concluded to assume the conduct of their own business, just as one hundred odd years before they had assumed the conduct of their own government, organizing now for industrial purposes on precisely the same grounds that they had then organized for political purposes. At last, strangely late in the world's history, the obvious fact was perceived that no business is so essentially the public business as the industry and commerce on which the people's livelihood depends, and that to entrust it to private persons to be managed for private profit is a folly similar in kind, though vast-

ly greater in magnitude, to that of surrendering the functions of political government to kings and nobles to be conducted for their personal glorification."

"Such a stupendous change as you describe," said I, "did not, of course, take place without great bloodshed and terrible convulsions."

"On the contrary," replied Dr. Leete, "there was absolutely no violence. The change had been long foreseen. Public opinion had become fully ripe for it, and the whole mass of the people was behind it. There was no more possibility of opposing it by force than by argument. On the other hand, the popular sentiment toward the great corporations and those identified with them had ceased to be one of bitterness, as they came to realize their necessity as a link, a transition phase, in the evolution of the true industrial system. The most violent foes of the great private monopolies were now forced to recognize how invaluable and indispensable had been their office in educating the people up to the point of assuming control of their own business.

"Fifty years before, the consolidation of the industries of the country under national control would have seemed a very daring experiment to the most sanguine. But by a series of object lessons, seen and studied by all men, the great corporations had taught the people an entirely new set of ideas on this subject. They had seen for many years syndicates handling revenues greater than those of states, and directing the labors of hundreds of thousands of men with an efficiency and economy unattainable in smaller operations. It had come to be recognized as an axiom that the larger the business, the simpler the principles that can be applied to it; that, as the machine is truer than the hand, so the system, which in a great concern does the work of the master's eye in a small business, turns out more accurate results. Thus it came about that, thanks to the corporations themselves, when it was proposed that the nation should assume their functions, the suggestion implied nothing which seemed impracticable even to the timid. To be sure it was a step beyond any yet taken, a broader generalization, but the very fact that the nation would be the sole corporation in the field would, it was seen, relieve the undertaking of many difficulties with which the partial monopolies had contended." . . .

"The national organization of labor under one direction was the complete solution of what was, in your day and under your system, justly regarded as the insoluble labor problem. When the nation became the sole employer, all the citizens, by virtue of their citizenship, became employees, to be distributed according to the needs of industry."

"That is," I suggested, "you have simply applied the principle of universal military service, as it was understood in our day, to the labor question."

"Yes," said Dr. Leete, "that was something which followed as a matter of course as soon as the nation had become the sole capitalist. The people were already accustomed to the idea that the obligation of every citizen, not physically disabled, to contribute his military services to the defense of the nation was equal and absolute. That it was equally the duty of every citizen to contribute his quota of industrial or intellectual services to the maintenance of the nation was equally evident, though it was not until the nation became the employer of labor that citizens were able to render this sort of service with any pretense either of universality or equity. No organization of labor was possible when the employing power was divided among hundreds or thousands of individuals and corporations, between which concert of any kind was neither desired, nor, indeed, feasible. It constantly happened then that vast numbers who desired to labor could find no opportunity, and on the other hand, those who

desired to evade a part or all of their debt could easily do so."

"Service, now, I suppose, is compulsory upon all," I suggested.

"It is rather a matter of course than of compulsion," replied Dr. Leete. "It is regarded as so absolutely natural and reasonable that the idea of its being compulsory has ceased to be thought of. He would be thought to be an incredibly contemptible person who should need compulsion in such a case. Nevertheless, to speak of service being compulsory would be a weak way to state its absolute inevitableness. Our entire social order is so wholly based upon and deduced from it that if it were conceivable that a man could escape it, he would be left with no possible way to provide for his existence. He would have excluded himself from the world, cut himself off from his kind, in a word, committed suicide."

"Is the term of service in this industrial army for life?"

"Oh, no; it both begins later and ends earlier than the average working period in your day. Your workshops were filled with children and old men, but we hold the period of youth sacred to education, and the period of maturity, when the physical forces begin to flag, equally sacred to ease and agreeable relaxation. The period of industrial service is twenty-four years, beginning at the close of the course of education at twenty-one and terminating at forty-five. After forty-five, while discharged from labor, the citizen still remains liable to special calls, in case of emergencies causing a sudden great increase in the demand for labor, till he reaches the age of fifty-five, but such calls are rarely, in fact almost never, made. The 15th day of October of every year is what we call Muster Day, because those who have reached the age of twenty-one are then mustered into the industrial service, and at the same time those who, after twenty-four years' service, have reached the age of forty-five, are honorably mustered

Edward Bellamy; etching by W. H. W. Bicknell

out. It is the great day of the year with us, whence we reckon all other events, our Olympiad, save that it is annual." . . .

"Surely," I said, "it can hardly be that the number of volunteers for any trade is exactly the number needed in that trade. It must be generally either under or over the demand."

"The supply of volunteers is always expected to fully equal the demand," replied Dr. Leete. "It is the business of the administration to see that this is the case. The rate of volunteering for each trade is closely watched. If there be a noticeably greater excess of volunteers over men needed in any trade, it is inferred that the trade offers greater attractions than others. On the other hand, if the number of volunteers for a trade tends to drop below the demand, it is inferred that it is thought more arduous. It is the business of the administration to seek constantly to equalize the attractions of the trades, so far as the conditions of labor in them are concerned, so that all trades shall be equally attractive to persons having natu-ral tastes for them. This is done by making the hours of labor in different trades to differ according to their arduousness. The lighter trades, prosecuted under the most agreeable circumstances, have in this way the longest hours, while an arduous trade, such as mining, has very short hours.

"There is no theory, no a priori rule by which the respective attractiveness of industries is determined. The administration, in taking burdens off one class of workers and adding them to other classes, simply follows the fluctuations of opinion among the workers themselves as indicated by the rate of volunteering. The principle is that no man's work ought to be, on the whole, harder for him than any other man's for him, the workers themselves to be the judges. There are no limits to the application of this rule. If any particular occupation is in itself so arduous or so oppressive that, in order to induce volunteers, the day's work in it had to be reduced to ten minutes, it would be done. If, even then, no man was willing to do it, it would remain undone. But of course, in point of fact, a moderate reduction in the hours of labor, or addition of other privileges, suffices to secure all needed volunteers for any occupation necessary to men.

"If, indeed, the unavoidable difficulties and dangers of such a necessary pursuit were so great that no inducement of compensating advantages would overcome men's repugnance to it, the administration would only need to take it out of the common order of occupations by declaring it "extra hazardous," and those who pursued it especially worthy of the national gratitude, to be overrun with volunteers. Our young men are very greedy of honor and do not let slip such opportunities. Of course you will see that dependence on the purely voluntary choice of avocations involves the abolition in all of anything like unhygienic conditions or special peril to life and limb. Health and safety are conditions common to all industries. The nation does not maim and slaughter its workmen by thousands as did the private capitalists and corporations of your day." . . .

"As an industrial system, I should think this might be extremely efficient," I said, "but I don't see that it makes any provision for the professional classes, the men who serve the nation with brains instead of hands. Of course you can't get along without the brain workers. How, then, are they selected from those who are to serve as farmers and mechanics? That must require a very delicate sort of sifting process, I should say."

"So it does," replied Dr. Leete; "the most delicate possible test is needed here, and so we leave the question whether a man shall be a brain or hand worker entirely to him to settle. At the end of the term of three years as a common laborer, which every man must serve, it is for him to choose, in accordance to his natural tastes, whether he will fit himself for an art or profession, or be a farmer or mechanic. If he feels that he can do better work with his brains than his muscles, he finds every facility provided for testing the reality of his supposed bent, of cultivating it, and, if fit, of pursuing it as his avocation. The schools of technology, of medicine, of art, of music, of histrionics, and of higher liberal learning are always open to aspirants without condition." . . .

"This opportunity for a professional training," the doctor continued, "remains open to every man till the age of thirty is reached, after which students are not received, as there would remain too brief a period before the age of discharge in which to serve the nation in their professions. In your day young men had to choose their professions very young, and, therefore, in a large proportion of instances, wholly mistook their vocations. It is recognized nowadays that the natural aptitudes of some are later than those of others in developing, and, therefore, while the choice of profession may be made as early as twenty-four, it remains open for six years longer." . . .

The conversation took another turn then, the point of ladies' fashions in the 19th century being raised, if I remember rightly, by Mrs. Leete, and it was not till after breakfast, when the doctor had invited me up to the housetop, which appeared to be a favorite resort of his, that he recurred to the subject.

"You were surprised," he said, "at my saying that we got along without money or trade, but a moment's reflection will show that trade existed and money was needed in your day simply because the business of production was left in private hands, and that, consequently, they are superfluous now."

"I do not at once see how that follows," I replied.

"It is very simple," said Dr. Leete. "When innumerable different and independent persons produced the various things needful to life and comfort, endless exchanges between individuals were requisite in order that they might supply themselves with what they desired. These exchanges constituted trade, and money was essential as their medium. But as soon as the nation became the sole producer of all sorts of commodities, there was no need of exchanges between individuals that they might get what they required. Everything was procurable from one source, and nothing could be procured anywhere else. A system of direct distribution from the national storehouses took the place of trade, and for this money was unnecessary."

"How is this distribution managed?" I asked.

"On the simplest possible plan," replied Dr. Leete. "A credit corresponding to his share of the annual product of the nation is given to every citizen on the public books at the beginning of each year, and a credit card issued him with which he procures at the public storehouses, found in every community, whatever he desires whenever he desires it. This arrangement, you will see, totally obviates the necessity for business transactions of any sort between individuals and consumers. Perhaps you would like to see what our credit cards are like.

"You observe," he pursued as I was curiously examining the piece of pasteboard he gave me, "that this card is issued for a certain number of dollars. We have kept the old word, but not the substance. The term, as we use it, answers to no real thing but merely serves as an algebraical symbol for comparing the values of products with one another. For this purpose they are all priced in dollars and cents, just as in your day. The value of what I procure on this card is checked off by the clerk, who pricks out of these tiers of squares the price of what I order."

"If you wanted to buy something of your neighbor, could you transfer part of your credit to him as consideration?" I inquired.

"In the first place," replied Dr. Leete, "our neighbors have nothing to sell us, but in any event our credit would not be transferable, being strictly personal. Before the nation could even think of honoring any such transfer as you speak of, it would be bound to inquire into all the circumstances of the transaction so as to be able to guarantee its absolute equity. It would have been reason enough, had there been no other, for abolishing money that its possession was no indication of rightful title to it. In the hands of the man who had stolen it or murdered for it, it was as good as in those which had earned it by industry. People nowadays interchange gifts and favors out of friendship, but buying and selling is considered absolutely inconsistent with the mutual benevolence and disinterestedness which should prevail between citizens and the sense of community of interest which supports our social system. According to our ideas, buying and selling is essentially antisocial in all its tendencies. It is an education in self-seeking at the expense of others, and no society whose citizens are trained in such a school can possibly rise above a very low grade of civilization."

"What if you have to spend more than your card in any one year?" I asked.

"The provision is so ample that we are more likely not to spend it all," replied Dr. Leete. "But if extraordinary expenses should exhaust it, we can obtain a limited advance on the next year's credit, though this practice is not encouraged, and a heavy discount is charged to check it. Of course, if a man showed himself a reckless spendthrift, he would receive his allowance monthly or weekly instead of yearly, or if necessary not be permitted to handle it at all."

"If you don't spend your allowance, I suppose it accumulates?"

"That is also permitted to a certain extent when a special outlay is anticipated. But unless notice to the contrary is given, it is presumed that the citizen who does not fully expend his credit did not have occasion to do so, and the balance is turned into the general surplus."

"Such a system does not encourage saving habits on the part of citizens," I said.

"It is not intended to," was the reply. "The nation is rich and does not wish the people to deprive themselves of any good thing. In your day, men were bound to lay up goods and money against coming failure of the means of support and for their children. This necessity made parsimony a virtue. But now it would have no such laudable object, and, having lost its utility, it has ceased to be regarded as a virtue. No man anymore has any care for the morrow, either for himself or his children, for the nation guarantees the nurture, education, and comfortable maintenance of every citizen from the cradle to the grave." . . .

"How, then, do you regulate wages?" I . . . asked.

Dr. Leete did not reply till after several

moments of meditative silence. "I know, of course," he finally said, "enough of the old order of things to understand just what you mean by that question; and yet the present order is so utterly different at this point that I am a little at loss how to answer you best. You ask me how we regulate wages; I can only reply that there is no idea in the modern social economy which at all corresponds with what was meant by wages in your day."

"I suppose you mean that you have no money to pay wages in," said I. "But the credit given the worker at the government storehouse answers to his wages with us. How is the amount of the credit given respectively to the workers in different lines determined? By what title does the individual claim his particular share? What is the basis of allotment?"

"His title," replied Dr. Leete, "is his humanity. The basis of his claim is the fact that he is a man."

"The fact that he is a man!" I repeated, incredulously. "Do you possibly mean that all have the same share?"

"Most assuredly."

The readers of this book never having practically known any other arrangement, or perhaps very carefully considered the historical accounts of former epochs in which a very different system prevailed, cannot be expected to appreciate the stupor of amazement into which Dr. Leete's simple statement plunged me.

"You see," he said, smiling, "that it is not merely that we have no money to pay wages in but, as I said, we have nothing at all answering to your idea of wages."

By this time I had pulled myself together sufficiently to voice some of the criticisms which, man of the 19th century as I was, came uppermost in my mind, upon this to me astounding arrangement. "Some men do twice the work of others!" I exclaimed. "Are the clever workmen content with a plan that ranks them with the indifferent?"

"We leave no possible ground for any complaint of injustice," replied Dr. Leete, "by requiring precisely the same measure of service from all."

"How can you do that, I should like to know, when no two men's powers are the same?"

"Nothing could be simpler," was Dr. Leete's reply. "We require of each that he shall make the same effort; that is, we demand of him the best service it is in his power to give."

"And supposing all do the best they can," I answered, "the amount of the product resulting is twice greater from one man than from another."

"Very true," replied Dr. Leete; "but the amount of the resulting product has nothing whatever to do with the question, which is one of desert. Desert is a moral question, and the amount of the product a material quantity. It would be an extraordinary sort of logic which should try to determine a moral question by a material standard. The amount of the effort alone is pertinent to the question of desert. All men who do their best, do the same. A man's endowments, however godlike, merely fix the measure of his duty. The man of great endowments who does not do all he might, though he may do more than a man of small endowments who does his best, is deemed a less deserving worker than the latter and dies a debtor to his fellows. The Creator sets men's tasks for them by the faculties He gives them; we simply exact their fulfillment. . . .

"It is most certain . . . that no able-bodied man nowadays can evade his share of work and live on the toil of others, whether he calls himself by the fine name of student or confesses to being simply lazy. At the same time, our system is elastic enough to give free play to every instinct of human nature which does not aim at dominating others or living on the fruit of others' labor. There is not only the remission by indemnification but the remission by abnegation. Any man in his thirty-third year, his term of service being then half-done, can obtain an honorable discharge from the army provided he accepts for the rest of his life one-half the rate of maintenance other citizens receive. It is quite possible to live on this amount, though one must forego the luxuries and elegancies of life, with some, perhaps, of its comforts." . . .

"Doctor," said I, in the course of our talk, "morally speaking, your social system is one which I should be insensate not to admire in comparison with any previously in vogue in the world, and especially with that of my own most unhappy century. If I were to fall into a mesmeric sleep tonight as lasting as that other, and meanwhile the course of time were to take a turn backward instead of forward, and I were to wake up again in the nineteenth century, when I had told my friends what I had seen, they would everyone admit that your world was a paradise of order, equity, and felicity. But they were a very practical people, my contemporaries, and after expressing their admiration for the moral beauty and material splendor of the system, they would presently begin to cipher and ask how you got the money to make everybody so happy; for certainly, to support the whole nation at a rate of comfort, and even luxury, such as I see around me must involve vastly greater wealth than the nation produced in my day.

"Now, while I could explain to them pretty nearly everything else of the main features of your system, I should quite fail to answer this question, and, failing there, they would tell me, for they were very close cipherers, that I had been dreaming; nor would they ever believe anything else. In my day, I know that the total annual product of the nation, although it might have been divided with absolute equality, would not have come to more than $300 or $400 per head, not very much more than

enough to supply the necessities of life with few or any of its comforts. How is it that you have so much more?"

"That is a very pertinent question, Mr. West," replied Dr. Leete, "and I should not blame your friends, in the case you supposed, if they declared your story all moonshine, failing a satisfactory reply to it. It is a question which I cannot answer exhaustively at any one sitting, and as for the exact statistics to bear out my general statements, I shall have to refer you for them to books in my library, but it would certainly be a pity to leave you to be put to confusion by your old acquaintances, in case of the contingency you speak of, for lack of a few suggestions.

"Let us begin with a number of small items wherein we economize wealth as compared with you. We have no national, state, county, or municipal debts, or payments on their account. We have no sort of military or naval expenditures for men or materials, no army, navy, or militia. We have no revenue service, no swarm of tax assessors and collectors. As regards our judiciary, police, sheriffs, and jailers, the force which Massachusetts alone kept on foot in your day far more than suffices for the nation now. We have no criminal class preying upon the wealth of society as you had. The number of persons, more or less absolutely lost to the working force through physical disability, of the lame, sick, and debilitated, which constituted such a burden on the able-bodied in your day, now that all live under conditions of health and comfort has shrunk to scarcely perceptible proportions, and with every generation is becoming more completely eliminated.

"Another item wherein we save is the disuse of money and the thousand occupations connected with financial operations of all sorts, whereby an army of men was formerly taken away from useful employments. Also consider that the waste of the very rich in your day on inordinate personal luxury has ceased, though, indeed, this item might easily be overestimated. Again, consider that there are no idlers now, rich or poor — no drones.

"A very important cause of former poverty was the vast waste of labor and materials which resulted from domestic washing and cooking and the performing separately of innumerable other tasks to which we apply the cooperative plan.

"A larger economy than any of these — yes, of all together — is effected by the organization of our distributing system by which the work done once by the merchants, traders, storekeepers, with their various grades of jobbers, wholesalers, retailers, agents, commercial travelers, and middlemen of all sorts, with an excessive waste of energy in needless transportation and interminable handlings, is performed by one-tenth the number of hands and an unnecessary turn of not one wheel. . . . Our statisticians calculate that one-eightieth part of our workers suffices for all the processes of distribution which in your day required one-eighth of the population, so much being withdrawn from the force engaged in productive labor."

"I begin to see," I said, "where you get your greater wealth."

"I beg your pardon," replied Dr. Leete, "but you scarcely do as yet. The economies I have mentioned thus far, in the aggregate, considering the labor they would save directly and indirectly through saving of material, might possibly be equivalent to the addition to your annual production of wealth of one-half its former total. These items are, however, scarcely worth mentioning in comparison with other prodigious wastes, now saved, which resulted inevitably from leaving the industries of the nation to private enterprise. However great the economies your contemporaries might have devised in the consumption of products, and however marvelous the progress of mechanical invention, they could never have raised themselves out of the slough of poverty so long as they held to that system.

"No mode more wasteful for utilizing human energy could be devised, and for the credit of the human intellect, it should be remembered that the system never was devised but was merely a survival from the rude ages when the lack of social organization made any sort of cooperation impossible."

"I will readily admit," I said, "that our industrial system was ethically very bad, but as a mere wealthmaking machine, apart from moral aspects, it seemed to us admirable."

"As I said," responded the doctor, "the subject is too large to discuss at length now, but if you are really interested to know the main criticisms which we moderns make on your industrial system as compared with our own, I can touch briefly on some of them.

"The wastes which resulted from leaving the conduct of industry to irresponsible individuals, wholly without mutual understanding or concert, were mainly four: first, the waste by mistaken undertakings; second, the waste from the competition and mutual hostility of those engaged in industry; third, the waste by periodical gluts and crises, with the consequent interruptions of industry; fourth, the waste from idle capital and labor, at all times. Any one of these four great leaks, were all the others stopped, would suffice to make the difference between wealth and poverty on the part of a nation."

1888

36.

THEODORE ROOSEVELT: The Issues of the Coming Election

Theodore Roosevelt's early political career included winning a place as delegate to the 1884 Republican National Convention, where he opposed the nomination of James G. Blaine and John A. Logan. Once they were nominated, however, Roosevelt engaged in a "most remarkable performance in the crow-eating line" and supported the ticket loyally. After Cleveland's victory over Blaine, Roosevelt spent the next four years on numerous writing projects, and in a losing mayoralty contest in New York City. The 1888 elections drew him once more into national politics, this time to support the successful candidate, Benjamin Harrison. In January of that election year, Roosevelt delivered these remarks on the coming election to the Union League Club of Washington, D.C.

Source: *Selections from the Correspondence of Theodore Roosevelt and Henry Cabot Lodge, 1884-1918*, New York, 1925, Vol. 1, pp. 62-65.

I DID NOT ORIGINALLY INTEND to speak to-night in reference to the report of your Committee; for I have been unable lately to attend the meetings of the Committee; and I have a very high regard for the gentlemen who have signed the report, both personally and politically, and dislike to differ from men with whom I usually agree. But as I am a member of the Committee, and as so much public attention has been attracted to the report, I feel that perhaps it is only proper that I should state to you the reasons why I cannot agree to it in its entirety.

That the internal revenue system is in many ways an objectionable one I admit, and I heartily concur in the recommendation to take the tax off tobacco. But I emphatically disbelieve in taking it off of spirits. It is a rudimentary axiom of political economy to raise revenue when practicable by a tax on mere luxuries and superfluities; and if there is a single article that it is right to tax, it is whisky. The people who drink and sell liquor are of all others those who should be made to contribute in every possible way to pay the running expenses of the state, for there can be no hardship involved in paying heavily for the use of what is at best a luxury, and frequently a pernicious luxury. The very fact that the third party Prohibitionists have declared in favor of removing the tax should make us set our faces against it; for experience has invariably shown that these same third party Prohibitionists are the most valuable allies the liquor sellers possess and are the consistent opponents of every rational scheme for dealing with the liquor question.

The Republican Party, and the Republican Party alone, has hitherto shown itself capable of grappling with the financial and business difficulties of the country, and I believe that its future will not belie its past. The question of the surplus must be met fairly and intelligently. The tax should be taken off tobacco and sugar. That is our first duty. In the next place, the possession of the surplus deprives us of all excuse for not attending to certain pressing national needs. It is a disgrace to us as a nation that we should have no warships worthy of the name and that our rich seaboard cities should lie at the mercy of any piratical descent from a hostile power. We are actually at the mercy of a tenth-rate country like Chile. Now, we have ample means wherewith to prepare a Navy capable of upholding the honor of the nation and a system of coast defense adequate to our needs. He is both a poor patriot and a short-sighted economist who longer opposes our doing so.

In the next place, we should meet the tariff question. The Republican Party, and the country at large as well, is definitely committed to the policy of protection; and unquestionably any reversal of that policy at present would do harm and produce widespread suffering. But for the Republican Party to announce that the inequalities and anomalies in the present tariff must not be touched, and that the high tariff is in itself something to which every other interest must yield, and to which every other issue must be subordinated, would be in my opinion a serious mistake. I think that there should be a prudent and intelligent revision

of the tariff on the lines indicated by the declarations of the last National Republican Convention and the official utterances of the last Republican President. I further believe that the Republican Party is alone capable of making such a revision. The last attempt of democracy to do so, under the guidance of Mr. Morrison was as ludicrous in conception as it was futile and contemptible in execution. Moreover, I do not think it wise to make our next fight purely on one issue, and that the issue of our opponents choosing; albeit as regards that, I think it not improbable that Mr. Cleveland can be beaten on the very points he has himself raised.

The Republican Party stands for other things in addition to protection. It stands for the national idea, for honest money, and for any honest civil service. I do not wonder that Mr. Cleveland in his last message forbore to touch on such points as these. An allusion to the first would come with bad grace from a President who has appointed to represent us at foreign capitals such avowed traitors as Keilly and Jackson. As for the other two, Mr. Cleveland evidently thought it worthwhile to ensure an identity in policy and utterance on the tariff between himself and Mr. Carlisle, but equally evidently he did not think it worth his while to try to prevent the Committee on Coinage being handed over to the apostle of the dishonest dollar, or to protest against the chairmanship of the Committee on Civil Service Reform being given to the man who had introduced the bill to repeal the Civil Service Act.

Nor indeed would such a protest have been taken seriously, coming from the President who wrote the Fellows letter; who appointed Higgins, Thomas, Raisin, and a host of their kind; who has made Senator Gorman the chief of his kitchen cabinet; who has retained Garland as his chief legal adviser; who has connived at the utter degradation and prostitution of the public service in Maryland and Indiana; and under whom the old spoils doctrine of "a clean sweep" among faithful public servants for merely partisan reasons has been applied almost throughout the country with a thoroughness that would have done no discredit to Andrew Jackson.

Doubtless President Cleveland meant to make good his original pledges concerning the civil service; doubtless no one regrets more than he himself his inability to stand up against the pressure of the spoilsmen within his own party; but the fact remains that he has signally failed thus to make good his pledges; that his acts have been absolutely at variance with his words; that hardly ever has an administration been more false to its promises on any subject than the administration has shown itself to be on the question of civil service reform.

When we can make a telling fight on so many issues the President fears to raise, it seems wise to do so, in addition to meeting him promptly on the one point he actually has raised. Above all, do not meet him on this question in a way that will tend to give the impression that the Republican Party is willing to subordinate all its other principles and all other considerations of public policy, to the single end of preserving untouched the present tariff, in its bad as well as in its good features. Let us make the next fight on the broad ground of Republicanism, with all, and not part merely, of what the name implies.

37.

James Bryce: Politics, Character, and Opinion in America

In contrast to observers of the American scene like Matthew Arnold, whose reports epitomized British aristocratic criticism, James Bryce (later British ambassador to the United States) wrote perceptively and sympathetically of the United States in the nineteenth century. The American Commonwealth, *from which several selections follow, was distinguished by Bryce's personal familiarity with the subject as well as scholarly research. The book received immediate acclaim and remains even in the twentieth century as one of the most penetrating analyses of American society and politics ever written. "No one can help admiring," Theodore Roosevelt wrote to Bryce, "the depth of your insight into our peculiar conditions, and the absolute fairness of your criticisms."*

Source: *The American Commonwealth*, 2nd edition, London, 1891, Vol. II, Chs. 58, 80, 109, 111, 112.

WHY THE BEST MEN DO NOT GO INTO POLITICS

There are several conditions present in the United States, conditions both constitutional and social, conditions independent either of political morality or of patriotism, which make the ablest citizens less disposed to enter political life than they would otherwise be, or than persons of the same class are in Europe. . . .

The want of a social and commercial capital is such a cause. To be a federal politician you must live in Washington, that is, abandon your circle of home friends, your profession or business, your local public duties. But to live in Paris or London is of itself an attraction to many Englishmen and Frenchmen.

There is no class in America to which public political life comes naturally as it still does to a certain class in England — no families with a sort of hereditary right to serve the state. Nobody can get an early and easy start on the strength of his name and connections as still happens in several European countries.

In Britain or France a man seeking to enter the higher walks of public life has more than 500 seats for which he may stand. If his own town or county is impossible, he goes elsewhere. In the United States he cannot. If his own district is already filled by a member of his own party, there is nothing to be done, unless he will condescend to undermine and supplant at the next nominating convention the sitting member. If he has been elected and happens to lose his own renomination or reelection, he cannot reenter Congress by any other door. The fact that a man has served gives him no claim to be allowed to go on serving. In the West, rotation is the rule. No wonder that, when a political career is so precarious, men of worth and capacity hesitate to embrace it. They cannot afford to be thrown out of their life's course by a mere accident.

Politics are less interesting than in Europe. The two kinds of questions which most attract eager or ambitious minds, questions of foreign policy and of domestic constitutional change, are generally absent — happily absent. Currency and tariff questions and financial affairs generally, internal improvements, the regulation of railways and so forth, are important no doubt, but to some minds not fascinating. How few people in the English or French legislatures

have mastered them, or would relish political life if it dealt with little else! There are no class privileges or religious inequalities to be abolished. Religion, so powerful a political force in Europe, is outside politics altogether.

In most European countries there has been for many years past an upward pressure of the poorer or the unprivileged masses, a pressure which has seemed to threaten the wealthier and more particularly the landowning class. Hence members of the latter class have had a strong motive for keeping tight hold of the helm of state. They have felt a direct personal interest in sitting in the legislature and controlling the administration of their country. This has not been so in America. Its great political issues have not been class issues. On the contrary there has been so great and general a sense of economic security, whether well or ill founded I do not now inquire, that the wealthy and educated have been content to leave the active work of politics alone.

The division of legislative authority between the federal Congress and the legislatures of the states further lessens the interest and narrows the opportunities of a political career. Some of the most useful members of the English Parliament have been led to enter it by their zeal for philanthropic schemes and social reforms. Others enter because they are interested in foreign politics or in commercial questions. In the United States, foreign politics and commercial questions belong to Congress, so no one will be led by them to enter the legislature of his state. Social reforms and philanthropic enterprises belong to the state legislatures, so no one will be led by them to enter Congress. The limited sphere of each body deprives it of the services of many active spirits who would have been attracted by it had it dealt with both these sets of matters or with the particular set of matters in which their own particular interest happens to lie.

In America there are more easy and at-

James Bryce

tractive openings into other careers than in most European countries. The settlement of the great West, the making and financing of railways, the starting of industrial or mercantile enterprises in the newer states, all offer a tempting field to ambition, ingenuity, and self-confidence. A man without capital or friends has a better chance than in Europe, and as the scale of undertakings is vaster, the prizes are more seductive. Hence much of the practical ability which in the Old World goes to parliamentary politics or to the civil administration of the state goes in America into business, especially into railways and finance. No class strikes one more by its splendid practical capacity than the class of railroad men. It includes administrative rulers, generals, diplomatists, financiers of the finest gifts. And in point of fact . . . the railroad kings have of late years swayed the fortunes of American citizens more than the politicians. . . .

It may however be alleged that I have omitted one significant ground for the dis-

taste of "the best people" for public life, viz., the bad company they would have to keep, the general vulgarity of tone in politics, the exposure to invective or ribaldry by hostile speakers and a reckless press. . . . The roughness of politics has, no doubt, some influence on the view which wealthy Americans take of a public career, but these are just the Americans who think that European politics are worked, to use the common phrase, "with kid gloves," and they are not the class most inclined anyhow to come to the front for the service of the nation. Without denying that there is recklessness in the American press and a want of refinement in politics generally, I do not believe that these phenomena have anything like the importance which European visitors are taught, and willingly learn, to attribute to them. Far more weight is to be laid upon the difficulties which the organization of the party system . . . throws in the way of men who seek to enter public life. There is . . . much that is disagreeable, much that is even humiliating in the initial stages of a political career, and doubtless many a pilgrim turns back after a short experience of this Slough of Despond.

To explain the causes which keep so much of the finest intellect of the country away from national business is one thing; to deny the unfortunate results would be quite another. Unfortunate they certainly are. But the downward tendency observable since the end of the Civil War seems to have been arrested. When the war was over, the Union saved, and the curse of slavery gone forever, there came a season of contentment and of lassitude. A nation which had surmounted such dangers seemed to have nothing more to fear. Those who had fought with tongue and pen and rifle might now rest on their laurels. After long-continued strain and effort, the wearied nerve and muscle sought repose. It was repose from political warfare only. For the end of the war coincided with the opening of a time of swift material growth and abounding material prosperity, in which industry and the development of the West absorbed more and more of the energy of the people. Hence a neglect of the details of politics such as had never been seen before.

The last few years have brought a revival of interest in public affairs, and especially in the management of cities. There is more speaking and writing and thinking, practical and definite thinking, upon the principles of government than at any previous epoch. Good citizens are beginning to put their hands to the machinery of government; and it is noticed than those who do so are, more largely than formerly, young men, who have not contracted the bad habits which the practice of politics has engendered among many of their elders, and who will in a few years have become an even more potent force than they are now. If the path to Congress and the state legislatures and the higher municipal offices were cleared of the stumbling blocks and dirt heaps which now encumber it, cunningly placed there by the professional politicians, a great change would soon pass upon the composition of legislative bodies and a new spirit be felt in the management of state and municipal as well as of national affairs.

NATIONAL CHARACTERISTICS AS MOLDING PUBLIC OPINION

As THE PUBLIC OPINION of a people is even more directly than its political institutions the reflection and expression of its character, it is convenient to begin the analysis of opinion in America by noting some of those general features of national character which give tone and color to the people's thoughts and feelings on politics. There are, of course, varieties proper to different classes and to different parts of the vast territory of the Union; but it is well to consider first such characteristics as belong to the nation as a whole and afterward to examine the various classes and districts of the country. And when I speak of the nation I mean the native Americans. What follows is not applicable to the recent immigrants from Europe, and, of course, even less applicable to the Southern Negroes; though both these elements are potent by their votes.

The Americans are a good-natured people, kindly, helpful to one another, disposed to take a charitable view even of wrongdoers. Their anger sometimes flames up, but the fire is soon extinct. Nowhere is cruelty more abhorred. Even a mob lynching a horse thief in the West has consideration for the criminal and will give him a good drink of whisky before he is strung up. Cruelty to slaves was rare while slavery lasted, the best proof of which is the quietness of the slaves during the war when all the men and many of the boys of the South were serving in the Confederate armies. As everybody knows, juries are more lenient to offenses of all kinds but one — offenses against women — than they are anywhere in Europe. The Southern "rebels" were soon forgiven; and though civil wars are proverbially bitter, there have been few struggles in which the combatants did so many little friendly acts for one another, few in which even the vanquished have so quickly buried their resentments.

It is true that newspapers and public speakers say hard things of their opponents; but this is a part of the game, and is besides a way of relieving their feelings — the bark is sometimes the louder in order that a bite may not follow. Vindictiveness shown by a public man excites general disapproval, and the maxim of letting bygones be bygones is pushed so far that an offender's misdeeds are often forgotten when they ought to be remembered against him.

All the world knows that they are a humorous people. They are as conspicuously the purveyors of humor to the nineteenth century as the French were the purveyors of wit to the eighteenth. Nor is this sense of the ludicrous side of things confined to a few brilliant writers. It is diffused among the whole people; it colors their ordinary life and gives to their talk that distinctively new flavor which a European palate enjoys. Their capacity for enjoying a joke against themselves was oddly illustrated at the outset of the Civil War, a time of stern excitement, by the merriment which arose over the hasty retreat of the federal troops at the Battle of Bull Run. When William M. Tweed was ruling and robbing New York, and had set on the bench men who were openly prostituting justice, the citizens found the situation so amusing that they almost forgot to be angry. Much of President Lincoln's popularity, and much also of the gift he showed for restoring confidence to the North at the darkest moments of the war, was due to the humorous way he used to turn things, conveying the impression of not being himself uneasy, even when he was most so.

That indulgent view of mankind which I have already mentioned, a view odd in a people whose ancestors were penetrated with the belief in original sin, is strengthened by this wish to get amusement out of everything. The want of seriousness which it produces may be more apparent than real. Yet it has its significance; for people become affected by the language they use, as we see men grow into cynics when they have acquired the habit of talking cynicism for the sake of effect.

They are a hopeful people. Whether or no they are right in calling themselves a new people, they certainly seem to feel in their veins the bounding pulse of youth. They see a long vista of years stretching out before them in which they will have time enough to cure all their faults, to overcome

all the obstacles that block their path. They look at their enormous territory with its still only half-explored sources of wealth; they reckon up the growth of their population and their products; they contrast the comfort and intelligence of their laboring classes with the condition of the masses in the Old World. They remember the dangers that so long threatened the Union from the slave power and the rebellion it raised, and see peace and harmony now restored, the South more prosperous and contented than at any previous epoch, perfect good feeling between all sections of the country. It is natural for them to believe in their star. And this sanguine temper makes them tolerant of evils which they regard as transitory, removable as soon as time can be found to root them up.

They have unbounded faith in what they call the "people" and in a democratic system of government. The great states of the European continent are distracted by the contests of Republicans and Monarchists, and of rich and poor — contests which go down to the foundations of government, and in France are further embittered by religious passions. Even in England the ancient constitution is always under repair; and while many think it is being ruined by changes, others hold that still greater changes are needed to make it tolerable. No such questions trouble American minds, for nearly everybody believes and everybody declares that the frame of government is in its main lines so excellent that such reforms as seem called for need not touch those lines, but are required only to protect the Constitution from being perverted by the parties. Hence a further confidence that the people are sure to decide right in the long run, a confidence inevitable and essential in a government which refers every question to the arbitrament of numbers.

There have, of course, been instances where the once insignificant minority proved to have been wiser than the majority of the moment. Such was eminently the case in the great slavery struggle. But here the minority prevailed by growing into a majority as events developed the real issues, so that this also has been deemed a ground for holding that all minorities which have right on their side will bring round their antagonists and in the long run win by voting power. If you ask an intelligent citizen why he so holds, he will answer that truth and justice are sure to make their way into the minds and consciences of the majority. This is deemed an axiom, and the more readily so deemed because truth is identified with common sense, the quality which the average citizen is most confidently proud of possessing.

This feeling shades off into another, externally like it but at bottom distinct — the feeling not only that the majority, be it right or wrong, will and must prevail but that its being the majority proves it to be right. This feeling appears in the guise sometimes of piety and sometimes of fatalism. Religious minds hold — you find the idea underlying many books and hear it in many pulpits — that Divine Providence has specially chosen and led the American people to work out a higher type of freedom and civilization than any other state has yet attained, and that this great work will surely be brought to a happy issue by the protecting hand which has so long guided it. Before others who are less sensitive to such impressions, the will of the people looms up like one of the irresistible forces of nature, which you must obey and which you can turn and use only by obeying. In the famous words of Bacon, *non nisi parendo vincitur* [there is no victory without preparation].

The Americans are an educated people, compared with the whole mass of the population in any European country except Switzerland, parts of Germany, Norway,

Iceland, and Scotland; that is to say, the average of knowledge is higher, the habit of reading and thinking more generally diffused than in any other country. (I speak, of course, of the native Americans, excluding Negroes and recent immigrants.) They know the Constitution of their own country, they follow public affairs, they join in local government and learn from it how government must be carried on, and in particular how discussion must be conducted in meetings and its results tested at elections. The town meeting has been the most perfect school of self-government in any modern country. They exercise their minds on theological questions, debating points of Christian doctrine with no small acuteness. Women in particular, though their chief reading is fiction and theology, pick up at the public schools and from the popular magazines far more miscellaneous information than the women of any European country possess, and this naturally tells on the intelligence of the men.

That the education of the masses is nevertheless a superficial education goes without saying. It is sufficient to enable them to think they know something about the great problems of politics; insufficient to show them how little they know. The public elementary school gives everybody the key to knowledge in making reading and writing familiar, but it has not time to teach him how to use the key, whose use is, in fact, by the pressure of daily work, almost confined to the newspaper and the magazine. So we may say that if the political education of the average American voter be compared with that of the average voter in Europe, it stands high; but if it be compared with the functions which the theory of the American government lays on him, which its spirit implies, which the methods of its party organization assume, its inadequacy is manifest.

This observation, however, is not so

much a reproach to the schools, which generally do what English schools omit — instruct the child in the principles of the Constitution — as a tribute to the height of the ideal which the American conception of popular rule sets up; for the functions of the citizen are not, as has hitherto been the case in Europe, confined to the choosing of legislators, who are then left to settle issues of policy and select executive rulers.

The American citizen is virtually one of the governors of the republic. Issues are decided and rulers selected by the direct popular vote. Elections are so frequent that to do his duty at them a citizen ought to be constantly watching public affairs with a full comprehension of the principles involved in them, and a judgment of the candidates derived from a criticism of their arguments as well as a recollection of their past careers. As has been said, the instruction received in the common schools and from the newspapers, and supposed to be developed by the practice of primaries and conventions, while it makes the voter deem himself capable of governing, does not completely fit him to weigh the real merits of statesmen, to discern the true grounds on which questions ought to be decided, to note the drift of events and discover the direction in which parties are being carried. He is like a sailor who knows the spars and ropes of the ship and is expert in working her but is ignorant of geography and navigation; who can perceive that some of the officers are smart and others dull but cannot judge which of them is qualified to use the sextant or will best keep his head during a hurricane.

They are a moral and well-conducted people. Setting aside the *colluvies gentium* which one finds in Western mining camps and which popular literature has presented to Europeans as far larger than it really is, setting aside also the rabble of a few great cities and the Negroes of the South, the average of temperance, chastity, truthfulness, and general probity is somewhat higher than in any of the great nations of Europe. The instincts of the native farmer or artisan are almost invariably kindly and charitable. He respects the law; he is deferential to women and indulgent to children; he attaches an almost excessive value to the possession of a genial manner and the observance of domestic duties.

They are also a religious people. It is not merely that they respect religion and its ministers, for that one might say of Russians or Sicilians, not merely that they are assiduous churchgoers and Sunday school teachers, but that they have an intelligent interest in the form of faith they profess, are pious without superstition and zealous without bigotry. The importance which they still, though less than formerly, attach to dogmatic propositions does not prevent them from feeling the moral side of their theology. Christianity influences conduct, not indeed half as much as in theory it ought, but probably more than it does in any other modern country, and far more than it did in the so-called ages of faith.

Nor do their moral and religious impulses remain in the soft haze of self-complacent sentiment. The desire to expunge or cure the visible evils of the world is strong. Nowhere are so many philanthropic and reformatory agencies at work. Zeal outruns discretion, outruns the possibilities of the case, in not a few of the efforts made, as well by legislation as by voluntary action, to suppress vice, to prevent intemperance, to purify popular literature.

Religion apart, they are an unreverential people. I do not mean irreverent — far from it — nor do I mean that they have not a great capacity for hero worship, as they have many a time shown. I mean that they are little disposed, especially in public questions — political, economical, or social — to defer to the opinions of those who are wiser or better instructed than themselves. Everything tends to make the individual independent and self-reliant. He goes early into the world; he is left to make his way alone; he tries one occupation after another, if the first or second venture does not prosper; he gets to think that each man is his own best helper and adviser. Thus he is led, I will not say to form his own opinions, for even in America few are those who do that, but to fancy that he has formed them, and to feel little need of aid from others toward correcting them.

There is, therefore, less disposition than in Europe to expect light and leading on public affairs from speakers or writers. Oratory is not directed toward instruction but toward stimulation. Special knowledge, which commands deference in applied science or in finance, does not command it in politics, because that is not deemed a special subject but one within the comprehension of every practical man. Politics is, to be sure, a profession, and so far might seem to need professional aptitudes. But the professional politician is not the man who has studied statesmanship, but the man who has practised the art of running conventions and winning elections.

Even that strong point of America, the completeness and highly popular character of local government, contributes to lower the standard of attainment expected in a public man, because the citizens judge of all politics by the politics they see first and know best — those of their township or city — and fancy that he who is fit to be selectman or county commissioner or alderman is fit to sit in the great council of the nation. Like the shepherd in Virgil, they think the only difference between their town and Rome is in its size, and believe that what does for Lafayetteville will do well enough for Washington. Hence when a man of statesmanlike gifts appears, he has little encouragement to take a high and statesmanlike tone, for his words do not necessarily receive weight from his position. He fears to be instructive or hortatory, lest such an attitude should expose him to ridicule; and in America ridicule is a terrible power. Nothing escapes it. Few have the courage to face it. In the indulgence of it even this humane race can be unfeeling.

They are a busy people. . . . The leisured class is relatively small, is in fact confined to a few Eastern cities. The citizen has little time to think about political problems. Engrossing all the working hours, his avocation leaves him only stray moments for this fundamental duty. It is true that he admits his responsibilities, considers himself a member of a party, takes some interest in current events. But although he would reject the idea that his thinking should be done for him, he has not leisure to do it for himself and must practically lean upon and follow his party. It astonishes an English visitor to find how small a part politics play in conversation among the wealthier classes and generally in the cities. . . . There is plenty of political chat round the store at the crossroads, and though it is rather in the nature of gossip than of debate, it seems, along with the practice of local government, to sustain the interest of ordinary folk in public affairs.

The want of serious and sustained thinking is not confined to politics. One feels it even more as regards economical and social questions. To it must be ascribed the vitality of certain prejudices and fallacies which could scarcely survive the continuous application of such vigorous minds as one finds among the Americans. Their quick perceptions serve them so well in business and in the ordinary affairs of private life that they do not feel the need for minute investigation and patient reflection on the underlying principles of things. They are apt to ignore difficulties, and when they can no longer ignore them, they will evade them rather than lay siege to them according to the rules of art. The sense that there is no time to spare haunts an American even when he might find the time, and would do best for himself by finding it.

Someone will say that an aversion to steady thinking belongs to the average man everywhere. Admitting this, I must repeat once more that we are now comparing the Americans, not with average men in other countries but with the ideal citizens of a democracy. We are trying them by the standard which the theory of their government assumes. In other countries, statesmen or philosophers do, and are expected to do, the solid thinking for the bulk of the people. Here the people are expected to do it for themselves. To say that they do it imperfectly is not to deny them the credit of doing it better than a European philosopher might have predicted.

They are a commercial people, whose point of view is primarily that of persons accustomed to reckon profit and loss. Their impulse is to apply a direct practical test to men and measures, to assume that the men who have got on fastest are the smartest men, and that a scheme which seems to pay well deserves to be supported. Abstract reasonings they dislike, subtle reasonings they suspect; they accept nothing as practical which is not plain, downright, apprehensible by an ordinary understanding. Although open-minded so far as willingness to listen goes, they are hard to convince, because they have really made up their minds on most subjects, having adopted the prevailing notions of their locality or party as truths due to their own reflection.

It may seem a contradiction to remark that with this shrewdness and the sort of hardness it produces they are nevertheless an impressionable people. Yet this is true. It is not their intellect, however, that is impressionable but their imagination and emotions, which respond in unexpected ways to appeals made on behalf of a cause which seems to have about it something noble or pathetic. They are capable of an ideality surpassing that of Englishmen or Frenchmen.

They are an unsettled people. In no state of the Union is the bulk of the population so fixed in its residence as everywhere in Europe; in many it is almost nomadic. Nobody feels rooted to the soil. Here today and gone tomorrow, he cannot readily contract habits of trustful dependence on his neighbors. Community of interest, or of belief in such a cause as temperance, or protection for native industry unites him for a time with others similarly minded, but congenial spirits seldom live long enough together to form a school or type of local opinion which develops strength and becomes a proselytizing force. Perhaps this tends to prevent the growth of variety in opinion. When a man arises with some power of original thought in politics, he is feeble if isolated and is depressed by his insignificance, whereas if he grows up in favorable soil with sympathetic minds around him, whom he can in prolonged intercourse permeate with his ideas, he learns to speak with confidence and soars on the wings of his disciples. Whether or no there be truth in this suggestion, one who considers the variety of conditions under which men live in America may find ground for surprise that there should be so few independent schools of opinion.

But even while an unsettled, they are nevertheless an associative, because a sympathetic people. Although the atoms are in constant motion, they have a strong attraction for one another. Each man catches his neighbor's sentiment more quickly and easily than happens with the English. That sort of reserve and isolation, that tendency rather to repel than to invite confidence which foreigners attribute to the Englishman, though it belongs rather to the upper and middle class than to the nation generally, is, though not absent, yet less marked in America. It seems to be one of the notes of difference between the two branches of the race.

In the United States, since each man likes to feel that his ideas raise in other minds the same emotions as in his own, a sentiment or impulse is rapidly propagated and quickly conscious of its strength. Add to this the aptitude for organization which their history and institutions have educed, and one sees how the tendency to form and the talent to work combinations for a political or any other object has become one of the great features of the country. Hence, too, the immense strength of party. It rests not only on interest and habit and the sense of its value as a means of working the government, but also on the sympathetic element and instinct of combination ingrained in the national character.

They are a changeful people. Not fickle, for they are if anything too tenacious of ideas once adopted, too fast-bound by party ties, too willing to pardon the errors of a cherished leader. But they have what chemists call low specific heat; they grow warm suddenly and cool as suddenly; they are liable to swift and vehement outbursts of feeling which rush like wildfire across the country, gaining glow like the wheel of a railway car by the accelerated motion. The very similarity of ideas and equality of conditions which makes them hard to convince at first makes a conviction once implanted run its course the more triumphantly. They seem all to take flame at once, because what has told upon one has told in the same way upon all the rest, and the obstructing and separating barriers which exist in Europe scarcely exist here.

Nowhere is the saying so applicable that nothing succeeds like success. The native American or so-called Know-Nothing Party had in two years from its foundation become a tremendous force, running, and seeming for a time likely to carry, its own presidential candidate. In three years more it was dead without hope of revival. Now

and then, as for instance in the elections of 1874-75, there comes a rush of feeling so sudden and tremendous that the name of tidal wave has been invented to describe it.

After this it may seem a paradox to add that the Americans are a conservative people. Yet anyone who observes the power of habit among them, the tenacity with which old institutions and usages, legal and theological formulas, have been clung to will admit the fact. A love for what is old and established is in their English blood. Moreover, prosperity helps to make them conservative. They are satisfied with the world they live in, for they have found it a good world, in which they have grown rich and can sit under their own vine and fig tree, none making them afraid. They are proud of their history and of their Constitution, which has come out of the furnace of civil war with scarcely the smell of fire upon it. It is little to say that they do not seek change for the sake of change, because the nations that do this exist only in the fancy of alarmist philosophers. There are nations, however, whose impatience of existing evils, or whose proneness to be allured by visions of a brighter future, makes them underestimate the risk of change, nations that will pull up the plant to see whether it has begun to strike root.

This is not the way of the Americans. They are no doubt ready to listen to suggestions from any quarter. They do not consider that an institution is justified by its existence, but admit everything to be matter for criticism. Their keenly competitive spirit and pride in their own ingenuity have made them quicker than any other people to adopt and adapt inventions: telephones were in use in every little town over the West, while in the city of London men were just beginning to wonder whether they could be made to pay. . . .

The fondness for trying experiments has produced a good deal of hasty legislation, especially in the newer states, and . . .

some of it has already been abandoned. But these admissions do not affect the main proposition. The Americans are at bottom a conservative people, in virtue both of the deep instincts of their race and of that practical shrewdness which recognizes the value of permanence and solidity in institutions. They are conservative in their fundamental beliefs, in the structure of their governments, in their social and domestic usages. They are like a tree whose pendulous shoots quiver and rustle with the lightest breeze, while its roots enfold the rock with a grasp which storms cannot loosen.

THE ABSENCE OF A CAPITAL

THE UNITED STATES are the only great country in the world which has no capital. . . . By a capital I mean a city which is not only the seat of political government but is also, by the size, wealth, and character of its population, the head and center of the country; a leading seat of commerce and industry; a reservoir of financial resources; the favored residence of the great and powerful; the spot in which the chiefs of the learned professions are to be found; where the most potent and widely read journals are published; whither men of literary and scientific capacity are drawn. The heaping together in such a place of these various elements of power, the conjunction of the forces of rank, wealth, knowledge, intellect, naturally makes such a city a sort of foundry in which opinion is melted and cast, where it receives that definite shape in which it can be easily and swiftly propagated and diffused through the whole country, deriving not only an authority from the position of those who form it but a momentum from the weight of numbers in the community whence it comes.

The opinion of such a city becomes powerful politically because it is that of the persons who live at headquarters, who hold the strings of government in their hands, who either themselves rule the state or are in close contact with those who do. It is true that, under a representative government, power rests with those whom the people have sent up from all parts of the country. Still these members of the legislature reside in the capital and cannot but feel the steady pressure of its prevailing sentiment which touches them socially at every point. It sometimes happens that the populace of the capital, by their power of overawing the rulers or perhaps of effecting a revolution, are able to turn the fortunes of the state. But even where no such peril is to be apprehended, any nation with the kind of a capital I am describing acquires the habit of looking to it for light and leading and is apt to yield to it an initiative in political movements.

In the field of art and literature, the influence of a great capital is no less marked. It gathers to a center the creative power of the country and subjects it to the criticism of the best instructed and most polished society. . . .

In the case both of politics and of literature, the existence of a capital tends to strengthen the influence of what is called society, that is to say, of the men of wealth and leisure who have time to think of other matters than the needs of daily life, and whose company and approval are apt to be sought by the men of talent. Thus, where the rich and great are gathered in one spot to which the nation looks, they effect more in the way of guiding its political thought and training its literary taste than is possible where they are dispersed over the face of a large country. In both points, therefore, it will evidently make a difference to a democratic country whether it has a capital and what degree of deference that capital receives. . . .

What are the cities of the United States which can claim to approach nearest to the sort of capital we have been considering? Not Washington, though it is the meeting place of Congress and the seat of federal administration. It has a relatively small population (in 1880, 147,293, of whom one-third were Negroes). Society consists of congressmen (for about half the year), officials, diplomatists, and some rich and leisured people who come to spend the winter. The leaders of finance, industry, commerce, and the professions are absent; there are few men of letters, no artists, hardly any journalists. What is called the "society" of Washington, which, being small, polished, and composed of people who constantly meet one another, is agreeable, and not the less agreeable because it has a peculiar flavor, is so far from aspiring to political authority as to deem it "bad form" to talk politics.

Not New York, though it is now by far the most populous city. It is the center of commerce, the sovereign of finance. But it has no special political influence or power beyond that of casting a large vote, which is an important factor in determining the thirty-six presidential votes of the state. Business is its main occupation: the representatives of literature are few; the journals, although certainly among the ablest and most widely read in the country are, after all, New York journals, and not, like those of Paris, London, or even Berlin, professedly written for the whole nation.

Next comes Philadelphia, once the first city in the Union, but now standing below New York in all the points just mentioned, with even less claim to be deemed a center of art or opinion. Boston was for a time the chosen home of letters and culture, and still contains, in proportion to her population, a larger number of men and women capable of making or judging good work than any other city. But she can no longer be said to lead abstract thought, much less current opinion.

Chicago combines a vast and growing population with a central position: she is in some respects more of a typical American city than any of the others I have named. But Chicago, so far as political initiative goes, has no more weight than what the number of her voters represents, and in art or literature is nowhere. Nor does any one of these cities seem on the way to gain a more commanding position. New York will probably retain her preeminence in population and commercial consequence, but she does not rise proportionately in culture, while the center of political gravity, shifting ever more and more to the West, will doubtless finally fix itself in the Mississippi Valley.

It deserves to be remarked that what is true of the whole country is also true of the great sections of the country. Of the cities I have named, none, except possibly Boston and San Francisco, can be said to be even a local capital, either for purposes of political opinion or of intellectual movement and tendency. Boston retains her position as the literary center of New England; San Francisco . . . has a preponderating influence on the Pacific Coast. But no other great city is regarded by the inhabitants of her own and the adjoining states as their natural head, to which they look for political guidance or from which they expect any intellectual stimulance. Even New Orleans, though by far the largest place in the South, is in no sense the metropolis of the South; and does little more for the South than set a conspicuous example of municipal misgovernment to the surrounding commonwealths. Though no Paris, no Berlin stands above them, these great American cities are not more important in the country, or even in their own sections of the country, than Lyons and Bordeaux are in France, Hamburg and Cologne in Germany. Even as between municipal communities, even in the sphere of thought and literary effort, equality and local independence have in America their perfect work. . . .

THE PLEASANTNESS
OF AMERICAN LIFE

PROBABLY the assertion of social equality was one of the causes which injured American manners forty years ago, for that they were then bad among townsfolk can hardly be doubted in face of the testimony, not merely of sharp tongues like Mrs. Trollope's but of calm observers like Sir Charles Lyell and sympathetic observers like Richard Cobden. In those days there was an obtrusive self-assertiveness among the less refined classes, especially toward those who, coming from the Old World, were assumed to come in a patronizing spirit. Now, however, social equality has grown so naturally out of the circumstances of the country, has been so long established, and is so ungrudgingly admitted that all excuse for obtrusiveness has disappeared. People meet on a simple and natural footing, with more frankness and ease than is possible in countries where everyone is either looking up or looking down.

There is no servility on the part of the humbler, and if now and then a little of the "I am as good as you" rudeness be perceptible, it is almost sure to proceed from a recent immigrant, to whom the attitude of simple equality has not yet become familiar as the evidently proper attitude of one man to another. There is no condescension on the part of the more highly placed, nor is there even that sort of scrupulously polite coldness which one might think they would adopt in order to protect their dignity. They have no cause to fear for their dignity, so long as they do not themselves forget it. And the fact that your shoemaker or your factory hand addresses you as an equal does not prevent him from respecting, and showing his respect for, all such superiority as

your birth or education or eminence in any line of life may entitle you to receive.

This naturalness of intercourse is a distinct addition to the pleasure of social life. It enlarges the circle of possible friendship, by removing the *gêne*, which in most parts of Europe persons of different ranks feel in exchanging their thoughts on any matters save those of business. It raises the humbler classes without lowering the upper; indeed, it improves the upper no less than the lower by expunging that latent insolence which deforms the manners of so many of the European rich or great.

It relieves women in particular, who in Europe are specially apt to think of class distinctions, from that sense of constraint and uneasiness which is produced by the knowledge that other women with whom they come in contact are either looking down on them or, at any rate, trying to gauge and determine their social position. It expands the range of a man's sympathies, and makes it easier for him to enter into the sentiments of other classes than his own. It gives a sense of solidarity to the whole nation, cutting away the ground for all sorts of jealousies and grudges which distract people, so long as the social pretensions of past centuries linger on to be resisted and resented by the leveling spirit of a revolutionary age. And I have never heard native Americans speak of any drawbacks corresponding to and qualifying these benefits. . . .

I come last to the character and ways of the Americans themselves, in which there is a certain charm, hard to convey by description, but felt almost as soon as one sets foot on their shore, and felt constantly thereafter. They are a kindly people. Good nature, heartiness, a readiness to render small services to one another, an assumption that neighbors in the country or persons thrown together in travel, or even in a crowd, were meant to be friendly rather than hostile to one another, seem to be everywhere in the air and in those who breathe it. Sociability is the rule; isolation and moroseness the rare exception. It is not merely that people are more vivacious or talkative than an Englishman expects to find them, for the Western man is often taciturn and seldom wreathes his long face into a smile. It is rather that you feel that the man next to you, whether silent or talkative, does not mean to repel intercourse or convey by his manner his low opinion of his fellow creatures.

Everybody seems disposed to think well of the world and its inhabitants, well enough at least to wish to be on easy terms with them and serve them in those little things whose trouble to the doer is small in proportion to the pleasure they give to the receiver. To help others is better recognized as a duty than in Europe. Nowhere is money so readily given for any public purpose; nowhere, I suspect, are there so many acts of private kindness done, such, for instance, as paying the college expenses of a promising boy or aiding a widow to carry on her husband's farm; and these are not done with ostentation. People seem to take their own troubles more lightly than they do in Europe and to be more indulgent to the faults by which troubles are caused. It is a land of hope, and a land of hope is a land of good humor. And they have also, though this is a quality more perceptible in women than in men, a remarkable faculty for enjoyment, a power of drawing more happiness from obvious pleasures, simple and innocent pleasures, than one often finds in overburdened Europe. . . .

THE UNIFORMITY OF AMERICAN LIFE

To the pleasantness of American life there is one, and only one, serious drawback — its uniformity. . . .

It is felt in many ways. I will name a few.

It is felt in the aspects of nature. . . . There are some extraordinary natural phenomena, such as Niagara, the Yellowstone geysers, and the great canyon of the Colorado River, which Europe cannot equal. But taking the country as a whole, and remembering that it is a continent, it is not more rich in picturesque beauty than the much smaller western half of Europe. . . . One finds, I think, less variety in the whole chain of the Rockies than in the comparatively short Pyrenees. . . . So the Atlantic Coast, though there are pretty bits between Newport and the New Brunswick frontier, cannot vie with the coasts of Scotland, Ireland, or Norway; while southward from New York to Florida it is everywhere flat and generally dreary. . . . The man who lives in the section of America which seems destined to contain the largest population, I mean the states on the Upper Mississippi, lives in the midst of a plain wider than the plains of Russia, and must travel hundreds of miles to escape from its monotony.

When we turn from the aspects of nature to the cities of men, the uniformity is even more remarkable. With five or six exceptions . . . American cities differ from one another only herein: that some of them are built more with brick than with wood, and others more with wood than with brick. In all else they are alike, both great and small. In all, the same wide streets, crossing at right angles, ill-paved, but planted along the sidewalks with maple trees, whose autumnal scarlet surpasses the brilliance of any European foliage. In all, the same shops, arranged on the same plan, the same Chinese laundries with Li Kow visible through the window, the same ice-cream stores, the same large hotels with seedy men hovering about in the dreary entrance hall, the same streetcars passing to and fro with passengers clinging to the doorstep, the same locomotives ringing their great bells as they clank slowly down the middle of the street. . . .

I return joyfully to the exceptions. Boston has a character of her own, with her beautiful Common, her smooth environing waters, her Beacon Hill crowned by the gilded dome of the State House, and Bunker Hill, bearing the monument of the famous fight. New York, besides a magnificent position, has in the grandeur of the buildings and the tremendous rush of men and vehicles along the streets as much the air of a great capital as London itself. Chicago, with her enormous size and the splendid warehouses that line her endless thoroughfares, leaves a strong though not wholly agreeable impression. Richmond has a quaint Old-World look which dwells in the memory. Few cities have a seafront equal in beauty to the lakefront of Cleveland. Washington, with its wide and beautifully graded avenues and the glittering white of the stately Capitol has become within the last twenty years a singularly handsome city.

And New Orleans — or rather the Creole quarter of New Orleans, for the rest of the city is commonplace — is delicious, suggesting old France and Spain, yet a France and Spain strangely transmuted in this new clime. I have seen nothing in America more picturesque than the Rue Royale, with its houses of all heights, often built round a courtyard, where a magnolia or an orange tree stands in the middle, and wooden external staircases lead up to wooden galleries, the house fronts painted of all colors and carrying double rows of balconies decorated with pretty ironwork, the whole standing languid and still in the warm soft air and touched with the subtle fragrance of decay. . . .

It is the absence in nearly all the American cities of anything that speaks of the past that makes their external aspect so unsuggestive. In pacing their busy streets and admiring their handsome city halls and churches, one's heart sinks at the feeling that nothing historically interesting ever has happened here, perhaps ever will happen. . . .

Nowhere, perhaps, does this sense of the absolute novelty of all things strike one so strongly as in San Francisco. Few cities in the world can vie with her either in the beauty or in the natural advantages of her situation; indeed, there are only two places in Europe — Constantinople and Gibraltar — that combine an equally perfect landscape with what may be called an equally imperial position. . . . San Francisco has had a good deal of history in her forty years of life; but this history does not, like that of Greece or Italy, write itself in stone, or even in wood.

Of the uniformity of political institutions over the whole United States, I have spoken already. Everywhere the same system of state governments, everywhere the same municipal governments, and almost uniformly bad or good in proportion to the greater or smaller population of the city; the same party machinery organized on the same methods, "run" by the same wirepullers and "workers." In rural local government there are some diversities in the names, areas, and functions of the different bodies, yet differences slight in comparison with the points of likeness. The schools are practically identical in organization, in the subjects taught, in the methods of teaching, though the administration of them is as completely decentralized as can be imagined, even the state commissioner having no right to do more than suggest or report. So it is with the charitable institutions, with the libraries, the lecture courses, the public amusements. All these are more abundant and better of their kind in the richer and more cultivated parts of the country, generally better in the North Atlantic than in the inland states, and in the West than in the South. But they are the same in type everywhere.

It is the same with social habits and usages. There are still some differences between the South and the North; and in the Eastern cities the upper class is more Europeanized in its code of etiquette and its ways of daily life. But even these variations tend to disappear. Eastern customs begin to permeate the West, beginning with the richer families; the South is more like the North than it was before the war. Travel where you will, you feel that what you have found in one place, that you will find in another. The thing which hath been, will be: you can no more escape from it than you can quit the land to live in the sea.

Last of all we come to man himself — to man and to woman, not less important than man. The ideas of men and women, their fundamental beliefs and their superficial tastes, their methods of thinking and their fashions of talking, are what most concern their fellowmen; and if there be variety and freshness in these, the uniformity of nature and the monotony of cities signify but little. . . .

I do not in the least mean that people are more commonplace in America than in England, or that the Americans are less ideal than the English. Neither of these statements would be true. On the contrary, the average American is more alive to new ideas, more easily touched through his imagination or his emotions than the average Englishman or Frenchman. I mean only that the native-born Americans appear to vary less, in fundamentals, from what may be called the dominant American type than Englishmen, Germans, Frenchmen, Spaniards, or Italians do from any type which could be taken as the dominant type in any of those nations. . . .

Those who have observed the uniformity I have been attempting to describe have commonly set it down, as Europeans do most American phenomena, to what they call democracy. Democratic government has in reality not much to do with it, except insofar as such a government helps to induce that deference of individuals to the mass which strengthens a dominant type, whether of ideas, of institutions, or of manners. More must be ascribed to the equality of material conditions, still more general than in Europe, to the fact that nearly everyone is engaged either in agriculture, or in commerce, or in some handicraft, to the extraordinary mobility of the population, which in migrating from one part of the country to another brings the characteristics of each part into the others, to the diffusion of education, to the cheapness of literature and universal habit of reading, which enable everyone to know what everyone else is thinking, but above all to the newness of the country, and the fact that four-fifths of it have been made all at a stroke, and therefore all of a piece, as compared with the slow growth by which European countries have developed. Newness is the cause of uniformity, not merely in the external aspect of cities, villages, farmhouses, but in other things also, for the institutions and social habits which belonged a century ago to a group of small communities on the Atlantic Coast have been suddenly extended over an immense area, each band of settlers naturally seeking to retain its customs and to plant in the new soil shoots from which trees like those of the old home might spring up. . . .

Doubtless many American institutions are old, and were old before they were carried across the Atlantic. But they have generally received a new dress, which, in adapting them to the needs of today, conceals their ancient character; and the form in which they have been diffused or reproduced in the different states of the Union is in all those states practically identical. . . .

In America a small race, of the same speech and faith, has spread itself out over an immense area and has been strong enough to impose its own type, not only on the Dutch and other early settlers of the middle states but on the immigrant masses which the last forty years have brought. May one, then, expect that, when novelty has worn off and America counts her life by centuries instead of by decades, variety will develop itself, and such complexities, or diversities, or incongruities (whichever one is to call them) as European countries present be deeper and more numerous?

As regards the outside of things, this seems unlikely. Many of the small towns of today will grow into large towns, a few of the large towns into great cities, but as they grow they will not become less like one another. There will be larger theaters and hotels, more churches (in spite of secularist lecturers) and handsomer ones; but what is to make the theaters and churches of one city differ from those of another? Fashion and the immense facilities of intercourse tend to wear down even such diversities in the style of building or furnishing, or in modes of locomotion, or in amusements and forms of social intercourse, as now exist.

As regards ideas and the inner life of men, the question is a more difficult one. At present there are only two parts of the country where one looks to meet with the well-marked individualities I refer to. One of these is New England, where the spirit of Puritanism, expressed in new literary forms by Emerson and his associates, did produce a peculiar type of thinking and discoursing, which has now, however, almost died out, and where one still meets, especially among the cultivated classes, a larger number than elsewhere of persons who have thought and studied for themselves and are unlike their fellows. The other part of the country is the Far West, where the wild life led by pioneers in exploration, or ranching, or gold mining has produced a number of striking figures, men of extraordinary self-reliance, with a curious mixture of geniality and reckless hardihood, no less indifferent to their own lives than to the lives of others. Of preserving this latter type there is, alas, little hope; the swift march of civilization will have expunged it in thirty years more.

When one sees millions of people thinking the same thoughts and reading the same books, and perceives that as the multitude grows its influence becomes always stronger, it is hard to imagine how new points of repulsion and contrast are to arise, new diversities of sentiment and doctrine to be developed. Nevertheless, I am inclined to believe that as the intellectual proficiency and speculative play of mind which are now confined to a comparatively small class become more generally diffused, as the pressure of effort toward material success is relaxed, as the number of men devoted to science, art, and learning increases, so will the dominance of what may be called the business mind decline, and, with a richer variety of knowledge, tastes, and pursuits, there will come also a larger crop of marked individualities and of divergent intellectual types.

Time will take away some of the monotony which comes from the absence of historical associations; for even if, as is to be hoped, there comes no war to make battlefields famous like those of twenty-five years ago, yet literature and the lives of famous men cannot but attach to many spots associations to which the blue of distance will at last give a romantic interest. No people could be more ready than are the Americans to cherish such associations. Their country has a short past, but they willingly revere and preserve all the memories the past has bequeathed to them.

38.

THEODORE ROOSEVELT: The Americanization of Immigrants

James Bryce, Oxford scholar and authority on civil law, drew from his numerous trips to the United States material for his classic work on American life and institutions, The American Commonwealth, *published in 1888. Theodore Roosevelt read the work and responded on January 6, 1888, with the following letter to Bryce. In his own work,* The Winning of the West, *Roosevelt traced the influence of immigration on American growth and development and agreed with Bryce that immigrants were so often persecuted because "there is a disposition in the United States to use the immigrants . . . much as the cat is used in the kitchen to account for broken plates and food which disappears."*

Source: *The Letters of Theodore Roosevelt*, Elting E. Morrison, ed., Cambridge, 1951, pp. 134-135.

YOU MUST by this time be tired of hearing your book compared to De Tocqueville's; yet you must allow me one brief allusion to the two together. When I looked over the proofs you sent me, I ranked your book and his together; now that I see your book as a whole, I feel that the comparison did it great injustice. It has all of De Tocqueville's really great merits; and has not got, as his book has, two or three serious and damaging faults. No one can help admiring the depth of your insight into our peculiar conditions and the absolute fairness of your criticisms.

Of course, there are one or two minor points on which I disagree with you; but I think the fact that you give a good view of all sides is rather funnily shown by the way in which each man who refuses to see any but one side quotes your book as supporting him. I was rather amused to see that the *Spectator* considered that the facts you gave told heavily against home rule, because our state legislatures were not ideal bodies,

and that similarly the *Saturday Review* had its worst suspicions of democracy amply confirmed.

I was especially pleased at the way in which you pricked certain hoary bubbles, notably the "tyranny of the majority" theory. You have also thoroughly understood that instead of the old American stock being "swamped" by immigration, it has absorbed the immigrants and remained nearly unchanged. Carl Schurz, even, hasn't imported a German idea into our politics; Albert Gallatin had something of the Swiss in his theories; our present Mayor Grant, of Irish blood, will serve New York, whether well or ill, solely by American principles.

But I do not think that the Irishman as a rule loses his active hatred of England till the third generation; and I fear that a good deal of feeling against England — mind you, none whatever against an Englishman — still foolishly exists in certain quarters of our purely American communities. But they are perfectly ready to elect Englishmen to office; relatively to the total number of immigrants many more English than Irish are sent to Congress, for instance.

Did you notice that this fall we, for the first time in five years, beat the Irish candidate for mayor in Boston, because the Irish were suspected of hostility to the public schools, though they warmly protested that the accusation was untrue?

It is very difficult for an outsider to tell how your politics are trending, nowadays.

39.

Seth Low: American City Government

Seth Low, municipal reformer and officer, prepared the following essay on problems of urban government as a chapter for the first edition of James Bryce's The American Commonwealth. *His experience in urban affairs encompassed charity work, president of the New York Republican Campaign Club, two terms as mayor of Brooklyn, and later a term as mayor of New York City. Low's essay was published at the end of his second term as mayor of Brooklyn. During his tenure of office he had instituted a civil service merit system, reformed the public school system, and reduced the city debt. In all his official activities and in his writings, Low stressed the idea that municipal government should be totally dissociated from national politics.*

Source: James Bryce, *The American Commonwealth,* 2nd edition revised, London, 1891, Vol. I, Ch. 52.

ANY EUROPEAN STUDENT of politics who wishes to understand the problem of government in the United States, whether of city government or any other form of it, must first of all transfer himself, if he can, to a point of view precisely the opposite of that which is natural to him. This is scarcely, if at all, less true of the English than of the continental student. In England, as upon the continent, from time immemorial, government has descended from the top down. Until recently society in Europe has accepted the idea, almost without protest, that there must be governing classes and that the great majority of men must be governed.

In the United States that idea does not obtain and, what is of scarcely less importance, it never has obtained. No distinction is recognized between governing and governed classes, and the problem of government is conceived to be this, that the whole of society should learn and apply to itself the art of government. Bearing this in mind, it becomes apparent that the immense tide of immigration into the United States is a continually disturbing factor. The immigrants come from many countries, a very large proportion of them being of the classes which, in their old homes from time out of mind, have been governed. Arriving in America, they shortly become citizens in a society which undertakes to govern itself.

However well-disposed they may be as a rule, they have not had experience in self-government, nor do they always share the ideas which have expressed themselves in the Constitution of the United States.

This foreign element settles largely in the cities of the country. It is estimated that the population of New York City contains 80 percent of people who either are foreign-born or who are the children of foreign-born parents. Consequently, in a city like New York, the problem of learning the art of government is handed over to a population that begins in point of experience very low down. In many of the cities of the United States, indeed in almost all of them, the population not only is thus largely untrained in the art of self-government but it is not even homogeneous; so that an American city is confronted, not only with the necessity of instructing large and rapidly growing bodies of people in the art of government but it is compelled at the same time to assimilate strangely different component parts into an American community. It will be apparent to the student that either one of these functions by itself would be difficult enough. When both are found side by side, the problem is increasingly difficult as to each. Together they represent a problem such as confronts no city in the United Kingdom or in Europe.

The American city has had problems to deal with also of a material character, quite different from those which have confronted the cities of the Old World. With the exception of Boston, Philadelphia, Baltimore, New Orleans, and New York, there is no American city of great consequence whose roots go back into the distant past, even of America. American cities as a rule have grown with a rapidity to which the Old World presents few parallels. London, in the extent of its growth but not in the proportions of it, Berlin since 1870, and Rome in the last few years are perhaps the only places in Europe which have been compelled to deal with this element of rapid growth in anything like a corresponding degree. All of these cities, London, Berlin, and Rome, are the seats of the national government and receive from that source more or less help and guidance in their development. In all of them an immense nucleus of wealth existed before this great and rapid growth began. The problem in America has been to make a great city in a few years out of nothing. There has been no nucleus of wealth upon which to found the structure which every succeeding year has enlarged. Recourse has been had of necessity, under these conditions, to the freest use of the public credit.

The city of Brooklyn and the city of Chicago, each with a population now of 750,000 people, are but little more than fifty years old. In that period everything now there has been created out of the fields. The houses in which the people live, the waterworks, the paved streets, the sewers, everything which makes up the permanent plant of a city, all have been produced while the city has been growing from year to year at a fabulous rate. Besides these things are to be reckoned the public schools, the public parks, and, in the case of Brooklyn, the great bridge connecting it with New York, two-thirds of the cost of which is borne by Brooklyn. Looked at in this light the marvel would seem to be, not so much that the American cities are justly criticizable for many defects but rather that results so great have been achieved in so short a time.

The necessity of doing so much so quickly has worked to the disadvantage of the American city in two ways. First, it has compelled very lavish expenditure under great pressure for quick results. This is precisely the condition under which the best trained businessmen make their greatest mistakes and are in danger of running into extravagance and wastefulness. No candid American will deny that American cities have suffered largely in this way, not alone from extravagance and wastefulness but also from dishonesty; but in estimating the extent of the reproach, it is proper to take into consideration these general conditions under which the cities have been compelled to work. The second disadvantage which American cities have labored under from this state of things has been their inability to provide adequately for their current needs, while discounting the future so freely in order to provide their permanent plant. When the great American cities have paid for the permanent plant which they have been accumulating during the last half century, so that the duty which lies before them is chiefly that of caring adequately for the current life of their population, a vast improvement in all these particulars may reasonably be expected.

In other words, time is a necessary element in making a great city as it is in every other great and enduring work. American cities are judged by their size rather than by the time which has entered into their growth. It cannot be denied that larger results could have been produced with the money expended if it always had been used with complete honesty and good judgment. But to make an intelligent criticism upon the American city, in its failures upon the material side, these elements of difficulty must be taken into consideration.

Another particular in which the American city may be thought to have come short of what might have been hoped for may be described in general terms as a lack of foresight. It would have been comparatively easy to have preserved in all of them small open parks, and generally to have made them more beautiful, if there had been a greater appreciation of the need for these things and of the growth the cities were to attain to. The Western cities probably have erred in this regard less than those upon the Atlantic Coast. But while it is greatly to be regretted that this large foresight has not been displayed, it is after all only repeating in America what has taken place in Europe.

The improvement of cities seems everywhere to be made by tearing down and replacing at great cost, rather than by a farsighted provision for the demands and opportunities of the future. These unfortunate

results in America have flowed largely from two causes: first, from inability on the part of the cities to appreciate in advance the phenomenal growth that is coming upon them; and, second, from the frequent tendency of population to grow in precisely the direction where it was not expected to. A singular illustration of this last factor is to be found in the city of Washington. The Capitol was made to face toward the east under the impression that population would settle in that direction; as a matter of fact, the city has grown toward the west, so that the Capitol stands with its back to the city and faces a district that is scarcely built upon at all.

Probably no detail strikes the eye of the foreigner more unfavorably in connection with the average American city than the poor paving of the streets and their lack of cleanliness. The comparison with cities of Europe in these respects is immensely to the disadvantage of the American city. But, in this connection, it is not unfair to call attention to the fact that the era of good paving and clean streets in Europe is scarcely more than thirty years old. Poor as is the condition of the streets in most American cities now, it would be risking very little to say that it would average much higher than ten years ago. There are several contributing causes which are reflected in this situation that represent difficulties from which most European cities are free. In the first place, frost strikes much deeper in America and is more trying to the pavements in every way. In the next place, the streets are more often disturbed in connection with gas pipes, steam pipes, and telegraph service than in European cities. But apart from these incidental difficulties the fundamental trouble in connection with the streets of American cities is the lack of sufficient appropriations to put them in first class condition and to keep them so, both as to paving and as to cleaning. The reason for this has been pointed out.

All the troubles, however, which have

marked the development of cities in the United States are not due to these causes. Cities in the United States as forms of government are of comparatively recent origin. The city of Boston, for example, in the state of Massachusetts, although the settlement was founded more than 250 years ago, received its charter as a city so recently as 1822. The city of Brooklyn received its charter from the state of New York in 1835. In other words, the transition from village and town government into government by cities has simply followed the transition of small places into large communities.

This suggests another distinction between the cities of the United States and those of Great Britain. The great cities of England and of Europe, with few exceptions, have their roots in the distant past. Many of their privileges and chartered rights were wrested from the Crown in feudal times. Some of these privileges have been retained and contribute to the income, the pride, and the influence of the municipality. The charter of an American city represents no element of prestige or inspiration. It is only the legal instrument which gives the community authority to act as a corporation and which defines the duties of its officers.

The motive for passing from town government to city government in general has been the same everywhere — to acquire a certain readiness of action and to make more available the credit of the community in order to provide adequately for its own growth. The town meeting, in which every citizen takes part, serves its purpose admirably in communities up to a certain size, or for the conducting of public work on not too large a scale. But the necessity for efficiency in providing for the needs of growth has compelled rapidly growing communities in all the states to seek the powers of a corporation as administered through a city government. Growing thus out of the town, it happened very naturally that the first conception of the city on the part of Ameri-

Art Commission of the City of New York

Seth Low, mayor of Brooklyn and New York City; portrait by William Merritt Chase

cans was that which had applied to the town and the village as local subdivisions of the commonwealth. Charters were framed as though cities were little states.

Americans are only now learning, after many years of bitter experience, that they are not so much little states as large corporations. Many of the mistakes which have marked the progress of American cities up to this point have sprung from that defective conception. The aim deliberately was to make a city government where no officer by himself should have power enough to do much harm. The natural result of this was to create a situation where no officer had power to do much good. Meanwhile, bad men united for corrupt purposes, and the whole organization of the city government aided such in throwing responsibility from one to another.

Many recent city charters in the United States proceed upon the more accurate theory that cities, in their organic capacity, are chiefly large corporations. The better results flowing from this theory are easily made clear. Americans are sufficiently adept in the administration of large business enterprises to understand that, in any such undertaking, some one man must be given the power of direction and the choice of his chief assistants; they understand that power and responsibility must go together from the top to the bottom of every successful business organization. Consequently, when it began to be realized that a city was a business corporation rather than an integral part of the state, the unwillingness to organize the city upon the line of concentrated power in connection with concentrated responsibility began to disappear.

40.

Matthew Arnold: Civilization in the United States

Matthew Arnold came to the United States in 1883, hoping to earn a little money from lectures and to learn a great deal about American life. Neither hope was completely fulfilled: the lecture series was only modestly successful, and Arnold's own prejudices — typical of many upper-class British — prevented his developing any serious appreciation of America's democratic government and customs. In the following selection from his 1888 work, Civilization in the United States, *Arnold discussed the lack of "interesting" things in America.*

Source: *Civilization in the United States,* Boston, 1889, pp. 180-190.

I ONCE DECLARED that in England the born lover of ideas and of light could not but feel that the sky over his head is of brass and iron. And so I say that, in America, he who craves for the *interesting* in civilization, he who requires from what surrounds him satisfaction for his sense of beauty, his sense for elevation, will feel the sky over his head to be of brass and iron. The human problem, then, is as yet solved in the United States most imperfectly; a great void exists in the civilization over there; a want of what is elevated and beautiful, of what is interesting. . . .

The want is such as to make any educated man feel that many countries, much less free and prosperous than the United States, are yet more truly civilized; have more which is interesting, have more to say to the soul; are countries, therefore, in which one would rather live. The want is graver because it is so little recognized by the mass of Americans; nay, so loudly denied by them.

If the community over there perceived the want and regretted it, sought for the right ways of remedying it, and resolved that remedied it should be; if they said, or even if a number of leading spirits among them said: "Yes, we see what is wanting to our civilization, we see that the average man is a danger, we see that our newspapers are a scandal, that bondage to the common and ignoble is our snare; but under the circumstances our civilization could not well have been expected to begin differently. What you see are *beginnings,* they are crude, they are too predominantly material, they omit much, leave much to be desired — but they could not have been otherwise, they have been inevitable, and we will rise above them"; if the Americans frankly said this, one would have not a word to bring against it.

One would *then* insist on no shortcoming, one would accept their admission that the human problem is at present quite insufficiently solved by them, and would press the matter no further. One would congratulate them on having solved the political problem and the social problem so successfully, and only remark, as I have said already, that in seeing clear and thinking straight on *our* political and social questions, we have great need to follow the example they set us on theirs.

But now the Americans seem, in certain matters, to have agreed, as a people, to deceive themselves, to persuade themselves that they have what they have not, to cover the defects in their civilization by boasting, to fancy that they well and truly solve, not only the political and social problem but the human problem too. One would say that they do really hope to find in tall talk and inflated sentiment a substitute for that real sense of elevation which human nature, as I have said, instinctively craves — and a substitute which may do as well as the genuine article. The thrill of awe, which Goethe pronounces to be the best thing humanity has, they would fain create by proclaiming themselves at the top of their voices to be "the greatest nation upon earth," by assuring one another, in the language of their national historian, that "American democracy proceeds in its ascent as uniformly and majestically as the laws of being and is as certain as the decrees of eternity."

Or, again, far from admitting that their newspapers are a scandal, they assure one another that their newspaper press is one of their most signal distinctions. Far from admitting that in literature they have as yet produced little that is important, they play at treating American literature as if it were a great independent power; they reform the spelling of the English language by the in-

sight of their average man. For every English writer they have an American writer to match; and him good Americans read. . . .

The worst of it is that all this tall talk and self-glorification meets with hardly any rebuke from sane criticism over there. I will mention, in regard to this, a thing which struck me a good deal. A Scotchman who has made a great fortune at Pittsburgh, a kind friend of mine, one of the most hospitable and generous of men, Mr. Andrew Carnegie, published a year or two ago a book called *Triumphant Democracy,* a most splendid picture of American progress. The book is full of valuable information, but religious people thought that it insisted too much on mere material progress and did not enough set forth America's deficiencies and dangers. And a friendly clergyman in Massachusetts, telling me how he regretted this, and how apt the Americans are to shut their eyes to their own dangers, put into my hands a volume written by a leading minister among the Congregationalists, a very prominent man, which he said supplied a good antidote to my friend Mr. Carnegie's book.

The volume is entitled *Our Country.* I read it through. The author finds in evangelical Protestantism, as the orthodox Protestant sects present it, the grand remedy for the deficiencies and dangers of America. On this I offer no criticism; what struck me, and that on which I wish to lay stress, is the writer's entire failure to perceive that such self-glorification and self-deception as I have been mentioning is one of America's dangers, or even that it *is* self-deception at all. He himself shares in all the self-deception of the average man among his countrymen; he flatters it. In the very points where a serious critic would find the Americans most wanting he finds them superior; only they require to have a good dose of evangelical Protestantism still added.

"Ours is the elect nation," preaches this reformer of American faults; "ours is the

Matthew Arnold, English critic who visited America in 1883 and 1884

elect nation for the age to come. We are the chosen people." Already, says he, we are taller and heavier than other men, longer-lived than other men, richer and more energetic than other men, above all, "of finer nervous organization" than other men. Yes, this people, who endure to have the American newspaper for their daily reading, and to have their habitation in Briggsville, Jacksonville, and Marcellus — this people is of finer, more delicate nervous organization than other nations! . . .

Undoubtedly the Americans are highly nervous, both the men and the women. A great Paris physician says that he notes a distinct new form of nervous disease produced in American women by worry about servants. But this nervousness, developed in the race out there by worry, overwork, want of exercise, injudicious diet, and a most trying climate — this morbid nervousness our friends ticket as the fine susceptibility of genius, and cite it as a proof of their distinction, of their superior capacity for civilization! "The roots of civilization

are the nerves," says our Congregationalist instructor, again; "and, other things being equal, the finest nervous organization will produce the highest civilization. Now, the finest nervous organization is ours."

The new West promises to beat in the game of brag even the stout champions I have been quoting. Those belong to the old Eastern states; and the other day there was sent to me a Californian newspaper which calls all the Easterners "the unhappy denizens of a forbidding clime," and adds: "The time will surely come when all roads will lead to California. Here will be the home of art, science, literature, and profound knowledge."

Common sense criticism, I repeat, of all this hollow stuff there is in America next to none. There are plenty of cultivated, judicious, delightful individuals there. They are our hope and America's hope; it is through their means that improvement must come. They know perfectly well how false and hollow the boastful stuff talked is; but they let the storm of self-laudation rage and say nothing. For political opponents and their doings there are in America hard words to be heard in abundance; for the real faults in American civilization, and for the foolish boasting which prolongs them, there is hardly a word of regret or blame, at least in public. Even in private, many of the most cultivated Americans shrink from the subject, are irritable and thin-skinned when it is canvassed. Public treatment of it, in a cool and sane spirit of criticism, there is none.

In vain I might plead that I had set a good example of frankness in confessing over here that, so far from solving our problems successfully, we in England find ourselves with an upper class materialized, a middle class vulgarized, and a lower class brutalized. But it seems that nothing will embolden an American critic to say firmly and aloud to his countrymen and to his newspapers that in America they do not solve the human problem successfully, and that with their present methods they never can. Consequently, the masses of the American people do really come to believe all they hear about their finer nervous organization, and the rightness of the American accent, and the importance of American literature; that is to say, they see things not as they are but as they would like them to be; they deceive themselves totally. And by such self-deception they shut against themselves the door to improvement, and do their best to make the reign of *das Gemeine* eternal.

In what concerns the solving of the political and social problem they see clear and think straight; in what concerns the higher civilization they live in a fools' paradise. This it is which makes a famous French critic speak of "the hard unintelligence of the people of the United States" — *la dure inintelligence des Américains du Nord* — of the very people who in general pass for being specially intelligent; and so, within certain limits, they are. But they have been so plied with nonsense and boasting that outside those limits and where it is a question of things in which their civilization is weak, they seem, very many of them, as if in such things they had no power of perception whatever, no idea of a proper scale, no sense of the difference between good and bad. And at this rate they can never, after solving the political and social problem with success, go on to solve happily the human problem too, and thus at last to make their civilization full and interesting.

41.

Machines and Apprentice Labor

The rapid advance of industrialism after the Civil War created problems with the system of apprenticeship. Whereas a boy had once learned all the facets of a trade, postwar improvements in technology brought specialization, which sharply limited what an individual needed to know to perform a task. In addition there were more technical schools where one could go to learn a trade. As opportunities increased boys were less willing to spend the amount of time required by the apprenticeship system. The following portion of the Annual Report of the Factory Inspectors of New York State in 1888 *deals with the new conditions that called for revising the apprenticeship laws.*

Source: *Third Annual Report of the Factory Inspectors of the State of New York, for the Year Ending December 1st, 1888*, Albany, 1889, pp. 68-74.

BY THE ACT of the legislature of 1888, the factory inspectors were required to enforce the law relating to the indenturing of apprentices (Chapter 934, Laws 1871). The industrial conditions existing at, and previously to, the time of the passage of the Law of 1871 are so completely revolutionized that the old form of apprenticeship has become almost obsolete. Where, in former times, boys were expected to learn a trade in all its features, they are now simply put at a machine or at one branch of the craft, and no understanding exists that they shall be taught any other branch or the use of any other machine. Employers claim that these boys are not apprentices, and even if they so desired, could not teach, in the broad sense formerly understood, an apprentice all the intricacies of a trade, for the reason that where the skill and intelligence of a journeyman workman were once essential, a simple machine now unerringly performs the service, and consequently there is no occasion for an apprentice to learn to do the labor by hand. These were the principal reasons given by employers as to why the law had become inoperative.

Parents also raised objections to binding their children to any one employer, maintaining that it was their right, if they saw fit, to take their children from one trade and put him at another without the interference or hindrance of the factory inspectors or of the law. The minors themselves objected to being bound to serve any particular length of time, insisting that they could not be prevented from quitting one employer and bettering themselves by going to another.

Thus it will be seen that the enforcement of the apprenticeship law was on every hand beset with difficulties. We can report no progress in obtaining general recognition for the act, and in but few cases were we called upon to enforce it. These cases were brought to our attention by parties other than those immediately interested, and consequently no test of the law could be brought before the courts. . . .

It will be seen that persons who employ minors to do any kind of work, where no understanding or agreement is made that they shall be taught all branches of the trade carried on by the employer, do not violate the apprenticeship law, and the minor and parent or guardian have neither source of redress nor counter responsibility. In plain language, the apprenticeship law is so easily evaded that for all practical good it is null and void. We must say that this is to be regretted. The proudest thing that an artisan can say is that he is a thorough mechanic, and the number who can truthfully make this assertion is growing smaller every year.

Slipshod and incompetent workmen overrun every trade. The superintendents, foremen, and responsible men in a majority of the manufacturing establishments in this state have been brought here from abroad, because of the thorough mastery of their trades obtained under the more rigorous apprenticeship laws of the Old World. The American children rarely obtain more than a superficial knowledge of a trade, and, as a matter of course, are not often capable of assuming the direction of an extensive establishment. Perhaps the law can be amended so as to produce a change in this condition of affairs; and the subject is important enough to warrant the most careful consideration.

There are only about four hundred people in fashionable New York society. If you go outside that number you strike people who are either not at ease in a ballroom or else make other people not at ease.

WARD McALLISTER, to Charles Crandall of the *New York Tribune*, 1888

42.

IRA ATEN: The Fence-Cutters

Barbed wire began to be widely used in Texas in the early 1880s, and with its use came the "wars" between the fence-cutters and the fence-users. Barbed wire meant the end of the open range, upon which many ranchers depended for grazing their herds. Fences meant injured animals, the end of the cattle drives, the need to patronize railroads to haul cattle. Fences also meant the end of heterogeneous herds. Thus the farmers could for the first time develop a blooded stock and operate within the confines of a specific ranch. The following letter by Texas Ranger Ira Aten, dated August 31, 1888, describes the fence-cutters and their activities.

Source: Walter Prescott Webb, *The Great Plains*, Boston, 1931, p. 314.

THE FENCE-CUTTERS here are what I would call cowboys or small cowmen that own cattle from 15 head all the way up to perhaps 200 head of cattle and a few cow ponies, etc. Some have a hundred acres of land, and some more, and some not so much, and perhaps a little field in cultivation. They hate the Granger, as they call them, for it is the Granger (or farmer) that have the pastures with the exception of Frost and Barry and a few others. In fact, they hate anybody that will fence land either for farming or pasture. They are a hard lot of men in here, and they are thieves as well as fence-cutters. . . .

Now for the good citizens, what do they deserve? I will simply state this, that a great many good citizens that don't own one-half as much as the parties that has been the instigator of all this fence-cutting in this section have had their fence cut from around their little horse pasture and even in several instances have had it cut from around their cultivated lands where corn and cotton was planted. They have quit cutting from around fields now but there are not a pasture of no kind up on the west side of the Houston & Texas Central Railway in this section where these wild and wooly wire-cutters operate.

I don't write all from hearsay, but from what I have seen myself. Small pastures that would not support but milk cows and work horses for a very small farm have been cut time and again until the owners have not the means to put up the wire any more and now all pastures are down and this is called the free-range country. Many have took down their wire and rolled it up to save it from being cut, etc. The fence-cutters themselves have told me that while a man was putting up his fence one day in a hollow a crowd of wire-cutters was cutting it back behind him in another hollow back over the hill. They delight in telling all such things and most of it is true also. The good citizens hold the wire-cutters in dread for they know they would not hesitate a moment to murder them.

1889

43.

Carl Schurz: The Need for a Rational Forest Policy

When Carl Schurz delivered the following address to the Forestry Associations on October 15, 1889, he tempered his dire predictions for the future of American forest lands with conservation proposals drawn from his experiences in Germany. As secretary of the interior in Rutherford B. Hayes's Cabinet, Schurz had determined to preserve the nation's forests for their threefold usefulness as sources of raw material, deterrents of soil erosion, and havens for recreation. Although Schurz's efforts met with violent opposition from railroad and timber interests, Congress eventually did enact the first federal conservation program in the first decade of the twentieth century.

Source: *Speeches, Correspondence and Political Papers of Carl Schurz,* Frederic Bancroft, ed., New York, 1913, Vol. V, pp. 22-33.

LET ME IN THE FIRST PLACE assure you of my most earnest sympathy in your efforts. I am heart and soul with you; nor is this to me a new subject. I know the advocates of the cause to which you are devoted are looked upon by many as a set of amiable sentimentalists who have fallen in love with the greenness of the woods and break out in hysteric wails when a tree is cut down. I assure you I have been led to take an earnest interest in this subject by considerations of an entirely unsentimental, practical nature, and this, no doubt, is the case with most of you. The more study and thought I have given the matter, the firmer has become my conviction that *the destruction of the forests of this country will be the murder of its future prosperity and progress.* This is no mere figure of speech, no rhetorical exag-

geration. It is simply the teaching of the world's history, which no fair-minded man can study without reaching the same conclusion.

I am aware that there are people who turn with a sneer from the expression of any fear that our country may become sterile; who profess to be highly amused when those countries in Asia are pointed out to them which once were called lands "flowing with milk and honey" . . . now in a great measure stripped bare, the old fertility gone, the people in large districts struggling with poverty and want.

Infatuated persons among us turn up their noses at these and similar lessons and superciliously exclaim: "What do we in this great and free country of ours care about abroad?" Let me say to you that the laws of nature are the same everywhere. Whoever violates them anywhere must always pay the penalty. No country ever so great and rich, no nation ever so powerful, inventive, and enterprising can violate them with impunity. We most grievously delude ourselves if we think that we can form an exception to the rule. And we have made already a most dangerous beginning, and more than a beginning, in the work of desolation. The destruction of our forests is so fearfully rapid that, if we go on at the same rate, men whose hair is already gray will see the day when in the United States from Maine to California and from the Mexican Gulf to Puget Sound there will be no forest left worthy of the name.

Who is guilty of that destruction? It is not merely the lumberman cutting timber on his own land for legitimate use in the pursuit of business gain; it is the lumberman who, in doing so, destroys and wastes as much more without benefit to anybody. It is not merely the settler or the miner taking logs for his cabin and fence rails and firewood, or timber for building a shaft, but it is the settler and the miner laying waste acres or stripping a mountain slope to get a few sticks. It is all these, serving indeed legitimate wants, but doing it with a wastefulness criminally reckless.

But it is not only these. It is the timber thief — making haste to strip the public domain of what he can lay his hands on lest another timber thief get ahead of him — and, in doing this, destroying sometimes far more than he steals. It is the tourist, the hunter, the mining prospector who, lighting his campfire in the woods to boil water for his coffee or to fry his bacon, and leaving that fire unextinguished when he proceeds, sets the woods in flames and delivers countless square miles of forest to destruction.

It is all these, but it is something more, and, let us confess it, something worse. It is a public opinion looking with indifference on this wanton, barbarous, disgraceful van-dalism. It is a spendthrift people recklessly wasting its heritage. It is a government careless of the future and unmindful of a pressing duty.

I have had some personal experience of this. The gentleman who introduced me did me the honor of mentioning the attention I devoted to this subject years ago as secretary of the interior. When I entered upon that important office, having the public lands in charge, I considered it my first duty to look around me and to study the problems I had to deal with. Doing so, I observed all the wanton waste and devastation I have described. I observed the notion that the public forests were everybody's property, to be taken and used or wasted as anybody pleased, everywhere in full operation. I observed enterprising timber thieves, not merely stealing trees but stealing whole forests. I observed hundreds of sawmills in full blast, devoted exclusively to the sawing up of timber stolen from the public lands. I observed a most lively export trade going on from Gulf ports as well as Pacific ports, with fleets of vessels employed in carrying timber stolen from the public lands to be sold in foreign countries, immense tracts being devastated that some robbers might fill their pockets.

I thought that this sort of stealing was wrong, in this country no less than elsewhere. Moreover, it was against the spirit and letter of the law. I, therefore, deemed it my duty to arrest that audacious and destructive robbery. Not that I had intended to prevent the settler and the miner from taking from the public lands what they needed for their cabins, their fields, or their mining shafts; but I deemed it my duty to stop at least the commercial depredations upon the property of the people. And to that end I used my best endeavors and the means at my disposal, scanty as they were.

What was the result? No sooner did my attempts in that direction become known than I was pelted with telegraphic dispatches from the regions most concerned, indignantly inquiring what it meant that an officer of the government dared to interfere with the legitimate business of the country! Members of Congress came down upon me, some with wrath in their eyes, others pleading in a milder way, but all solemnly protesting against my disturbing their constituents in this peculiar pursuit of happiness. I persevered in the performance of my plain duty. But when I set forth my doings in my annual report and asked Congress for rational forestry legislation, you should have witnessed the sneers at the outlandish notions of this "foreigner" in the Interior Department; notions that, as was said, might do for a picayunish German principality but were altogether contemptible when applied to this great and free country of ours.

By the way, some of the gentlemen who sneered so greatly might learn some lessons from those picayunish German principalities, which would do them much good. I recently revisited my native land and saw again some of the forests I had known in my younger days — forests which in the meantime had yielded to their owners or to the government large revenues from the timber cut, but were now nevertheless as stately as they had been before, because the cutting had been done upon rational principles and the forests had been steadily improved by scientific cultivation. I passed over a large tract I had known as a barren heath, the heath of Lüneburg, which formerly, as the saying was, sustained only the "Heidschnucken," a species of sheep as little esteemed for their wool as their mutton — the same heath now covered with a dense growth of fine forest. Instead of sneering, our supercilious scoffers would do better for themselves as well as for the country if they devoted their time a little more to studying and learning the valuable lessons with which the experience of other countries abound.

What the result of my appeals was at the time I am speaking of, you know. We suc-

ceeded in limiting somewhat the extent of the depredations upon the public forests and in bringing some of the guilty parties to justice. A few hundred thousand dollars were recovered for timber stolen, but the recommendations of rational forestry legislation went for nothing. Some laws were indeed passed, but they appeared rather to favor the taking of timber from the public lands than to stop it. Still, I persevered, making appeal after appeal, in public and in private, but I found myself standing almost solitary and alone. Deaf was Congress, and deaf the people seemed to be. Only a few still voices rose up here and there in the press in favor of the policy I pursued.

Thank heaven, the people appear to be deaf no longer. It is in a great measure owing to your wise and faithful efforts that the people begin to listen, and that in several states practical steps have already been taken in the right direction. . . .

I do not hesitate to say that the money spent for the Army, the police, and public schools is not spent to greater public advantage than the money spent for the introduction of a rational forestry system would be. However, a part of the public service already existing might well be used for the purpose of guarding at least the forests belonging to the public domain of the United States. It may well be assumed that although trifling Indian disturbances may still occur here and there, the danger of Indian wars on a large scale is now behind us. If a wise, just, and humane Indian policy be followed, we may be sure that it is altogether over. Not a few of our outlying military posts may then be abandoned, and a part of our Army will become disposable for other purposes. Why should not two or three battalions be organized as forest guards or forest rangers; the men, perhaps, also to receive some useful instruction to fit them for their new duties? Surely, no soldier could, in time of peace and there being no prospect of war, be more usefully employed.

Of the influence of forests on climate and

of the necessity of planting or replanting them where they fall below the proportion which the area of forest should bear to the aggregate area of the country, men more competent than I am have spoken and will speak to you. We are all agreed also on the necessity of spreading information on this important subject. No respectable university or agricultural college should be without a department in which forestry as a science is taught; and most of us will no doubt see the day when the importance of that science will be recognized by every thinking American. Let us hope that this appreciation will come in time.

I regret we cannot forcibly enough impress upon the American people the necessity of speedy measures looking to the preservation of our mountain forests which, when once destroyed, cannot be renewed. Unless this be done in time, our children will curse the almost criminal improvidence of their ancestors; but if it is done in time, those who are instrumental in doing it will deserve and will have the blessings of future generations.

44.

Hamilton S. Wicks: The Oklahoma Land Rush

The "unassigned lands" of the Oklahoma Territory encompassed approximately 2,000,000 acres near the center of the state not occupied by the Indian nations known as the Five Civilized Tribes. When these lands were opened to settlement under the terms of the Homestead Act, some 50,000 persons started out at noon on April 22, 1889, to vie for the tracts (160 acres to a person) of free land. Hamilton Wicks participated in the famous "land rush" and recorded the following account of that chaotic scene.

Source: *Cosmopolitan*, September 1889: "The Opening of Oklahoma."

A CITY ESTABLISHED AND POPULATED in half a day, in a remote region of country and many miles distant from the nearest civilized community, is a marvel that could have been possible in no age but our own, and in no land except the United States.

The opening of Oklahoma was indeed one of the most important events that has occurred in the development of the West. It marks an epoch in the settlement of the unoccupied lands owned by the government of the United States. Never before has there been such a general uprising of the common people seeking homesteads upon the few remaining acres possessed by Uncle Sam. The conditions and circumstances of the settlement of Oklahoma were widely different from those of the settlement of any other section of the United States. This new territory is surrounded by thoroughly settled and well-organized commonwealths. It is a region containing an area of 69,000 square miles, having an average width of 470 miles, and an average length of 210 miles, being much larger than Ohio, or Indiana, or Kentucky, or Illinois, or "the Virginias," or even the whole of New England.

No method can so clearly bring before the public the actual facts of this wonderful opening as the narration, by one who participated in it, of his experience. . . .

As our train slowly moved through the

Cherokee Strip, a vast procession of "boomers" was seen moving across the plains to the Oklahoma lines, forming picturesque groups on the otherwise unbroken landscape. The wagon road through the "Strip," extemporized by the boomers, ran for long distances parallel with the railway, and the procession that extended the whole distance illustrated the characteristics of Western American life. Here, for instance, would be a party consisting of a "prairie schooner" drawn by four scrawny, rawboned horses, and filled with a tatterdemalion group, consisting of a shaggy bearded man, a slatternly looking woman, and several girls and boys, faithful images of their parents, in shabby attire, usually with a dog and a coop of chickens. In striking contrast to this frontier picture, perhaps a couple of flashy real estate men from Wichita would come jogging on a short distance behind, driving a spanking span of bays, with an equipage looking for all the world as though it had just come from a fashionable livery stable.

Our train, whirling rapidly over the prairie, overtook many such contrasted pictures. There were single rigs and double rigs innumerable; there were six-mule teams and four-in-hands, with here and there parties on horseback, and not a few on foot trudging along the wayside. The whole procession marched, rode, or drove, as on some gala occasion, with smiling faces and waving hands. Everyone imagined that Eldorado was just ahead, and I dare say the possibility of failure or disappointment did not enter into the consideration of a single individual on that cool and delightful April day. For many, alas, the anticipations were "April hopes, the fools of chance."

As our train neared the Oklahoma border, the "procession" became more dense and in some instances clogged the approaches to the fords of the small streams that crossed its pathway. When we finally slowed up at the dividing line, the camps of the "boomers" could be seen extending in every direction, and a vast amount of stock was strewn over the green prairie.

And now the hour of twelve was at hand, and everyone on the *qui vive* for the bugle blast that would dissolve the chain of enchantment hitherto girding about this coveted land. Many of the "boomers" were mounted on high-spirited and fleet-footed horses, and had ranged themselves along the territorial line, scarcely restrained even by the presence of the troop of cavalry from taking summary possession. The better class of wagons and carriages ranged themselves in line with the horsemen, and even here and there mule teams attached to canvascovered vehicles stood in the front ranks, with the reins and whip grasped by the "boomers" wives. All was excitement and expectation. Every nerve was on tension and every muscle strained. The great event for which these brawny noblemen of the West have been waiting for years was on the point of transpiring.

Suddenly the air was pierced with the blast of a bugle. Hundreds of throats echoed the sound with shouts of exultation. The quivering limbs of saddled steeds, no longer restrained by the hands that held their bridles, bounded forward simultaneously into the "beautiful land" of Oklahoma; and wagons and carriages and buggies and prairie schooners and a whole congregation of curious equipages joined in this unparalleled race, where every starter was bound to win a prize — the "Realization Stakes" of home and prosperity.

Here was a unique contest in which thousands participated and which was to occur but once for all time. Truly an historical event! We, the spectators, witnessed the spectacle with most intense interest. Away dashed the thoroughbreds, the broncos, the pintos, and the mustangs at a breakneck pace across the uneven surface of the prairie. It was amazing to witness the recklessness of those cowboy riders. They jumped obstacles; they leaped ditches; they cantered with no diminution of speed through water pools; and when they came to a ravine too wide to leap, down they would go with a rush, and up the other side with a spurt of energy, to scurry once more like mad over the level plain. This reckless riding was all very well at the fore part of the race, but it could not prevail against the more discreet maneuverings of several elderly "boomers" who rode more powerful and speedy horses.

One old white-bearded fellow especially commanded attention. He was mounted on a coal black thoroughbred, and avoided any disaster by checking the pace of his animal when ravines had to be crossed. But his splendid bursts of speed when no obstructions barred the way soon placed him far in advance of all his competitors. It took but a short time to solve this question of speed among the riders, and after a neck-and-neck race for half a mile or more, they spread like a fan over the prairie, and were eventually lost to our vision among the rolling billows of Oklahoma's far-expanding prairie. . . .

The race was not over when you reached the particular lot you were content to select for your possession. The contest still was who should drive their stakes first, who would erect their little tents soonest, and then, who would quickest build a little wooden shanty.

The situation was so peculiar that it is difficult to convey correct impressions of the situation. It reminded me of playing blindman's buff. One did not know how far to go before stopping; it was hard to tell when it was best to stop; and it was a puzzle whether to turn to the right hand or the left. Everyone appeared dazed, and all for the most part acted like a flock of stray sheep. Where the boldest led, many others followed. I found myself, without exactly knowing how, about midway between the government building and depot. It occurred to me that a street would probably run past the depot.

I accosted a man who looked like a deputy, with a piece of white cord in his hands,

and asked him if this was to be a street along here.

"Yes," he replied. "We are laying off four corner lots right here for a lumber yard."

"Is this the corner where I stand?" I inquired.

"Yes," he responded, approaching me.

"Then I claim this corner lot!" I said with decision, as I jammed my location stick in the ground and hammered it securely home with my heel. "I propose to have one lot at all hazards on this town site, and you will have to limit yourself to three, in this location at least."

An angry altercation ensued, but I stoutly maintained my position and my rights. I proceeded at once to unstrap a small folding cot I brought with me, and, by standing it on its end, it made a tolerable center pole for a tent. I then threw a couple of my blankets over the cot and staked them securely into the ground on either side. Thus I had a claim that was unjumpable because of substantial improvements, and I felt safe and breathed more freely until my brother arrived on the third train, with our tent and equipments.

Not long after his arrival, an enterprising individual came driving by with a plow, and we hired him for a dollar to plow around the lot I had stepped off, 25 feet in front and 140 feet in depth. Before dusk we had a large wall tent erected on our newly acquired premises, with a couple of cots inside and a liberal amount of blankets for bedding. Now we felt doubly secure in our possession; and as night approached, I strolled up on the eminence near the Land Office and surveyed the wonderful cyclorama spread out before me on all sides.

Ten thousand people had "squatted" upon a square mile of virgin prairie that first afternoon, and as the myriad of white tents suddenly appeared upon the face of the country, it was as though a vast flock of huge white-winged birds had just settled down upon the hillsides and in the valleys.

Here indeed was *a city laid out and popu-lated in half a day*. Thousands of campfires sparkled upon the dark bosom of the prairie as far as the eye could reach, and there arose from this huge camp a subdued hum declaring that this almost innumerable multitude of the brave and self-reliant men had come to stay and work and build in that distant Western wilderness a city that should forever be a trophy to American enterprise and daring. . . .

On the morning of April 23, a city of 10,000 people, 500 houses, and innumerable tents existed where twelve hours before was nothing but a broad expanse of prairie. The new city changed its appearance every twenty-four hours, as day by day the work of construction went on. The tents were rapidly superseded by small frame structures, until at the end of a month there were scarcely any tents to be seen. The small frame structures in turn gave place to larger ones, and a number of fine two-story frame buildings were erected on the principal thoroughfares before the end of the first sixty days. The cost of these two-story frame buildings ranged from $700 to $2,000, where lumber was purchased at $30 per thousand and carpenters charged $3 a day.

As soon as it became apparent to capitalists that this enterprise was in reality the beginnings of a great city, preparations were made for the erection of a number of brick blocks; and at the time of writing this article — less than one hundred days from the date of the opening — Guthrie presents the appearance of a model Western city, with broad and regular streets and alleys; with handsome store and office buildings; with a system of parks and boulevards, unsurpassed in point of number, extent, and beauty by any city of twice its size and population in the West; with a number of fine iron bridges spanning the Cottonwood River, which runs through its midst; with a system of waterworks that furnishes hydrants at the corners of all the principal streets and keeps several large sprinkling carts continually busy; with an electric light plant on the Westinghouse system of alternating currents, capable not only of thoroughly lighting the whole city but of furnishing the power for running an electric railway, for which the charter has already been granted by the City Council, and a large sum of money put up as a forfeiture by the company that accepted it. . . .

I was witness of all this magical municipal development and could scarcely realize the miracle that was unfolding before me. There was no pretense that any person was there except for his individual self-interest; but the energy that the individual members of the community displayed, each for himself, resulted in the greatest benefit for the community as a whole. The wealth-creating force that was displayed in the building up of Guthrie cannot be better illustrated than in the fact that lots which had no value prior to April 22 sold in the center of the business movement as high as $500 within a week thereafter, and a number changed hands before the expiration of the first month for $1,500 each; while to my own knowledge a few sold, before sixty days had elapsed, for prices ranging from $1,700 to $5,000 per lot of 25 by 140 feet.

The law west of the Pecos.

ROY BEAN, sign over saloon in West Texas, 1880s

45.

THEODORE ROOSEVELT: False Sentimentality About the Indians

Theodore Roosevelt favored a rational and equitable Indian policy, but he firmly believed that the Indian nations had no claim to the land they inhabited and were in fact nomadic people who by temperament had no desire to hold property. Roosevelt, disdainful of such zealous reformers as novelist Helen Hunt Jackson because he felt they distorted the character of Indian-white relations, dubbed the entire group "foolish sentimentalists." He gave his own interpretation of government dealings with the Indians in the following passage from The Winning of the West *(1889-1896).*

Source: *The Winning of the West,* Homeward Bound Edition, Vol. I, New York, 1910, Appendix A to Chapter 4.

IT IS GREATLY TO BE WISHED that some competent person would write a full and true history of our national dealings with the Indians. Undoubtedly the latter have often suffered terrible injustice at our hands. A number of instances, such as the conduct of the Georgians to the Cherokees in the early part of the present century, or the whole treatment of Chief Joseph and his Nez Percés, might be mentioned, which are indelible blots on our fair fame; and yet, in describing our dealings with the red men as a whole, historians do us much less than justice.

It was wholly impossible to avoid conflicts with the weaker race, unless we were willing to see the American continent fall into the hands of some other strong power; and even had we adopted such a ludicrous policy, the Indians themselves would have made war upon us. It cannot be too often insisted that they did not own the land; or, at least, that their ownership was merely such as that claimed often by our own white hunters. If the Indians really owned Kentucky in 1775, then in 1776 it was the property of Boone and his associates; and to dispossess one party was as great a wrong as to dispossess the other. To recognize the Indian ownership of the limitless prairies and forests of this continent — that is, to consider the dozen squalid savages who hunted at long intervals over a territory of 1,000 square miles as owning it outright — necessarily implies a similar recognition of the claims of every white hunter, squatter, horse thief, or wandering cattleman.

Take as an example the country round the Little Missouri. When the cattlemen, the first actual settlers, came into this land in 1882, it was already scantily peopled by a few white hunters and trappers. The latter were extremely jealous of intrusion; they had held their own in spite of the Indians, and, like the Indians, the inrush of settlers and the consequent destruction of the game meant their own undoing; also, again like the Indians, they felt that their having hunted over the soil gave them a vague prescriptive right to its sole occupation, and they did their best to keep actual settlers out. In some cases, to avoid difficulty, their nominal claims were bought up; generally and rightly, they were disregarded. Yet they certainly had as good a right to the Little Missouri country as the Sioux have to most of the land on their present reservations.

In fact, the mere statement of the case is sufficient to show the absurdity of asserting that the land really belonged to the Indians. The different tribes have always been utterly unable to define their own boundaries. Thus the Delawares and Wyandots, in 1785, though entirely separate nations, claimed and, in a certain sense, occupied almost exactly the same territory.

Moreover, it was wholly impossible for our policy to be always consistent. Nowadays we undoubtedly ought to break up the great Indian reservations, disregard the tribal governments, allot the land in severalty (with, however, only a limited power of alienation), and treat the Indians as we do other citizens, with certain exceptions, for their sakes as well as ours.

But this policy, which it would be wise to follow now, would have been wholly impracticable a century since. Our central government was then too weak either effectively to control its own members or adequately to punish aggressions made upon them; and even if it had been strong, it would probably have proved impossible to keep entire order over such a vast, sparsely peopled frontier, with such turbulent elements on both sides. The Indians could not be treated as individuals at that time. There was no possible alternative, therefore, to treating their tribes as nations, exactly as the French and English had done before us. Our difficulties were partly inherited from these, our predecessors; were partly caused by our own misdeeds; but were mainly the inevitable result of the conditions under which the problem had to be solved — no human wisdom or virtue could have worked out a peaceable solution.

As a nation, our Indian policy is to be blamed because of the weakness it displayed, because of its shortsightedness and its occasional leaning to the policy of the sentimental humanitarians; and we have often promised what was impossible to perform; but there has been little willful wrongdoing. Our government almost always tries to act fairly by the tribes; the governmental agents (some of whom have been dishonest and others foolish, but who as a class have been greatly traduced) in their reports are far more apt to be unjust to the whites than to the reds; and the federal authorities, though unable to prevent much of the injustice, still did check and control the white borderers very much more effectually than the Indian sachems and war chiefs controlled their young braves.

The tribes were warlike and bloodthirsty, jealous of each other and of the whites; they claimed the land for their hunting grounds, but their claims all conflicted with one another; their knowledge of their own boundaries was so indefinite that they were always willing, for inadequate compensation, to sell land to which they had merely the vaguest title; and yet, when once they had received the goods, were generally reluctant to make over even what they could; they coveted the goods and scalps of the whites, and the young warriors were always on the alert to commit outrages when they could do it with impunity.

On the other hand, the evil-disposed whites regarded the Indians as fair game for robbery and violence of any kind; and the far larger number of well-disposed men, who would not willingly wrong any Indian, were themselves maddened by the memories of hideous injuries received. They bitterly resented the action of the government which, in their eyes, failed to properly protect them, and yet sought to keep them out of waste, uncultivated lands which they did not regard as being any more the property of the Indians than of their own hunters. With the best intentions, it was wholly impossible for any government to evolve order out of such chaos without resort to the ultimate arbitrator — the sword.

The purely sentimental historians take no account of the difficulties under which we labored, nor of the countless wrongs and provocations we endured, while grossly magnifying the already lamentably large number of injuries for which we really deserve to be held responsible. To get a fair idea of the Indians of the present day and of our dealings with them, we have fortunately one or two excellent books, notably *Hunting Grounds of the Great West* and *Our Wild Indians,* by Col. Richard I. Dodge (Hartford, 1882), and *Massacres of the Mountains,* by J. P. Dunn (New York, 1886). As types of the opposite class, which are worse than valueless and which nevertheless might cause some hasty future historian, unacquainted with the facts, to fall into grievous error, I may mention, *A Century of Dishonor,* by H. H. (Mrs. Helen Hunt Jackson), and *Our Indian Wards* (George W. Manypenny).

Theodore Roosevelt photographed while hunting in the West

The latter is a mere spiteful diatribe against various Army officers, and neither its manner nor its matter warrants more than an allusion. Mrs. Jackson's book is capable of doing more harm because it is written in good English, and because the author, who had lived a pure and noble life, was intensely in earnest in what she wrote, and had the most praiseworthy purpose — to prevent our committing any more injustice to the Indians. This was all most proper; every good man or woman should do whatever is possible to make the government treat the Indians of the present time in the fairest and most generous spirit, and to provide against any repetition of such outrages as were inflicted upon the Nez Percés and upon part of the Cheyennes, or the wrongs with which the civilized nations of the Indian territory are sometimes threatened.

The purpose of the book is excellent, but the spirit in which it is written cannot be called even technically honest. As a polemic, it is possible that it did not do harm (though the effect of even a polemic is marred by hysterical indifference to facts). As a history it would be beneath criticism were it not that the high character of the author and her excellent literary work in other directions have given it a fictitious value and made it much quoted by the large class of amiable but maudlin fanatics concerning whom it may be said that the excellence of their intentions but indifferently atones for the invariable folly and ill effect of their actions. It is not too much to say that the book is thoroughly untrustworthy from cover to cover, and that not a single statement it contains should be accepted without independent proof; for even those that are not absolutely false are often as bad on account of so much of the truth having been suppressed.

One effect of this is of course that the author's recitals of the many real wrongs of Indian tribes utterly fail to impress us because she lays quite as much stress on those that are nonexistent and on the equally numerous cases where the wrongdoing was wholly the other way. To get an idea of the value of the work, it is only necessary to compare her statements about almost any tribe with the real facts, choosing at random; for instance, compare her accounts of the Sioux and the Plains tribes generally with those given by Colonel Dodge in his two books; or her recital of the Sandy Creek massacre with the facts as stated by Mr. Dunn, who is apt, if anything, to lean to the Indian's side.

These foolish sentimentalists not only write foul slanders about their own countrymen but are themselves the worst possible advisers on any point touching Indian management. They would do well to heed General Sheridan's bitter words, written when many Easterners were clamoring against the Army authorities because they took partial vengeance for a series of brutal outrages: "I do not know how far these humanitarians should be excused on account of their ignorance; but surely it is the only excuse that can give a shadow of justification for aiding and abetting such horrid crimes."

46.

Lewis H. Blair: Southern Treatment of the Negro

The process of Negro enfranchisement, in full momentum directly after the Civil War, came to a virtual halt by the end of the century. Southern racists became less discreet about their hatreds and Northern egalitarians relaxed their guard; spurious "scientific" treatises "proving" Negro inferiority had appeared, and sectional strife wearied Northern zeal for equality. "The supremacy of the white race of the South must be maintained forever," remarked Henry W. Grady, the editor of the Atlanta Constitution, *in 1887, ". . . because the white race is the superior race." Lewis Blair's* The Prosperity of the South, *a chapter of which is reprinted here, is an atypical Southern attempt to combat race prejudice against the Negro.*

Source: *The Prosperity of the South Dependent Upon the Elevation of the Negro*, Richmond, Va., 1889, Ch. 10.

If the Negro is not to be elevated to the full standard, then clap on the shackles again and reduce him speedily to bondage when he can be made to work; no, not reduce him to slavery, because all history proves that slavery is finally destructive of the master caste, but put him between the upper and the nether millstone, turn on the water, and quickly grind him out of existence; for otherwise he must necessarily become a thorn in the side of society, for, having once tasted the sweets of partial enfranchisement, he will not cease his efforts to obtain complete enfranchisement and equality until they are crowned with success or until he is again reduced to abject submission. This period of trial or probation may continue for a few years, or it may be indefinitely, but whether it lasts for centuries or merely for years, it must be a period of anxiety and impoverishment for the whites.

But the South *must* do something; it can't say I won't do anything, or I will fold my hands and see what will happen. The South, impelled by the current of events, has done a great deal, and it is still doing much; but a vast deal yet remains to be done, and the point is to prove to the South that it is its interest to do this great deal more, and to do it without unnecessary delay.

The first, the most important and the most difficult step to take is to mollify and finally to obliterate race and color prejudice, a prejudice by no means peculiar to the South or to white and black races; for until very recent years the Frenchman had neither charity nor justice for the Englishman, though separated only by a narrow strip of water, and the Englishman reciprocated in kind and with usurious interest; and although divided by only an imaginary line, the prejudices between Englishman and Scotchman were notorious; and even today the Englishman is ruled by prejudice when Ireland and her claims are in question. But these race prejudices have now measurably disappeared, and they will finally become practically extinct as intercourse, commercial and otherwise, makes nations mutually acquainted.

And not only national but personal prejudices of all kinds also disappear as intelligence is disseminated. Prejudice against color itself has quite disappeared among Latin nations and is quite unknown in Great Britain, our worthy exemplar in so many respects, where a Negro stands on his merits like other people. But a general exclamation will arise that prejudice against color is ineradicable and that we can never, never overcome it.

Such a confession involves two contradictory assertions, both of which are equally erroneous. It implies that we are superior to the great European nations, and in the same breath that we are inferior to them — superior in that we are too wise to follow their example and divest ourselves of prejudice against color, and inferior in that we

are unwilling or unable to do so. Neither is true; and if European nations have found it wise to break down the prejudice against color, it will not be wise, but foolish, for us not to follow their example; and if they have been able and willing to throw off the shackles of prejudice, we are dishonoring ourselves to say or to think that we cannot do so likewise.

Many glory in prejudice, foolishly thinking it a mark of superiority; but prejudice is always a weakness, and when it is extreme it is a badge of dishonor. The prejudiced are as they are because they do not see things in their true light, and are like a horse that shies and throws its rider to death because it sees in the simple clod, stone, or stump a frightful specter about to spring upon and devour him. The clearer one sees and the more enlightened he is, the freer he is from prejudice, which may be termed seeing things in a false light. And for so many generations past we have been looking upon the Negro in a false light [that] we cannot see him and his rights in their true light, and we shy violently and run the risk of wrecking our whole material welfare at the ideas of elevation, equality, manhood, etc., for the Negro. Southerners cannot be true to their lofty character to be either unwilling or incapable of overcoming color prejudice, nor true to their interests either.

And while mollifying and finally correcting our prejudices, we must also modify our actions before we can inspire the Negro with the self-respect and hope that are essential to making him a good citizen and an efficient producer of wealth. And the first duty resting upon us in this respect is to see that in criminal matters — that is to say, in matters of life and liberty — the scales of justice hang more level between whites and blacks; that the hand of justice bears more equally upon the two colors, and that both are punished alike for similar offenses, although it would seem reasonable to inflict heavier penalties upon the whites because they occupy a much higher plane morally, socially, and intellectually, and are therefore less excusable for violating law. And we must see that our courts of justice, the most august and beneficent product of civilization, are an equal refuge for the wronged of all colors, and an equal terror to all wrongdoers, irrespective of previous condition.

And is not the law the same for all; and does it make any distinction between rich and poor, white and black? Literally, the law is the same for all. Then what more can be desired? The trouble is not that the laws are partial, though some of [their] enactments — namely, the whipping post, chain gang, and poll tax laws — were aimed principally against the Negro; but the trouble is with the interpretation of the laws by the juries, who merely voice public sentiment, which is superior to the law itself.

The average jury is a whimsical creature, subject to all kinds of influences, though mostly of a sentimental character. In criminal matters where whites are concerned, it seems ever to lean to the defense; and the strongest arguments of the prosecution are easily offset and upset by appeals on behalf of youth, family, station, respectability, etc.; or perhaps the whole family, weeping, is placed in full view of the jury; and the susceptible jury — sure at least in such cases to weep with them that weep — speedily brings in a verdict of acquittal where guilt is clearly manifest; or it says jail where it ought to say penitentiary; or one year where it ought to say ten, and ten years where it ought to pronounce death.

But the Negro has none of these sentimental advantages. Too poor to employ competent counsel, his liberty and life are necessarily committed to incompetent hands, when the proverb of "Poor pay — poor preach" becomes reality. But more unfortunate still, what sentiment can a poor, ignorant, unkempt Negro inspire, who thinks of his family, of his wife bowed down with grief, of his little ones deprived of a father's support and suffering for bread? The idea is preposterous, and so the jury, without difficulty, brings in its verdict of jail, penitentiary, or even death. The Negro may be rightly punished, and he may receive no more than his just deserts; but if this is so, then the white receives less than his due deserts; or if the white is judged none too leniently, then the Negro is judged altogether too harshly.

As long as the Negro sees this state of affairs continue; as long as justice appears to him to slip aside her bandage when he is brought before her august tribunal, and judge him according to his previous and present condition, he must be bowed down with dread and humiliation, and whatever hope he may have nourished must die within him. But when he sees that similar offenses meet with equal punishments, irrespective of color or previous condition, then however severely he may be chastised, his self-respect and hope will not be offended; but on the contrary, they will spring up and strengthen and make him a man — make him an efficient agent in promoting that prosperity of which we are ever dreaming but never behold. In civil suits, where the judges, in Virginia at least, practically, through their instructions, decide the case, the Negro receives substantial justice.

But are Negroes treated unfairly by juries and public opinion? Yes, and the experience and observation of every fair-minded man will confirm the assertion. One cardinal proof is that a white man seldom receives punishment for assault, however brutal, however unprovoked, however cowardly — be it maiming, homicide, or murder upon a Negro — unless, forsooth, the assailant be some degraded creature, disowned by his own caste. Of the numberless instances — running into the thousands during the past twenty-three years — of homicides and murder of blacks by whites, there is no single instance of capital punishment and few, very few, instances of imprisonment beyond a few months in jail or a slight fine. The fact is the juries, which are the sole judges of the evidence, will accept testimony against a Negro that they would reject in the case of whites; and, on the other hand, they will frequently reject, or at least discredit, testimony of the Negro against the white man, however well supported it may be.

But to compound for sins we are inclined to by damning those we have no mind to, in case of any difficulty between white and black, and the former is injured or loses his life; lucky is the latter if the homicide is not declared by the crowd to be murder — when courts of justice, though sure to inflict the highest penalty in his case, are found to be too slow, and he is dragged forth and slain, unshrived and unshriven, as if he were a monstrous wild beast of whose presence earth could not be rid too quickly.

As bearing on this point, the following is copied from the *Richmond Dispatch* as I am writing this chapter. Many other examples could be selected in the course of any month. All these wretches were Negroes, whom justice, entirely untempered by mercy, would not have suffered to escape, and there was therefore absolutely no excuse and no necessity for these assassinations:

[Special telegram to the *Dispatch*.]

RALEIGH, N.C., September 14 — News was received here tonight of another lynching, which is the *thirteenth* this year. It occurred at Whiteville, Columbus County, night before last. A body of masked men, a hundred or more, entered the jail and demanded the keys from the jailer. With a score of revolvers pointed at him, he surrendered the keys, and the lynchers went to the cell where Sherman Farrier (colored) was confined for an outrage committed on an aged white woman, took him and departed. Yesterday, suspended to the limb of a large oak about one mile from the jail, the body of Sherman Farrier was found with a placard pinned on his breast bearing the words: "We protect the virtue of our women. Beware." Farrier was a man of bad character and had repeatedly been engaged in robbery. He was given a preliminary hearing before two magistrates last Monday and was committed to jail to await trial. The evidence against him was conclusive.

We will here mention a singular phase of Southern white life, and that is, the slain or injured is *always* the guilty party, and nowhere else in the wide world does justice so accurately apportion penalty. The slain *must* be the guilty party, for the white slayer of his white brother is never punished, or hardly ever, and is almost always acquitted with honor. Acquittal usually means innocence, but universal acquittal can only mean universal innocence, and universal guilt of the maimed or slain. As a matter of fact, it is safer in the South for a respectable white man to slay his neighbor than to kill his neighbor's dog; for killing the man rarely means more than a short time in jail, a feeble trial, and an acquittal with eclat, of course a round legal fee; but killing the dog means almost as generally an accounting with the owner of the dog, in which case the murderous revolver may take an active part.

But let it not be supposed from the foregoing that the whites individually are not just to the Negro; they are much more considerate of his wants and feelings than are Northern people. But as a rule our kindness is bestowed as condescension, and it must be received with all due humility and with a tacit acknowledgment of inferiority of status; for let the Negro betray even a moderate sense of equality or manhood, he is then thought "impudent" and our kindness takes affront. Until the Negro sees and feels that the community fully recognizes that courts of justice are as much a refuge for him and as much a bulwark of his life and liberty as for the highest and the proudest, he can never feel sure of his position; and as long as what he enjoys is by favor or condescension, he can never be certain that what he enjoys today may not be arbitrarily wrested from him tomorrow; and [not] until he sees that what he enjoys is by inalienable right can he have that sense of security and manhood that [is] essential for an efficient wealth producer.

47.

JOHN E. BRUCE: Negro Plea for Organized Resistance to White Men

When reactionary white supremacists regained political power in the South after Reconstruction, they imposed upon Negroes a regime of terror and disenfranchisement calculated to override the legal provisions of the Fourteenth and Fifteenth Amendments to the Constitution. Although Negro moderates proposed numerous programs to challenge the economic, social, and political policies of the reactionaries, the general mood of the Negro became one of helplessness. Under these conditions, there was a certain appeal in proposals for direct retaliation such as those in the following speech by Negro journalist John Bruce. The manuscript is dated October 5, 1889.

Source: Manuscript in John E. Bruce Collection, Folder No. 7, Shomburg Collection, New York Public Library, 103 West 135th Street, New York, N.Y.

I FULLY REALIZE THE DELICACY of the position I occupy in this discussion and know too well that those who are to follow me will largely benefit by what I shall have to say in respect to the application of force as one of the means to the solution of the problem known as the "Negro problem."

I am not unmindful of the fact that there are those living who have faith in the efficacy of submission, who are still pregnated with the slavish fear which had its origin in oppression and the peculiar environments of the slave period. Those who are thus minded will advise a pacific policy in order as they believe to affect a settlement of this question, with which the statesmanship of a century has grappled without any particularly gratifying results. Agitation is a good thing, organization is a better thing. The million Negro voters of Georgia, and the undiscovered millions in other Southern states — undiscovered so far as our knowledge of their numbers exists — could, with proper organization and intelligent leadership, meet force with force with most beneficial results.

The issue upon us cannot be misunderstood by those who are watching current events. To us it is not a theory (to quote a distinguished Democrat), but a condition that confronts us; a condition big with hope and fear; a condition where cowards quail and brave men stand their ground; a condition demanding the highest courage, the greatest sacrifices, the noblest ambition to overcome, and to set forever at rest the question of the Negro's right to the titles of manhood, self-respect, and honor. The man who will not fight for the protection of his wife and children is a *coward* and deserves to be ill-treated. The man who takes his life in his hand and stands up for what he knows to be right will always command the respect of his enemy.

Submission to the *dicta* of Southern bulldozers is the basest cowardice, and there is no just reason why manly men of any race should allow themselves to be continually outraged and oppressed by their equals before the law. . . . In all our homogeneous population no race or class has been more loyal, has shown a greater respect for law and order, has been more willing to write its benefits in marble and its injuries in dust than the Negroes of the United States. . . .

Under the present condition of affairs the only hope, the only salvation for the Negro is to be found in a resort to force under wise and discreet leaders. He must sooner or later come to this in order to set at rest, for all time to come, the charge that he is a moral coward. . . . I hate namby-pambyism, or anything that looks like temporizing, when duty calls.

To settle this Southern problem, the Negro must not be rash and indiscreet either in action or in words, but he must be very determined and terribly in earnest, and of one mind to bring order out of chaos and to convince Southern rowdies and cutthroats that more than two can play at the game with which they have amused their fellow conspirators in crime for nearly a quarter of a century.

Under the Mosaic dispensation, it was the custom to require an eye for an eye and a tooth for a tooth. Under a no less barbarous civilization than that which existed at that period of the world's history, let the Negro require at the hands of every white murderer in the South or elsewhere a life for a life. If they burn our houses, burn theirs; if they kill our wives and children, kill theirs; pursue them relentlessly, meet force with force everywhere it is offered. If they demand blood, exchange with them until they are satiated. By a vigorous adherence to this course the shedding of human blood by white men will soon become a thing of the past.

Wherever and whenever the Negro shows himself to be a man, he can always command the respect even of a cutthroat. Organized resistance to organized resistance is the best remedy for the solution of the vexed problem of the century, which to me seems practicable and feasible; and I submit this view of the question, ladies and gentlemen, for your careful consideration.

Sometimes I feel like a motherless child,
A long ways from home.

48.

WILLIAM BROUGH: "Let Us All Speak Our Minds"

From the time of the first American Rights Convention in 1848, suffragettes such as Elizabeth Cady Stanton and Lucretia Mott stirred sympathy for — and ardent opposition to — the cause of women's rights with parades, pamphlets, and propaganda songs like "Let Us All Speak Our Minds." Rather than the heavy sentimentality of most of the songs, "Let Us All Speak Our Minds" leavens its message with a bit of humor, and is generally considered the best of its kind.

LET US ALL SPEAK OUR MINDS

Men tell us 'tis fit that wives should submit
To their husbands submissively, weakly;
That whatever they say, their wives should obey,
Unquestioning, stupidly, meekly.
Our husbands would make us their own dictum take
Without ever a wherefore or why for it;
But I don't and I can't and I won't and I shan't;
No, I will speak my mind if I die for it.

For we know it's all fudge to say man's the best judge
Of what should be and shouldn't, and so on,
That woman should bow, nor attempt to say how
She considers that matters should go on.
I never yet gave up myself thus a slave,
However my husband might try for it;
For I can't and I won't and I shan't and I don't;
But I will speak my mind if I die for it!

And all ladies I hope who've with husbands to cope,
With the rights of the sex will not trifle.
We all, if we choose our tongues but to use,
Can all opposition soon stifle.
Let man, if he will, then bid us be still
And silent, a price he'll pay high for it;
For we won't and we can't and we don't and we shan't —
Let us all speak our minds if we die for it!

49.

ANDREW CARNEGIE: The Birth and Growth of Trusts in a Free Market

Andrew Carnegie's career took him from a job as a telegraph boy paying $2.50 a week through railroad and iron foundry enterprises to the presidency of the Carnegie Company, which he sold for $250 million in gold bonds at his retirement in 1901. Carnegie believed American capitalism to be the most efficient and productive economic order in the world. He subscribed wholeheartedly to laissez faire economic policies and credited his own success to an understanding of and adeptness in free competitive practices. In the following article, Carnegie dismissed the trusts as "vain devices" that would shortly fail the test of free competition.

Source: *North American Review*, February 1889.

WE MUST ALL HAVE OUR TOYS; the child his rattle, the adult his hobby, the man of pleasure the fashion, the man of art his master; and mankind in its various divisions requires a change of toys at short intervals. The same rule holds good in the business world. We have had our age of "consolidations" and "watered stocks." Not long ago everything was a "syndicate"; the word is already becoming obsolete and the fashion is for "trusts," which will in turn no doubt give place to some new panacea, that is in turn to be displaced by another, and so on without end.

The great laws of the economic world, like all laws affecting society, being the genuine outgrowth of human nature, alone remain unchanged through all these changes. Whenever consolidations, or watered stocks, or syndicates, or trusts endeavor to circumvent these, it always has been found the result is that, after the collision, there is nothing left of the panaceas, while the great laws continue to grind out their irresistible consequences as before.

It is worthwhile to inquire into the appearance and growth of trusts and learn what environments produce them. Their genesis is as follows: a demand exists for a certain article beyond the capacity of existing works to supply it. Prices are high and profits tempting. Every manufacturer of that article immediately proceeds to enlarge his works and increase their producing power. In addition to this, the unusual profits attract the attention of his principal managers or those who are interested to a greater or less degree in the factory. These communicate the knowledge of the prosperity of the works to others. New partnerships are formed, and new works are erected, and before long the demand for the article is fully satisfied, and prices do not advance.

In a short time the supply becomes greater than the demand, there are a few tons or yards more in the market for sale than required, and prices begin to fall. They continue falling until the article is sold at cost to the less favorably situated or less ably managed factory; and even until the best managed and best equipped factory is not able to produce the article at the prices at which it can be sold. Political economy says that here the trouble will end. Goods will not be produced at less than cost. This was true when Adam Smith wrote, but it is not quite true today.

When an article was produced by a small manufacturer, employing, probably at his own home, two or three journeymen and an apprentice or two, it was an easy matter for him to limit or even to stop production. As manufacturing is carried on today, in enormous establishments with $5 million or $10 million of capital invested and with thousands of workers, it costs the manufacturer much less to run at a loss per ton or per yard than to check his production. Stoppage would be serious indeed. The condition of cheap manufacture is running full. Twenty sources of expense are *fixed charges,* many of which stoppage would only increase. Therefore the article is produced for months, and in some cases that I have known for years, not only without profit or without interest upon capital but to the impairment of the capital invested. Manufacturers have balanced their books year after year only to find their capital reduced at each successive balance.

While continuing to produce may be costly, the manufacturer knows too well that stoppage would be ruin. His brother manufacturers are of course in the same situation. They see the savings of many years, as well perhaps as the capital they have succeeded in borrowing, becoming less and less, with no hope of a change in the situation. It is in soil thus prepared that anything promising relief is gladly welcomed. The manufacturers are in the position of patients that have tried in vain every doctor of the regular school for years, and are now

liable to become the victims of any quack that appears. Combinations — syndicates — trusts — they are willing to try anything. A meeting is called, and, in the presence of immediate danger, they decide to take united action and form a trust. Each factory is rated as worth a certain amount. Officers are chosen, and through these the entire product of the article in question is to be distributed to the public, at remunerative prices. Such is the genesis of "trusts" in manufactured articles.

In transportation the situation, while practically the same, differs in some particulars. Many small railway lines are built under separate charters. A genius in affairs sees that the eight or ten separate organizations, with as many different ideas of management, equipment, etc., are as useless as were the 250 petty kings in Germany, and, Bismarck-like, he sweeps them out of existence, creates a great through line, doubles the securities or stock, the interest upon which is paid out of the saving effected by consolidation, and all is highly satisfactory, as in the case of the New York Central.

Or a line is built and managed with such sagacity as distinguishes the Pennsylvania Railroad, and it succeeds in developing the resources of the state so extensively that upon a line of 350 miles between Pittsburgh and Philadelphia, it nets about $13 million per annum. Twelve million dollars of this it shows upon its books. From $1 million to $2 million extra are expended in making one of the best lines in the world out of a road which was originally designed as a horse railroad. We do not call our railroad combinations trusts, but they are substantially such, since they aim at raising and maintaining transportation rates in certain districts. They are "combinations" or "systems" which aim at monopolies within these districts. . . .

There is one huge combination classed with trusts which is so exceptional in its origin and history that it deserves a separate paragraph. I refer to the Standard Oil Company. So favorable an opportunity to control a product perhaps never arose as in the case of petroleum. At an early stage a few of the ablest business men that the world has ever seen realized the importance of the discovery and invested largely in the purchase of property connected with it. The success of the petroleum business was phenomenal, and so was the success of these people. The profits they made and, no doubt, as much capital as they could borrow were fearlessly reinvested, and they soon became the principal owners and, finally, substantially the only owners of the territory which contained this great source of wealth. The Standard Oil Company would long ago have gone to pieces had it not been managed, upon the whole, in harmony with the laws which control business.

It is generally admitted that the prices of oil to the consumer are as low today, and many think that they are even lower, than could have been attained had the business not been grouped and managed as one vast concern in the broad spirit for which the Standard Oil managers are famous. They are in the position somewhat of the Colemans, of Pennsylvania, who possess the chief source of the ore supply in the East. They own the Cornwall deposit of ore as the Standard Oil Company owns the source of the oil deposit. But as the company has continually to deal with the finding of oil in other localities, the price of its existence and success is the continuance of that exceptional ability in its councils and management displayed by its founders. Threatened opposition arises every now and then, and the chances are greatly in favor of the Standard Oil Company losing its practical monopoly and going the way of all huge combinations. It is a hundred to one whether it will survive when the present men at the head retire; or perhaps I should say when the present man retires, for wonderful organizations imply a genius at the head, a commander in chief, with exceptionally able corps commanders no doubt, but still a Grant at the head.

To those who quote the Standard Oil Company as an evidence that trusts or combinations can be permanently successful, I say wait and see. I have spoken thus freely of that company because I am ignorant of its management, profits, and modes of action. I view it from the outside, as a student of political economy only, and as such have endeavored to apply to it the principles which I know *will* have their way no matter how formidable the attempt made to defeat their operation.

We have given the genesis of trusts and combinations in their several forms. The question is — Do they menace the permanent interest of the nation? Are they a source of serious danger? Or are they to prove, as many other similar forms have proved, mere passing phases of unrest and transition? To answer this question let us follow the operation of the manufacturing trust which we have in imagination created, salt or sugar, nails, beams, or lead or copper; it is all the same.

The sugar refiners, let us say, have formed a trust after competing one with another through years of disastrous business, and all the sugar manufactured in the country in existing factories is sold through one channel at advanced prices. Profits begin to grow. Dividends are paid, and those who before saw their property vanishing before their eyes are now made happy. The dividends from that part of a man's capital invested in the sugar business yield him profit far above the capital he has invested in various other affairs. The prices of sugar are such that the capital invested in a new factory would yield enormously.

He is perhaps bound not to enlarge his factory or to enter into a new factory, but his relatives and acquaintances soon discover the fresh opportunity for gain. He can advise them to push the completion of a small factory, which, of course, must be taken into the trust. Or, even if he does not give his friends this intimation, capital is always upon the alert, especially when it is bruited about that a trust has been formed, as in the case of sugar, and immediately new sugar manufactories spring up, as if by magic. The more successful the trust, the surer these offshoots are to sprout. Every victory is a defeat. Every factory that the trust buys is the sure creator of another, and so on, *ad infinitum,* until the bubble bursts.

The sugar refiners have tried to get more from capital in a special case than capital yields in general. They have endeavored to raise a part of the ocean of capital above the level of the surrounding waters, and over their bulwarks the floods have burst, and capital, like water, has again found its level. It is true that to regain this level a longer or a shorter period may be required, during which the article affected may be sold to the consumer in limited quantities at a higher rate than before existed. But for this the consumer is amply recompensed in the years that follow, during which the struggle between the discordant and competitive factories becomes severer than it ever was before, and lasts till the great law of the survival of the fittest vindicates itself. Those factories and managers that can produce to the best advantage eventually close the less competent. Capital wisely managed yields its legitimate profit. After a time, the growth of demand enables capital to receive an unusual profit. This in turn attracts fresh capital to the manufacture, and we have a renewal of the old struggle, the consumer reaping the benefit.

Such is the law, such has been the law, and such promises to be the law for the future; for, so far, no device has yet been devised that has permanently thwarted its operation. Given freedom of competition, and all combinations or trusts that attempt to exact from the consumer more than a le-

gitimate return upon capital and services write the charter of their own defeat.

We have many proofs that this great law does not sleep and that it will not be suppressed. Some time ago . . . the steel rail manufacturers of Europe formed a trust and advanced the price of rails to such an extent that American manufacturers were able for the first and perhaps for the last time to export steel rails to Canada in competition with the European. But the misunderstandings and quarrels, inseparable from these attempted unions of competitors, soon broke the trust. With vindictive feelings, added to what was before business rivalry, the struggle was renewed, and the steel-rail industry of Europe has never recovered. It was found that the advance of prices had only galvanized into life concerns which never should have attempted to manufacture rails; and so that trust died a natural death. . . .

The Sugar Trust has already a noted competitor at its heels. The Copper Trust is in danger. All stand prepared to attack a "trust" or "combine" if it proves itself worth attacking; in other words, if it succeeds in raising its profits above the natural level of profits throughout the country, it is subject to competition from every quarter and must finally break down. It is unnecessary to devote much attention to the numerous trusts in minor articles which one reads of, a new one appearing every few days and others passing out of existence, because they are all subject to the great law. The newspapers charge that trusts exist or have existed in wallpaper, shoe laces, lumber, coal, coke, brick, screw, rope, glass, schoolbooks, insurance, and hardware, and twenty more articles; but the fitting epitaph for these ephemeral creations is

If I was so soon to be done for,
I wonder what I was begun for! . . .

The people of America can smile at the

efforts of all her railway magnates and of all her manufacturers to defeat the economic laws by trusts or combinations, or pools, or "differentials," or anything of like character. Only let them hold firmly to the doctrine of free competition. Keep the field open. Freedom for all to engage in railroad building when and where capital desires subject to conditions open to all. Freedom for all to engage in any branch of manufacturing under like conditions.

There can then be no permanent extortion of profit beyond the average return from capital, nor any monopoly, either in transportation or manufacturing. Any attempt to maintain either must end in failure, and failure ultimately disastrous just in proportion to the temporary success of the foolish effort. It is simply ridiculous for a party of men to meet in a room and attempt by passing resolutions to change the great laws which govern human affairs in the business world, and this, whether they be railway presidents, bankers, or manufacturers.

The fashion of trusts has but a short season longer to run, and then some other equally vain device may be expected to appear when the next period of depression arrives; but there is not the slightest danger that serious injury can result to the sound principles of business from any or all of these movements. The only people who have reason to fear trusts are those foolish enough to enter into them. The consumer and the transporter, not the manufacturer and the railway owner, are to reap the harvest.

Even since the foregoing was written, a new form has appeared upon the stage in the shape of "The Presidents' Agreement — an agreement among gentlemen," in which the parties engage to control, strangle, and restrict the future development of our magnificent railway system under the laws of natural growth at a time when the country requires this development as much as it ever did. These gentlemen are not going to engage in building lines which will give the public the benefit of healthy competition, or permit such to be built hereafter. It is safe to say that very soon this toy will be discarded, like its predecessors, for another, and that the very men apparently most pleased with this new rattle will then regard it with the greatest contempt and go forward in the good work, as hitherto, developing the railway system wherever and whenever they think they see a fair chance for profit.

Whenever existing railways exact from the public more than a fair return upon the actual capital invested, or upon the capital which would be required to duplicate existing lines, competing lines will be built — fortunately for the interests of the country — which is much more concerned in getting cheap transportation than it is in insuring dividends for capitalists; and whenever a percentage is to be obtained by the negotiation of railway securities, bankers will be found — also fortunately for the best interests of the country — who will gladly find a market for them without stopping to inquire whether monopolies are to be overthrown by the new lines.

It is not in the power of man to exact for more than a brief season, and a very brief season indeed, unusual profit upon actual capital invested either in transportation or manufacture so long as all are free to compete, and this freedom, it may safely be asserted, the American people are not likely to restrict.

50.

Andrew Carnegie: Private Fortunes for Public Benefit

Andrew Carnegie combined his enormously profitable business career with philanthropic activities inspired by a belief that wealth entailed social obligations. In the following passage from "Wealth," an article published in 1889 and later known as "The Gospel of Wealth," Carnegie expressed his feelings about philanthropy. In accord with the principles embodied in the article, Carnegie spent $350 million in various philanthropies, including gifts of public libraries and church organs, grants to colleges and universities, the Hero Funds, the Carnegie Foundation for the Advancement of Teaching, and the Endowment for International Peace.

Source: *North American Review*, June 1889.

We accept and welcome . . . as conditions to which we must accommodate ourselves great inequality of environment, the concentration of business — industrial and commercial — in the hands of a few, and the law of competition between these as being not only beneficial but essential for the future progress of the race. Having accepted these, it follows that there must be great scope for the exercise of special ability in the merchant and in the manufacturer who has to conduct affairs upon a great scale. That this talent for organization and management is rare among men is proved by the fact that it invariably secures for its possessor enormous rewards, no matter where or under what laws or conditions. The experienced in affairs always rate the *man* whose services can be obtained as a partner as not only the first consideration but such as to render the question of his capital scarcely worth considering, for such men soon create capital; while, without the special talent required, capital soon takes wings.

Such men become interested in firms or corporations using millions; and estimating only simple interest to be made upon the capital invested, it is inevitable that their income must exceed their expenditures and that they must accumulate wealth. Nor is there any middle ground which such men can occupy, because the great manufacturing or commercial concern which does not earn at least interest upon its capital soon becomes bankrupt. It must either go forward or fall behind: to stand still is impossible. It is a condition essential for its successful operation that it should be thus far profitable, and even that, in addition to interest on capital, it should make profit. It is a law, as certain as any of the others named, that men possessed of this peculiar talent for affairs, under the free play of economic forces, must, of necessity, soon be in receipt of more revenue than can be judiciously expended upon themselves; and this law is as beneficial for the race as the others.

Objections to the foundations upon which society is based are not in order because the condition of the race is better with these than it has been with any others which have been tried. Of the effect of any new substitutes proposed, we cannot be sure. The socialist or anarchist who seeks to overturn present conditions is to be regarded as attacking the foundation upon which civilization itself rests, for civilization took its start from the day that the capable, industrious workman said to his incompetent and lazy fellow, "If thou dost not sow, thou shalt not reap," and thus ended primitive Communism by separating the drones from the bees. One who studies this subject will soon be brought face to face with the conclusion that upon the sacredness of property civilization itself depends — the right of the laborer to his $100 in the savings bank, and equally the legal right of the millionaire to his millions.

To those who propose to substitute Communism for this intense individualism the answer, therefore, is: The race has tried that. All progress from that barbarous day to the present time has resulted from its displacement. Not evil, but good, has come to the race from the accumulation of wealth by those who have the ability and energy that produce it. But even if we admit for a moment that it might be better for the race to discard its present foundation, individualism — that it is a nobler ideal that man should labor, not for himself alone but in and for a brotherhood of his fellows and share with them all in common, realizing Swedenborg's idea of heaven, where, as he says, the angels derive their happiness, not from laboring for self but for each other — even admit all this, and a sufficient answer is: This is not evolution, but revolution.

It necessitates the changing of human nature itself — a work of aeons, even if it were good to change it, which we cannot know. It is not practicable in our day or in our age. Even if desirable theoretically, it belongs to another and long-succeeding sociological stratum. Our duty is with what is practicable now; with the next step possible in our day and generation. It is criminal to waste our energies in endeavoring to uproot, when all we can profitably or possibly accomplish is to bend the universal tree of humanity a little in the direction most favorable to the production of good fruit under existing circumstances.

We might as well urge the destruction of the highest existing type of man because he failed to reach our ideal as to favor the destruction of individualism, private property, the law of accumulation of wealth, and the law of competition; for these are the highest results of human experience, the soil in which society so far has produced the best fruit. Unequally or unjustly, perhaps, as these laws sometimes operate, and imperfect as they appear to the idealist, they are, nevertheless, like the highest type of man, the best and most valuable of all that humanity has yet accomplished.

We start, then, with a condition of affairs under which the best interests of the race are promoted, but which inevitably gives wealth to the few. Thus far, accepting conditions as they exist, the situation can be surveyed and pronounced good. The question then arises — and, if the foregoing be correct, it is the only question with which we have to deal — What is the proper mode of administering wealth after the laws upon which civilization is founded have thrown it into the hands of the few? And it is of this great question that I believe I offer the true solution. It will be understood that *fortunes* are here spoken of, not moderate sums saved by many years of effort, the returns from which are required for the comfortable maintenance and education of families. This is not *wealth* but only *competence*, which it should be the aim of all to acquire.

There are but three modes in which surplus wealth can be disposed of. It can be left to the families of the decedents; or it can be bequeathed for public purposes; or, finally, it can be administered during their lives by its possessors. Under the first and second modes most of the wealth of the world that has reached the few has hitherto been applied. Let us in turn consider each of these modes.

The first is the most injudicious. In monarchical countries, the estates and the greatest portion of the wealth are left to the first son that the vanity of the parent may be gratified by the thought that his name and title are to descend to succeeding generations unimpaired. The condition of this class in Europe today teaches the futility of such hopes or ambitions. The successors have become impoverished through their follies or from the fall in the value of land. Even in Great Britain the strict law of entail has been found inadequate to maintain the status of an hereditary class. Its soil is rapidly passing into the hands of the stranger. Under republican institutions the division of property among the children is much fairer, but the question which forces itself upon thoughtful men in all lands is: Why should men leave great fortunes to their children? If this is done from affection, is it not misguided affection? Observation teaches that, generally speaking, it is not well for the children that they should be so burdened. Neither is it well for the state. Beyond providing for the wife and daughters moderate sources of income, and very moderate allowances indeed, if any, for the sons, men may well hesitate, for it is no longer questionable that great sums bequeathed oftener work more for the injury than for the good of the recipients. Wise men will soon conclude that, for the best interests of the members of their families and of the state, such bequests are an improper use of their means.

It is not suggested that men who have failed to educate their sons to earn a livelihood shall cast them adrift in poverty. If any man has seen fit to rear his sons with a view to their living idle lives, or, what is highly commendable, has instilled in them the sentiment that they are in a position to labor for public ends without reference to pecuniary considerations, then, of course, the duty of the parent is to see that such are provided for *in moderation*. There are instances of millionaires' sons unspoiled by wealth, who, being rich, still perform great services in the community. Such are the very salt of the earth, as valuable as, unfor-

tunately, they are rare; still it is not the exception but the rule that men must regard, and, looking at the usual result of enormous sums conferred upon legatees, the thoughtful man must shortly say, "I would as soon leave to my son a curse as the almighty dollar," and admit to himself that it is not the welfare of the children but family pride which inspires these enormous legacies.

As to the second mode, that of leaving wealth at death for public uses, it may be said that this is only a means for the disposal of wealth, provided a man is content to wait until he is dead before it becomes of much good in the world. Knowledge of the results of legacies bequeathed is not calculated to inspire the brightest hopes of much posthumous good being accomplished. The cases are not few in which the real object sought by the testator is not attained, nor are they few in which his real wishes are thwarted. In many cases the bequests are so used as to become only monuments of his folly.

It is well to remember that it requires the exercise of not less ability than that which acquired the wealth to use it so as to be really beneficial to the community. Besides this, it may fairly be said that no man is to be extolled for doing what he cannot help doing, nor is he to be thanked by the community to which he only leaves wealth at death. Men who leave vast sums in this way may fairly be thought men who would not have left it at all had they been able to take it with them. The memories of such cannot be held in grateful remembrance, for there is no grace in their gifts. It is not to be wondered at that such bequests seem so generally to lack the blessing.

The growing disposition to tax more and more heavily large estates left at death is a cheering indication of the growth of a salutary change in public opinion. The state of Pennsylvania now takes — subject to some exceptions — one-tenth of the property left by its citizens. The budget presented in the British Parliament the other day proposes to increase the death duties; and, most significant of all, the new tax is to be a graduated one. Of all forms of taxation, this seems the wisest. Men who continue hoarding great sums all their lives, the proper use of which for public ends would work good to the community, should be made to feel that the community, in the form of the state, cannot thus be deprived of its proper share. By taxing estates heavily at death the state marks its condemnation of the selfish millionaire's unworthy life.

It is desirable that nations should go much further in this direction. Indeed, it is difficult to set bounds to the share of a rich man's estate which should go at his death to the public through the agency of the state, and by all means such taxes should be graduated, beginning at nothing upon moderate sums to dependents and increasing rapidly as the amounts swell, until, of the millionaire's hoard as of Shylock's, at least

Andrew Carnegie; photo by Handy

——— The other half
Comes to the privy coffer of the state.

This policy would work powerfully to induce the rich man to attend to the administration of wealth during his life, which is the end that society should always have in view, as being that by far most fruitful for the people. Nor need it be feared that this policy would sap the root of enterprise and render men less anxious to accumulate, for to the class whose ambition it is to leave great fortunes and be talked about after their death, it will attract even more attention, and, indeed, be a somewhat nobler ambition to have enormous sums paid over to the state from their fortunes.

There remains, then, only one mode of using great fortunes; but in this we have the true antidote for the temporary unequal distribution of wealth, the reconciliation of the rich and the poor — a reign of harmony — another ideal, differing, indeed, from that of the Communist in requiring only the further evolution of existing conditions,

not the total overthrow of our civilization. It is founded upon the present most intense individualism, and the race is prepared to put it in practice by degrees whenever it pleases. Under its sway we shall have an ideal state in which the surplus wealth of the few will become, in the best sense, the property of the many, because administered for the common good; and this wealth, passing through the hands of the few, can be made a much more potent force for the elevation of our race than if it had been distributed in small sums to the people themselves. Even the poorest can be made to see this and to agree that great sums gathered by some of their fellow citizens and spent for public purposes, from which the masses reap the principal benefit, are more valuable to them than if scattered among them through the course of many years in trifling amounts. . . .

Poor and restricted are our opportunities in this life; narrow our horizon; our best work most imperfect; but rich men should be thankful for one inestimable boon. They have it in their power during their lives to busy themselves in organizing benefactions from which the masses of their fellows will derive lasting advantage, and thus dignify their own lives. The highest life is probably to be reached, not by such imitation of the life of Christ as Count Tolstoï gives us but, while animated by Christ's spirit, by recognizing the changed conditions of this age and adopting modes of expressing this spirit suitable to the changed conditions under which we live; still laboring for the good of our fellows, which was the essence of his life and teaching, but laboring in a different manner.

This, then, is held to be the duty of the man of wealth: first, to set an example of modest, unostentatious living, shunning display or extravagance; to provide moderately for the legitimate wants of those dependent upon him; and after doing so to consider all surplus revenues which come to him simply as trust funds which he is called upon to administer, and strictly bound as a matter of duty to administer in the manner which, in his judgment, is best calculated to produce the most beneficial results for the community — the man of wealth thus becoming the mere agent and trustee for his poorer brethren, bringing to their service his superior wisdom, experience, and ability to administer, doing for them better than they would or could do for themselves. . . .

In bestowing charity, the main consideration should be to help those who will help themselves; to provide part of the means by which those who desire to improve may do so; to give those who desire to rise the aids by which they may rise; to assist, but rarely or never to do all. Neither the individual nor the race is improved by almsgiving. Those worthy of assistance, except in rare cases, seldom require assistance. The really valuable men of the race never do, except in cases of accident or sudden change. Everyone has, of course, cases of individuals brought to his own knowledge where temporary assistance can do genuine good, and

these he will not overlook. But the amount which can be wisely given by the individual for individuals is necessarily limited by his lack of knowledge of the circumstances connected with each. He is the only true reformer who is as careful and as anxious not to aid the unworthy as he is to aid the worthy, and, perhaps, even more so, for in almsgiving more injury is probably done by rewarding vice than by relieving virtue. . . .

Thus is the problem of rich and poor to be solved. The laws of accumulation will be left free; the laws of distribution free. Individualism will continue, but the millionaire will be but a trustee for the poor; entrusted for a season with a great part of the increased wealth of the community, but administering it for the community far better than it could or would have done for itself. The best minds will thus have reached a stage in the development of the race in which it is clearly seen that there is no mode of disposing of surplus wealth creditable to thoughtful and earnest men into whose hands it flows save by using it year by year for the general good.

This day already dawns. But a little while, and although, without incurring the pity of their fellows, men may die sharers in great business enterprises from which their capital cannot be or has not been withdrawn, and is left chiefly at death for public uses, yet the man who dies leaving behind him millions of available wealth, which was his to administer during life, will pass away "unwept, unhonored, and unsung," no matter to what uses he leaves the dross which he cannot take with him. Of such as these the public verdict will then be: "The man who dies thus rich dies disgraced."

Such, in my opinion, is the true gospel concerning wealth, obedience to which is destined some day to solve the problem of the rich and the poor, and to bring "Peace on earth, among men goodwill."

51.

DAVID A. WELLS: Machines and Economic Change

David Wells's experiences as an inventor, writer of texts in natural science and philosophy, and economic adviser to Presidents Lincoln, Garfield, and Cleveland gave him a distinctive vantage point from which to survey the changes in the nation's economic system brought on by the advent of modern industrial techniques. Wells was one of the first economists to recognize the problem of technological unemployment — unemployment created by innovations in production methods — and he gave special attention to the effects of technological progress on workers in Recent Economic Changes.

Source: *Recent Economic Changes*, New York, 1889, pp. 91-113.

MACHINERY IS NOW RECOGNIZED as essential to cheap production. Nobody can produce effectively and economically without it, and what was formerly known as domestic manufacture is now almost obsolete. But machinery is one of the most expensive of all products, and its extensive purchase and use require an amount of capital far beyond the capacity of the ordinary individual to furnish. There are very few men in the world possessed of an amount of wealth sufficient to individually construct and own an extensive line of railway or telegraph, a first-class steamship, or a great factory. It is also to be remembered that, for carrying on production by the most modern and effective methods, large capital is needed, not only for machinery but also for the purchasing and carrying of extensive stocks of crude material and finished products.

Sugar can now be, and generally is, refined at a profit of an eighth of a cent a pound, and sometimes as low as a sixteenth; or, in other words, from 8 to 16 pounds of raw sugar must now be treated in refining in order to make a cent; from 800 to 1,600 pounds to make a dollar; from 80,000 to 160,000 pounds to make a hundred dollars, and so on. The mere capital requisite for providing and carrying the raw material necessary for the successful prosecution of this business, apart from all other conditions, places it, therefore, of necessity beyond the reach of any ordinary capitalist or producer. . . . In the manufacture of jewelry by machinery, one boy can make up 9,000 sleeve buttons per day; four girls also, working by modern methods, can put together in the same time 8,000 collar buttons. But to run an establishment with such facilities the manufacturer must keep constantly in stock $30,000 worth of cut ornamental stones and a stock of cuff buttons that represents 9,000 different designs and patterns.

Hence, from such conditions have grown up great corporations or stock companies, which are only forms of associated capital organized for effective use and protection. They are regarded to some extent as evils; but they are necessary, as there is apparently no other way in which the work of production and distribution, in accordance with the requirements of the age, can be prosecuted. The rapidity, however, with which such combinations of capital are organizing for the purpose of promoting industrial and commercial undertakings on a scale heretofore wholly unprecedented, and the tendency they have to crystallize into something far more complex than what has been familiar to the public as corporations, with the impressive names of syndicates, trusts, etc., also constitute one of the remarkable features of modern business methods. It must also be admitted that the whole tendency of recent economic development is in the direction of limiting the area within which the influence of competition is effective.

And when once a great association of capital has been effected, it becomes necessary to have a mastermind to manage it — a man who is competent to use and direct other men, who is fertile in expedient and quick to note and profit by any improvements in methods of production and variations in prices. Such a man is a general of industry, and corresponds in position and functions to the general of an army.

What, as a consequence, has happened to the employees? Coincident with and as a result of this change in the methods of production, the modern manufacturing system has been brought into a condition analogous to that of a military organization, in which the individual no longer works as independently as formerly, but as a private in the ranks, obeying orders, keeping step, as it were, to the tap of the drum, and having nothing to say as to the plan of his work, of its final completion, or of its ultimate use and distribution. In short, the people who work in the modern factory are, as a rule, taught to do one thing — to perform one, and generally a simple, operation; and when there is no more of that kind of work to do, they are in a measure helpless.

The result has been that the individualism or independence of the producer in manufacturing has been in a great degree destroyed, and with it has also in a great degree been destroyed the pride which the workman formerly took in his work — that fertility of resource which formerly was a special characteristic of American workmen, and that element of skill that comes from long and varied practice and reflection and responsibility. Not many years ago every shoemaker was or could be his own employer. The boots and shoes passed directly from an individual producer to the consumer. Now this condition of things has passed away. Boots and shoes are made in large factories; and machinery has been so utilized, and the division of labor in connection with it has been carried to such an extent, that the process of making a shoe is said to be divided into sixty-four parts, or the shoemaker of today is only the sixty-fourth part of what a shoemaker once was. It is also asserted that "the constant employment at one sixty-fourth part of a shoe not only offers no encouragement to mental activity but dulls by its monotony the brain of the employee to such an extent that the power to think and reason is almost lost."

As the division of labor in manufacturing — more especially in the case of textiles — is increased, the tendency is to supplement the employment of men with the labor of women and children. The whole number of employees in the cotton mills of the United States, according to the census of 1880, was 172,544; of this number, 59,685 were men and 112,859 women and children. In Massachusetts, out of 61,246 employees in the cotton mills, 22,180 are males; 31,496, women; and 7,570, children. In the latter state certain manufacturing towns, owing to the disparity in the numbers of men and women employed, and in favor of the latter, are coming to be known by the appellation of "she-towns." . . .

Another exceedingly interesting and developing feature of the new situation is that, as machinery has destroyed the handicrafts and associated capital has placed individual capital at a disadvantage, so machinery and associated capital in turn, guided by the same common influences, now war upon machinery and other associated capital. Thus the now well-ascertained and accepted fact, based on long experience, that power is most economically applied when applied on the largest possible scale, is rapidly and inevitably leading to the concentration of manufacturing in the largest establishments and the gradual extinction of those which are small. Such also has already been, and such will continue to be, the outcome of railroad, telegraph, and steamship development and experience; and another quarter of a century will not unlikely see all of the numerous companies that at present make up the vast railroad system of the United States consolidated, for sound economic reasons, under a comparatively few organizations or companies. . . .

Such changes in the direction of the concentration of production by machinery in large establishments are, moreover, in a certain and large sense, not voluntary on the part of the possessors and controllers of capital but necessary or even compulsory. If an eighth or a sixteenth of a cent a pound is all the profit that competition and modern improvements will permit in the business of refining sugar, such business has got to be conducted on a large scale to admit of the realization of any profit. An establishment fitted up with all modern improvements and refining the absolutely large but comparatively small quantity of a million pounds per annum, could realize, at a sixteenth of a cent a pound profit on its work, but $625. Accordingly, the successful refiner

of sugars of today, in place of being as formerly a manufacturer exclusively, must now, as a condition of full success, be his own importer, do his own lighterage, own his own wharfs and warehouses, make his own barrels and boxes, prepare his own bone black, and ever be ready to discard and replace his expensive machinery with every new improvement. But to do all this successfully requires not only the command of large capital but of business qualifications of the very highest order — two conditions that but comparatively few can command. It is not, therefore, to be wondered at that, under the advent of these new conditions, one-half of the sugar refineries that were in operation in the seaboard cities of the United States in 1875 have since failed or discontinued operations.

In the great beef slaughtering and packing establishments at Chicago, which slaughter 1,000 head of cattle and upward in a day, economies are effected which are not possible when this industry is carried on, as usual, upon a very small scale. Every part of the animal — hide, horns, hoofs, bones, blood, and hair — which in the hands of the ordinary butcher are of little value or a dead loss, are turned to a profit by the Chicago packers in the manufacture of glue, bone dust, fertilizers, etc.; and accordingly the great packers can afford to and do pay more for cattle than would otherwise be possible — an advance estimated by the best authorities at $2 a head. Nor does this increased price which Western stock growers receive come out of the consumer of beef. It is made possible only by converting the portions of an ox that would otherwise be sheer waste into products of value. . . .

It was a matter of congratulation after the conclusion of the American War in 1865 that the large plantation system of cotton raising would be broken up, and a system of smaller crops, by small and independent farmers or yeomanry, would take its place. Experience has not, however, verified this expectation; but, on the contrary, has shown that it is doubtful whether any profit can accrue to a cultivator of cotton whose annual crop is less than fifty bales.

> Cotton (at the South) is made an exclusive crop because it can be sold for cash — for an actual and certain price in gold. It is a mere trifle to get 8 or 9 cents for a pound of cotton, but for a bale of 450 pounds it is $40. The bale of cotton is therefore a reward which the anxious farmer works for during an entire year and for which he will spend half as much in money before the cotton is grown, besides all his labor and time. And the man who cannot make eight or ten bales at least has almost no object in life, and nothing to live on. — *Bradstreet's Journal.*

About fifteen years ago the new and so-called roller process for crushing and separating wheat was discovered and brought into use. Its advantages over the old method of grinding by millstones were that it separated the flour more perfectly from the hull or bran of the berry of the wheat, gave more flour to a bushel of wheat, and raised both its color and strength (nutriment). As soon as these facts were demonstrated, the universal adoption of the roller mills and the total abolition of the stone mills became only a question of time, as the latter could not compete with the former. The cost of building mills to operate by the roller process is, however, much greater than that of the old stone mills. Formerly, from $25,000 to $50,000 was an ample capital with which to engage in flour milling in the United States, where waterpower only was employed; but at the present time from $100,000 to $150,000 is required to go into the business upon a basis with any promise of success, even with a small mill; while the great mills of Minneapolis, St. Louis, and Milwaukee cost from $250,000 to $500,000 each, and include steam as well as waterpower.

The consequence of requiring so much more capital to participate in the flour business now than formerly is that the smaller flour mills in the United States are being crushed, or forced into consolidation with the larger companies, the latter being able, from dealing in such immense quantities, to buy their wheat more economically, obtain lower rates of freight, and, by contracting ahead, keep constantly running. At the same time, there is a tendency to drive the milling industry from points in the country to the larger cities, and central grain and flour markets where cheap freights and large supplies of wheat are available. As might have been anticipated, therefore, the Milwaukee *Directory of American Millers* for 1886 shows a decrease in the number of flour mills in the United States for that year, as compared with 1884, of 6,812, out of a total in the latter year of 25,079, but an increase at the same time in capacity for flour production. . . .

Attention is next asked to the economic — industrial, commercial, and financial — disturbances that have also resulted in recent years from changes, in the sense of improvements, in the details of the distribution of products; and as the best method of showing this, the recent course of trade in respect to the practical distribution and supply of one of the great articles of commerce, namely, tinplate, is selected.

Before the days of the swift steamship and the telegraph, the business of distributing tinplate for consumption in the United States was largely in the hands of one of the great mercantile firms of New York, who brought to it large enterprise and experience. At every place in the world where tin was produced and tinplate manufactured, they had their confidential correspondent or agent, and every foreign mail brought to them exclusive and prompt returns of the state of the market. Those who dealt with such a firm dealt with them under conditions which, while not discriminating unfavorably to any buyer, were certainly extraordinarily favorable to the seller, and great fortunes were amassed.

But, today, how stands that business? There is no man, however obscure he may be, who wants to know any morning the state of the tinplate market in any part of the world but can find it in the mercantile journals. If he wants to know more in detail, he joins a little syndicate for news, and then he can be put in possession of every transaction of importance that took place the day previous in Cornwall, Liverpool, in the Strait of Sunda, in Australia, or South America. What has been the result? There are no longer great warehouses where tin in great quantities and of all sizes, waiting for customers, is stored. The business has passed into the hands of men who do not own or manage stores. They have simply desks in offices.

They go round and find who is going to use tin in the next six months. They hear of a railroad bridge which is to be constructed; of a certain number of cars which are to be covered; that the salmon canneries on the Columbia River or Puget Sound are likely to require 70,000 boxes of tin to pack the catch of this year, as compared with a requirement of 60,000 last year — a business, by the way, which a few years ago was not in existence — and they will go to the builders, contractors, or business managers and say to them: "You will want at such a time so much tin. I will buy it for you at the lowest market price, not of New York but of the world, and I will put it in your possession, in any part of the continent, on a given day, and you shall cash the bill and pay me a percentage commission" — possibly a fraction of one percent; thus bringing a former great and complicated business of importing, warehousing, selling at wholesale and retail, and employing many middlemen, clerks, bookkeepers, and large capital to a mere commission business, which dispenses to a great extent with the employment of

intermediates and does not necessarily require the possession or control of any capital.

Let us next go one step further and see what has happened at the same time to the man whose business it has been not to sell but to manufacture tinplate into articles for domestic use, or for other consumption. Thirty or forty years ago the tinman, whose occupation was mainly one of handicraft, was recognized as one of the leading and most skillful mechanics in every village, town, and city. His occupation has, however, now well-nigh passed away. For example, a townsman and a farmer desires a supply of milk cans. He never thinks of going to his corner tinman, because he knows that in New York and Chicago and Philadelphia and other large towns and cities there is a special establishment fitted up with special machinery which will make his can better and 50 percent cheaper than he can have it made by hand in his own town. And so in regard to almost all the other articles which the tinman formerly made. He simply keeps a stock of machine-made goods, as a small merchant, and his business has come down from that of a general, comprehensive mechanic to little other than a tinker and mender of pots and pans.

Where great quantities of tinplate are required for a particular use, as, for example, the canning of salmon or lobsters, of biscuit, or of fruit and vegetables, the plates come direct from the manufactory to the manufacturer of cans or boxes, in such previously agreed-upon sizes and shapes as will obviate any waste of material and reduce to a minimum the time and labor necessary to adapt them to their respective uses. And by this arrangement alone, in one cracker (biscuit) bakery in the United States, consuming 40,000 tin boxes per month, forty men are now enabled to produce as large a product of boxes in a given time as formerly required fifty men; and, taken in connection with machinery, the labor of twenty-five men in the entire business has become equivalent to that of the fifty who until recently worked by other methods.

And what has been thus affirmed of tinplate might be equally affirmed of a great variety of other leading commodities. The blacksmith, for example, no longer making but buying his horseshoes, nails, nuts, and bolts; the carpenter, his doors, sash, blinds, and moldings; the wheelwright, his spokes, hubs, and felloes; the harness maker, his straps, girths, and collars; the painter, his paints, ground and mixed; and so on — the change in methods of distribution and preparation for final consumption having been equally radical in almost every case, though varying somewhat in respect to particulars.

The same influences have also to a great degree revolutionized the nature of retail trade, which has been aptly described as, "until lately, the recourse of men whose character, skill, thrift, and ambition won credit and enabled them to dispense with large capital." Experience has shown that, under a good organization of clerks, shopmen, porters, and distributors, it costs much less proportionally to sell a large amount of goods than a small amount; and that the buyer of large quantities can, without sacrifice of satisfactory profit, afford to offer to his retail customers such advantages in respect to prices and range of selection as almost to preclude competition on the part of dealers operating on a smaller scale, no matter how otherwise capable, honest, and diligent they may be. The various retail trades in the cities and larger towns of all civilized countries are accordingly being rapidly superseded by vast and skillfully organized establishments — and in Great Britain and Europe by cooperative associations — which can sell at little over wholesale prices a great variety of merchandise, dry goods, manufactures of leather, books, stationery, furs, ready-made clothing, hats and caps, and sometimes groceries and hardware, and at the same time give their customers far greater conveniences than can be offered by the ordinary shopkeeper or tradesman. . . .

The spirit of progress conjoined with capital, and having in view economy in distribution and the equalization of values, is therefore controlling and concentrating the business of retailing in the same manner as the business of wholesale distribution and transportation, and of production by machinery, is being controlled and concentrated, and all to an extent never before known in the world's experience. And in both wholesale and retail operations the reduction of profits is so general that it must be accepted as a permanent feature of the business situation and a natural result of the new conditions that have been noted.

Keeping economy in distribution constantly in view as an essential for material progress, the tendency is also everywhere to dispense to the greatest extent with the "middleman," and put the locomotive and the telegraph in his place. Retail grocers . . . now buy their teas directly of the Chinaman and dispense with the services of the East Indian merchant and his warehouses. Manufacturers deal more directly with retailers, with the result, it is claimed, of steadying supply and demand and preventing the recurrence of business crises. The English cotton spinner at Manchester buys his raw cotton by cable in the interior towns of the cotton-growing states of North America and dispenses with the services of the American broker or commission merchant. European manufacturers now send their agents with samples of merchandise to almost every locality in America, Asia, and the Pacific Islands, where commerce is protected and transportation practicable, and offer supplies, even in comparatively small quantities, on better terms than dealers and consumers can obtain from the established wholesale or retail merchants of their vicinity.

A woolen manufacturer, for example, prepares a set of patterns for an ensuing season, sends his agent around the world with them, and makes exactly as many pieces as his customers want, not weaving a single yard for chance sale. A great importing house will take orders for goods to be delivered two or three months afterward, and import exactly what is ordered and no more. Rent, insurance, handling, and profits are thus minimized. Before the days of railroad extension, country buyers used to have to come to the centers of trade in spring and fall to lay in their supplies; now they come every month, if they wish, to assort a stock which is on an average much less heavy than it used to be and can be replenished by the dealer at very short notice by telegraph to the manufacturer, whether he resides at home or beyond an ocean.

The great dry-goods houses of the large commercial cities are in turn reducing their storage and becoming mere salesrooms, the merchandise marketed by them being forwarded directly from the point of manufacture to that of distribution. A commission house may, therefore, carry on a large business and yet not appear to the public to be extensively occupied. One not inconsiderable gain from such a change in goods distribution accrues from a consequent reduction in the high rates and aggregates of city fire insurances.

From these specimen experiences it is clear that an almost total revolution has taken place, and is yet in progress, in every branch and in every relation of the world's industrial and commercial system. Some of these changes have been eminently destruc-

tive, and all of them have inevitably occasioned, and for a long time yet will continue to occasion, great disturbances in old methods and entail losses of capital and changes of occupation on the part of individuals. And yet the world wonders, and commissions of great states inquire, without coming to definite conclusions, why trade and industry in recent years have been universally and abnormally disturbed and depressed.

There is one curious example in which improvement is being sought for at the present time, though what at first seems to be retrogression. With the great extension and perfecting of the railway system, and the consequent great reduction in the cost of merchandise carriage through its agency, it has been generally assumed that there was no longer any necessity for long lines of canals, or profit in their maintenance and operation; and, as a matter of fact, many canals of expensive construction in England and the United States have been absolutely abandoned. But at the present time there is a tendency — especially in Europe — to return to the use of inland navigation — canals and rivers — for the purpose of still further cheapening transportation. . . .

In the United States the resuscitation of the decayed canal system of transportation has not as yet been considered as desirable, and probably because the average charges for railroad freight service is considerably below the average rates of any other country in the world; although other nations have nominally cheaper labor and far denser populations.

Typewriters quotha! They are as bad as postal cards. Both of them are unclean things I have never touched. . . . I could never say what I would if I had to pick out my letters like a learned pig.
JAMES RUSSELL LOWELL, letter to Mrs. W. K. Clifford, June 11, 1889

52.

Richard T. Ely: The Needs of the City

Reform of municipal government was a principal concern of the late nineteenth century Progressive movement. Rapid growth and poor organization, coupled with large immigrant communities loyal to powerful political bosses, created in city government seemingly endless opportunities for corruption and graft. The cities of that era, Andrew White charged in 1890, were "the worst in Christendom — the most expensive, the most inefficient, and the most corrupt." In December 1889, Richard Ely, a dissenter from the classical school of economics and laissez faire policy, addressed himself to urban problems in a lecture given at the Boston Conference of the Evangelical Alliance, entitled The Needs of the City, *parts of which follow.*

Source: *The Needs of the City,* n.p., n.d., pp. 3-14.

WHAT ARE THE NEEDS OF THE CITY?

1. First of all, I would mention this need, a profound revival of religion, not in any narrow or technical sense but in the broadest, largest, fullest sense; a great religious awakening which shall shake things, going down into the depths of men's lives and modifying their character. The city needs religion, and without religion the salvation of the city is impossible. . . .

2. The second great need of the city — which is the first need restated from a different point of view — is a renaissance of nationalism, or, if you will to narrow it down to our present theme, *municipalism.* Government is the God-given agency through which we must work. To many, I am aware, this is not a welcome word, but it is a true word. We may twist and turn as long as we please, but we are bound to come back to a recognition of this truth. Societies have failed. Society, particularly as organized in city councils or city governments — to adopt what is with us the more comprehensive designation — must

recognize the work we want done as the concern of the community and must themselves do it. . . .

Societies have failed and will fail. They cannot, acting simply as societies, do the work. Their resources are inadequate, the territory they can cover is too small, and their power is insufficient. The Evangelical Alliance simply as such can never do the work. The Evangelical Alliance, like other societies, must put itself behind municipal government and recognize the reform and elevation of municipal government as one of the chief features of its work. It must strive to establish among us true cities of God. There is plenty of room for the individual and for individual activity. Not all the work can be done by government, although without government very little can be accomplished. But in addition to strictly private work, there is room for any amount of individual work in stimulating official work and in cooperation with official work.

We must recognize this, and the sooner we recognize it the better. This doctrine was long resisted in the matter of popular education, but now its recognition in this department of life is universal. In all the world's history we have never had anything like universal education, save when and where government has furnished it. How long and arduously have people with us (and more arduously and still longer in England) tried with private means to educate the people, and how ineffectually! But when your Horace Mann comes forward and convinces the people that "voluntary work is most effective when it is in connection with official work," then indeed the people's cause moves forward.

We need today in our cities new men to arise and to preach this doctrine with the apostolic zeal of Horace Mann. Not more private schools are needed but the better maintenance of such as exist, and otherwise the use of private means to stimulate public endeavor. This is, I am happy to say, being done to some extent. As I understand it, this is what the trustees of the Peabody and Slater funds are most wisely trying to do.

It takes a great effort and persistent, unflagging zeal to keep alive a few industrial schools like those which Mr. Brace has established in New York. He has my admiration for his great work, but I cannot help asking the question, if a little more energy had been used in stimulating public authorities and cooperating with them, would not greater things have been accomplished? Shameful, incredibly disgraceful as it may be to the authorities of New York City, 14,000 children in that city were this fall turned from the doors of the public schools because there was not room for them. Now, with 200 children to a school, it would take 70 private schools to educate these children, whereas the energy and zeal necessary to support ten such schools, expended in enlightening the public and stimulating the conscience of the municipal authorities, would have rendered this criminal record an impossibility.

Mr. Jacob A. Riis has written an article on the tenement-house population of New York, which appeared in *Scribner's Magazine* for December 1889. It is called "How the Other Half Lives," and is a noteworthy article. One passage in it shows the ineffectiveness of private work dissociated from official work or inadequately supported by legislation and administration. It is as follows: "The ten-cent lodging houses more than counterbalance the good done by the free reading room, lectures, and all other agencies of reform. Such lodging houses have caused more destitution, more beggary and crime than any other agency I know of." Mr. Riis quotes this from one of the justices on the Police Court bench.

Now these lodging houses can never in the world be abolished by private effort. Insufficient as it has been, public authority, I believe, has already done more to improve the dwellings of the poor than all private agencies combined. But we want a cooperation of both. "The first practical work is to rouse the town councils to the sense of their powers; to make them feel that their duty is not to protect the pockets of the rich (by reducing taxes and turning children away from public schools as in New York) but to save the people." And "the care of the people is the care of the community and not of any philanthropic section." . . .

We need, then, two things, religion and nationalism. Put these together and we have religious nationalism. But is this not Christian socialism? Yes, it is in a certain sense, and I rejoice in the growth here in Boston — I may say frankly — of nationalism and Christian socialism. It is not that I accept all the principles of those who support these movements. I must with equal frankness say that I can only go part way with them, for I think they go too far. I do think, however, and I do not hesitate to say that I think that today they are the leaven which is needed in American society, and as I fear nothing from those doctrines of theirs which strike me as extreme, I rejoice in their activity. Christian socialism — if you will take it in my conservative sense — is what I think we need; that is, religion coupled with true nationalism.

An objection may be raised here on account of the poor character of our government of cities. Of course our governments are poor. Why should they not be? We have done everything to make them so. We have been taught to turn away from government for the accomplishment of business purposes and for social improvement. We have been trying to reduce government to a contemptible insignificance, and in many cases have succeeded in reducing it to contemptible impotence. Lest men should do some wrong thing, we have made it impossible for them to do any good thing. We have succeeded in turning the energy and talent of the community, for the most part, away from public life and diverted the great bulk of talent and energy into private life. We have reaped the legitimate fruits that might have been expected, one is tempted to say, which have been deserved.

Government never in the world's history has been made good government by the application of the maxim, "That is the best government that governs least." It never will be made good by reducing it to insignificance. It is, as a matter of fact, the opposite policy which has made good government whenever and wherever good government has existed.

You have read about the cathedral building 400, 500, and 600 years ago. How could our ancestors in those times, in some respects so rude, accomplish such matchless marvels in cathedral building? Simply by putting their souls into the work. Similarly, when we put some portion of our intellectual and spiritual resources into the duties of government, recognizing the nation as church, we shall have good government.

We are considering the needs of the city. But this means an increasing proportion of the population, and, on the whole, I think we may rejoice that it does mean an ever increasing proportion of the population. The statistics of the increasing urban population throughout the civilized world have often been presented. We all know that one hundred years ago a thirtieth of the population of our country lived in cities, that now one-fourth live in cities, and that presently half of our population will be urban. This movement is inevitable. It is not due, as some think, in any considerable degree to the inclinations and desires of the people, but it is due to an economic force which is well-nigh as irresistible as the movements of the tide.

Let us cherish no utopian schemes of turning people back to the rural districts. Every new good road, every new canal, every new railway, every new invention, every economic improvement, in short, nearly all industrial progress centralizes the population in cities. It is on the whole good because man finds his welfare in association with his fellows; by nature, as Aristotle says, he is a social being; and city life makes a higher degree of association possible. This means progress of all kinds, if we are but equal to the increasing strains city life puts upon our civilization. . . .

ENUMERATION OF THINGS
NEEDED BY THE CITY

1. Let me first mention the means of education which should be liberally provided and which should, for the most part, be gratuitously offered. I do not speak simply of schools of the lower grades but of schools of all grades and of much besides schools. I would thus broaden the way to success and utilize all talent in the community. With these schools I would establish a sifting process so that only the more gifted should advance to higher grades. Such a scheme has already been working in New York state for some time. There are state scholarships, entitling the recipients to free tuition in Cornell University, and one of

them is offered for competition in each assembly district, each year. There are thus over 500 all told.

It may be that the ideal thing is a public educational system comprising all grades of school up to and inclusive of the university. . . . It seems, however, that in a state like Massachusetts the proper course is by means of such scholarships to connect the public schools with your academies, colleges, and universities, institutions like Amherst College, Clarke and Harvard universities, which are private foundations. I think a beginning has already been made in the Massachusetts Institute of Technology.

But public education does not begin early enough for the needs of the city. The majority of children in cities are under bad home influences, and free kindergartens should be a part of the school system. It is all very well to talk about the work of the family, but what about the majority of children in large cities for whom no wholesome family life exists? . . .

Industrial training ought to be made important everywhere, and I note with satisfaction the progress it is making in Boston. Mr. Brace speaks of industrial schools as the best agency for reforming the worst class of children in cities, and the experience of the Elmira Reformatory in New York shows that a majority even of young convicted criminals can be reformed by it when coupled with good discipline. We find that many criminals and paupers are uneducated and untrained in any trade. The apprenticeship system is antiquated, and city dwellings furnish no opportunity for girls to learn womanly occupations. Preparation for life must for all come from the school; for the many it is the only place whence it can come.

But our educational system should not cease to provide for people when they leave school. Education ought to end only with life. This brings me to mention such educational facilities as free libraries, free reading

Library of Congress

Richard T. Ely

rooms within convenient distance of every part of the city, perhaps in many cases attached to schoolhouses, and open after school hours.

University extension lectures ought to be provided, and Mr. Dewey of New York has been working on some large plans for extension lectures to be connected with the public schools of New York state and to be conducted under the auspices of the Board of Regents. Private undertakings, like Chautauqua, could well supplement whatever public authority does.

Schoolhouses should be better utilized as gathering places for clubs, debating societies, and all bodies of men who would give guarantee of proper behavior. Open in the evening, they would help to counteract the baleful influences of the saloon.

Art galleries and museums — which may multiply the value of pictures and other enjoyable articles a hundredfold by rendering them accessible to all — may be mentioned under this general head, and, in my opinion, they ought all to be open on Sunday. I do not believe in leaving a free field to the devil every seventh day.

It goes without the saying that religious education is an important part of all education and that the church should become more active than ever, and become to a greater extent than at present a real people's church. Church buildings also are not as fully utilized as they might be.

2. As a second item, and one closely connected, I mention playgrounds, parade grounds, playrooms, and gymnasiums. I would include universal military drill for boys and young men. Experienced educators will tell you what a remarkable agency physical drill is for the cultivation of good morals; half of the wrongdoings of young rascals in cities is due to the fact that they have no innocent outlet for their animal spirits.

3. The third item is free public baths and public washhouses like those which in Glasgow have proved so successful.

4. The fourth item is public gardens and parks and good open-air music.

5. Very important in all large cities is an improvement of artisans' dwellings and the housing of the poor generally. All those who work among the poor, speak about the great obstacle to reform and improvement found in rent. . . . A lady working in connection with the charity organization of Baltimore spoke of it thus a few days since in conversation: "Rent, oh, that is the dreadful thing! The rent of the poor just goes on increasing all the time. So do their appetites, but these have to wait while the rent has to be paid!"

I cannot speak of the many things which can be done and which are being done to improve the housing of the poorer urban classes. One of the most promising reforms, it seems to me, is to obey the law and assess all unimproved city land up to its full value, the very last dollar of its value, and then exempt all new dwellings from taxation for a period of five years. A somewhat similar plan appears to have produced excellent results in Vienna. Of course, this alone is not sufficient.

6. My sixth item is complete municipalization of markets and slaughterhouses, rendering food inspection easier and more thorough.

7. The seventh item is organized medical relief, rendering medical attendance and medicines accessible to the poor without a sacrifice of self-respect and independence. . . . I think the Johns Hopkins Hospital in Baltimore is likely to contribute something to the solution of this problem.

8. Poor relief ought to be better organized, almshouses should be workhouses and workhouses should be industrial schools. We may consider in this connection an extension of public and private pensions, and I was glad recently to notice remarks on this subject by President Eliot of Harvard University. Anyone may witness in Germany the beneficial effects of an extensive pension system. It is a great economy of resources, as smaller salaries are sufficient under a pension system; it diminishes poverty and pauperism and thus relieves the public treasuries. It prevents anxiety and checks the greed begotten of uncertainty. An extension of the principle of insurance is desirable for similar reasons.

9. The ninth item is improved sanitary legislation and administration. Great strides have already been made in this direction, but probably the urban death rate among children of the poor under five years of age could still be reduced one-half.

10. The next item is a better regulation of the liquor traffic where its suppression is impossible. I think something better than high license is practicable, and I have worked out a system, which I have called modified prohibition, and I must be allowed on account of lack of time to refer you to my treatment of this subject in my book, *Taxation in American States and Cities.* I would include local option in wards

and full payment for every privilege to sell intoxicating beverages. To limit the number of saloons, as in Boston, Pittsburgh, and elsewhere, and then to give licenses for a fixed sum is a crying injustice to all who are refused licenses. Such licenses should be sold at auction.

But temperance reform ought to include positive measures as well as negative, and how effective positive measures are, Mr. Brace's book amply demonstrates. The use of town halls and schoolrooms for political and other gatherings in England has proved a good temperance measure. Do not simply drive out the saloon; replace it.

11. Municipal savings banks. Such institutions have produced most gratifying results in many German cities. Deposits should be invested in city bonds and other good securities. The investment in city bonds would tend to give depositors a realizing sense of what they have at stake in municipal government.

12. Ownership and management by the city of natural monopolies of a local character, like electric lights, gasworks, streetcar lines, docks, etc. Read Dr. Shaw on the excellent results accomplished elsewhere, notably in Glasgow, by this policy.

I will not enumerate further items in this connection. I have already said that the individual force and energy of citizens should be used to inaugurate and carry out these reforms. I would utilize in a higher degree than heretofore the help of women. Police matrons have done something for one class of our urban population in several American cities, and in Glasgow, lady health inspectors have proved an efficient adjunct to the Health Department. Lady members of school boards have done good service in several cities.

We should also have private associations of women to insist on the enforcement of law. Something has been done in New York by The Ladies Health Protective Association, which aims to secure enforcement of sanitary legislation and to insist on a proper street-cleaning service. We ought also to have in every city ladies' public educational associations to stimulate the educational authorities and to see that the last letter of the law is obeyed; in New York, for instance, see that schoolhouses are provided for all children and that the compulsory educational law is enforced.

We should also have businessmen's associations, clergymen's associations, and the like, all to help to make the life of public servants who neglect their duty a burden to them.

RESOURCES FOR THESE REFORMS

WHENCE SHALL COME the resources for these reforms? I have already given the answer. A moderate and conservative nationalism will provide resources. It is simply necessary to utilize public resources. Comptroller Myers of New York recently said that he could pay all the expenses of the city government from dock rents, miscellaneous receipts, and the annual value of streetcar and other similar franchises. Berlin pays over 15 percent of its expenses from the profits of gasworks; Richmond, Va., when I last looked at the report, about 7 percent. We have also electric lighting as a source of revenue. Then we have plans . . . for securing a portion of the increment of city real estate for the public, and that without depriving anyone of his property rights. Inheritances, and particularly collateral inheritances, may be taxed, and intestate collateral inheritances might be even abolished.

Resources for every needed reform can be found in abundance whenever any honest search is made for them. We have yet no adequate idea of the public resources of a great city.

1889-1890

53.

The Negro in the Post-Reconstruction Era

*The period of Reconstruction, which was effectively terminated by the recall of the
last federal troops from the Southern states in 1877, saw only a slight improvement
of economic conditions from the all but total devastation left by the Civil War.
By 1890 the white "Bourbon" class had regained political control of many state
legislatures from the Negroes and sought to revitalize the Southern economy through
partnership with the North, diversification of agriculture, and development of untapped
natural resources. Henry W. Grady, editor of the* Atlanta Constitution *and a leading
proponent of what he called the "New South," courted the industrialists in a number of
speeches delivered in large Northern cities. In the speech reprinted here, addressed
in December 1889 to the Boston Merchants' Association, Grady outlined the role of
the Southern free Negro in this "new" economy. Grady's thinly veiled belief in the
natural inferiority of the Negro prompted the Reverend Joshua A. Brockett, of
St. Paul's A.M.E. Church, Cambridge, to reply to Grady's address in January 1890.*

Source: *The Complete Orations and Speeches of Henry W. Grady,*
Edwin DuBois Shurter, ed., New York, 1910, pp. 192-220.
Philadelphia Christian Recorder, January 16, 1890.

I.

Henry W. Grady:
The New South

Happy am I that this mission has brought
my feet at last to press New England's historic soil and my eyes to the knowledge of
her beauty and her thrift. Here, within
touch of Plymouth Rock and Bunker Hill,
where Webster thundered and Longfellow
sang, Emerson thought and Channing
preached, here in the cradle of American
letters, and almost of American liberty, I
hasten to make the obeisance that every
American owes New England when first he
stands uncovered in her mighty presence.
Strange apparition! This stern and unique
figure, carved from the ocean and the wilderness, its majesty kindling and growing
amid the storms of winters and of wars, until at last the gloom was broken, its beauty
disclosed in the sunshine, and the heroic
workers rested at its base, while startled
kings and emperors gazed and marveled
that from the rude touch of this handful,

cast on a bleak and unknown shore, should have come the embodied genius of human government and the perfected model of human liberty! God bless the memory of those immortal workers and prosper the fortunes of their living sons and perpetuate the inspirations of their handiwork.

Two years ago, sir, I spoke some words in New York that caught the attention of the North. As I stand here to reiterate, as I have done everywhere, every word I then uttered — to declare that the sentiments I then avowed were universally approved in the South — I realize that the confidence begotten by that speech is largely responsible for my presence here tonight. I should dishonor myself if I betrayed that confidence by uttering one insincere word or by withholding one essential element of the truth.

Apropos of this last, let me confess, Mr. President — before the praise of New England has died on my lips — that I believe the best product of her present life is the procession of 17,000 Vermont Democrats, that for twenty-two years, undiminished by death, unrecruited by birth or conversion, have marched over their rugged hills, cast their Democratic ballots, and gone back home to pray for their unregenerate neighbors, and awake to read the record of 25,000 Republican majority. May God of the helpless and the heroic help them, and may their sturdy tribe increase!

Far to the South, Mr. President, separated from this section by a line, once defined in irrepressible difference, once traced in fratricidal blood, and now, thank God, but a vanishing shadow, lies the fairest and richest domain of this earth. It is the home of a brave and hospitable people. There, is centered all that can please or prosper humankind. A perfect climate above a fertile soil yields to the husbandman every product of the Temperate Zone. There, by night, the cotton whitens beneath the stars, and, by day, the wheat locks the sunshine in its

bearded sheaf. In the same field the clover steals the fragrance of the wind, and the tobacco catches the quick aroma of the rains. There, are mountains stored with exhaustless treasures; forests, vast and primeval, and rivers that, tumbling or loitering, run wanton to the sea.

Of the three essential items of all industries — cotton, iron, and wool — that region has easy control. In cotton, a fixed monopoly; in iron, proven supremacy; in timber, the reserve supply of the republic. From this assured and permanent advantage, against which artificial conditions cannot much longer prevail, has grown an amazing system of industries. Not maintained by human contrivance of tariff or capital, afar off from the fullest and cheapest source of supply, but resting in divine assurance, within touch of field and mine and forest; not set amid costly farms from which competition has driven the farmer in despair, but amid cheap and sunny lands, rich with agriculture, to which neither season nor soil has set a limit — this system of industries is mounting to a splendor that shall dazzle and illumine the world.

That, sir, is the picture and the promise of my home — a land better and fairer than I have told you, and yet but fit setting, in its material excellence, for the loyal and gentle quality of its citizenship. Against that, sir, we have New England, recruiting the republic from its sturdy loins, shaking from its overcrowded hives new swarms of workers, and touching this land all over with its energy and its courage. And yet, while in the El Dorado of which I have told you, but 15 percent of lands are cultivated, its mines scarcely touched, and its population so scant that, were it set equidistant, the sound of the human voice could not be heard from Virginia to Texas.

While on the threshold of nearly every house in New England stands a son, seeking with troubled eyes some new land to which to carry his modest patrimony, the strange fact remains that in 1880 the South had fewer Northern-born citizens than she had in 1870; fewer in '70 than in '60. Why is this? Why is it, sir, though the sectional line be now but a mist that the breath may dispel, fewer men of the North have crossed it over to the South than when it was crimson with the best blood of the republic, or even when the slaveholder stood guard every inch of its way?

There can be but one answer. It is the very problem we are now to consider. The key that opens that problem will unlock to the world the fairer half of this republic, and free the halted feet of thousands whose eyes are already kindled with its beauty. Better than this, it will open the hearts of brothers for thirty years estranged, and clasp in lasting comradeship a million hands now withheld in doubt. Nothing, sir, but this problem, and the suspicions it breeds, hinders a clear understanding and a perfect union. Nothing else stands between us and such love as bound Georgia and Massachusetts at Valley Forge and Yorktown, chastened by the sacrifices at Manassas and Gettysburg, and illumined with the coming of better work and a nobler destiny than was ever wrought with the sword or sought at the cannon's mouth.

If this does not invite your patient hearing tonight, hear one thing more. My people, your brothers in the South — brothers in blood, in destiny, in all that is best in our past and future — are so beset with this problem that their very existence depends upon its right solution. Nor are they wholly to blame for its presence. The slave ships of the republic sailed from your ports, the slaves worked in our fields. You will not defend the traffic, nor I the institution. But I do hereby declare that in its wise and humane administration, in lifting the slave to heights of which he had not dreamed in his savage home, and giving him a happiness he has not yet found in

freedom, our fathers left their sons a saving and excellent heritage. In the storm of war this institution was lost. I thank God as heartily as you do that human slavery is gone forever from the American soil.

But the freedman remains. With him a problem without precedent or parallel. Note its appalling conditions. Two utterly dissimilar races on the same soil; with equal political and civil rights, almost equal in numbers but terribly unequal in intelligence and responsibility; each pledged against fusion, one for a century in servitude to the other and freed at last by a desolating war; the experiment sought by neither, but approached by both with doubt — these are the conditions. Under these, adverse at every point, we are required to carry these two races in peace and honor to the end. Never, sir, has such a task been given to mortal stewardship. Never before in this republic has the white race divided on the rights of an alien race. The red man was cut down as a weed because he hindered the way of the American citizen. The yellow man was shut out of this republic because he is an alien and inferior. The red man was owner of the land, the yellow man highly civilized and assimilable — but they hindered both sections and are gone!

But the black man, affecting but one section, is clothed with every privilege of government and pinned to the soil, and my people commanded to make good at any hazard and at any cost, his full and equal heirship of American privilege and prosperity. . . . It matters not that wherever the whites and blacks have touched, in any era or any clime, there has been irreconcilable violence. It matters not that no two races, however similar, have lived anywhere, at any time, on the same soil with equal rights in peace. In spite of these things we are commanded to make good this change of American policy which has not perhaps changed American prejudice; to make certain here what has elsewhere been impossible between whites and blacks; and to reverse, under the very worst conditions, the universal verdict of racial history. And driven, sir, to this superhuman task with an impatience that brooks no delay, a rigor that accepts no excuse, and a suspicion that discourages frankness and sincerity.

We do not shrink from this trial. It is so interwoven with our industrial fabric that we cannot disentangle it if we would; so bound up in our honorable obligation to the world, that we would not if we could. Can we solve it? The God who gave it into our hands, He alone can know. But this the weakest and wisest of us do know; we cannot solve it with less than your tolerant and patient sympathy — with less than the knowledge that the blood that runs in your veins is our blood — and that when we have done our best, whether the issue be lost or won, we shall feel your strong arms about us and hear the beating of your approving hearts.

The resolute, clear-headed, broad-minded men of the South — the men whose genius made glorious every page of the first seventy years of American history, whose courage and fortitude you tested in five years of the fiercest war, whose energy has made bricks without straw and spread splendor amid the ashes of their war-wasted homes — these men wear this problem in their hearts and their brains, by day and by night. They realize, as you cannot, what this problem means, what they owe to this kindly and dependent race, the measure of their debt to the world in whose despite they defended and maintained slavery. And though their feet are hindered in its undergrowth and their march encumbered with its burdens, they have lost neither the patience from which comes clearness nor the faith from which comes courage. Nor, sir, when in passionate moments is disclosed to them that vague and awful shadow, with its lurid abysses and its crimson stains, into which I pray God they may never go, are they

struck with more of apprehension than is needed to complete their consecration!

Such is the temper of my people. But what of the problem itself? Mr. President, we need not go one step further unless you concede right here the people I speak for are as honest, as sensible, and as just as your people, seeking as earnestly as you would in their place rightly to solve the problem that touches them at every vital point. If you insist that they are ruffians, blindly striving with bludgeon and shotgun to plunder and oppress a race, then I shall sacrifice my self-respect and tax your patience in vain. But admit that they are men of common sense and common honesty, wisely modifying an environment they cannot wholly disregard, guiding and controlling as best they can the vicious and irresponsible of either race, compensating error with frankness and retrieving in patience what they lose in passion, and conscious all the time that wrong means ruin — admit this and we may reach an understanding tonight.

The President of the United States in his late message to Congress, discussing the plea that the South should be left to solve this problem, asks: "Are they at work upon it? What solution do they offer? When will the black man cast a free ballot? When will he have the civil rights that are his?" I shall not here protest against the partisanry that, for the first time in our history in time of peace, has stamped with the great seal of our government a stigma upon the people of a great and loyal section; though I gratefully remember that the great dead soldier, who held the helm of state for the eight stormy years of Reconstruction, never found need for such a step; and though there is no personal sacrifice I would not make to remove this cruel and unjust imputation on my people from the archives of my country!

But, sir, backed by a record on every page of which is progress, I venture to make earnest and respectful answer to the questions that are asked. I bespeak your patience, while with vigorous plainness of speech, seeking your judgment rather than your applause, I proceed step by step.

We give to the world this year a crop of 7,500,000 bales of cotton, worth $45 million, and its cash equivalent in grain, grasses, and fruit. This enormous crop could not have come from the hands of sullen and discontented labor. It comes from peaceful fields, in which laughter and gossip rise above the hum of industry and contentment runs with the singing plow.

It is claimed that this ignorant labor is defrauded of its just hire. I present the tax books of Georgia, which show that the Negro, twenty-five years ago a slave, has in Georgia alone $10 million of assessed property, worth twice that much. Does not that record honor him and vindicate his neighbors? What people, penniless, illiterate, has done so well? For every Afro-American agitator, stirring the strife in which alone he prospers, I can show you a thousand Negroes, happy in their cabin homes, tilling their own land by day, and at night taking from the lips of their children the helpful message their state sends them from the schoolhouse door.

And the schoolhouse itself bears testimony. In Georgia we added last year $250,000 to the school fund, making a total of more than $1 million — and this in the face of prejudice not yet conquered — of the fact that the whites are assessed for $368 million, the blacks for $10 million, and yet 49 percent of the beneficiaries are black children — and in the doubt of many wise men if education helps, or can help, our problem. Charleston, with her taxable values cut half in two since 1860, pays more in proportion for public schools than Boston. Although it is easier to give much out of much than little out of little, the South, with one-seventh of the taxable property of the country, with relatively larger debt, hav-

ing received only one-twelfth as much public land, and having back of its tax books none of the $500 million of bonds that enrich the North — and though it pays annually $26 million to your section as pensions — yet gives nearly one-sixth of the public-school fund. The South since 1865 has spent $122 million in education, and this year is pledged to $37 million for state and city schools, although the blacks, paying one-thirtieth of the taxes, get nearly one-half of the fund.

Go into our fields and see whites and blacks working side by side, on our buildings in the same squad, in our shops at the same forge. Often the blacks crowd the whites from work, or lower wages by greater need or simpler habits, and yet are permitted because we want to bar them from no avenue in which their feet are fitted to tread. They could not there be elected orators of the white universities, as they have been here, but they do enter there a hundred useful trades that are closed against them here. We hold it better and wiser to tend the weeds in the garden than to water the exotic in the window.

In the South, there are Negro lawyers, teachers, editors, dentists, doctors, preachers, multiplying with the increasing ability of their race to support them. In villages and towns they have their military companies equipped from the armories of the state, their churches and societies built and supported largely by their neighbors. What is the testimony of the courts? In penal legislation we have steadily reduced felonies to misdemeanors, and have led the world in mitigating punishment for crime that we might save, as far as possible, this dependent race from its own weakness. In our penitentiary record 60 percent of the prosecutors are Negroes, and in every court the Negro criminal strikes the colored juror, that white men may judge his case. In the North, one Negro in every 466 is in jail; in the South only one in 1,865. In the North the percentage of Negro prisoners is six times as great as native whites; in the South, only four times as great. If prejudice wrongs him in Southern courts, the record shows it to be deeper in Northern courts.

I assert here, and a bar as intelligent and upright as the bar of Massachusetts will solemnly endorse my assertion, that in the Southern courts, from highest to lowest, pleading for life, liberty, or property, the Negro has distinct advantage because he is a Negro, apt to be overreached, oppressed; and that this advantage reaches from the juror in making his verdict to the judge in measuring his sentence. Now, Mr. President, can it be seriously maintained that we are terrorizing the people from whose willing hands come every year $1 billion of farm crops? Or have robbed a people, who twenty-five years from unrewarded slavery have amassed in one state $20 million of property?

Or that we intend to oppress the people we are arming every day? Or deceive them when we are educating them to the utmost limit of our ability? Or outlaw them when we work side by side with them? Or reenslave them under legal forms when for their benefit we have even imprudently narrowed the limit of felonies and mitigated the severity of law? My fellow countryman, as you yourself may sometimes have to appeal to the bar of human judgment for justice and for right, give to my people tonight the fair and unanswerable conclusion of these incontestible facts.

But it is claimed that under this fair-seeming there is disorder and violence. This I admit. And there will be until there is one ideal community on earth after which we may pattern. But how widely it is misjudged! It is hard to measure with exactness whatever touches the Negro. His helplessness, his isolation, his century of servitude — these dispose us to emphasize and magnify his wrongs. This disposition inflamed by prejudice and partisanry has led to injustice and delusion. Lawless men may ravage a county in Iowa and it is accepted as an incident; in the South a drunken row is declared to be the fixed habit of the community. Regulators may whip vagabonds in Indiana by platoons and it scarcely arrests attention; a chance collision in the South among relatively the same classes is gravely accepted as evidence that one race is destroying the other. We might as well claim that the Union was ungrateful to the colored soldiers who followed its flag because a Grand Army post in Connecticut closed its doors to a Negro veteran, as for you to give racial significance to every incident in the South or to accept exceptional grounds as the rule of our society.

I am not one of those who becloud American honor with the parade of the outrages of either section, and belie American character by declaring them to be significant and representative. I prefer to maintain that they are neither, and stand for nothing but the passion and the sin of our poor fallen humanity. If society, like a machine, were no stronger than its weakest part, I should despair of both sections. But, knowing that society, sentient and responsible in every fiber, can mend and repair until the whole has the strength of the best, I despair of neither.

These gentlemen who come with me here, knit into Georgia's busy life as they are, never saw, I dare assert, an outrage committed on a Negro! And if they did, not one of you would be swifter to prevent or punish. It is through them, and the men who think with them — making nine-tenths of every Southern community — that these two races have been carried thus far with less of violence than would have been possible anywhere else on earth. And in their fairness and courage and steadfastness — more than in all the laws that can be passed or all the bayonets that can be mustered — is the hope of our future.

When will the black cast a free ballot?

When ignorance anywhere is not dominated by the will of the intelligent; when the laborer anywhere casts a vote unhindered by his boss; when the vote of the poor anywhere is not influenced by the power of the rich; when the strong and the steadfast do not everywhere control the suffrage of the weak and shiftless — then and not till then will the ballot of the Negro be free.

The white people of the South are banded, Mr. President, not in prejudice against the blacks, not in sectional estrangement, not in the hope of political dominion, but in a deep and abiding necessity. Here is this vast ignorant and purchasable vote — clannish, credulous, impulsive, and passionate — tempting every art of the demagogue, but insensible to the appeal of the statesman. Wrongly started, in that it was led into alienation from its neighbor and taught to rely on the protection of an outside force, it cannot be merged and lost in the two great parties through logical currents, for it lacks political conviction and even that information on which conviction must be based. It must remain a faction, strong enough in every community to control on the slightest division of the whites. Under that division it becomes the prey of the cunning and unscrupulous of both parties. Its credulity is imposed on, its patience inflamed, its cupidity tempted, its impulses misdirected, and even its superstition made to play its part in a campaign in which every interest of society is jeopardized and every approach to the ballot box debauched.

It is against such campaigns as this — the folly and the bitterness and the danger of which every Southern community has drunk deeply — that the white people of the South are banded together. Just as you in Massachusetts would be banded if 300,000 black men — not one in a hundred able to read his ballot — banded in a race instinct, holding against you the memory of a century of slavery, taught by your late conquerors to distrust and oppose you,

had already travestied legislation from your statehouse, and in every species of folly or villainy had wasted your substance and exhausted your credit.

But admitting the right of the whites to unite against this tremendous menace, we are challenged with the smallness of our vote. This has long been flippantly charged to be evidence, and has now been solemnly and officially declared to be proof of political turpitude and baseness on our part. Let us see. Virginia — a state now under fierce assault for this alleged crime — cast, in 1888, 75 percent of her vote. Massachusetts, the state in which I speak, 60 percent of her vote. Was it suppression in Virginia and natural causes in Massachusetts? Last month Virginia cast 69 percent of her vote, and Massachusetts, fighting in every district, cast only 49 percent of hers. If Virginia is condemned because 31 percent of her vote was silent, how shall this state escape in which 51 percent was dumb?

Let us enlarge this comparison. The sixteen Southern states in 1888 cast 67 percent of their total vote, the six New England states but 63 percent of theirs. By what fair rule shall the stigma be put upon one section, while the other escapes? A congressional election in New York last week, with the polling place within touch of every voter, brought out only 6,000 votes of 28,000, and the lack of opposition is assigned as the natural cause. In a district in my state, in which an opposition speech has not been heard in ten years, and the polling places are miles apart, under the unfair reasoning of which my section has been a constant victim, the small vote is charged to be proof of forcible suppression. In Virginia an average majority of 10,000 under hopeless division of the minority, was raised to 42,000; in Iowa, in the same election, a majority of 32,000 was wiped out, and an opposition majority of 8,000 was established. The change of 42,000 votes in Iowa is accepted as political revolution, in Virginia an increase of 30,000 on a safe majority is declared to be proof of political fraud.

I charge these facts and figures home, sir, to the heart and conscience of the American people, who will not assuredly see one section condemned for what another section is excused! If I can drive them through the prejudice of the partisan, and have them read and pondered at the fireside of the citizen, I will rest on the judgment there formed and the verdict there rendered!

It is deplorable, sir, that in both sections a larger percentage of the vote is not regularly cast, but more inexplicable that this should be so in New England than in the South. What invites the Negro to the ballot box? He knows that, of all men, it has promised him most and yielded him least. His first appeal to suffrage was the promise of "forty acres and a mule." His second, the threat that Democratic success meant his reenslavement. Both have proved false in his experience. He looked for a home, and he got the freedman's bank. He fought under the promise of the loaf, and in victory was denied the crumbs. Discouraged and deceived, he has realized at last that his best friends are his neighbors, with whom his lot is cast, and whose prosperity is bound up in his, and that he has gained nothing in politics to compensate the loss of their confidence and sympathy that is at last his best and his enduring hope. And so, without leaders or organization — and lacking the resolute heroism of my party friends in Vermont that makes their hopeless march over the hills a high and inspiring pilgrimage — he shrewdly measures the occasional agitator, balances his little account with politics, touches up his mule, and jogs down the furrow, letting the mad world jog as it will!

The Negro vote can never control in the South, and it would be well if partisans in the North would understand this. I have seen the white people of a state set about by black hosts until their fate seemed

sealed. But, sir, some brave man, banding them together, would rise, as Elisha rose in beleaguered Samaria, and touching their eyes with faith, bid them look abroad to see the very air "filled with the chariots of Israel and the horsemen thereof." If there is any human force that cannot be withstood, it is the power of the banded intelligence and responsibility of a free community. Against it, numbers and corruption cannot prevail. It cannot be forbidden in the law or divorced in force. It is the inalienable right of every free community, and the just and righteous safeguard against an ignorant or corrupt suffrage. It is on this, sir, that we rely in the South. Not the cowardly menace of mask or shotgun; but the peaceful majesty of intelligence and responsibility, massed and unified for the protection of its homes and the preservation of its liberty. That, sir, is our reliance and our hope, and against it all the powers of the earth shall not prevail.

It was just as certain that Virginia would come back to the unchallenged control of her white race, that before the moral and material power of her people once more unified, opposition would crumble until its last desperate leader was left alone vainly striving to rally his disordered hosts, as that night should fade in the kindling glory of the sun. You may pass force bills, but they will not avail. You may surrender your own liberties to federal election law, you may submit, in fear of a necessity that does not exist, that the very form of this government may be changed, this old state that holds in its charter the boast that "it is a free and independent commonwealth," it may deliver its election machinery into the hands of the government it helped to create, but never, sir, will a single state of this Union, North or South, be delivered again to the control of an ignorant and inferior race. We wrested our state government from Negro supremacy when the federal drumbeat rolled closer to the ballot box and federal bayonets hedged it deeper about than will ever again be permitted in this free government. But, sir, though the cannon of this republic thundered in every voting district of the South, we still should find in the mercy of God the means and the courage to prevent its reestablishment!

I regret, sir, that my section, hindered with this problem, stands in seeming estrangement to the North. If, sir, any man will point out to me a path down which the white people of the South divided may walk in peace and honor, I will take that path though I take it alone — for at the end, and nowhere else, I fear, is to be found the full prosperity of my section and the full restoration of this Union. But, sir, if the Negro had not been enfranchised, the South would have been divided and the republic united. . . . What solution, then, can we offer for this problem? Time alone can disclose it to us. We simply report progress and ask your patience. If the problem be solved at all — and I firmly believe it will, though nowhere else has it been — it will be solved by the people most deeply bound in interest, most deeply pledged in honor to its solution. I had rather see my people render back this question rightly solved than to see them gather all the spoils over which the faction has contended since Catiline conspired and Caesar fought.

Meantime we treat the Negro fairly, measuring to him justice in the fullness the strong should give to the weak, and leading him in the steadfast ways of citizenship that he may no longer be the prey of the unscrupulous and the sport of the thoughtless. We open to him every pursuit in which he can prosper, and seek to broaden his training and capacity. We seek to hold his confidence and friendship, and to pin him to the soil with ownership, that he may catch in the fire of his own hearthstone that sense of responsibility the shiftless can never know. And we gather him into that alliance of intelligence and responsibility that, though it now runs close to racial lines, welcomes the

responsible and intelligent of any race. By this course, confirmed in our judgment and justified in the progress already made, we hope to progress slowly but surely to the end.

The love we feel for that race you cannot measure nor comprehend. As I attest it here, the spirit of my old black mammy from her home up there looks down to bless, and through the tumult of this night steals the sweet music of her croonings as thirty years ago she held me in her black arms and led me smiling into sleep. This scene vanishes as I speak, and I catch a vision of an old Southern home, with its lofty pillars, and its white pigeons fluttering down through the golden air. I see women with strained and anxious faces and children alert yet helpless. I see night come down with its dangers and its apprehensions, and in a big homely room I feel on my tired head the touch of loving hands — now worn and wrinkled, but fairer to me yet than the hands of mortal woman, and stronger yet to lead me than the hands of mortal man — as they lay a mother's blessing there while at her knees, the truest altar I yet have found; I thank God that she is safe in her sanctuary, because her slaves, sentinel in the silent cabin or guard at her chamber door, put a black man's loyalty between her and danger.

I catch another vision. The crisis of battle: a soldier struck, staggering, fallen. I see a slave scuffling through the smoke, winding his black arms about the fallen form, reckless of the hurtling death, bending his trusty face to catch the words that tremble on the stricken lips, so wrestling meantime with agony that he would lay down his life in his master's stead. I see him by the weary bedside, ministering with uncomplaining patience, praying with all his humble heart that God will lift his master up, until death comes in mercy and in honor to still the soldier's agony and seal the soldier's life. I see him by the open grave, mute, motionless, uncovered, suffering for the death of him who in life fought against his freedom. I see him when the mound is heaped and the great drama of his life is closed, turn away and with downcast eyes and uncertain step start out into new and strange fields, faltering, struggling, but moving on, until his shambling figure is lost in the light of this better and brighter day. And from the grave comes a voice saying: "Follow him! Put your arms about him in his need, even as he put his about me. Be his friend as he was mine." And out into this new world — strange to me as to him, dazzling, bewildering both — I follow! And may God forget my people, when they forget these.

Whatever the future may hold for them, whether they plod along in the servitude from which they have never been lifted since the Cyrenian was laid hold upon by the Roman soldiers and made to bear the cross of the fainting Christ; whether they find homes again in Africa, and thus hasten the prophecy of the psalmist who said: "And suddenly Ethiopia shall hold out her hands unto God"; whether, forever dislocated and separated, they remain a weak people beset by stronger, and exist as the Turk, who lives in the jealousy rather than in the conscience of Europe; or whether in this miraculous republic they break through the caste of twenty centuries and, belying universal history, reach the full stature of citizenship, and in peace maintain it; we shall give them uttermost justice and abiding friendship. And whatever we do, into whatever seeming estrangement we may be driven, nothing shall disturb the love we bear this republic, or mitigate our consecration to its service.

I stand here, Mr. President, to profess no new loyalty. When General Lee, whose heart was the temple of our hopes and whose arm was clothed with our strength, renewed his allegiance to the government at Appomattox, he spoke from a heart too great to be false, and he spoke for every honest man from Maryland to Texas. From that day to this, Hamilcar has nowhere in the South sworn young Hannibal to hatred and vengeance — but everywhere to loyalty and to love. Witness the soldier standing at the base of a Confederate monument above the graves of his comrades, his empty sleeve tossing in the April wind, adjuring the young men about him to serve as honest and loyal citizens the government against which their fathers fought. This message, delivered from that sacred presence, has gone home to the hearts of my fellows! And, sir, I declare here, if physical courage be always equal to human aspiration, that they would die, sir, if need be, to restore this republic their fathers fought to dissolve!

Such, Mr. President, is this problem as we see it; such is the temper in which we approach it; such the progress made. What do we ask of you? First, patience; out of this alone can come perfect work. Second, confidence; in this alone can you judge fairly. Third, sympathy; in this you can help us best. Fourth, give us your sons as hostages. When you plant your capital in millions send your sons that they may help know how true are our hearts and help swell the Anglo-Saxon current until it can carry without danger this black infusion. Fifth, loyalty to the republic, for there is sectionalism in loyalty as in estrangement. This hour little needs the loyalty that is loyal to one section and yet holds the other in enduring suspicion and estrangement. Give us the broad and perfect loyalty that loves and trusts Georgia alike with Massachusetts, that knows no South, no North, no East, no West; but endears with equal and patriotic love every foot of our soil, every state of our Union.

A mighty duty, sir, and a mighty inspiration impels every one of us tonight to lose in patriotic consecration whatever estranges, whatever divides. We, sir, are Americans, and we fight for human liberty. The uplifting force of the American idea is under every throne on earth. France, Brazil: these are our victories. To redeem the earth from kingcraft and oppression: this is our mission. And we shall not fail. God has sown in our soil the seed of this millennial harvest, and he will not lay the sickle to the ripening crop until his full and perfect day has come. Our history, sir, has been a constant and expanding miracle from Plymouth Rock and Jamestown all the way, aye, even from the hour when, from the voiceless and trackless ocean, a new world rose to the sight of the inspired sailor.

As we approach the fourth centennial of that stupendous day — when the Old World will come to marvel and to learn, amid our gathered treasures — let us resolve to crown the miracles of our past with the spectacle of a republic compact, united, indissoluble in the bonds of love — loving from the lakes to the Gulf — the wounds of war healed in every heart as on every hill — serene and resplendent at the summit of human achievement and earthly glory — blazing out the path, and making clear the way up which all the nations of the earth must come in God's appointed time.

II.

JOSHUA A. BROCKETT:
Reply to Grady

HENRY W. GRADY, of Atlanta, Ga., delivered an address before the Boston Merchants' Association at their annual banquet, on Thursday evening, December 13, 1889. That speech, because of its eloquence and significance, has aroused an unusual amount of earnest discussion in all circles and in all grades of society. All just minds of all classes and of all races will freely acknowledge that it was an eloquent address, by which fact the power of the individual mind is hindered for a moment in passing an ac-

curate opinion upon its veracity, justice, and motive. But, upon reflection, judgment returns, and notwithstanding that Mr. Grady is the exponent of the doctrine of a so-called new South, finds nothing new presented by him as the solution of the Negro problem. In that address, beneath the glamor of eloquence, the old rebel spirit, and the old South is seen throughout.

In every expression of every line in which the Negro is mentioned the old spirit of Negro hatred is manifest. The beautifully phrased compliments so charmingly paid the North are but a disguise to conceal the hand which once strove to stab it. That hand still holds the knife, kept bright and keen by disappointed hopes of twenty years and more. This is readily seen through the crafty thrusts it deals to New England's deserted or artificially made farms. In that man's veins courses the blood of generations of traffickers in human slavery. His fathers engaged in that work of hell, so foul and dark. Mr. Grady declares his love for the blacks! Can he, a most loyal son of such fathers, reverse nature's law, and love those whom they hated? The Negro is said because of slavery to be mentally, morally, and spiritually depraved. Now taking into consideration who the man is, whence he came, his surroundings and training, it would be as difficult for Mr. Grady to reverse the laws of heredity, and cherish that great and abiding love for the Negro which he professes to have, as it would be for the Negro in the brief and recent space of his freedom to remove from himself all traces of mental, moral, and spiritual imperfections which generations of bondage left upon him.

The gentleman asks the question when will the black cast a free ballot? His reply is, when ignorance anywhere is not dominated by the will of the intelligent; when the laborer casts his vote unhindered by his boss; when the strong and steadfast do not everywhere control the suffrage of the weak and shiftless. Then and not till then will the Negro be free. He also says that the Negro vote can never again control in the South. He asks of the North, "Can we solve this question?" and answers, "God knows."

Consistency, thou art a jewel! It is declared that the Negro is peaceful and industrious on the one hand, weak and shiftless on the other. If he is peaceful surely the South has small need to fear an uprising. Politics, then, is the only source whence danger can come to the whites. If the black vote is never to control again, why should Mr. Grady state that the condition of the people is fraught with danger from the presence of a shiftless people? Whence the need of that wail for sympathy, if, as Mr. Grady says, the colored man must down, and the white partisan might as well understand it? If the colored man is never to rise, why waste so much eloquence upon a useless subject? The problem is already solved.

Mr. Grady asserts that nearly one-half of the school fund is used to educate the Negro. If the South is leagued together to maintain itself against this beleaguering black host, why educate it?

Has Mr. Grady to learn that education and power are inseparable? I will give Mr. Grady fair warning if they continue to give one-half or thereabouts to the school fund to educate a black man, then he will rise against the greatest odds that the South can oppose; not God alone, but even I know when the black man will be free.

Mr. Grady says that the Negro has not a basis upon which to rest his political conviction, and that of 300,000 voters, not 1 in 100 can read his ballot. That is a splendid compliment to the educational system which costs the South so dear. Either the South is amazingly stupid to pay so dearly for such meager results, or the Negro is incapable of learning, or the money is not paid.

Mr. Grady states that the Negro, by every species of villainy and folly, has wasted his substance and exhausted his credit. By the side of that statement I will place another of Mr. Grady's statements, namely, that from the Negroes' willing hands comes $1 billion of farm crops. If the latter statement is true, then the character of the Negro in the former statement has been falsified. Does Mr. Grady desire to make a strong case against this villainous race at the expense of the truth? And if the former statement is true, that the Negro is villainously wasteful, the $1 billion crops are but a creation of fancy, and the Northern sons with their modest patrimony would do well to remain standing in their doors, or turn their gaze in any direction but southward.

Again, with childlike innocence, Mr. Grady asks, can it be seriously maintained that we are terrorizing the people from whose willing hands comes every year $1 billion in crops? Or that we have robbed a people who, twenty-five years from unrewarded slavery, have amassed in one state $20 million worth of property?

In Georgia, Mr. Grady's own state, the Negro's real wealth accumulated since the war, is $20 million. Its population of Negroes is 725,132. Twenty millions of dollars divided among that number will give to each person $27.58. Upon the same basis of calculation the total wealth of the Negro in the 15 Southern states, including the District of Columbia, is $146,189,834. The colored population of these states is 5,305,149. It seems an enormous sum. In those 15 states the Negro has, by the exceedingly friendly aid of their best friends, amassed a fortune of $1 a year.

Should they not, because of this rapid accumulation of wealth, balance their little account, clutch to the mule, jog down the furrow, and let the world wag on?

Look now for a moment at those billion-dollar yearly crops accumulating for 27 years, giving us the almost inconceivable sum of $27 billion, which, divided between a number of whites equal to that of blacks, each one would from this $27 billion, receive $5,089.39. Thus the blacks receive for their willing toil through 27 years $27.58, while the whites receive $5,089.39. These are both sides of the Grady picture of Negro wealth which was intended to deceive the North. Gaze upon it.

Mr. Grady manifested the love he bears us by arousing the public sentiment to riot in Atlanta because the postmaster had appointed a colored man to a clerkship in the post office.

Why, if the blacks are contented and happy in their cabin homes, did New Bedford look upon the pitiful sight, but three winters ago, of a black man with barefooted and ragged wife and children trudging along its streets in the dead of winter?

The man who thus led his family had in the South worked while daylight lasted, yet had received but 40 cents in money the year before. His wife, a cook, received $2 a month for her labor.

Brought from that land in childhood by loyal white friends, one of whom today is in the city, another in Springfield, other in different states; reared and trained here, I little dreamed that in after years I should be returned at the command of my parents. Such, however, was the case. Then I learned that though cotton may whiten beneath the stars, horny handed and slavish toil has most to do with its growth and whitening. The wheat may lack the sunshine in its bearded sheaf, but if it listens to the prayers of the oppressed it shrinks within its sheaf and turns black with horror of great grief. The mountains may be stored with exhaustless treasure, and the swamps charged with exhaustless death. There are rivers that, tumbling or loitering, run wanton to the sea, and creeks, stagnant and sluggish, and ponds green with malarious

infection where moccasins disport themselves.

Again Mr. Grady says of the three essentials, iron, cotton, wood, that region has easy control. Make the list of essentials four, and add unpaid colored labor. He also says in cotton they have a fixed monopoly; in iron a proven supremacy; in timber, the reserved supply of the republic. They have also the Negro, the foundation of their institutions.

Upon that land there rests a curse, which can only be removed by and through the redemption of the Negro.

Again Mr. Grady describes a scene of his old black mammy as she held him in her black arms and led him smilingly to sleep. I can easily conjure up a scene of those old white-aproned nurses as they, in the long watches of the night, led those fractious young ones in to sleep. In helplessness that black mammy was compelled to nurse the young vulture whose wings of thought would soon bear him with crooked beak and whetted talons from the milk of the mother to the blood of her children.

From your loins, my people, a race shall spring that shall possess the land in which their fathers' bones repose; a race which for manliness no race shall surpass; a race that shall know no fear but that of wrong; that shall laugh scornful defiance in the rebel face, and demand restitution for the centuries of their fathers' unrequited toil. In peace and justice we will work out our own redemption, and in that redemption present to the world the solution of the Negro problem. If peace and justice be denied, we will suffer on and multiply until God's own time will have fully come; then we shall stand forth as terrible as an army with banners, and the South shall shake with the power of the Negro's tread.

Sitting Bull with his last squaw and three of their children, photographed in 1882

END OF THE FRONTIER

The year 1890 is usually given as a convenient figure for the end of the frontier period of American history, and it is accurate as far as the massive physical movement of frontier is concerned. The persistence and effect of the psychological aspects of the frontier are still a matter of debate. But by 1890, though small pockets of land remained to be settled, the last large areas of desirable land had been opened; the country was covered and ready to turn inward. Hasty settlers in the plains regions had made little allowance for the very different conditions there; the relatively austere soil and climate forced many to desert their claims, particularly in the aftermath of the blizzard and dry summer of 1887. The full development of the new territories depended upon a genuine containment and consolidation of the area and new techniques of exploitation such as large-scale irrigation and dry farming. Applied technology and economic integration were the new order of the day; with them came new balances of power. The exploitation of the West came to be the task of the West itself.

(Above) Geronimo and three warriors at the 1886 conference in the Sierra Madres with Gen. George Crook (left)

The final defeat of the Indians was an inevitable if costly step in the containment of the West. The later Indian troubles stemmed mainly from older leaders unreconciled to the reservation. Geronimo left his to terrorize the Southwest from 1882 to 1886. The Sioux, driven by the messiah craze, made one last stand in 1889-91. When Sitting Bull died, hundreds fled the reservation; they were defeated at the Battle of Wounded Knee, the last major battle between Indians and white men.

Council between Geronimo (left center) and Gen. Crook (second from right)

(Above) Gen. Miles and his staff viewing a hostile Indian camp near Pine Ridge, South Dakota, 1891; photo by Grabill

(Right) Two of the surviving Mandans after most of the tribe was wiped out in a smallpox epidemic; (far right) Red Cloud and American Horse; photo by Grabill, 1891

Arapaho braves resting during the Ghost Dance, ritual which was widely popular among Indians resisting suppression by the United States Army during the 1880s

View of Front Street in Dodge City, Kansas, 1879

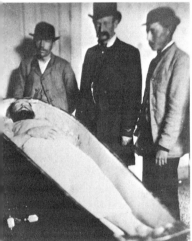

The "Wild West" that has become so large a part of popular American folklore was seldom if ever the reality of life in the Western settlements. Most of the characters were real but rather mundane and short-lived; the whole period lasted probably less than a decade. Wild Bill Hickok was shot in 1876, Billy the Kid in 1881, Jesse James in 1882; there was evidently not enough adventure to hold Bat Masterson — he left Dodge and Tombstone to become a sports writer for a New York newspaper and died at his desk in 1921. The more common way of Western life was the difficult, day-to-day drudgery of eking out a subsistence on the dry, inhospitable plains. Until methods of dry farming were discovered and hard winter and spring wheats were introduced, life in the West was usually nearly impossible.

(Above) Three men viewing the body of Jesse James; (right) Peace Commission in Kansas, including (front row left to right) Charles Bassett, Wyatt Earp, M. F. McClain and Neal Brown; (back row left to right) W. H. Harris, Luke Short, Bat Masterson, and W. F. Petillon

(Above) Western ranch house in Dakota, 1882; photo by Grabill; (left) people of Deadwood celebrating the completion of the railroad to Lead City in 1888; (below) Deadwood and Delaware Smelter in 1890

(Above) Rawding family sod house home, north of Sargent in Custer County, Neb., about 1886; (left) wedding of a couple in Custer County, Neb., 1889; (below) sheep ranch near Coburg, Neb., photo by Butcher, 1887

(Above) Harrowing on a farm in the Dakotas, 1877; from a stereograph by Haynes; (below) thrashing on another Dakota farm during the same year; Haynes photo

Branding calves during a roundup on the Salt Fork in Barber County, Kan., 1890s

Another symbol of the wide-open West was the cattle drive. Great herds were driven from Texas and the Southwest to railheads in Kansas and Missouri along the famous Chisholm, Goodnight Loving, and Santa Fe trails. Trail drives, and the colorful cowboys that made them, came to a virtual end by 1895; extended railroads, barbed wire, and the huge influx of farming settlers effectively eliminated the entire operation. The Oklahoma land rush of 1889 and the Cherokee Strip rush of 1893 were among several such runs into former Indian reservation lands which lasted until 1895 and settled the Oklahoma and Indian territories. The later rushes were small, however, compared with the great "Harrison's Hoss Race" of 1889, run by 20,000 prospective landowners.

(Left) Jesse Chisholm, Scotch-Cherokee Indian trader. His wagon route in the Oklahoma Indian Territory became the trail followed by cowboys bringing longhorns from Texas to Kansas in the 1870s. (Below) Cowboys at "mess" during a roundup; photo by Grabill in 1887

(Above) View of Prescott, Ariz., about 1866; (right) residents of Santa Fe, N.M., photographed on San Francisco Street in 1885; (below) street scene in Santa Fe Mexican quarter

(Above) Supply train through a mountain pass in Colorado; (below) street scene in Aspen, Colo., in the 1890s; photo by Kilburn

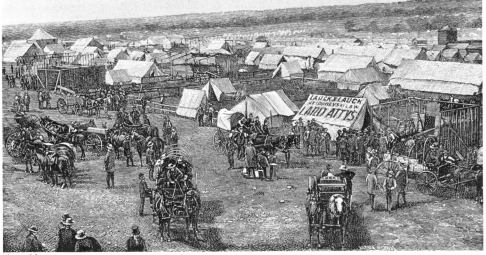

(Above) Guthrie, Oklahoma Territory, five days after the 1889 land rush; (below) Rock Island train at the Kansas state line just prior to opening Cherokee Strip to settlement, 1893

Land rush in the Cherokee Strip, Sept. 16, 1893

Kearney Street, San Francisco, during a Fourth of July celebration

When the fever of the gold rush and vigilante days was gone, San Francisco proceeded to develop itself and became the industrial and financial center of the region. The San Joaquin Valley, with San Francisco at its head, became at the same time one of the most productive farming areas in the world.

(Left) Street scene in San Francisco, about 1880; (below) the Charles Crocker residence in San Francisco in the 1880s

(Above) Superintendent's cottage on the Buena Vista Ranch in California about 1890; (left) Calloway Canal in Kern Co.; (below) barnyard of the Lakeside Ranch. Irrigation was bringing vast areas of California's arid interior valleys under cultivation

(Above) Bakersfield, Cal., in 1890; (left) Indian corn raised on the Buena Vista Ranch; (right) a portion of the orange orchard on the Tejon Ranch; (below) stacking alfalfa during a harvest on the Stockdale Ranch. All of these farms were photographed by Watkins for a survey of Kern County, Cal., 1890

1890

54.

Robert G. Ingersoll: The Absurdity of Religion

In the storm of controversy following the publication of Charles Darwin's Origin of Species, *lawyer Robert G. Ingersoll became known as "the great agnostic." Only Ingersoll's great personal charm and the propriety of his personal conduct saved him from social ostracism and perhaps physical harm. Nevertheless, his career suffered; at his death the* Chicago Tribune *commented that "splendidly endowed as he was he could have won great distinction in the field of politics had he so chosen. But he determined to enlighten the world concerning the 'Mistakes of Moses.' That threw him out of the race." The following selection is from one of Ingersoll's most famous lectures, "Why Am I an Agnostic?"*

Source: *Works*, Clinton P. Farrell, ed., New Dresden Edition, New York, 1900, Vol. XI, pp. 237-259.

THE SAME RULES OR LAWS of probability must govern in religious questions as in others. There is no subject — and can be none — concerning which any human being is under any obligation to believe without evidence. Neither is there any intelligent being who can, by any possibility, be flattered by the exercise of ignorant credulity. The man who, without prejudice, reads and understands the Old and New Testaments will cease to be an orthodox Christian. The intelligent man who investigates the religion of any country without fear and without prejudice will not and cannot be a believer.

Most people, after arriving at the conclusion that Jehovah is not God, that the Bible is not an inspired book, and that the Christian religion, like other religions, is the creation of man, usually say: "There must be a Supreme Being, but Jehovah is not his name and the Bible is not his word. There must be somewhere an overruling Providence or Power."

This position is just as untenable as the other. He who cannot harmonize the cruelties of the Bible with the goodness of Jehovah cannot harmonize the cruelties of nature with the goodness and wisdom of a supposed Deity. He will find it impossible to account for pestilence and famine, for earthquake and storm, for slavery, for the triumph of the strong over the weak, for the countless victories of injustice. He will find it impossible to account for martyrs — for the burning of the good, the noble, the loving, by the ignorant, the malicious, and the infamous.

How can the deist satisfactorily account for the sufferings of women and children?

In what way will he justify religious persecution — the flame and sword of religious hatred? Why did his God sit idly on His throne and allow his enemies to wet their swords in the blood of his friends? Why did He not answer the prayers of the imprisoned, of the helpless? And when He heard the lash upon the naked back of the slave, why did He not also hear the prayer of the slave? And when children were sold from the breasts of mothers, why was He deaf to the mother's cry?

It seems to me that the man who knows the limitations of the mind, who gives the proper value to human testimony, is necessarily an agnostic. He gives up the hope of ascertaining first or final causes, of comprehending the supernatural, or of conceiving of an infinite personality. From out the words "Creator," "Preserver," and "Providence," all meaning falls.

The mind of man pursues the path of least resistance, and the conclusions arrived at by the individual depend upon the nature and structure of his mind, on his experience, on hereditary drifts and tendencies, and on the countless things that constitute the difference in minds. One man, finding himself in the midst of mysterious phenomena, comes to the conclusion that all is the result of design; that back of all things is an infinite personality — that is to say, an infinite man; and he accounts for all that is by simply saying that the universe was created and set in motion by this infinite personality, and that it is miraculously and supernaturally governed and preserved. This man sees with perfect clearness that matter could not create itself, and therefore he imagines a creator of matter. He is perfectly satisfied that there is design in the world, and that, consequently, there must have been a designer.

It does not occur to him that it is necessary to account for the existence of an infinite personality. He is perfectly certain that there can be no design without a designer, and he is equally certain that there can be a designer who was not designed. The absurdity becomes so great that it takes the place of a demonstration. He takes it for granted that matter was created and that its creator was not. He assumes that a creator existed from eternity, without cause, and created what is called "matter" out of nothing; or, whereas there was nothing, this creator made the something that we call substance.

Is it possible for the human mind to conceive of an infinite personality? Can it imagine a beginningless being, infinitely powerful and intelligent? If such a being existed, then there must have been an eternity during which nothing did exist except this being; because, if the universe was created, there must have been a time when it was not, and back of that there must have been an eternity during which nothing but an infinite personality existed.

Is it possible to imagine an infinite intelligence dwelling for an eternity in infinite nothing? How could such a being be intelligent? What was there to be intelligent about? There was but one thing to know — namely, that there was nothing except this being. How could such a being be powerful? There was nothing to exercise force upon. There was nothing in the universe to suggest an idea. Relations could not exist — except the relation between infinite intelligence and infinite nothing.

The next great difficulty is the act of creation. My mind is so that I cannot conceive of something being created out of nothing. Neither can I conceive of anything being created without a cause. Let me go one step further. It is just as difficult to imagine something being created with, as without, a cause. To postulate a cause does not in the least lessen the difficulty. In spite of all, this lever remains without a fulcrum. We cannot conceive of the destruction of substance. The stone can be crushed to powder, and the powder can be ground to such a fineness that the atoms can only be distinguished by the most powerful microscope, and we can then imagine these atoms being divided and subdivided again and again and again; but it is impossible for us to conceive of the annihilation of the least possible imaginable fragment of the least atom of which we can think. Consequently, the mind can imagine neither creation nor destruction. From this point it is very easy to reach the generalization that the indestructible could not have been created.

These questions, however, will be answered by each individual according to the structure of his mind, according to his experience, according to his habits of thought, and according to his intelligence or his ignorance, his prejudice or his genius.

Probably a very large majority of mankind believe in the existence of supernatural beings, and a majority of what are known as the civilized nations in an infinite personality. In the realm of thought, majorities do not determine. Each brain is a kingdom, each mind is a sovereign. . . .

If the average Christian had been born in Turkey, he would have been a Mohammedan; and if the average Mohammedan had been born in New England and educated at Andover, he would have regarded the damnation of the heathen as the "tidings of great joy."

Nations have eccentricities, peculiarities, and hallucinations, and these find expression in their laws, customs, ceremonies, morals, and religions. And these are in great part determined by soil, climate, and the countless circumstances that mold and dominate the lives and habits of insects, individuals, and nations. The average man believes implicitly in the religion of his country because he knows nothing of any other, and has no desire to know. It fits him because he has been deformed to fit it, and he regards this fact of fit as an evidence of its inspired truth.

Has a man the right to examine, to investigate the religion of his own country — the religion of his father and mother? Christians admit that the citizens of all countries not Christian have not only this right but that it is their solemn duty. Thousands of missionaries are sent to heathen countries to persuade the believers in other religions, not only to examine their superstitions but to renounce them and to adopt those of the missionaries. It is the duty of a heathen to disregard the religion of his country and to hold in contempt the creed of his father and of his mother. If the citizens of heathen nations have the right to examine the foundations of their religion, it would seem that the citizens of Christian nations have the same right.

Christians, however, go further than this. They say to the heathen: You must examine your religion, and not only so, but you must reject it; and, unless you do reject it, and, in addition to such rejection, adopt ours, you will be eternally damned. Then these same Christians say to the inhabitants of a Christian country: You must not examine; you must not investigate; but, whether you examine or not, you must believe or you will be eternally damned.

If there be one true religion, how is it possible to ascertain which of all the religions the true one is? There is but one way. We must impartially examine the claims of all. The right to examine involves the necessity to accept or reject. Understand me, not the right to accept or reject, but the necessity. From this conclusion there is no possible escape. If, then, we have the right to examine, we have the right to tell the conclusion reached. Christians have examined other religions somewhat, and they have expressed their opinion with the utmost freedom — that is to say, they have denounced them all as false and fraudulent, have called their gods idols and myths, and their priests impostors.

The Christian does not deem it worthwhile to read the Koran. Probably not one Christian in a thousand ever saw a copy of that book. And yet all Christians are perfectly satisfied that the Koran is the work of an impostor. No Presbyterian thinks it is worth his while to examine the religious systems of India; he knows that the Brahmins are mistaken and that all their miracles are falsehoods. No Methodist cares to read the life of Buddha, and no Baptist will waste his time studying the ethics of Confucius. Christians of every sort and kind take it for granted that there is only one true religion, and that all except Christianity are absolutely without foundation.

The Christian world believes that all the prayers of India are unanswered; that all the sacrifices upon the countless altars of Egypt, of Greece, and of Rome were without effect. They believe that all these mighty nations worshiped their gods in vain; that their priests were deceivers or deceived; that their ceremonies were wicked or meaningless; that their temples were built by ignorance and fraud, and that no god heard their songs of praise, their cries of despair, their words of thankfulness; that on account of their religion no pestilence was stayed; that the earthquake and volcano, the flood and storm went on their ways of death, while the real God looked on and laughed at their calamities and mocked at their fears.

We find now that the prosperity of nations has depended, not upon their religion, not upon the goodness or providence of some god, but on soil and climate and commerce, upon the ingenuity, industry, and courage of the people, upon the development of the mind, on the spread of education, on the liberty of thought and action; and that in this mighty panorama of national life, reason has built and superstition has destroyed.

Being satisfied that all believe precisely as they must and that religions have been naturally produced, I have neither praise nor blame for any man. Good men have had bad creeds, and bad men have had good ones. Some of the noblest of the human race have fought and died for the wrong. The brain of man has been the trysting place of contradictions. Passion often masters reason, and "the state of man, like to a little kingdom, suffers then the nature of an insurrection."

In the discussion of theological or religious questions, we have almost passed the personal phase, and we are now weighing arguments instead of exchanging epithets and curses. They who really seek for truth must be the best of friends. Each knows that his desire can never take the place of fact, and that, next to finding truth, the greatest honor must be won in honest search.

We see that many ships are driven in many ways by the same wind. So men, reading the same book, write many creeds and lay out many roads to heaven. To the best of my ability, I have examined the religions of many countries and the creeds of many sects. They are much alike, and the testimony by which they are substantiated is of such a character that to those who believe is promised an eternal reward. In all the sacred books there are some truths, some rays of light, some words of love and hope. The face of savagery is sometimes softened by a smile — the human triumphs and the heart breaks into song. But in these books are also found the words of fear and hate, and from their pages crawl serpents that coil and hiss in all the paths of men.

For my part, I prefer the books that inspiration has not claimed. Such is the nature of my brain that Shakespeare gives me greater joy than all the prophets of the ancient world. There are thoughts that satisfy the hunger of the mind. I am convinced that Humboldt knew more of geology than the author of Genesis; that Darwin was a greater naturalist than he who told the story of the Flood; that Laplace was better acquainted with the habits of the sun and moon than Joshua could have been; and that Haeckel, Huxley, and Tyndall know more about the earth and stars, about the history of man, the philosophy of life — more that is of use, ten thousand times — than all the writers of the sacred books.

I believe in the religion of reason — the gospel of this world; in the development of the mind, in the accumulation of intellectual wealth, to the end that man may free himself from superstitious fear, to the end that he may take advantage of the forces of nature to feed and clothe the world.

Let us be honest with ourselves. In the presence of countless mysteries; standing beneath the boundless heaven sown thick with constellations; knowing that each grain of sand, each leaf, each blade of grass, asks of every mind the answerless question; knowing that the simplest thing defies solution; feeling that we deal with the superficial and the relative, and that we are forever eluded by the real, the absolute — let us admit the limitations of our minds, and let us have the courage and the candor to say: We do not know.

55.

RUSSELL H. CONWELL: Acres of Diamonds

Baptist minister, pastor of Temple Baptist Church in Philadelphia, and founder of Temple University, Russell Conwell first delivered his sermon-lecture Acres of Diamonds *in 1861, as an eighteen-year-old boy. The exhortation was a success from the beginning, and Conwell repeated it some 6,000 times during the next fifty years, with total proceeds, including royalties on the printed version, of more than $8 million. The actual text was always different, Conwell once observed, depending on the place where it was given, but its idea was always the same — "that in this country of ours every man has the opportunity to make more of himself than he does in his own environment, with his own skill, with his own energy, and with his own friends." We reprint here one version of the sermon, placing it chronologically at about the middle of Conwell's career.*

Source: *Acres of Diamonds,* Cleveland, 1905.

THE ACRES OF DIAMONDS of which I propose to speak today are to be found in your homes, or near to them, and not in some distant land. I cannot better introduce my thought than by the relation of a little incident that occurred to a party of American travelers beyond the Euphrates River. We passed across the great Arabian Desert, coming out at Baghdad, passed down the river to the Arabian Gulf, and on our way down we hired an Arabian guide to show us all the wonderful things connected with the ancient history and scenery. And that guide was very much like the barbers . . . in this country today; that is, he thought it was not only his duty to guide us but also to entertain us with stories both curious and weird, and ancient and modern, many of which I have forgotten; and I am glad I have, but there is one I remember today. The old guide led the camel along by his halter, telling various stories, and once he took his Turkish cap from his head and swung it high in the air to give me to understand that he had something especially important to communicate, and then he told me this beautiful story.

"There once lived on the banks of the Indus River an ancient Persian by the name of Al Hafed. He owned a lovely cottage on a magnificent hill, from which he could look down upon the glittering river and the glorious sea; he had wealth in abundance, fields, grain, orchards, money at interest, a beautiful wife and lovely children, and he was contented. Contented because he was wealthy, and wealthy because he was contented. And one day there visited this Al Hafed an ancient priest, and that priest sat down before the fire and told him how diamonds were made, and said the old priest, 'If you had a diamond the size of your thumb you could purchase a dozen farms like this, and if you had a handful you could purchase the whole county.'

"Al Hafed was at once a poor man; he had not lost anything, he was poor because he was discontented, and he was discontented because he thought he was poor. He said: 'I want a mine of diamonds; what is the use of farming a little place like this? I want a mine and I will have it.' He could hardly sleep that night, and early in the morning he went and wakened the priest, and said: 'I want you to tell me where you can find diamonds.' Said the old priest: 'If you want diamonds, go and get them.'

'Won't you please tell me where I can find them?'

'Well, if you go and find high mountains, with a deep river running between them, over white sand, in this white sand you will find diamonds.'

'Well,' said he, 'I will go.'

"So he sold his farm, collected his money, and went to hunt for diamonds. He began, very properly, with the Mountains of the Moon, and came down through Egypt and Palestine. Years passed. He came over through Europe, and, at last, in rags and hunger, he stood a pauper on the shores of the great Bay of Barcelona; and when that great tidal wave came rolling in through the Pillars of Hercules, he threw himself into the incoming tide and sank beneath its foaming crest, never again to rise in this life."

Here the guide stopped to fix some dislo-

cated baggage, and I said to myself, "What does he mean by telling me this story! It was the first story I ever read in which the hero was killed in the first chapter." But he went on:

"The man who purchased Al Hafed's farm led his camel one day out to the stream in the garden to drink. As the camel buried his nose in the water, the man noticed a flash of light from the white sand and reached down and picked up a black stone with a strange eye of light in it which seemed to reflect all the hues of the rainbow. He said, 'It's a wonderful thing,' and took it in his house, where he put it on his mantel and forgot all about it. A few days afterwards the same old priest came to visit Al Hafed's successor. He noticed a flash of light from the mantel, and taking up the stone, exclaimed:

'Here is a diamond! Has Al Hafed returned!!'

'Oh, no, that is not a diamond, that is nothing but a stone that we found out in the garden.'

'But,' said the priest, 'that is a diamond!' And together they rushed out into the garden and stirred up the white sands with their fingers, and there came up other more beautiful gems, and more valuable than the first."

And that was the guide's story. And it is, in the main, historically true. Thus were discovered the wonderful mines of Golconda. Again the guide swung his cap, and said: "Had Al Hafed remained at home and dug in his own cellar or garden, or under his own wheat fields, he would have found Acres of Diamonds." And this discovery was the founding of the line of the Great Moguls, whose magnificent palaces are still the astonishment of all travelers. He did not need to add the moral.

But that I may teach by illustration, I want to tell you the story that I then told him. We were sort of exchanging works; he would tell me a story and I would tell him one, and so I told him about the man in

California, living on his ranch there, who read of the discovery of gold in the southern part of the state. He became dissatisfied and sold his ranch and started for new fields in search of gold. His successor, Colonel Sutter, put a mill on the little stream below the house, and one day, when the water was shut off, his little girl went down to gather some of the white sand in the raceway; and she brought some of it into the house to dry it. And while she was sifting it through her fingers, a gentleman, a visitor there, noticed the first shining sands of gold ever discovered in Upper California. That farm that the owner sold to go somewhere else to find gold has added $18 million to the circulating medium of the world; and they told me there sixteen years ago that the owner of one-third of the farm received a $20 gold piece for every fifteen minutes of his life.

That reminds me of what Professor Agassiz told his summer class in mineralogy in reference to Pennsylvania. I live in Pennsylvania, but, being a Yankee, I enjoy telling this story. This man owned a farm, and he did just what I would do if I owned a farm in that state — sold it. Before he sold it, he concluded that he would go to Canada to collect coal oil. The professors will tell you that this stuff was first found in connection with living springs, floating on the water. This man wrote to his cousin in Canada asking for employment collecting this oil. The cousin wrote back that he did not understand the work. The farmer then studied all the books on coal oil, and when he knew all about it, and the theories of the geologists concerning it from the formation of primitive coal beds to the present day, he removed to Canada to work for his cousin, first selling his Pennsylvania farm for $1,833.

The old farmer who purchased his estate went back of the barn one day to fix a place for the horses to drink and found that the previous owner had already arranged that matter. He had fixed some plank edgewise, running from one bank toward the other and resting edgewise a few inches into the water, the purpose being to throw over to one side a dreadful looking scum that the cattle would not put their noses in, although they would drink the water below it. That man had been damming back for twenty-one years that substance, the discovery of which the official geologist pronounced to be worth to the state the sum of $100 million. Yet that man had sold his farm for $1,833. He sold one of the best oil-producing farms and went somewhere else to find — nothing.

That story brought to my mind the incident of the young man in Massachusetts. There was a young man in college studying mining and mineralogy, and while he was a student they employed him for a time as a tutor and paid him $15 a week for the special work. When he graduated they offered him a professorship and $45 a week. When this offer came, he went home and said to his mother:

"Mother, I know too much to work for $45 a week; let us go out to California, and I will stake out gold mines and copper and silver mines, and we will be rich."

His mother said it was better to stay there. But as he was an only son he had his way, and they sold out and started. But they only went to Wisconsin, where he went into the employ of the Superior Copper Mining Company, at a salary of $15 a week. He had scarcely left the old estate before the farmer who bought it was digging potatoes and bringing them through the yard in a large basket. The farms there are almost all stone wall, and the gate was narrow, and as he was working his basket through, pulling first one side then the other, he noticed in that stone wall a block of native silver about eight inches square. This professor of mining and mineralogy was born on that place, and when he sold out he sat on that very stone while he was making the bargain. He had passed it again and again. He had rubbed it with his sleeve until it had reflected his countenance and said: "Come, now, here is $100,000 for digging — dig me."

I should enjoy exceedingly telling these stories, but I am not here to relate incidents so much as to bring lessons that may be helpful to you. I love to laugh at the mistakes of these men until the thought comes to me, "How do you know what that man in Wisconsin is doing — and that man in Canada?" It may be that he sits by his hearth today and shakes his sides and laughs at us for making the same mistakes and feels that after all he is in comparatively good company. We have all made the same mistakes. Is there anyone here that has not? If there is one that says you have never made such a blunder, I can argue with you that you have. You may not have had the acres of diamonds and sold them. You may not have had wells of oil and sold them, and yet you may have done so. A teacher in the Wilkes-Barre schools came to me after one of my lectures and told me that he owned a farm of fifty acres that he sold for $5 an acre, and a few weeks before my lecture it was sold for $38,000 because they had found a silver mine on it.

You say you never have made any such mistakes. Are you rich today? Are you worth $5 million? Of course not!

Why not? "I never had opportunity to get it."

Now you and I can talk. Let us see!

Were you ever in the mercantile business? Why didn't you get rich? "Because I couldn't, there was so much competition and all that." Now, my friend, didn't you carry on your store just as I carried on my father's store? I don't like to tell how I conducted my father's store. But when he went away to purchase goods, he would sometimes leave me in charge; and a man would come in and say: "Do you keep jackknives?" "No, we don't keep jackknives." Then another would come in and ask: "Do you keep jackknives?" "No, we

don't!!" And still another. "No, we don't keep jackknives; why are you all bothering me about jackknives!!!"

Did you keep store in that way? Do you ask me what was the fault? The difficulty was that I never had learned by bitter experience the foundation of business success; and that it is the same foundation that underlies all true success, the foundation that underlies Christianity and morality. That it is the whole of man's life to live for others; and he that can do the most to elevate, enrich, and inspire others shall reap the greatest reward himself. Not only so says the Holy Book but so says business common sense.

I will go into your store and ask: "Do you know neighbor A that lives over a couple of squares from your store?" "Yes, he deals here." "Where did he come from?" "I don't know." "Has he any children?" "I don't know." "Does he have a school in his district? Does he go to church?" "I don't know." "Is he a married man?" "I don't know." "What ticket does he vote?" "I don't know, and I don't care!"

Is that the way you do business? If it is, then you have been conducting your business as I carried on my father's store! And you do not succeed and are poor? I understand it. You can't succeed and I am glad of it, and I will give $5 to see your failure announced in the newspaper tomorrow morning. The only way to succeed is to take an interest in the people around you and honestly work for their welfare.

"But," you say, "I have no capital." I am glad you haven't. I am sorry for the rich men's sons. Young man, if you have no capital, there is hope for you. According to the statistics collected in the city of Boston twenty years ago, ninety-six of every one hundred successful merchants were born poor; and trustworthy statistics also show that of the rich men's sons not one in a thousand dies rich. I am sorry for the rich men's sons unless their fathers be wise enough to bring them up like poor children. If you haven't any capital, life is full of hope to you.

A. T. Stewart started out with a dollar and a half to begin on and he lost all but sixty-two and a half cents the first afternoon. That was before he was a school teacher. He purchased things the people did not want. He said, "I will never do that again," and he went around to the doors and found what the people wanted and invested his sixty-two and a half cents safely, for he knew what people wanted, and went on until he was worth $42 million. And what man has done, men can do again. You may say: "I can't be acquainted with every man in the county and know his wife and children in order to succeed." If you know a few fairly well, you may judge the world by them.

John Jacob Astor is said by one of his latest biographers to have had a mortgage on a millinery establishment. I always think when I reach this point that the ladies will say: "Fools rush in where angels fear to tread." They could not pay the interest on the mortgage and he foreclosed and took possession. He went into partnership with the same man who failed and kept the old clerks and retained the old stock. He went out and set down on a bench in Union Park. What was he doing there? He was watching the women as they passed by, and when he saw a lady with her shoulders thrown back and her head up as if she didn't care if all the world was looking at her, he studied that bonnet; and before it was out of sight he knew every feather and ribbon and all about the frame; and — and — some men may be able to describe a bonnet, but I cannot. I don't believe there are words in the English language to do it. Then he went to the store and said: "Put such and such a bonnet in the window, for I know that there is one woman that likes it." And then he would go and watch for another style and return and have that put

in the window with the other. And success came.

Some years ago I went into that store to find out about it for myself, and there I found the descendants of that man doing business, and it is the largest millinery firm in the world, with branch houses in all the large cities on the globe. That success was made because Astor studied into the matter and knew what the women wanted before he had the articles made.

But you say, "I cannot do it." You can do it. You say you have no capital — but you have a jackknife. I could not sleep if I did not have a jackknife in my pocket — a Yankee cannot. In Massachusetts, there lived a man who was a carpenter and who was out of work. He sat around the stove until his wife told him to go outdoors, and he did — every man in Massachusetts is compelled by law to obey his wife! He sat down on the shore of the bay and whittled a soaked oak shingle, until he made a chain that his children quarreled over. Then he whittled another.

Then a neighbor, coming in, advised him to whittle toys, for sale. "I can't make toys," said he. "Yes, you can." "But I wouldn't know what to make." There is the whole thing; not in having the machinery or the capital but in knowing what the people want; and so his friend said to the carpenter: "Why don't you ask your own children? See what they like, and perhaps other children will like the same thing." He concluded to do so; and, when his little girl came down, he said: "Mary, what kind of a toy would you like to have me make?" "Oh, a little doll cradle, and carriage, and horse," and a dozen other things.

He began with his jackknife and made up these rough, unpainted toys. A friend of his sold them in a Boston shoe store at first, and brought back 25 and 50 cents at a time, and then his wife began to be better-natured. The wife always does get better-natured when there is a prospect of money to divide. She came out and split up the wood while he made up the toys. The last case I had as a lawyer before I entered the ministry that man was on the stand, and I said to him: "When did you commence to whittle those toys?" "In 1870." "How much are the patents on those toys worth?" His answer was, their actual value, to him, was $78,000; and it was a little less than seven years after the time when he began with his jackknife; and today I know that he is worth $100,000, and he has received it all from having consulted his own children and judging from them what other people's children wanted and trying to supply the demand. If a man takes an interest in people, and knows what they need, and endeavors to supply it, he must succeed.

Some of you who sit before me, thinking you are poor, are actually in possession of wealth; like the Baltimore lady, who, fourteen years after her father's failure, found a costly diamond bracelet he had lost seventeen years before.

Many of you smile at the thought that you are in the actual possession of wealth. A shoemaker in Massachusetts sat around in the house until his wife drove him out with a broom, and then he went out into the backyard and sat down on an ash barrel. Nearby was a beautiful mountain stream but I don't suppose that he thought of Tennyson's beautiful poem —

I chatter, chatter, as I flow,
    To join the brimming river;
Men may come, and men may go,
    But I go on forever.

It was not a poetical situation, sitting on an ash barrel and his wife in the kitchen with a mop.

Then he saw a trout flash in the stream and hide under the bank, and he reached down and got the fish and took it into the house; and his wife took it and sent it to a friend in Worcester. The friend wrote back that he would give $5 for another such a trout, and our shoemaker and his wife immediately started out to find it — man and wife now perfectly united. A $5 bill in prospect! They went up the stream to its source and followed it down to the brimming river, but there was not another trout to be found. Then he went to the minister. That minister didn't know how trout grew, but he told them to go to the public library and, under a pile of dime novels, he would find Seth Green's book, and that would give them the information they wanted. They did so, and found out all about the culture of trout, and began operations.

They afterwards moved to the banks of the Connecticut River and then to the Hudson, and now that man sends trout, fresh and packed in ice, all over the country, and is a rich man. His wealth was in that backyard just as much twenty years before. But he did not discover it until his repeated failures had made his wife imperious.

I remember meeting, in western Pennsylvania, a distinguished professor who began as a country school teacher. He was determined to know his district, and he learned that the father of one of the boys was a maker of wagon wheels. He studied up all about making wagon wheels, and when that man's boy came to school he told him all about it; and the boy went home and told his father: "I know more about wagon wheels than you do!" "That teacher is teaching that boy wonderfully," said the father. He told a farmer's boy all about the value of fertilizer for the soil, and he went home and told his father, and the old gentleman said: "How that boy is learning!" That teacher is now the president of a college, and is a D.D., an LL.D., and a Ph.D. He taught what the people wanted to know, and that made him successful.

Once I went up into the mountain region of New Hampshire to lecture, and I suffered a great deal from the cold. When I came back to Harvard, I said to a friend, who was a scientific man of great culture:

"Professor, I am never going into New Hampshire to lecture again, never!" "Why?" "Because I nearly shivered the teeth out of my head." "And why did you shiver?" "Because the weather was cold." "Oh, no, no!" said my friend. "Then it was because I did not have bedclothes enough!" "No, no, it wasn't that." "Well," I said, "you are a scientific man, and I wish you would tell me, then, just why I shivered?" "Well, sir," he replied, "it was because you didn't know any better." Said he: "Didn't you have in your pocket a newspaper?" "Oh, yes." "Well, why didn't you spread that over your bed? If you had you would have been as warm as the richest man in America under all his silk coverlids; and you shivered because you did not know enough to put the two-cent paper over your bed." ·

How many women want divorces — and ought to have them, too! How many divorces originate something like this: A workingman comes in haste to his supper and sits down to eat potatoes that are about as hard as the rocks beside which they grew. He will chop them up and eat them in a hurry, and they won't digest well. They make him cross. He frets and scolds, and perhaps he swears, he scarcely knows why, and then there is trouble. If the good woman had only known enough of science to put in a pinch of salt, they would have come out mealy and luscious and eatable and ready to laugh themselves to pieces in edible joy; and he would have eaten them down in peace and satisfaction and with good digestion; and he would have arisen from the table with a smile on his face; and there would have been joy in that family — and all because of a pinch of salt. The lack in appreciating the value of little things often keeps us in poverty.

I want to ask the audience — Who are the great inventors of the world? Many will answer that it is a peculiar race of men, with intellects like lightning flashes and heads like bushel measures. But, in fact, inventors are usually ordinary practical thinkers. You may invent as much as they if you study on the question — What does the world need? It is not so difficult to prepare a machine, after all, as it is to find out just what people want. The Jacquard loom was invented by a workingwoman. So was the printing roller. So was the second-best cotton gin. So was the mowing machine. I am out of all patience with myself because I did not invent the telephone. I had the same opportunity that the other boy had; I put my ear down to the rail and heard the rumbling of the engine through the miles of track, and arose and threw snowballs — the other boy arose and asked — Why? He discovered that it was caused by the generation of electricity by the wheels, and, when he saw Edison's speaking machine, he had the whole matter at a glance.

There was a congressman once who resolved to talk sense; of course, he was an exception to the general rule. He was one day walking through the Treasury Department, when a clerk said to him that it was a fine day. As he met other clerks, they remarked the same thing, and at last our congressman said: "Why do you tell me that it is a fine day? I know that already. Now, if you could tell me what the weather will be tomorrow, it would be of some importance." A clerk caught the idea and began to think it over, and entered into correspondence with the professor at Cincinnati. That was the origin of our signal service. Soon we will know what the weather will be a week ahead. Yes, not many years hence, we will decide what weather we will have by a popular vote. How simple all these mighty improvements and inventions seem when we study the simple steps of their evolution!

Yet civilized men and women are greater today than ever before. We often think all great men are dead, and the longer they are dead the greater they appear to have been. But, in fact, men are greater and women are nobler than ever before. We are building on the foundations of the past, and we must be exceeding small if we are not greater than they who laid them. The world knows nothing of its greatest men. Some young man may say: "I am going to be great." "How?" "How? By being elected to an office." Shall the man be greater than the men who elect him? Shall the servant be greater than his master? That a man is in public office is no evidence of greatness. Even if you are great when you are in office, they will not call you great till after you die. Another young man says: "I am going to be great when there comes a war." But success in war is not always an evidence of greatness.

Historians are apt to credit a successful man with more than he really does and with deeds that were performed by subordinates. General Thomas was one of the greatest generals of the war, yet an incident in his life illustrates this thought. After the Battle of Nashville, the soldiers, seeing him, cheered the hero and shouted, "Hurrah for the hero of Lookout Mountain." This was distasteful to the General, and he ordered it to be stopped. Said he: "Talk about the hero of Lookout Mountain! Why, I was ordered by General Grant to keep my troops at the foot of the mountain, and the enemy began to drop their shells among us, and I ordered my men to retreat, but they would not do it; and they charged and captured the works against my positive orders. Now they talk about the hero of Lookout Mountain!" Yet as he was in command of that corps he would naturally be credited with the victory of that charge, while the daring private or subordinate may never be mentioned in history.

You can be as great at home and in private life as you can on fields of awful carnage. Greatness, in its noblest sense, knows no social or official rank.

I can see again a company of soldiers in the last war going home to be received by their native town officers. Did you ever think you would like to be a king or queen? Go and be received by your town officers, and you will know what it means. I shall never see again so proud a moment as that when, at the head of a company of troops, we were marching home to be received. I was but a boy in my teens. I can hear now distinctly the band playing and see the people that were waiting. We marched into their town hall and were seated in the center. Then I was called to take a position on the platform with the town officers. Then came the address of welcome. The old gentleman had never made a speech before, but he had written this, and walked up and down the pasture until he had committed it to memory. But he had brought it with him and spread it out on the desk. The delivery of the speech by that good but nervous town official went something like this:

"Fellow Citizens — fellow citizens. We are — we are — we are very happy — we are — we are very happy to welcome back to our native town — these soldiers. Fellow citizens, we are very happy to welcome back to our native town these soldiers who have — who have — who have fought — who have fought and bled — and come back to their native town again. We are — we are — we are especially — especially pleased to see with us today this young hero. This young hero — to see this young hero — in imagination we have seen — (remember that he said "in imagination") we have seen him leading his troops on to battle. We have seen his — his — his shining sword, flashing in the sunshine, as he shouted to his troops, 'Come on!' "

Oh, dear, dear, dear! What did he know about war? That captain, with his shining sword flashing in air, shouting to his troops, *"Come on!"* He never did it, never. If there had not often been a double line of flesh and blood between him and the enemy, he would not have been there that day to be received. If he had known anything about war he would have known what any soldier in this audience can tell you that it was next to a crime for an officer of infantry in time of danger to go ahead of his men! Do you suppose he is going out there to be shot in front by the enemy and in the back by his own men? That is no place for him. And yet the hero of the reception hour was that boy. There stood in that house, unnoticed, men who had carried that boy on their backs through deep rivers, men who had given him their last draft of coffee; men who had run miles to get him food. And some were not there; some were sleeping their last sleep in their unknown graves. They had given their lives for the nation, but were scarcely noticed in the good man's speech. And the boy was the hero of the reception hour. Why? For no other reason under heaven but because he was an officer and these men were only private soldiers. Human nature often estimates men's greatness by the office they hold; yet office cannot make men great, nor noble, nor brave.

Any man may be great, but the best place to be great is at home. All men can make their kind better; they can labor to help their neighbors and instruct and improve the minds of the men, women, and children around them; they can make holier their own locality; they can build up the schools and churches around them; and they can make their own homes bright and sweet. These are the elements of greatness; it is here greatness begins; and if a man is not great in his own home or in his own school district, he will never be great anywhere.

56.

WARD McALLISTER: How "The Four Hundred" Lives

"There are only about four hundred people in fashionable New York society," Ward McAllister told Charles Crandall of the New York Tribune *in 1888. "If you go outside that number you strike people who are either not at ease in a ballroom or else make other people not at ease." The phrase caught on and became the symbol of the aristocracy of wealth that ruled, if it did not grace, the Gilded Age. McAllister was the spokesman and, some said, the court jester of this closed society, whose entertainments were extravaganzas and whose ostentation contrasted glaringly with the poverty that surrounded it. Excerpts from McAllister's account of this society that he so much admired appear below.*

Source: *Society As I Have Found It*, New York, 1890, pp. 157-162, 335-363.

AT THIS TIME there were not more than one or two men in New York who spent, in living and entertaining, over $60,000 a year. There were not half a dozen chefs in private families in this city. Compare those days to these and see how easily one or two men of fortune could then control, lead, and carry on society, receive or shut out people at their pleasure. If distinguished strangers failed to bring letters to them, they were shut out from everything. Again, if, though charming people, others were not in accord with those powers, they could be passed over and left out of society. All this many of us saw, and saw how it worked, and we resolved to band together the respectable element of the city and by this union make such strength that no individual could withstand us. The motto, we felt, must be *nous nous soutenons.* This motto we then assumed, and we hold it to this day, and have found that the good and wise men of this community could always control society. This they have done and are still doing. Our first step then in carrying out these views was to arrange for a series of "cotillon dinners."

I must here explain that behind what I call the "smart set" in society there always stood the old, solid, substantial, and respected people. Families who held great social power as far back as the birth of this country, who were looked up to by society, and who always could, when they so wished, come forward and exercise their power, when, for one reason or another, they would take no active part, joining in it quietly, but not conspicuously. Ordinarily, they preferred, like the gods, to sit upon Olympus. I remember a lady, the head of one of these families, stating to me that she had lived longer in New York society than any other person. This point, however, was not yielded or allowed to go undisputed, for the daughter of a rival house contended that *her* family had been longer in New York society than any other family, and though she had heard the assertion, as I gave it, she would not admit its correctness.

What I intend to convey is that the heads of these families, feeling secure in their position, knowing that they had great power when they chose to exercise it, took no leading part in society's daily routine. They gave handsome dinners and perhaps, once a year, a fine ball. I know of one or two families who have scrupulously all their lives avoided display, anything that could make fashionable people of them, holding their own, esteemed and respected; and when they threw open their doors to society, all made a rush to enter. To this day, if one of these old families, even one of its remotest branches, gives a day reception, you will find the street in which they live blockaded with equipages.

For years we have literally had but one *salon* in this city — a gathering in the evening of all the brilliant and cultivated people, both young and old, embracing the distinguished strangers. A most polished and cultivated Bostonian, a brilliant woman, was the first, in my day, to receive in this way weekly. During her life she held this *salon,* both here and all through the summer in Newport. "The robe of Elijah fell upon Elisha" in an extremely talented woman of the world, who has most successfully held, and now holds, this *salon* on the first day of every week during the winter and at Newport in summer.

The mistake made by the world at large is that fashionable people are selfish, frivolous, and indifferent to the welfare of their fellow creatures; all of which is a popular error, arising simply from a want of knowledge of the true state of things. The elegancies of fashionable life nourish and benefit art and artists; they cause the expenditure of money and its distribution; and they really prevent our people and country from settling down into a humdrum rut and becoming merely a money-making and money-saving people, with nothing to brighten up and enliven life; they foster all the fine arts; but for fashion what would become of them? They bring to the front merit of every kind; seek it in the remotest corners, where it modestly shrinks from observation, and force it into notice; adorn their houses with works of art and themselves with all the taste and novelty they can find in any quarter of the globe, calling forth talent and ingenuity.

Fashionable people cultivate and refine themselves, for fashion demands this of them. Progress is fashion's watchword; it never stands still; it always advances, it values and appreciates beauty in woman and talent and genius in man. It is certainly always most charitable; it surrounds itself with the elegancies of life; it soars, it never crawls. I know the general belief is that all fashionable people are hollow and heartless.

My experience is quite the contrary I have found as warm, sympathetic, loving hearts in the garb of fashion as out of it. A thorough acquaintance with the world enables them to distinguish the wheat from the chaff, so that all the good work they do is done with knowledge and effect. The world could not dispense with it. Fashion selects its own votaries. You will see certain members of a family born to it, as it were; others of the same family with none of its attributes. You can give no explanation of this: "One is taken, the other left." Such and such a man or woman are cited as having been always fashionable. The talent of and for society develops itself just as does the talent for art.

The next great event in the fashionable world was a Newport ball. A lady who had married a man of cultivation and taste, a member of one of New York's oldest families, who had inherited from her father an enormous fortune, was at once seized with the ambition to take and hold a brilliant social position, to gratify which she built one of the handsomest houses in this city, importing interiors from Europe for it and such old Spanish tapestries as had never before been introduced into New York; after which she went to Newport and bought a beautiful villa on Bellevue Avenue, and there gave, in the grounds of that villa, the handsomest ball that had ever been given there.

The villa itself was only used to receive and sup the guests in, for a huge tent, capable of holding 1,500 people, had been spread over the entire villa grounds, and in it was built a platform for dancing. The approaches to this tent were admirably designed, and produced a great effect. On entering the villa itself, you were received by the hostess and then directed by liveried servants to the two improvised *salons* of the tent. The one you first entered was the Japanese room, adorned by every conceivable kind of old Japanese objects of art, couches, hangings of embroideries, cunning cane

houses — all illuminated with Japanese lanterns — and the ceiling canopied with Japanese stuffs, producing, with its soft reddish light, a charming effect; then, behind tables scattered in different parts of the room, stood Japanese boys in costume serving fragrant tea. Every possible couch, lounge, and easy chair was there to invite you to sit and indulge yourself in ease and repose.

Leaving this anteroom, you entered still another *salon*, adorned with modern and Parisian furniture, but furnished with cunningly devised corners and nooks for "flirtation couples"; and from this you were ushered into the gorgeous ballroom itself — an immense open tent, whose ceiling and sides were composed of broad stripes of white and scarlet bunting. Then, for the first time at a ball in this country, the electric light was introduced, with brilliant effect. Two grottoes of immense blocks of ice stood on either side of the ballroom, and a powerful jet of light was thrown through each of them, causing the ice to resemble the prisms of an illuminated cavern, and fairly to dazzle one with their coloring. Then, as the blocks of ice would melt, they would tumble over each other in charming glacierlike confusion, giving you winter in the lap of summer; for every species of plant stood around this immense floor, as a flowering border, creeping quite up to these little improvised glaciers. The light was thrown and spread by these two powerful jets, sufficiently strong to give a brilliant illumination to the ballroom. The only criticism possible was that it made deep shadows.

All Newport was present to give brilliancy to the scene. Everything was to be European, so one supped at small tables as at a ball in Paris, all through the night. Supper was ready at the opening of the ball, and also as complete and as well served at the finish, by daylight. Newport had never seen before, and has never since seen, anything as dazzling and brilliant, as well conceived, and as well carried out in every detail.

Desirous of obtaining an office from the

administration of President Arthur, I went to Washington with letters to the President and his attorney general. On my arrival, depositing my luggage in my room at Willard's, I descended to the modest little barbershop of that hotel, and there, in the hands of a colored barber, I saw our distinguished secretary of state, the Hon. Frederick T. Frelinghuysen, who, on catching sight of me, exclaimed:

"Halloa, my friend! What brings you here?" He had for years been my lawyer in New Jersey.

I replied: "I want an office."

"Well, what office?"

I told him what I wanted.

"I hope you do not expect me to get it for you!" he exclaimed.

"Not exactly," I answered. "My man is the attorney general, and I want you to tell me where I can find him."

"Find him! Why, that's easy enough; there is not another such man in Washington. Where do you dine?"

"Here, in this house, at seven."

"He dines here at the same hour. All you have to do is to look about you then, and when you see an old-fashioned, courtly gentleman of the Benjamin Franklin style, you will see Brewster," said Mr. Frelinghuysen.

While quietly taking my soup, I saw an apparition! In walked a stately, handsome woman, by her side an old-fashioned, courtly gentleman in a black velvet sack coat, ruffled shirt, and ruffled wristbands, accompanied by a small boy, evidently their son. "There he is," I said to myself. Now, I make it a rule never to disturb anyone until they have taken off the edge of their appetite. I stealthily viewed the man on whom my hopes hinged. Remarkable to look at he was. A thoroughly well-dressed man, with the unmistakable air of a gentleman and a man of culture. As he spoke he gesticulated, and even with his family, he seemingly kept up the liveliest of conversations. No sooner had he reached his coffee than I reached him. In five minutes I was as much at home with him as if I had known him for five years.

"Well, my dear sir," he said, "what made you go first to Frelinghuysen? Why did you not come at once to me? I know all about you; my friends are your friends. I know what you want. The office you wish, I will see that you get. Our good President will sanction what I do. The office is yours. Say no more about it." From that hour this glorious old man and myself were sworn friends; I was here simply carrying out the axiom to keep one's friendships in repair; and, as he had done so much for me, I resolved, in turn, to do all I could for him, and I know I made the evening of his life, at least, one of pleasurable and quiet enjoyment.

He came to me that summer at Newport, and the life he there led among fashionable people seemed to be a new awakening to him of cultivated and refined enjoyment. He found himself among people there who appreciated his well-stored mind and his great learning. He was the brightest and best conversationalist I have ever met with. His memory was marvelous; every little incident of everyday life would bring forth some poetical illustrations from his mental storehouse.

At a large dinner I gave him, to which I had invited General Hancock and one of the judges of the Supreme Court of the United States, the question of precedence presented itself. I sent in the judge before the general, and being criticized for this, I appealed to the general himself. "In Washington," he said, "I have been sent in to dinner on many occasions before our Supreme Court judges, and again on other occasions they have preceded me. There is no fixed rule; but I am inclined to think I have precedence."

During this summer, a young friend of mine was so charmed with the attorney general that he advised with me about giving him an exceptionally handsome entertainment. This idea took shape the following winter, when he came and asked me to assist him in getting up for him a superb banquet at Delmonico's. He wanted the brilliant people of society to be invited to it and no pains or expense to be spared to make it the affair of the winter. I felt that our distinguished citizen, the ex-secretary of state and ex-governor, who had so long held political as well as social power, and his wife, should be asked to preside over it, and thus expressed myself to him, and was requested to ask them to do so. I presented myself to this most affable and courtly lady in her sunshiny drawing room on Second Avenue and proffered my request. She graciously accepted the invitation, saying she well knew the gentleman and his family as old New Yorkers, and to preside over a dinner given to her old friend Mr. Brewster would really give her the greatest pleasure.

Great care was taken in the selection of the guests. New York sent to this feast the brilliant men and women of that day, and the feast was worthy of them. The "I" table (shape of letter *I*) was literally a garden of superb roses; a border of heartsease, the width of one's hand, encircled it, and was most artistic. Delmonico's ballroom, where we dined, had never been so elaborately decorated. The mural decorations were superb; plaques of lilies of the valley, of tulips, and of azaleas adorned the walls; and the dinner itself was pronounced the best effort of Delmonico's chefs. What added much to the general effect was, on leaving the table for a short half hour, to find the same dining room, in that short space of time, converted into a brilliant ballroom, all full of the guests of the patriarchs, and a ball under full headway.

We here reach a period when New York society turned over a new leaf. Up to this time, for one to be worth $1 million was to be rated as a man of fortune, but now, bygones must be bygones. New York's ideas as to values, when fortune was named, leaped boldly up to $10 million, $50 million, $100 million, and the necessities and luxuries followed suit. One was no longer content with a dinner of a dozen or more to be served by a couple of servants. Fashion demanded that you be received in the hall of the house in which you were to dine by from five to six servants, who, with the butler, were to serve the repast. The butler, on such occasions, to do alone the headwork, and under him he had these men in livery to serve the dinner — he to guide and direct them. Soft strains of music were introduced between the courses, and in some houses gold replaced silver in the way of plate, and everything that skill and art could suggest was added to make the dinners not a vulgar display but a great gastronomic effort, evidencing the possession by the host of both money and taste.

The butler from getting a salary of $40 a month received then from $60 to $75 a month. The second man jumped up from $20 to $35 and $40; and the extra men, at the dinner of a dozen people or more, would cost $24. Then the orchids, being the most costly of all flowers, were introduced in profusion. The canvasback, that we could buy at $2.50 a pair, went up to $8 a pair; the terrapin were $4 apiece. Our forefathers would have been staggered at the cost of the hospitality of these days. . . .

The six quadrilles were really the event of the ball, consisting of "The Hobby-horse Quadrille," the men who danced in it being dressed in "pink," and the ladies wearing red hunting coats and white satin skirts, all of the period of Louis XIV. In the "Mother Goose Quadrille" were "Jack and Jill," "Little Red Riding-Hood," "Bo-Peep," "Goody Two-Shoes," "Mary, Mary, Quite Contrary," and "My Pretty Maid." The "Opera Bouffe Quadrille" was most successful; but of all of them, "The Star Quadrille," containing the youth and beauty of the city, was the most brilliant. The ladies in it were arrayed as twin stars, in four different colors — yellow, blue, mauve, and white. Above the forehead of each lady, in her hair, was worn an electric light, giving a fairy- and elflike appearance to each of them. "The Dresden Quadrille," in which the ladies wore white satin, with powdered hair, and the gentlemen, white satin knee breeches and powdered wigs, with the Dresden mark, crossed swords, on each of them, was effective.

The hostess appeared as a Venetian princess, with a superb jeweled peacock in her hair. The host was the Duke de Guise for that evening. The host's eldest brother wore a costume of Louis XVI. His wife appeared as "The Electric Light," in white satin, trimmed with diamonds, and her head one blaze of diamonds. The most remarkable costume, and one spoken of to this day, was that of a cat; the dress being of cats' tails and white cats' heads, and a bell with "Puss" on it in large letters. A distinguished beauty, dressed as a Phoenix, adorned with diamonds and rubies, was superb, and the Capuchin Monk, with hood and sandals, inimitable; but to name the most striking would be to name all.

The great social revolution that had occurred in New York this winter, like most revolutionary waves, reached Newport. Our distinguished New York journalist then made Newport his summer home, buying the fine granite house that for years had been first known as "The Middleton Mansion," afterwards the "Sidney Brooks residence," and filling it with distinguished Europeans. His activity and energy gave new life to the place.

One fine summer morning, one of his guests, an officer in the English Army, a bright spirit and admirable horseman, riding on his polo pony up to the Newport Reading Room, where all the fossils of the place, the nobs, and the swells daily gossiped, he

was challenged to ride the pony into the hall of this revered old club, and, being bantered to do it, he actually did ride the pony across the narrow piazza and into the hall of the club itself. This was enough to set Newport agog. What sacrilege! An Englishman to ride in upon us, not respecting the sanctity of the place! It aroused the old patriots who were members of that Institution with the spirit of '76, and a summary note was sent to the great journalist withdrawing the invitation the club had previously given his guest. The latter, in turn, felt aggrieved and retaliated with this result: building for Newport a superb casino, embracing a club, a ballroom, and a restaurant, opposite his own residence. All this evidencing that agitation of any kind is as beneficial in social circles as to the atmosphere we breathe.

Then our journalist conceived and gave a handsome Domino ball. All the ladies in Domino, much after the pattern of the one previously given by the Duchess de Dino, and in many respects resembling it, having a huge tent spread behind the house, and all the rooms on the first floor converted into a series of charming supper rooms, each table decorated most elaborately with beautiful flowers — as handsome a ball as one could give. I took the wife of the attorney general to it in Domino, who, after her life in Washington, was amazed at the beauty of the scene. The grounds, which were very handsome, were all, even the plants themselves, illuminated with electric lights — that is, streams of electric light were cunningly thrown under the plants, giving an illumination à giorno, and producing the most beautiful effect.

At this ball there appeared a Blue Domino that set all the men wild. Coming to the ball in her own carriage (her servants she felt she could trust not to betray her), she dashed into the merry throng and, gliding from one to the other, whispered airy nothings into men's ears. But they contained enough to excite the most intense curiosity as to who she was. She was the belle of the evening; she became bold and daring at times, attacking men of and about the inmost secrets of their hearts, so as to alarm them; and when she had worked them all up to a fever heat, she came to me to take her to the door that she might make good her escape. A dozen men barricaded the way, but with the rapidity of a deer she dashed through them, reached the sidewalk, and her footman literally threw her into the carriage. Her coachman, well drilled, dashed off at a furious rate, and to this day no one has ever found out who the fair creature was. . . .

Hearing that President Arthur would visit Newport, as I felt greatly in his debt I resolved to do my share in making his visit pleasant and agreeable. He was to be the guest of Governor Morgan, whom I at once buttonholed and to him gave the above views. I found, like all these great political magnates, that he preferred to have the President to himself, and rather threw cold water on my attempting anything in my humble way at entertaining him. "Why, my dear sir," he replied, "the President will not go to one of your country picnics. It is preposterous to think of getting up such a rural thing for him. I shall, of course, dine him and give him a fete, and have already sent to New York for my Madeira."

"Sent for your Madeira!" I exclaimed. "Why, my dear Governor, it will not be fit to drink when it reaches you."

"Why not?" he asked.

"Because it will be so shaken up, it will be like tasting bad drugs. Madeira of any age, if once moved, cannot be tasted until it has had at least a month's repose. President Arthur is a good judge of Madeira, and he would not drink your wine."

"Well, what am I to do?" said he.

"Why, my dear Governor, I will myself carry to your house for him a couple of bottles of my very best Madeira." This I did, sitting in the middle of the carriage, one bottle in each hand (it having been first carefully decanted), and into the governor's parlor I was ushered, and then placed my offering before the President, telling him that I well knew he loved women, as well as song and wine; prayed him to honor me with his presence at a Newport picnic, promising to cull a bouquet of such exotics as are only grown in a Newport hothouse.

The invitation he at once accepted, much, I thought, to the chagrin of the governor, who, accompanying me to his front door, said: "My dear sir, one must remember that he is the President of the United States, ruling over 60 million people. He is here as my guest, and now to go off and dine on Sunday with a leader of fashion, and then to follow this up by attending one of your open-air lunches, seems to me not right." (I must here say in his defense that the governor had never been to one of my "open-air lunches" and knew not of what he spoke.)

I then resolved to make this picnic worthy of our great ruler, and at once invited to it a beautiful woman, one who might have been selected for a Madonna. This is the first time I have made mention of her; she possessed that richness of nature you only see in Southern climes; one of the most beautiful women in America. She promised to go to this country party and bring her court with her.

I selected the loveliest spot on Newport Island, known as "The Balch Place," near "The Paradise and Purgatory Rocks," for this fete. The Atlantic Ocean, calm and unruffled, lay before us; all the noise it made was the gentle ripple of the waves as they kissed the rocky shore. Giving the President our great beauty, he led the way to the collation, partaken of at little tables under the sparse trees that the rough winter barely permitted to live, and then we had a merry dance on the green, on an excellent platform fringed with plants.

At a subsequent breakfast, I was intensely gratified to have the President say to me, before the whole company, "McAllister, you did indeed redeem your promise. The beauty of the women at your picnic, the beauty of the place, and its admirable arrangement made it the pleasantest party I have had at Newport" — and this was said before my friend the governor. Grand, elaborate entertainments are ofttimes not as enjoyable as country frolics.

57.

Jacob Riis: Racial Groups Among the New York Tenements

One of the most obvious social problems of the American city during the late nineteenth century was wretched housing conditions. For the first time, slums became a fixture of city life. The influx of immigrants and factory workers created such acute housing shortages that greedy landlords could easily fill to overflow their decaying tenement buildings. A newspaperman, Jacob Riis, led the crusade for housing reform in New York City. His vivid articles depicting tenement life stimulated the demand for improved housing for the poor; even Theodore Roosevelt joined the campaign. One of Riis's best-known works was How the Other Half Lives *(1890), portions of which are reprinted here.*

Source: *How the Other Half Lives*, New York, 1914, pp. 21-27, 48-49, 104-107, 136-140, 148-151.

THE MIXED CROWD

WHEN once I asked the agent of a notorious Fourth Ward alley how many people might be living in it I was told: One hundred and forty families, one hundred Irish, thirty-eight Italian, and two that spoke the German tongue. Barring the agent herself, there was not a native-born individual in the court. The answer was characteristic of the cosmopolitan character of lower New York, very nearly so of the whole of it, wherever it runs to alleys and courts. One may find for the asking an Italian, a German, a French, African, Spanish, Bohemian, Russian, Scandinavian, Jewish, and Chinese colony. Even the Arab, who peddles "holy earth" from the Battery as a direct importation from Jerusalem, has his exclusive preserves at the lower end of Washington Street. The one thing you shall vainly ask for in the chief city of America is a distinctively American community. There is none; certainly not among the tenements.

Where have they gone to, the old inhabitants? I put the question to one who might fairly be presumed to be of the number, since I had found him sighing for the "good old days" when the legend "no Irish need apply" was familiar in the advertising columns of the newspapers. He looked at me with a puzzled air. "I don't know," he said. "I wish I did. Some went to California in '49, some to the war and never came back. The rest, I expect, have gone to Heaven, or somewhere. I don't see them 'round here."

Whatever the merit of the good man's conjectures, his eyes did not deceive him. They are not here. In their place has come this queer conglomerate mass of heterogeneous elements, ever striving and working like whisky and water in one glass, and with the like result: final union and a prevailing taint of whisky. The once unwelcome Irishman has been followed in his turn by the Italian, the Russian Jew, and the Chinaman, and has himself taken a hand at opposition, quite as bitter and quite as ineffectual, against these later hordes. Wherever these have gone, they have crowded him out, possessing the block, the street, the ward with their denser swarms. But the Irishman's revenge is complete. Victorious in defeat over his recent as over his more ancient foe, the one who opposed his coming no less than the one who drove him out, he dictates to both their politics, and, secure in possession of the offices, returns the native his greeting with interest, while collecting the rents of the Italian whose house he has bought with the profits of his saloon.

As a landlord he is picturesquely autocratic. An amusing instance of his methods came under my notice while writing these lines. An inspector of the Health Department found an Italian family paying a man with a Celtic name $25 a month for three small rooms in a ramshackle rear tenement — more than twice what they were worth — and expressed his astonishment to the tenant, an ignorant Sicilian laborer. He replied that he had once asked the landlord to reduce the rent, but he would not do it.

"Well! What did he say?" asked the inspector.

" 'Damma, man!' he said; 'if you speaka thata way to me, I fira you and your things in the streeta.' " And the frightened Italian paid the rent.

In justice to the Irish landlord it must be said that like an apt pupil he was merely showing forth the result of the schooling he had received, reenacting, in his own way, the scheme of the tenements. It is only his frankness that shocks. The Irishman does not naturally take kindly to tenement life, though with characteristic versatility he adapts himself to its conditions at once. It does violence, nevertheless, to the best that is in him, and for that very reason of all who come within its sphere soonest corrupts him. The result is a sediment, the product of more than a generation in the city's slums, that, as distinguished from the larger body of his class, justly ranks at the foot of tenement dwellers the so-called "low Irish."

It is not to be assumed, of course, that the whole body of the population living in the tenements, of which New Yorkers are in the habit of speaking vaguely as "the poor," or even the larger part of it, is to be classed as vicious or as poor in the sense of verging on beggary.

New York's wage earners have no other place to live, more is the pity. They are truly poor for having no better homes; waxing poorer in purse as the exorbitant rents to which they are tied, as ever was serf to soil, keep rising. The wonder is that they are not all corrupted, and speedily, by their surroundings. If, on the contrary, there be a steady working up, if not out of the slough, the fact is a powerful argument for the optimist's belief that the world is, after all, growing better, not worse, and would go far toward disarming apprehension, were it not for the steadier growth of the sediment of the slums and its constant menace. Such an impulse toward better things there certainly is. The German ragpicker of thirty years ago, quite as low in the scale as his Italian successor, is the thrifty tradesman or prosperous farmer of today.

The Italian scavenger of our time is fast graduating into exclusive control of the corner fruit stands, while his black-eyed boy monopolizes the bootblacking industry, in which a few years ago he was an intruder. The Irish hod carrier in the second generation has become a brick layer, if not the alderman of his ward; while the Chinese coolie is in almost exclusive possession of the laundry business. The reason is obvious. The poorest immigrant comes here with the purpose and ambition to better himself, and, given half a chance, might be reasonably expected to make the most of it. To the false plea that he prefers the squalid homes in which his kind are housed there could be no better answer. The truth is, his half chance has too long been wanting, and for the bad result he has been unjustly blamed.

As emigration from East to West follows the latitude, so does the foreign influx in New York distribute itself along certain well-defined lines that waver and break only under the stronger pressure of a more gregarious race or the encroachments of inexorable business. A feeling of dependence upon mutual effort, natural to strangers in a strange land, unacquainted with its language and customs, sufficiently accounts for this.

The Irishman is the true cosmopolitan immigrant. All-pervading, he shares his lodging with perfect impartiality with the Italian, the Greek, and the "Dutchman," yielding only to sheer force of numbers, and objects equally to them all. A map of the city, colored to designate nationalities, would show more stripes than on the skin of a zebra, and more colors than any rainbow. The city on such a map would fall into two great halves, green for the Irish prevailing in the West Side tenement districts, and blue for the Germans on the East Side. But intermingled with these ground colors would be an odd variety of tints that would give the whole the appearance of an extraordinary crazy quilt.

From down in the Sixth Ward, upon the site of the old Collect Pond, that in the days of the fathers drained the hills which are no more, the red of the Italian would be seen forcing its way northward along the line of Mulberry Street to the quarter of the French purple on Bleecker Street and South Fifth Avenue, to lose itself and reappear, after a lapse of miles, in the "Little Italy" of Harlem, east of Second Avenue. Dashes of red, sharply defined, would be seen strung through the Annexed District, northward to the city line. On the West Side the red would be seen overrunning the old Africa of Thompson Street, pushing the black of the Negro rapidly uptown, against querulous but unavailing protests, occupying his home, his church, his trade and all, with merciless impartiality.

There is a church in Mulberry Street that has stood for two generations as a sort of milestone of these migrations. Built originally for the worship of staid New Yorkers of the "old stock," it was engulfed by the colored tide, when the draft riots drove the Negroes out of reach of Cherry Street and the Five Points. Within the past decade the advance wave of the Italian onset reached it, and today the arms of United Italy adorn its front. The Negroes have made a stand at several points along Seventh and Eighth Avenues; but their main body, still pursued by the Italian foe, is on the march yet, and the black mark will be found overshadowing today many blocks on the East Side, with One Hundredth Street as the center, where colonies of them have settled recently.

Hardly less aggressive than the Italian, the Russian and Polish Jew, having overrun the district between Rivington and Division Streets, east of the Bowery, to the point of suffocation, is filling the tenements of the old Seventh Ward to the river front, and disputing with the Italian every foot of available space in the back alleys of Mulberry Street. The two races, differing hopelessly in much, have this in common: they carry their slums with them wherever they go, if allowed to do it. Little Italy already rivals its parent, the "Bend," in foulness. Other nationalities that begin at the bottom make a fresh start when crowded up the ladder. Happily both are manageable — the one by rabbinical, the other by the civil, law.

Between the dull gray of the Jew, his favorite color, and the Italian red, would be seen squeezed in on the map a sharp streak of yellow, marking the narrow boundaries of Chinatown. Dovetailed in with the German population, the poor but thrifty Bohemian might be picked out by the somber hue of his life as of his philosophy, struggling against heavy odds in the big human beehives of the East Side. Colonies of his people extend northward, with long lapses of space, from below the Cooper Institute more than three miles. The Bohemian is the only foreigner with any considerable representation in the city who counts no wealthy man of his race, none who has not to work hard for a living, or has got beyond the reach of the tenement.

Down near the Battery, the West Side emerald would be soiled by a dirty stain, spreading rapidly like a splash of ink on a sheet of blotting paper, headquarters of the Arab tribe, that in a single year has swelled from the original dozen to twelve hundred, intent, every mother's son, on trade and barter. Dots and dashes of color here and there would show where the Finnish sailors worship their *djumala* (God); the Greek peddlers, the ancient name of their race, and the Swiss the goddess of thrift. And so on to the end of the long register, all toiling together in the galling fetters of the tenement.

Were the question raised who makes the most of life thus mortgaged, who resists most stubbornly its leveling tendency — knows how to drag even the barracks upward a part of the way at least toward the ideal plane of the home — the palm must be unhesitatingly awarded the Teuton. The Italian and the poor Jew rise only by compulsion. The Chinaman does not rise at all; here, as at home, he simply remains stationary. The Irishman's genius runs to public affairs rather than domestic life; wherever he is mustered in force the saloon is the gorgeous center of political activity. The German struggles vainly to learn his trick; his Teutonic wit is too heavy, and the political ladder he raises from his saloon usually too short or too clumsy to reach the desired goal. The best part of his life is lived at home, and he makes himself a home independent of the surroundings, giving the lie to the saying, unhappily become a maxim of social truth, that pauperism and drunkenness naturally grow in the tenements. He makes the most of his tenement, and it should be added that, whenever and as soon as he can save up money enough, he gets out and never crosses the threshold of one again. . . .

THE ITALIAN IN NEW YORK

CERTAINLY A PICTURESQUE, if not very tidy, element has been added to the population in the "assisted" Italian immigrant who claims so large a share of public attention, partly because he keeps coming at such a tremendous rate; but chiefly because he elects to stay in New York, or near enough for it to serve as his base of operations; and here promptly reproduces conditions of destitution and disorder which, set in the framework of Mediterranean exuberance, are the delight of the artist, but in a matter-of-fact American community become its danger and reproach. The reproduction is made easier in New York because he finds the material ready to hand in the worst of the slum tenements; but even where it is not he soon reduces what he does find to his own level, if allowed to follow his natural bent.

The Italian comes in at the bottom, and, in the generation that came over the sea, he stays there. In the slums he is welcomed as a tenant who "makes less trouble" than the contentious Irishman or the order-loving German; that is to say, is content to live in a pig sty and submits to robbery at the hands of the rent collector without murmur. Yet this very tractability makes of him in good hands, when firmly and intelligently managed, a really desirable tenant. But it is not his good fortune often to fall in with other hospitality upon his coming than that which brought him here for its own profit, and has no idea of letting go its grip upon him as long as there is a cent to be made out of him.

Recent congressional inquiries have shown the nature of the "assistance" he receives from greedy steamship agents and "bankers," who persuade him by false promises to mortgage his home, his few belongings, and his wages for months to come for a ticket to the land where plenty of work is to be had at princely wages. The padrone — the "banker" is nothing else — having made his 10 percent out of him en route, receives him at the landing and turns him to double account as a wage earner and a rent payer. In each of these roles he is made to yield a profit to his unscrupulous countryman, whom he trusts implicitly with the instinct of utter helplessness. The man is so ignorant that, as one of the sharpers who prey upon him put it once, it "would be downright sinful not to take him in." His ignorance and unconquerable suspicion of strangers dig the pit into which he falls.

He not only knows no word of English but he does not know enough to learn. Rarely only can he write his own language. Unlike the German, who begins learning English the day he lands as a matter of duty, or the Polish Jew, who takes it up as soon as he is able as an investment, the Italian learns slowly, if at all. Even his boy, born here, often speaks his native tongue indifferently. He is forced, therefore, to have constant recourse to the middleman,

who makes him pay handsomely at every turn. He hires him out to the railroad contractor, receiving a commission from the employer as well as from the laborer, and repeats the performance monthly, or as often as he can have him dismissed. . . .

JEWTOWN

THE TENEMENTS GROW TALLER, and the gaps in their ranks close up rapidly as we cross the Bowery and, leaving Chinatown and the Italians behind, invade the Hebrew quarter. Baxter Street, with its interminable rows of old-clothes shops and its brigades of pullers-in — nicknamed "the Bay" in honor, perhaps, of the tars who lay to there after a cruise to stock up their togs, or maybe after the "schooners" of beer plentifully bespoke in that latitude — Bayard Street, with its synagogues and its crowds, gave us a foretaste of it. No need of asking here where we are. The jargon of the street, the signs of the sidewalk, the manner and dress of the people, their unmistakable physiognomy betray their race at every step. Men with queer skull caps, venerable beard, and the outlandish long-skirted caftan of the Russian Jew, elbow the ugliest and the handsomest women in the land. The contrast is startling. The old women are hags; the young, houris. Wives and mothers at sixteen, at thirty they are old. So thoroughly has the chosen people crowded out the gentiles in the Tenth Ward that, when the great Jewish holidays come around every year, the public schools in the district have practically to close up. Of their thousands of pupils scarce a handful come to school. Nor is there any suspicion that the rest are playing hookey. They stay honestly home to celebrate. There is no mistaking it: we are in Jewtown.

It is said that nowhere in the world are so many people crowded together on a square mile as here. The average five-story tenement adds a story or two to its stature in Ludlow Street and an extra building on the rear lot, and yet the sign "To Let" is the rarest of all there. Here is one seven stories high. The Sanitary policeman, whose beat this is, will tell you that it contains thirty-six families, but the term has a widely different meaning here and on the avenues. In this house, where a case of smallpox was reported, there were fifty-eight babies and thirty-eight children that were over five years of age. In Essex Street, two small rooms in a six-story tenement were made to hold a "family" of father and mother, twelve children, and six boarders. The boarder plays as important a part in the domestic economy of Jewtown as the lodger in the Mulberry Street Bend. These are samples of the packing of the population that has run up the record here to the rate of 330,000 per square mile. The densest crowding of Old London . . . never got beyond 175,000. Even the alley is crowded out.

Through dark hallways and filthy cellars, crowded, as is every foot of the street, with dirty children, the settlements in the rear are reached. Thieves know how to find them when pursued by the police, and the tramps that sneak in on chilly nights to fight for the warm spot in the yard over some baker's oven. They are out of place in this hive of busy industry, and they know it. It has nothing in common with them or with their philosophy of life that the world owes the idler a living. Life here means the hardest kind of work almost from the cradle. The world as a debtor has no credit in Jewtown. Its promise to pay wouldn't buy one of the old hats that are hawked about Hester Street, unless backed by security representing labor done at lowest market rates. But this army of workers must have bread. It is cheap and filling, and bakeries abound. Wherever they are in the tenements the tramp will skulk in, if he can.

There is such a tramps' roost in the rear of a tenement near the lower end of Ludlow Street that is never without its tenants in winter. By a judicious practice of flopping over on the stone pavement at intervals and thus warming one side at a time, and with an empty box to put the feet in, it is possible to keep reasonably comfortable there even on a rainy night. In summer the yard is the only one in the neighborhood that does not do duty as a public dormitory.

Thrift is the watchword of Jewtown, as of its people the world over. It is at once its strength and its fatal weakness, its cardinal virtue and its foul disgrace. Become an overmastering passion with these people who come here in droves from Eastern Europe to escape persecution, from which freedom could be bought only with gold, it has enslaved them in bondage worse than that from which they fled. Money is their God. Life itself is of little value compared with even the leanest bank account. In no other spot does life wear so intensely bald and materialistic an aspect as in Ludlow Street. Over and over again I have met with instances of these Polish or Russian Jews deliberately starving themselves to the point of physical exhaustion, while working night and day at a tremendous pressure to save a little money. An avenging Nemesis pursues this headlong hunt for wealth; there is no worse paid class anywhere. I once put the question to one of their own people, who, being a pawnbroker, and an unusually intelligent and charitable one, certainly enjoyed the advantage of a practical view of the stituation: "Whence the many wretchedly poor people in such a colony of workers, where poverty, from a misfortune, has become a reproach, dreaded as the plague?"

"Immigration," he said, "brings us a lot. In five years it has averaged 25,000 a year, of which more than 70 percent have stayed in New York. Half of them require and receive aid from the Hebrew Charities from

Jacob Riis

the very start, lest they starve. That is one explanation. There is another class than the one that cannot get work: those who have had too much of it; who have worked and hoarded and lived, crowded together like pigs, on the scantiest fare and the worst to be got, bound to save whatever their earnings, until, worn out, they could work no longer. Then their hoards were soon exhausted. That is their story." And I knew that what he said was true. . . .

THE BOHEMIANS —
TENEMENT-HOUSE
CIGARMAKING

EVIL as the part is which the tenement plays in Jewtown as the pretext for circumventing the law that was made to benefit and relieve the tenant, we have not far to go to find it in even a worse role. If the tenement is here continually dragged into the eye of public condemnation and scorn, it is be-

cause in one way or another it is found directly responsible for, or intimately associated with, three-fourths of the miseries of the poor. In the Bohemian quarter it is made the vehicle for enforcing upon a proud race a slavery as real as any that ever disgraced the South. Not content with simply robbing the tenant, the owner, in the dual capacity of landlord and employer, reduces him to virtual serfdom by making his becoming *his* tenant, on such terms as he sees fit to make, the condition of employment at wages likewise of his own making. It does not help the case that this landlord employer, almost always a Jew, is frequently of the thrifty Polish race just described.

Perhaps the Bohemian quarter is hardly the proper name to give to the colony, for, though it has distinct boundaries, it is scattered over a wide area on the East Side, in wedgelike streaks that relieve the monotony of the solid German population by their strong contrasts. The two races mingle no more on this side of the Atlantic than on the rugged slopes of the Bohemian mountains; the echoes of the Thirty Years' War ring in New York, after two centuries and a half, with as fierce a hatred as the gigantic combat bred among the vanquished Czechs. A chief reason for this is doubtless the complete isolation of the Bohemian immigrant. Several causes operate to bring this about: his singularly harsh and unattractive language, which he can neither easily himself unlearn nor impart to others, his stubborn pride of race, and a popular prejudice which has forced upon him the unjust stigma of a disturber of the public peace and an enemy of organized labor.

I greatly mistrust that the Bohemian on our shores is a much-abused man. To his traducer, who casts up anarchism against him, he replies that the last census (1880) shows his people to have the fewest criminals of all in proportion to numbers. In New York a Bohemian criminal is such a rarity that the case of two firebugs of several years ago is remembered with damaging distinctness. The accusation that he lives like the "rat" he is, cutting down wages by his underpaid labor, he throws back in the teeth of the trades unions with the countercharge that they are the first cause of his attitude to the labor question.

A little way above Houston Street the first of his colonies is encountered, in Fifth Street and thereabouts. Then for a mile and a half scarce a Bohemian is to be found, until Thirty-eighth Street is reached. Fifty-fourth and Seventy-third Streets in their turn are the centers of populous Bohemian settlements. The location of the cigar factories, upon which he depends for a living, determines his choice of home, though there is less choice about it than with any other class in the community, save perhaps the colored people. Probably more than half of all the Bohemians in this city are cigarmakers, and it is the herding of these in great numbers in the so-called tenement factories, where the cheapest grade of work is done at the lowest wages, that constitutes at once their greatest hardship and the chief grudge of other workmen against them.

The manufacturer who owns, say, from three or four to a dozen or more tenements contiguous to his shop, fills them up with these people, charging them outrageous rents, and demanding often even a preliminary deposit of $5 "key money"; deals them out tobacco by the week, and devotes the rest of his energies to the paring down of wages to within a peg or two of the point where the tenant rebels in desperation. When he does rebel, he is given the alternative of submission, or eviction with entire loss of employment. His needs determine the issue. Usually he is not in a position to hesitate long. Unlike the Polish Jew, whose example of untiring industry he emulates, he has seldom much laid up against a rainy day. He is fond of a glass of beer, and

likes to live as well as his means will permit. The shop triumphs, and fetters more galling than ever are forged for the tenant. In the opposite case, the newspapers have to record the throwing upon the street of a small army of people, with pitiful cases of destitution and family misery.

Men, women, and children work together seven days in the week in these cheerless tenements to make a living for the family, from the break of day till far into the night. Often the wife is the original cigarmaker from the old home, the husband having adopted her trade here as a matter of necessity, because, knowing no word of English, he could get no other work. As they state the cause of the bitter hostility of the trade unions, she was the primary bone of contention in the day of the early Bohemian immigration. The unions refused to admit the women, and, as the support of the family depended upon her to a large extent, such terms as were offered had to be accepted. The manufacturer has ever since industriously fanned the antagonism between the unions and his hands, for his own advantage. The victory rests with him, since the Court of Appeals decided that the law, passed a few years ago, to prohibit cigarmaking in tenements was unconstitutional, and thus put an end to the struggle.

While it lasted, all sorts of frightful stories were told of the shocking conditions under which people lived and worked in these tenements, from a sanitary point of view especially, and a general impression survives to this day that they are particularly desperate. The Board of Health, after a careful canvass, did not find them so then. I am satisfied from personal inspection, at a much later day, guided in a number of instances by the union cigarmakers themselves to the tenements which they considered the worst, that the accounts were greatly exaggerated. Doubtless the people are poor, in many cases very poor; but they are not uncleanly, rather the reverse; they live much better than the clothing makers in the Tenth Ward, and in spite of their sallow look, that may be due to the all-pervading smell of tobacco, they do not appear to be less healthy than other indoor workers.

I found on my tours of investigation several cases of consumption, of which one at least was said by the doctor to be due to the constant inhalation of tobacco fumes. But an examination of the death records in the Health Department does not support the claim that the Bohemian cigarmakers are peculiarly prone to that disease. On the contrary, the Bohemian percentage of deaths from consumption appears quite low. This, however, is a line of scientific inquiry which I leave to others to pursue, along with the more involved problem whether the falling off in the number of children, sometimes quite noticeable in the Bohemian settlements, is, as has been suggested, dependent upon the character of the parents' work. The sore grievances I found were the miserable wages and the enormous rents exacted for the minimum of accommodation. And surely these stand for enough of suffering. . . .

THE COLOR LINE
IN NEW YORK

THE COLOR LINE must be drawn through the tenements to give the picture its proper shading. The landlord does the drawing, does it with an absence of pretense, a frankness of despotism, that is nothing if not brutal. The czar of all the Russias is not more absolute upon his own soil than the New York landlord in his dealings with colored tenants. Where he permits them to live, they go; where he shuts the door, stay out. By his grace they exist at all in certain localities; his ukase banishes them from others. He accepts the responsibility, when laid at his door, with unruffled complacency. It is business, he will tell you. And it is. He

makes the prejudice, in which he trafficks, pay him well, and that, as he thinks it quite superfluous to tell you, is what he is there for.

That his pencil does not make quite as black a mark as it did, that the hand that wields it does not bear down as hard as only a short half dozen years ago, is the hopeful sign of an awakening public conscience under the stress of which the line shows signs of wavering. But for this the landlord deserves no credit. It has come, is coming about despite him. . . . Natural selection will have more or less to do beyond a doubt in every age with dividing the races; only so, it may be, can they work out together their highest destiny. But with the despotism that deliberately assigns to the defenseless black the lowest level for the purpose of robbing him there that has nothing to do. Of such slavery, different only in degree from the other kind that held him as a chattel, to be sold or bartered at the will of his master, this century, if signs fail not, will see the end in New York.

Ever since the war New York has been receiving the overflow of colored population from the Southern cities. In the last decade this migration has grown to such proportions that it is estimated that our blacks have quite doubled in number since the Tenth Census. Whether the exchange has been of advantage to the Negro may well be questioned. Trades of which he had practical control in his Southern home are not open to him here. I know that it may be answered that there is no industrial proscription of color; that it is a matter of choice. Perhaps so. At all events he does not choose then. How many colored carpenters or masons has anyone seen at work in New York? In the South there are enough of them, and, if the testimony of the most intelligent of their people is worth anything, plenty of them have come here. As a matter of fact, the colored man takes in New York, without a struggle, the lower level of menial service for which his past traditions and natural love of ease perhaps as yet fit him best. Even the colored barber is rapidly getting to be a thing of the past. Along shore, at any unskilled labor, he works unmolested; but he does not appear to prefer the job.

His sphere thus defined, he naturally takes his stand among the poor, and in the homes of the poor. Until very recent times — the years since a change was wrought can be counted on the fingers of one hand — he was practically restricted in the choice of a home to a narrow section on the West Side, that nevertheless had a social top and bottom to it — the top in the tenements on the line of Seventh Avenue as far north as Thirty-second Street, where he was allowed to occupy the houses of unsavory reputation which the police had cleared and for which decent white tenants could not be found; the bottom in the vile rookeries of Thompson Street and South Fifth Avenue, the old "Africa" that is now fast becoming a modern Italy. Today there are black colonies in Yorkville and Morrisania. The encroachment of business and the Italian below, and the swelling of the population above, have been the chief agents in working out his second emancipation, a very real one, for with his cutting loose from the old tenements there has come a distinct and gratifying improvement in the tenant, that argues louder than theories or speeches the influence of vile surroundings in debasing the man. The colored citizen whom this year's census man found in his Ninety-ninth Street "flat" is a very different individual from the "nigger" his predecessor counted in the black-and-tan slums of Thompson and Sullivan Streets.

There is no more clean and orderly community in New York than the new settlement of colored people that is growing up on the East Side from Yorkville to Harlem. Cleanliness is the characteristic of the Negro in his new surroundings, as it was his virtue in the old. In this respect he is immensely the superior of the lowest of the whites, the Italians, and the Polish Jews, below whom he has been classed in the past in the tenant scale. Nevertheless, he has always had to pay higher rents than even these for the poorest and most stinted rooms. The exceptions I have come across, in which the rents, though high, have seemed more nearly on a level with what was asked for the same number and size of rooms in the average tenement, were in the case of tumbledown rookeries in which no one else would live, and were always coupled with the condition that the landlord should "make no repairs." It can readily be seen that his profits were scarcely curtailed by his "humanity." The reason advanced for this systematic robbery is that white people will not live in the same house with colored tenants, or even in a house recently occupied by Negroes, and that consequently its selling value is injured. The prejudice undoubtedly exists, but it is not lessened by the house agents, who have set up the maxim "once a colored house, always a colored house."

———————◆———————

Have you not learned that not stocks or bonds or stately homes, or products of mill or field are our country? It is the splendid thought that is in our minds.

BENJAMIN HARRISON

58.

JOHN IRELAND: State Schools and Religious Instruction

When the National Educational Association met in St. Paul in 1890, Archbishop John Ireland of that city spoke to the convention on the perennial American question about the relations between parochial and public education. Catholic leaders were opposed to the children of their church attending public schools where, at best, the religious atmosphere was neutral, at worst, pointedly anti-Catholic. Archbishop Ireland's proposal that the state subsidize regular instruction at parochial schools and leave the church to deal with religious education, touched off a furor both within his church and among public school supporters. Out of his proposals came the Faribault Plan, by which school boards of two Minnesota communities operated the parochial schools and left religious instruction of the students in the hands of the local clergy. Owing to the public controversy over the plan, it was abandoned in a few years without an adequate trial.

Source: *The Church and Modern Society,* Chicago, 1896, Vol. I, pp. 217-232.

I BEG LEAVE TO MAKE at once my profession of faith. I declare unbounded loyalty to the Constitution of my country. I desire no favors; I claim no rights that are not in consonance with its letter and spirit. The rights which the Constitution guarantees I do claim, and, in doing so, I am but the truer and more loyal American. In what I am about to say to this distinguished audience, the principles of our common American citizenship will inspire my words. I beg you to listen to me and to discuss my arguments in the light of those principles.

I am a friend and an advocate of the state school. In the circumstances of the present time, I uphold the parish school. I sincerely wish that the need for it did not exist. I would have all schools for the children of the people to be state schools.

The accusation has gone abroad that Catholics are bent on destroying the state school. Never was accusation more unfounded. I will summarize the articles of my school creed; they follow all the lines upon which the state school is built.

The right of the state school to exist is, I consider, a matter beyond the stage of discussion. I fully concede it. I go farther: I concede the necessity of the state school. The child must have instruction, and in no mean degree, if the man is to earn for himself an honest competence and acquit himself of the duties which, for its own life and prosperity, society exacts from all its members. This proposition, which is true in any country of modern times, is peculiarly true in America. The imparting of such instruction is primarily the function of the parent.

The divine appointment is that under the care and direction of the parent the child shall grow in mind as well as in body. But, as things are, tens of thousands of children will not be instructed if parents solely remain in charge of the duty. The state must come forward as an agent of instruction; else ignorance will prevail. Indeed, in the absence of state action there never was that universal instruction which we have so nearly attained and which we deem so necessary. In the absence of state action, universal instruction would, I believe, never have been possible in any country.

Universal instruction implies free schools in which knowledge is to be had for the asking; in no other manner can instruction be brought within the reach of all children. Free schools! Blest indeed is the nation whose vales and hillsides they adorn, and blest the generations upon whose souls are poured their treasures! No tax is more legitimate than that which is levied in order to dispel mental darkness and build up within the nation's bosom intelligent manhood and womanhood. The question should not be raised: How much good accrues to the individual taxpayer? It suffices that the general welfare is promoted. It is scarcely necessary to add that the money paid in school tax is the money of the state and is to be disbursed only by the officials of the state, and only for the specific purposes for which it was collected.

I am unreservedly in favor of state laws making instruction compulsory. Instruction is so much needed by the citizen for his own sake and for that of society that the parent who neglects to provide for the education of the child sins against the child and against society, and should be punished by the state. First principles, of course, must not be forgotten. Since instruction is primarily the function of the parent, the parent possesses the right to educate his child in the manner agreeable to himself, provided always that the education given in this manner suffices to fit the child for his ulterior duties to society. Only when children do not attend other schools known to be competent to impart instruction should compulsory education demand attendance in state schools. The compulsory laws recently enacted in certain states of the Union are, in my judgment, objectionable in a few of their incidental clauses. These clauses will, I am confident, be readily altered in future legislative sessions. With the body of the laws and their general intent to ensure universal instruction, I am in most hearty accord.

It were idle for me to praise the work of the state school of America in imparting secular instruction. We all recognize its value. It is our pride and our glory. The republic of the United States has solemnly affirmed its resolve that within its borders no clouds of ignorance shall settle upon the minds of the children of its people. In furnishing the means to accomplish this result, its generosity knows no limit. The free school of America! Withered be the hand raised in sign of its destruction!

Can I be suspected of enmity to the state school because I would fain widen the expanse of its wings until all the children of the people find shelter beneath their cover; because I tell of defects which for very love of the state school I seek to remedy?

I turn to the denominational or parish school. It exists. I again express my regret that there is a necessity for its existence. In behalf of the state school I call upon my fellow Americans to aid in the removal of this necessity.

Catholics are foremost in establishing parish schools — 750,000 children, it is estimated, are educated in their parish schools. Only a lack of material means prevents them from housing the full number of their children. Lutherans, also, exhibit great zeal for parish schools. Many Episcopalians, and not a few of other Protestant denominations, commend and organize parish schools. The various denominational colleges of the country are practically parish schools for the children of the richer classes. The spirit of the parish school, if not the school itself, is widespread among American Protestants and is made manifest by their determined opposition to the exclusion of Scripture reading and other devotional exercises from the schoolroom.

There is dissatisfaction with the state school as it is at present organized. The state school tends to eliminate religion from the minds and hearts of the youth of the country. This is my grievance against the state school of today.

Believe me, my Protestant fellow citizens, I am absolutely sincere when I declare that I speak for the weal of Protestantism as well as for that of Catholicism. I am a Catholic, of course, to the tiniest fiber of my heart, unflinching and uncompromising in my faith. But God forbid that I should desire to see in America the ground which Protestantism now occupies swept by the devastating blast of unbelief. Let me be your ally in warding off from the country irreligion, the destroyer of Christian life and of Christian civilization.

What we have to fear is the materialism that does not see beyond the universe a living personal God, and the agnosticism that reduces Him to an unknown perhaps. Irreligion is abroad, scorning the salvation which is offered in the teachings and graces of Christ Jesus, sneering at the biblical page, warring upon the sacredness of the Christian Sabbath and the music of its church bells that tell of Heaven and of the hopes of immortal souls. Let us be on our guard. In our fear lest Protestants gain some advantage over Catholics, or Catholics over Protestants, we play into the hands of unbelievers and secularists. We have given over to them the school, the nursery of thought. Are we not securing to them the mastery of the future?

The state school is nonreligious. There never can be positive religious teaching where the principle of nonsectarianism rules. What is the result? The school deals with immature, childish minds, upon which silent facts and examples make deepest impression. It claims nearly all the time remaining to pupils outside of rest and recreation. It treats of land and sea, but not of Heaven; it speaks of statesmen and warriors, but not of God and Christ; it tells how to attain success in this world, but says nothing about the world beyond the grave. The pupil sees and listens and insensibly forms the conclusion that religion is of minor importance.

Religious indifference becomes his creed; his manhood will be, as was his childhood in the school, estranged from God and the positive influences of religion. The brief and hurried lessons of the family fireside and the Sunday school will be of slight avail. At best, the time is too short for that most difficult of lessons, religion. The child is weary after the exacting drill of the schoolroom and does not relish an extra task, of the necessity of which the teacher, in whom he confides most trustingly, has said nothing. The great mass of children receive no fireside lessons and attend no Sunday school, and the great mass of the children of America are growing up without religion.

Away with theories and dreams: let us read the facts. In 10,000 homes of the land, the father hastens to his work at early dawn before his children have risen from their slumbers, and at night an exhausted frame bids him seek repose, with scarcely time to kiss his little ones. The mother toils all day that her children may eat and be clothed; it is mockery to ask her to be their teacher! What may we expect from the Sunday school? An hour in the week to study religion is as nothing, and during that hour the small number only will be present. The churches are open and the teachers are at hand, but the nonreligious school has engrossed the attention and the energies of the child during five days of the week; he is unwilling to submit to the drudgery of a further hour's work on Sunday. Accidentally it may be, and unintentionally, but, in fact, most certainly, the state school crowds out the church.

The teaching of religion is not a function of the state; but the state should, for the sake of its people and for its own sake, permit and facilitate the teaching of religion by the church. This the state does not do; rather, it hinders and prevents the work of the church. The children of the masses are learning no religion. The religion of thousands who profess some form of religion is the merest veneering of mind and heart. Its doctrines are vague and chaotic notions as to what God is and what our relations to Him are. Very often it is mere sentimentality, and its precepts are the decorous rulings of natural culture and natural prudence. This is not the religion that built up our Christian civilization in the past and that will maintain it in the future. This is not the religion that will subjugate passion and repress vice. It is not the religion that will guard the family and save society.

Let the state look to itself. The mind which it polishes is a two-edged sword — an instrument for evil as well as for good; it were fatal to polish it without the assurance that in all likelihood it shall become an instrument for good. I am not questioning how far we may lay at the door of the nonreligious school the breaking up of Christian creeds, the growth of agnosticism and unbelief, the weakening of public and private morals, and the almost complete estrangement from church organizations of the poor and the working classes. But I do submit that these dreaded evils of our day should awaken us from our lethargy and stimulate us to bestow more than ordinary care upon the religious instruction of the children of the land, that they may have the strength to withstand the fierce temptations which await them.

Do not say that the state school teaches morals. Christians demand religion. From

John Ireland, archbishop of St. Paul, Minn.

the principles of religion, morals derive power and vitality. Separated from a belief in God and in the existence of the soul beyond the present life, morals are vague and weak commands which passion is not slow to scorn. What seems to be morals without religion are often but the blossomings of fortunate and kindly natures, or habits, which, fashioned upon Christian traditions, grow weak as the traditions become remote.

To the American people — religious-minded and God-fearing as I know them to be — I put the question: Ought we not to have religious instruction in connection with the school? There are, I confess, serious difficulties in the way. But are we to be stopped by difficulties when it is incumbent upon us to reach the goal? Secularists and unbelievers will demand their rights. I concede their rights. I will not impose upon them my religion, which is Christianity. But let them not impose upon me and my fellow Christians their religion, which is secularism. Secularism is a religion of its kind, and usually a very loud-spoken and intolerant religion. Nonsectarianism is not secularism, and when nonsectarianism is intended, the secularist sect must not claim for itself the field which it refuses to others. I am taking my stand upon our common American citizenship. The liberty I claim, that I grant.

I come to the chief difficulty. The American people at large are Christians; but they are divided among themselves. Not to speak of other differences, there is the vital and radical one between Catholicism and Protestantism of all forms. I am not arguing; I am stating facts. Well-meaning men propose as a remedy to teach a common Christianity in the schools. This will not do. In loyalty to their principles, Catholics cannot and will not accept a common Christianity. To Catholics, what does not bear on its face the stamp of Catholicity is Protestant in form and in implication, even if it be Catholic in substance. This being a settled fact, American Catholics will not, of course, impose Catholicism upon Protestant children, and, with similar fair-mindedness, American Protestants will not impose Protestantism upon Catholic children. A compromise becomes necessary. Is it not a thousand times better to make a compromise than to allow secularism to triumph and own the country?

I turn to all Americans — secularists as well as Christian believers — I address them in the name of American citizenship. We are a practical people, and when we find facts before us, whether we like or dislike them, we look at them with an eye to the general good. Now it is manifest that dissatisfaction exists with the state school because of its exclusion of religion. This dissatisfaction, moreover, is founded on conscience and will continue until the cause of it is removed.

Is not the fact that dissatisfaction exists sufficient for Americans to set to work earnestly, and with a goodwill, to remove the cause of it? The welfare of the country demands peace and harmony among citizens. Let us put an end to the constant murmurings and bitter recriminations with which our school war fills the land. Since we prize the advantages of our state school, let us enable all the children of the people to enjoy those advantages. Since there is such a public institution as the state school, supported by all the people, let us see that all may use it — let there be no taxation without representation in the enjoyment of the benefits of it.

I invoke the spirit of American liberty and American institutions. Citizens of the republic may differ diametrically in their views of policies and measures; some may deem the views of others to be utterly wrong. Still, is it not the duty of all to promote peace, and, as far as possible, to make concessions so that none be dissatisfied or disturbed in their rights of conscience? It matters not that one of the parties to a controversy comprises the majority of the voters of the state. The force of numbers may prevail in civil law; it is not always justice. Minorities have rights, and those rights the majority should recognize as speedily as may be consistent with the public weal.

It is no honor to America that 10 million of its people are forced by law to pay taxes for the support of schools to which their conscience does not give approval, and are, furthermore, compelled by their zeal for the religious instruction of their children to build schoolhouses of their own and pay their own teachers. It is no honor for the 50 million to profit by the taxes paid by the 10 million. The cry that the state schools are open to Catholics if they silence their conscience is not a defense that will hold before the bar of justice. This aspect of the case is the more serious when we consider that the 10 million are largely the poorer classes of the population and that they are sincerely and loyally desiring to obtain the benefits of the state school if only the obstacles be removed. It is no honor to the American republic that she, more than any other nation, be eager to keep religion away from schools. No nation goes in this direction so far as ours.

It is a terrible experiment upon which we have entered; the very life of our civilization and of our country is at stake. I know not how to account for this condition of things. Neither the genius nor the history of the country gives countenance to it. The American people are naturally reverent and religious. Their laws and public observances breathe forth the perfume of religion. The American school, as it first reared its log walls amid the villages of New England, was religious through and through. The favor with which a nonreligious school is now regarded is, I verily believe, due to the thoughtlessness of a moment and will not last.

I solve the difficulty by submitting it to the calm judgment of the country. No question is insoluble to Americans if truth and justice press it home to them. Other countries, whose civilization we do not despise, have found a solution. I instance England and Prussia. We are not inferior to those countries in practical legislation and in the spirit of peaceful compromise. Suggestions of mine must necessarily be crude in form and local and temporary in application. I will, however, lay them before you.

I would permeate the regular state school with the religion of the majority of the children of the land, be this religion as Protestant as Protestantism can be, and I would, as is done in England, pay for the secular instruction given in denominational schools according to results; that is, every pupil passing the examination before state officials, and in full accordance with the state program, would secure to his school the cost of the tuition of a pupil in the state school. This is not paying for religious instruction but for the secular instruction demanded by the state and given to the pupil as thoroughly as he could have received it in the state school.

Another plan: I would do as Protestants and Catholics in Poughkeepsie and other places in the United States have agreed to do, to the entire satisfaction of all citizens and the great advancement of educational interests. In Poughkeepsie the city School Board rents the buildings formerly used as parish schools, and from the hour of 9 A.M. to that of 3 P.M. the school is in every respect a state school — teachers being engaged and paid by the board, teachers and pupils being examined, state books being used, the door being always open to superintendent and members of the board. There is simply the tacit understanding that so long as the teachers, Catholic in faith, pass their examinations and do their work as efficiently and as loyally as other teachers under the control of the board, they shall not be replaced by teachers of another faith. During school hours no religious instruction is given. Christian doctrine is taught outside the hours for which the buildings are leased to the board. The state pays not one cent for the religious instruction of the pupils. In the other schools, Protestant devotional exercises take place in fullest freedom before the usual school hour.

Do not tell me of difficulties of detail in the working out of either of my schemes. There are difficulties; but will not the result be ample compensation for the struggle to overcome them? Other schemes, more perfect in conception and more easy of application, will, perhaps, be presented later; meanwhile, let trial be made of those which I have submitted.

Allow me one word as a Catholic. I have sought to place on the precise line where it belongs the objection which Catholics have to the state school. Is it fair, is it honest to raise the cry that Catholics are opposed to education, to free schools, to the American school system? I lose patience with adversaries who seek to place us in this false position, so opposed to all our convictions and resolves. In presence of this vast and distinguished assembly, I protest with all the energy of my soul against the charge that the schools of the nation have their enemies among Catholics. Not one stone of the wondrous edifice which Americans have reared in their devotion to education would Catholics remove or permit to be removed. They would fain add to its splendor and majesty by putting side by side religious and secular instruction, neither of them interfering with the other, each of them borrowing from the other aid and dignity. Do the schools of America fear contact with religion? Catholics demand the Christian state school. In so doing, they prove themselves truest friends of the school and of the state.

59.

Calvin M. Woodward: The Educational Value of Manual Training

An educational reform frequently discussed in the late nineteenth century was the development of a manual arts program for boys disinclined or unsuited to study the liberal arts. C. M. Woodward, dean of the polytechnic school of Washington University in St. Louis, founded the St. Louis Manual Training School under the auspices of the university in 1880. The school, an educational innovation, was designed to provide a "systematic study of tools, processes, and materials." Woodward thought all boys might benefit from such an education by discovering their "inborn capacities and aptitudes whether in the direction of literature, science, engineering or the practical arts." The following selection is from a book first published in 1890.

Source: *Manual Training in Education*, London, 1898, pp. 125-146.

THE VALUE OF MANUAL TRAINING when properly combined with literary, scientific, and mathematical studies is shown in various ways. I do not find it easy to classify these fruits under such heads as economic, mental, and moral; for a benefit conferred may fall under two or even all three heads. I will, however, adopt a certain order. I speak of manual training as a feature of the higher grades and within the reach of all boys. It bears fruit only in proportion to its adoption.

1. *It keeps boys longer at school.* This result is very quickly noticed and fully appreciated. One superintendent says: "Manual training has increased the attendance of boys in the high school fully 33 percent." . . . Everyone knows how classes of boys diminish as they approach and pass through the high school. . . . The superintendent of a large city says that of 108 pupils (boys and girls) entering the primary school only *20* finish the grammar, *4* are found in the second class of the high, and *1 graduates.*

For boys alone the showing would be worse. Not one-half of those who finish the grammar enter the high, and not 20 percent of those who enter complete the course. Several hundred pupils have entered the St.

Louis Manual Training School. A large proportion of these would not have gone to school elsewhere, I am certain, and yet 50 percent of them complete the course. . . .

2. *It awakens a lively interest in school and invests dull subjects with new life.* This is akin to the first point. "My son never was so interested in his school, never studied so hard, and never had so much to tell about schoolwork as now." That is the way scores of parents have reported. "My son got his start and taste for study in the manual training school." The habit of applying what one reads or hears to what one does makes things interesting.

3. *It keeps boys out of mischief, both in and out of school.* This result is most marked. I am a teacher of wide experience, in schools classical, semi-classical, and scientific, besides ten years director of the manual. I have never seen a school so easy to manage as the manual training school. The pupils are so earnest, so impressed with the value of what they are receiving that mischief and foolishness seem rather out of place. Fellow principals in other cities bear the same testimony. One says that the moral influence of manual training, as evidenced in the school itself, is worth all the manual training costs. . . .

4. *It gives boys with strong mechanical aptitudes, but who are slow of speech an equal chance with boys with glib tongues and good memories.* What we call scholarship and rank is based on success in all the five features of the program. Shopwork and drawing count equally with mathematics, science, and literature. A boy who cannot do well on some of these lines must be mentally deficient. Few boys can at the start do equally well in all, but success in shop and drawing (and here good judgment, close observation, and a firm hand avail more than fluent speech) has often the effect of arousing ambition and awakening dormant powers. I have seen boys almost made anew by the realization that they were not dunces after

all, and that there was more than one criterion of success.

Perhaps a majority of healthy boys are so constituted that their controlling interests are not in the study of words, the forms of speech, or the boundless mass of information which is given in books; and I would give such boys a fair chance of adequate development. Such boys are not necessarily blockheads, nor even dull. Their intellectual powers may be strong, though their strength lies not in the direction of memory. . . .

5. Manual training stimulates a *love for truth, simplicity,* and *intellectual honesty.* The comparative worthlessness of inaccuracy, of a want of agreement between the thought and the deed that was to realize the thought is made as manifest as sunlight. If a fitting is not true; if a device is not just what it seems to be, it is a failure and a sham, and the boy learns to rate them as such. Professor Eggleston says that the boy who learns to despise "work out of truth," who will not "tell a lie in wood," will by necessary and unconscious process of reasoning despise in a greater degree a lie in words. Simplicity is the greatest possible merit in a mechanical device or process. Everything must be direct, straightforward, with the least noise, and a minimum waste of effort. A high appreciation of this quality in manual work cannot but tend toward a similar quality in character, conversation, and life. In like manner, honesty finds expression in deed as much as in word. The inexorable and unchanging laws of physics and mechanics admit no bribe and connive at no deception. The pupil is stimulated to love and respect honesty, not by resisting but by seeing that dishonesty is a sign of weakness and incompetency.

6. *Correct notions of things, relations, and forces* derived from actual personal experience go far toward a comprehension of the language employed by others to express their thoughts and experiences. Correct use

of language depends not so much upon what one has read as upon the extent of his intercourse with correctly speaking people. Nearly all our forcible words are derived from the physical world, where they cannot be defined by other words but must be felt and experienced to be known. In this respect the activities of the shop serve to supplement the science laboratories, nature, and art. Among all these the industrial interests are not to be overlooked.

7. Science and mathematics profit from a better understanding of *forms, materials, and processes,* and from the readiness with which their principles may be illustrated. This advantage is very noticeable to teachers. Definitions are quickly grasped by shopworkers and geometrical constructions are easily seen.

In devising and constructing apparatus, manual training is invaluable. I have seen hundreds of well-made, serviceable pieces made by students to illustrate the various departments of physics. Hydraulics, hydrostatics, pneumatics, acoustics, heat, light, electricity, and magnetism are best taught by beginning with school-made and then school-used apparatus. Nothing so stimulates an interest in physics as laboratory work, and without some manual training the best part of laboratory work is almost impossible. The ability to think out a piece of apparatus, make a scale drawing of it, showing all details, including joints and methods of support, and then to construct it in proper material is exceedingly valuable. Chemistry is somewhat dependent upon manual skill, though to a less extent than physics.

Passing now beyond the school, I come to its fruits outside.

8. It aids one who must *choose his occupation.* Most children step from the schoolroom into the working world with no just conception of what the world is nor what it is doing. In a great majority of cases one's occupation is the result of chance or environment. There is no intelligent choice because there is no intelligence in such matters. Boys who live near the wharves become sailors; the son of the schoolmaster teaches school, etc. If they break away from the influences that would thus hedge them in, they are apt to take their chances with the odds against them. It is more than likely that the square plug gets into the round hole. To change the figure, the boy fresh from school sees a variety of roads before him. How is he to know which to choose unless he knows not only the roads but himself? Clearly, intelligent choice can be exercised only when the chief characteristics of both roads and traveler are fairly comprehended. Education, then, must be "all around" and many-sided unless the right of choice is denied. . . .

It occasionally happens that the student who has special aptitudes in certain directions finds great difficulty in mastering subjects in other directions. In such cases it is often the best course to yield to natural tastes and to assist the student in finding his proper sphere of work and study. A decided aptitude for handicraft is sometimes coupled with a strong aversion to and unfitness for literary work, which largely taxes the memory. There can be no doubt that in such cases more time should be spent in the laboratory and less in the library and recitation room. On the other hand, great facility in the acquisition and use of language is often accompanied by a great lack of mechanical interest or power. When such a bias is discovered, the lad should unquestionably be sent to his grammar and dictionary rather than to the laboratory or drafting room. It is confidently believed that the developments of the manual training school will prevent those serious errors in the choice of a vocation which often prove so fatal to the fondest hopes.

It is highly desirable that a larger proportion of intelligent and well-educated youth should devote their energies to manual pursuits or to the development of mechanical industries, both for their own sakes and for the sake of the occupations and for society.

Undoubtedly the common belief is that it requires no great amount of brains or intelligence to be a mechanic; and those who go through ordinary higher schools are not expected by their teachers to be mechanics. Every bright farmer's boy, every gifted son of a mechanic, if he but stay in school is sure to be stolen away from the occupation of his father and led into the ranks of the "learned professions."

This loss of the best minds and the lack of the results of a generous education does much to give color to popular prejudice and to keep down mechanic arts in the estimation of all. This result is most unfortunate for society. It creates distinctions which ought not to exist and gives rise to false estimates of the comparative value of the various kinds of intellectual culture. Hitherto, men who have cultivated their minds have neglected their hands; and those who have labored with their hands have found no opportunity to generously cultivate their brains. The crying demand today is for intellectual combined with manual training. It is this want that the Manual Training School aims to supply. Its motto is: "The cultured mind, the skillful hand."

9. It raises the *standards of attainment in mechanical occupations* and invests them with new dignity. Man became man when he made his first tool, and he becomes more manly as he continues to invent and use more tools. Man subdues nature and develops art through the instrumentality of tools. To turn a crank one needs only muscular power. But to devise and build the light engine which, under the direction of a single intelligent master spirit shall lift the burden of a thousand men requires a high degree of intelligence and manual skill.

There are now no hewers of wood or drawers of water. That menial work is now done by machinery. Even the streets are swept by horsepower, and the best bricks are made without the touch of man's hands. Through the instrumentality of tools, the intellect is gradually doing away with the lower forms of labor. Every occupation becomes ennobled by the transforming influence of thought and skill. The farmer of old yoked his wife with his cow, and together they dragged the clumsy plow or transported the scanty harvest. Down to fifty years ago the life of a farmer was associated with unceasing, stupefying toil. What will it be when every farmer's boy is properly educated and trained? Farming is rapidly becoming a matter of horsepower, steam power, and machinery. The farmer will rise in dignity when he is able to intelligently direct such appliances and to manage them well.

Instead of preparing men to bear more cheerfully the drudgery of toil, we should enable them to overcome toil by a degree of skill which raises a trade to the rank of a profession. The profession of dentistry has developed from a mere trade by the use of scientific methods. When to the skill of the machinist we add drawing, mathematics, and science, including theoretical mechanics, we have an accomplished mechanical engineer. A few days ago I met a graduate of a manual training school. We were both inspecting the massive machinery of a "powerhouse" of an electric railway. Said he, "When the manual boys go into mechanics they help the crafts. They bring education, intelligence, and habits of systematic study. They lift up the business and win a degree of respect that the old shophands never got and never deserved."

What that young man said has wide application. Only a small part of the students can be expected to become mechanics, for their aptitudes and their opportunities will carry them in a great variety of ways; but wherever they go they are likely to come in contact with industrial work. If they are true to their teachings they will affect all such work favorably. The habit of working on an exact plan, of analyzing an apparently complicated operation into a series of simple steps enables one to solve many a new problem, even with new material and under entirely novel circumstances.

10. It enables an employer of labor to better estimate the comparative value of skilled and unskilled labor, and to exercise a higher consideration for the laboring man. Too often there is a great gulf between employer and employee; neither knows enough of the experiences of the other to furnish common standing ground, their educations have been on totally different planes. Give to the literary and scientific training of the one a fair allowance of manual training, and to the unscientific and narrow toolwork of the other something of letters, mathematics, science, and drawing, and the two understand each other at once. . . .

11. *It stimulates invention.* We are apt to fancy that the age of invention is nearly over. On the contrary, it has barely dawned. What has been done in the past has been in spite of the education of the schools. The educated man, so-called, rarely makes a practical invention, so deficient is he in a knowledge of essential conditions. The practical mechanic rarely invents because he cannot calculate and cannot draw. Add to their educations the missing elements in either case and you have a vantage ground that to no great extent has ever been occupied. Already I have seen its fruits. One of our students invented a new tool that enabled him to double the amount of turning he could do in a day. Another invented a method of forcing water from a tank below the floor of a palace car to the faucets of the washstand. Another invented an automatic air brake for a streetcar. And another has greatly improved the details of an electric plant — and all are yet boys. When manual training has been generally adopted for boys in their teens, the world will see a

multiplication of useful inventions such as not even the past twenty-five years can parallel. The era of invention is now in its infancy.

12. It increases the *breadwinning and homemaking power* of the average boy. The average boy has his bread to win and his home to make. It is of the utmost importance that his education should fit him for his work. Three out of four of the boys in a great city are practically thrown upon their own resources the moment they leave school. Their degree of preparation for life's work and duties is a matter of no small concern to themselves and to the state. There is, there can be no sort of doubt about the ability and the disposition of this average boy to make and maintain a good home if he will secure a manual-training-school education with its full complement of studies. . . .

13. It adds to the efficiency of school work by *making school attractive;* by arousing the enthusiasm of pupils; by making the work more intelligible; by making pupils more manageable. These results manifest themselves most clearly to the teachers who are in daily contact with the pupils. I have been witness of this kind of fruit from the beginning and have not hesitated to speak of it; but cautious people have been prone to suspect that the color of my glasses had much to do with the complexion of what I saw. . . .

14. The last fruit I shall name is that of *intelligent citizenship.* I am aware that this will excite some surprise. The opponents, or rather the critics, of manual training are apt to assert with some emphasis that the object of public education is to produce a high grade of citizenship, and they generally claim that the traditional course of study is well fitted to that end, while manual training, insofar as it enters into education, tends toward narrow selfishness and away from an interest in the commonwealth. On the contrary, I claim that the effects are more

than likely to be transposed, and I am confident that longer experience will show that I am right.

There are several reasons for such a result.

a. People well-versed in the principles which underlie the mechanical operations of a majority of our citizens are much more likely to take an intelligent interest in the people themselves, in their condition and needs. Franklin said he had always noticed

that "among workmen, good apprentices made good citizens."

b. They are more likely to discuss questions of public improvements with judgment.

c. They are less visionary, more matter-of-fact, and consequently better prepared to deal with actual people under actual conditions. Of course, I am comparing manual-training-school pupils with those of other schools.

60.

ALFRED THAYER MAHAN: Sea Power and History

The trend toward expansionism in American foreign policy was stimulated by men such as Alfred Thayer Mahan, president of the Naval War College and author of The Influence of Sea Power Upon History, 1660-1783, *published in 1890. In this work, Mahan related military to political history and argued that the key to national greatness was the development of sea power in combination with a strong industrial economy. He was supported in these views by Theodore Roosevelt, who declared that he shared with Mahan "precisely the same idea of patriotism." Portions of Mahan's classic work are reprinted here.*

Source: *The Influence of Sea Power Upon History, 1660-1783*, Boston, 1890, pp. 1-4, 25-29, 50-59, 81-88.

THE HISTORY OF SEA POWER is largely, though by no means solely, a narrative of contests between nations, of mutual rivalries, of violence frequently culminating in war. The profound influence of sea commerce upon the wealth and strength of countries was clearly seen long before the true principles which governed its growth and prosperity were detected. To secure to one's own people a disproportionate share of such benefits, every effort was made to exclude others, either by the peaceful legislative methods of monopoly or prohibitory regulations or, when these failed, by direct violence.

The clash of interests, the angry feelings roused by conflicting attempts thus to appropriate the larger share, if not the whole, of the advantages of commerce, and of distant unsettled commercial regions, led to wars. On the other hand, wars arising from other causes have been greatly modified in their conduct and issue by the control of the sea. Therefore the history of sea power, while embracing in its broad sweep all that tends to make a people great upon the sea or by the sea, is largely a military history; and it is in this aspect that it will be mainly, though not exclusively, regarded in the following pages.

A study of the military history of the past, such as this, is enjoined by great military leaders as essential to correct ideas and to the skillful conduct of war in the future. Napoleon names among the campaigns to be studied by the aspiring soldier those of Alexander, Hannibal, and Caesar, to whom gunpowder was unknown; and there is a substantial agreement among professional writers that, while many of the conditions of war vary from age to age with the progress of weapons, there are certain teachings in the school of history which remain constant and, being, therefore, of universal application can be elevated to the rank of general principles. For the same reason the study of the sea history of the past will be found instructive, by its illustration of the general principles of maritime war, notwithstanding the great changes that have been brought about in naval weapons by the scientific advances of the past half century and by the introduction of steam as the motive power.

It is doubly necessary thus to study critically the history and experience of naval warfare in the days of sailing ships, because, while these will be found to afford lessons of present application and value, steam navies have as yet made no history which can be quoted as decisive in its teaching. Of the one, we have much experimental knowledge; of the other, practically none. Hence theories about the naval warfare of the future are almost wholly presumptive; and although the attempt has been made to give them a more solid basis by dwelling upon the resemblance between fleets of steamships and fleets of galleys moved by oars, which have a long and well-known history, it will be well not to be carried away by this analogy until it has been thoroughly tested.

The resemblance is indeed far from superficial. The feature which the steamer and the galley have in common is the ability to move in any direction independent of the wind. Such a power makes a radical distinction between those classes of vessels and the sailing ship; for the latter can follow only a limited number of courses when the wind blows and must remain motionless when it fails. But, while it is wise to observe things that are alike, it is also wise to look for things that differ; for when the imagination is carried away by the detection of points of resemblance — one of the most pleasing of mental pursuits — it is apt to be impatient of any divergence in its new-found parallels and so may overlook or refuse to recognize such. Thus the galley and the steamship have in common, though unequally developed, the important characteristic mentioned, but in at least two points they differ; and in an appeal to the history of the galley for lessons as to fighting steamships, the differences as well as the likeness must be kept steadily in view or false deductions may be made.

The motive power of the galley when in use necessarily and rapidly declined because human strength could not long maintain such exhausting efforts, and consequently tactical movements could continue but for a limited time; and, again, during the galley period, offensive weapons were not only of short range but were almost wholly confined to hand-to-hand encounter. These two conditions led almost necessarily to a rush upon each other, not, however, without some dexterous attempts to turn or double on the enemy, followed by a hand-to-hand melee. In such a rush and such a melee, a great consensus of respectable, even eminent, naval opinion of the present day finds the necessary outcome of modern naval weapons — a kind of Donnybrook Fair, in which, as the history of melees shows, it will be hard to know friend from foe.

Whatever may prove to be the worth of this opinion, it cannot claim an historical basis in the sole fact that galley and steamship can move at any moment directly upon the enemy, and carry a beak upon their prow, regardless of the points in which galley and steamship differ. As yet this opinion is only a presumption, upon which final judgment may well be deferred until the trial of battle has given further light. Until that time there is room for the opposite view — that a melee between numerically equal fleets, in which skill is reduced to a minimum, is not the best that can be done with the elaborate and mighty weapons of this age. The surer of himself an admiral is, the finer the tactical development of his fleet, the better his captains, the more reluctant must he necessarily be to enter into a melee with equal forces, in which all these advantages will be thrown away, chance reign supreme, and his fleet be placed on terms of equality with an assemblage of ships which have never before acted together. History has lessons as to when melees are, or are not, in order.

The galley, then, has one striking resemblance to the steamer but differs in other important features which are not so immediately apparent and are therefore less accounted of. In the sailing ship, on the contrary, the striking feature is the difference between it and the more modern vessel; the points of resemblance, though existing and easy to find, are not so obvious and therefore are less heeded. This impression is enhanced by the sense of utter weakness in the sailing ship as compared with the steamer owing to its dependence upon the wind; forgetting that, as the former fought with its equals, the tactical lessons are valid. The galley was never reduced to impotence by a calm, and hence receives more respect in our day than the sailing ship; yet the latter displaced it and remained supreme until the utilization of steam. The powers to injure an enemy from a great distance, to maneuver for an unlimited length of time without wearing out the men, to devote the greater part of the crew to the offensive weapons instead of to the oar, are common to the sailing vessel and the steamer, and are at least as important, tactically considered, as the power of the galley to move in a calm or against the wind.

THE FIRST AND MOST OBVIOUS LIGHT in which the sea presents itself from the political and social point of view is that of a great highway; or better, perhaps, of a wide common, over which men may pass in all directions but on which some well-worn paths show that controlling reasons have led them to choose certain lines of travel rather than others. These lines of travel are called trade routes; and the reasons which have determined them are to be sought in the history of the world. . . .

Under modern conditions . . . home trade is but a part of the business of a country bordering on the sea. Foreign necessaries or luxuries must be brought to its ports, either in its own or in foreign ships, which will return bearing in exchange the products of the country, whether they be the fruits of the earth or the works of men's hands; and it is the wish of every nation that this shipping business should be done by its own vessels. The ships that thus sail to and fro must have secure ports to which to return and must, as far as possible, be followed by the protection of their country throughout the voyage. . . .

The needs of commerce, however, were not all provided for when safety had been secured at the far end of the road. The voyages were long and dangerous, the seas often beset with enemies. In the most active days of colonizing there prevailed on the sea a lawlessness, the very memory of which is now almost lost, and the days of settled peace between maritime nations were few and far between. Thus arose the demand for stations along the road, like the Cape of Good Hope, St. Helena, and Mauritius, not primarily for trade but for defense and war; the demand for the possession of posts like Gibraltar, Malta, Louisburg, at the entrance of the Gulf of St. Lawrence — posts whose value was chiefly strategic, though not necessarily wholly so. Colonies and colonial posts were sometimes commercial, sometimes military in their character; and it was exceptional that the

Alfred Thayer Mahan, naval officer and historian who wrote several books on the role of sea power in history

same position was equally important in both points of view, as New York was.

In these three things — production, with the necessity of exchanging products; shipping, whereby the exchange is carried on; and colonies, which facilitate and enlarge the operations of shipping and tend to protect it by multiplying points of safety — is to be found the key to much of the history, as well as of the policy, of nations bordering upon the sea. The policy has varied both with the spirit of the age and with the character and clear-sightedness of the rulers; but the history of the seaboard nations has been less determined by the shrewdness and foresight of governments than by conditions of position, extent, configuration, number, and character of their people — by what are called, in a word, natural conditions.

It must however be admitted . . . that the wise or unwise action of individual men has at certain periods had a great modifying influence upon the growth of sea power in the broad sense, which includes not only the military strength afloat that rules the sea or any part of it by force of arms but also the peaceful commerce and shipping from

which alone a military fleet naturally and healthfully springs and on which it securely rests.

The principal conditions affecting the sea power of nations may be enumerated as follows: (1) geographical position; (2) physical conformation, including, as connected therewith, natural productions and climate; (3) extent of territory; (4) number of population; (5) character of the people; (6) character of the government, including therein the national institutions.

Geographical Position. It may be pointed out, in the first place, that if a nation be so situated that it is neither forced to defend itself by land nor induced to seek extension of its territory by way of the land, it has, by the very unity of its aim directed upon the sea, an advantage as compared with a people one of whose boundaries is continental. This has been a great advantage to England over both France and Holland as a sea power. The strength of the latter was early exhausted by the necessity of keeping up a large army and carrying on expensive wars to preserve her independence; while the policy of France was constantly diverted, sometimes wisely and sometimes most foolishly, from the sea to projects of continental extension. These military efforts expended wealth; whereas a wiser and consistent use of **her** geographical position would have added to it. . . .

National Character. If sea power be really based upon a peaceful and extensive commerce, aptitude for commercial pursuits must be a distinguishing feature of the nations that have at one time or another been great upon the sea. History almost without exception, affirms that this is true. . . .

The tendency to trade, involving of necessity the production of something to trade with, is the national characteristic most important to the development of sea power. Granting it and a good seaboard, it is not likely that the dangers of the sea, or any aversion to it, will deter a people from seeking wealth by the paths of ocean commerce. Where wealth is sought by other means, it may be found; but it will not necessarily lead to sea power. . . .

The tendency to save and put aside, to venture timidly and on a small scale may lead to a general diffusion of wealth on a like small scale, but not to the risks and development of external trade and shipping interests. . . . As regards the stability of a man's personal fortunes, this kind of prudence is doubtless wise; but when excessive prudence or financial timidity becomes a national trait, it must tend to hamper the expansion of commerce and of the nation's shipping. The same caution in money matters, appearing in another relation of life, has checked the production of children and keeps the population of France nearly stationary. . . .

In yet another way does the national genius affect the growth of sea power in its broadest sense; and that is insofar as it possesses the capacity for planting healthy colonies. Of colonization, as of all other growths, it is true that it is most healthy when it is most natural. Therefore colonies that spring from the felt wants and natural impulses of a whole people will have the most solid foundations; and their subsequent growth will be surest when they are least trammeled from home if the people have the genius for independent action. Men of the past three centuries have keenly felt the value to the mother country of colonies as outlets for the home products and as a nursery for commerce and shipping; but efforts at colonization have not had the same general origin, nor have different systems all had the same success. The efforts of statesmen, however far-seeing and careful, have not been able to supply the lack of strong natural impulse; nor can the most minute regulation from home produce as good results as a happier neglect, when the germ of self-development is found in the national character.

There has been no greater display of wisdom in the national administration of successful colonies than in that of [the] unsuccessful. Perhaps there has been even less. If elaborate system and supervision, careful adaptation of means to ends, diligent nursing could avail for colonial growth, the genius of England has less of this systematizing faculty than the genius of France; but England, not France, has been the great colonizer of the world. Successful colonization, with its consequent effect upon commerce and sea power, depends essentially upon national character; because colonies grow best when they grow of themselves, naturally. The character of the colonist, not the care of the home government, is the principle of the colony's growth.

This truth stands out the clearer because the general attitude of all the home governments toward their colonies was entirely selfish. However founded, as soon as it was recognized to be of consequence, the colony became to the home country a cow to be milked; to be cared for, of course, but chiefly as a piece of property valued for the returns it gave. Legislation was directed toward a monopoly of its external trade; the places in its government afforded posts of value for occupants from the mother country; and the colony was looked upon, as the sea still often is, as a fit place for those who were ungovernable or useless at home. The military administration, however, so long as it remains a colony, is the proper and necessary attribute of the home government.

The fact of England's unique and wonderful success as a great colonizing nation is too evident to be dwelt upon; and the reason for it appears to lie chiefly in two traits of the national character. The English colonist naturally and readily settles down in his new country, identifies his interest with it, and, though keeping an affectionate remembrance of the home from which he came, has no restless eagerness to return. In the second place, the Englishman at once and instinctively seeks to develop the resources of the new country in the broadest sense. In the former particular he differs from the

French, who were ever longingly looking back to the delights of their pleasant land; in the latter, from the Spaniards, whose range of interest and ambition was too narrow for the full evolution of the possibilities of a new country. . . .

Before quitting this head of the inquiry, it is well to ask how far the national character of Americans is fitted to develop a great sea power, should other circumstances become favorable. It seems scarcely necessary, however, to do more than appeal to a not very distant past to prove that, if legislative hindrances be removed and more remunerative fields of enterprise filled up, the sea power will not long delay its appearance. The instinct for commerce, bold enterprise in the pursuit of gain, and a keen scent for the trails that lead to it all exist; and if there be in the future any fields calling for colonization, it cannot be doubted that Americans will carry to them all their inherited aptitude for self-government and independent growth.

Character of the Government. In discussing the effects upon the development of a nation's sea power exerted by its government and institutions, it will be necessary to avoid a tendency to over-philosophizing, to confine attention to obvious and immediate causes and their plain results without prying too far beneath the surface for remote and ultimate influences.

Nevertheless, it must be noted that particular forms of government with their accompanying institutions and the character of rulers at one time or another have exercised a very marked influence upon the development of sea power. The various traits of a country and its people which have so far been considered constitute the natural characteristics with which a nation, like a man, begins its career; the conduct of the government in turn corresponds to the exercise of the intelligent willpower, which, according as it is wise, energetic, and persevering, or the reverse, causes success or failure in a man's life or a nation's history.

It would seem probable that a government in full accord with the natural bias of its people would most successfully advance its growth in every respect; and, in the matter of sea power, the most brilliant successes have followed where there has been intelligent direction by a government fully imbued with the spirit of the people and conscious of its true general bent. Such a government is most certainly secured when the will of the people, or of their best natural exponents, has some large share in making it; but such free governments have sometimes fallen short, while on the other hand despotic power, wielded with judgment and consistency, has created at times a great sea commerce and a brilliant navy with greater directness than can be reached by the slower processes of a free people. The difficulty in the latter case is to insure perseverance after the death of a particular despot. . . .

To turn now from the particular lessons drawn from the history of the past to the general question of the influence of government upon the sea career of its people, it is seen that that influence can work in two distinct but closely related ways.

First, in peace. The government by its policy can favor the natural growth of a people's industries and its tendencies to seek adventure and gain by way of the sea; or it can try to develop such industries and such seagoing bent when they do not naturally exist; or, on the other hand, the government may by mistaken action check and fetter the progress which the people left to themselves would make. In any one of these ways the influence of the government will be felt, making or marring the sea power of the country in the matter of peaceful commerce; upon which alone, it cannot be too often insisted, a thoroughly strong navy can be based.

Second, for war. The influence of the government will be felt in its most legitimate manner in maintaining an armed navy of a size commensurate with the growth of its shipping and the importance of the interests connected with it. More important even than the size of the navy is the question of its institutions, favoring a healthful spirit and activity and providing for rapid development in time of war by an adequate reserve of men and of ships and by measures for drawing out that general reserve power which has before been pointed to, when considering the character and pursuits of the people.

Undoubtedly under this second head of warlike preparation must come the maintenance of suitable naval stations in those distant parts of the world to which the armed shipping must follow the peaceful vessels of commerce. The protection of such stations must depend either upon direct military force, as do Gibraltar and Malta, or upon a surrounding friendly population, such as the American colonists once were to England and, it may be presumed, the Australian colonists now are. Such friendly surroundings and backing, joined to a reasonable military provision, are the best of defenses, and, when combined with decided preponderance at sea, make a scattered and extensive empire, like that of England, secure; for while it is true that an unexpected attack may cause disaster in some one quarter, the actual superiority of naval power prevents such disaster from being general or irremediable. History has sufficiently proved this. England's naval bases have been in all parts of the world; and her fleets have at once protected them, kept open the communications between them, and relied upon them for shelter.

Colonies attached to the mother country afford, therefore, the surest means of supporting abroad the sea power of a country. In peace, the influence of the government should be felt in promoting by all means a warmth of attachment and a unity of interest which will make the welfare of one the welfare of all, and the quarrel of one the quarrel of all; and in war, or rather for war, by inducing such measures of organization and defenses as shall be felt by all to be a fair distribution of a burden of which each reaps the benefit.

Such colonies the United States has not and is not likely to have. As regards purely military naval stations, the feeling of her people was probably accurately expressed by a historian of the English Navy 100 years ago, speaking then of Gibraltar and Port Mahon. "Military governments," said he, "agree so little with the industry of a trading people and are in themselves so repugnant to the genius of the British people that I do not wonder that men of good sense and of all parties have inclined to give up these as Tangiers was given up." Having therefore no foreign establishments, either colonial or military, the ships of war of the United States, in war, will be like land birds, unable to fly far from their own shores. To provide resting places for them, where they can coal and repair, would be one of the first duties of a government proposing to itself the development of the power of the nation at sea.

As the practical object of this inquiry is to draw from the lessons of history inferences applicable to one's own country and service, it is proper now to ask how far the conditions of the United States involve serious danger and call for action on the part of the government in order to build again her sea power. It will not be too much to say that the action of the government since the Civil War, and up to this day, has been effectively directed solely to what has been called the first link in the chain which makes sea power. Internal development, great production, with the accompanying aim and boast of self-sufficingness, such has been the object, such to some extent the result. In this the government has faithfully reflected the bent of the controlling elements of the country, though it is not always easy to feel that such controlling elements are truly representative, even in a free country. However that may be, there is no doubt that, besides having no colonies, the intermediate link of a peaceful shipping and the interests involved in it are now likewise lacking. In short, the United States has only one link of the three.

The circumstances of naval war have changed so much within the last hundred years that it may be doubted whether such disastrous effects on the one hand, or such brilliant prosperity on the other, as were seen in the wars between England and France, could now recur. In her secure and haughty sway of the seas, England imposed a yoke on neutrals which will never again be borne; and the principle that the flag covers the goods is forever secured. The commerce of a belligerent can therefore now be safely carried on in neutral ships, except when contraband of war or to blockaded ports; and as regards the latter, it is also certain that there will be no more paper blockades.

Putting aside, therefore, the question of defending her seaports from capture or contribution, as to which there is practical unanimity in theory and entire indifference in practice, what need has the United States of sea power? Her commerce is even now carried on by others; why should her people desire that which, if possessed, must be defended at great cost? So far as this question is economical, it is outside the scope of this work; but conditions which may entail suffering and loss on the country by war are directly pertinent to it. Granting, therefore, that the foreign trade of the United States, going and coming, is on board ships which an enemy cannot touch except when bound to a blockaded port, what will constitute an efficient blockade? The present definition is, that it is such as to constitute a manifest danger to a vessel seeking to enter or leave the port.

This is evidently very elastic. Many can remember that during the Civil War, after a night attack on the United States fleet off Charleston, the Confederates next morning sent out a steamer with some foreign consuls on board, who so far satisfied themselves that no blockading vessel was in sight

that they issued a declaration to that effect. On the strength of this declaration, some Southern authorities claimed that the blockade was technically broken and could not be technically reestablished without a new notification. Is it necessary, to constitute a real danger to blockade runners, that the blockading fleet should be in sight? Half a dozen fast steamers, cruising twenty miles offshore between the New Jersey and Long Island coast, would be a very real danger to ships seeking to go in or out by the principal entrance to New York; and similar positions might effectively blockade Boston, the Delaware, and the Chesapeake. The main body of the blockading fleet, prepared not only to capture merchant ships but to resist military attempts to break the blockade, need not be within sight, nor in a position known to the shore. . . .

It may be urged that, with the extensive seacoast of the United States, a blockade of the whole line cannot be effectively kept up. No one will more readily concede this than officers who remember how the blockade of the Southern coast alone was maintained. But in the present condition of the Navy, and, it may be added, with any additions not exceeding those so far proposed by the government, the attempt to blockade Boston, New York, the Delaware, the Chesapeake, and the Mississippi, in other words, the great centers of export and import, would not entail upon one of the large maritime nations efforts greater than have been made before. . . .

The question is eminently one in which the influence of the government should make itself felt, to build up for the nation a navy which, if not capable of reaching distant countries, shall at least be able to keep clear the chief approaches to its own. The eyes of the country have for a quarter of a century been turned from the sea; the results of such a policy and of its opposite will be shown in the instance of France and of England. Without asserting a narrow parallelism between the case of the United

States and either of these, it may safely be said that it is essential to the welfare of the whole country that the conditions of trade and commerce should remain, as far as possible, unaffected by an external war. In order to do this, the enemy must be kept not only out of our ports but far away from our coasts.

Can this navy be had without restoring the merchant shipping? It is doubtful. History has proved that such a purely military sea power can be built up by a despot, as was done by Louis XIV; but though so fair seeming, experience showed that his navy was like a growth which, having no root, soon withers away. But in a representative government any military expenditure must have a strongly represented interest behind it, convinced of its necessity. Such an interest in sea power does not exist, cannot exist here without action by the government.

How such a merchant shipping should be built up, whether by subsidies or by free trade, by constant administration of tonics or by free movement in the open air, is not a military but an economical question. Even had the United States a great national shipping, it may be doubted whether a sufficient navy would follow; the distance which separates her from other great powers, in one way a protection, is also a snare. The motive, if any there be, which will give the United States a navy is probably now quickening in the Central American isthmus. Let us hope it will not come to the birth too late.

61.

Edward Everett Hale: A High Court for the Americas

An objective of the International Conference of American States, which convened at Washington, D.C., in 1889-1890, was the formulation of a plan for arbitration of disputes between the republics of the Western Hemisphere. One plan urged upon the meeting was advanced by Edward Everett Hale, pastor of the South Congregational Church of Boston and later chaplain of the U.S. Senate. Although the conference did little to solve the arbitration problem other than adopt a resolution declaring illegal acts of conquest in defiance of arbitration, elements of Hale's plan were realized in the 1948 Pact of Bogotá, which called for giving the International Court of Justice jurisdiction in certain disputes between American states. Hale's humanitarian principles and devotion to international peace were embodied in the following call for a high court for the Americas.

Source: *A New England Boyhood and Other Bits of Autobiography*, Boston, 1905, pp. 401-405.

THE MEETING OF THE AMERICAN CONGRESS has no object so important as the establishment of a system of arbitration as to any questions which may arise between the different states of North and South America. What must be attempted is the establishment of a system. Discussion is not enough. Resolutions are not enough, nor any professions. It is possible to establish a system, and a long period must pass before so favorable an opportunity can occur again.

It is too much forgotten that an essential part of the prosperity and success of the United States as a nation is the system by which questions between the states are adjusted. Difficulties, indeed, are brought to an end almost as soon as they begin. Many a contest between neighboring and rival states has been adjusted by the Supreme Court while most of the citizens of each state did not know that there was any question. Thus the Supreme Court adjusted a boundary question between Massachusetts and Rhode Island, of more importance than many boundary questions which have plunged Europe in war. And it would be fair to say that half the people of both states did not know that there had been any controversy.

It is not enough for the Congress to vote that, in the future, questions of dispute shall be referred to courts of arbitration. When questions assume importance, after they have been neglected, and when they have had a chance to grow in consequence, it may be too late to constitute a proper court of arbitration. The demand of our time is that a permanent court of arbitration shall be appointed at once, and shall be in readiness to receive all such questions as soon as they arise. Indeed, it may be possible for such a court to give such counsel as shall solve the question at its very birth.

The court should *exist* and hold its sessions from time to time, ready to receive inquiries and to solve doubts as to international law, and ready at any moment to hear an international question as soon as it arises.

Such a court should consist of statesmen and jurists of the very highest rank — men who have distinguished themselves before the world by their equity and wisdom in public affairs. Its establishment should be on such a scale of dignity and the powers conferred on it should be so high that even a justice of the Supreme Court of the United States should feel honored by an appointment to serve on it, or such a statesman as John Quincy Adams after he had left the presidential chair.

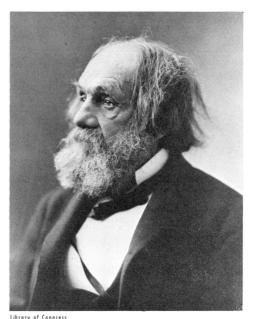

Edward Everett Hale

It should meet quarterly, at least, for regular sessions, now at one of the cities of North America, now at one of South America, as convenience might order. There is no reason, indeed, why it should not meet in Europe, or in one of the West India islands. It would have permanent clerks and reporters of its decisions.

At first, probably, no questions would be referred to it except, perhaps, a few trifles of form. But it should be required to publish from time to time opinions, in the line of *obiter dicta*, its members devoting themselves exclusively to the study of international law and the study of such principles as shall bring in the reign of justice among men.

The several states should have a right to submit to it, in advance, questions as to public policy as governed by international law. And to such questions it should give immediate attention and return short rescripts in the form of practical answers.

Before such a tribunal, sooner or later, two states, in contest with each other, would bring the subject of their debate. The court would hear them by counsel and would give its decision. To enforce that decision, it is perfectly true, it would not have a musket nor a ship. But the moral weight of its decision would be absolute. No state in America is so strong that it could stand against it. The legislation of every state and its conduct would, sooner or later, comply with the court's decision.

Take, for instance, the question now existing as the preservation of seals in the northern waters. No nation concerned wishes to do wrong in the matter. No intelligent person wishes to see this race of animals annihilated. It is a subject eminently fit to be presented to such a court, that it may say what the laws of nations, or the eternal justice, would command in that affair. And England, Canada, or the United States would have to obey the decision.

The manner of composing such a court is rather a matter of detail. Our experience in the Supreme Court of the United States would suggest a tribunal of seven or nine jurists. They should be selected from the different nations, so that all parts of America might be represented, and authority might be given to appoint one or two "assessors" from the most distinguished jurists of Europe. The honors and emoluments of the court should be such that any man in the world might be proud and glad to hold a place on it.

The appointments should be for good behavior, to cease at the age, say, of sixty-five or seventy years, with a handsome retiring pension.

The judges might be appointed by such a Congress as now is in session, with a provision that their successors should be named in rotation by the several nations. It might be well that the name of a new candidate should be selected from a list drawn up by the other members of the tribunal. The judges should appoint their own secretaries and other officers.

Their salaries should be paid from a common treasury established for the purpose. This treasury should be kept full by contributions assessed on the several states in proportion to their wealth or population. The expenses might mount to a quarter of a million dollars annually, or even half a million; but this is nothing for the object in view.

It is difficult to estimate the value of such a tribunal, in its everyday duty of working on the international law of the world and answering its demands. And so soon as one of the exigencies arise which create wars between nations, its worth would be more than can be told.

We trust that the American Congress, representing North and South America, will address itself squarely to some such practicable system, not content with general statements, which are, after all, merely declamatory, of the folly and cost and horror of war.

The purification of politics is an iridescent dream. Government is force. . . . The Decalogue and the Golden Rule have no place in a political campaign. The commander who lost the battle through the activity of his moral nature would be the derision and jest of history.

JOHN JAMES INGALLS, *New York World,* 1890

62.

Hannis Taylor: The Growing Inefficiency of the House of Representatives

The unprecedented assumption of power by Congress after the Civil War placed the real governing authority in the hands of congressional committees, especially the House Rules Committee, which was able to block almost any legislation it chose. In addition, any member of the House could, under the rules then in effect, refuse to answer a roll call even though present in the chamber, with the result that a minority was often able to keep a majority from enacting legislation owing to the lack of a quorum. Thomas B. Reed, the Republican Speaker of the House, determined to change the rules, and over a period of several years, from 1890 to 1895, was largely successful. In 1890, when the House seemed at a hopeless impasse, the article from which the following selection is taken appeared in the Atlantic Monthly. *Its author, Hannis Taylor, president of the Alabama Bar Association, thought Reed's reforms necessary but insufficient, and proposed additional changes modeled on British parliamentary practice.*

Source: *Atlantic Monthly,* June 1890: "The National House of Representatives: Its Growing Inefficiency as a Legislative Body."

Those who have carefully observed the procedure of our national House of Representatives during the last twenty years can hardly differ as to the fact that it is yearly becoming more and more unequal to the task of discharging the vast and intricate duties which are cast upon it by the ever increasing wants of our complex national life. That this inadequacy will increase as our domain widens and as our population increases can scarcely be doubted, provided no way can be found to remove the impediments which now choke up the main channel of national legislation. The public generally understands that at every session, after 10,000 or more bills and joint resolutions have been dumped in upon the House, it goes through a protracted period of outward activity, during which it deliberates very little, and legislates less, so far as vital national interests are concerned.

The House is thus beginning to be looked upon as a vast graveyard, in which all serious national business is laid to rest. The conviction is every day deepening that the overshadowing questions touching taxation, finance, the public defense, and the like enter its portals only to perish in a despairing struggle with the elements of political obstruction, which even their urgency has no power to overcome. In this way the House is ceasing to be the workshop of the Constitution; it is degenerating into an expensive and unwieldy machine, which does little or no business of real value and importance. . . .

These well-known facts have for a long time been the subject of satire and of invective, to the detriment of the reputation of the House, both at home and abroad. One of the profoundest and most partial of our foreign critics (Mr. Freeman), after carefully observing the procedure of both houses, wrote not long ago as follows:

I may here quote the remark of an acute American friend, that the Senate is as much superior to the House of Lords as the House of Representatives is inferior to the House of Commons. . . . The Senate seemed truly a senate; the House of Representatives struck me as a scene of mere hubbub rather than of real debate.

However this may be, one thing is certain, and that is that the inefficiency of the House does not grow out of any inferiority of its membership to that of the Senate, but rather out of the cumbersome and unwieldy parliamentary system by which its energies are paralyzed.

The root of the evil lies in the absence of an efficient and organized connection between the Cabinet and the members of the political party in the House which the Cabinet represents; in the absence of the right of the Cabinet to appear upon the floor of the House, and to lift up out of the mass of legislations the vital and urgent national questions upon which the legislative mind should be concentrated. There is no effective fighting force in the House, armed with the power to take the initiative and to force the great questions to an issue. The right of initiative in legislation is really reduced to zero by being subdivided among the forty or more standing committees of the House, to which was referred "all proposed legislation," under the old eleventh rule.

The single question which the writer of this article desires to propound is this: Cannot the practical working of the legislative department of our federal Constitution, *constructed after the English model as it existed a century ago,* be improved in the light of the invaluable changes which have been made in the old machine since that time? In other words, if our fathers were wise enough in their day to adapt to the wants of the newborn republic the very best of everything which then existed in the English political system, should not the present generation be fertile enough in political resources to utilize and adapt to our present needs a most valuable improvement in the old system, which is in successful daily operation before our eyes?

A fortunate thing it is that a growing reverence for the Constitution of the United States is ever present to thwart the empirics who are continually proposing to amend some vital part of its organic structure. But it is one thing to alter the organic structure of a system and quite another to devise expedients by which the practical operation of that system may be rendered more harmonious. . . .

The framers of the Constitution wisely left to congressional and party action a wide domain, in which it is practicable to devise, in the light of experience, methods and expedients by which the daily working of the federal system may be rendered more prompt and efficacious. There is no organic defect in the Constitution itself, but there is a lack of cohesion and adjustment between the legislative department and the political force which puts it in motion. Ours is a government of parties, a system which presupposes compact party organization and efficient party leadership.

It is an historical fact that, from the foundation of the government, the politics of the country have been dominated by one or the other of two great political organizations with more or less definite political creeds. In every national contest each party undertakes to formulate its convictions and to announce them in the party platform which emanates from the leading minds that dominate the convention. Upon these platforms, presidential candidates are nominated, and each party pledges itself, in the event of success, to give effect to its policy through practical legislation.

Down to this point our system of party organization works well. The trouble begins when the newly elected President and his Cabinet, as the ostensible leaders of the successful party, undertake to give effect to the program upon which it has triumphed. The fact that the Cabinet has neither place nor voice in the popular chamber renders it unnecessary, in fact inexpedient, for the President to form his Cabinet council out of the real leaders of his party. Thus, unknown and untried men — sometimes ambitious plutocrats who have simply made large gifts to the party chest — are often for the first time brought to the front as pilots of the ship of state.

As the administration has neither place nor voice in either house, it can offer in neither, in its own name, any scheme of legislation designed to carry out a definite policy. In this way, the President and his Cabinet are driven to the humiliating necessity of appealing to this or that party leader in the Senate or House to get up something in the way of a bill or bills to redeem the pledges of the party platform. The great magnates thus appealed to do not always agree with the administration even as to what their own party teaches; each one is apt to have his own personal "views," and before long he begins to talk about "my policy." Hampered by this impotent system of personalism, of organized confusion, the party in possession of the executive power soon begins to drift helplessly upon a sea of troubles. If any great party measure is formulated, it must be the work of some self-constituted individual who gives the measure his name; and if by chance it passes all the rocks and shoals in its path, he becomes at last one of the immortals.

The great defect in this eccentric and personal system is that no one can now acquire sufficient personal authority for the end in view. What man in the House today, on either side, can demand that it pause and listen to him while he presses upon it the urgent national questions which should first be disposed of? Here the question may be asked — How is it that we have gone on so well under the old system for so long a time? The answer is that that time has passed; our legislative business has so increased that the time has now come when we must have greater facilities and more ef-

ficient methods. There was a time when England had no cabinet, in the modern sense of that term, to take the lead in the Commons, and there direct and drive the business of the kingdom. But that was when Parliament was little more than the local legislature of Great Britain, and not the supreme council of an empire.

The business of our House of Representatives has grown until it is nearly, if not quite, as vast and complex as that of the House of Commons. Under the pressure of it the primitive system has broken down, and we must now devise new expedients adequate to changed conditions. The practical question, therefore, is this: How can we so change our political and parliamentary methods as to obtain all the real advantages of the English cabinet system? If the end can be obtained at all, it must be through the adoption of two simple expedients.

First, the starting point should be a bill which would confer upon the Cabinet the right to a place and voice in each house, *with the right to offer in each such schemes of legislation as it might see fit to advocate.* Some years ago, Mr. Pendleton took a timid step in the right direction when he offered a bill which proposed to give to the Cabinet the right to appear in each house, and to debate pending questions. The fatal defect in that bill was its failure to authorize the ministers to submit to the houses formulated measures of legislation. The end in view cannot be attained unless we vest in the administration the right to take the initiative, so as to force to an issue all the great questions upon which the public mind is divided. It is not necessary that the ministers should have the right to vote; it is only necessary that they should have the right to submit bills and to debate them.

Here it may be asked — What practical good would be accomplished if the administration could not command a majority in either house? The answer is that the executive government would possess the power to lift up out of the bog in which they now lie each one of the great questions as to which legislation is most needed; it could then force their consideration upon the House until definite action was had; and then in the first congressional election that followed the people could vote indirectly, in choosing their representatives, upon every question upon which the House had acted or refused to act. When a period of ten years is taken, we have quite as many, if not more, appeals to the people than usually occur in that length of time in England. The trouble is that in these elections the people are not permitted to pass upon definite propositions. Our congressional elections are therefore ceasing to be what they should be, occasions upon which the people can express their views upon urgent and practical questions.

It may also be asked, if the ministers are defeated in the House, should they be forced, as under the present French parliamentary system, to resign office before the constitutional term of the President expires? The answer is that under our Constitution no such provision would be either necessary or desirable. From the history of the Swiss cabinet system, which seems to stand midway between the parliamentary and congressional systems, we learn that a ministry with a definite term works well in practice. In a recent article in the *Nation*, entitled "The Swiss Cabinet," the writer has this to say:

> When, however, bills urged or approved by the council are rejected by the legislature, the ordinary parliamentary result does not take place. No one feels obliged to resign. The cabinet is elected for a given time, and, being thus established, sudden and frequent crises are avoided. . . . The chief objection to party government — violent and rapid changes of ministries — would seem to be overcome by a compromise which secures both responsibility to the majority in the legislature and a known tenure of office.

The great end to be attained is an investing of the Cabinet with the power to force

Hannis Taylor

every great national question to an issue in the House of Representatives so that the people may pass directly upon the result in the next congressional election. The party that undertook to oppose the measures of the administration would of course be forced to propose better ones in order to maintain itself in the confidence of the people. Issues would thus be clearly defined, definite results would be reached, questions would be settled, and business would be disposed of.

Second, to vest in the Cabinet the right to appear in both houses, initiate legislation, and then debate it would be simply to make of them a dumb show, unless they go armed as the authorized and official representatives of the party to which they belong. The mere right to appear in the houses is a matter of no moment whatever unless the cabinet can represent, in its corporate person, the political force which alone can make its presence effective. Nothing could be more simple than for each of the great parties, by a resolution of its national convention, to vest in its presidential candidate and his Cabinet, in the event of success, the official party leadership, according to the English practice. In that way, the whole vexatious and inefficient system of personal dictatorship could be cut up by the roots and supplanted by an impersonal system, which would be not only more effective but more agreeable to the sensibilities of the average American.

Nothing is easier for an American party man to understand than that the business and policy of his party are in the hands of a committee in whose selection he has had a voice. No party that has confidence enough in a man to elect him President should be unwilling to entrust to him the selection of the committee which shall shape the conduct of the party during his administration. From this condition of things two good results would follow: first, no party would dare to nominate any but its real chief for the presidential office; second, no President would dare to select any but the real party leaders as his Cabinet ministers. The lead in public affairs would thus pass neither to accidents nor to personal favorites and friends but to the real leaders of the people.

If a readjustment is ever brought about, upon the lines indicated in this article, between the driving force of the political party in possession of the executive power and the legislative machinery which such force is expected to put in motion, the House of Representatives will of course become, in a sense in which it never was before, the workshop of the Constitution. It will be, more than ever before, a place in which the party which possesses a majority will be expected to enact legislation without unreasonable or vexatious obstruction from the minority. Our whole system of representative government rests upon the principle that the majority, after patiently listening to the minority, shall possess the ultimate power to decide what law or policy shall prevail.

For years the two great parties have divided the votes of the House in such equal proportions that it has become the fashion for the minority systematically to pursue such a plan of obstruction as to make all legislation upon contested questions practically impossible. Under this system of obstruction, for which both parties are equally responsible, the usefulness of the House has in a great measure disappeared, and the country is left to suffer the consequences. Although we are groaning under a war tariff, which both parties admit should be reduced and reformed, no legislation even on that subject is possible.

The first mutterings of the storm have been heard. The party now in possession of a scant majority in the House has made a revolutionary effort so to weaken the opposition as to enable it to do business. Certain rulings of Speaker Reed have no doubt been revolutionary, if a departure from settled parliamentary precedent in the effort to do business can be called revolution. The most significant fact which the pending contest has so far developed is embodied in the statement which Speaker Reed is said to have made to the Associated Press in explanation or apology for his conduct. The substance of this statement, as reported, is that the members of the House cannot be permitted to stand idly by and draw their pay; that every legitimate resource must be exhausted in the effort to expedite the public business.

The public demand is becoming so imperious that the internal contentions of the House, which have for so long hindered and delayed urgent legislation upon a series of great national questions, shall cease that the dominant party has been compelled to resort even to revolutionary tactics in the effort to obtain the power to act. If the next congressional election shall put the Democratic Party, as it possibly will, in possession of a bare majority, the same deadlock will recur, and the same imperious voice will demand that the majority shall be armed with the power to act. As the grievance which this unfortunate condition of things produces is national, the demand for its removal extends far beyond the limits of party. No reform will come from within until the leaders of both parties in the House are made to understand that there is an imperious popular demand that the Lower House must so reform its procedure as permanently to vest in the majority of the dominant party, whichever it may be, the power to act.

It may be claimed that the Republican majority, by the adoption of the new rules, has already accomplished that result. If it has, a starting point only has been gained.

No decided and lasting change for the better can be brought about until there is established a real and practical connection between the working majority in the House and the executive government. The old worn-out congressional system, under which the initiative in legislation is vested in a large number of committees without any common leadership, can never be made adequate to the present wants of the country until it is so remodeled as to vest the initiative in legislation touching great national questions in a single grand committee, the Cabinet, which should be clothed with the official leadership of the party which it represents.

63.

The Sherman Antitrust Act

The enormous success of the Standard Oil Trust stimulated similar agreements in other American industries in the 1870s and 1880s. After state attempts to control the growth of monopolies had proved ineffective, some federal restraint was provided by passage of the Sherman Antitrust Act of 1890. The Act was inadequate in that it did not define "trusts," provide for practical means of "restraint," or indicate whether labor combinations as well as industrial were to be subject to its provisions. The vagueness of the Act itself, plus subsequent Supreme Court rulings, deprived it of any real effectiveness against the trusts, although it was used effectively against labor organizations on several occasions.

Source: *Statutes,* XXVI, pp. 209-210.

An act to protect trade and commerce against unlawful restraints and monopolies.

Be it enacted by the Senate and House of Representatives of the United States of America in Congress assembled:

Section 1. Every contract, combination in the form of trust or otherwise, or conspiracy in restraint of trade or commerce among the several states or with foreign nations is hereby declared to be illegal. Every person who shall make any such contract or engage in any such combination or conspiracy shall be deemed guilty of a misdemeanor, and on conviction thereof shall be punished by fine not exceeding $5,000 or by imprisonment not exceeding one year, or by both said punishments, in the discretion of the court.

Section 2. Every person who shall monopolize, or attempt to monopolize, or combine or conspire with any other person or persons to monopolize any part of the trade or commerce among the several states or with foreign nations shall be deemed guilty of a misdemeanor, and on conviction thereof shall be punished by fine not exceeding $5,000 or by imprisonment not exceeding one year, or by both said punishments, in the discretion of the court.

Section 3. Every contract, combination in form of trust or otherwise, or conspiracy in restraint of trade or commerce in any territory of the United States or of the District of Columbia, or in restraint of trade or commerce between any such territory and another, or between any such territory or territories and any state or states or the District of Columbia, or with foreign nations, or between the District of Columbia and any state or states or foreign nations is hereby declared illegal. Every person who shall make any such contract or engage in any such combination or conspiracy shall be deemed guilty of a misdemeanor, and on conviction thereof shall be punished by fine not exceeding $5,000 or by imprisonment not exceeding one year, or by both said punishments, in the discretion of the court.

Section 4. The several Circuit courts of the United States are hereby invested with jurisdiction to prevent and restrain violations of this act; and it shall be the duty of the several district attorneys of the United States, in their respective districts, under the direction of the attorney general, to institute proceedings in equity to prevent and restrain such violations. Such proceedings may be by way of petition setting forth the case and praying that such violations shall be enjoined or otherwise prohibited. When the parties complained of shall have been duly notified of such petition, the court shall proceed, as soon as may be, to the hearing and determination of the case; and, pending such petition and before final de-

cree, the court may at any time make such temporary restraining order or prohibition as shall be deemed just in the premises.

Section 5. Whenever it shall appear to the court before which any proceeding under Section 4 of this act may be pending, that the ends of justice require that other parties should be brought before the court, the court may cause them to be summoned, whether they reside in the district in which the court is held or not; and subpoenas to that end may be served in any district by the marshal thereof.

Section 6. Any property owned under any contract or by any combination, or pursuant to any conspiracy (and being the subject thereof) mentioned in Section 1 of this act, and being in the course of transportation from one state to another or to a foreign country, shall be forfeited to the United States, and may be seized and condemned by like proceedings as those provided by law for the forfeiture, seizure, and condemnation of property imported into the United States contrary to law.

Section 7. Any person who shall be injured in his business or property by any other person or corporation by reason of anything forbidden or declared to be unlawful by this act may sue therefor in any Circuit Court of the United States in the district in which the defendant resides or is found, without respect to the amount in controversy, and shall recover threefold the damages by him sustained, and the costs of suit, including a reasonable attorney's fee.

Section 8. That the word "person," or "persons," wherever used in this act, shall be deemed to include corporations and associations existing under or authorized by the laws of either the United States, the laws of any of the territories, the laws of any state, or the laws of any foreign country.

64.

Benjamin R. Tucker: The State and Anarchism

Benjamin Tucker, the most prominent American exponent of philosophical anarchism, participated in the movement as a lecturer and editor of the Radical Review *and* Liberty. *He espoused passive resistance and deplored the tactics of anarchists in the Haymarket riot and of President Garfield's assassin, Charles Guiteau, his antipathy to violence perhaps being the result of a Unitarian upbringing and his education at a Friends Academy. The following article was adapted from a speech delivered October 14, 1890.*

Source: *Instead of a Book, By A Man Too Busy To Write One,* New York, 1893, pp. 21-27: "Relation of the State to the Individual."

PRESUMABLY THE HONOR which you have done me in inviting me to address you to-day upon "The Relation of the State to the Individual" is due principally to the fact that circumstances have combined to make me somewhat conspicuous as an exponent of the theory of modern anarchism — a theory which is coming to be more and more regarded as one of the few that are tenable as a basis of political and social life. In its name, then, I shall speak to you in discussing this question, which either underlies or closely touches almost every practical problem that confronts this generation. The future of the tariff, of taxation, of finance, of property, of woman, of marriage, of the family, of the suffrage, of education, of invention, of literature, of science, of the arts, of personal habits, of private character, of ethics, of religion will be determined by the conclusion at which mankind shall arrive as to whether and how far the individual owes allegiance to the State.

Anarchism, in dealing with this subject, has found it necessary, first of all, to define its terms. Popular conceptions of the terminology of politics are incompatible with the rigorous exactness required in scientific investigation. To be sure, a departure from the popular use of language is accompanied by the risk of misconception by the multitude, who persistently ignore the new definitions; but, on the other hand, conformity thereto is attended by the still more deplorable alternative of confusion in the eyes of the competent, who would be justified in attributing inexactness of thought where there is inexactness of expression.

Take the term "State," for instance, with which we are especially concerned today. It is a word that is on every lip. But how many of those who use it have any idea of what they mean by it? And, of the few who have, how various are their conceptions! We designate by the term "State" institutions that embody absolutism in its extreme form and institutions that temper it with more or less liberality. We apply the word alike to institutions that do nothing but aggress and to institutions that, besides aggressing, to some extent protect and defend. But which is the State's essential function, aggression or defense, few seem to know or care.

Benjamin R. Tucker

Some champions of the State evidently consider aggression its principle, although they disguise it alike from themselves and from the people under the term "administration," which they wish to extend in every possible direction. Others, on the contrary, consider defense its principle, and wish to limit it accordingly to the performance of police duties. Still others seem to think that it exists for both aggression and defense, combined in varying proportions according to the momentary interests, or maybe only whims, of those happening to control it. Brought face to face with these diverse views, the Anarchists, whose mission in the world is the abolition of aggression and all the evils that result therefrom, perceived that, to be understood, they must attach some definite and avowed significance to the terms which they are obliged to employ, and especially to the words "State" and "government."

Seeking, then, the elements common to all the institutions to which the name "State" has been applied, they have found

them two in number: first, aggression; second, the assumption of sole authority over a given area and all within it, exercised generally for the double purpose of more complete oppression of its subjects and extension of its boundaries. That this second element is common to all States, I think, will not be denied — at least, I am not aware that any State has ever tolerated a rival State within its borders; and it seems plain that any State which should do so would thereby cease to be a State and to be considered as such by any. The exercise of authority over the same area by two States is a contradiction. That the first element, aggression, has been and is common to all States will probably be less generally admitted. Nevertheless, I shall not attempt to re-enforce here the conclusion of [Herbert] Spencer, which is gaining wider acceptance daily — that the State had its origin in aggression, and has continued as an aggressive institution from its birth.

Defense was an afterthought, prompted by necessity; and its introduction as a State function, though effected doubtless with a view to the strengthening of the State, was really and in principle the initiation of the State's destruction. Its growth in importance is but an evidence of the tendency of progress toward the abolition of the State. Taking this view of the matter, the Anarchists contend that defense is not an essential of the State, but that aggression is.

Now, what is aggression? Aggression is simply another name for government. Aggression, invasion, government are interconvertible terms. The essence of government is control, or the attempt to control. He who attempts to control another is a governor, an aggressor, an invader, and the nature of such invasion is not changed, whether it is made by one man upon another man, after the manner of the ordinary criminal; or by one man upon all other men, after the manner of an absolute monarch; or by all other men upon one man, after the manner of a modern democracy. On the other hand, he who resists another's attempt to control is not an aggressor, an invader, a governor, but simply a defender, a protector; and the nature of such resistance is not changed whether it be offered by one man to another man, as when one repels a criminal's onslaught; or by one man to all other men, as when one declines to obey an oppressive law; or by all other men to one man, as when a subject people rises against a despot; or as when the members of a community voluntarily unite to restrain a criminal.

This distinction between invasion and resistance, between government and defense, is vital. Without it there can be no valid philosophy of politics. Upon this distinction and the other considerations just outlined, the Anarchists frame the desired definitions. This, then, is the Anarchistic definition of government: the subjection of the noninvasive individual to an external will. And this is the Anarchistic definition of the State: the embodiment of the principle of invasion in an individual, or a band of individuals, assuming to act as representatives or masters of the entire people within a given area.

As to the meaning of the remaining term in the subject under discussion, the word "individual," I think there is little difficulty. Putting aside the subtleties in which certain metaphysicians have indulged, one may use this word without danger of being misunderstood. Whether the definitions thus arrived at prove generally acceptable or not is a matter of minor consequence. I submit that they are reached scientifically, and serve the purpose of a clear conveyance of thought. The Anarchists, having by their adoption taken due care to be explicit, are entitled to have their ideas judged in the light of these definitions.

Now comes the question proper: what relations should exist between the State and the individual? The general method of determining these is to apply some theory of ethics involving a basis of moral obligation. In this method the Anarchists have no confidence. The idea of moral obligation, of inherent rights and duties, they totally discard. They look upon all obligations, not as moral but as social, and even then not really as obligations except as these have been consciously and voluntarily assumed. If a man makes an agreement with men, the latter may combine to hold him to his agreement; but, in the absence of such agreement, no man, so far as the Anarchists are aware, has made any agreement with God or with any other power of any order whatsoever. The Anarchists are not only utilitarians but egoists, in the farthest and fullest sense. So far as inherent right is concerned, might is its only measure.

Any man, be his name Bill Sykes or Alexander Romanoff, and any set of men, whether the Chinese highbinders or the Congress of the United States, have the right, if they have the power, to kill or coerce other men and to make the entire world subservient to their ends. Society's right to enslave the individual and the individual's right to enslave society are unequal only because their powers are unequal. This position being subversive of all systems of religion and morality, of course I cannot expect to win immediate assent thereto from the audience which I am addressing today; nor does the time at my disposal allow me to sustain it by an elaborate or even a summary examination of the foundations of ethics. Those who desire a greater familiarity with this particular phase of the subject should read a profound German work, *Der Einzige und sein Eigenthum,* written years ago by a comparatively unknown author, Dr. Caspar Schmidt, whose nom de plume was Max Stirner. Read only by a few scholars, the book is buried in obscurity, but is destined to a resurrection that perhaps will mark an epoch.

If this, then, were a question of right, it would be, according to the Anarchists, purely a question of strength. But fortunately it is not a question of right; it is a question of expediency, of knowledge, of science — the science of living together, the science of society. The history of humanity has been largely one long and gradual discovery of the fact that the individual is the gainer by society exactly in proportion as society is free, and of the law that the condition of a permanent and harmonious society is the greatest amount of individual liberty compatible with equality of liberty. The average man of each new generation has said to himself more clearly and consciously than his predecessor: "My neighbor is not my enemy, but my friend, and I am his, if we would but mutually recognize the fact. We help each other to a better, fuller, happier living; and this service might be greatly increased if we would cease to restrict, hamper, and oppress each other. Why can we not agree to let each live his own life, neither of us transgressing the limit that separates our individualities?"

It is by this reasoning that mankind is approaching the real social contract, which is not, as Rousseau thought, the origin of society but rather the outcome of a long social experience, the fruit of its follies and disasters. It is obvious that this contract, this social law, developed to its perfection, excludes all aggression, all violation of equality of liberty, all invasion of every kind. Considering this contract in connection with the Anarchistic definition of the State as the embodiment of the principle of invasion, we see that the State is antagonistic to society; and, society being essential to individual life and development, the conclusion leaps to the eyes that the relation of the State to the individual and of the individual to the State must be one of hostility, enduring till the State shall perish.

"But," it will be asked of the Anarchists at this point in the argument, "what shall be done with those individuals who un-

doubtedly will persist in violating the social law by invading their neighbors?" The Anarchists answer that the abolition of the State will leave in existence a defensive association resting no longer on a compulsory but on a voluntary basis, which will restrain invaders by any means that may prove necessary. "But that is what we have now," is the rejoinder. "You really want, then, only a change of name?" Not so fast, please. Can it be soberly pretended for a moment that the State, even as it exists here in America, is purely a defensive institution? Surely not, save by those who see of the State only its most palpable manifestation — the policeman on the street corner. And one would not have to watch him very closely to see the error of this claim.

Why, the very first act of the State, the compulsory assessment and collection of taxes is itself an aggression, a violation of equal liberty, and, as such, vitiates every subsequent act, even those acts which would be purely defensive if paid for out of a treasury filled by voluntary contributions. How is it possible to sanction, under the law of equal liberty, the confiscation of a man's earnings to pay for protection which he has not sought and does not desire? And, if this is an outrage, what name shall we give to such confiscation when the victim is given, instead of bread, a stone; instead of protection, oppression? To force a man to pay for the violation of his own liberty is indeed an addition of insult to injury. But that is exactly what the State is doing.

Read the *Congressional Record*; follow the proceedings of the state legislatures; examine our statute books; test each act separately by the law of equal liberty — you will find that a good nine-tenths of existing legislation serves, not to enforce that fundamental social law but either to prescribe the individual's personal habits or, worse still, to create and sustain commercial, industrial, financial, and proprietary monopolies which deprive labor of a large part of the reward that it would receive in a perfectly free market. "To be governed," says Proudhon, "is to be watched, inspected, spied, directed, law-ridden, regulated, penned up, indoctrinated, preached at, checked, appraised, sized, censured, commanded, by beings who have neither title nor knowledge nor virtue. To be governed is to have every operation, every transaction, every movement noted, registered, counted, rated, stamped, measured, numbered, assessed, licensed, refused, authorized, endorsed, admonished, prevented, reformed, redressed, corrected. To be governed is, under pretext of public utility and in the name of the general interest, to be laid under contribution, drilled, fleeced, exploited, monopolized, extorted from, exhausted, hoaxed, robbed; then, upon the slightest resistance, at the first word of complaint, to be repressed, fined, vilified, annoyed, hunted down, pulled about, beaten, disarmed, bound, imprisoned, shot, mitrailleused [machine-gunned], judged, condemned, banished, sacrificed, sold, betrayed, and, to crown all, ridiculed, derided, outraged, dishonored."

And I am sure I do not need to point out to you the existing laws that correspond to and justify nearly every count in Proudhon's long indictment. How thoughtless, then, to assert that the existing political order is of a purely defensive character instead of the aggressive State which the Anarchists aim to abolish!

This leads to another consideration that bears powerfully upon the problem of the invasive individual, who is such a bugbear to the opponents of Anarchism. Is it not such treatment as has just been described that is largely responsible for his existence? I have heard or read somewhere of an in-

scription written for a certain charitable institution:

This hospital a pious person built,
But first he made the poor wherewith to fill't.

And so, it seems to me, it is with our prisons. They are filled with criminals which our virtuous State has made what they are by its iniquitous laws, its grinding monopolies, and the horrible social conditions that result from them. We enact many laws that manufacture criminals, and then a few that punish them. Is it too much to expect that the new social conditions which must follow the abolition of all interference with the production and distribution of wealth will in the end so change the habits and propensities of men that our jails and prisons, our policemen and our soldiers — in a word, our whole machinery and outfit of defense — will be superfluous? That, at least, is the Anarchists' belief. It sounds Utopian, but it really rests on severely economic grounds.

Today, however, time is lacking to explain the Anarchistic view of the dependence of usury, and therefore of poverty, upon monopolistic privilege, especially the banking privilege, and to show how an intelligent minority, educated in the principle of Anarchism and determined to exercise that right to ignore the State upon which Spencer, in his *Social Statics,* so ably and admirably insists, might, by setting at defiance the National and State banking prohibitions, and establishing a Mutual Bank in competition with the existing monopolies, take the first and most important step in the abolition of usury and of the State. Simple as such a step would seem, from it all the rest would follow.

65.

Oliver Wendell Holmes: The American Appetite for Old World Titles

Oliver Wendell Holmes held liberal views in matters of intellectual freedom, and his criticisms of the nineteenth-century remnants of Calvinism were notably caustic. Yet on issues of social reform he was a conservative, reflecting his position as "a man of family," or, as he defined it, one "who inherits family traditions and the cumulative humanities of at least five generations." In the following selection from Over the Teacups, *Holmes used satire as a means to discredit labor organizations and the poorer classes they were attempting to reach.*

Source: *Over the Teacups*, London, 1890, pp. 218-223.

ONE OF MY NEIGHBORS, a thorough American, is much concerned about the growth of what he calls the "hard-handed aristocracy." He tells the following story:

"I was putting up a fence about my yard, and employed a man of whom I knew something — that he was industrious, temperate, and that he had a wife and children to support — a worthy man, a native New Englander. I engaged him, I say, to dig some postholes. My employee bought a new spade and scoop on purpose, and came to my place at the appointed time, and began digging. While he was at work, two men came over from a drinking saloon, to which my residence is nearer than I could desire. One of them I had known as Mike Fagan, the other as Hans Schleimer. They looked at Hiram, my New Hampshire man, in a contemptuous and threatening way for a minute or so, when Fagan addressed him:

" 'And how much does the man pay yez by the hour?'

" 'The gentleman doesn't pay me by the hour,' said Hiram.

" 'How mosh does he bay you by der veeks?' said Hans.

" 'I don' know as that's any of your business,' answered Hiram.

" 'Faith, we'll make it our business,' said Mike Fagan. 'We're Knoights of Labor, we'd have yez to know, and ye can't make yer bargains jist as ye loikes. We manes to know how many hours ye worrks, and how much ye gets for it.'

" '*Knights* of Labor!' said I. 'Why, that is a kind of title of nobility, isn't it? I thought the laws of our country didn't allow titles of that kind. But if you have a right to be called knights, I suppose I ought to address you as such. Sir Michael, I congratulate you on the dignity you have attained. I hope Lady Fagan is getting on well with my shirts. Sir Hans, I pay my respects to your title. I trust that Lady Schleimer has got through that little difficulty between Her Ladyship and yourself in which the Police Court thought it necessary to intervene.'

"The two men looked at me. I weigh about a hundred and eighty pounds, and am well put together. Hiram was noted in his village as a 'rahstler.' But my face is rather pallid and peaked, and Hiram had something of the greenhorn look. The two men, who had been drinking, hardly knew what ground to take. They rather liked the sound of *Sir* Michael and *Sir* Hans. They did not know very well what to make of their wives as 'ladies.' They looked doubtful whether to take what had been said as a *casus belli* [occasion of war] or not, but they wanted a pretext of some kind or other. Presently one of them saw a label on the scoop, or long-handled, spoonlike shovel, with which Hiram had been working.

" 'Arrah, be jabers!' exclaimed Mike Fagan, 'but hasn't he been a-tradin' wid Brown, the hardware fellah that we boycotted! Grab it, Hans, and we'll carry it off and show it to the brotherhood.'

"The men made a move toward the implement.

" 'You let that are scoop shovel alone,' said Hiram.

"I stepped to his side. The Knights were combative, as their noble predecessors with the same title always were, and it was necessary to come to a *voie de fait* [act of violence]. My straight blow from the shoulder did for Sir Michael. Hiram treated Sir Hans to what is technically known as a cross-buttock.

" 'Naow, Dutchman,' said Hiram, 'if you don't want to be planted in that are posthole, y'd better take y'rself out o' this here piece of private property. Dangerous passin, as the signposts say, abaout these times.'

"Sir Michael went down, half-stunned by my expressive gesture; Sir Hans did not know whether his hip was out of joint or he had got a bad sprain; but they were both out of condition for further hostilities. Perhaps it was hardly fair to take advantage of their misfortunes to inflict a discourse upon them, but they had brought it on themselves, and we each of us gave them a piece of our mind.

" 'I tell you what it is,' said Hiram, 'I'm a free and independent American citizen, and I an't a-gon' to hev no man tyrannize over me, if he doos call himself by one o' them noblemen's titles. Ef I can't work jes' as I choose, fur folks that wants me to work fur 'em and that I want to work fur, I might jes' as well go to Sibery and done with it. My gran'f'ther fit in Bunker Hill

battle. I guess if our folks in them days didn't care no great abaout Lord Percy and Sir William Haowe, we an't a-gon' to be scart by Sir Michael Fagan and Sir Hans What's-his-name, nor no other fellahs that undertakes to be noblemen, and tells us common folks what we shall dew an' what we sha'n't. No, *sir!'*

"I took the opportunity to explain to Sir Michael and Sir Hans what it was our fathers fought for and what is the meaning of liberty. If these noblemen did not like the country, they could go elsewhere. If they didn't like the laws, they had the ballot box and could choose new legislators. But as long as the laws existed they must obey them. I could not admit that, because they called themselves by the titles the Old World nobility thought so much of, they had a right to interfere in the agreements I entered into with my neighbor. I told Sir Michael that if he would go home and help Lady Fagan to saw and split the wood for her fire, he would be better employed than in meddling with my domestic arrangements. I advised Sir Hans to ask Lady Schleimer for her bottle of spirits to use as an embrocation for his lame hip. And so my two visitors with the aristocratic titles staggered off and left us plain, untitled citizens, Hiram and myself, to set our posts and consider the question whether we lived in a free country or under the authority of a self-constituted order of quasi-nobility."

It is a very curious fact that, with all our boasted "free and equal" superiority over the communities of the Old World, our people have the most enormous appetite for Old World titles of distinction. Sir Michael and Sir Hans belong to one of the most extended of the aristocratic orders. But we have also "Knights and Ladies of Honor," and, what is still grander, "Royal Conclave of Knights and Ladies," "Royal Arcanum," and "Royal Society of Good Fellows," "Supreme Council," "Imperial Court," "Grand Protector," and "Grand Dictator," and so on. Nothing less than "Grand" and

"Supreme" is good enough for the dignitaries of our associations of citizens. Where does all this ambition for names without realities come from? . . .

It appears to be a peculiarly American weakness. The French republicans of the earlier period thought the term "citizen" was good enough for anybody. At a later period, "le Roi Citoyen" — the citizen king — was a common title given to Louis Philippe. But nothing is too grand for the American, in the way of titles. The proudest of them all signify absolutely nothing. They do not stand for ability, for public service, for social importance, for large possessions; but, on the contrary, are oftenest found in connection with personalities to which they are supremely inapplicable. We can hardly afford to quarrel with a national habit which, if lightly handled, may involve us in serious domestic difficulties. The "Right Worshipful" functionary whose equipage stops at my back gate, and whose services are indispensable to the health and comfort of my household, is a dignitary whom I must not offend. I must speak with proper deference to the lady who is scrubbing my floors when I remember that her husband, who saws my wood, carries a string of high-sounding titles which would satisfy a Spanish nobleman.

66.

JOHN WESLEY POWELL: Institutions for the Arid Lands

In the westward movement of the post-Civil War years the plains region east of the Rocky Mountains, known as the Great American Desert, was usually bypassed in favor of the more fertile regions of the West Coast. Farmers were generally convinced that lack of rainfall made the Great Plains useless for agriculture. It was left to such men as John Wesley Powell, explorer and director of the United States Geological Survey from 1880 to 1894, to demonstrate the potentiality of the plains region. In Powell's notable 1878 report, Lands of the Arid Region, *he described the uses to which the varying areas of the Plains could be put. Powell recognized that the region could not be dealt with by Congress under the terms of the Homestead Act of 1862, for small farming was not suitable there, and the mineral deposits clearly were worth more than the stipulated price homesteaders paid for land. The following article by Powell, published in 1890, outlined his proposals for development of the region.*

Source: *Century Magazine*, May 1890.

INDUSTRIAL CIVILIZATION IN AMERICA began with the building of log cabins. Where Piedmont plain merges into coastal plain, there rivers are transformed — dashing waters are changed to tidal waters and navigation heads, and there "powers" are found. Beside these transformed waters, in a narrow zone from north to south across the United States, the first real settlement of the country began by the building of log-cabin homes. This first cabin zone ultimately became the site of the great cities of the

East — Boston, New York, Philadelphia, Baltimore, Washington, Richmond, Charleston, and Augusta; and steadily, while the cities were growing, the log-cabin zone moved westward, until it reached the border of the Great Plains, which it never crossed.

The arid region of the West was settled by gold and silver hunters aggregated in comparatively large bodies. Their shanties of logs, slabs, boards, and adobes were speedily replaced by the more costly structures of towns and cities which suddenly sprang into existence where gold or silver was found. These towns and cities were thus scattered promiscuously through the mountainland. In them, avenues of trees were planted and parks were laid out, and about them, gardens, vineyards, and orchards were cultivated. From this horticulture sprang the agriculture of the region.

In the East the log cabin was the beginning of civilization; in the West, the miner's camp. In the East agriculture began with the settler's clearing; in the West, with the exploitation of wealthy men. In the log-cabin years a poor man in Ohio might clear an acre at a time and extend his potato patch, his cornfield, and his meadow from year to year, and do all with his own hands and energy, and thus hew his way from poverty to plenty. At the same time, his wife could plant hollyhocks, sweet williams, marigolds, and roses in boxed beds of earth around the cabin door. So field and garden were all within the compass of a poor man's means, his own love of industry, and his wife's love of beauty.

In western Europe, where our civilization was born, a farmer might carry on his work in his own way, on his own soil or on the land of his feudal lord, and in the higher phases of this industry he could himself enjoy the products of his labor, subject only to taxes and rents. Out of this grew the modern agriculture with which we are so familiar in America, where the farmer owns his land, cultivates the soil with his own hands, and reaps the reward of his own toil, subject only to the conditions necessary to the welfare of the body politic.

The farming of the arid region cannot be carried on in this manner. Individual farmers with small holdings cannot sustain themselves as individual men; for the little farm is, perchance, dependent upon the waters of some great river that can be turned out and controlled from year to year only by the combined labor of many men. And in modern times great machinery is used, and dams, reservoirs, canals, and many minor hydraulic appliances are necessary. These cost large sums of money, and in their construction and maintenance many men are employed. In the practice of agriculture by irrigation in high antiquity, men were organized as communal bodies or as slaves to carry on such operations by united labor. Thus the means of obtaining subsistence were of such a character as to give excuse and cogent argument for the establishment of despotism. The soil could be cultivated, great nations could be sustained only by the organization of large bodies of men working together on the great enterprises of irrigation under despotic rulers. But such a system cannot obtain in the United States, where the love of liberty is universal.

What, then, shall be the organization of this new industry of agriculture by irrigation? Shall the farmers labor for themselves and own the agricultural properties severally? Or shall the farmers be a few capitalists, employing labor on a large scale, as is done in the great mines and manufactories of the United States? The history of two decades of this industry exhibits this fact: that, in part, the irrigated lands are owned and cultivated by men having small holdings, but in larger part they are held in great tracts by capitalists, and the tendency to this is on the increase. When the springs and creeks are utilized, small holdings are developed;

but when the rivers are taken out upon the lands, great holdings are acquired; and thus the farming industries of the West are falling into the hands of a wealthy few.

Various conditions have led to this. In some portions of the arid region, especially in California, the Spanish land grants were utilized for the purpose of aggregating large tracts for wholesale farming. Sometimes the lands granted to railroads were utilized for the same purpose. Then, to promote the irrigation of this desert land, an act was passed by Congress giving a section of land for a small price to any man who would irrigate it. Still other lands were acquired under the Homestead Act, the Preemption Act, and the Timber-Culture Act. Through these privileges, title could be secured to two square miles of land by one individual. Companies wishing to engage in irrigation followed, in the main, one of two plans: they either bought the lands and irrigated their own tracts, or they constructed irrigating works and supplied water to the farmers. Through the one system, land monopoly is developed; through the other, water monopoly.

Such has been the general course of the development of irrigation. But there are three notable exceptions. The people of the Southwest came originally by the way of Mexico from Spain, where irrigation and the institutions necessary for its control had been developing from high antiquity, and these people well understood that their institutions must be adapted to their industries; and so they organized their settlements as pueblos, or "irrigating municipalities," by which the lands were held in severalty while the tenure of waters and works was communal or municipal. The Mormons, settling in Utah, borrowed the Mexican system. The lands in small tracts were held in severalty by the people, but the waters were controlled by bishops of the church, who among the "Latter-day Saints"

are priests of the "Order of Aaron" and have secular functions. In southern California, also, many colonies were planted in which the lands were held in severalty and in small parcels.

Gradually in these communities the waters are passing from the control of irrigating corporations into the control of the municipalities which the colonies have formed. Besides these three great exceptions there are some minor ones, which need not here be recounted. In general, farming by irrigation has been developed as wholesale farming in large tracts or as wholesale irrigating by large companies. Some of these water companies are foreign, others are capitalists of the Eastern cities, while a few are composed of capitalists of the West.

Where agriculture is dependent upon an artificial supply of water, and where there is more land than can be served by the water, values inhere in water, not in land; the land without the water is without value. A stream may be competent to irrigate 100,000 acres of land, and there may be 500,000 acres of land to which it is possible to carry the water. If one man holds that water he practically owns the land; whatever value is given to any portion of it is derived from the water owned by the one person. In the far West, a man may turn a spring or a brook upon a little valley stretch and make him a home with his own resources, or a few neighbors may unite to turn a small creek from its natural channel and gradually make a cluster of farms. This has been done, and the available springs and brooks are almost exhausted. But the chief resource of irrigation is from the use of the rivers and from the storage of waters which run to waste during a greater part of the year; for the season of irrigation is short, and during most of the months the waters are lost unless held in reservoirs.

In the development of these water companies, there has been much conflict. In the main, improvident franchises have been granted, and, when found onerous, the people have impaired or more or less destroyed them by unfriendly legislation and administration. The whole subject, however, is in its infancy, and the laws of the Western territory are inadequate to give security to capital invested in irrigating works on the one hand and protection to the farmer from extortion on the other. For this reason the tendency is to organize land companies. At present there is a large class of promoters who obtain options on lands and make contracts to supply water, and then enlist capital in the East and in Europe and organize and control construction companies, which, sometimes at least, make large profits.

There seems to be little difficulty in interesting capitalists in these enterprises. The great increase in value given to land through its redemption by irrigation makes such investments exceedingly attractive. But, at present, investors and farmers are alike badly protected, and the lands and waters are falling into the hands of "middlemen." If the last few years' experience throws any light upon the future, the people of the West are entering upon an era of unparalleled speculation, which will result in the aggregation of the lands and waters in the hands of a comparatively few persons. Let us hope that there is wisdom enough in the statesmen of America to avert the impending evil.

Whence, then, shall the capital come? And how shall the labor be organized by which these 100 million acres of land are to be redeemed? This is the problem that today confronts our statesmen and financiers. Capital must come, for the work is demanded and will pay. Let us look at the statistics of this subject in round numbers, and always quite within probable limits. Let us speak of 100 million acres of land to be redeemed by the use of rivers and reservoirs. This will cost about $10 per acre, or $1 billion. In the near future a demand for this amount will be made, and it will be forthcoming beyond a peradventure. The experience obtained by the redemption of 6 million acres of land already under cultivation abundantly warrants the statement that an average of $50 per acre is a small estimate to be placed upon the value of the lands yet to be redeemed as they come to be used. Thus there is a prize to be secured of $5 billion by the investment of $1 billion. Such vast undertakings will not be overlooked by the enterprising men of America.

In a former article on "The Irrigable Lands of the Arid Region," in the *Century Magazine* for March 1890, it was explained that the waters of the arid lands flowing in the great rivers must somehow be divided among the states, and that in two cases important international problems are involved. It was also shown that contests are arising between different districts of the same state. But the waters must be still further subdivided in order that they may be distributed to individual owners. How can this be done? Lands can be staked out, cornerposts can be established, dividing lines can be run, and titles to tracts in terms of metes and bounds can be recorded. But who can establish the cornerposts of flowing waters? When the waters are gathered into streams they rush on to the desert sands or to the sea; and how shall we describe the metes and bounds of a wave? The farmer may brand his horses, but who can brand the clouds or put a mark of ownership on the current of a river? The waters of today have values and must be divided; the waters of the morrow have values, and the waters of all coming time, and these values must be distributed among the people. How shall it be done?

It is proposed to present a plan for the solution of these problems, and others con-

John Wesley Powell, first to navigate the Grand Canyon, and Tau-Gu, Great Chief of the Pai-Utes, 1872; from a stereograph by John K. Hillers

nected therewith, in an outline of institutions necessary for the arid lands. Some of these problems have been discussed in former articles, and it may be well to summarize them all once more, as follows:

First, the capital to redeem by irrigation 100 million acres of land is to be obtained, and $1 billion is necessary.

Second, the lands are to be distributed to the people, and, as yet, we have no proper system of land laws by which it can be done.

Third, the waters must be divided among the states, and, as yet, there is no law for it, and the states are now in conflict.

Fourth, the waters are to be divided among the people so that each man may have the amount necessary to fertilize his farm, each hamlet, town, and city the amount necessary for domestic purposes, and that every thirsty garden may quaff from the crystal waters that come from the mountains.

Fifth, the great forests that clothe the hills, plateaus, and mountains with verdure must be saved from devastation by fire and preserved for the use of man, that the sources of water may be protected, that farms may be fenced and homes built, and that all this wealth of forest may be distributed among the people.

Sixth, the grasses that are to feed the flocks and herds must be protected and utilized.

Seventh, the great mineral deposits — the fuel of the future, the iron for the railroads, and the gold and silver for our money — must be kept ready to the hand of industry and the brain of enterprise.

Eighth, the powers of the factories of that great land are to be created and utilized that the hum of busy machinery may echo among the mountains — the symphonic music of industry.

A thousand millions of money must be used; who shall furnish it? Great and many industries are to be established; who shall control them? Millions of men are to labor; who shall employ them? This is a great nation, the government is powerful; shall it engage in this work? So dreamers may dream, and so ambition may dictate, but in the name of the men who labor I demand that the laborers shall employ themselves; that the enterprise shall be controlled by the men who have the genius to organize and whose homes are in the lands developed, and that the money shall be furnished by the people; and I say to the government: Hands off! Furnish the people with institutions of justice and let them do the work for themselves. The solution to be propounded, then, is one of institutions to be organized for the establishment of justice, not of appropriations to be made and offices created by the government.

In a group of mountains a small river has its source. A dozen or a score of creeks unite to form the trunk. The creeks higher up divide into brooks. All these streams combined form the drainage system of a hydrographic basin, a unit of country well-defined in nature, for it is bounded above and on each side by heights of land that rise as crests to part the waters. Thus, hydraulic basin is segregated from hydraulic basin by nature herself, and the landmarks are practically perpetual. In such a basin of the arid region the irrigable lands lie below; not chiefly by the river's side but on the mesas and low plains that stretch back on each side. Above these lands the pasturage hills and mountains stand, and there the forests and sources of water supply are found.

Such a district of country is a commonwealth by itself. The people who live therein are interdependent in all their industries. Every man is interested in the conservation and management of the water supply, for all the waters are needed within the district. The men who control the farming below must also control the upper regions where the waters are gathered from the heavens and stored in the reservoirs. Every farm and garden in the valley below is dependent upon each fountain above.

All of the lands that lie within the basin above the farming districts are the catchment areas for all the waters poured upon the fields below. The waters that control these works all constitute one system, are dependent one upon another, and are independent of all other systems. Not a spring or a creek can be touched without affecting the interests of every man who cultivates the soil in the region. All the waters are common property until they reach the main canal, where they are to be distributed among the people. How these waters are to be caught and the common source of wealth utilized by the individual settlers interested therein is a problem for the men of the district to solve, and for them alone.

But these same people are interested in the forests that crown the heights of the hydrographic basin. If they permit the forests to be destroyed, the source of their water supply is injured and the timber values are wiped out. If the forests are to be guarded, the people directly interested should perform the task. An army of aliens set to watch the forests would need another army of aliens to watch them, and a forestry organization under the hands of the general government would become a hotbed of corruption; for it would be impossible to fix responsibility and difficult to secure integrity of administration because ill-defined values in great quantities are involved.

Then the pasturage is to be protected. The men who protect these lands for the water they supply to agriculture can best protect the grasses for the summer pasturage of the cattle and horses and sheep that are to be fed on their farms during the months of winter. Again, the men who create waterpowers by constructing dams and digging canals should be permitted to utilize these powers for themselves, or to use the income from these powers which they themselves create for the purpose of constructing and maintaining the works necessary to their agriculture.

Thus it is that there is a body of interdependent and unified interests and values, all collected in one hydrographic basin and all segregated by well-defined boundary lines from the rest of the world. The people in such a district have common interests, common rights, and common duties, and must necessarily work together for common purposes. Let such a people organize, under national and state laws, a great irrigation district, including an entire hydrographic basin; and let them make their own laws for the division of the waters, for the protection and use of the forests, for the protection of the pasturage on the hills, and for the use of the powers. This, then, is the proposition I make: that the entire arid region be organized into natural hydrographic districts, each one to be a commonwealth within itself for the purpose of controlling and using the great values which have been pointed out. There are some great rivers where the larger trunks would have to be divided into two or more districts, but the majority would be of the character described. Each such community should possess its own irrigation works; it would have to erect diverting dams, dig canals, and construct reservoirs; and such works would have to be maintained from year to year. The plan is to establish local self-government by hydrographic basins.

Let us consider next the part which should be taken by the local governments, the state governments, and the general government in the establishment and maintenance of these institutions. Let there be established in each district a court to adjudicate questions of water rights, timber rights, pasturage rights, and power rights in compliance with the special laws of the community and the more general laws of the state and the nation. Let there be appeal from these lower courts to the higher courts. Let the people of the district provide their own officers for the management and control of the waters, for the protection and utilization of the forests, for the protection and management of the pasturage, and for the use of the powers; and with district courts, water masters, foresters, and herders, they would be equipped with the local officers necessary for the protection of their own property and the maintenance of individual rights.

The interests are theirs, the rights are theirs, the duties are theirs; let them control their own actions. To some extent this can be accomplished by cooperative labor; but ultimately and gradually great capital must be employed in each district. Let them obtain this capital by their own enterprise as a community. Constituting a body corporate, they can tax themselves and they can borrow moneys. They have a basis of land titles, water rights, pasturage rights, forest

rights, and power rights; all of these will furnish ample security for the necessary investments; and these district communities, having it in their power to obtain a vast increment by the development of the lands, and to distribute it among the people in severalty, will speedily understand how to attract capital by learning that honesty is the best policy.

Each state should provide courts for the adjudication of litigation between people of different districts and courts of appeal from the irrigation district courts. It should also establish a general inspection system and provide that the irrigation reservoirs shall not be constructed in such a manner as to menace the people below and place them in peril from floods. And, finally, it should provide general statutes regulating water rights.

But the general government must bear its part in the establishment of the institutions for the arid regions. It is now the owner of most of the lands, and it must provide for the distribution of these lands to the people in part, and in part it must retain possession of them and hold them in trust for the districts. It must also divide the waters of the great rivers among the states. All this can be accomplished in the following manner. Let the general government make a survey of the lands, segregating and designating the irrigable lands, the timber lands, the pasturage lands, and the mining lands; let the general government retain possession of all except the irrigable lands, but give these to the people in severalty as homesteads. Then let the general government declare and provide by statute that the people of each district may control and use the timber, the pasturage, and the water powers under specific laws enacted by themselves and by the states to which they belong. Then let the general government further declare and establish by statute how the waters are to be divided among the districts and used on the lands segregated as irrigable lands, and then provide that the waters of each district may be distributed among the people by the authorities of each district under state and national laws. By these means the water would be relegated to the several districts in proper manner, interstate problems would be solved, and the national courts could settle all interstate litigation.

But the mining industries of the country must be considered. Undeveloped mining lands should remain in the possession of the general government, and titles thereto should pass to individuals, under provisions of statutes already existing, only where such lands are obtained by actual occupation and development, and then in quantities sufficient for mining purposes only. Then mining regions must have mining towns. For these the town-site laws already enacted provide ample resource.

It is thus proposed to divide responsibility for these institutions between the general government, the state governments, and the local governments. Having done this, it is proposed to allow the people to regulate their own affairs in their own way — borrow money, levy taxes, issue bonds, as they themselves shall determine; construct reservoirs, dig canals, when and how they please; make their own laws and choose their own officers; protect their own forests, utilize their own pasturage, and do as they please with their own powers; and to say to them that "with wisdom you may prosper, but with folly you must fail."

It should be remembered that the far West is no longer an uninhabited region. Towns and cities are planted on the mountainsides, and stupendous mining enterprises are in operation. On the streams, sawmills have been erected, and the woodsman's ax echoes through every forest. In many a valley and by many a stream may be found a field, a vineyard, an orchard, and a garden; and the hills are covered with flocks and herds. In almost every hydrographic basin there is already found a population sufficient for the organization of the necessary irrigation districts. The people are intelligent, industrious, enterprising, and wide-awake to their interests. Their hearts beat high with hope, and their aspirations are for industrial empire. On this round globe and in all the centuries of human history there has never before been such a people. Their love of liberty is unbounded, their obedience to law unparalleled, and their reverence for justice profound; every man is a freeman king with power to rule himself, and they may be trusted with their own interests.

Many of the great industrial undertakings of mankind require organized labor, and this demand grows with the development of inventions and the use of machinery. The transfer of toil from the muscles of men to the sinews of nature has a double result — social solidarity is increased and mind is developed. In the past, civilization has combined the labor of men through the agency of despotism; and this was possible when the chief powers were muscular. But when the physical powers of nature are employed and human powers engaged in their control, men cannot be enslaved; they assert their liberty, and despotism falls. Under free governments the tendency is to transfer power from hereditary and chosen rulers to money kings, as the integration of society in industrial operations is accomplished through the agency of capital.

This organization of physical power with human industry for great ends by the employment of capital is accomplished by instituting corporations. Corporations furnish money and machinery and employ men organized under superintendents to accomplish the works necessary to our modern civilization. Gradually society is being organized into a congeries of such corporations to control the leading industries of the land.

Hitherto agriculture in this country has not come under the domination of these modern rulers. Throughout all the humid regions the farmer is an independent man, but in the arid regions corporations have sought to take control of agriculture. This is rendered possible by the physical conditions under which the industry is carried on. Sometimes the corporations have attempted to own the lands and the water, and to construct the great works and operate them as part and parcel of wholesale farming. In other cases the corporations have sought to construct the works and sell the water to individual farmers with small holdings. By neither of these methods has more than partial success been achieved. There is a sentiment in the land that the farmer must be free, that the laborer in the field should be the owner of the field. Hence, by unfriendly legislation and by judicial decision — which ultimately reflect the sentiment of the people — these farming corporations and water corporations of the West have often failed to secure brilliant financial results, and many have been almost destroyed.

Thus there is a war in the West between capital and labor — a bitter, relentless war, disastrous to both parties. The effort has been made to present a plan by which the agriculture of the arid lands may be held as a vast field of exploitation for individual farmers who cultivate the soil with their own hands; and at the same time and by the same institutions to open to capital a field for safe investment and remunerative return, and yet to secure to the toiling farmers the natural increment of profit which comes from the land with the progress of industrial civilization.

The great enterprises of mining, manufacturing, transporting, exchanging, and financiering in which the business kings of America are engaged challenge admiration, and I rejoice at their prosperity and am glad that blessings thus shower upon the people; but the brilliancy of great industrial operations does not daze my vision. I love the cradle more than the bank counter. The cottage home is more beautiful to me than the palace. I believe that the schoolhouse is primal, the university, secondary; and I believe that the justice's court in the hamlet is the only permanent foundation for the Supreme Court at the capital. Such are the interests which I advocate. Without occult powers of prophecy, the man of common sense sees a wonderful future for this land. Hard is the heart, dull is the mind, and weak is the will of the man who does not strive to secure wise institutions for the developing world of America.

The lofty peaks of the arid land are silvered with eternal rime; the slopes of the mountains and the great plateaus are covered with forest groves; the hills billow in beauty; the valleys are parks of delight; and the deep canyons thrill with the music of laughing waters. Over them all a clear sky is spread through which the light of heaven freely shines. Clouds rarely mask the skies but come at times like hosts of winged beauty floating past, as they change from gray to gold, to crimson, and to gorgeous purple. The soul must worship these glories, yet, with the old Scotch poet, I can exclaim:

> It's rare to see the morning bleeze,
> Like a bonfire frae the sea;
> It's fair to see the burnie kiss
> The lip o' the flow'ry lea;
> An' fine it is on green hillside,
> Where hums the bonnie bee,
> But rarer, fairer, finer far
> Is the ingleside for me.

Kodak snapshot taken at the White House egg roll, 1889

FRUITS OF INDUSTRY

The recovery from the depression of the 1870s brought unparalleled prosperity as the returns from the heavy investment in industrialization began to roll in. New inventions and techniques seemed endless and contributed greatly to the booming economy — the telephone, the electric light, and the camera were not only extremely useful additions to existing industry but began great industries of their own. Under the natural laissez faire capitalism of the day, the nearly unrestricted operation of capital tended strongly to concentrate wealth in relatively few hands — hands that were often unprepared for wealth and that became the unrefined, laughable nouveau riche of the Gilded Age.

Atrocious taste in architecture and decoration and nearly everything else became common among the upper strata as the newly arrived vied for attention in their new game of conspicuous — and generally outrageous — consumption. It was in this period that the exploitative nature of the absolutely free play of capital was first found wanting in justice.

(Above) Cyrus Field, supervisor of construction of the first transatlantic telegraph cable; (below) landing the French transoceanic telegraph cable on the beach at Duxbury, Mass., 1869

(Above) Machinery used in paying out the first Atlantic cable from the frigate "Niagara," 1857; (below) central operating department of the Western Union Telegraph Company's New York office, about 1880

Between 1840 and 1850, the United States Patent Office granted 6,480 patents; between 1890 and 1900 the number was over 221,000. This was the golden age of the independent inventor, the backyard engineers who produced and improved the technology of the country. The telegraph was made international with Cyrus Field's transatlantic cable in 1866. Bell's telephone of 1876 spread rapidly across the nation. Edison's electric light in 1879, his phonograph, motion picture, and countless other innovations made him the inventor's inventor. George Eastman followed his first dry plate of 1880 with the first transparent film in 1884 and built a fortune on a virtual monopoly of photographic equipment. The automobile is of disputed origin, but its essential development occupied the 1890s.

(Above) Bell demonstrating the telephone's ability to transmit sound by electricity from Salem to Boston, Mass., to a group of scientists, 1887; (center) photo of Alexander Graham Bell taken in 1876, the year he invented the first telephone; (left) a telephone "central"

(Above) Interior of the first electrical exposition in America, sponsored by the Franklin Institute in 1884; (right) photograph of Thomas Alva Edison in his laboratory; (below left) electric reflector constructed in San Jose, Calif.; (below right) sketch of an electrical generator built by Edison

George Eastman with a Kodak #2 camera on the S.S."Gallia," 1890; photo by Fred Church

Photograph of George Eastman made using experimental film in place of plates, 1884

Four photographers on an outing at Enfield Glen in New York, 1885

Rear view of "The Breakers" in Nantucket, R.I., one of the most luxurious homes of the 1890s

(Above left) Open carriage popular in 1881; (above right) "To the stars through difficulties"; satirical drawing by W. H. Hyde for "Life," 1883; (below) room in the Stanford House, California

(Above) Interior of the Anchor Liner, "City of St. Louis," 1888; (center) "The George Washington Jones family returns from Paris"; drawing by A. B. Frost for "Harper's Weekly"

Dining room of the S.S. "City of Rome"; photographed in the 1880s

Bar Harbor, Maine, in 1883; photo from a dry plate negative by S. Fisher Corlies

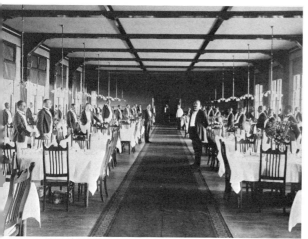

Sports and recreation on a large scale came with affluence and an increase in leisure time. Baseball, dating from the 1850s, became a popular spectator sport; the National League, devoted to making professional baseball respectable, was founded in 1876. Football became the great intercollegiate sport. Coastal or mountain resorts with large hotels and recreational facilities were built for those not quite rich enough for a private "cottage" in Newport.

(Left) Dining room of the Hotel Champlain in Glens Falls, N.Y., 1890; photo by S. R. Stoddard

View of the Grand Hotel, a resort in the Catskill Mountains; photographed by J. J. Kirkbride

Saranac Lake House, a resort in the Adirondacks; photo by S. R. Stoddard, 1890

(Above left) Cookout at Williams Stream; (above right) boating on Moosehead Lake; photos by Kirkbride, 1885; (below) couples at Lake View House in Bolton on Lake George, 1889

(Above) Hunting party in 1882; (right) knock-
down blow during the Sullivan-Kilrain fight,
1889; photo by George Barker; (below) John L.
Sullivan, lithograph, 1887; (bottom right) group
of hunters camping at Norcross Brook, Maine,
1886; photo by Kirkbride

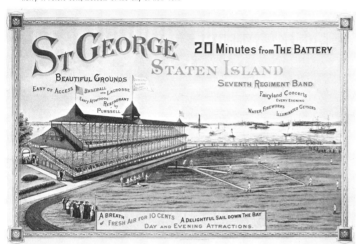

(Above) "Five Seconds for Refreshments"; a Currier and Ives view of the service on a "Limited Express" in 1884; (left) advertisement for a Staten Island amusement park, 1886

(Left) Early baseball player in uniform; (below) contestants lined up at the start of a bicycle race, 1890. Cycling's popularity increased greatly when a bicycle with identical wheels was introduced in the 1890s

(Above) Baxter Street Court, New York City; photographed by Jacob Riis; (below) baby in a slum tenement; Riis photo, 1888-89

Unauthorized lodging in a Bayard Street tenement, New York, 1890; Riis photo

All the praise of capitalism and all the Horatio Alger stories together couldn't hide the fact that industry rested on the exploited laborer. Large-scale immigration, in particular, aided in keeping wages down and in stifling the growth of protective labor unions. Insecurity and defensive clannishness led directly to the growth of the city slums. Disorganized and disoriented, the immigrant laborer was easily held down to subsistence wages; isolated in the slum, his existence was habitually ignored.

(Right) Children playing on a garbage pile in Mulberry Road, New York; (below) interior of a New York dive; photo by Riis

Women's quarters at the West 47th Street police station in New York City, 1891; photographed by Riis

(Right) McAuley's Mission in the Bowery in New York City, ministering to the material and spiritual wants of the "Bowery Bums"; (bottom) Sister Irene with her flock at the Foundling Asylum in New York, 1888

67.

"The Farmer Is the Man"

In the midst of a society generally unsympathetic to their needs, farmers in the 1880s and 1890s found themselves embroiled in disputes with the railroads over rates and service, with grain and livestock dealers over the low prices received for produce, with merchants over the high cost of necessary supplies, and with each other over solutions to their problems. Eventually the overwhelming nature of those problems led to the great farmers' revolt of the 1890s and the rise of the Populist Party. "The Farmer Is the Man" became a rallying song of that revolt, reminding one and all that the farmer population was indispensable.

THE FARMER IS THE MAN

When the farmer comes to town
With his wagon broken down,
Oh, the farmer is the man who feeds
    them all.
If you'll only look and see
I think you will agree
That the farmer is the man who feeds
    them all.

The farmer is the man,
The farmer is the man,
Lives on credit till the fall;
Then they take him by the hand
And they lead him from the land —
The middleman's the one who gets it all.

When the butcher hangs around,
While the butcher cuts a pound,
Oh, the farmer is the man who feeds
    them all;
And the preacher and the cook
Go a-strolling by the brook,
Oh, the farmer is the man who feeds
    them all.

Oh, the farmer is the man,
The farmer is the man,
Lives on credit till the fall;
And his pants are wearing thin,
His condition, it's a sin,
He's forgot that he's the man who feeds
    them all.

When the banker says he's broke,
And the merchant's up in smoke,
They forget that it's the farmer feeds
    them all.
It would put them to the test
If the farmer took a rest,
Then they'd know that it's the farmer feeds
    them all.

The farmer is the man,
The farmer is the man,
Lives on credit till the fall;
With the int'rest rate so high
It's a wonder he don't die,
For the mortgage man's the one who gets
    it all.

68.

Washington Gladden: The Embattled Farmers

Mechanization of farming methods in the last third of the nineteenth century dramatically increased crop yields, but such production required expensive machinery, and the price received for produce kept dropping as the cost of farmers' purchases rose. Thus the farmers added to their list of old enemies — drought and floods, crop disease and pestilence — new problems of production and price control. Reform movements arose; one of the most prominent was the Populist Party, organized in 1891 as political successor to the Granger movement of the 1870s and the Farmers' Alliances of the 1880s. A Congregational minister, Washington Gladden, discussed those groups and the farmers' welfare in the following article of November 1890.

Source: *Forum*, November 1890.

THE FARMERS OF THE UNITED STATES are up in arms. They are the bone and sinew of the nation; they produce the largest share of its wealth; but they are getting, they say, the smallest share for themselves. The American farmer is steadily losing ground. His burdens are heavier every year and his gains are more meager; he is beginning to fear that he may be sinking into a servile condition. He has waited long for the redress of his grievances; he purposes to wait no longer. Whatever he can do by social combinations or by united political action to remove the disabilities under which he is suffering, he intends to do at once and with all his might.

There is no doubt at all that the farmers of this country are tremendously in earnest just now, and they have reason to be. Beyond question they are suffering sorely. The business of farming has become, for some reasons, extremely unprofitable. With the hardest work and with the sharpest economy, the average farmer is unable to make both ends meet; every year closes with debt, and the mortgage grows till it devours the land. The Labor Bureau of Connecticut has shown, by an investigation of 693 representative farms, that the average annual reward of the farm proprietor of that state for his expenditure of muscle and brain is $181.31, while the average annual wages of the ordinary hired man is $386.36. Even if the price of board must come out of the hired man's stipend, it still leaves him a long way ahead of his employer. In Massachusetts the case is a little better; the average farmer makes $326.49, while his hired man gets $345.

In a fertile district in the state of New York, a few weeks ago, an absentee landlord advertised for a man to manage his farm. The remuneration offered was not princely. The farm manager was to have his rent, his garden, pasturage for one cow, and a salary of $250 a year for his services and those of his wife. There was a rush of applicants for the place. Who were they? Many of them were capable and intelligent farmers who had lost their own farms in the hopeless struggle with adverse conditions and who were now well content to exchange their labor and their experience against a yearly reward of $250. The instance is typical. Throughout the Eastern states, with the home market which protection is supposed to have built up at their very doors, the farmers are falling behind.

Says Professor C. S. Walker:

A careful study of New England farming in the light of all points of view, carried on for the past ten years by means of statistical investigation, personal observation during carriage drives from Canada to Long Island Sound and intimate association with all classes of farmers assures one that the man who cultivates an average farm and depends upon its profits alone for the support of himself and family, if he pay his taxes and debts, cannot compete with his brothers or attain to their standard of living, who, with equal powers, employ them in other walks of life.

The same story is heard in the Central states. In Ohio, farms are offered for beggarly rents, and even on these favorable terms farming does not pay. Tenant farmers are throwing up their leases and moving into the cities, well content to receive as common laborers $1.25 a day, and to pay such rents and to run such risks of enforced idleness as the change involves. At the South the case is even worse. Under a heavy burden of debt the farmer struggles on from year to year, the phenomenal growth of the manufacturing interests in his section seeming to bring him but slight relief. And even in the West we find the same state of things. A large share of recent corn crops has been consumed for fuel; and over vast areas, Mr. C. Wood Davis tells us, "wheat sells at from 40 to 50 cents, oats at from 9 to 12 cents, and corn at from 10 to 13 cents a bushel, and fat cattle at from 1½ to 3 cents a pound." Under such conditions the life of the Western farmer cannot be prosperous. From Kansas and Nebraska and Dakota the cry is no less loud and bitter than from Connecticut and New York and North Carolina.

The causes of this lamentable state of things are many. Who shall estimate them? Mr. Davis gives this list: "Monometallism, deficient or defective circulating medium, protective tariffs, trusts, dressed-beef combinations, speculation in farm products, overgreedy middlemen, and exorbitant transportation rates." These are a few of the disadvantages of which the farmers now complain. Doubtless several of these causes are working against them. Whether, in their diagnosis of the disease, they always put their finger on the right spot may be doubted. People cannot always be trusted to tell what ails them. The patient knows that he is suffering, but he does not always discover the nature of his malady. Mr. Davis gives strong reasons for the belief that the root of the difficulty is overproduction; that there are too many farms, and that more corn, wheat, oats, beef, and pork have been raised than the country can use.

There is the foreign market, to be sure; but in that the farmer of the West must compete with the low-priced labor of India and of Russia. If his product is very greatly in excess of the wants of his own country, he will be forced to sell at very low prices. The fact seems to be that the less of these staples the farmers raise, the more they get for them. The short crops of this year may, very likely, bring them more money than the enormous crops of 1889. The comforting assurance of Mr. Davis that the acreage of farms cannot increase so rapidly in the future, and that the population will soon grow up to the food supply and will redress the balance in the farmer's favor, is one that may well be cherished.

But granting that this is the chief cause of the depression of agriculture, other causes of considerable importance should not be overlooked. The enormous tribute which the farmers of the West are paying to the moneylenders of the East is one source of their poverty. Scarcely a week passes that does not bring to me circulars from banking firms and investment agencies all over the

West begging for money to be loaned on farms at 8 or 9 percent net. The cost of negotiation and collection, which the farmer must pay, considerably increases these rates. The descriptive lists of farms which accompany these circulars show that the mortgages are not all given for purchase money.

I find in one of the agricultural papers the following figures indicating the increase in farm mortgages in Dane County, Wisconsin, during the year 1889. The number of mortgages filed was 467; the average amount of each, $1,252; the total amount, $584,727.80; the number of mortgages given for purchase money, only 9. But whether the mortgages represent debts incurred in the purchase of the land or those incurred for other purposes, it is evident that when they bear such rates of interest they constitute a burden under which no kind of business can be profitably carried on. The farmer who voluntarily pays such tribute as this to the moneylenders is quite too sanguine. Other businessmen will not handicap themselves in this way. But probably the larger proportion of these mortgages are extorted from the farmers by hard necessity. Not their hope of increased prosperity makes them incur these debts so often as the pressure of obligations which have been incurred and which must be met.

The steady and increasing migration from the farms to the cities is in part an effect of the depression of agriculture and in part a cause of that depression. If a large part of the most vigorous and enterprising members of the farmers' families leave the farms, it is evident that the farms will not be carried on with the enterprise and vigor which are necessary to the success of any business. Is it not true that less ingenuity and less invention have been developed in this business than in most other occupations? There is plenty of money in the country; might not the farmer, by the application of brains to his calling, get a little more of it? Of the great staples, the country can consume only

a limited quantity; but the country is ready to take all sorts of fancy food products — delicacies, luxuries, gastronomic novelties — and to pay good prices for them. . . .

Along some such lines as these the farmers will most surely draw to themselves a larger share of the surplus wealth of the country. That surplus is abundant, but all sorts of people with keen wits and strenuous energies are competing for it. Those who have it are ready to exchange it for gratifications of various sorts. The problem is to please them. Within the bounds of innocent and wholesome delectation, there is a wide range for the exercise of invention by the food producers of the nation. If they confine themselves to the business of raising corn and wheat and pork and beef, their market will be narrow. They can widen it almost indefinitely if they will devote to their business the same kind of ingenuity that manufacturers of all classes are constantly exercising in their efforts to attract to their own coffers the abundance of the land.

Such methods, however, are not those by which the farmers now hope to better their condition. They are organized mainly for other purposes. They believe that the miseries under which they are suffering are largely due to political causes and can be cured by legislation. They have found out that of the 20 million breadwinners they comprise 8 or 9 million, and they think that if they stand together they can get such legislation as they desire. The old Grange kept pretty well out of politics; the new Farmers' Alliance and its affiliated organizations intend to work the political placer for all that it can be made to yield. Hear them:

> The prime object of this association is to better the condition of the farmers of America, mentally, morally, and financially; to suppress personal, sectional, and national prejudices, all unhealthful rivalry and selfish ambition; to return to the principles on which the government was founded by adhering to the doctrine of

equal rights and equal chances to all and special privileges to none; to educate and commingle with those of the same calling to the end that country life may become less lonely and more social; to assist the weak with the strength of the strong, thereby rendering the whole body more able to resist; and to bequeath to posterity conditions that will enable them, as honest, intelligent, industrious producers, to cope successfully with the exploiting class of middlemen.

For the promotion of these objects three methods are named — "social, business, and political." The social feature is easily understood; the business methods involve various forms of cooperative buying and selling; and the political methods are defined only by saying that they are strictly nonpartisan, and that they must ever remain so. This seems to mean that the farmers decline to attach themselves to either political party, but that they will try to make both parties serve them.

All questions in political economy will be thoroughly discussed, and when the order can agree on a reform as necessary, they will demand it of the government and of every political party; and if the demand goes unheeded, they will find ways to enforce it. The most essential reforms must come from legislation,. but that does not necessarily compel the necessity of choosing candidates and of filling the offices. Such a course may become necessary, but it will not be resorted to under any other circumstances.

This is pretty explicit, and it is beginning to exert a solemnizing influence in the councils of the politicians. The Farmers' Alliance is not unconscious of its power. The movement is running like wildfire over all our hills and prairies, and it is claimed that forty members of the next Congress will be pledged to support its demands. What will be its demands?

1. Cheap money, to begin with. The farmers are generally debtors; they want cheap money wherewith to pay their debts.

Of course the cheaper the money, the less groceries and clothing and machinery can be bought with it; but the farmers think of their debts more than of their necessities, and the longing of their souls is for cheap money. They are therefore in favor of the free coinage of silver; but they insist that even this would be an ineffectual remedy, since only about $45 million a year, at the utmost, could thus be added to the currency of the country, and this amount, they think, would be ridiculously inadequate.

2. The subtreasury plan, so called, by which warehouses are to be built in every county where they are demanded, wherein the farmers may deposit cotton, wheat, corn, oats, or tobacco, receiving in return a Treasury note for 80 percent of the value of the product so deposited, at the current market price. These Treasury notes are to be legal tender for debts and receivable for customs. A warehouse receipt, also, is to be given to the depositor, designating the amount and grade of the product deposited and the amount of money advanced upon it, and indicating that interest upon the money thus advanced is to be paid by the depositor at the rate of 1 percent per annum. These receipts are to be negotiable by endorsement.

The holder of a receipt, by presenting it at the warehouse, returning the money advanced, and paying interest and charges, may obtain the product deposited; and the money thus returned is to be destroyed by the secretary of the Treasury. This scheme for getting an ample supply of money directly into the hands of the farmers, at a nominal rate of interest, appears to have the endorsement of the Alliance. The journals of the organization are discussing it freely and are adducing various historical instances to show that the principle involved in it has been tested and found valid; but the verdict of most economists and financiers is strongly against the measure.

3. The ownership by the government of

all the railroads, telegraphs, and telephones is another plank in the platform of the Alliance. Here is a measure which is certainly debatable; let us hope that the farmers will secure for it a thorough discussion.

4. The prohibition of gambling in stocks and that of alien ownership of land are propositions which will also receive considerable support outside the Alliance.

5. The abolition of national banks and the substitution of legal-tender Treasury notes for national-bank notes, will not, probably, command universal assent.

6. The adoption of a constitutional amendment requiring the choice of United States senators by the people seems to be a popular measure among the members of the Alliance. To this they will be able to rally a strong support.

With these and other demands inscribed upon their banners, the farmers are in the field. They will make lively work for the politicians in the West and in the South during the pending campaign. No small amount of dodging and ducking on the part of these worthies may be looked for. Several of the strong agricultural districts will return to Congress men pledged to advocate the measures of the Alliance. Already they have picked out the place which they wish their contingent to occupy on either side of the center aisle in the House of Representatives, where they expect to hold the balance of power and to take the place of the Center in the French Assembly.

How long they will hold together is difficult to predict. It may be that the discussions in which they must take part will show them that some of the measures of direct relief on which they are chiefly depending are impracticable; and it is conceivable that this discovery will tend to demoralize them. That they can become a permanent political force is not likely, for parties which represent only classes cannot live in a republic. But several results, by no means undesirable, may be looked for as the outcome of this farmers' uprising.

1. They will secure a thorough discussion of some important economical questions. They will force the people to consider carefully the problem of the state ownership of the great public highways. It is not absurd to demand that the state should own and control, even if it does not operate, the railroads; and that it should own and operate the telegraphs. The conclusion to which such an experienced railway manager as the president of the Chicago and Alton Railway has already come is one to which many other people are likely to come in the course of this debate. If the farmers can stick together and can stick to their text long enough to get this business thoroughly ventilated, they will do a good service.

2. They are loosening the bands of partisanship and are opening the way for a rational cooperation of citizens for all desirable purposes. "The most hopeful feature of this whole uprising," writes a shrewd observer, "is the smashing of the old party shackles that goes along with it." That it may lead to a reconstruction of parties is not improbable.

3. They are helping to make an end of the sectionalism which has been a large part of the capital of a certain class of politicians. Their manifestoes point to this as the one striking result of their work thus far. "Scarcely a vestige," they say, "of the old sectional prejudice of a few years ago is now visible within our ranks." The South and the West are coming into fraternal relations. Mr. Lodge has already discovered that the West is not supporting his Force Bill. "The demagogue politician who now attempts to array sectional prejudice in order that he may keep farmers equally divided on important questions," is admonished that he is about to confront "a superior intelligence that will soon convince him that his occupation is gone."

The farmers' movement is not, probably, the deluge; but it will prove to be something of a shower — in some quarters, a cyclone — and it will clear the atmosphere.

1891

69.

William A. Peffer: The Rise of Farmer Organizations

Organized efforts to improve the lot of farmers flourished in the Mississippi Valley during the 1860s and 1870s, but groups such as the Grange and Farmers' Alliances fell victim to their own accomplishments and declined as conditions improved. The settlement of the Middle Border states, however, brought new problems with taxes, land prices, and exorbitant fees charged by middlemen for procuring loans and selling crops; in Kansas alone, 11,000 mortgages were foreclosed between 1889 and 1893. These frustrations soon gave rise to new calls to organize for mutual assistance. The following account by Senator William A. Peffer of Kansas appeared in 1891.

Source: *The Farmer's Side,* New York, 1891, pp. 148-161.

THE GRANGE

The Patrons of Husbandry, commonly known as the Grange, began their organization about twenty-four years ago in the city of Washington. The Grange grew rapidly about nine years, then quite as rapidly for a time receded from view; but in the meantime it had accomplished a noble work, much wider in its scope and grander in its proportions than people generally have ever been willing to admit. From the Grange came what is known as the "Granger" railroad legislation, the establishment in our laws of the principle that transportation belongs to the people, that it is a matter for the people themselves to manage in their own way, and that the Congress of the United States, under authority vested in that body by the Constitution, is authorized and empowered to regulate commerce among the several states as well as with foreign nations. That principle, once advocated and urged by the Grange, finally became permanently ingrafted in our laws.

Then came the Interstate Commerce Commission; that was another outcome of the Grange movement. Opposition to conspiracies of wealth against the rights of farmers — of labor in general, but of farmers in particular — was among the first and best works of the Grange. The footprints of that first and best organization of farmers ever effected up to that time — are seen plainly in much of the legislation of this country during the last twenty years. Grange influence revived in recent years, and is again growing. It is now one of the most earnest, active, and efficient agencies in the agitation of measures in the interest of agriculture. It lacks but one element of strength, and that will come in due time —

namely, the uniting with other bodies of organized farmers in one great political movement to enforce themselves what they have long been trying ineffectually to enforce through their separate party organizations — the dethronement of the money power.

Aside from the political influence of the Grange, it has been a powerful factor in the social development of farmers. Go into a Grange neighborhood any place where the members have maintained their organization during all the troublesome, trying years that followed their first organization, and you find a neighborhood of thrifty, intelligent, well-advanced farmers, their wives and daughters enjoying all of the comforts and conveniences which have been brought into use through the multiplication of inventions for the saving of labor and the production of wealth. Their meetings have been schools in which the best sort of education comes; and now the Grange as a body is one of the most fruitful social institutions in the country. As fast as its members see their way clear to a union with their fellow farmers generally for political purposes, they will have accomplished a grand mission, and they will finally come to that.

THE FARMERS' ALLIANCE

THE FARMERS' ALLIANCE is a body in many respects quite similar to that of the Grange. In both bodies women are equal with men in all of the privileges of the association. They are fast training women in channels of political thought. Many of the best essays and addresses read and delivered in their meetings are prepared by women, and it is beginning to dawn upon the minds of men long encrusted by custom and usage that the women who were chosen in early life as partners and companions — women who first became wives and then mothers and guardians of the best families upon earth, women who have nurtured children and trained them up to useful manhood and

womanhood, looked after their interests when the days of childhood were numbered, and never forgot them "even until death" — these same women, who of all persons have a fonder attachment, a warmer affection, and a deeper love for their children, in the midst of mature life as well as in childhood, are quite as capable of looking after the interests of men and women when they are grown as while they are prattling infants about the playgrounds of the old homestead.

These social bodies of farmers, where men and women are at last made equal in public affairs, even though to a limited degree, are fast, very fast, educating the rural mind to the belief that women are as necessary in public affairs as they are in private affairs. Their influence is constantly growing stronger as the years come and go, and, strange as it may seem to some persons, they are losing none of their womanhood, but are constantly adding graces to lives already beautiful and useful.

The Farmers' Alliance was organized primarily — just as the Grange had been — for social purposes; but yet immediately in connection with its inception was an effort to defeat the absorption of state lands of Texas by speculators. One great object of the association was to save the public lands for the people. It has always been a leading idea among farmers that the public lands ought to be saved for homes for the people. They foresaw what the end would be in case speculators, whether individual or corporate, were allowed to monopolize the land. In time, settlers would be required to pay exorbitant prices for what they are entitled to at cost. The Homestead Law embodies the true theory of government disposition of the public lands. They belong to the people, in the right of the people.

Whatever they cost in money, if anything, was paid by the money of the people through a system of taxation, which was supposed to be just, bearing equally, as far as possible, upon all classes and conditions of the people. It was, as the farmers believed, a stupendous wrong inflicted upon the people of the country generally when lands were given away in immense quantities to corporations. All of that was so much money thrown into the coffers of rich men and wealthy corporations, and taken away from the poor. And now that our public lands are so much curtailed as that there is hardly room enough in fertile areas left to locate a single homestead, a great question comes up of taxing the people to inaugurate a general system of irrigation to reclaim arid lands, and to supply the demand for homes by increasing the productiveness of the public lands which are yet left for the use of the people; and this idea of "land for the landless and homes for the homeless" — once so noisy a party war cry — will again be made part of the platform of a national party which will rise into view within the next year or two.

The Farmers' Alliance is in two bodies now. One was begun in Texas about the year 1875; it is known as the "Southern Alliance." It has absorbed the "Farmers' Union" of Louisiana, the "Agricultural Wheel" of Arkansas, and some other local organizations of farmers in different parts of the Southern states, with Kansas, Missouri, and Kentucky. It has a very large membership in Iowa, Ohio, and New York, and is spreading into all the other states. Thirty-five states now have organized alliances. While the body is strongest in Southern states, if its growth in the Northern and Western states continues to be as rapid the next year or two as it has been in the last two years, it will soon have a large membership in every state in the Union.

Its principles, socially and politically, are almost exactly the same as those taught by the Grange; namely, good fellowship and obliteration of sectional prejudices, a nationalizing of the people, a spirit of friendly feeling among the masses, abandonment of old issues, with the discussion of new problems of the present and the future, all based upon the fundamental idea which angels sang to shepherds when the Babe of Bethlehem was born — "Peace on earth, goodwill toward men." The "Southern Alliance," as it is commonly called by outsiders, is the "Farmers' Alliance and Industrial Union"; it is built upon principles broad and deep as humanity.

NATIONAL FARMERS' ALLIANCE

THEN THERE IS ANOTHER BODY, known as the National Farmers' Alliance. It originated about the year 1877 in Illinois. It differs from the Southern Alliance practically only in this, that the Southern Alliance has a "secret work"; it transacts all of its business with closed doors; the members know one another outside as well as inside by means of "grips" and "passwords," just as Masons and Odd Fellows do. This is true likewise of the Grange. The National Farmers' Alliance, commonly known as the Northern Alliance, transacts its business openly, the same as any ordinary public assembly. The objects and aims of both bodies are practically the same — opposition to all private monopolies and the better dispensing of justice among the people. One of the tenets of all these organizations is "equal rights to all, special privileges to none."

FARMERS' MUTUAL BENEFIT ASSOCIATION

THERE IS ANOTHER rapidly growing body of farmers. It took form in the southern part of Illinois about four years ago. It is known as the Farmers' Mutual Benefit Association, with objects the same as the other bodies before named. It, too, has a secret work, but it differs from the Alliance and the Grange in that it does not admit women to membership; that will doubtless come later, for it seems that no considerable body of men in the discussion of matters which are largely social to begin with can very well get along without the help of women, who have been so serviceable to them in their home life.

There is a considerable number of other local bodies of farmers, as the Farmers' League, the Farmers' Union, the Farmers' Protective Association, Anti-Monopoly League, etc. These are mostly in Ohio and states to the eastward. The difference between the Alliance and other bodies of farmers named is about this: The Alliance is more aggressive along political lines than any of the others, and the Alliance has taken more advanced grounds in favor of independent political action. Alliance men and women in very large numbers have come to the conclusion that they have exhausted all of their means for effecting, through the agency of the old political parties, the needed changes in our legislation and customs.

THE KANSAS MOVEMENT

THE LESSON LEARNED by the movement of Alliance men in Kansas in 1890 has been one of very great profit to the brethren in other parts of the country. It was discovered in Kansas that the party machinery was so completely in the hands of a few men as to make the party's policy simply what was dictated by the little circle of leaders, and it was evident that they were completely wedded to the power which has been absorbing the substance of the toilers. Kansas is an agricultural state, one of the most beautiful regions under heaven; with soil rich as any that the sun shines upon; with a climate salubrious; with an atmosphere balmy; with bright skies bending over a landscape delightful in its magnificent proportions; peopled by a rugged yeomanry — industrious, enterprising, sober, intelligent — a body of men and women unsurpassed anywhere in disposition to move forward and upward; men and women who in less than the period of a genera-

tion have built an empire, have produced 50 million bushels of wheat and 250 million bushels of corn in one year, have opened 200,000 farms, have built 9,000 miles of railroad and 8,000 schoolhouses.

And the farmers of that state came to the conclusion that they were entitled to at least a fair share in the benefits of legislation. They found, however, that it was practically impossible to control the course of political parties, for the reason that the machinery was in the hands of men living in the towns, and connected in one way or another, to a greater or less degree, with railroads and with corporations engaged in the business of lending money for people in the East, deeply immersed in real-estate transactions, and in one way or another interested in matters that were directly and continually and powerfully in opposition to the interests of the farmers.

Looking the situation over carefully and deliberately, they came to the conclusion that the best way out of their troubles was through an independent political movement; so the Alliance submitted that proposition to their fellow workers inside and outside of the Alliance, to members of the Grange and of the Farmers' Mutual Benefit Association, to the Knights of Labor, to the Federation of Labor, and to other workers in different departments. The result was the formation of a political party known locally as the People's Party; and when the votes were counted after election day it appeared that the party was made up about as follows: Republicans, 45,000 voters; Democrats, 35,000 voters; Union-Labor men, 33,000 voters; Prohibitionists, 2,000 voters — making a total vote of 115,000.

The political complexion of the state was changed in six months to the extent of 100,000 votes. At the election in 1888 the Republican majority over all opposition was about 42,000 votes; at the election in 1890 that party fell short of a majority sixty-odd thousand votes. The People's Party in Kansas elected one state officer; attorney general; 5 out of the 7 members of Congress; 95 of the 125 members of the Lower House of the legislature (the senators elected in 1888 holding over to 1892); and secured the election of a United States senator on the 28th day of January following. . . .

THE CINCINNATI CONFERENCE

THE RESULT IN KANSAS encouraged farmers in other states, and soon a movement was set on foot looking to the organization of an independent political movement covering the whole country. The first step in that direction was the National Union Conference, held at Cincinnati, May 19, 1891, composed of nearly 1,500 delegates representing thirty-two states and two territories — Alabama, Arkansas, California, Colorado, Connecticut, Florida, Illinois, Indiana, Iowa, Kansas, Kentucky, Louisiana, Maine, Massachusetts, Michigan, Minnesota, Missouri, Nebraska, New York, North Carolina, North Dakota, Ohio, Pennsylvania, Rhode Island, South Carolina, South Dakota, Tennessee, Texas, Washington, West Virginia, Wisconsin, Wyoming, Oklahoma, and District of Columbia.

A National Central Committee was appointed and arrangements made for a general union of all the industrial forces of the country in a convention in 1892 for the purpose of completing organization and putting a national ticket in the field.

70.

GROVER CLEVELAND: Against a Free Silver Policy

Congress attempted to end bimetallism in 1853 by abolishing silver coins, but neglected to mention silver dollars in its bill, so the country remained on a two-metal standard until a revision of the law in 1873. Advocates of a "free silver" policy — coinage of silver to gold at a ratio of 16 to 1 — opposed both measures and defended their position with four arguments: that the single-standard law of 1873 had been railroaded through Congress; that silver "hard money" was the coin of the common people; that the Panic of 1873 was brought on by the "demonetization" of silver; and that the institution of a free silver policy would increase the supply of money and end the depression. These theories had special appeal for the poorer classes and the economically unsophisticated, and the Democratic Party gave enough support to pass a free silver bill in the Senate in January 1891. Most observers expected Democrat Grover Cleveland to join the silver cause, but he stated his refusal to do so in the following letter of February 10, 1891, addressed to E. Ellery Anderson of the Reform Club of New York.

Source: *The Writings and Speeches of Grover Cleveland*, George F. Parker, ed., New York, 1892, p. 374.

Dear Sir:

I have this afternoon received your note inviting me to attend tomorrow evening the meeting called for the purpose of voicing the opposition of the businessmen of our city to "the free coinage of silver in the United States."

I shall not be able to attend and address the meeting as you request, but I am glad that the business interests of New York are at last to be heard on this subject. It surely cannot be necessary for me to make a formal expression of my agreement with those who believe that the greatest peril would be invited by the adoption of the scheme, embraced in the measure now pending in Congress, for the unlimited coinage of silver at our mints.

If we have developed an unexpected ca-pacity for the assimilation of a largely increased volume of this currency, and even if we have demonstrated the usefulness of such an increase, these conditions fall far short of insuring us against disaster if, in the present situation, we enter upon the dangerous and reckless experiment of free, unlimited, and independent silver coinage.

71.

WILLIAM DEAN HOWELLS: Democratic Art

William Dean Howells' polite realism was unusually candid for a novelist of his time, representing as it did a striking dissent from the school of romantic fiction. His prestigious career as novelist, critic, and editor in chief of the Atlantic Monthly *was enhanced by encouraging young artists and producing lengthy commentaries on the American novel. The best examples of the latter were collected in* Criticism and Fiction, *including the following selection, which reflects Howells' confidence in the future of American literature.*

Source: *Criticism and Fiction*, New York, 1891, pp. 137-140.

FOR OUR NOVELISTS to try to write Americanly, from any motive, would be a dismal error; but being born Americans, I would have them use "Americanisms" whenever these serve their turn; and when their characters speak, I should like to hear them speak true American, with all the varying Tennesseean, Philadelphian, Bostonian, and New York accents. If we bother ourselves to write what the critics imagine to be "English," we shall be priggish and artificial, and still more so if we make our Americans talk "English." There is also this serious disadvantage about "English," that if we wrote the best "English" in the world, probably the English themselves would not know it, or, if they did, certainly would not own it.

It has always been supposed by grammarians and purists that a language can be kept as they find it; but languages, while they live, are perpetually changing. God apparently meant them for the common people — whom Lincoln believed God liked because He had made so many of them; and the common people will use them freely as they use other gifts of God. On their lips our continental English will differ more and more from the insular English, and I believe that this is not deplorable, but desirable.

In fine, I would have our American novelists be as American as they unconsciously can. Matthew Arnold complained that he found no "distinction" in our life, and I would gladly persuade all artists intending greatness in any kind among us that the recognition of the fact pointed out by Mr. Arnold ought to be a source of inspiration to them, and not discouragement.

We have been now some hundred years building up a state on the affirmation of the essential equality of men in their rights and duties, and whether we have been right or been wrong, the gods have taken us at our word and have responded to us with a civilization in which there is no "distinction" perceptible to the eye that loves and values it. Such beauty and such grandeur as we have is common beauty, common grandeur, or the beauty and grandeur in which the quality of solidarity so prevails that neither distinguishes itself to the disadvantage of anything else. It seems to me that these conditions invite the artist to the study and the appreciation of the common, and to the portrayal in every art of those finer and higher aspects which unite rather than sever humanity, if he would thrive in our new order of things.

The talent that is robust enough to front the everyday world and catch the charm of its workworn, careworn, brave, kindly face, need not fear the encounter, though it

Library of Congress

William Dean Howells

seems terrible to the sort nurtured in the superstition of the romantic, the bizarre, the heroic, the distinguished, as the things alone worthy of painting or carving or writing. The arts must become democratic, and then we shall have the expression of America in art; and the reproach which Mr. Arnold was half right in making us shall have no justice in it any longer; we shall be "distinguished."

———————◆———————

If you say a true and important thing once, in the most striking way, people read it, and say to themselves, "That is very likely so," and forget it. If you keep on saying it, over and over again, even with less felicity of expression, you'll hammer it into their heads so firmly that they'll say, "It is so"; and they'll remember forever it is so.

CHARLES A. DANA

1892

72.

RICHARD OLNEY: On the Interstate Commerce Commission

Railroad owners disliked the Interstate Commerce Commission, regarding it as a potential threat to their property and to their prerogatives. The owners hoped that an administration in Washington friendly to business would eliminate the commission or at least nullify its efforts at railroad regulation. Grover Cleveland's victory in November 1892 led the owners to believe that the commission could now be gotten rid of, and Charles Perkins, president of the Burlington Railroad, asked his corporation counsel, Richard Olney, to see what he could do. Olney, who was shortly to be named attorney general in the new administration, wrote the following reply to Perkins on December 28, 1892. The letter expresses with extraordinary frankness the attitude of many business leaders in the 1890s toward any government interference with free enterprise.

Source: Olney Papers, Library of Congress (353-354).

My Dear Mr. Perkins:

I have yours of the 22nd instant enclosing the newspaper paragraphs about the Interstate Commerce Commission.

My impression would be that, looking at the matter from a railroad point of view exclusively, it would not be a wise thing to undertake to abolish the Commission. The attempt would not be likely to succeed — if it did not succeed and were made on the ground of the inefficiency and uselessness of the Commission, the result would very probably be giving it the powers it now lacks.

The Commission, as its functions have now been limited by the courts, is, or can be made, of great use to the railroads. It satisfies the popular clamor for a government supervision of railroads, at the same time that that supervision is almost entirely nominal. Further, the older such a commission gets to be, the more inclined it will be found to be to take the business and railroad view of things. It thus becomes a sort of barrier between the railroad corporations and the people and a sort of protection against hasty and crude legislation hostile to railroad interests.

The Commission costs something, of course. But so long as its powers are advisory merely, for the reasons just stated, it strikes me it is well worth the money. The part of wisdom is not to destroy the Commission but to utilize it.

I make the foregoing suggestions for your consideration and perhaps without having given sufficient thought to the matter. But they certainly point out one view of it which is well worth reflecting upon.

73.

JAMES BAIRD WEAVER: Wealth, Poverty, and Monopoly

James Baird Weaver of Iowa, Greenback Party candidate for President in 1880, helped form the Populist Party, which nominated him for the presidency in 1892. In the course of the campaign, Weaver published a tract, A Call to Action, *that stated his social and economic philosophy and included a strong denunciation of monopolies and of the creditor class as controllers of the nation's finances. Weaver ran a poor third in the election, but the growing strength of the Populists was indicated by the fact that he received over a million popular votes and twenty-two electoral votes. Portions of two chapters — "Dives and Lazarus" and "Danger and Duty" — of the tract are reprinted here.*

Source: *A Call to Action*, Des Moines, 1892, pp. 362-378, 441-445.

CONTRASTS

IF THE MASTER BUILDERS of our civilization one hundred years ago had been told that at the end of a single century American society would present such melancholy contrasts of wealth and poverty, of individual happiness and widespread infelicity as are to be found today throughout the republic, the person making the unwelcome prediction would have been looked upon as a misanthropist and his loyalty to democratic institutions would have been seriously called in question. Our federal machine, with its delicate interlace work of national, state, and municipal supervision, each intended to secure perfect individual equality, was expected to captivate the world by its operation and insure domestic contentment and personal security to a degree never before realized by mankind.

But there is a vast difference between the generation which made the heroic struggle for self-government in colonial days and the third generation which is now engaged in a mad rush for wealth. The first took its stand upon the inalienable rights of man and made a fight which shook the world. But the leading spirits of the latter are entrenched behind class laws and revel in special privileges. It will require another revolution to overthrow them. That revolution is upon us even now.

Two representative characters — Dives

and Lazarus — always make their appearance side by side in disturbing contrast just before the tragic stage of revolution is reached. They were present at the overthrow of ancient civilizations; the hungry multitude stood outside the gates when Belshazzar's impious feast was spread; they were both at the cave of Adullam when the scepter was about to depart from the tyrant Saul to the hands of the youthful David; they stood side by side when Alaric thundered at the gates of Rome; they confronted one another in the fiery tempest of the French Revolution, and they are sullenly face to face in our own country today. We will devote a few pages to the delineation of these forces as they appear in our civilization at the present period.

SOCIAL EXTRAVAGANCE

In the year 1884, as we are told by Ward McAllister in his book entitled *Society as I Found It,* a wealthy gentleman gave a banquet at Delmonico's at which the moderate number of seventy-two guests, ladies and gentlemen, were entertained. The gentleman giving the banquet had unexpectedly received from the Treasury of the United States a rebate of $10,000 for duties which had been exacted from him through some alleged misconception of the law. He resolved to spend the entire sum in giving a single dinner which should excel any private entertainment ever given in New York. He consulted Charles Delmonico, who engaged to carry out his wishes. The table was constructed with a miniature lake in the center thirty feet in length, enclosed by a network of golden wire which reached to the ceiling, forming a great cage. Four immense swans were secured from one of the parks and placed in this lake. High banks of flowers of every hue surrounded the lake and covered the entire table, leaving barely enough room for the plates and wine glasses. The room was festooned with flowers in every direction. Miniature mountains and valleys with carpets of flowers made vocal with sparkling rivulets met the eye on every hand.

Golden cages filled with sweet singing birds hung from the ceiling and added their enchantment to the gorgeous spectacle. Soft, sweet music swept in from adjoining rooms, and all that art, wealth, and imagination could do was done to make the scene one of unexampled beauty. And then the feast! All the dishes which ingenuity could invent or the history of past extravagance suggest were spread before the guests. The oldest and costliest wines known to the trade flowed like the water that leaped down the cascades in the banqueting hall. The guests were wild with exultation and delight and tarried far into the night. But in a few brief hours the romanticism had passed, the carousal was broken, and the revelers were face to face with the responsibilities which none of us can evade. The fool and his money had parted.

SILVER, GOLD, AND DIAMOND DINNERS

Some time after the "swan dinner" was given, three of the swell leaders of New York society planned to give each a handsome entertainment which should set all New York talking. Each instructed the head of the celebrated cafe to spare no expense and to make his dinner the best of the three. So magnificent were these entertainments that Lorenzo Delmonico designated them as the silver, gold, and diamond dinners. Each had peculiarities which distinguished it from the others. At one of them each lady found snugly concealed in her napkin a gold bracelet with the monogram of Jerome Park in the center in chased gold.

DIAMOND VESTURE

At one of the stated receptions given at the Executive Mansion during the first session of the Forty-ninth Congress, there appeared among the throng of exquisitely attired guests the wife of a noted New York millionaire. She was accompanied by two trusted attendants, handsomely dressed in citizens' garb, who remained constantly with her, but slightly to the rear so as to keep perfect watch over her drapery. As she swept through the hall with her train and into the great East Room, her raiment glistened until it almost seemed that a celestial constellation had descended from the skies to attend this reception. Her vesture was studded with a vast number of diamonds and other precious stones, valued above $1 million! The climax of absurdity was reached and the utmost height of folly scaled. Does the reader for a moment think that the circle of wealthy snobs to which this lady belongs has any regard to republican institutions? On the contrary, every sensible person knows that they are the bitter foes to every democratic impulse, and their extreme wealth enables them to make their hostility aggressive and effective.

PRINCE ASTOR'S WEDDING

IN THE YEAR 1890, young Astor, a scion of the celebrated family which has so long been prominent in New York financial circles, was married. Both the groom and the bride represented millions of wealth and the wedding was an imposing and gorgeous affair. Twenty-five thousand dollars were expended on the day's ceremony. The presents were valued at $2 million, and the couple and their attendants and a number of friends immediately departed on an expensive yachting cruise which was to cost them $10,000 a month to maintain. In speaking of these nuptials, the *Christian Union* said: "When we read this we are reminded of Thackeray's description of the extravagance of the Prince Regent during the Napoleonic Wars:

> If he had been a manufacturing town, or a populous rural district, or an army of 5,000 men, he would not have cost

more. The nation gave him more money, and more and more. The sum is past counting.

Looked at soberly, the sums lavished upon our American commoners are as disgraceful to our institutions as were the squanderings of the Prince Regent to those of England. If the scandal is less it is because the disastrous concentration of hereditary wealth has as yet awakened less serious thought among us than the disastrous concentration of hereditary power had awakened in England. In the case of the Astors, quite as much as of the Prince Regent, the enormous sums expended are the gift of the nation, obtained without compensating service on the part of the recipients. The burden upon the labor of the country is as great. . . .

AT THE RICH MAN'S GATE

ABOUT THE TIME these princely entertainments were given, and in the same year with some of them, one of the metropolitan journals caused a careful canvass to be made of the unemployed of that city. The number was found to be *150,000 persons who were daily unsuccessfully seeking work within the city limits of New York.* Another 150,000 earn less than 60 cents per day. Thousands of these are poor girls who work from eleven to sixteen hours per day. In the year 1890, over 23,000 families, numbering about 100,000 people, were forcibly evicted in New York City owing to their inability to pay rent; and one-tenth of all who died in that city during the year were buried in the Potters Field. . . .

AT CHICAGO

IN THE LATTER PART of the year 1891, a committee from a Chicago Trade and Labor Assembly, at the request of a body of striking cloakmakers, made an investigation of the condition of that class of workers in the city. They were accompanied by an officer of the City Health Department, the city attorney, and artists and reporters of the local press. They found that 13,000 persons were engaged in the manufacture of clothing in Chicago, over one-half of whom were females. In order to reduce the cost of production, the firms engaged in the manufacture of clothing have adopted the European sweating system, which is, in brief, as follows: The material for garments is cut to size and shape and delivered by the large firms to individual contractors known as sweaters, who relieve the firm of all other care or expense, taking the goods to what are known as sweating dens, usually located in the poorest neighborhoods of the great city. These sweaters are employed by the most opulent firms.

The committee visited a large number of these dens, nearly all of which were dwelling houses which served as living and sleeping rooms for the sweater's family and the employees. In one room ten feet by forty, they found thirty-nine young girls, twelve children between ten and twelve years of age, eleven men, and the sweater and his wife. The room and all the surroundings were filthy in the extreme. The rates of wages were of course very low, and yet the fear of discharge rendered it almost impossible to obtain satisfactory information.

The committee found 2,100 children at work in these dismal places who were underage and employed in violation of existing laws against child labor. Sanitary laws were also overridden in all of these miserable abodes. . . . And yet in the face of these glaring conditions, which are common in all of our populous cities, empty-headed political charlatans still vex the public with their puerile rant about protection for American labor. . . .

AND HAS IT COME TO US SO SOON?

ABOUT THE CLOSE of the recent Jackson Park World's Fair strike, we clipped from the columns of one of the Chicago dailies the following local editorial. Speaking of the poor strikers the paper said:

The outlook discouraged them. None had any great supply of money and few had places to sleep. The outlook was altogether discouraging and was made even more so by the action of the police, who broke up the picket lines as fast as they were formed, and even refused to allow them to congregate in any numbers.

About 9 o'clock in the morning a hundred or so weary strikers were stretched in the sun on the prairie near Parkside endeavoring to get some sleep, when word was passed for a meeting at 67th Street and Stony Island Avenue. By 9:30 o'clock, 200 men had congregated there and Dr. Willoughby, the owner of the lot, objected. He notified the police that he did not want any trespassing on his premises, and Lieutenant Rehm and a squad of ten officers were dispatched to the scene. He ordered the strikers to disperse, but they failed to obey with alacrity, and the police had to drive them off. There was some slight resistance, and several heads suffered in consequence from contact with policemen's batons.

We trust the brief pages of this chapter may suffice to call the attention of the reader to the ghastly condition of American society and to remind him of the imperative call which is made upon him as an individual to do all in his power to arrest the alarming tendencies of our times. In the opinion of the writer, unless the people of America shall immediately take political matters into their own hands, the contrasts suggested in this chapter portend a tragic future. The millionaire and the pauper cannot, in this country, long dwell together in peace, and it is idle to attempt to patch up a truce between them. Enlightened self-respect and a quickened sense of justice are impelling the multitude to demand an interpretation of the anomalous spectacle constantly presented before their eyes, of a world filled with plenty and yet multitudes of people suffering for all that goes to make life desirable. They are calling to know why idleness should dwell in luxury and those who toil in want; and they are inquiring why one-half of God's children should be deprived of homes upon a planet which is large enough for all.

The world will find a solution for these insufferable afflictions in the glorious era but just ahead. Even now the twilight discloses the outlines of a generous inheritance for all and we hear the chirping of sweet birds making ready to welcome with melody and gladness the advent of the full-orbed day.

DANGER AND DUTY

THE AMERICAN PEOPLE have entered upon the mightiest civic struggle known to their history. Many of the giant wrongs which they are seeking to overthrow are as old as the race of man and are rock-rooted in the ignorant prejudices and controlling customs of every nation in Christendom. We must expect to be confronted by a vast and splendidly equipped army of extortionists, usurers, and oppressors marshaled from every nation under heaven. Every instrumentality known to man — the state with its civic authority, learning with its lighted torch, armies with their commissions to take life, instruments of commerce essential to commercial intercourse, and the very soil upon which we live, move, and have our being — all these things and more are being perverted and used to enslave and impoverish the people. The Golden Rule is rejected by the heads of all the great departments of trade, and the law of Cain, which repudiates the obligations that we are mutually under to one another, is fostered and made the rule of action throughout the world. Corporate feudality has taken the place of chattel slavery and vaunts its power in every state. . . .

But thanks to the all-conquering strength of Christian enlightenment, we are at the dawn of the golden age of popular power.

We have unshaken faith in the integrity and final triumph of the people. But their march to power will not be unobstructed. The universal uprising of the industrial forces will result in unifying the monopolistic and plutocratic elements also, and through the business and social influences of these potential and awakened forces, thousands of well-meaning professional and businessmen of all classes will be induced, for a time, to make common cause against us. This makes it necessary for the friends of reform to put forth herculean efforts to disabuse the minds of well-meaning people concerning the underlying objects of the movement, and this calls for systematic, energetic, and constant educational work, covering the whole range of the reforms proposed. It is also the surest method of overcoming the obstacle of indifference among the people.

We must also be prepared to see the two well-organized and equipped political parties march to the assistance of each other at critical points along the line. The leaders will spare no effort to accomplish this end. Two influences, now at work are ample to at least partially precipitate this result — the use of money and the community of danger inspired by the appearance of the new political force. The great mass of voters should be faithfully warned of this danger before designing leaders have made the attempt to mislead them. In this manner the evil consequences of their efforts can be largely averted.

THE GREAT DANGER

IF THE ECONOMIC REVOLUTION now in progress in the United States is not speedily successful, the industrial people will have no one to blame but themselves. Through suffering and research they have learned the causes of their distress. They have organized, decided upon remedies, and made known their demands. They have the numbers to make their wishes effective. The

Constitution and laws of the country place the whole matter within their hands. The great initial battles have been fought in the courts and this constitutes their Gibraltar and impregnable vantage ground. Nothing is now needed but a proper use of the ballot.

If the friends of reform will make one united and fearless effort, the victory will be won. Fidelity to truth, to home, to family, and to the brotherhood of purpose is all that is required. Capital possesses one thing which labor does not — ready cash. They will not hesitate to make the best possible use of it. But labor possesses that which capital does not — numbers. They should be made effective. Will they longer refuse to make use of the peaceful weapon which their fathers placed in their hands? If we will not with courage and conscience choose the methods of peace, the sword is inevitable. Persistent oppression on the one hand and neglect to make proper use of the ballot on the other, in the very nature of things, call for the application of force as the only solution. Avenging armies always follow close upon the heels of legalized injustice. If we would escape the sword, we must at once conquer through the power of truth and through knowledge incarnated and set in motion.

Let us all remember that the various organizations now so powerful cannot always be maintained. They will decay with time and fall to pieces from lack of purpose or the discouragements of defeat. Our enemies well understand this and are urging procras-

tination and pleading for time. As well might the general of an army send a bearer of dispatches, under a flag of truce, to ask the commander of the opposing forces when he would like to have the engagement brought on. If the general consulted were weak in numbers, he would decide to postpone the battle until such time as the forces of his adversary could be wasted by death, disease, and desertion.

STRIKE NOW!

WE HAVE CHALLENGED the adversary to battle and our bugles have sounded the march. If we now seek to evade or shrink from the conflict, it will amount to a confession of cowardice and a renunciation of the faith. Let us make the year 1892 memorable for all time to come as the period when the great battle for industrial emancipation was fought and won in the United States. It is glorious to live in this age and to be permitted to take part in this heroic combat is the greatest honor that can be conferred upon mortals. It is an opportunity for every man, however humble, to strike a blow that will permanently benefit his race and make the world better for his having lived. Throughout all history we have had ample evidence that the New World is the theater upon which the great struggle for the rights of man is to be made, and the righteous movement now in progress should again forcibly remind us of our enviable mission, under Providence, among the nations of the earth.

I fought once too often. But I'm glad that it was an American who beat me and that the championship stays in this country.
JOHN L. SULLIVAN, spoken from the ring after the loss of his title to "Gentleman Jim" Corbett, Sept. 7, 1892

74.

Illinois Sweatshops

The impact of industrial growth on American life during the Gilded Age was nowhere so apparent as in the large cities, and particularly in the sections inhabited by low-income, working-class people. Many of those people, unskilled in any craft, were desperately poor and easy prey for mercenary manufacturers and "middlemen." One of the institutions peculiar to the era, born of the poverty of the workers, the avarice of manufacturers, and the insatiable demands of machinery, was the sweatshop. The following extract from an 1893 report by the Illinois Bureau of Labor Statistics is a singularly vivid account of life in the sweatshops.

Source: *Seventh Biennial Report of the Bureau of Labor Statistics of Illinois,* Springfield, 1893, pp. 357-402: "The Sweating System."

ANY INQUIRY into the occupations of working women in Chicago, or in any other of the larger cities, must lead the inquirer, sooner or later, to the so-called sweating system, under which the manufacture of ready-made clothing is chiefly conducted. The peculiarities of this phase of industrial life are, however, so marked, and have recently attracted so much attention, that it has been deemed proper to extend the observations of the bureau in this matter beyond the women employed under this system and to gather whatever facts or figures were available concerning all the shops of this kind, and all the people, both men and women, employed in them in Chicago. This has involved the collection of some memoranda as to the distinctive features of the system as well as the statistics of its present development in this state.

The "sweating system" is one of respectable antiquity and is a surviving remnant of the industrial system which preceded the factory system, when industry was chiefly conducted on the piece-price plan in small shops or the homes of the workers. Machinery developed the modern factory and concentrated labor, but in the tailoring trades, the practice of sending out garments, ready-cut, to be made by journeymen at their homes and at a price-per-garment, has survived and is still maintained in custom work, in which the journeyman is still a skilled tailor who makes the whole garment. The modern demand for ready-made clothing in great quantities and of the cheaper grades has, however, led to much subdivision of the labor on garments and, with it, to the substitution of the contractor, or sweater, with groups of employees in separate processes for the individual tailor skilled in all of them.

The odious but expressive name "sweating" has been attached to the business because of its evil nature and consequences. In its worst form, and there are doubtless degrees in its development, it is simply extortion practised upon people whose environment prevents their escape from it; in other words, it is a deliberate preying upon the necessities of the poor. In its economical aspect it is the culmination and final fruit of the competitive system in industry.

In practice, sweating consists of the farming out by competing manufacturers to competing contractors the material for garments, which, in turn, is distributed among competing men and women to be made up. The middleman, or contractor, is the sweater (though he also may be himself subjected to pressure from above) and his employees are the sweated or oppressed. He contracts to make up certain garments, at a given price per piece, and then hires other people to do the work at a less price. His profit lies in the difference between the two prices. In the process he will furnish shop room and machines to some, and allow others, usually the finishers, to take the work to their living and lodging rooms in tenements.

The sweater may be compelled to underbid his fellow contractor in order to get work, but he can count with a degree of certainty on the eagerness of the people who work for him to also underbid each other, so as to leave his margin of profit but little impaired. The system thrives upon the increasing demand for cheap, ready-made clothing, cheap cloaks, and cheap suits for children, which demand springs in turn from the rivalry of competing dealers and producers. Thus each class preys upon the other, and all of them upon the last and weakest.

Such is the logic and the operation of the process called sweating; it is practised somewhat in other industries, but finds its fullest scope in the garment trade, because the articles can readily, and with comparative safety, be distributed to the shops and abodes of the workers. But the system is not new, except in new countries and new cities, and it is now hardly new in Chicago. . . .

In this country the whole ready-made clothing trade rests upon the sweating system in some of its various forms. From Boston, for many years, garments have been sent throughout New England to be made by the wives and daughters of the country people, but the more recent migration of Poles and Italians to that city has introduced a new form of cheap labor, and much clothing of the poorer grades goes to their shops and is finished in their homes. Recent legislation and tenement inspection has, however, done much to improve sanitary conditions among them and remove much of the danger from infectious diseases.

From Philadelphia, garments are sent into New Jersey and Delaware, as well as throughout the farming districts of Pennsylvania, to be stitched by women. Vast quantities of clothing, such as cotton and woolen shirts and women's underwear, are farmed out under contract to charitable and other institutions, while clothing for the Army and Navy and for the postal service is largely made under the sweating system, both in Philadelphia and Baltimore.

The great center of the clothing trade is, however, in New York City. There, whole streets are reported as having shops or home finishers in every house. It is particularly difficult to ascertain the number of persons thus employed in that city because it is augmented by every shipload of emigrants from Russia, Bohemia, Scandinavia, and Italy, and again reduced by deportations to the West. Sweaters' shops are now scattered even among those villages of Long Island and New Jersey which are easily accessible by ferryboat from New York. No successful check upon the system has yet been accomplished by legislation in that state. A measure recently passed embraces somewhat trenchant provisions, but its results remain as yet to be seen. The reports of the factory inspector reveal a state of things not surpassed by the English reports.

In Chicago, where it dates back scarcely a generation, the sweating system seems to be a direct outgrowth of the factory system; that is, the sweatshops have gradually superseded the manufacturers' shops. It increases, with the demand for cheap clothing, the influx of cheap labor and the consequent subdivision of the processes of manufacture. In the clothing trades in Chicago, three different sorts of shops have been developed, known among the employees as the "inside shops," or those conducted on the factory system by the manufacturers themselves; the "outside shops," or those conducted by the contractors; and the "home shops," or family groups.

In the inside shops the manufacturer deals with his employees through foremen and forewomen instead of contractors. These shops are in large buildings, steam is provided for motive power, the sanitary ordinances are, in a measure, observed, and the establishments, being large and permanent, are known to the municipal authorities and are subject to inspection. Even these shops, in which there is, strictly, no subletting, are pervaded and dominated by the influence of the sweating system. There is but little uniformity of hours, wages, rules, length of season, or proportion of men to women and children. The competition of the outside contractors renders the position of employees constantly more precarious, and the inside shops which thrive are those which approximate most closely to the organization of the sweaters' shops, substituting many subdivisions of labor for the skilled workman.

Formerly, these shops employed cutters, buttonholers and tailors or cloakmakers who did the whole work, taking the garment from the cutter and completing it, doing both machine and handwork. To increase their speed, these skilled hands now have "hand girls" who do the simple sewing, put on buttons, draw basting threads, etc. Formerly, the skilled tailors or cloakmakers constituted a large majority of the employees, but with the growth of the sweating system the cutters alone increase in number and their speed is multiplied by the use of steam machinery. All goods not needed to fill urgent orders are now given direct from the cutters to the sweaters' shops. Some manufacturers have modified their own shops to mere cutters' shops and send all their garments to the contractors; others have found it unprofitable to manufacture for themselves and have resorted to the sweaters entirely. Thus the sweating system strengthens itself and eliminates the clothing factory proper. Very few of these remain, and those which were found are not enumerated as sweating shops.

Substantially all manufacturers employ a number of sweaters who conduct small shops on their own account. These underbid each other to obtain work. They do not make common cause against the manufacturers, either by combining among themselves or by uniting with their employees. On the contrary, they exploit their employees to the utmost to compensate themselves for the exactions of the manufacturers and the competition among themselves.

The economic position of the sweater is anomalous. He has no commercial risks; he gives the manufacturer no considerable security for the goods entrusted to his care, and rarely has more than a wagonload of them in his possession; he pays one week's rent in advance for his shop (which may also be his dwelling) and buys his sewing machines on the installment plan, paying for them 75 cents a week each; or, he may still further reduce his investment by requiring his operators to furnish their own machines. Finally, he does not pay his employees until he receives his money for the finished lot.

In the small shops the characteristics of the sweating system are accentuated, and the most marked of these are disorder and instability. The latter results from the irresponsibility of the sweater and the facility with which he may either establish himself or change his location. This has very much embarrassed the process of enumeration. A man may work in his bedroom today, in another man's shop tomorrow, in his own shop in a month, and, before the end of the season, abandon that for a place in a factory. If an inspector orders sanitary changes to be made within a week the sweater may prefer to disappear before the close of the week and open another shop in another place. Such easy evasion of the authorities places the sweater almost beyond official control, and many of them overcrowd their shops, overwork their employees, hire small children, keep their shops unclean, and their sanitary arrangements foul and inadequate.

The provisional nature of the small shops also accounts largely for the absence of steam motive power for the sewing machines, though it is also explained by the statement that "leg power is cheaper than steam." The increasing employment of girls aged from twelve to sixteen years as machine operators is making this motive power still cheaper and at the same time more destructive of health and life.

The minute subdivision of the work in the sweaters' shops reduces the skill required to the lowest point. The whole number of employees, therefore, in all the outside shops includes, besides a few of the skilled, who would, under the old system, be employed in the inside shops, a majority of unskilled hands of both sexes, earning low wages, easily replaced, and wholly at the mercy of the sweater. Subdivision thus reaches its highest development; operators stitch, pressers press, basters baste, button girls sew on buttons, others draw basting threads, and finishers finish. Sometimes one girl, with a buttonhole machine, makes a specialty of the inside bands of knee pants, making buttonholes by the thousand gross. On the other hand, coats requiring buttonholes made in cloth, and with more skill, are sent by the contractor to a buttonhole shop, where two or three young men work machines, and where small boys or girls smear the holes in preparation for them.

In nearly every small shop there are some finishers, but in the case of knee pants, trousers, cloaks, and vests, the garments, after being cut, basted, stitched and buttonholed, are given out to have all that remains, the felling and handstitching, done at home before the garment is pressed and sent to the factory.

These tenement workers are known as "finishers." They are generally associated with some one of the shops, but will take work from any of them. Hundreds of women and girls compete among themselves, keeping their names on the contractors' lists, as the contractors compete among themselves for work from the manufacturers.

These women sew in the intervals of their housework and the garments lie about the living rooms, across greasy chairs and tables, upon filthy floors and vermin-infested beds. Soils upon garments are so common that the presser in the shops is also a cleaner, provided with benzene, alcohol, etc., for the removal of grease and stains. The competition of the home finishers constantly presses upon the wages of the shop hands. In some localities nearly every house contains some of these home finishers; our enumerators have located a total of 1,836 of them in the several districts; and they increase as the shops increase and as immigration increases.

Many of the Bohemians and Scandinavians have acquired their own homes and their own shops, which are usually built upon the same premises, and are properly lighted and ventilated. Very few of the Scandinavians have shops in their dwellings. They prefer to combine, in groups of from three to eight, and rent a large building, which is then partitioned off according to their needs. There are of course exceptions even among these people, and some of them set up shops in places wholly unfit for such uses; but the baser localities and shops are usually occupied by Russian Jews, Poles, and Italians. In the regions occupied by these, unclean and offensive conditions are not confined to the shops; they are equally features of the dwellings and persons and habits of the people. In these districts the worst of the shops are found located often in basements, and on alleys, or in wholly inadequate and unsanitary rooms in the dilapidated structures of these neighborhoods.

A few examples may be cited illustrating what some of these places are like. In one case, several men were found at work pressing knee pants in a low basement room, poorly lighted and ventilated by two small windows. There was no floor in this room, and the people were living on the bare earth, which was damp and littered with every sort of rubbish. In another case, seven persons were at work in a room 12 by 15 feet in dimensions and with but two windows. These people, with the sewing machines of operators and the tables used by the pressers, so filled this meager space that it was impossible to move about. Charcoal was used for heating the pressers' irons, and the air was offensive and prostrating to a degree. Separated from this shop room by a frail partition which did not reach to the ceiling was a bedroom about 7 by 15 feet in size, containing two beds, for the use of the family of the sweater. In another instance, in a small basement room which measured only 7 feet 10 inches by 6 feet 6 inches, and without door or window opening to the outer air, a man was at work pressing knee pants by the light of a very poor gasoline lamp and using a gasoline stove for heating his irons.

One of the principal aims of the sweater is the avoidance of rent; hence the only requirement for a sweaters' shop is that the structure must be strong enough to sustain the jar of the machines. This condition being filled, any tenement room is available, whether in loft, or basement, or stable. Fire escapes in such buildings are unknown; water for flushing closets is rarely found, and

the employees are equally at the mercy of fire and disease. Frequently the sweater's home is his shop, with a bed among the machines; or, the family sleeps on cots, which are removed during the day to make room for employees. Sometimes two or three employees are also boarders or lodgers, and the tenement dwelling is the shop; and cooking, sleeping, sewing, and the nursing of the sick are going on simultaneously.

A shop was found in which twelve persons lived in six rooms, of which two were used as a shop. Knee pants in all stages of completion filled the shop, the bedrooms, and kitchen. Nine men were employed at machines in a room 12 by 14, and there knee pants were being manufactured by the thousand gross. This is in the rear of a swarming tenement in a wretched street. Sometimes the landlord is the sweater, using his own basement or outhouse for a shop and renting his rooms to his employees for dwellings. Only one case was found in which a tailor, not a sweater, had acquired a house. He is a skilled tailor, still doing "the whole work" at home assisted by his wife. For nineteen years he has lived and worked in two wretched rear tenement rooms, paying by installments for his house, which is still encumbered. All others in the trade who owned houses were found to be either sweaters or women finishers, whose able-bodied husbands follow other occupations, such as teaming, peddling, ditching, street cleaning, etc.

But the worst conditions of all prevail among the families who finish garments at home. Here the greatest squalor and filth abounds and the garments are of necessity exposed to it and a part of it during the process of finishing. A single room frequently serves as kitchen, bedroom, living room, and working room. In the Italian quarter, four families were found occupying one four-room flat, using one cook stove, and all the women and children sewing in the bedrooms. For this flat they pay $10 a month, each family contributing $2.50 a month. Another group was found consisting of thirteen persons, of whom four were fathers of families and five were women and girls sewing on cloaks at home. These thirteen people pay $8 per month rent, each family contributing $2.

A house-to-house canvass in this district establishes the fact that it is only the poorest of the poor who finish garments at home, only the worst tenements being occupied by them, or the worst rooms of the better houses. A widow, who is a finisher, and two children were found in a rear shanty, in one room, below the street grade, and with only a narrow slit in the wall for a window. For this she pays $3 a month. Another was finishing knee pants in a room so dark it required some time to discern her. This room was lighted by a single window obscured by an adjacent four-story building. She also pays $3 a month rent. One of the vilest tenements in Chicago is owned by a woman whose husband is an Italian street sweeper. She lives on the premises and sews cloaks at 8 cents apiece, collects rent from thirty families under one roof, and tolerates a wretched sweatshop on her top floor. Eight of her tenants sew cloaks or knee pants in their living rooms. They pay $3 a month for the worst apartments and $10 for the best. . . .

Wages are paid by the piece and by the week; by the piece to skilled hands and to the home finishers; by the week uniformly to beginners and usually to shop hands; but all employees, whether paid by the piece or by the week, are subject to the "task" system; that is, they must accomplish a certain amount of work in a given time or forfeit their places. The best rates of wages are naturally found in the manufacturers' "inside" shops and in the better contractors shops, in both of which the employees are usually of the more skilled class who speak some English and have some trade organization. . . .

The people who are found in sweatshops are rarely illiterate in their own languages, with perhaps the exception of the Italian peasants. Every Hebrew is taught to read his own literature in childhood, though very few of them can write and still fewer can keep books of account. Almost none of them can read or write in the English language. The Scandinavians and Germans are all educated in excellent schools in their own countries, and read, write and keep accounts in their own language. Wholly illiterate are the Italians. Women finishers are found by scores who cannot count the pennies due them. None of them can read or write in any language.

The ability and desire to learn English varies with the nationality. Bohemians and many Poles send their children to parochial schools, but they learn neither to speak nor read English. Hebrew children go to the public schools, but, like many others, get only half-time instruction for want of school accommodations. Italian parents gladly avail themselves of this excuse and do not attempt to send their children to school at all. Italians do not learn English in the first generation, and in the second their children learn only what can be picked up in the streets. The boys are newsboys, ragpickers, and shoe blacks; the girls are ragpickers or button girls, and even begin to sew on cloaks at a very early age.

In the matter of religion, the sweaters' employees are either Catholics, Hebrews, or Lutherans, the latter both Scandinavian and German, and principally women. The Hebrews are usually strictly Orthodox and are held together in swarming colonies by the need of having their own butchers. Sweaters' victims all keep the church holidays, except during the busy season, when work is frequently continued through seven days in the week. At other times the Italians, particularly, are punctilious about the observance of their *festas*, and the Hebrews in the observance of their holy days. To many of them amusement is almost unknown. They sleep late on Sundays and holidays, and sit listlessly about the rest of the day, except when in church. Young men and girls are disposed to attend night schools, or other free or cheap classes, when out of work or the opportunity is afforded.

There are a number of organizations among the more intelligent and self-helpful in the garment trades, among which are unions of the cutters, the custom tailors, the ladies'-garment tailors, the cloakmakers, the women cloakmakers, cloak cutters, and cloak pressers. The differences of race, language, and religion prove an obstacle to the growth of organization.

The food and clothing of these communities is necessarily simple and meager. Among the Italians, bread and macaroni, with stale fruit and vegetables, constitute the diet, almost to the exclusion of meat. Among the Hebrews, the Mosaic prescription is some protection against the sale and use of improper meats, but in general the groceries and meat shops in these districts deal only in goods of defective and, consequently, cheap quality. There is nothing fresh and good offered for sale. Milk is conspicuously absent even from the diet of little children, and every winter there are long periods of rye bread and water in hundreds of families where the father is an operator without work in the shop or credit at the store.

In the matter of clothing, all sorts of makeshifts are resorted to, except the appropriation of the garments they make. Italian women wear the peasant costumes with which they come to this country as long as possible, which is usually very long, and

buy secondhand clothing for their children. Shoes are a very heavy item of expense among these people, especially if they have far to walk to their work, or run sewing machines after they get there. In many small shops, men dispense with all clothing except trousers and short-sleeved gauze undershirts, even in the presence of women, and work in their bare feet. Girls who are thrown upon their own resources were found still wearing the clothing brought from the Old Country, and with small prospect of buying any other as the earnings of the busy season are otherwise absorbed during the dull season.

Very few sweaters' victims accumulate any savings. When they do they become sweaters themselves. So far as observation extended, no disposition was discovered among them to return to the countries whence they came, even when they became able to do so. On the other hand, they manifest great desire to see their children attain some degree of prosperity greater than their own. Unfortunately, their eagerness in this particular frequently defeats itself, for they send their young children to the shop instead of to the school. Here their health is undermined; their presence in the shop reduces the wages of adults, and both parents and children become involved in a common struggle for existence. The result is that discontent is universal. The sweater complains of increased competition and reduced prices and profits; the victims complain of low wages, of poor pay, of the long dull season, of the heat and overcrowding in the busy season, and of the poverty and toil from which they cannot escape.

———————◆———————

I know of no profession, art, or trade that women are working in today, as taxing on mental resource as being a leader of society.
MRS. OLIVER HAZARD PERRY BELMONT, one of the queens of Newport

75.

Howell Davies: Convict Labor for Strikebreaking

The convict-lease system of labor came into existence following the Civil War in the poorer regions of the country, especially the South. Farmers, businessmen, and other property owners became amenable to any scheme that would promise to lower their taxes. The practice of having a state hire out convicts as a conscript labor force decreased taxes by making the penitentiaries nearly self-supporting. Factory and mine owners found the system ideal, for the labor cost them only a few cents per man per day, thus saving wages they would otherwise pay to free workers. As the convict labor system grew, penalties for offenses increased, thereby greatly adding to the number of men available for cheap labor. Convict laborers were also used as strikebreakers, as is shown by the following letter, written on January 11, 1892, by Howell Davies, a Welsh immigrant.

Source: *The Welsh in America*, Alan Conway, ed., Minneapolis, 1961, pp. 201-204.

Coal Creek and Briceville are two famous coal villages in the eastern part of the above state [Tennessee] about three miles from each other. There is a bed of excellent steam coal here, about four feet thick. At the end of the war in 1865, they started working coal here. Two Welsh brothers, Joseph and David Richards, opened the first coal mine and built log houses. Three of the coal mines were opened by other companies soon afterward. A large community of Welsh settled in the place and chapels were built to hold religious services in Welsh. There are very few of the old settlers left here now. Within a few years Messrs. Richards sold their interests to the Knoxville Iron Company.

The wages for cutting coal at that time were 4 cents a bushel. The wages for cutting coal now is 50 cents a ton. At the beginning of 1877 the owners demanded a lowering in wages. The colliers stood firm and the strike lasted for a long time. In the end the Knoxville Iron Company made an agreement with the governor of the state to get convicts to work in their mines, and this agreement was to last for six or seven years. The agreement was carried out and about 140 to 160 criminals sentenced to hard labor for their wicked deeds, such as thieves, housebreakers, murderers, etc. came to work in the valley. This strange migration forced the first settlers to sell their houses and land and to go elsewhere.

There was bitter strife in the district when the end of the first agreement came. The state government was approached and a number of major accusations about the barbaric cruelty used toward the prisoners were brought forward. A commission was appointed and a great number of witnesses were questioned, but the end was to legalize the institution of putting convicts to work in the coal mines. Consequently, the convicts were kept working there until last summer.

In 1888, the railroad was extended for three miles to the south of Coal Creek and three additional collieries were opened in the valley. A village called Briceville was built containing many hundreds of houses, and a great number of them together with the plots on which they stood belonged to the inhabitants. One of the chief shareholders and a governor of the colliery at the end of the railroad is a Welshman, raised in America. At the beginning of 1890 there was a series of complaints and misunderstandings between the employers and employees of this colliery, and sometime last summer a stockade was built and about 120 to 140 convicts were put to work in the mine with two or three armed guards of the state of Tennessee to watch over them. This caused bitterness and uneasiness among the inhabitants of Briceville and in the district for twenty miles around because of the loss in the trading sense and the notoriety in the social sense.

At last, at the end of July, the colliers and their supporters gathered together in a band of about 2,500. They surrounded the stockade of the Tennessee mines and sent a deputation to the officer of the guards ordering him to leave and to take the convicts in orderly fashion with him to the state prison. If he refused to obey, the men would attack and let every convict go where he wished and the stockade would be smashed to pieces. The officer of the guards saw that it would be foolish to stand out against such a daring band and left in peace for the railroad station in Coal Creek, keeping watch on the prisoners. The collier army followed them shouting victoriously.

After going three miles and coming by the Knoxville Iron Company coal mine, the miners split into two parts, one-half to follow the Briceville convicts to the station and the other to order the convicts at Coal Creek and their guard to follow their fellow convicts. Those in charge at this settlement also obeyed without opposition, and soon two groups of convicts and guards could be seen on the railroad coal cars and the engine taking them safely to the prison in Knoxville.

After that the colliers met in council and twenty were put to guard the Knoxville Iron Company property so that there should be no damage done to it. Everyone else went home without firing a shot. No drinking was permitted and no one lost a pennyworth of his possessions. The governor called out the state militia and headed for Coal Creek but fortunately he left the soldiers in Knoxville and boldly went among the citizens whom he considered mob leaders and rebels against the government. He came to Coal Creek and a crowd gathered to meet him. His reception was polite but not enthusiastic.

It was decided to have arbitration on the matter, and within a week it was decided that the arbitration should last sixty days, on condition that the governor should summon the legislature immediately to discuss the matter. In the meantime, the convicts should return to the coal mines. The legislature met and sat for four weeks in September. A deputation of colliers went to Nashville to plead the injustice of the convict law, but the members, two-thirds of whom were farmers, would not give them a hearing. The state senators encouraged the governor to use every means to compel obedience to the law although the press throughout all the states demanded that the complaints of the colliers should be heard.

When the deputation returned from Nashville, it was obvious that loyalty to the government had declined rapidly; but to stop the trouble, the colliers raised the legal issue that the present agreement on convict labor was contrary to the laws of the United States, and they won their case in the county court; but an appeal was lodged with a higher court in the state and judgment was given against the colliers. The Supreme Court's decision was published in the last week of October.

On Thursday night of the same week, armed bands gathered around the two prisons in Coal Creek and Briceville, firing sticks of dynamite, and holes were blown in the stout wooden walls. The guards were frightened and the convicts were allowed to go where they wanted, and Briceville Prison was burned to the ground. It is said that the reason why the Knoxville Iron Company's prison was saved and not burned was that the works manager's house was attached to the prison and the convicts that were released pleaded that the kind wife of the manager should not be frightened or put in danger. She is a gentle and kind Welsh woman.

The following Sunday they attacked in the same fashion the Olive Springs Prison, a coal village about fifteen miles south of Briceville. The convicts were set free and the prison burned. By the beginning of spring, Briceville was again free of convicts. After these disturbances, the governor offered large rewards for evidence against anyone who took part in the disturbances, but not one accuser has come forward yet. The coal mines were run excellently in the last two months of the year by employing free labor. Everyone was fully and regularly employed. The only uneasy people were the owners of the two collieries and the government officers.

The week before Christmas it was judged that harsher measures were being prepared by the government, and, on the morning of the last day of the year, twenty-two fully armed soldiers, one cannon, one Gatling gun, and tons of equipment, together with balls and powder, arrived on a special train at Coal Creek station. Nobody knew of their coming. They went quickly into camp on top of the hill near the convict prison of the Knoxville Iron Company coal mine. On Saturday morning, the second day of the year, a band of 125 convicts, together with 25 armed guards, were moved in railroad carriages near to the coal works.

The colliers and their supporters were angry and threatening. The following letter was distributed among the people of the neighborhood:

> The convicts shall not stay here again. We pray for blessing on our people, destruction on the convicts, destruction on the instigators, destruction on the militia. We must attack. It makes no difference what the consequences may be, death, destruction, anarchy! One hundred and sixty-seven people think they can frighten us! Will we put up with this? No! Never! The time has come to rush to the defense of our families and our homes!

76.

Charles K. Harris: "After the Ball"

The Gay Nineties saw Americans emerge from the strictness of Victorian mores and enjoy such new forms of entertainment as vaudeville and musical comedies. "After the Ball," the first really successful popular song of the era, helped establish Tin Pan Alley as an institution. After being introduced in the musical A Trip to Chinatown, *the song sold over a million copies of sheet music. Charles K. Harris, the composer of "After the Ball," wrote the words for the song after seeing two lovers quarrel at a dance in Chicago.*

AFTER THE BALL

A little maiden climbed an old man's knees —
Begged for a story: "Do uncle, please!
Why are you single, why live alone?
Have you no babies, have you no home?"
"I had a sweetheart, years, years ago,
Where she is now, pet, you will soon know;
List to the story, I'll tell it all:
I believed her faithless after the ball."

"Bright lights were flashing in the grand ballroom,
Softly the music playing sweet tunes.
There came my sweetheart, my love, my own,
'I wish some water; leave me alone.'
When I returned, dear, there stood a man
Kissing my sweetheart as lovers can.
Down fell the glass, pet, broken, that's all —
Just as my heart was after the ball."

"Long years have passed, child, I have never wed,
True to my lost love though she is dead.
She tried to tell me, tried to explain —
I would not listen, pleadings were vain.
One day a letter came from that man;
He was her brother, the letter ran.
That's why I'm lonely, no home at all —
I broke her heart, pet, after the ball."

Chorus:
After the ball is over, after the break of morn,
After the dancers' leaving, after the stars are gone,
Many a heart is aching, if you could read them all —
Many the hopes that have vanished after the ball.

77.

WALTER B. HILL: A Nation of Presidents

The magazine article that appears below, written in 1892 by a Georgia educator, lawyer, and occasional essayist, describes a special characteristic of Americans that it would probably be wrong to say no longer obtains. Although an unsympathetic observer might count the penchant for titles as evidence of the peculiar naiveté of a people without a titled aristocracy, the phenomenon is — or at least was — a relatively harmless accompaniment of the proclivity to form associations that is basic to American political life.

Source: *Century Magazine,* July 1892: "The Great American Safety-Valve."

THE REPUBLIC IS OPPORTUNITY. It is the birthright of every American boy to have the chance to be President and of every American girl to have the chance to be the President's wife. The atmosphere is stimulating to ambition. The desire inspired by the genius of American institutions is "to be equal to our superiors and superior to our equals." But in the midst of universal suggestions prompting the citizen to high ambitions, the ugly fact remains that the positions of political distinction are relatively very few compared to the vast multitude of possible aspirants. The practical politician confesses this in the wail, "There ain't offices enough to go round among the boys."

The intelligent foreigner is much perplexed by this problem. He can understand why the undistinguished classes on the continent submit contentedly to obscure conditions of life. It is the lot to which they are born. But here every schoolboy is taught that the highest stations are open to him; and in a thousand papers, books, lectures, speeches, and sermons he is told that perseverance alone will put the highest prizes within his grasp. What, then, can explain the contentedness of the millions who, as the French say, never "pierce" the level of mediocrity? What is the great American safety valve for these ambitions for precedence which our national life generates, fosters, and stimulates, without adequate provision for their gratification?

A friend from abroad, without the philosophic insight of Mr. Bryce or the illuminating wit of Max O'Rell, was once presenting to me what seemed to him the serious phases of this problem. I thought myself competent to make the explanation; but I did not know how to take hold of the subject. We were standing in the office of a large hotel at the time, when an incident gave me the clue.

There walked up to the register a sturdy American citizen, who seized the pen as if he were about to sign some momentous document. Bending over the open page of the book, he scrawled his name, his mouth moving and writhing with every twist of the pen. It occurred to me to look at the record of this new arrival, and this is what I saw: "Hon. Sock Bruitt, Chairman of the Committee on Pumps, Whiskyville, Texas."

Seizing this thread, I proceeded to unravel as best I could the tangled skein of American life as it is organized into social, business, religious, and other associations, all of them elaborately officered. Until I made the effort to explain the matter to "an alien to the commonwealth," I had never realized the full significance of the nonpolitical, officeholding class in our country as a factor in the national life.

Take a city directory and examine the list of organizations usually printed in such a publication. You will see ample provision for the local ambitions of all the inhabitants. Take one of the books issued by a "live" church; examine the list of societies, devotional, missionary, temperance, young people's, Sunday-school, charitable, etc.

The matter will be made clearer still if you study the subject in a small village where universal acquaintance is possible. I made a test case of one small town and found that every man, woman, and child (above ten years of age) in the place held an office, with the exception of a few scores of flabby, jellyfish characters, whose lack of ambition or enterprise removes them from consideration as elements of the problem.

But mere local precedence does not satisfy the more aspiring minds; hence, nearly all of the thousand and one societies have state and national organizations. Here is an enormous supply of official positions. Every trade, every profession, every benevolence,

every sport, every church furnishes distinctions commensurate in territorial magnitude with our great country.

And still the full measure of American officialism is not attained. There must be international organization. The earth must be girdled; and so, every society aims to plant a few lodges, or posts, or bands, or auxiliaries, or unions, or chapters (as they may be styled) beyond the seas. It little matters how few or scattered or insignificant these foreign plants may be. It is enough that "international organization has been accomplished," and with it a new set of officials having worldwide jurisdiction.

The grandeur of all these distinctions suffers no diminution in their names. The chief officer is ruler, chancellor, commander, seigneur, president, potentate, with many superlative and worshipful prefixes. And in the rituals of the numerous orders, the Almighty is habitually referred to as the Supreme Commander, Ruler, Potentate, or otherwise, as the case may be. By this means the American imagination accomplishes an interuniversal as well as an international organization.

A few years ago, in a little country village, there was instituted a chapter of a certain benevolent insurance order. The Chancellor was subsequently elected Grand Chancellor of the State. Afterward, at a national convention, he was made Supreme Grand Chancellor of the United States. The next year he was elected Most Supreme Grand Chancellor of the World; and it became his duty, the order paying his expenses, to make an international visitation to the three chapters in Australia, New Zealand, and England that composed the aforesaid "world."

When that triumphal tour was completed, his return home was heralded, and the chapter of his village arranged for a reception of the honorable dignitary. Never shall I forget the feeling of solemn awe that settled down upon the little community as the evening approached when the Most Supreme Grand Chancellor of the World was to arrive. This favored American was a "bigger man than old Grant."

Not only are there offices enough to "go round" but the really capable and pushing American is generally honored with a score.

I have heard a busy and overworked man decline to be at the head of an organization because he was at the head of twenty-five already.

Here then we have the great American safety valve — we are a nation of presidents.

78.

George Bird Grinnell: The Last of the Buffalo

"Indians and buffalo," John C. Frémont wrote in 1845, "make the poetry and life of the prairie." Forty-five years later little of either poetry or life had survived the advance of civilization. When Frémont wrote, Indians still freely roamed the West and the supply of buffalo seemed inexhaustible. The destruction of the herds coincided with the coming of the railroad to the Midwest. The Union Pacific, completed in 1869, brought not only settlers but also professional game hunters, who slaughtered the beasts at such a rate that George Grinnell could report in 1892 that the herds that once had appeared as massive as stands of timber had dwindled to a few hundred head. His article for Scribner's *magazine appears here in part.*

Source: *Scribner's,* September 1892.

ON THE FLOOR, on either side of my fireplace, lie two buffalo skulls. They are white and weathered, the horns cracked and bleached by the snows and frosts and the rains and heats of many winters and summers. Often, late at night, when the house is quiet, I sit before the fire and muse and dream of the old days; and as I gaze at these relics of the past, they take life before my eyes. The matted brown hair again clothes the dry bone, and in the empty orbits the wild eyes gleam. Above me curves the blue arch; away on every hand stretches the yellow prairie, and scattered near and far are the dark forms of buffalo. They dot the rolling hills, quietly feeding like tame cattle, or lie at ease on the slopes, chewing the cud and half asleep. The yellow calves are close by their mothers; on little eminences the great bulls paw the dust, and mutter and moan, while those whose horns have grown one, two, and three winters are mingled with their elders.

Not less peaceful is the scene near some river bank when the herds come down to water. From the high prairie on every side they stream into the valley, stringing along in single file, each band following the deep trail worn in the parched soil by the tireless feet of generations of their kind. At a quick walk they swing along, their heads held low. The long beards of the bulls sweep the ground; the shuffling tread of many hoofs marks their passing, and above each long line rises a cloud of dust that sometimes obscures the westering sun.

Life, activity, excitement mark another memory as vivid as these. From behind a near hill, mounted men ride out and charge down toward the herd. For an instant the buffalo pause to stare and then crowd together in a close throng, jostling and pushing each other, a confused mass of horns, hair, and hoofs. Heads down and tails in air, they rush away from their pursuers, and as they race along, herd joins herd, till the black mass sweeping over the prairie numbers thousands. On its skirts hover the active, nimble horsemen, with twanging bowstrings and sharp arrows piercing many fat cows. The naked Indians cling to their naked horses as if the two were parts of one incomparable animal, and swing and yield to every motion of their steeds with the grace of perfect horsemanship. The ponies, as quick and skillful as the men, race up beside the fattest of the herd, swing off to avoid the charge of a maddened cow, and, returning, dart close to the victim, whirling hither and yon, like swallows on the wing. And their riders, with the unconscious skill, grace, and power of matchless archery, are drawing their bows to the arrow's head, and driving the feathered shaft deep through the bodies of the buffalo. Returning on their tracks, they skin the dead, then load the meat and robes on their horses, and with laughter and jest ride away.

After them, on the deserted prairie, come the wolves to tear at the carcasses. The rain and the snow wash the blood from the bones and fade and bleach the hair. For a few months the skeleton holds together; then it falls down, and the fox and the badger pull about the whitening bones and scatter them over the plain. So this cow and this bull of mine may have left their bones on the prairie where I found them and picked them up to keep as mementoes of the past, to dream over, and in such reverie to see again the swelling hosts which

yesterday covered the plains and today are but a dream.

So the buffalo passed into history. Once an inhabitant of this continent from the Arctic slope to Mexico, and from Virginia to Oregon, and, within the memory of men yet young, roaming the plains in such numbers that it seemed that it could never be exterminated, it has now disappeared as utterly as has the bison from Europe. For it is probable that the existing herds of that practically extinct species, now carefully guarded in the forests of Grodno, about equal in numbers the buffalo in the Yellowstone Park; while the wild bison in the Caucasus may be compared with the "wood" buffalo which survive in the Peace River district. In view of the former abundance of our buffalo, this parallel is curious and interesting.

The early explorers were constantly astonished by the multitudinous herds which they met with, the regularity of their movements, and the deep roads which they made in traveling from place to place. Many of the earlier references are to territory east of the Mississippi, but even within the last fifteen years buffalo were to be seen on the Western plains in numbers so great that an entirely sober and truthful account seems like fable. Describing the abundance of buffalo in a certain region, an Indian once said to me, in the expressive sign language of which all old frontiersmen have some knowledge, "The country was one robe."

Much has been written about their enormous abundance in the old days, but I have never read anything that I thought an exaggeration of their numbers as I have seen them. Only one who has actually spent months in traveling among them in those old days can credit the stories told about them. The trains of the Kansas Pacific Railroad used frequently to be detained by herds which were crossing the tracks in front of the engines, and in 1870, trains on which I was traveling were twice so held, in one case for three hours. When railroad travel first began on this road, the engineers tried the experiment of running through these passing herds, but, after their engines had been thrown from the tracks, they learned wisdom and gave the buffalo the right of way.

Two or three years later, in the country between the Platte and Republican rivers, I saw a closely massed herd of buffalo so vast that I dare not hazard a guess as to its numbers; and in later years I have traveled for weeks at a time in northern Montana, without ever being out of sight of buffalo. These were not in close herds, except now and then when alarmed and running, but were usually scattered about, feeding or lying down on the prairie at a little distance from one another, much as domestic cattle distribute themselves in a pasture or on the range. As far as we could see on every side of the line of march, and ahead, the hillsides were dotted with dark forms, and the field glass revealed yet others stretched out on every side in one continuous host, to the most distant hills. Thus was gained a more just notion of their numbers than could be had in any other way, for the sight of this limitless territory occupied by these continuous herds was more impressive than the spectacle of a surging, terrified mass of fleeing buffalo, even though the numbers which passed rapidly before one's gaze in a short time were very great. . . .

They were a wandering race, sometimes leaving a district and being long absent, and again returning and occupying it for a considerable period. What laws or what impulses governed these movements we cannot know. Their wandering habits were well understood by the Indians of the Western plains, who depended upon the buffalo for food. It was their custom to follow the herds about, and when, as sometimes occurred, these moved away and could not be found, the Indians were reduced to great straits for food, and sometimes even starved to death.

Under natural conditions the buffalo was an animal of rather sluggish habits, mild, inoffensive, and dull. In its ways of life and intelligence, it closely resembled our domestic cattle. It was slow to learn by experience, and this lack of intelligence greatly hastened the destruction of the race. Until the very last years of its existence as a species, it did not appear to connect the report of firearms with any idea of danger to itself, and, though constantly pursued, did not become wild. If he used skill and judgment in shooting, a hunter who had "got a stand" on a small bunch could kill them all before they had moved out of rifle shot. It was my fortune, one summer, to hunt for a camp of soldiers, and more than once I have lain on a hill above a little herd of buffalo, shot down what young bulls I needed to supply the camp, and then walked down to the bunch and, by waving my hat and shouting, driven off the survivors, so that I could prepare the meat for transportation to camp. This slowness to take the alarm, or indeed to realize the presence of danger, was characteristic of the buffalo almost up to the very last. A time did come when they were alarmed readily enough, but this was not until all the large herds had been broken up and scattered, and the miserable survivors had been so chased and harried that at last they learned to start and run even at their own shadows. . . .

When the first telegraph line was built across the continent, the poles used were light and small, for transportation over the plains was slow and expensive, and it was not thought necessary to raise the wires high above the ground. These poles were much resorted to by the buffalo to scratch against, and before long a great many of them were pushed over. A story, now of considerable antiquity, is told of an ingenious employee of the telegraph company who devised a plan for preventing the buffalo from disturbing the poles. This he expected to accomplish by driving into them spikes which should prick the animals when they rubbed against them. The result somewhat astonished the inventor, for it was discovered that, where formerly one buffalo rubbed against the smooth telegraph poles, ten now struggled and fought for the chance to scratch themselves against the spiked poles, the iron furnishing just the irritation which their tough hides needed. . . .

It was once thought that the buffalo performed annually extensive migrations, and it was even said that those which spent the summer on the banks of the Saskatchewan wintered in Texas. There is no reason for believing this to have been true. Undoubtedly there were slight general movements north and south, and east and west, at certain seasons of the year, but many of the accounts of these movements are entirely misleading, because greatly exaggerated. In one portion of the northern country I know that there was a decided east and west seasonal migration, the herds tending in spring away from the mountains, while in the autumn they worked back again, no doubt seeking shelter in the rough, broken country of the foothills from the cold west winds of the winter. . . .

Apart from man, the buffalo had but few natural enemies. Of these, the most destructive were the wolves, which killed a great many of them. These, however, were principally old, straggling bulls, for the calves were protected by their mothers, and the females and young stock were so vigorous and so gregarious that they had but little to fear from this danger. It is probable that, notwithstanding the destruction which they wrought, the wolves performed an important service for the buffalo race, keeping it vigorous and healthy by killing weak, disabled, and superannuated animals which could no longer serve any useful purpose in the herd and yet consumed the grass which would support a healthy breeding animal. It is certainly true that sick buffalo, or those out of condition, were rarely seen. . . .

To the Indians the buffalo was the staff of life. It was their food, clothing, dwellings, tools. The needs of a savage people are not many, perhaps, but whatever the Indians of the Plains had, that the buffalo gave them. It is not strange, then, that this animal was reverenced by most Plains tribes, nor that it entered largely into their sacred ceremonies, and was in a sense worshiped by them. The Pawnees say "Through the corn and the buffalo we worship the Father." The Blackfeet ask, "What one of all the animals is most sacred?" and the reply given is "The buffalo."

The robe was the Indian's winter covering and his bed, while the skin, freed from the hair and dressed, constituted his summer sheet or blanket. The dressed hide was used for moccasins, leggings, shirts, and women's dresses. Dressed cowskins formed their lodges, the warmest and most comfortable portable shelters ever devised. Braided strands of rawhide furnished them with ropes and lines, and these were made also from the twisted hair. The green hide was sometimes used as a kettle in which to boil meat, or, stretched over a frame of boughs, gave them coracles, or boats, for crossing rivers. The tough, thick hide of the bull's neck, allowed to shrink smooth, made a shield which would turn a lance thrust, an arrow, or even the ball from an old-fashioned smooth-bore gun. From the rawhide, the hair having been shaved off, were made parfleches — envelopelike cases which served for trunks or boxes — useful to contain small articles. The cannon bones and ribs were used to make implements for dressing hides; the shoulder blades lashed to sticks made hoes and axes, and the ribs, runners for small sledges drawn by dogs.

The hoofs were boiled to make a glue for fastening the feathers and heads on their arrows, the hair used to stuff cushions, and later saddles, strands of the long black beard to ornament articles of wearing apparel and implements of war, such as shields and quivers. The sinews lying along the back gave them thread and bowstrings, and backed their bows. The horns furnished spoons and ladles, and ornamented their war bonnets. Water buckets were made from the lining of the paunch. The skin of the hind leg cut off above the pastern, and again a short distance above the hock, was once used for a moccasin or boot. Fly brushes were made from the skin of the tail dried on sticks. Knife sheaths, quivers, bow cases, gun covers, saddlecloths, and a hundred other useful and necessary articles all were furnished by the buffalo.

The Indians killed some smaller game, as elk, deer, and antelope, but for food their dependence was on the buffalo. But before the coming of the whites, their knives and arrowheads were merely sharpened stones, weapons which would be inefficient against such great, thick-skinned beasts. Even under the most favorable circumstances, with these primitive implements, they could not kill food in quantities sufficient to supply their needs. There must be some means of taking the buffalo in considerable numbers. Such wholesale capture was accomplished by traps or surrounds, which all depended for success on one characteristic of the animal — its curiosity.

The Blackfeet, Plains Crees, Gros Ventres of the Prairie, Sarcees, some bands of the Dakotas, Snakes, Crows, and some others, drove the herds of buffalo into pens from above, or over high cliffs, where the fall killed or crippled a large majority of the herd. The Cheyennes and Arapahoes drove them into pens on level ground; the Blackfeet, Aricaras, Mandans, Gros Ventres of the Village, Pawnees, Omahas, Otoes, and others surrounded the herds in great circles on the prairie, and then, frightening them so that they started running, kept them from breaking through the line of men and made them race round and round in a circle until they were so exhausted that they could not run away and were easily killed. . . .

To the white travelers on the plains in early days, the buffalo furnished support and sustenance. Their abundance made fresh meat usually obtainable, and the early travelers usually carried with them bundles of dried meat, or sacks of pemmican, food made from the flesh of the buffalo, that contained a great deal of nutriment in very small bulk. Robes were used for bedding, and, in winter, buffalo moccasins were worn for warmth, the hair side within. Coats of buffalo skin are the warmest covering known, the only garment which will present an effective barrier to the bitter blasts that sweep over the plains of the Northwest.

Perhaps as useful to early travelers as any product of the buffalo was the "buffalo chip," or dried dung. This, being composed of comminuted woody fiber of the grass, made an excellent fuel, and in many parts of the treeless plains was the only substance which could be used to cook with.

The dismal story of the extermination of the buffalo for its hides has been so often told that I may be spared the sickening details of the butchery which was carried on from the Mexican to the British boundary line in the struggle to obtain a few dollars by a most ignoble means. As soon as railroads penetrated the buffalo country, a market was opened for their hides. Men too lazy to work were not too lazy to hunt, and a good hunter could kill in the early days from thirty to seventy-five buffalo a day, the hides of which were worth from $1.50 to $4 each. This seemed an easy way to make money, and the market for hides was unlimited. Up to this time the trade in robes had been mainly confined to those dressed by the Indians, and these were for the most part taken from cows. The coming of the railroad made hides of all sorts marketable, and even those taken from naked old bulls found a sale at some price.

The butchery of buffalo was now something stupendous. Thousands of hunters followed millions of buffalo and destroyed them wherever found and at all seasons of the year. They pursued them during the day, and at night camped at the watering places and built lines of fires along the streams to drive the buffalo back so that they could not drink. It took less than six years to destroy all the buffalo in Kansas, Nebraska, Indian Territory, and northern Texas. The few that were left of the southern herd retreated to the waterless plains of Texas, and there for a while had a brief respite. Even here the hunters followed them, but as the animals were few and the territory in which they ranged vast, they held out here for some years. It was in this country, and against the very last survivors of this southern herd, that "Buffalo Jones" made his very successful trips to capture calves.

The extirpation of the northern herd was longer delayed. No very terrible slaughter occurred until the completion of the Northern Pacific Railroad; then, however, the same scenes of butchery were enacted. Buffalo were shot down by tens of thousands, their hides stripped off, and the meat left to the wolves. The result of the crusade was soon seen: the last buffalo were killed in the Northwest near the boundary line in 1883, and that year may be said to have finished up the species, though some few were killed in 1884 to 1885.

After the slaughter had been begun, but years before it had been accomplished, the subject was brought to the attention of Congress, and legislation looking to the preservation of the species was urged upon that body. Little general interest was taken in the subject, but in 1874, after much discussion, Congress did pass an act providing for the protection of the buffalo. The bill, however, was never signed by the President.

During the last days of the buffalo, a remarkable change took place in its form, and this change is worthy of consideration by naturalists, for it is an example of specialization — of development in one particular direction — which was due to a change in the environment of the species, and is interesting because it was brought about in a very few years and indicates how rapidly, under favoring conditions, such specialization may take place.

This change was noticed and commented on by hunters who followed the northern buffalo, as well as by those who assisted in the extermination of the southern herd. The southern hunters, however, averred that the "regular" buffalo had disappeared — gone off somewhere — and that their place had been taken by what they called the southern buffalo, a race said to have come up from Mexico, and characterized by longer legs and a longer, lighter body than the buffalo of earlier years, and which was also peculiar in that the animals never became fat. Intelligent hunters of the northern herd, however, recognized the true state of the case, which was that the buffalo, during the last years of their existence, were so constantly pursued and driven from place to place that they never had time to lay on fat as in earlier years, and that, as a consequence of this continual running, the animal's form changed, and instead of a fat, short-backed, short-legged animal, it became a long-legged, light-bodied beast, formed for running.

This specialization in the direction of speed at first proceeded very slowly, but at last, as the dangers to which the animals were subjected became more and more pressing, it took place rapidly, and as a consequence the last buffalo killed on the plains were extremely long-legged and rangy, and were very different in appearance — as they were in their habits — from the animals of twenty years ago.

Buffalo running was not a sport that required much skill, yet it was not without its dangers. Occasionally a man was killed by the buffalo, but deaths from falls and from bursting guns were more common. Many curious stories of such accidents are told by the few real old-timers whose memory goes back fifty years, to the time when flintlock guns were in use. A mere fall from a horse is lightly regarded by the practised rider; the danger to be feared is that in such a fall the horse may roll on the man and crush him. Even more serious accidents occurred when a man fell upon some part of his equipment, which was driven through his body. Hunters have fallen in such a way that their whipstocks, arrows, bows, and even guns have been driven through their bodies. The old flintlock guns, or "fukes," which were loaded on the run, with powder poured in from the horn by guess and a ball from the mouth, used frequently to burst, causing the loss of hands, arms, and even lives. . . .

In the early days when the game was plenty, buffalo running was exhilarating sport. Given a good horse, the only other requisite to success was the ability to remain on his back till the end of the chase. No greater degree of skill was needed than this, and yet the quick motion of the horse, the rough ground to be traversed, and the feeling that there was something ahead that must be overtaken and stopped made the ride attractive. There was the very slightest spice of danger, for while no one anticipated an accident, it was possible that one's horse might step into a badger hole, in which case his rider would get a fall that would make his bones ache.

The most exciting, and by far the most interesting, hunts in which I ever took part were those with the Indians of the Plains. They were conducted almost noiselessly, and no ring of rifle shot broke the stillness of the air nor puff of smoke rose toward the still, gray autumn sky. The consummate grace and skill of the naked Indians, and the speed and quickness of their splendid ponies, were well displayed in such chases as these. More than one instance is recorded where an Indian has sent an arrow entirely through the bodies of two buffalo. Sometimes such a hunt was signalized by some

feat of daring bravado that, save in the seeing, was scarcely credible, as when the Cheyenne Big Ribs rode his horse close up to the side of a huge bull, and, springing on his back, rode the savage beast for some distance, and then, with his knife, gave it its death stroke.

Or a man might find himself in a position of comical danger, as did "the Trader," who was thrown from his horse on to the horns of a bull without being injured. One of the horns passed under his belt and supported him, and at the same time prevented the bull from tossing him. In this way he was carried for some distance on the animal's head, when the belt gave way and he fell to the ground unhurt, while the bull ran on. There were occasions when buffalo or horses fell in front of horsemen riding at full run and when a fall was avoided only by leaping one's horse over the fallen animal. In the buffalo chase of old days it was well for a man to keep his wits about him, for, though he might run buffalo a thousand times without accident, the moment might come when only instant action would save him his life, or at least an ugly hurt.

In the early days of the first Pacific Railroad, and before the herds had been driven back from the track, singular hunting parties were sometimes seen on the buffalo range. These hunters were capitalists connected with the newly constructed roads, and some of them now for the first time bestrode a horse, while few had ever used firearms. On such a hunt, one well-known railroad director, eager to kill a buffalo, declined to trust himself on horseback, preferring to bounce over the rough prairie in an ambulance driven by an alarmed soldier, who gave less attention to the mules he was guiding than to the loaded and cocked pistol which his excited passenger was brandishing.

These were amusing excursions where a merry party of pleasant officers from a frontier post and their guests, a jolly crowd of merchants, brokers, and railroad men from the East, start out to have a buffalo hunt. With them go the post guide and a scout or two, the escort of soldiers, and the great blue army wagons, under whose white tilts are piled all the comforts that the post can furnish — unlimited food and drink and many sacks of forage for the animals. Here all was mirth and jest and good fellowship, and except that canvas covered them while they slept, the hunters lived in as much comfort as when at home. The killing of buffalo was to them only an excuse for their jolly outing amid novel scenes. . . .

Of the millions of buffalo which even in our own time ranged the plains in freedom, none now remain. From the prairies which they used to darken, the wild herds, down to the last straggling bull, have disappeared. In the Yellowstone National Park, protected from destruction by United States troops, are the only wild buffalo which exist within the borders of the United States. These are mountain buffalo, and, from their habit of living in the thick timber and on the rough mountainsides, they are only now and then seen by visitors to the Park. It is impossible to say just how many there are, but from the best information that I can get, based on the estimates of reliable and conservative men, I conclude that the number was not less than 400 in the winter of 1891-92. Each winter or spring the government scout employed in the Park sees one or more herds of these buffalo, and as such herds are usually made up in part of young

animals and have calves with them, it is fair to assume that they are steadily if slowly increasing. The report of a trip made last January speaks of four herds seen in the Hayden Valley, which numbered respectively 78, 50, 110, and 15. Besides these, a number of single animals and of scattering groups were seen at a distance, which would perhaps bring the total number up to 300. Of course, it is not to be supposed that all the buffalo in the Park were at that time collected in this one valley.

In the far Northwest, in the Peace River district, there may still be found a few wood buffalo. Judging from reports of them which occasionally reach us from Indians and Hudson's Bay men, their habits resemble those of the European bison. They are seldom killed, and the estimate of their numbers varies from 500 to 1500. This cannot be other than the merest guess, since they are scattered over many thousand square miles of territory, which is without inhabitants and for the most part unexplored.

On the Great Plains is still found the buffalo skull half buried in the soil and crumbling to decay. The deep trails once trodden by the marching hosts are grass-grown now and fast filling up. When these most enduring relics of a vanished race shall have passed away, there will be found, in all the limitless domain once darkened by their feeding herds, not one trace of the American buffalo.

79.

JOSEPH MAYER RICE: The Absurdity of Primary Education

The series of articles on the U.S. public school system that were commissioned by Walter Hines Page, editor of the Forum, *and that appeared in his magazine from October 1892 to June 1893, marked the beginning of the sustained public protest that, under the name of progressive education, transformed the character of public school education. Joseph Rice, who has been called the first of the muckrakers, spent six months touring thirty-six cities and interviewing 1,200 teachers in preparation for his exposé. He criticized the rigidity of teaching methods that made a mockery of individuality and revealed the regrettable alliance between teacher appointments and the patronage on which local ward politics thrived. Rice pointed to exceptions, too (notably Francis Parker's Cook County Normal School), but this did not avert the unprecedented furor aroused among educators when the articles appeared, and that continued when they were published in book form in 1893. "The Public-School System of New York City," the first chapter of the book, is reprinted in part here.*

Source: *The Public-School System of the United States,* New York, 1893, Ch. 1.

IN DESCRIBING THE SCHOOLS of our cities, I begin with the discussion of the schools of New York City because they represent a condition that may be regarded, in many respects, as typical of the schools of all of our large cities. They show clearly the elements that lead to an inferior order of schools; and, further, the remedy that I propose for the eradication of their evils is applicable to the school system of every large city.

Before entering on the discussion of these schools, however, I desire, in order to prevent misunderstandings . . . to call attention to the fact that the degree of excellence of a school system is represented not by what is done by those teachers who are sufficiently interested to do more than is required of them but by the degree of inferi-

ority that the teaching may reach and yet be accepted as satisfactory. Therefore, in pronouncing a school system unscientific, I by no means desire to imply that no good schools can be found in that system, but simply that the good schools that do exist have been developed, not as a result of the system but in spite of it.

Now, what is the character of the instruction that will be passed as satisfactory by the superintendents of the public schools of New York City? Surely no one can call me unjust when I answer this question by describing the work of a school whose principal has been marked uniformly "excellent" during the twenty-five years or more that she has held her present position. I cannot say that this school is a typical New York primary school. . . . But I do most positively assert that the mere fact that a superintendent is permitted to give a school of this nature his warmest endorsement is sufficient to prove that the school system of New York is not conducted for the benefit of the child alone.

The principal of this school has pedagogical views and a maxim peculiarly her own. She believes that when a child enters upon school life his vocabulary is so small that it is practically worthless and his power to think so feeble that his thoughts are worthless. She is consequently of the opinion that what the child knows and is able to do on coming to school should be entirely disregarded, that he should not be allowed to waste time, either in thinking or in finding his own words to express his thoughts, but that he should be supplied with ready-made thoughts as given in a ready-made vocabulary. She has therefore prepared sets of questions and answers so that the child may be given in concise form most of the facts prescribed in the course of study for the three years of primary instruction.

The instruction throughout the school consists principally of grinding these answers verbatim into the minds of the children. The principal's ideal lies in giving each child the ability to answer without hesitation, upon leaving her school, every one of the questions formulated by her. In order to reach the desired end, the school has been converted into the most dehumanizing institution that I have ever laid eyes upon, each child being treated as if he possessed a memory and the faculty of speech, but no individuality, no sensibilities, no soul.

So much concerning the pedagogical views on which this school is conducted; now as to the maxim. This maxim consists of three short words, "Save the minutes." The spirit of the school is, "Do what you like with the child, immobilize him, automatize him, dehumanize him, but save, save

the minutes." In many ways the minutes are saved. By giving the child ready-made thoughts, the minutes required in thinking are saved. By giving the child ready-made definitions, the minutes required in formulating them are saved. Everything is prohibited that is of no measurable advantage to the child, such as the movement of the head or a limb when there is no logical reason why it should be moved at the time. I asked the principal whether the children were not allowed to move their heads. She answered, "Why should they look behind when the teacher is in front of them?" — words too logical to be refuted.

During the recitations many minutes are saved. The principal has indeed solved the problem of how the greatest number of answers may be given in the smallest number of minutes. In the first place, no time is spent in selecting pupils to answer questions, every recitation being started by the first pupil in the class, the children then answering in turn, until all have recited. Second, time is economized in the act of rising and sitting during the recitations, the children being so drilled that the child who recites begins to fall back into his seat while uttering the last word of a definition, the next succeeding child beginning his ascent while the one before him is in the act of descending. Indeed, things appear as if the two children occupying adjoining seats were sitting upon the opposite poles of an invisible seesaw, so that the descending child necessarily raises the pupil next to him to his feet.

Then, again, the minutes are saved by compelling the children to unload their answers as rapidly as possible, distinctness of utterance being sacrificed to speed, and to scream their answers at the tops of their voices, so that no time may be wasted in repeating words inaudibly uttered. For example, the principal's definition of a note — "A note is a sign representing to the eye the length or duration of time" — is ideally delivered when it sounds something like "Notsinrepti length d'ration time." Another way in which time is saved is by compelling the children to stare fixedly at the source whence the wisdom flows. When the teacher is the source of wisdom, all the children in the room stare fixedly in the direction of the teacher; when a word on the blackboard is the source of wisdom, all eyes stare fixedly at a point on the blackboard.

There is one more peculiarity. When material, of whatever nature, is handed to the children, enough to supply a whole row is given to the end child. The material is then passed along sideways, until each child in the row has been supplied. During this procedure the children are compelled to look straight in front of them and to place their hands sidewise in order to receive the material without looking whence it comes. The pupils are thus obliged to grope, as if they were blind, for the things passed to them. The principal assured me, however, that to drill the children in this groping is not attended with much difficulty, the pupils in the lowest primary grade — the little five-year-olds — learning to take and pass things like blind people during the first week or two of their school life.

Sense training is a special feature of the school, and at least a half-dozen different methods, nearly all of which are original, are used for the purpose. The first of these methods is one by means of which form and color are studied in combination. I witnessed such a lesson in the lowest primary grade. Before the lesson began there was passed to each child a little flag on which had been pasted various forms and colors, such as a square piece of green paper, a triangular piece of red paper, etc. When each child had been supplied, a signal was given by the teacher. Upon receiving the signal, the first child sprang up, gave the name of the geometrical form upon his flag, loudly

and rapidly defined the form, mentioned the name of the color, and fell back into his seat to make way for the second child, thus: "A square; a square has four equal sides and four corners; green" (down). Second child (up): "A triangle; a triangle has three sides and three corners; red" (down). Third child (up): "A trapezium; a trapezium has four sides, none of which are parallel, and four corners; yellow" (down). Fourth child (up): "A rhomb; a rhomb has four sides, two sharp corners and two blunt corners; blue." This process was continued until each child in the class had recited. The rate of speed maintained during the recitation was so great that seventy children passed through the process of defining in a very few minutes. The children are drilled in these definitions as soon as they enter the school, and the definitions are repeated from week to week and from year to year, until the child has finished his primary-school education. . . .

In no single exercise is a child permitted to think. He is told just what to say, and he is drilled not only in what to say but also in the manner in which he must say it. As the principal succeeds, however, in putting the children through the work of the grades, the superintendents see no reason why they should not criticize her most favorably.

The typical New York City primary school, although less barbarous and absurd than the one just described, is nevertheless a hard, unsympathetic, mechanical-drudgery school, a school into which the light of science has not yet entered. Its characteristic feature lies in the severity of its discipline, a discipline of enforced silence, immobility, and mental passivity. The differences found in going from room to room and from school to school — I have seen many of them — are differences in degree only, and not in kind. One teacher will allow her pupils to move their heads a little more freely than the standard, another will allow a little more freedom to the shoulder joints but less freedom in moving the head, and a third will require the children to keep their hands in their laps instead of behind their backs.

The character of the instruction is identical with that found wherever this false system of discipline prevails, being of that form which appeals to the memory alone. The aim of the teacher is simply to secure results by drilling the pupils in the facts prescribed for the grade. The public-school system of New York City offers, therefore, a striking example of how, under unwise management, a trained teacher may be reduced to the level of one who has had no training. Many New York schoolteachers have told me that the New York school gave them no opportunity to put their knowledge of psychology and pedagogy to practical use, and that they consequently felt the normal-school influence vanish soon after beginning to teach.

As the methods are unscientific, little can be gained by dilating upon them. Reading is taught by the combined word and spelling method; that is, the child is taught to recognize a word at sight and to spell the word as soon as he is able to read it. Each new word is taught by the above-mentioned development method. For example, if the teacher desires to develop the word "boat," she will say in substance: "The other day I went down to the river and I saw something with a whole lot of people on it floating on the water." She then writes the word "boat" on the blackboard and asks the pupils, "What do you think this word is?" One child will say, "ship"; another will say, "steamer"; and a third will say "boat." Many teachers really believe that when the child thus reads the word "boat" he has succeeded in finding it out by himself. The word "dog" is developed by telling the children that it is something that says "bow-wow," and the word "cow" by in-forming them that it is an animal with horns and says "moo."

By the use of this method the child is actually prevented from exercising his reasoning faculties, and reading is converted into a pure and simple process of memorizing word forms. I have always found the results of the exclusive use of the combined word and spelling method to be very inferior. In New York City the primary reading is, as a rule, so poor that the children are scarcely able to recognize new words at sight at the end of the second school year. Even the third-year reading is miserable. In many cities the children read better at the end of the second year than they do in New York at the end of the third. Indeed, I feel as if I could truthfully say that in Minneapolis the pupils read as well at the end of the first year as they do in New York at the end of the third, and this in spite of the fact that the Minneapolis schools are charming and the pupils — even those from the poorest of homes — governed by love and sympathy. In these schools many methods — the word method, the sentence method, phonics, word building, etc. — are used in teaching reading. . . .

It is not difficult to account for the low standard of the New York schools; indeed, under existing conditions, it would be surprising if the instruction were of a higher order. In the first place, there is absolutely no incentive to teach well. If mechanical teaching be in general deemed satisfactory, why should the teacher trouble with the preparation of lessons and the study of educational methods and principles, and then teach upon scientific principles at the risk of not covering the work of the grade? Further, a teacher scarcely imperils her position by doing exceedingly poor work, the only penalty being that an incompetent teacher cannot claim the maximum salary after she has taught the required fourteen years. In New York City teachers are very rarely discharged, even for the grossest negligence and incompetency. In order that a principal may be discharged, sixteen of the twenty-one members of the Board of Education must vote against her, and for many reasons it is practically impossible to secure that number of adverse votes.

To discharge a teacher is also a matter attended with considerable difficulty. Before a teacher can be removed, a number of barriers must be passed. The majority of the members of the Board of Trustees of any ward can recommend the removal of a teacher in the ward, but before she can be removed the consent of the majority of the inspectors of the district must be obtained in writing. But even after the consent of three trustees out of five and two inspectors out of three has been obtained — and this consent is not easy to obtain — the teacher can appeal to the Board of Education, that body having the power to reverse the decision of the trustees and inspectors and to order her reinstatement.

Second, there is no source of inspiration, practically nothing being done by the supervising officers to raise the standard of the teachers. Indeed, the supervision as now conducted is little more than a farce. The superintendent of schools may be said to be simply an executive officer. What he does, beyond meeting the assistant superintendents once a month and the principals three or four times annually, and keeping certain sets of books, is a question that no one as yet appears to have answered.

Besides the chief officer, eight assistant superintendents are employed to supervise the work of 4,000 teachers. Though some of them possess expert qualifications and the ability to educate teachers, the circumstances under which they labor appear to be such as to render their services of very little value. Even under the most favorable circumstances, a single supervising officer cannot successfully direct the work of 500 teachers. But, in addition, the method of supervision — if indeed there be a method — is so unsystematic as apparently to render their services of least value. Each classroom in the city is supposed to be visited and examined by several of the supervisors once a year. But there are no district lines, and the visits are consequently very irregularly arranged. Further, the visits are too few to be of real benefit to the teacher and yet frequent enough to disturb the teacher's mental equilibrium during the intervening period. Under the circumstances, it were better for all concerned if there were no supervision at all, and this is doubly true for the reason that whether or not the supervisors find the teachers competent is a matter of very little practical consequence. Besides examining classes, the assistant superintendents lecture from time to time. Each teacher attends in all three or four such lectures annually.

The argument is used that the duty of instructing the teachers does not devolve upon the supervisors but upon the principals. The principals of the New York schools do not teach, and it is believed that their time should be devoted to the training of their teachers. But when we consider that in selecting principals expert qualifications are not taken into account, the argument becomes worthless. Indeed, as a rule, the newly appointed teachers are better qualified professionally than the principals. While the new teachers are normal-school graduates, many of the principals have had no professional training whatever, nor have they at any time, either with or without guidance, devoted a sufficient amount of time to professional studies to learn the *ABC* of scientific pedagogy. Some principals read enough educational matter to pick up a few devices, but those who may be said to be experts are very rare exceptions.

In the grammar departments quite a number of alive and active principals, who exert an excellent influence over their teachers, may be found. Some of these have, indeed, succeeded in developing comparatively good schools. I have not, however, as yet found a single primary school conducted on modern educational principles. The typical primary principal does not appear to know that education means anything beyond cramming into the minds of the pupils a certain number of cut-and-dried facts. What the average principal does beyond keeping an accurate account of the attendance of pupils and teachers, and listening to complaints from parents and teachers, is also a matter that has puzzled more than one intimately acquainted with the New York public schools.

Now, a word concerning those who are responsible for the condition of the schools, the members of the various boards of education. The Board of Education, properly speaking, consists of three independent bodies. The first of these is the central board, known as the Board of Education. It consists of twenty-one members, appointed by the mayor. Second, there are eight boards of inspectors, each of which has three members, who exercise a sort of supervision over the schools of three wards. Inspectors also are appointed by the mayor. Third, there are twenty-four boards of trustees — one for each ward — each of which has five members. The trustees are appointed by the Board of Education. There are, therefore, in all, 165 persons directly connected with the management of the schools.

Things appear to be arranged among these bodies on the principle of power without responsibility. When anything goes amiss, it is impossible to discover which one of these 165 persons is responsible. "No one is responsible for anything," has become a byword among those who in any way seek to fix responsibility. In many of the schools a most horribly unsanitary condition of affairs prevails, for which, however, no one appears to be responsible. The course of studies is highly unscientific, but no one has constructed it, and no one is responsible for it. When appointments are to be made, everyone is on the alert; when responsibility is to be fixed, no one is in readiness to step forward. Everything appears to be involved in a most intricate muddle.

The power to appoint the teachers is vested in the Board of Trustees, while the appointment of superintendents and principals lies in the hands of the Board of Education. In no way has anyone connected with the educational side of the system a word to say concerning the appointment or discharge of principals or teachers. Nearly all appointments are made by "pulls," merit being a side issue. The superintendents should naturally be held responsible for poor teaching, but justly they cannot be so held for the reason that it is almost impossible for them to have incompetents discharged. Indeed, the superintendent has said that he has given up, as a hopeless task, attempting to have incompetent principals and teachers discharged. Therefore the supervisors can justly lay the blame of poor teaching on the members of the Board of Education, while the Board of Education can justly throw this responsibility on the shoulders of those whose duty it is to secure proper teaching. So things have always been, and so they will remain until a radical change is effected. Meanwhile, none suffer but those for whom the millions are appropriated — the children.

In regard to the public, the mere fact that things are muddled as they are proves that the citizens take no active interest in the schools. As for the parents in particular, the fact that they send their children to unsanitary schools — indeed, so unsanitary as to be unfit for the habitation of human beings — is of itself sufficient to prove that they are in no way concerned with what the schools do with their children. This does not apply alone to the more ignorant classes, some of the most unhealthful schools in the city being attended by children from the best of homes.

Now, how may the evils be eradicated and the schools improved? That the schools of small cities may be improved in a comparatively small time is a matter that has been repeatedly demonstrated; but how to improve the schools of large cities is a problem that has never been solved. The large cities should therefore learn the lesson taught by the small ones — namely, that if the superintendent is an educator, spares no pains in endeavoring to improve the minds of his teachers, and is unhampered in his labors by the Board of Education, a few years will suffice to raise the standard of the schools, *provided the number of teachers in his charge be not too large.*

This principle might be applied to a large city by treating it as a collection of small ones. A superintendent cannot well care for more than 150, or at most 200, teachers; in other words, he cannot properly care, without assistance, for a city of more than 75,000 inhabitants at the utmost. As New York City has 20 times 200 teachers, 20 times 75,000 inhabitants, its schools should be divided into at least 20 independent districts, each one of which should be placed in charge of a superintendent having all the powers and responsibilities of a city superintendent. In the appointment of special supervisors, such as supervisors of drawing, music, etc., these district lines should be strictly observed, so that each district superintendent might be held responsible in every way for the schools of his district. The district superintendent should be required to devote all his working hours to visiting classes for the purpose of aiding the teachers and to meeting teachers in order to instruct them in educational methods and principles as well as in their grade work.

Under an arrangement of this nature, provided the right sort of superintendents be secured, there is no reason why the schools of each district should not improve as rapidly as the schools of a small city when in good hands. Though each district would in great part be independent, it should nevertheless be regarded as but a part of a large system. Unity can and must be preserved. How, under these conditions, it may be preserved, I shall now endeavor to show.

In the first place, there should then, as now, be a city superintendent responsible for the general condition of the schools throughout the city. The city superintendent should take an active part in improving the minds of the teachers. All his time should be devoted to visiting classes and to teaching teachers. One day in each month might be spent by him in one of the districts, and this would enable him to make his rounds once a month. Three or four hours might readily be spent daily by the city superintendent in visiting classes, and the hours from four to six in the afternoon in meeting the teachers. He might meet the 200 teachers of a district in a body for the purpose of conducting an educational conference. This would enable him to meet all his 4,000 teachers once a month. Three or four hours devoted to visiting the schools of each district once a month would be sufficient to enable the superintendent to judge how things in any particular district were progressing. Such visits should be suggestive, and not examinational.

The city superintendent should be in every sense an educator, and as such he would seek unity rather than uniformity, and he would give to each district superintendent liberty to develop his pedagogical powers, but would check that which partakes of the nature of license. The superintendent, principals, and teachers of each district would now be likely to do their utmost to develop the best schools in the city, and a healthful competitive spirit might readily be maintained. In four or five years marked differences in regard to the degree of excellence of the schools of the various districts would appear. The schools of the incompetent and nonenergetic superintendents would be likely to fall so far behind the best that such officers could not well retain their positions, and a natural weeding out of incompetent persons would ensue.

Second, a board of superintendents, of which each district superintendent should be a member and the city superintendent the presiding officer, should be formed. This board should meet frequently for educational discussions, and all important matters concerning the pedagogical management of the schools should be brought before it. The course of studies should result from the conferences of this board. Above all, the power to appoint principals and teachers should be vested in this board of superintendents. As each district superintendent would be held responsible for the condition of the schools of his district, his wishes concerning the persons to be appointed should be respected; he should be allowed to nominate the teachers, but the board of superintendents should confirm the nominations and retain a veto power. Under these conditions, appointments would be made for merit alone, and each district superintendent would certainly do his utmost to find proper persons to fill vacancies. Also, the power to discharge principals and teachers should be vested in the board of superintendents. The city superintendent should be appointed by the Board of Education, but as he would be held responsible for the schools of all the districts, he should have the power to nominate his assistants, and not more than a veto power should be vested in the Board of Education.

The financial management of the schools should remain in the hands of businessmen, but all matters pertaining to the educational part of the system — the construction of the course of studies, the appointment and discharge of principals and teachers — should be in the hands of the board of experts.

The additional expense that would be incurred under this plan would be, comparatively speaking, only nominal. An allowance of $4,000 for a district superintendent and $10,000 to each district for special supervisors would require an additional expenditure of less than $200,000 a year, an increase of only 5 percent over that now incurred by the maintenance of the corps of teachers.

When I was a boy of fourteen, my father was so ignorant I could hardly stand to have the old man around. But when I got to be twenty-one, I was astonished at how much the old man had learned in seven years.

SAMUEL L. CLEMENS ("MARK TWAIN")

80.

Charles W. Eliot: Failures of Popular Education

President Charles W. Eliot of Harvard proposed reforms affecting education, not only at its highest levels but also in the primary and secondary schools. In an article prepared for the December 1892 edition of the Forum *and reprinted here in part, Eliot described the faults of popular education with criticisms similar to those made by reformers like Joseph Mayer Rice: i.e., the practice of teaching by memorization neglected the most important function of all educational institutions — developing the student's ability to think.*

Source: *Forum*, December 1892: "Wherein Popular Education Has Failed."

IT CANNOT BE DENIED that there is serious and general disappointment at the results of popular education up to this date. Elementary instruction for all children and more advanced instruction for some children have been systematically provided in many countries for more than two generations at great cost and with a good deal of enthusiasm, though not always on wise plans.

Many of the inventions of the same rich period of seventy years have greatly promoted the diffusion of education by cheapening the means of communicating knowledge. Cheap books, newspapers, and magazines, cheap postage, cheap means of transportation, and free libraries have all contributed to the general cultivation of intelligence, or at least to the wide use of reading matter and the spread of information. In spite, however, of all these efforts to make education universal, all classes complain more than ever before of the general conditions of society.

Now, if general education does not promote general contentment, it does not promote public happiness; for a rational contentment is an essential element in happiness, private or public. To this extent universal education must be admitted to have failed at the end of two generations of sincere and strenuous, if sometimes misdirected, effort. Perhaps it is too soon to expect from public education any visible increase of public contentment and happiness. It may be that general discontent is a necessary antecedent of social improvement and a preliminary manifestation of increased knowledge and wisdom in all classes of the community.

Yet after two whole generations it seems as if some increase of genuine reasonableness of thought and action in all classes of the population ought to be discernible. Many persons, however, fail to see in the actual conduct of the various classes of society the evidence of increasing rationality. These skeptical observers complain that people in general, taken in masses with proper exclusion of exceptional individuals, are hardly more reasonable in the conduct of life than they were before free schools, popular colleges, and the cheap printing press existed. They point out that when the vulgar learn to read they want to read trivial or degrading literature, such as the common newspapers and periodicals which are mainly devoted to accidents, crimes, criminal trials, scandals, gossip, sports, prizefights, and low politics. Is it not the common school and the arts of cheap illustration, they say, that have made obscene books, photographs and pictures, low novels, and all the literature which incites to vice and crime, profitable, and therefore abundant and dangerous to society?

They complain that in spite of every effort to enlighten the whole body of the people, all sorts of quacks and imposters thrive, and that one popular delusion or sophism succeeds another, the best-educated classes contributing their full proportion of the deluded. Thus the astrologer in the Middle Ages was a rare personage and usually a dependent of princes; but now he advertises in the popular newspapers and flourishes as never before. Men and women of all classes, no matter what their education, seek advice on grave matters from clairvoyants, seers, Christian Scientists, mind-cure practitioners, bonesetters, Indian doctors, and fortune-tellers. The ship of state barely escapes from one cyclone of popular folly, like the fiat-money delusion or the Granger legislation of the seventies, when another blast of ill-formed opinion comes down on it, like the actual legislation which compels the buying and storing of silver by government, or the projected legislation which would compel government to buy cotton, wheat, or corn and issue paper money against the stock.

The educated critics of the practical results of public education further complain that lawless violence continues to break out just as it did before common schools were thought of, that lynch law is familiar in the United States, riots common from Berlin to Seattle, and assassination an avowed means of social and industrial regeneration. Even

religious persecution, these critics say, is rife. The Jews are ostracized in educated Germany and metropolitan New York, and in Russia are robbed and driven into exile by thousands. Furthermore, in spite of the constant inculcation of the principles of civil and religious liberty, new tyrannies are constantly arising. The tyrant, to be sure, is no longer an emperor, a king, or a feudal lord but a contagious public opinion, a majority of voters inclined to despotism, or an oppressive combination of owners, contractors, or workmen. From time to time the walking delegate seems to be a formidable kind of tyrant, all the more formidable because his authority is but brief and his responsibility elusive.

Popular elections and political conventions and caucuses provide another set of arguments for the skeptics about the results of universal education. Have these not been carried on with combined shoutings, competitive, prolonged howlings, banners, torches, uniforms, parades, misrepresentations, suppressions of truth, slanders, and vituperation, rather than with arguments and appeals to enlightened self-interest, benevolence, patriotism, and the sense of public duty? Are votes less purchasable now than they were before the urban graded school and the state university were known? How irrational is the preparation made by the average voter for the exercise of the function of voting! He reads steadily one intensely partisan newspaper, closes his mind to all information and argument which proceed from political opponents, distrusts independent newspapers and independent men, and is afraid of joint debates. Such are some of the allegations and doubts of the educated critics with regard to the results of popular education.

On the other hand, the least educated and most laborious classes complain that in spite of universal elementary education, society does not tend toward a greater equality of condition; that the distinctions between rich and poor are not diminished but intensified, and that elementary education does not necessarily procure for the wage earner any exemption from incessant and exhausting toil. They recognize, indeed, that machine labor has in many cases been substituted for hand labor; but they insist that the direction of machines is more exacting than old-fashioned hand work, and that the extreme division of labor in modern industries is apt to make the life of the operative or mechanic monotonous and narrowing.

They complain that the rich, though elaborately instructed in school and church, accept no responsibilities with their wealth, but insist on being free to break up their domestic or industrial establishments at their pleasure, or, in other words, to give or withhold employment as they find it most convenient or profitable. They allege that the rich man in modern society does not bear, either in peace or in war, the grave responsibilities which the rich man of former centuries, who was a great landowner, a soldier, and a magistrate, was compelled to bear; and that education, whether simple or elaborate, has not made the modern rich man less selfish and luxurious than his predecessor in earlier centuries who could barely sign his name.

They admit that the progress of science has made mankind safer from famine and pestilence than it used to be, but they point out that wars are more destructive than ever, this century being the bloodiest of all the centuries; that European armies are larger and more expensively equipped than ever before, and hence are more burdensome to the laboring populations which support them; while in the American republic the annual burden of paying the military and naval pensions which result from a single great war is heavier, twenty-seven years after the war ended, than the annual burden of maintaining the largest standing army in Europe. Clearly, the spread of edu-

cation has not enabled the nations to avoid war or to diminish its cost, either in blood or treasure. If universal education cannot abolish, or even abate, in seventy years the horrible waste and cruelty of war, can anything great be hoped from it for the laboring classes?

They complain also that the education of the employer and the employed has not made the conditions of employment more humane and comfortable; that almost all services and industries — agricultural, domestic, and manufacturing — are organized on the brutal principle of dismissal on the instant or with briefest notice, and that assured employment during good behavior and efficiency, which is almost a prerequisite of happiness for a reasonable and provident person, remains the privilege of an insignificant minority of well-to-do people, like judges, professors, and officers of financial and industrial corporations. How much has all this boasted education increased the intelligence and insight of even the best-educated and most capable people if they still cannot devise just and satisfying conditions of employment in their own households, shops, ships, and factories?

It is much more important that fidelity, constancy, loyalty, and mutual respect and affection between employer and employed should be fostered by the prevailing terms of employment than that more yards of cotton cloth or more tons of steel should be produced, more miles of railroad maintained, or more bushels of wheat raised. Those fine human qualities are the ultimate product to be desired. Have they been developed and fostered during the two generations of popular education? Or have dishonesty in labor, disloyalty, mutual jealousy, and distrust between employer and employed, and general discontent increased?

These indictments against universal education as a cure for ancient wrongs and evils are certainly formidable; but they exaggerate existing evils and leave out of sight great improvements in social condition which the last two generations have seen. It is only necessary for us to call to mind a few of the beneficent changes which the past seventy years have wrought to assure ourselves that some powerful influences for good have been at work in the best-educated nations. Consider, for example, the mitigation of human miseries which the reformation of penal codes and of prisons, the institution of reformatories, the building of hospitals, asylums, and infirmaries, and the abolition of piracy and slavery have brought about. Consider the positive influence toward the formation of habits of industry and frugality exerted by such institutions as savings banks, mutual-benefit societies, and life insurance corporations.

Harvard University

Charles W. Eliot, president of Harvard

Unanswerable statistics show that during the past seventy years there has been a steady improvement in the condition of the most laborious classes in modern society, the wage earners, and this improvement touches their earnings, their hours of labor, their lodgings, their food and clothing, and the means of education for their children. Consider how step by step terrors have been disarmed, superstitions abolished, the average duration of human life lengthened, and civil order extended over regions once desolate or dangerous. Think how family and school discipline have been mitigated within two generations, and how all sorts of abuses and cruelties are checked and prevented by the publicity of modern life, a publicity which depends on the universal capacity to read.

Let us remember that almost all business is nowadays conducted on trust — trust that the seller will deliver his goods according to sample and promise, and trust that the buyer will pay at the time appointed. Now, this general trustworthiness is of course based on moral qualities which inhere in the race, but these qualities are ef-

fectively reinforced and protected by the publicity which general education has made possible. Consider how freedom of intercourse between man and man, tribe and tribe, nation and nation has been developed, even within a single generation; how the United States have spread across the continent, how Italy has been made one nation, and Germany one, and the Austrian Empire confederated from three distinct nationalities. Every one of these great expansions or consolidations has resulted in greater freedom of intercourse and in the removal of barriers and of causes of strife and ill-will.

Moreover, on taking a broad view of the changes in civilized society since 1830, do we not see that there has been great progress toward unity — not indeed toward uniformity, but toward a genuine unity? The different classes of society and the different nations are still far from realizing the literal truth of the New Testament saying, "We are members one of another," but they have lately made some approach to realizing that truth. Now, unity of spirit with diversity of gifts is the real end to be attained in social organization. It would not be just to contend that popular education has brought to pass all these improvements and ameliorations; but it has undoubtedly contributed to them all.

Moreover, we find on every hand evidences of increased intelligence in large masses of people. If war has not ceased, soldiers are certainly more intelligent than they used to be, else they could not use the arms of precision with which armies are now supplied. The same is true of all industry and trade — they require more intelligence than formerly in all the work people. While, therefore, we must admit that education has not accomplished all that might fairly have been expected of it, we may believe that it has had some share in bringing about many of the ameliorations of the social state in the past two generations.

It is somewhat comforting to recall, as we confess to disappointment with the results of universal education, that modern society has had several disappointments before of a nature similar to that it now experiences. There was a time when it was held that a true and universally accepted religious belief would bring with it an ideal state of society; but this conviction resulted in sanguinary persecutions and desolating wars, for to attain the ideal state of society through one true religion was an end so lofty as to justify punishing and even exterminating all who did not accept the religion.

Again, when modern representative institutions were first put into practice it seemed as if the millennium were near — popular government seemed of infinite promise for the happiness of mankind. Were not all despotisms to be done away with? Were not all men to enjoy liberty, equality, and fraternity? It was a painful surprise to discover that under a regime of general liberty a few could so use their freedom as to gain undue advantages over the many. It was a disappointment to find that superior shrewdness and alertness could secure, under public freedom and public law, a lordship such as superior force could hardly win when there was little freedom and little law. How high were the expectations based on universal suffrage, that exaltation of man as man without regard to his social condition, that strong expression of the equality of all men in political power! Yet all these successive hopes have proved in a measure delusive.

On the whole, the most precious and stable result of the civilized world's experience during the past 300 years is the doctrine of universal toleration, or liberty for all religious opinions under the protection of the state, there being as yet no such thing in Christian society as one true and universal religion. We have all had to learn that representative institutions do not at present necessarily produce good government — in many American cities they coexist with bad government — and that universal suffrage is not a panacea for social ills but simply the most expedient way to enlist the interest and support of us all in the government of us all. Never yet has society succeeded in embodying in actual institutions a just liberty, a real equality, or a true fraternity.

Training is everything. The peach was once a bitter almond; cauliflower is nothing but cabbage with a college education.
SAMUEL L. CLEMENS ("MARK TWAIN"), *"Pudd'nhead Wilson's Calendar,"* 1894

Carson Mansion, Eureka, California; perhaps the ultimate triumph of the eclectic mode

"TASTE" AND THE ARTS

Romanticism flourished in the United States a generation later than it had in Europe — and only when Americans had time for it. As great wealth poured from the postwar industrial boom and the cities mushroomed, houses and public buildings took on all the embellishments of monumental sculpture — cupolas, pillars, porticos, and elaborate trim. Garish interiors predominated. Even modest homes emphasized eclectic clutter. But it was not all wasted money and effort; as personal art galleries became a fashion for the immensely wealthy, paintings by the "masters," mainly contemporary French mannerists whose names are all but forgotten, were bought up uncritically, and shiploads of artifacts, whole castles and churches were sent back to America. Much of this wholesale acquisition of "culture" was tasteless and quantities of artistic trash were accumulated, but this private collecting later formed the basis for every great museum collection in the country. The millionaire buyers soon learned to seek expert advice. Unfortunately, it was not until the turn of the century that collectors and museums began to give any significant attention to domestic genius.

Interpretations of Gothic styles succeeded neo-classical interpretations as suitable for monumental buildings: Broad Street Station, Philadelphia, and a design for the Washington Monument

Madison Square Garden was designed by Stanford M. White with a taste for Oriental opulence. The White building has been twice succeeded by newer halls; (right) County Jail, Galveston, Texas

Early examples of the townhouse design that was
the standard in New York for many years; (right)
example of simple design popular at mid-century

Advertisement from "Harper's Weekly" for a book of
"artistic designs" for cottages, containing suggestions
for embellishments; (below) Mills residence, Millbrae,
California, an example of more restrained embellish-
ment in a mansion

Drawing room in the Tiffany House, 1887 — Oriental opulence not without taste

Dining room of the Tiffany House; (right) main hall, looking toward music room of the Villard House; (below) front hall of the Stanford House, San Francisco, a tasteless marbled palace

Private picture gallery in the Stanford House, apparently containing Bierstadt landscapes

Although there were a number of art schools and museums operating by that time, the Centennial Exposition in Philadelphia is generally credited with arousing in Americans a "taste" for art. For the wealthy this meant a consciousness of styles in building and an interest in collecting, if not a trained sensitivity to the value of what was built or collected. As the collections grew, so did the notion of bringing "culture" to the public. The Metropolitan Museum in New York, the Boston Fine Arts Museum, and the Chicago Art Institute were founded in the 1870s. In each case, the impetus came from private citizens fulfilling a new-found duty to bring culture to the masses.

Photograph by Thomas Eakins of a painting class at the Art Students' League, New York; (below) new building for the Metropolitan Museum

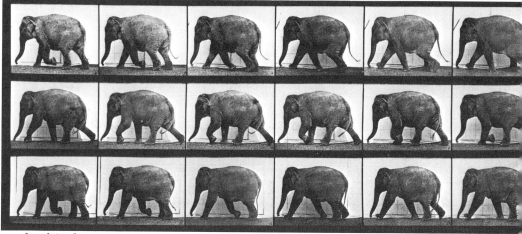

One of a large number of motion study photographs taken by Eadweard Muybridge in the 1880s

(Right) One segment of a Muybridge series of men wrestling; (above) a time-lapse study by Thomas Eakins of a man pole-vaulting

Nude study by Eakins. His technical, realistic approach to painting brought him to photography as a means of studying motion and the human form. Eakins spent some time with Muybridge

"The Nantucket School of Philosophy" by Eastman Johnson, 1887

Following the Civil War painting in America resumed, unsteadily, the course charted by the earlier "genre" and Hudson River schools. In some cases these old styles and perspectives were adopted intact, as in the romantic and sentimental genre paintings of Eastman Johnson (1824-1906) or the pastoral landscapes of John F. Kensett. Sentiment and romance were what the public wanted, by and large, and while Johnson and others were skilled and popular, they did little to extend either the vision or the technical insight of American painting.

(Right) "Banjo Lesson" by Henry O. Tanner and (below) "Pastoral Visit" by Richard Brooke, the two leading Negro artists of the day

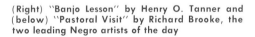

(Above) "Tenafly Autumn" by George Inness; (below) Inness, portrait by William M. Chase

(Below) "Merced River, Yosemite Valley" by Albert Bierstadt, 1866; (above) Yosemite Valley, photographed by Charles Bierstadt, brother of the painter, on one of their trips to the Rockies

Museum of Fine Arts, Boston, Karolik Collection

"Approaching Storm: Beach Near Newport" by Martin Johnson Heade (1819-1903); (below) "River Scene," 1870, painted by John Frederick Kensett (1818-1872)

Drawing on the tradition of the Hudson River School, a number of landscape painters enjoyed considerable popular success in the postwar years. Albert Bierstadt (1830-1902) amassed a modest fortune from the popularity of his immense, detailed Rocky Mountain romances. He and a number of other landscape painters brought great technical skill to their interpretations, recreating the light and feel of the outdoors with affecting fidelity. George Inness stands out, however, with a sophisticated technique particularly suited to the soft moods of summer. His uniquely lyrical style gives the paintings a striking charm and originality.

Metropolitan Museum, Collis P. Huntington gift

"Haying Near New Haven" by Frederick E. Church (1826-1900)

New Britain Museum of American Art

"Long Branch, New Jersey" by Winslow Homer

(Above) "Visit From the Old Mistress", 1876, and "Maine Coast" (below), 1895, both by Homer

The initial vision of these native American perspectives was brought to maturity by Winslow Homer and Thomas Eakins. They painted in markedly different styles but they came to share an explicit contempt for the vulgar sentimentality of current tastes and for the mannered aesthetics of European academies. Homer in particular struggled to develop a more fluid and intuitive style that would do justice to the older vision. Eakins, meanwhile, approached the same problem with mathematical precision in composition and a clinical study of anatomy. In the end, the dogged integrity of the two men brought both to the forefront of naturalist painting.

Four paintings by Thomas Eakins: (above) "Chess Players," 1876; (center right) "Between Rounds," 1899

(Center left) Henry Rowlands, professor of physics at Johns Hopkins and a leading experimental physicist; (below) David H. Agnew, noted surgeon and professor of surgery, University of Pennsylvania

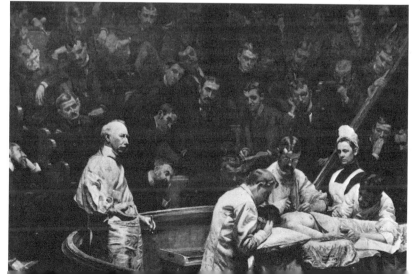

Mr. and Mrs. I. N. Phelps Stokes (left) painted by John Singer Sargent, 1897; (above) self-portrait of the artist in his studio

(Right) Sargent portrait of William Merritt Chase; (below) "The Open Air Breakfast" by Chase, 1888. Chase was particularly noted as a teacher, at the Art Students' League and elsewhere. He acquired his impressionist style only gradually after returning to America from study abroad.

"The Morning Toilet" by Mary Cassatt

Most of the dozens of artists who studied abroad returned after a few years. They stirred vigorous aesthetic arguments and dominated artists' organizations and schools, trying to bring the conventions of European academies to America. Some, however, never came back. The dean of expatriates was James A. M. Whistler, who emigrated at 21, acquired a contempt for middle-class society in Paris and developed an artistic doctrine to fit his situation.

(Above) "Beach at Selsey Bill" and (below left) Miss Cicely Alexander by Whistler; Whistler painted by William M. Chase

(Above) "The Tempest" by Albert Pinkham Ryder (1847-1917); (right) Ryder, portrait by J. A. Weir; (below) "Moonlight" by Ralph Albert Blakelock (1847-1919)

The brooding strength of Albert Pinkham Ryder's unique style foreshadowed a major direction of 20th-century painting. Entirely subjective, Ryder's essential elements were rhythm and expressive force. The paintings throb with the vision of his solitary intelligence which shows through both the literary interpretations and the nature studies. Ryder lived alone in a squalid apartment, working and reworking his canvases. This constant revision left some of the paintings with thick layers of badly mixed paint that has cracked and faded over the years.

1893

81.

David J. Brewer: An Independent Judiciary as the Salvation of the Nation

David Brewer spent twenty-one years of his long judicial career as an associate justice of the U.S. Supreme Court, to which he was appointed by President Harrison in 1889. His opinions, of which 70 of the 526 he delivered for the Court dealt with constitutional questions, marked him as a conservative defender of the rights of property and of the wealthy few. He viewed any scheme that would redistribute the wealth with suspicion and opposed the position that Congress could assume powers not designated by the Constitution in dealing with national economic problems. Brewer's eloquence kept him in high demand as a public speaker. The address, a portion of which is reprinted here, was delivered to an audience of New York lawyers in January 1893.

Source: *Proceedings of the New York State Bar Association,* New York, 1893, pp. 37-47.

THREE THINGS differentiate the civilized man from the savage — that which he knows, that which he is, and that which he has.

That which he knows: the knowledge of the savage is limited to the day and bounded by the visible horizon. The civilized man looks backward through all history and beholds the present limits of the universe. The accumulations of the centuries are his. . . . That which he knows he can never be despoiled of, and he carries its glory and its joy as safe in his soul as the secrets of eternity in the consciousness of omnipotence.

That which he is: all passions riot in the savage. He grovels through things of earth to satisfy the lusts of the body; and the height of his morality is an eye for an eye and a tooth for a tooth. Civilization lifts the soul above the body and makes character the supreme possession. It reads into human history the glory and value of self-denial. It catches from the Divine One of Nazareth the nobility of helpfulness and teaches that the externals are not the man; that accumulations and accomplishments only suggest that which makes both valuable; and that the poet's divination, "a man's a man for a' that," is the ultimate fact.

That also which a man is, is not the subject of larceny; nor can it be wrested from him by king or mob. The unavailing tortures of the Inquisition, the gloom of the dungeon, the awful silence of the scaffold, and the blazing splendors of the martyr's fires attest the words of Him who said, "Fear not them which kill the body, but are not able to kill the soul"; and affirm the inalienable immortality of that which a man is.

That which he has: a hut for a home; a blanket and a breech clout for his apparel; a bow and arrow for his means of support; a canoe and a horse for his travel; and seashells for his jewels — these are the possessions of the savage. But for the child of civilization, all continents bring food to his table and decorations to his home. . . .

But that which he has lies within the reach of others. Given power and willingness on the part of those about him, and a man may be stripped of all his material possessions. Hence the Eighth and Tenth Commandments: "Thou shalt not steal"; "Thou shalt not covet." Only under their sanction is society possible.

I am not here this evening to defend the Eighth Commandment or to denounce its grosser violators. I do not propose to discuss the footpad or the burglar; they are vulgar and brutal criminals, in whose behalf there has as yet been organized no political party. I wish rather to notice that movement which may be denominated the movement of "coercion," and which by the mere force of numbers seeks to diminish protection to private property. It is a movement which in spirit, if not in letter, violates both the Eighth and Tenth Commandments; a movement which, seeing that which a man has, attempts to wrest it from him and transfer it to those who have not.

It is the unvarying law that the wealth of a community will be in the hands of a few; and the greater the general wealth, the greater the individual accumulations. The large majority of men are unwilling to endure that long self-denial and saving which makes accumulation possible; they have not the business tact and sagacity which brings about large combinations and great financial results; and hence it always has been, and until human nature is remodeled always will be, true that the wealth of a nation is in the hands of a few, while the many subsist upon the proceeds of their daily toil. But security is the chief end of government; and other things being equal, that government is best which protects to the fullest extent each individual, rich or poor, high or low, in the possession of his property and the pursuit of his business.

It was the boast of our ancestors in the Old Country that they were able to wrest from the power of the king so much security for life, liberty, and property. . . . Here, there is no monarch threatening trespass upon the individual. The danger is from the multitudes — the majority, with whom is the power. . . .

The property of a great railroad corporation stretches far away from the domicile of its owner, through state after state, from ocean to ocean; the rain and the snow may cover it; the winds and the storms may wreck it; but no man or multitude dare touch a car or move a rail. It stands as secure in the eye and in the custody of the law as the purposes of justice in the thought of God.

This movement expresses itself in two ways: First, in the improper use of labor organizations to destroy the freedom of the laborer and control the uses of capital. I do not care to stop to discuss such wrongs as these — preventing one from becoming a skilled laborer by forbidding employers to take more than a named number of apprentices; compelling equal wages for unequal skill and labor; forbidding extra hours of labor to one who would accumulate more than the regular stipend. That which I particularly notice is the assumption of control over the employer's property, and blocking the access of laborers to it. The common rule as to strikes is this: Not merely do the employees quit the employment, and thus handicap the employer in the use of his property, and perhaps in the discharge of duties which he owes to the public; but they also forcibly prevent others from taking their places. It is useless to say that they only advise — no man is misled.

When a thousand laborers gather around a railroad track and say to those who seek employment that they had better not, and when that advice is supplemented every little while by a terrible assault on one who disregards it, everyone knows that something more than advice is intended. It is coercion, force; it is the effort of the many, by the mere weight of numbers, to compel the one to do their bidding. It is a proceeding outside of the law, in defiance of the law; and in spirit and effect an attempt to strip from one that has that which of right belongs to him — the full and undisturbed use and enjoyment of his own. It is not to be wondered at that deeds of violence and cruelty attend such demonstrations as these; nor will it do to pretend that the wrongdoers are not the striking laborers, but lawless strangers who gather to look on. . . .

In the state of Pennsylvania, only last year, to such an extent was this attempt of an organization to control both employee and employer carried that there is now pending in the courts of the state, upon the concurrent advice of all the justices of its Supreme Court, an inquiry as to whether this disturbance of social order did not amount to treason. And this is but one type of multitudes of cases all over the land. This is the struggle of irresponsible persons and organizations to control labor. It is not in the interest of liberty — it is not in the interest of individual or personal rights. It is the attempt to give to the many a control over the few — a step toward despotism. Let the movement succeed, let it once be known that the individual is not free to contract for his personal services, that labor is to be farmed out by organizations, as today by the Chinese companies, and the next step will be a direct effort on the part of the many to seize the property of the few.

The other form of this movement assumes the guise of a regulation of the charges for the use of property subjected, or supposed to be, to a public use. This acts in two directions: One by extending the list of those things, charges for whose use the government may prescribe; until now we hear it affirmed that, whenever property is devoted to a use in which the public has an interest, charges for that use may be fixed by law. And if there be any property in the use of which the public or some portion of it has no interest, I hardly know what it is or where to find it. And, second, in so reducing charges for the use of property, which in fact is subjected to a public use, that no compensation or income is received by those who have so invested their property. By the one it subjects all property and its uses to the will of the majority; by the other it robs property of its value. Statutes and decisions both disclose that this movement, with just these results, has a present and alarming existence. . . .

There are today $10 billion invested in railroad property, whose owners in this country number less than 2 million persons. Can it be that whether that immense sum shall earn a dollar, or bring the slightest recompense to those who have invested perhaps their all in that business, and are thus aiding in the development of the country, depends wholly upon the whim and greed of that great majority of 60 million who do not own a dollar? It may be said that that majority will not be so foolish, selfish, and cruel as to strip that property of its earning capacity. I say that so long as constitutional guarantees lift on American soil their buttresses and bulwarks against wrong, and so long as the American judiciary breathes the free air of courage, it cannot.

It must not be supposed that the forms in which this movement expresses itself are in themselves bad. Indeed, the great danger is in the fact that there is so much of good in them. If the livery of heaven were never stolen, and all human struggles were between obvious right and conceded wrong, the triumph of the former would be sure and speedy. Labor organizations are the needed and proper complement of capital organizations. They often work wholesome restraints on the greed, the unscrupulous rapacity which dominates much of capital; and the fact that they bring together a multitude of tiny forces, each helpless in a solitary struggle with capital, enables labor to secure its just rights.

So also, in regulating the charges of property which is appropriated to a public use, the public is but exercising a legitimate function, and one which is often necessary to prevent extortion in respect to public uses. Within limits of law and justice, labor organizations, and state regulation of charges for the use of property which is in fact devoted to public uses are commendable. But with respect to the proposition that the public may rightfully regulate the charges for the use of any property in whose use it has an interest, I am like the lawyer who, when declared guilty of contempt, responded promptly that he had shown no contempt, but on the contrary had carefully concealed his feelings.

Now conceding that there is this basis of wisdom and justice, and that within these limits the movement in both directions will work good to society, the question is how can its excesses, those excesses which mean peril to the nation, be stayed? Will the many who find in its progress temporary and apparent advantages so clearly discern the ultimate ruin which flows from injustice as voluntarily to desist; or must there be some force, some tribunal, outside, so far as possible, to lift the restraining hand? The answer is obvious.

Power always chafes at but needs restraint. This is true whether that power be in a single monarch or in a majority. All history attests the former. We are making that which proves the latter. The triple subdivision of governmental powers into legislative, executive, and judicial recognizes the truth, and has provided in this last coordinate department of government the restraining force. And the question which now arises is whether, in view of this exigency, the functions of the judiciary should be strengthened and enlarged, or weakened and restricted.

As might be expected, they who wish to push this movement to the extreme, who would brook no restraint on aught that seems to make for their gain, are unanimous in crying out against judicial interference, and are constantly seeking to minimize the power of the courts. Hence the demand for arbitrators to settle all disputes between employer and employees, for commissions to fix all tariffs for common carriers. The argument is that judges are not adapted by their education and training to settle such matters as these; that they lack acquaintance with affairs and are tied to precedents; that the procedure in the courts is too slow and that no action could be had therein until long after the need of action has passed. It would be folly to assert that this argument is barren of force. There are judges who never move a step beyond what has been; who would never adjudge the validity of the plan of salvation without a prior decision of the Master of the Rolls or the Queen's Bench in favor of the doctrine of vicarious sacrifice; and it is true that proceedings in the law courts do not anticipate the flight of time.

But the great body of judges are as well versed in the affairs of life as any; and they who unravel all the mysteries of accounting between partners, settle the business of the largest corporations and extract all the truth from the mass of scholastic verbiage that falls from the lips of expert witnesses in patent cases, will have no difficulty in determining what is right and wrong between employer and employees, and whether proposed rates of freight and fare are reasonable as between the public and the owners. While as for speed, is there anything quicker than a writ of injunction?

But the real objection lies deeper. Somehow or other men always link the idea of justice with that of judge. It matters not that an arbitrator or commissioner may perform the same function, there is not the same respect for the office nor the same feeling that justice only can be invoked to control the decision. The arbitrator and commission will be approached with freedom by many with suggestions that the public or the party, or certain interests, demand or will be profited by a decision in one way; but who thus comes near to the court or offers those suggestions to the judge? There is the tacit but universal feeling that justice, as he sees it, alone controls the decision.

It is a good thing that this is so; that in the common thought the idea of justice goes hand in hand with that of judge; and that when anything is to be wrought out which it is feared may not harmonize with eternal principles of right and wrong, the cry is for arbitration or commission, or something else whose name is not symbolical or suggestive. I would have it always kept so, and kept so by the very force of the work and life of him who is a judge. It is an Anglo-Saxon habit to pay respect to the judicial office; and it is also an Anglo-Saxon demand that he who holds that office shall so bear himself as to be worthy of respect.

So it is that the mischief makers in this movement ever strive to get away from courts and judges, and to place the power of decision in the hands of those who will the more readily and freely yield to the pressure of numbers, that so-called demand of the majority. But the common idea of justice is that the judge should be indifferent between the litigants — as free as possible from the influence of either; and no temporary arbitrator or political commission can ever equal in these respects the established courts and regular judges.

And so it is that because of the growth of this movement — of its development in many directions and the activity of those who are in it, and especially because of the further fact that, carrying votes in its hand, it ever appeals to the trimming politician and time-serving demagogue and thus en-

Library of Congress

David J. Brewer

ters into so much of legislation — arises the urgent need of giving to the judiciary the utmost vigor and efficiency. Now, if ever in the history of this country, must there be somewhere and somehow a controlling force which speaks for justice and for justice only. Let this movement sweep on with no restraining force. And it is the rule of all such movements that, unchecked, they grow in violence. . . .

What, then, ought to be done? My reply is, strengthen the judiciary. How? Permanent tenure of office accomplishes this. If a judge is to go out of office in a few months, the litigant will be more willing to disobey and take the chances of finally escaping punishment by delaying the proceedings until a new judge shall take the place — one whom his vote may select and from whom, therefore, he will expect slight if any punishment — while if the incumbent holds office for life, the duration of that life being uncertain, whether one or thirty years, no litigant wants to take the risk of disobedience with a strong probability that a punishment, though it may be delayed, will come and come with a severity equal to the wrong of the disobedience. . . . So if you would give the most force and effect to the decisions of your courts, you must give to the judges a permanent tenure of office.

Again, it will give greater independence of action. Judges are but human. If one must soon go before the people for reelection, how loath to rule squarely against public sentiment! There is no need of imputing conscious dishonesty; but the inevitable shrinking from antagonizing popular feeling or the wishes or interests of some prominent leader or leaders tends to delay or modify the due decision, while the judge who knows nothing can disturb his position does not hesitate promptly and clearly to "lay judgment to the line and righteousness to the plummet." "Let the jury determine," is the motto of one tribunal; "The court must decide," is the rule of the other. Cases at law and a jury are favored in the one; equity and its singleness of responsibility is the delight of the other.

Far be it from me to intimate aught against the character or ability of that larger number of elective judges in this country who secure continuation in office only through the well-earned confidence of the people. The bulk of my judicial life has been spent in such tribunals and under such experiences, and I know the worth and prize the friendship of these men. I am simply comparing system with system. It is a significant fact that some of the older states which have the elective system are lengthening the terms of judicial office. The judges of your highest court hold office for fourteen years, and in the sister state of Pennsylvania for twenty-one years. And this is almost equivalent to a life tenure, for it will be found that the term of office of a justice of the Supreme Court of the United States (taking all who have held that office, including the present incumbents) averages less than fifteen years.

It is said that the will of the people would often be delayed or thwarted, and that this is against the essential idea of government of and by the people. But for what are written constitutions? They exist, not simply to prescribe modes of action but because of the restraints and prohibitions they contain. Popular government may imply, generally speaking, that the present will of the majority should be carried into effect; but this is true in no absolute or arbitrary sense, and the limitations and checks which are found in all written constitutions are placed there to secure the rights of the minority.

Constitutions are generally, and ought always to be, formed in times free from excitement. They represent the deliberate judgment of the people as to the provisions and restraints which, firmly and fully enforced, will secure to each citizen the greatest liberty and utmost protection. They are rules prescribed by Philip sober to control Philip drunk. When difficulties arise, when the measures and laws framed by a majority are challenged as a violation of these rules and a trespass upon the rights of the minority, common justice demands that the tribunal to determine the question shall be as little under the influence of either as is possible.

Burke says:

> Society requires not only that the possessions of individuals should be subjected, but that even in the mass and body, as well as in the individuals, the inclinations of men should be thwarted, their wills controlled and their passions brought into subjection. This can only be done by a power out of themselves and not in the exercise of its functions subject to that will and those passions which it is his office to bridle and subdue. In this sense the restraints on men, as well as their liberties, are to be reckoned among their rights.

And surely, if the judges hold office by a life tenure and with a salary which cannot be disturbed, it would seem as though we had a tribunal as far removed from disturbing influences as possible. Though if I were to perfect the judiciary system I would add a provision that they should also be ineligible to political office and to that extent free from political ambition.

It may be said that this is practically substituting government by the judges for government by the people, and thus turning back the currents of history. The world has seen government by chiefs, by kings and emperors, by priests and by nobles. All have failed, and now government by the people is on trial. Shall we abandon that and try government by judges? But this involves a total misunderstanding of the relations of judges to government. There is nothing in this power of the judiciary detracting in the least from the idea of government of and by the people. The courts hold neither purse nor sword; they cannot corrupt nor arbitrarily control. They make no laws, they establish no policy, they never enter into the domain of popular action. They do not govern. Their functions in relation to the state are limited to seeing that popular action does not trespass upon right and justice as it exists in written constitutions and natural law.

So it is that the utmost power of the courts and judges works no interference with true liberty, no trespass on the fullest and highest development of government of and by the people; it only means security to personal rights — the inalienable rights, life, liberty, and the pursuit of happiness; it simply nails the Declaration of Independence, like Luther's theses against indulgences upon the doors of the Wittenberg church, of human rights and dares the anarchist, the socialist, and every other assassin of liberty to blot out a single word. . . .

Magnifying, like the apostle of old, my office, I am firmly persuaded that the salvation of the nation, the permanence of government of and by the people rests upon the independence and vigor of the judiciary. To stay the waves of popular feeling, to restrain the greedy hand of the many from filching from the few that which they have

honestly acquired, and to protect in every man's possession and enjoyment, be he rich or poor, that which he has, demands a tribunal as strong as is consistent with the freedom of human action and as free from all influences and suggestions other than is compassed in the thought of justice, as can be created out of the infirmities of human nature. To that end the courts exist, and for that let all the judges be put beyond the reach of political office and all fear of losing position or compensation during good behavior.

It may be that this is not popular doctrine today, and that the drift is found in such declarations as these — that the employee has a right to remain on his employer's property and be paid wages, whether the employer wishes him or no; that the rights of the one who uses are more sacred than of him who owns property; and that the Dartmouth College case, though once believed to be good in morals and sound in law, is today an anachronism and a political outrage. The black flag of anarchism, flaunting destruction to property, and therefore relapse of society to barbarism; the red flag of socialism, inviting a redistribution of property which, in order to secure the vaunted equality, must be repeated again and again at constantly decreasing intervals, and that colorless piece of baby cloth which suggests that the state take all property and direct all the life and work of individuals as if they were little children, may seem to fill the air with their flutter.

But as against these schemes, or any other plot or vagary of fiend, fool, or fanatic, the eager and earnest protest and cry of the Anglo-Saxon is for individual freedom and absolute protection of all his rights of person and property; and it is the cry which, reverberating over this country from ocean to ocean, thank God, will not go unheeded. That personal independence which is the lofty characteristic of our race will assert itself, and no matter what may stand in the way or who may oppose, or how much of temporary miscarriage or disappointment there may be, it will finally so assert itself in this land that no man or masses shall dare to say to a laborer he must or must not work, or for whom or for how much he shall toil; and that no honest possessor of property shall live in fear of the slightest trespass upon his possessions.

And to help and strengthen that good time, we shall yet see in every state an independent judiciary, made as independent of all outside influences as is possible, and to that end given a permanent tenure of office and an unchangeable salary; and above them that court, created by the fathers, supreme in fact as in name, holding all, individuals and masses, corporations and states — even the great nation itself — unswervingly true to the mandates of justice; that justice which is the silver sheen and the golden band in the jeweled diadem of Him to whom all nations bow and all worlds owe allegiance.

82.

James B. Thayer: The American Doctrine of Judicial Review

A major obstacle to reform efforts at the end of the nineteenth century was the conservatism of the courts. Jurists like Supreme Court Justice David J. Brewer maintained that the courts had a duty to protect private property, while reform leaders charged that the courts' interpretations were influenced by the judges' anti-progressive politics. In the course of this discussion Professor James Thayer of Harvard published what Felix Frankfurter later termed "the most important single essay" in American constitutional law: a clear and logical statement of the nature and limits of judicial power concluding that the courts' function was to fix "the outside border of reasonable legislative action." The essay is reprinted here in part.

Source: *Harvard Law Review*, October 25, 1893: "The Origin and Scope of the American Doctrine of Constitutional Law."

How did our American doctrine, which allows to the judiciary the power to declare legislative acts unconstitutional and to treat them as null, come about, and what is the true scope of it?

It is a singular fact that the state constitutions did not give this power to the judges in express terms; it was inferential. In the earliest of these instruments no language was used from which it was clearly to be made out. Only after the date of the federal Constitution was any such language to be found; as in Article XII of the Kentucky constitution of 1792. The existence of the power was at first denied or doubted in some quarters; and so late as the year 1825, in a strong dissenting opinion, Mr. Justice Gibson, of Pennsylvania, one of the ablest of American judges, and afterward the chief justice of that state, wholly denied it under any constitution which did not expressly give it. He denied it, therefore, under the state constitutions generally, while admitting that in that of the United States the power was given; namely, in the second clause of Article VI, when providing that the Constitution, and the laws and treaties made in pursuance thereof, "shall be the supreme law of the land; and the judges in every state shall be bound thereby, anything in the constitution or laws of any state to the contrary notwithstanding."

So far as the grounds for this remarkable power are found in the mere fact of a constitution being in writing, or in judges being sworn to support it, they are quite inadequate. Neither the written form nor the oath of the judges necessarily involves the right of reversing, displacing, or disregarding any action of the legislature or the executive which these departments are constitutionally authorized to take, or the determination of those departments that they are so authorized. . . .

It is plain that where a power so momentous as this primary authority to interpret is given, the actual determinations of the body to whom it is entrusted are entitled to a corresponding respect; and this not on mere grounds of courtesy or conventional respect but on very solid and significant grounds of policy and law. The judiciary may well reflect that if they had been regarded by the people as the chief protection against legislative violation of the Constitution, they would not have been allowed merely this incidental and postponed control. They would have been let in, as it was sometimes endeavored in the conventions to let them in, to a revision of the laws before they began to operate. As the opportunity of the judges to check and correct unconstitutional acts is so limited, it may help us to understand why the extent of their control, when they do have the opportunity, should also be narrow.

It was, then, all along true, and it was foreseen, that much which is harmful and unconstitutional may take effect without any capacity in the courts to prevent it, since their whole power is a judicial one. Their interference was but one of many safeguards, and its scope was narrow.

The rigor of this limitation upon judicial action is sometimes freely recognized, yet in a perverted way, which really operates to extend the judicial function beyond its just bounds. The court's duty, we are told, is the mere and simple office of construing two writings and comparing one with another, as two contracts or two statutes are construed and compared when they are said to conflict; of declaring the true meaning of each, and, if they are opposed to each other, of carrying into effect the Constitution as being of superior obligation — an ordinary and humble judicial duty, as the courts sometimes describe it. This way of putting it easily results in the wrong kind of disregard of legislative considerations; not merely in refusing to let them directly operate as grounds of judgment but in refusing to consider them at all.

Instead of taking them into account and allowing for them as furnishing possible grounds of legislative action, there takes place a pedantic and academic treatment of the texts of the Constitution and the laws. And so we miss that combination of a lawyer's rigor with a statesman's breadth of view which should be found in dealing with this class of questions in constitutional law. Of this petty method we have many specimens; they are found only too easily today in the volumes of our current reports.

In order, however, to avoid falling into these narrow and literal methods, in order to prevent the courts from forgetting, as Marshall said, that "it is a constitution we are expounding," these literal precepts about the nature of the judicial task have been accompanied by a rule of administration which has tended, in competent hands, to give matters a very different complexion.

Let us observe the course which the courts, in point of fact, have taken in administering this interesting jurisdiction.

They began by resting it upon the very simple ground that the legislature had only a delegated and limited authority under the constitutions; that these restraints, in order to be operative, must be regarded as so much law; and, as being law, that they must be interpreted and applied by the court. This was put as a mere matter of course. The reasoning was simple and narrow. . . .

The people, it was said, have established written limitations upon the legislature; these control all repugnant legislative acts; such acts are not law; this theory is essentially attached to a written constitution; it is for the judiciary to say what the law is, and if two rules conflict, to say which governs; the judiciary are to declare a legislative act void which conflicts with the constitution, or else that instrument is reduced to nothing. And then, it was added, in the federal instrument, this power is expressly given.

Nothing could be more rigorous than all this. As the matter was put, the conclusions were necessary. Much of this reasoning, however, took no notice of the remarkable peculiarities of the situation; it went forward as smoothly as if the Constitution were a private letter of attorney and the court's duty under it were precisely like any of its most ordinary operations. . . .

The courts have perceived with more or less distinctness that this exercise of the judicial function does in truth go far beyond the simple business which judges sometimes describe. If their duty were in truth merely and nakedly to ascertain the meaning of the text of the Constitution and of the impeached act of the legislature, and to determine, as an academic question, whether in the court's judgment the two were in conflict, it would, to be sure, be an elevated and important office, one dealing with great matters, involving large public consider-

ations, but yet a function far simpler than it really is.

Having ascertained all this, yet there remains a question — the really momentous question — whether, after all, the court can disregard the act. It cannot do this as a mere matter of course, merely because it concluded that upon a just and true construction the law is unconstitutional. That is precisely the significance of the rule of administration that the courts lay down. It can only disregard the act when those who have the right to make laws have not merely made a mistake but have made a very clear one — so clear that it is not open to rational question. That is the standard of duty to which the courts bring legislative acts; that is the test which they apply, not merely their own judgment as to constitutionality but their conclusion as to what judgment is permissible to another department which the Constitution has charged with the duty of making it.

This rule recognizes that, having regard to the great, complex, ever unfolding exigencies of government, much which will seem unconstitutional to one man, or body of men, may reasonably not seem so to another; that the Constitution often admits of different interpretations; that there is often a range of choice and judgment; that in such cases the Constitution does not impose upon the legislature any one specific opinion, but leaves open this range of choice; and that whatever choice is rational is constitutional. This is the principle which the rule that I have been illustrating affirms and supports.

The meaning and effect of it are shortly and very strikingly intimated by a remark of Judge Cooley, to the effect that one who is a member of a legislature may vote against a measure as being, in his judgment, unconstitutional; and, being subsequently placed on the bench, when this measure, having been passed by the legislature in spite of his opposition, comes before him judicially, may there find it his duty, although he has in no degree changed his opinion, to declare it constitutional.

Will anyone say, "You are overemphasizing this matter and making too much turn upon the form of a phrase"? No, I think not. I am aware of the danger of doing that. But whatever may be said of particular instances of unguarded or indecisive judicial language, it does not appear to me possible to explain the early, constant, and emphatic statements upon this subject on any slight ground. The form of it is in language too familiar to courts, having too definite a meaning, adopted with too general an agreement, and insisted upon quite too emphatically to allow us to think it a mere courteous and smoothly transmitted platitude. . . .

What really took place in adopting our theory of constitutional law was this: We introduced for the first time into the conduct of government through its great departments a judicial sanction, as among these departments — not full and complete, but partial. The judges were allowed, indirectly and in a degree, the power to revise the action of other departments and to pronounce it null. In simple truth, while this is a mere judicial function, it involves, owing to the subject matter with which it deals, taking a part, a secondary part, in the political conduct of government. If that be so, then the judges must apply methods and principles that befit their task.

In such a work there can be no permanent or fitting *modus vivendi* between the different departments unless each is sure of the full cooperation of the others, so long as its own action conforms to any reasonable and fairly permissible view of its constitutional power. The ultimate arbiter of what is rational and permissible is indeed always the courts, so far as litigated cases bring the question before them. This leaves to our courts a great and stately jurisdiction. It will only imperil the whole of it if it is sought

to give them more. They must not step into the shoes of the lawmaker. . . .

Finally, let me briefly mention one or two discriminations which are often overlooked, and which are important in order to a clear understanding of the matter. Judges sometimes have occasion to express an opinion upon the constitutionality of a statute, when the rule which we have been considering has no application, or a different application from the common one. There are at least three situations which should be distinguished: (1) where judges pass upon the validity of the acts of a coordinate department; (2) where they act as advisers of the other departments; (3) where, as representing a government of paramount authority, they deal with acts of a department which is not coordinate.

(1) The case of a court passing upon the validity of the act of a coordinate department is the normal situation to which the previous observations mainly apply. I need say no more about that.

(2) As regards the second case, the giving of advisory opinions; this, in reality, is not the exercise of the judicial function at all, and the opinions thus given have not the quality of judicial authority. A single exceptional and unsupported opinion upon this subject, in the state of Maine, made at a time of great political excitement, and a doctrine in the state of Colorado, founded upon considerations peculiar to the constitution of that state, do not call for any qualification of the general remark, that such opinions, given by our judges — like that well-known class of opinions given by the judges in England when advising the House of Lords, which suggested our own practice — are merely advisory and in no sense authoritative judgments. Under our constitutions such opinions are not generally given. In the six or seven states where the constitutions provide for them, it is the practice to report these opinions among the regular decisions, much as the responses of the

judges in Queen Caroline's Case, and in MacNaghten's Case, in England, are reported, and sometimes cited, as if they held equal rank with true adjudications. As regards such opinions, the scruples, cautions, and warnings of which I have been speaking, and the rule about a reasonable doubt, which we have seen emphasized by the courts as regards judicial decisions upon the constitutionality of laws, have no application. What is asked for is the judge's own opinion.

(3) Under the third head come the questions arising out of the existence of our double system, with two written constitutions, and two governments, one of which, within its sphere, is of higher authority than the other. The relation to the states of the paramount government as a whole, and its duty in all questions involving the powers of the general government to maintain that power as against the states in its fullness, seem to fix also the duty of each of its departments; namely, that of maintaining this paramount authority in its true and just proportions, to be determined by itself.

If a state legislature passes a law, which is impeached in the due course of litigation before the national courts, as being in conflict with the supreme law of the land, those courts may have to ask themselves a question different from that which would be applicable if the enactments were those of a coordinate department. When the question relates to what is admitted not to belong to the national power, then whoever construes a state constitution, whether the state or national judiciary, must allow to that legislature the full range of rational construction. But when the question is whether state action be or be not conformable to the paramount Constitution, the supreme law of the land, we have a different matter in hand.

Fundamentally, it involves the allotment of power between the two governments —

where the line is to be drawn. True, the judiciary is still debating whether a legislature has transgressed its limit; but the departments are not coordinate, and the limit is at a different point. The judiciary now speaks as representing a paramount Constitution and government, whose duty it is, in all its departments, to allow to that Constitution nothing less than its just and true interpretation; and having fixed this, to guard it against any inroads from without.

I have been speaking of the national judiciary. As to how the state judiciary should treat a question of the conformity of an act of their own legislature to the paramount Constitution, it has been plausibly said that they should be governed by the same rule that the federal courts would apply. Since an appeal lies to the federal courts, these two tribunals, it has been said, should proceed on the same rule, as being parts of one system. But under the Judiciary Act an appeal does not lie from every decision; it only lies when the state law is *sustained* below. It would perhaps be sound on general principles, even if an appeal were allowed in all cases, here also to adhere to the general rule that judges should follow any permissible view which the coordinate legislature has adopted. At any rate, under existing legislation, it seems proper in the state court to do this, for the practical reason that this is necessary in order to preserve the right of appeal.

The view which has thus been presented seems to me highly important. I am not stating a new doctrine, but attempting to restate more exactly and truly an admitted one. If what I have said be sound, it is greatly to be desired that it should be more emphasized by our courts, in its full significance. It has been often remarked that private rights are more respected by the legislatures of some countries which have no written constitution than by ours. No doubt our doctrine of constitutional law has had a tendency to drive out questions of justice and right and to fill the mind of legislators with thoughts of mere legality of what the Constitution allows. And moreover, even in the matter of legality, they have felt little responsibility; if we are wrong, they say, the courts will correct it. If what I have been saying is true, the safe and permanent road toward reform is that of impressing upon our people a far stronger sense than they have of the great range of possible harm and evil that our system leaves open, and must leave open, to the legislatures and

of the clear limits of judicial power; so that responsibility may be brought sharply home where it belongs.

The checking and cutting down of legislative power, by numerous detailed prohibitions in the Constitution, cannot be accomplished without making the government petty and incompetent. This process has already been carried much too far in some of our states. Under no system can the power of courts go far to save a people from ruin; our chief protection lies elsewhere. If this be true, it is of the greatest public importance to put the matter in its true light.

83.

Edward C. Billings: Labor and the Antitrust Laws

The Sherman Antitrust Law of 1890 forbade "every contract, combination in the form of trust or otherwise, or conspiracy, in restraint of trade or commerce among the several States, or with foreign nations. . . ." The Act did not indicate, however, whether labor unions were to be subject to its terms. The question came before the courts in the case of United States v. Workingmen's Amalgamated Council of New Orleans et al. *A portion of Judge Billings' decision is reprinted here.*

Source: 54 Fed. 994.

District Judge Billings. This cause is submitted upon an application for an injunction on the bill of complaint, answer, and numerous affidavits and exhibits. The bill of complaint in this case is filed by the United States under the act of Congress entitled "An act to protect trade and commerce against unlawful restraint and monopolies." . . . The substance of the bill is that there is a gigantic and widespread combination of the members of a multitude of separate organizations for the purpose of restraining the commerce among the several states and with foreign countries.

It avers that a disagreement between the warehousemen and their employes and the principal draymen and their subordinates had been adopted by all the organizations named in the bill, until, by this vast combination of men and of organizations, it was threatened that, unless there was an acquiescence in the demands of the subordinate workmen and draymen, all the men in all of the defendant organizations would leave work and would allow no work in any department of business; that violence was threatened and used in support of this demand; and that this demand included the interstate and foreign commerce which flows through the city of New Orleans. The bill further states that the proceedings on the part of the defendants had taken such a vast and ramified proportion that, in consequence of the threats of the defendants, the whole business of the city of New Orleans was paralyzed, and the transit of goods and merchandise which was being conveyed through it from state to state, and to and from foreign countries, was totally interrupted. . . .

The defendants urge . . . that, the strike or cessation of labor being ended and labor resumed throughout all branches of business, there is no need for an injunction. I know of no rule which is better settled than that the question as to the maintenance of a bill and the granting of relief to a complainant is to be determined by the status existing at the time of filing the bill. Rights do not ebb and flow. If they are invaded and recourse to courts of justice is rendered necessary, it is no defense to the invasion of a right, either admitted or proved, that since the institution of the suit the invasion has ceased. With emphasis would this be true where, as here, the right to invade is not disclaimed. The question, then, is what was the state of facts at the time of and prior to the filing of the bill; or whether, if the facts alleged in the bill were true at that time, there was need of an injunction.

The defendants urge . . . that the right of the complainants depends upon an unsettled question of law. The theory of the defense is that this case does not fall within the purview of the statute; that the statute prohibited monopolies and combinations which, using words in a general sense, were of capitalists and not of laborers. I think the congressional debates show that the statute had its origin in the evils of massed capital;

but, when the Congress came to formulating the prohibition which is the yardstick for measuring the complainant's right to the injunction, it expressed it in these words: "Every contract or combination in the form of trust, or otherwise in restraint of trade or commerce among the several states or with foreign nations, is hereby declared to be illegal."

The subject had so broadened in the minds of the legislators that the source of the evil was not regarded as material, and the evil in its entirety is dealt with. They made the interdiction include combinations of labor as well as of capital; in fact, all combinations in restraint of commerce, without reference to the character of the persons who entered into them. It is true this statute has not been much expounded by judges, but, as it seems to me, its meaning, as far as relates to the sort of combinations to which it is to apply, is manifest and that it includes combinations which are composed of laborers acting in the interest of laborers. . . .

The defendants urge . . . that the corporations of the various labor associations made defendants are in their origin and purposes innocent and lawful. I believe this to be true. But associations of men, like individuals, no matter how worthy their general character may be, when charged with unlawful combinations and when the charge is fully established, cannot escape liability on the ground of their commendable general character. In determining the question of sufficiency of proof of an accusation of unlawful intent, worth in the accused is to be weighed; but when the proof of the charge is sufficient — overwhelmingly sufficient — the original purpose of an association has ceased to be available as a ground of defense.

The defendants urge . . . that the combination to secure or compel the employment of none but union men is not in the restraint of commerce. To determine whether the proposition urged as a defense can apply to this case, the case must first be stated as it is made out by the established facts. The case is this: The combination setting out to secure and compel the employment of none but union men in a given business as a means to effect this compulsion finally enforced a discontinuance of labor in all kinds of business, including the business of transportation of goods and merchandise which were in transit through the city of New Orleans, from state to state, and to and from foreign countries. When the case is thus stated — and it must be so stated to embody the facts here proven — I do not think there can be any question but that the combination of the defendants was in restraint of commerce.

I have thus endeavored to state and deal with the various grounds of defense urged before me. I shall now, as briefly as possible, state the case as it is established in the voluminous record.

A difference had sprung up between the warehousemen and their employes and the principal draymen and their subordinates. With the view and purpose to compel an acquiescence on the part of the employers in the demands of the employed, it was finally brought about by the employed that all the union men — that is, all the members of the various labor associations — were made by their officers, clothed with authority under the various charters, to discontinue business, and one of these kinds of business was transporting goods which were being conveyed from state to state, and to and from foreign countries. In some branches of business the effort was made to replace the union men by other workmen.

This was resisted by the intimidation springing from vast throngs of the union men assembling in the streets, and in some instances by violence; so that the result was that, by the intended effects of the doings of these defendants, not a bale of goods constituting the commerce of the country could be moved.

The question simply is: Do these facts establish a case within the statute? It seems to me this question is tantamount to the question: Could there be a case under the statute? It is conceded that the labor organizations were at the outset lawful. But, when lawful forces are put into unlawful channels — i.e., when lawful associations adopt and further unlawful purposes and do unlawful acts — the associations themselves become unlawful. The evil, as well as the unlawfulness, of the act of the defendants consists in this: that, until certain demands of theirs were complied with, they endeavored to prevent, and did prevent, everybody from moving the commerce of the country. . . .

It is the successful effort of the combination of the defendants to intimidate and overawe others who were at work in conducting or carrying on the commerce of the country in which the court finds their error and their violation of the statute. One of the intended results of their combined action was the forced stagnation of all the commerce which flowed through New Orleans. This intent and combined action are none the less unlawful because they included in their scope the paralysis of all other business within the city as well.

For these reasons I think the injunction should issue.

84.

JOHN PETER ALTGELD: Reasons for Pardoning the Haymarket Rioters

The Haymarket meeting of May 4, 1886, called to protest the deaths of six men in the previous day's fight at the McCormick Harvesting Machine Company, turned into a riot when a bomb was thrown into the crowd massed in Chicago's Haymarket Square, killing seven police and throwing most of Chicago into near hysteria. Eight men — all anarchists — were arrested, tried before Judge Joseph E. Gary, and convicted of the murder of one of the policemen although no evidence connected them with the bombing. The Illinois and United States Supreme Courts affirmed the convictions, which sentenced seven of the men to death and one to prison. In 1887 Governor Richard J. Oglesby commuted two of the death sentences to life imprisonment, four of the men were hanged, and one committed suicide. A new petition for clemency for the remaining three was presented to Governor Altgeld in 1893. The governor granted executive pardons — at the cost of his own political future — and issued the following explanation.

Source: *The Chicago Martyrs,* San Francisco, 1899, pp. 131-159.

ON THE NIGHT OF MAY 4, 1886, a public meeting was held on Haymarket Square in Chicago; there were from 800 to 1,000 people present, nearly all being laboring men. There had been trouble, growing out of the effort to introduce an eight-hour day, resulting in some collisions with the police, in one of which several laboring people were killed, and this meeting was called as a protest against alleged police brutality.

The meeting was orderly and was attended by the mayor, who remained until the crowd began to disperse and then went away. As soon as Capt. John Bonfield of the Police Department learned that the mayor had gone, he took a detachment of police and hurried to the meeting for the purpose of dispersing the few that remained, and, as the police approached the place of meeting, a bomb was thrown by some unknown person, which exploded and wounded many and killed several police-

men, among the latter being one Mathias Degan.

A number of people were arrested, and, after a time, August Spies, Albert R. Parsons, Louis Lingg, Michael Schwab, Samuel Fielden, George Engel, Adolph Fischer, and Oscar Neebe were indicted for the murder of Mathias Degan. The prosecution could not discover who had thrown the bomb and could not bring the really guilty man to justice; and, as some of the men indicted were not at the Haymarket meeting and had nothing to do with it, the prosecution was forced to proceed on the theory that the men indicted were guilty of murder because it was claimed they had at various times in the past uttered and printed incendiary and seditious language, practically advising the killing of policemen, of Pinkerton men, and others acting in that capacity, and that they were therefore responsible for the murder of Mathias Degan.

The public was greatly excited, and after a prolonged trial all the defendants were found guilty; Oscar Neebe was sentenced to fifteen years imprisonment and all of the other defendants were sentenced to be hanged. The case was carried to the Supreme Court and was there affirmed in the fall of 1887. Soon thereafter Lingg committed suicide. The sentence of Fielden and Schwab was commuted to imprisonment for life, and Parsons, Fischer, Engel, and Spies were hanged, and the petitioners now ask to have Neebe, Fielden, and Schwab set at liberty.

The several thousand merchants, bankers, judges, lawyers, and other prominent citizens of Chicago who have by petition, by letter, and in other ways urged executive clemency mostly base their appeal on the ground that, assuming the prisoners to be guilty, they have been punished enough; but a number of them who have examined the case more carefully and are more familiar with the record and with the facts disclosed by the papers on file base their appeal on entirely different grounds. They assert:

First, that the jury which tried the case was a packed jury selected to convict.

Second, that according to the law as laid down by the Supreme Court, both prior to and again since the trial of this case, the jurors, according to their own answer, were not competent jurors, and the trial was, therefore, not a legal trial.

Third, that the defendants were not proven to be guilty of the crime charged in the indictment.

Fourth, that, as to the defendant Neebe, the state's attorney had declared at the close of the evidence that there was no case against him, and yet he has been kept in prison all these years.

Fifth, that the trial judge was either so prejudiced against the defendants or else so determined to win the applause of a certain class in the community that he could not and did not grant a fair trial.

Upon the question of having been punished enough, I will simply say that if the defendants had a fair trial, and nothing has developed since to show that they were not guilty of the crime charged in the indictment, then there ought to be no executive interference, for no punishment under our laws could then be too severe. Government must defend itself; life and property must be protected, and law and order must be maintained; murder must be punished, and if the defendants are guilty of murder, either committed by their own hands or by someone else acting on their advice, then, if they have had a fair trial, there should be in this case no executive interference. The soil of America is not adapted to the growth of anarchy. While our institutions are not free from injustice, they are still the best that have yet been devised, and therefore must be maintained.

The record of the trial shows that the jury in this case was not drawn in the manner that juries usually are drawn; that is, instead of having a number of names drawn out of a box that contained many hundred names, as the law contemplates shall be done in order to insure a fair jury and give neither side the advantage, the trial judge appointed one Henry L. Ryce as a special bailiff to go out and summon such men as he (Ryce) might select to act as jurors. While this practice has been sustained in cases in which it did not appear that either side had been prejudiced thereby, it is always a dangerous practice, for it gives the bailiff absolute power to select a jury that will be favorable to one side or the other.

Counsel for the state, in their printed brief, say that Ryce was appointed on motion of defendants. While it appears that counsel for the defendants were in favor of having someone appointed, the record has this entry: "Mr. Grinnell (the state's attorney) suggested Mr. Ryce as special bailiff, and he was accepted and appointed." But it makes no difference on whose motion he was appointed if he did not select a fair jury. It is shown that he boasted while selecting jurors that he was managing this case; that these fellows would hang as certain as death; that he was calling such men as the defendants would have to challenge peremptorily and waste their challenges on, and that when their challenges were exhausted they would have to take such men as the prosecution wanted.

It appears from the record of the trial that the defendants were obliged to exhaust all of their peremptory challenges, and they had to take a jury, almost every member of which stated frankly that he was prejudiced against them. On page 133 of Volume I of the record, it appears that when the panel was about two-thirds full, counsel for defendants called attention of the court to the fact that Ryce was summoning only prejudiced men, as shown by their examinations. Further, that he was confining himself to particular classes, i.e., clerks, merchants, manufacturers, etc. Counsel for defendants then moved the court to stop this and direct Ryce to summon the jurors from the body of the people; that is, from the community at large and not from particular classes; but the court refused to take any notice of the matter.

For the purpose of still further showing the misconduct of Bailiff Ryce, reference is made to the affidavit of Otis S. Favor. Mr. Favor is one of the most reputable and honorable businessmen in Chicago; he was himself summoned by Ryce as a juror but was so prejudiced against the defendants that he had to be excused, and he abstained from making any affidavit before sentence because the state's attorney had requested him not to make it, although he stood ready to go into court and tell what he knew if the court wished him to do so, and he naturally supposed he would be sent for. But after the Supreme Court had passed on the case and some of the defendants were about to be hanged, he felt that an injustice was being done, and he made the following affidavit.

Otis S. Favor, being duly sworn, on oath says that he is a citizen of the United States and of the State of Illinois, residing in Chicago, and a merchant doing business at Numbers 6 and 8 Wabash Avenue, in the city of Chicago, in said county. That he is very well acquainted with Henry L. Ryce, of Cook County, Illinois, who acted as special bailiff in summoning jurors in the case of *The People, etc.* v. *Spies et al.,* indictment for murder, tried in the Criminal Court of Cook County, in the summer of 1886. That affiant was himself summoned by said Ryce for a juror in said cause but was challenged and excused therein because of his prejudice. That on several occasions in conversation between affiant and said Ryce touching the summoning of the jurors by said Ryce, and while said Ryce was so acting as special bailiff as aforesaid, said Ryce said to this affiant and to other persons in affiant's presence, in substance and effect as follows, to wit:

"I (meaning said Ryce) am managing this case (meaning this case against *Spies et al.*) and know what I am about. Those fellows (meaning the defendants, *Spies et al.*) are going to be hanged as certain as death. I am calling such men as the defendants will have to challenge peremptorily and waste their time and challenges. Then they will have to take such men as the prosecution wants."

That affiant has been very reluctant to make any affidavit in this case, having no sympathy with anarchy nor relationship to or personal interest in the defendants or any of them, and not being a Socialist, Communist, or anarchist; but affiant has an interest as a citizen in the due administration of the law, and that no injustice should be done under judicial procedure, and believes that jurors should not be selected with reference to their known views or prejudices. Affiant further says that his personal relations with said Ryce were at said time and for many years theretofore had been most friendly and even intimate, and that affiant is not prompted by any ill will toward anyone in making this affidavit, but solely by a sense of duty and a conviction of what is due to justice.

Affiant further says that about the beginning of October 1886, when the motion for a new trial was being argued in said cases before Judge Gary, and when, as he was informed, application was made before Judge Gary for leave to examine affiant in open court touching the matters above stated, this affiant went, upon request of State's Attorney Grinnell, to his office during the noon recess of the court and there held an interview with said Grinnell, Mr. Ingham, and said Ryce, in the presence of several other persons, including some police officers, where affiant repeated substantially the matters above stated, and the said Ryce did not deny affiant's statements, and affiant said he would have to testify thereto if summoned as a witness but had refused to make an affidavit thereto, and affiant was then and there asked and urged to persist in his refusal and to make no affidavit. And affiant further saith not. . . .

So far as shown, no one connected with the state's attorney's office has ever denied the statements of Mr. Favor as to what took place in that office, although his affidavit was made in November 1887.

As to Bailiff Ryce, it appears that he has made an affidavit in which he denies that he made the statements sworn to by Mr. Favor, but, unfortunately for him, the record of the trial is against him, for it shows conclusively that he summoned only the class of men mentioned in Mr. Favor's affidavit. According to the record, 981 men were examined as to their qualifications as jurors, and most of them were either employers or men who had been pointed out to the bailiff by their employer. . . .

Again, it is shown that various attempts were made to bring to justice the men who wore the uniform of the law while violating it, but all to no avail; that the laboring people found the prisons always open to receive them but the courts of justice were practically closed to them; that the prosecuting officers vied with each other in hunting them down but were deaf to their appeals; that in the spring of 1886 there were more labor disturbances in the city, and particularly at the McCormick factory; that under the leadership of Captain Bonfield

the brutalities of the previous year were even exceeded. Some affidavit and other evidence is offered on this point which I cannot give for want of space.

It appears that this was the year of the eight-hour agitation, and efforts were made to secure an eight-hour day about May 1, and that a number of laboring men, standing not on the street but on a vacant lot, were quietly discussing the situation in regard to the movement, when suddenly a large body of police, under orders from Bonfield, charged on them and began to club them; that some of the men, angered at the unprovoked assault, at first resisted but were soon dispersed; that some of the police fired on the men while they were running and wounded a large number who were already 100 feet or more away and were running as fast as they could; that at least four of the number so shot down died; that this was wanton and unprovoked murder, but there was not even so much as an investigation.

While some men may tamely submit to being clubbed and seeing their brothers shot down, there are some who will resent it and will nurture a spirit of hatred and seek revenge for themselves, and the occurrences that preceded the Haymarket tragedy indicate that the bomb was thrown by someone who, instead of acting on the advice of anybody, was simply seeking personal revenge for having been clubbed, and that Captain Bonfield is the man who is really responsible for the death of the police officers. . . .

It is further shown here that much of the evidence given at the trial was a pure fabrication; that some of the prominent police officials, in their zeal, not only terrorized ignorant men by throwing them into prison and threatening them with torture if they refused to swear to anything desired but that they offered money and employment to those who would consent to do this. Further, that they deliberately planned to have fictitious conspiracies formed in order that they might get the glory of discovering them. In addition to the evidence in the record of some witnesses who swore that they had been paid small sums of money, etc., several documents are here referred to.

First, an interview with Captain Ebersold, published in the *Chicago Daily News,* May 10, 1889. Ebersold was chief of the police of Chicago at the time of the Haymarket trouble, and for a long time before and thereafter, so that he was in a position to know what was going on, and his utterances upon this point are therefore important. Among other things he says:

> It was my policy to quiet matters down as soon as possible after the 4th of May. The general unsettled state of things was an injury to Chicago. On the other hand, Captain Schaack wanted to keep things stirring. He wanted bombs to be found here, there, all around, everywhere. I thought people would lie down and sleep better if they were not afraid that their homes would be blown to pieces any minute. But this man Schaack, this little boy who must have glory or his heart would be broken, wanted none of that policy.
>
> Now, here is something the public does not know. After we got the anarchist societies broken up, Schaack wanted to send out men to again organize new societies right away. You see what this would do. He wanted to keep the thing boiling — keep himself prominent before the public. Well, I sat down on that; I didn't believe in such work, and of course Schaack didn't like it.
>
> After I heard all that, I began to think there was, perhaps, not so much to all this anarchist business as they claimed, and I believe I was right. Schaack thinks he knew all about those anarchists. Why, I knew more at that time than he knows today about them. I was following them closely. As soon as Schaack began to get some notoriety, however, he was spoiled.

This is a most important statement, when a chief of police, who has been watching the anarchists closely, says that he was convinced that there was not so much in all their anarchist business as was claimed, and that a police captain wanted to send out

men to have other conspiracies formed in order to get the credit of discovering them and keep the public excited; it throws a flood of light on the whole situation and destroys the force of much of the testimony introduced at the trial; for, if there has been any such extensive conspiracy as the prosecution claims, the police would have soon discovered it.

No chief of police could discover a determination on the part of an individual, or even a number of separate individuals, to have personal revenge for having been maltreated, nor could any chief discover a determination by any such individual to kill the next policeman who might assault him. Consequently, the fact the the police did not discover any conspiracy before the Haymarket affair shows almost conclusively that no such extensive combination could have existed. . . .

At the conclusion of the evidence for the state, the Hon. Carter H. Harrison, then mayor of Chicago, and F. S. Winston, then corporation counsel for Chicago, were in the courtroom and had a conversation with Mr. Grinnell, the state's attorney, in regard to the evidence against Neebe, in which conversation, according to Mr. Harrison and Mr. Winston, the state's attorney said that he did not think he had a case against Neebe and that he wanted to dismiss him but was dissuaded from doing so by his associate attorneys, who feared that such a step might influence the jury in favor of the other defendants.

Mr. Harrison, in a letter, among other things said:

> I was present in the courtroom when the state closed its case. The attorney for Neebe moved his discharge on the ground that there was no evidence to hold him on. The state's attorney, Mr. Julius S. Grinnell, and Mr. Fred S. Winston, corporation counsel for the city, and myself, were in earnest conversation when the motion was made. Mr. Grinnell stated to us that he did not think

there was sufficient testimony to convict Neebe. I thereupon earnestly advised him, as the representative of the state, to dismiss the case as to Neebe, and, if I remember rightly, he was seriously thinking of doing so, but, on consultation with his assistants, and on their advice, he determined not to do so lest it would have an injurious effect on the case as against the other prisoners. . . . I took the position that such discharge, being clearly justified by the testimony, would not prejudice the case as to the others.

Mr. Winston adds the following to Mr. Harrison's letter:

March 21, 1889

I concur in the statement of Mr. Harrison; I never believed there was sufficient evidence to convict Mr. Neebe, and so stated during the trial.

F. S. WINSTON

In January 1890, Mr. Grinnell wrote a letter to Governor Fifer, denying that he had ever made any such statement as that mentioned by Mr. Harrison and Mr. Winston; also that he did believe Neebe guilty; that Mr. Harrison suggested the dismissal of the case as to Neebe; and, further, that he would not have been surprised if Mr. Harrison had made a similar suggestion as to others. And then he says: "I said to Mr. Harrison at that time, substantially, that I was afraid that the jury might not think the testimony presented in the case sufficient to convict Neebe, but that it was in their province to pass upon it."

Now, if the statement of Messrs. Harrison and Winston is true, then Grinnell should not have allowed Neebe to be sent to the penitentiary, and even if we assume that both Mr. Harrison and Mr. Winston are mistaken, and that Mr. Grinnell simply used the language he now says he used, then the case must have seemed very weak to him. If, with a jury prejudiced to start with, a judge pressing for conviction, and amid the almost irresistible fury with which the trial was conducted, he still was afraid

the jury might not think the testimony in the case was sufficient to convict Neebe, then the testimony must have seemed very weak to him, no matter what he may now protest about it.

When the motion to dismiss the case as to Neebe was made, defendants' counsel asked that the jury might be permitted to retire while the motion was being argued, but the court refused to permit this and kept the jury present where it could hear all that the court had to say; then, when the argument on the motion was begun by defendants' counsel, the court did not wait to hear from the attorneys for the state but at once proceeded to argue the points itself with the attorneys for the defendants, so that while the attorneys for the state made no argument on the motion, twenty-five pages of the record are filled with the colloquy or sparring that took place between the court and the counsel for the defendants, the court in the presence of the jury making insinuations as to what inference might be drawn by the jury from the fact that Neebe owned a little stock in a paper called the *Arbeiter-Zeitung* and had been seen there, although he took no part in the management until after the Haymarket troubles, it appearing that the *Arbeiter-Zeitung* had published some very seditious articles, with which, however, Neebe had nothing to do.

Finally, one of the counsel for the defendants said: "I expected that the representatives of the state might say something, but as Your Honor saves them that trouble, you will excuse me if I reply briefly to the suggestions you have made." Some other remarks were made by the court, seriously affecting the whole case and prejudicial to the defendants, and then, referring to Neebe, the court said: "Whether he had anything to do with the dissemination of advice to commit murder is, I think, a debatable question which the jury ought to pass on." Finally the motion was overruled.

Now, with all the eagerness shown by

the court to convict Neebe, it must have regarded the evidence against him as very weak, otherwise it would not have made this admission, for if it was a del 'le question whether the evidence tended to show guilt, then that evidence must have been far from being conclusive upon the question as to whether he was actually guilty; this being so, the verdict should not have been allowed to stand, because the law requires that a man shall be proven to be guilty beyond a reasonable doubt before he can be convicted of criminal offense. I have examined all of the evidence against Neebe with care, and it utterly fails to prove even the shadow of a case against him. Some of the other defendants were guilty of using seditious language, but even this cannot be said of Neebe.

It is further charged, with much bitterness, by those who speak for the prisoners, that the record of this case shows that the judge conducted the trial with malicious ferocity and forced eight men to be tried together; that in cross-examining the state's witnesses, he confined counsel to the specific points touched on by the state, while in the cross-examination of the defendants' witnesses, he permitted the state's attorney to go into all manner of subjects entirely foreign to the matters on which the witnesses were examined in chief; also, that every ruling throughout the long trial on any contested point was in favor of the state; and, further, that page after page of the record contains insinuating remarks of the judge, made in the hearing of the jury, and with the evident intent of bringing the jury to his way of thinking; that these speeches, coming from the court, were much more damaging than any speeches from the state's attorney could possibly have been; that the state's attorney often took his cue from the judge's remarks; that the judge's magazine article recently published, although written nearly six years after the trial, is yet full of venom; that, pretending to simply review the case, he had to drag into his article a letter written by an excited woman to a newspaper after the trial was over, and which therefore had nothing to do with the case, and was put into the article simply to create a prejudice against the woman, as well as against the dead and the living; and that, not content with this, he, in the same article, makes an insinuating attack on one of the lawyers for the defense, not for anything done at the trial but because more than a year after the trial, when some of the defendants had been hung, he ventured to express a few kind, if erroneous, sentiments over the graves of his dead clients, whom he at least believed to be innocent. It is urged that such ferocity of subserviency is without a parallel in all history; that even Jeffreys in England contented himself with hanging his victims and did not stoop to berate them after death.

These charges are of a personal character, and, while they seem to be sustained by the record of the trial and the papers before me and tend to show the trial was not fair, I do not care to discuss this feature of the case any further because it is not necessary. I am convinced that it is clearly my duty to act in this case for the reasons already given; and I, therefore, grant an absolute pardon to Samuel Fielden, Oscar Neebe, and Michael Schwab, this 26th day of June, 1893.

85.

John Peter Altgeld: The Choice Before Labor — Organization or Annihilation

John Peter Altgeld, the "eagle forgotten" of Vachel Lindsay's impassioned memorial poem, was the first Democratic governor of Illinois after the Civil War. His enlightened efforts on behalf of the surviving anarchists of the Haymarket Riot, along with his opposition to the use of federal troops in the Pullman Strike of 1894, subjected him to public abuse that terminated his public life. An active reformer as well as a jurist, Altgeld in an 1884 publication, Our Penal Machinery and Its Victims, *had stated his belief that the poor did not receive a fair chance in American life, and he favored the activities of labor unions in behalf of workingmen. The following address at an 1893 Labor Day observance in Chicago was delivered during the worst depression of the nineteenth century.*

Source: *Live Questions*, Chicago, 1899, pp. 340-347: "Address to the Laboring Order of Chicago."

YOU ARE TO BE CONGRATULATED on the success of your celebration. Two great demonstrations in Chicago alone are vying with each other in honoring Labor Day. These vast assemblages represent sturdy manhood and womanhood. They represent honest toil of every kind, and they represent strong patriotism and desirable citizenship. The law has set apart this day in recognition of the nobility of labor, and, as the governor of this great state, I have come to pay homage to that force which lays the foundation of empires, which builds cities, builds railroads, develops agriculture, supports schools, founds industries, creates commerce, and moves the world.

It is wisely directed labor that has made our country the greatest ever known and has made Chicago the wonder of mankind. I say wisely directed labor, for without wise direction labor is fruitless. The pointing out and the doing are inseparably connected. More than this, ahead of the directing, there must go the genius which originates and conceives, the genius which takes the risk and moves a league forward. All three are necessary to each other. Weaken either, and there are clouds in the sky. Destroy either, and the hammer of industry ceases to be heard.

Glance over this majestic city, see its workshops, its warehouses, its commercial palaces, its office temples, and the thousand other structures that show the possibilities of human achievement and tell who did all this. You say the laboring men; yes, that is correct. But I tell you that if the gods keep a record of our doings, they have set down the men who originated all this, and then dared to make a forward step in building, as among the greatest of laborers.

We are at present in the midst of a great industrial and commercial depression. Industry is nearly at a standstill all over the earth. The consumptive power, or rather the purchasing power, of the world has been interfered with, producing not only a derangement but a paralysis, not only stopping further production but preventing the proper distribution of what there is already created; so that we have the anomalous spectacle of abundant food products, on the one hand, and hungry men without bread, on the other; abundant fabrics, on the one hand, and industrious, frugal men going half-clad, on the other. Employer and employee are affected alike.

There are thousands of honest, industrious, and frugal men who walk the streets all day in search of work, and even bread, and there are many hundreds of the most enterprising employers who sweat by day and walk the floor by night trying to devise means to keep the sheriff away from the establishment. You are not responsible for this condition. Men here and in Europe who call themselves statesmen have inaugurated policies of which this is a natural result. Considering the increase in population, the increase in the industries and commercial activity of the world, as well as the increased area over which business was done, there has in recent years been a practical reduction in the volume of the money of the world of from 33 to 40 percent, and there had of necessity to follow a shrinkage in the value of property to a corresponding extent.

This has been going on for a number of years, and as it has progressed it has become harder and harder for the debtor to meet his obligations; for the value of his property kept falling while his debt did not fall. Consequently, every little while, a lot of debtors who could no longer stand the strain succumbed. The result was that each time there was a flurry in financial circles. By degrees these failures became more frequent, until, finally, people who had money took alarm and withdrew it from circulation. This precipitated a panic and with it a harvest of bankruptcy. No doubt there were secondary causes that contributed, but this one cause was sufficient to create the distress that we see.

If for some years to come there should not be sufficient blood in the industrial and commercial world to make affairs healthy, then you must console yourselves with the thought that our country, with all the other great nations, has been placed on a narrow gold basis, and you will not be troubled with any of these cheap dollars that the big newspapers claim you did not want. The present depression, resulting from a lack of ready money in the world, shows how indispensable capital is to labor — all the wheels of industry stand still the moment it is withdrawn. It also shows that, while the interests of the employer and the employee may be antagonistic on the subject of wages, they are the same in every other respect; neither can do anything without the other — certain it is that the employee cannot prosper unless the employer does. On the other hand, if the purchasing power of the employee is destroyed, the employer must soon be without a market for his goods.

The great American market was due to the purchasing power of the laboring classes. If this should in the end be destroyed, it will change entirely the character of our institutions. Whenever our laboring classes are reduced to a condition where they can buy only a few coarse articles of food and clothing, then our glory will have departed.

Still another thing has been made more clear than before, and that is that the employers, as a rule, are not great capitalists of the country. As a rule, they are enterprising men who borrow idle capital and put it to some use; and whenever they are suddenly called on to pay up and are not able to borrow elsewhere, they are obliged to shut down.

There are many advanced thinkers who look forward to a new industrial system that shall be an improvement on the present and under which the laborer shall come nearer getting his share of the benefits resulting from invention and machinery than under the present system. All lovers of their kind would hail such a system with joy. But we are forced to say that it is not yet at hand. As we must have bread and must have clothing, we are obliged to cling to the old system for the present, and probably for a long time to come, until the foundations can be laid for a better one by intelligent progress. Classes, like individuals, have their bright and their dark days, and just now there seems to be a long, dark day ahead of you. It will be a day of suffering and distress, and I must say to you there seems to be no way of escaping it, and I therefore counsel you to face it squarely and bear it with that heroism and fortitude with which an American citizen should face and bear calamity.

It has been suggested that the state and different branches of government should furnish employment during the winter to idle men. Certainly everything that can be done in this line will be done, but I must warn you not to expect too much from this source. The powers of government are so hedged about with constitutional provisions that much cannot be done. The state at present has no work to do. The parks can employ only a few men. The city has work for more men, but it is also limited in its funds. The great drainage canal may, and probably will, give employment to a considerable number of men; but, after all, you must recognize that these things will be only in the nature of makeshifts; only to tide over; only to keep men and their families from starving. And on this point let me say it will be the duty of all public officials to see to it that no man is permitted to starve on the soil of Illinois, and provision will be made to that end.

But all this is temporary. The laborer must look to ways and means that are permanent for the improvement of his condition when the panic is over, and these measures must be along the line of and in harmony with the institutions of this century and must move by a gradual and steady development. Nothing that is violently done is of permanent advantage to the workingman. He can only prosper when his labor is in demand, and his labor can be in demand only when his employer prospers and there is nothing to interfere with consumption.

The world has been slow to accord labor its due. For thousands of years pillage, plunder, and organized robbery, called warfare, were honorable pursuits, and the man who toiled in order that all might live was despised. In the flight of time, it was but yesterday that the labor of the earth was driven with the lash and either sold on the block like cattle or tied by an invisible chain to the soil, and was forbidden to even wander outside his parish. In the yesterday of time, even the employers of labor were despised. The men who conducted great industries, who carried on commerce, who practised the useful arts, the men who made the earth habitable were looked down upon by a class that considered it honorable to rob the toiler of his bread — a class which, while possessing the pride of the eagle, had only the character of the vulture.

Great has been the development since then. This century brought upon its wings higher ideas, more of truth and more of common sense, and it announced to mankind that he is honorable who creates; that he should be despised who can only consume; that he is the benefactor of the race who gives it additional thought, an additional flower, an additional loaf of bread, an additional comfort; and he is a curse to his kind who tramples down what others build or, without compensation, devours what others create. The century brought with it still greater things. Not only did it lift the employer to a position of honor, influence, and power but it tore away parish boundaries, it cut the chains of the serf, it burned the auction block, where the laborer and his children were sold. And it brought ideas; it taught the laboring man to extend his hand to his fellow laborer; it taught him to organize and not only to read but to investigate, to inquire, to discuss, to consider, and to look ahead; so that today the laborer and his cause, at least theoretically, command the homage of all civilized men, and the greatest states in Christendom have set apart a day to be annually observed as a holiday in honor of labor.

The children of Israel were forty years in marching from the bondage of Egypt to the freer atmosphere of Palestine, and a halo of glory envelops their history. In the last forty years the children of Toil have made a forward march which is greater than any ever made in the wilderness. True, the land is not conquered. You have simply camped upon that higher plane where you can more clearly see the difficulties of the past, and where, in the end, you may hope for a higher justice and a happier condition for yourselves and your children; but a great deal remains to be done. In a sense, you are just out of the wilderness.

You ask along what lines, then, shall we proceed when the times get better in order to improve our condition? I answer along lines which harmonize, not only with nature's laws but with the laws of the land. Occupying, as I do, a position which makes me in a sense a conservator of all interests and classes, I desire to see the harmonious prosperity of all; and let me say to you that, until all the active interests of the land prosper again, there can be no general demand for your services and, consequently, no healthy prosperity. What I wish to point out is the absolute necessity of each class or interest being able to take care of itself in the fierce struggle for existence. You have not yet fully reached this state.

In the industrial world, as well as in the political world, only those forces survive which can maintain themselves and which are so concentrated that their influence is immediately and directly felt. A scattered force, no matter how great, is of no account in the sharp contests of the age. This is an age of concentration. Everywhere there is concentration and combination of capital and of those factors which today rule the world. The formation of corporations has greatly accelerated this movement, and no matter what is said about it, whether we approve it or not, it is the characteristic feature of our civilization and grows out of increased invention, the speedy communication between different parts of the world, and the great industrial generalship and enterprise of the time. It is questionable whether this tendency to combination could have been stopped in any way. It is certain, without this concentration of force, the gigantic achievements of our times would have been an impossibility. Combination and concentration are the masters of the age.

Let the laborer learn from this and act accordingly. Faultfinding and idle complaint are useless. Great forces, like great rivers, cannot be stopped. You must be able to fight your own battles. For the laborer to stand single-handed before giant combinations of power means annihilation. The world gives only when it is obliged to and respects only those who compel its respect.

Government was created by power and has always been controlled by power. Do not imagine that it is sufficient if you have justice and equity on your side, for the earth is covered with the graves of justice and equity that failed to receive recognition because there was no influence or force to compel it, and it will be so until the millennium. Whenever you demonstrate that you are an active, concentrated power, moving along lawful lines, then you will be felt in government. Until then, you will not. This is an age of law as well as of force, and no force succeeds that does not move along legal lines.

The laboring men of the world always have been, and are today, the support and principal reliance of the government. They support its flags in time of war, and their hands earn the taxes in time of peace. Their voice is for fair play, and no great government was ever destroyed by the laboring classes. Treason and rebellion never originated with them but always came from the opposite source.

Early in our history there occurred what was called Shays's Rebellion, but they were not wageworkers who created it. Then came the so-called Whisky Rebellion, created not by day laborers. During the War of 1812, a convention was held in the East which practically advocated a dissolution of the Union, but wageworkers were not among its members. The great rebellion of 1861 was not fomented by the laboring classes but by those classes which ate the bread that others toiled for. It was a rebellion by those who had long been prominent as leaders, who largely controlled the wealth of the country, who boasted of aristocratic society, and many of whom had been educated at the expense of the country whose flag they fired on. While, on the other hand, the great armies which put down this rebellion and supported the flag were composed of men who had literally earned their bread by the sweat of their brows.

It is true that at times a number of laborers, more or less ignorant, who thought they were being robbed of the fruits of their toil have indulged in rioting; and, while they have always lost by it and while they cannot be too severely condemned, yet they do not stand alone in this condemnation; for there have been many broadcloth mobs in this country, and in different sections of it, whose actions were lawless and as disgraceful as that of any labor mob that ever assembled. I must congratulate organized labor upon its freedom from turbulence. Rioting is nearly always by an ignorant class outside of all organizations and which, in most cases, was brought into the community by conscienceless men to defeat

organized labor. There should be a law compelling a man who brings this class of people into our midst to give bond for their support and their good behavior, for at present they are simply a disturbing element. They threaten the peace of society and bring reproach on the cause of labor.

The lesson I wish to impress upon you is that in business, in the industries, in government, everywhere, only those interests and forces survive that can maintain themselves along legal lines; and if you permanently improve your condition it must be by intelligently and patriotically standing together all over the country. Every plan must fail unless you do this.

At present you are to a great extent yet a scattered force, sufficiently powerful, if collected, to make yourselves heard and felt; to secure not only a fair hearing but a fair decision of all questions. Unite this power and you will be independent; leave it scattered and you will fail. Organization is the result of education as well as an educator. Let all the men of America who toil with their hands once stand together and no more complaints will be heard about unfair treatment. The progress of labor in the future must be along the line of patriotic association, not simply in localities but everywhere. And let me caution you that every act of violence is a hindrance to your progress.

There will be men among you ready to commit it. They are your enemies. There will be sneaks and Judas Iscariots in your ranks, who will for a mere pittance act as spies and try to incite some of the more hotheaded of your number to deeds of violence in order that these reptiles may get the credit of exposing you. They are your enemies. Cast them out of your ranks. Remember that any permanent prosperity must be based upon intelligence and upon conditions which are permanent.

And let me say to you again, in conclusion, this fall and this winter will be a trying time to you. The record of the laborers of the earth is one of patriotism. They have maintained the government, they have maintained the schools and churches, and it behooves you now to face the hardships that are upon you and see that your cause is not injured by grave indiscretions. Make the ignorant understand that government is strong and that life and property will be protected and law and order will be maintained, and that, while the day is dark now, the future will place the laborer in a more exalted position than he has ever occupied.

86.

JOSIAH STRONG: The Discontent of the Working Classes

Josiah Strong, a leader of the movement known as Christian Socialism, came to national prominence with the publication of Our Country *in 1885. His second book,* The New Era, *a portion of which is reprinted here, was published simultaneously in England and America. His thought was not strikingly original and bore the marks of the popular intellectual movements of the time. An evolutionist who believed in progress and a pioneer sociologist who believed in the possibility of reform, he was also an enthusiast for human welfare who believed in exporting (imperialistically if need be) the American way of life. It is not surprising to find him asserting, as he does here, that the Kingdom of God could be realized on earth.*

Source: *The New Era, or The Coming Kingdom,* New York, 1893, pp. 135-163.

THE FACT OF POPULAR DISCONTENT is too obvious to require proof. Its extent may be briefly noticed before we consider its causes and its significance.

It prevails chiefly among artisans and farmers, and shows itself in the numerous organizations among these classes which have sprung into existence in recent years. Among the former the most powerful organization is the American Federation of Labor, which has over 6,000 local unions with an aggregate membership of 675,000; while the various granges, associations, leagues, and alliances of farmers have a combined membership, it is said, of not less than 3 million. This discontent has framed the platforms of new political parties, has found many organs in the press, and further utters itself in numerous strikes and serious riots. In this country, from 1881 to 1886 inclu-

sive, 1,323,203 employees were involved in strikes directly affecting 22,304 establishments. In the summer of 1892, within a few days of each other, the states of New York, Pennsylvania and Tennessee ordered out their militia, while Idaho called on the United States government for troops to suppress labor riots. In Europe, like discontent finds like expression among the same classes.

First, let us look at the causes of this discontent.

To some it seems causeless, or at least without excuse, because workingmen are now better fed, better clothed, better housed than ever before; while many workingmen believe that their condition is growing constantly worse.

Whether the industrial classes are any happier now than they were a half-century ago may well be doubted, but beyond question their condition is improved. The American economist, Mr. David A. Wells, thinks that, taking into account hours, wages, and prices of food, the average farm laborer in the United States is twice as well off as he was thirty or forty years ago.

In Mr. Mulhall's *History of Prices* he shows that "the condition of the working classes has so much improved that they now consume in all countries twice as much as in 1850." Textile fabrics are 11 percent cheaper than they were in 1860, books and newspapers 33 percent, and the same amount of labor will now buy the workingman of Europe 140 pounds of bread as against 77 pounds in the decade ending 1860. The deductions of this statistician are that "15 shillings will now buy as much manufactures as 20 in the years 1841-50, but in matters of food we should require 22 shillings"; and that, taking increased wages and food values together, the English workingman is able to purchase 21 percent more of the necessaries of life in beef, butter, sugar, wheat, and coal than in 1840. Enhanced rent reduces his ability considerably, yet after allowing for this there is still a gain of at least 10 percent.

Another English statistician, Mr. Giffen, is of the opinion that there has been such a change in the textile, house-building, and engineering trades during the past fifty years that the British workman now gets from 50 to 100 percent more money for 20 percent less work. And for that period the rise of wages has been greater in France than in either England or America.

No doubt the condition of the workingman has improved, but it by no means follows that he should be any better contented. A savage of the South Sea Islands, being presented with a yard of cloth and a few fishhooks, may be much more satisfied with his lot than a mechanic who owns his home and has all the necessaries and many of the comforts of civilized life. We must take into consideration the widely different standards of living. There has been a change

for the better in the circumstances of workingmen, but there has been a still greater change in the *men themselves,* which is the secret of increasing popular discontent amid improving conditions. Evidently the problem has two factors both of which must be taken into consideration, viz., the men and their circumstances. . . .

In considering how great has been the change in workingmen, mark the increase of popular intelligence during the past century. . . .The average laborer in the United States today is more intelligent than many a great noble a few centuries ago. . . .

There has occurred in our own times an event, scarcely less important to the world than the invention of printing itself, which has lifted the sun high in the heavens and flooded the very foundations of society with light. I refer to the successful application of steam to the printing press. Few appreciate the tremendous significance of this event. It meant the enlightenment of the *many* for the first time in the world's history. . . .

Second only to the influence of the press on popular intelligence has been that of travel. . . .The average workingman two or three generations ago would no doubt have been well content with the hours, wages, food, lodgings, and clothes of the average workingman today, but, during the nineteenth century, public schools, public libraries, art galleries, museums, expositions, public parks, newspapers, and travel have all become common. Advertising, which is the art of making people want things, appeals to all classes alike. There has been a wonderful leveling up of the "common" people. Once, great men were gods, and slaves were less than human. Now all alike are *men,* having much the same wants and quite the same rights.

The spread of democracy, the growth of individualism, the equality of all men before the law have suggested the idea of equality of condition and made the masses feel that they are as capable of enjoying the good things of life as the classes. All these have contributed powerfully to increase the intelligence and wants of workingmen, and the resulting elevation of the standard of living has made a home, a table, a coat seem almost intolerable which once would have been deemed comfortable and even luxurious. The workingman of today may have, if you please, twice as much as his grandfather had, but he knows, say, ten times as much and wants ten times as much; hence his discontent. . . .

We have glanced at the man; let us now look at his circumstances.

The conditions under which he works are radically different from what they were a hundred years ago. Profound economic changes have attended the transition in the world's methods of production and distribution which has taken place during this century and more especially during the past twenty-five or thirty years. It is to this source we must look for some of the principal causes of popular discontent which has been pronounced ever since the commencement of the industrial depression which began in 1873 and affected all classes, but more especially laboring men.

In the "age of homespun," industry was individual; it has now become organized. This organization first extended from the home to the factory. Soon the factory became a part of a larger system, including in its organization the town, the province or region, then the whole country; and now we have entered on the last great stage, viz., that of organizing the industries of the world.

Each new stage in this development has necessarily disturbed industry and required a more or less extended readjustment of labor. Every great laborsaving invention has of course thrown thousands out of employment, though every such mechanical triumph has ultimately given employment to many for every one that it has robbed of work. . . .

The progress of invention, by causing a continual "dropping" of men, produces among operatives a feeling of insecurity which ministers to discontent. Everyone knows he is liable to learn any day that his strength or technical skill has been made useless by a new machine. Moreover, the introduction of machinery and the division of labor have rendered much work irksome by making it mechanical and monotonous.

Thus the various steps which have attended the great revolution in the world's methods of production have occasioned much discontent and not a little distress. The changes which have more recently taken place in the world's methods of distribution have been equally great and equally productive of far-reaching results. . . .

One result was that in our great West a territory larger than that of the thirteen original states was settled in half a dozen years, thus making a vast addition to the world's agricultural products, and bringing the cheap lands of the West into damaging competition not only with New England but with Old England and continental Europe as well. A leading farmer of Devonshire testified before the British commission in 1886: "I have calculated that the produce of five acres of wheat can be brought from Chicago to Liverpool at less than the cost of manuring one acre for wheat in England." This fact has sent thousands of farm laborers into English cities, there to lower wages by competing for work.

> Indian corn has been extensively raised in Italy. But Indian corn grown in the valley of the Mississippi, a thousand miles from the seaboard, has been transported in recent years to Italy and sold in her markets at a lower cost than the corn of Lombardy and Venetia, where the wages of the agriculturist are not one-third of the wages paid in the United States for corresponding labor. And one not surprising sequel of this is that 77,000 Italian laborers emigrated to the United States in 1885.

This immigration affects unfavorably the price of labor here and so ministers to popular discontent in this country. Thus these economic changes consequent upon new methods of distribution act and react all over the civilized world.

We are evidently being forced into something larger than national life. A *world* life is becoming apparent, as yet very imperfect but distinctly real. The great movements of commerce and of immigration are a part of that life. The industrial and economic disturbances of the past twenty years, which have been well-nigh or quite coextensive with civilization, are appropriately called "growing pains" naturally attendant on the process by which the nations adjust themselves to closer relations and new conditions in the world's progress. And these readjustments, with their accompanying disturbances, will continue to recur until there is at length effected a complete coordination of the world's industries, which will enable each people to render to mankind the greatest service of which they are capable and which will insure to all the largest possible returns for their service.

This coordination of industries will be effected slowly, of course, and it will require many years for the nations to gain the full consciousness of a world life. Popular discontent, therefore, will by no means be temporary; it will continue as long as these disturbing causes operate.

But let us look more closely at the circumstances of the workingman. He finds himself belonging to a system which, as we saw in the preceding chapter, is essentially unchristian because essentially selfish. He finds his labor rated as a commodity whose price is determined solely by the law of supply and demand. He believes that under the existing system he is the victim of the "iron law" of Ricardo, according to which wages are reduced to the lowest point at which the laborer can sustain life and reproduce his kind. . . .

Again, the workingman feels that he is not sharing equitably in the general prosperity.

The spirit of American civilization is eminently progressive. The increase of our population, the springing up of new cities and the growth of old ones, the extension of our railway and telegraph systems, the increase of our agricultural, manufacturing, and mining products, the development of our natural resources, the accumulation of our national wealth — all these are simply enormous. Such are the progress of invention and the increase of knowledge, and such is the rapidity with which important changes jostle each other, that years seem like generations.

In the midst of all this progress the workingman feels that he is practically standing still, or worse. He sees many belonging to other classes waxing rich, while he is perhaps unable to support his family. If he could feed and fatten himself and family on the east wind and lay by all his wages, it would take a lifetime to save as much as many business and professional men make in a single year.

His wants are increasing with his intelligence, but there is no corresponding increase of his means. We hear it often said and often denied that while the rich are growing richer the poor are growing poorer. The poor are not growing poorer in the sense that their wages will buy less of the necessaries of life or that they are rated lower on the tax list, but it is true in the sense that there is a greater disparity now between the workingman's income and his wants than ever before and that is the only sense worth considering in this connection. . . .

Now here is the point of my contention: the question whether the condition of the workingman has *materially* improved in this century is stoutly debated, *but the question whether there has been most wonderful material progress in general is not debatable;* no one doubts it. Evidently, then, the progress of the workingman is not proportionate to the general material progress. And this fact gives him just ground for complaint.

Mr. Giffen thinks that "the poor have had almost all the benefit of the great material advance of the last fifty years." But it would be quite impossible to convince the workingman of this in the face of many facts with which he is familiar. He knows, for instance, that a carload of coal can be mined, made ready for market, and loaded in one-half the time now that it required ten years ago; but he knows that the miner's wages have not been doubled in ten years. He knows that in cotton factories the operative produces nearly four times as much as he did fifty or sixty years ago, while his wages have been increased only 80 percent. He knows that in the flouring mill one man now does the work formerly done by four, but he does not receive the wages of four. A woman with a sewing machine can do probably six times as much work as could a needlewoman fifty years ago; but the seamstress of today does not receive six times as much as her mother did or work only one-sixth as many hours. She works quite as hard and quite as long, and in many cases for wages quite as small. In the manufacture of shoes an operative now does the work formerly done by five or six or even ten; and in the manufacture of wallpaper the workman's effectiveness has been increased a hundredfold.

A few years ago a skilled workman could make up three dozen pairs of sleeve buttons per day. Now, by the aid of the most improved machinery, a boy can make up 9,000 pairs, or 250 times as many. The inventions which make this possible have neither reduced the workman's toil nor increased his wages. When he set up thirty-six pairs a day, he received $2.50 or $3 for it. Now the boy, who does as much as 250 men could then, receives less than 90 cents for it. True, improved methods and machinery have both reduced prices and raised wages, but is it strange if many believe that those who are exploiting labor get the greater share of the benefit?

No one would pretend that workingmen

in the United States are 25 percent better off now than they were ten years ago; and yet from 1880 to 1890 the average wealth of American families rose from $4,000 to $5,000.

In view of the fact just mentioned; in view of our marvelous mechanical progress, which enables one man now to do as much as four, six, ten, and in some instances even a hundred men or more, twenty years ago; and in view of the fact that the intelligence and wants of workingmen have increased severalfold, does it not seem somewhat puerile to urge that workingmen have had their share of the general progress because, taking into account both wages and prices, they have made "a gain of at least 10 percent in half a century"?

The real question is not whether the laborer is receiving the larger wages than formerly, nor even whether his increase is proportionate to the general increase of wealth, but whether he is receiving his *just dues*. It is often claimed that all wealth really belongs to him because he has produced it all. This is absurd. Besides the skill, time, and strength of the workman, several other factors enter into the cost of the product, viz., the material, tools, machinery, and perhaps building. Without these the workman can do nothing. If he furnishes all of these as well as the work, then the product is wholly his. If capital furnishes a part, then a part of the product belongs to capital. Precisely how much is the fair share of each is the difficult question.

But thus much is clear — capital and labor together produce sufficient wealth every year, in this country, to lift laborer as well as capitalist above want for a year. Over and above all expenditure and all waste, our average annual increase of wealth from 1880 to 1890 was $1,781,700,000. If, then, the industrious and economical laborer has not been lifted above want, he evidently has not had his due share and ought not to be satisfied until justice is done him.

Workingmen will not deny that different

services have different values. But in view of the fact that capital is as helpless without labor as labor is without capital, that both are alike necessary to society, it is difficult, and becoming increasingly so as working-men grow more intelligent, to convince them that there is any justice in so wide a disparity as exists between their condition and that of capitalists. The limits of such a work as this permit us to note but few of the many lights and shadows which mark the strong contrasts of the social picture. . . .

Wealth is often a well-earned reward and poverty is sometimes a well-deserved penalty, but they are becoming more and more in this country a matter of inheritance — a distinction which finds no shadow of justification in the character of those whose circumstances point so strong a contrast.

Our discussion thus far has related more especially to the artisan class; some attention must be given to the complaint of the farmer.

In many parts of the United States there has been a notable decline in the value of agricultural lands. Many farms in New England can be bought for less than the cost of the buildings and walls on them. There is excellent land in the heart of Massachusetts whose market value has depreciated one-half in sixty years. Governor Foraker said in 1887 that farm property in Ohio was then from 25 to 50 percent cheaper than it was in 1880. During the same interval the value of agricultural land in the ten cotton states declined $459 million, or 31 percent. . . .

This general depression of agriculture is due to the radical changes in the methods of production and distribution which have taken place, especially during the last third of a century. The disturbances and consequent discontent in the industrial world which resulted from invention appeared much earlier among artisans than among farmers because machinery was applied to manufactures much earlier than to agricul-

ture. Our Civil War, which took so many men from the farms, greatly stimulated the invention and introduction of agricultural machinery. Then, following close on the war, came the great changes in the method of distribution — the transcontinental railways, which opened up a vast territory to settlement and cultivation; and the compound marine engine, which brought our Western products into most damaging competition with the agriculture of Europe. And of course the Middle States and New England farmers also suffered from the same competition.

One might suppose that with the European and American markets delivered over to them the Western farmers might have flourished beyond all precedent; but they complain that all profits and in many cases even their farms have been eaten up by interest, the railways, and the middlemen.

During the era of rapid settlement after the war, the farmers borrowed vast sums of money, often at exorbitant rates of interest, to enable them to improve their land and to buy machinery which had now become a necessity, while the planters of the cotton states probably became more generally and more deeply involved than the farmers; the fall in the prices of produce practically increased their indebtedness; the railways, at whose mercy the farmers were, charged "all that the traffic would bear," and a swarm of middlemen left for the producers but a small fraction of the prices paid by the consumers. Thus, notwithstanding the Mississippi Valley has become the granary of the world, its farmers and planters have become painfully embarrassed, and many of them, through mortgages, have suffered the loss of everything. Investigations of the last census made in ten counties in Kansas showed that less than 24 percent of the farmers held their farms unencumbered.

The deep discontent of the farmers will be by no means temporary, since it has been produced by causes which will continue operative for years to come. The changes in the methods of production are not yet complete. Mr. D. A. Wells says that it is coming to be the opinion of many of the best authorities, both in the United States and Europe, that the only possible future for agriculture is to be found in large farms, worked with ample capital, especially in the form of machinery and with labor organized somewhat after the factory system. Moreover, though most of the public agricultural lands are taken, less than one-fifth of our arable land is under actual cultivation. So far as agriculture is concerned, therefore, the greater part of our territory is practically unoccupied. Furthermore, according to Mr. Edward Atkinson, we could double our produce without putting another acre under the plow, "by merely bringing our product up to our average standard of reasonably good agriculture." All of which means that our farm products are capable of being increased some tenfold.

Thus it appears that the causes which have produced the discontent of the farmers — the changed methods of production, the great increase of agricultural products, the existence of mortgages, and the exactions of railways and middlemen — are all likely to continue for some time to come.

No doubt the condition of the farmer and of the workingman will improve in the future, but as improvement of condition has been accompanied by increasing discontent during the past century, we cannot infer that future improvement, under the existing organization of society, will allay discontent.

Second, having examined the causes of popular discontent, we are now prepared to consider very briefly its significance.

This is not the first age of the world when there has been a widespread discontent, but it means more in this age than it ever meant before because there is greater popular intelligence. An intelligent discontent will not suffer in dumb despair; it has resources, means of expressing itself and of enforcing its demands. It can agitate and educate public opinion. It knows enough of the progress of the world in the past to hope for the future, and it is easy for hope to purpose and achieve.

Again, popular discontent means more in this age than ever before because it appeals to more tender sensibilities. There have been greater miseries in other ages, but in this day those who suffer are not paralyzed by despair, and those who witness suffering are not frozen with indifference. Conditions which a few centuries since were taken for granted and caused no comment now excite indignation and horror. Once, men were insensible to the sufferings of strangers; now, a calamity by fire or flood or pestilence or famine brings quick relief from distant parts of the world. Once, gentlefolk found amusement in sights of blood and horror and death; now, cruelty, even to animals, is a crime. Once, human suffering was a matter of course and the misery of the many was deemed the will of God; today, all suffering is seen to imply something abnormal, and all agree that if possible its cause must be removed.

Perhaps there is no better illustration of the change in the world's sensibilities than that which is afforded by the punishment of criminals now and a few centuries ago. Once, the death penalty was inflicted by slowly immersing the victim in a caldron of boiling oil. Harrison, the regicide, was sentenced to be hanged, then revived, maimed, drawn, and hanged again — and this torture, remember, was *judicial,* inflicted by the highest court of the most Christian nation in the world. Now, public opinion insists that the death penalty, when inflicted, be as nearly painless and instantaneous as possible. As the world's nerves are refined, suffering of every sort becomes more and more intolerable.

Moreover, as society becomes more highly organized and intimate relations are multiplied, it is becoming more and more true that its different classes are members one of another, and when one member suffers all the members suffer with it. One class *cannot* remain indifferent to the wrongs of another.

Again, the discontent of the people is more significant now than ever before because now the people rule. When they were slaves, crushed under law, custom, institutions, and all the rigid strata of the social structure, their discontent signified little until it gathered the might of an earthquake sufficient to shatter society with its upheaval. Now, numbers possess the power and can exercise it through the established channels of the law. What king or emperor or aristocracy may think or propose is to us of no consequence, but what the masses think or propose is of utmost consequence, for they are to determine the future of civilization. The rich and powerful are naturally conservative. It is of course those who are discontented with their lot who want a change; hence it is that new ideas, whether political or religious, generally gain currency first among the poor. Evidently, popular discontent has profound significance. What *is* that significance?

It is as true of society as of the individual that self-dissatisfaction is a sign of upward, not downward, movement. Popular contentment marks a stagnant civilization —

China; popular restlessness marks a progressive civilization — Japan. New wants are rungs in the ladder of progress; and civilization, reaching up to them, mounts to something higher.

The discontent of the masses means that they feel the pulsations of a new life born of increased intelligence. As we have seen, to add to a man's knowledge is to enlarge his horizon, to make him conscious of new wants, and to show him new possibilities. The popular ferment of today means a struggle to realize the possibilities of a new and larger life. . . .

Does it not look as if there were about to be a new evolution of civilization? If this evolution is to bring the solution of our great sociological problems, it must be along Christian lines. Men are unconsciously seeking to harmonize in modern society the two great principles of individualism and organization and so to readjust our social and economic relations as to coordinate these two seemingly conflicting principles. . . . This must be done by the application of the teachings of Christ. Surely, if the new era is to mark an advance in the coming of the kingdom, the multitude that is being quickened with a new life and is to fashion our unfolding civilization must be brought under the power of Christian truth.

87.

LESTER F. WARD: Competition and Society

*Lester Frank Ward is best known as a pioneer American sociologist, although he was
also a noted geologist and paleobotanist in his own time. Taking off from the
strict Darwinian view of evolution as a purely natural process, he argued that the human
mind is a factor in man's biological evolution, which, he held, could be to some extent
controlled and directed by wise policy. Possessing a thoroughly democratic and
humanitarian point of view, Ward maintained that education and freedom from economic
pressures are essential elements in human progress. Governments, therefore, should
work to abolish poverty and to create national systems of education geared to develop
both the genius and the average mind. Ward advanced many of these views in an early
work from which the following selection is taken.*

Source: *The Psychic Factors of Civilization*, Boston, 1893, pp. 259-275.

THE ENVIRONMENT, though ever changing, does not change to conform to the structures but in the contrary direction, always rendering the partly adapted structures less adapted, and the only organic progress possible is that which accrues through changes of structure that tend to enable organic beings to cope with sterner and ever harder conditions. In any and every case it is the environment that works the changes and the organism that undergoes them.

But the most important factor in the environment of any species is its organic environment. The hardest pressure that is brought to bear upon it comes from the living things in the midst of which it lives, and, though paradoxical, it is those beings which most resemble it that crowd it most severely. The least advantage gained by one species from a favorable change of structure tends to make it spread and infringe upon others and soon to acquire, if not strenuously resisted, a complete monopoly of all things that are required for its support. Any

other species that consumes the same elements must, unless equally vigorous, be crowded out. This is the true meaning of the survival of the fittest. It is essentially a process of *competition*, but it is competition in its purest form, wholly unmixed with either moral or intellectual elements, which is never the case with competition in human society.

The prevailing idea is wholly false which claims that it is the fittest possible that survive in this struggle. The effect of competition is to prevent any form from attaining its maximum development and to maintain a certain comparatively low level of development for all forms that succeed in surviving. This is a normal result of the rhythmic character of all purely natural, *i.e.*, not rational or teleological, phenomena. . . . The greater part of what is gained in the flood tide is lost in the ebb. Wherever competition is wholly removed, as through the agency of man in the interest of any one form, great strides are immediately made by the form thus protected, and it soon outstrips all those that depend upon competition for their motive to advancement. Such has been the case with the cereals and fruit trees, and with domestic animals, in fact, with all the forms of life that man has excepted from the biologic law and subjected to the law of mind.

The supposed tendency of such forms to revert to their original wild state, about which so much has been said, is simply their inability when remanded to their pristine competitive struggle to maintain the high position which they had acquired during their halcyon days of exemption from that struggle, which they can no more do than they can attain that position while subjected to it. Competition, therefore, not only involves the enormous waste which has been described but it prevents the maximum development, since the best that can be attained under its influence is far inferior to that which is easily attained by the artificial, *i.e.,* the rational and intelligent, removal of that influence.

Hard as it seems to be for modern philosophers to understand this, it was one of the first truths that dawned upon the human intellect. Consciously or unconsciously, it was felt from the very outset that the mission of mind was to grapple with the law of competition and as far as possible to resist and defeat it. This iron law of nature, as it may be appropriately called (Ricardo's "iron law of wages" is only one manifestation of it), was everywhere found to lie athwart the path of human progress, and the whole upward struggle of rational man, whether physical, social, or moral, has been with this tyrant of nature — the law of competition. And insofar as he has progressed at all beyond the purely animal stage, he has done so through triumphing little by little over this law and gaining somewhat the mastery in this struggle.

In the physical world he has accomplished this so far as he has been able through invention, from which have resulted the arts and material civilization. Every implement or utensil, every mechanical device, every object of design, skill, and labor, every artificial thing that serves a human purpose is a triumph of mind over the physical forces of nature in ceaseless and aimless competition. The cultivation and improvement of economic plants and the domestication of useful animals involve the direct control of biologic forces and the exemption of these forms of life from the operation of the great organic law which dwarfs their native powers of development. All human institutions — religion, government, law, marriage, custom — together with innumerable other modes of regulating social, industrial, and commercial life, are, broadly viewed, only so many ways of meeting and checkmating the principle of competition as it manifests itself in society. And, finally, the ethical code and the moral law of enlightened man are nothing else than the means adopted by reason, intelligence, and refined sensibility for suppressing and crushing out the animal nature of man — for chaining the competitive egoism that all men have inherited from their animal ancestors.

One important fact has thus far been left out of view. Man, it is true, is a rational being, but he is also still an animal. He has struggled manfully against the iron law of nature, but he is far from having overcome it. He has met with wonderful success in this direction in his dealings with it in the physical world; he has laid a firm hand upon it in the domain of organic life; by the aid of well-ordained institutions he has dealt it heavy blows in its social aspects; and the suicidal tendency which it exhibits when operating upon dense masses of people has enlisted against it with telling effect the counterlaw of ethics. But all this has fallen far short of completely eradicating the deep-seated principle that lies at the foundation of animal economics. Aside from these few directions in which he has succeeded in partially supplanting the competitive economics of life by the cooperative economics of mind, he is still as completely under the dominion of the former as is any other organic being. . . .

The competition which we see in the social and industrial world, competition aided and modified by reason and intelligence, while it does not differ in either its principle or its purpose from the competition among animals and plants, differs widely in its methods and its effects. We see in it the same soulless struggle, the same intense egoism, the same rhythm by which existing inequalities are increased, the same sacrifice of the weaker to the stronger, and the same frenzy of the latter to possess and monopolize the earth. But along with this the antagonistic principle is also in active operation. This is the law of mind making for a true economy of energy. It is mind alone that perceives that competition is wasteful of energy, and, therefore, in the interest of the very success that competition seeks, it proceeds to antagonize competition and to substitute for it art, science, and cooperation. By the aid of these the success of those who use them is increased many hundredfold.

In society, therefore, competition tends to defeat itself by inciting against it the power of thought. It cannot endure. It is at best only a temporary condition or transition state. On the one hand, the competition between men resolves itself into a competition between machines, and instead of the fittest organism it is the fittest mechanism that survives. On the other hand, the competition between individuals becomes a competition between associations of individuals. Such associations are the result of cooperation, which is the opposite of competition. Economists talk of free competition, but in society this is scarcely possible. Only the simplest operations, those conducted with the least intelligence, can continue for any length of time to compete. The least skilled forms of labor approach this condition most closely, but freedom is here limited by the relations that labor sustains to capital.

The chief difference between employers and employed until recently has been that the former have used the rational method, while the latter have used the natural method. Capital has always combined and cooperated, while labor has only competed. But such is the power of the former method and its superiority over the latter that competing labor has had no chance in the struggle with combining capital. Latterly, however, labor has begun in a small way to call to its aid the psychological economy of cooperation. So strange and unexpected did this seem that it was at first looked upon as a crime against society, and many still so regard it. Indeed, all the laws of modern nations are framed on the assumption that capital naturally combines, while labor naturally competes, and attempts on the part of labor to combine against capital are usually suppressed by the armed force of the state, while capitalists are protected by the civil and military authority of the state against such assumed unlawful attempts. This enormous odds against which labor struggles in its effort to adopt and apply the economics of mind will greatly retard the progress of industrial reform which aims to place labor on an equal footing with capital in this respect.

Competition between industrial associations, or corporations, follows the law of competition among rational beings in general and is only a brief transition stage, to be quickly followed by further combination. Just as competition among individuals soon resulted in that combination by which corporations were formed, so competition between corporations soon results in the amalgamation of all in any one industry into one great compound corporation, now commonly under the form of a "trust." This process of compound cooperation does not stop until the whole product of the given industry is controlled by a single body of men. Such a body thus acquires absolute power over the price of the commodity produced, the only limit being that of the maximum profit that it can be made to yield.

Thus, for example, all the petroleum a country produces may be under the control of a single trust, and in order to secure for the members of that association of capitalists the maximum return for the petroleum, its price will be placed at the highest figure that consumers of petroleum will pay rather than, in whole or in part, return to candles or resort to gas or electricity. There is no necessary relation that this price shall bear to the cost of production. It may be twenty or it may be a hundred times that cost, and the profits accruing to the trust will be proportional. The same may be true of coal or iron or sugar or cotton, and even in the case of breadstuffs something analogous can occur through the device which is known as "cornering." All monopolies rest on the same principle, and they are as common in the industries of transportation and exchange as in that of production. Not only do the railroad and telegraph systems furnish illustrations but they may be found in the mercantile business of every country, in all of which competition is short, heated, and fitful, ending in the swallowing up of the small industries by the great ones in ever widening cycles. . . .

The reader cannot have failed to perceive the fundamental difference between the social phenomena above reviewed and those that take place everywhere in nature below the level of man's rational faculty, and hence, even when dealing with the universal law of competition, an entirely different set of principles must be applied to man from those which can be applied to irrational life. There competition is free, or rather it is pure. It continues as long as the weaker can survive it, and when these at last go to the

wall and the better adapted structures survive and triumph, it is the triumph of a real superiority, and the strong and robust alone are left to recruit the earth. But when mind enters into the contest, the character of competition is at first completely changed, and later competition itself is altogether crushed out; and while it is still the strong that survive, it is a strength which comes from indirection, from deception, artfulness, cunning, and shrewdness, necessarily coupled with stunted moral qualities, and largely aided by the accident of position.

In no proper sense is it true that the fittest survive. If this were their only function, it is evident that brains would be a positive detriment to society. Pure animal competition would be far better. It is probably the contemplation of the hopelessness of this state of things which has given the gloomy cast to Oriental philosophy, and it is no wonder that those moderns who consider the present order unalterable should maintain that we live in the worst possible universe. Those who can see a surplus of good in things as they are, or can hope for their improvement under the laws of evolution unaided by social intelligence, must be set down as hopelessly blinded by the great optimistic illusion of all life.

While competition is not to be looked upon as a social desideratum, even in its pure animal form, much less in its aggressive human form, free individual activity under the full play of all natural motives is of the utmost importance. Among these motives those of friendly rivalry and honest emulation are legitimate, harmless, and powerful. These competition suppresses; it tends to choke individual freedom and clog the wheels of social progress. How can this true individualism be secured and complete freedom of individual action be vouchsafed? Herein lies a social paradox.

It is clear from what has been said that this will never bring itself about. The tendencies are strongly in the opposite direction. Competition is growing more and more aggressive, heated, and ephemeral. Combination is growing more and more universal, powerful, and permanent. This is the result of the most complete laissez-faire policy. The paradox therefore is that *individual freedom can only come through social regulation*. The cooperative effects of the rule of mind which annihilate competition can only be overcome by that still higher form of cooperation which shall stay the lower form and set free the normal faculties of man. Free competition that shall be both innocent and beneficial may be secured to a limited extent in this way and in no other way.

88.

FREDERICK JACKSON TURNER: The Significance of the Frontier in American History

It is now almost a commonplace to speak of the effects of an open frontier on American national development, but the first man to assess its importance was the historian Frederick Jackson Turner, who read a short paper on the subject to a special meeting of the American Historical Association held during the World's Columbian Exposition on July 12, 1893. Turner's thesis had the simplicity that marks all revolutionary doctrines. His main point was that the sustained availability of "free land" had provided the equality of opportunity that, in his view, had made possible the development (almost unique in the world) of democratic political institutions. If he was right, it meant not only that an era had ended but also that all future developments would have to take a different form. Turner's paper, reprinted here in its entirety, inaugurated a new period in American historiography. Its thesis has been often opposed, but its brilliance never has been contested.

Source: *Proceedings of the State Historical Society of Wisconsin*, Madison, 1894, pp. 79-112.

IN A RECENT BULLETIN of the superintendent of the census for 1890 appear these significant words:

Up to and including 1880 the country had a frontier of settlement, but at present the unsettled area has been so broken into by isolated bodies of settlement that there can hardly be said to be a frontier line. In the discussion of its extent, its westward movement, etc., it cannot, therefore, any longer have a place in the census reports.

This brief official statement marks the closing of a great historic movement. Up to our own day, American history has been in a large degree the history of the colonization of the Great West. The existence of an area of free land, its continuous recession, and the advance of American settlement westward explain American development. Behind institutions, behind constitutional forms and modifications lie the vital forces that call these organs into life and shape them to meet changing conditions. Now, the peculiarity of American institutions is the fact that they have been compelled to adapt themselves to the changes of an expanding people — to the changes involved in crossing a continent, in winning a wilderness, and in developing at each area of this progress out of the primitive economic and political conditions of the frontier into the complexity of city life.

Said Calhoun in 1817, "We are great, and rapidly — I was about to say fearfully — growing!" So saying, he touched the distinguishing feature of American life. All peoples show development: the germ theory of politics has been sufficiently emphasized. In the case of most nations, however, the development has occurred in a limited area; and if the nation has expanded, it has met other growing peoples whom it has conquered. But in the case of the United States we have a different phenomenon.

Limiting our attention to the Atlantic Coast, we have the familiar phenomenon of the evolution of institutions in a limited area, such as the rise of representative government; the differentiation of simple colonial governments into complex organs; the progress from primitive industrial society, without division of labor, up to manufacturing civilization. But we have in addition to this *a recurrence of the process of evolution in each Western area reached in the process of expansion.* Thus American development has exhibited not merely advance along a single line but a return to primitive conditions on a continually advancing frontier line, and a new development for that area.

American social development has been continually beginning over again on the frontier. This perennial rebirth, this fluidity of American life, this expansion westward with its new opportunities, its continuous touch with the simplicity of primitive society, furnish the forces dominating American character. The true point of view in the history of this nation is not the Atlantic Coast, it is the Great West. Even the slavery struggle, which is made so exclusive an object of attention by writers like Professor Von Holst, occupies its important place in American history because of its relation to westward expansion.

In this advance, the frontier is the outer edge of the wave — the meeting point between savagery and civilization. Much has been written about the frontier from the point of view of border warfare and the chase, but as a field for the serious study of the economist and the historian it has been neglected.

What is the frontier? It is not the European frontier — a fortified boundary line running through dense populations. The most significant thing about it is that it lies at the hither edge of free land. In the census reports it is treated as the margin of that settlement which has a density of two or more to the square mile. The term is an elastic one, and for our purpose does not need sharp definition. We shall consider the whole frontier belt, including the Indian country and the outer margin of the "settled area" of the census reports. This paper will make no attempt to treat the subject exhaustively; its aim is simply to call attention to the frontier as a fertile field for investigation, and to suggest some of the problems which arise in connection with it.

In the settlement of America we have to observe how European life entered the continent, and how America modified and developed that life and reacted on Europe. Our early history is the study of European germs developing in an American environment. Too exclusive attention has been paid by institutional students to the Germanic origins, too little to the American factors.

Now, the frontier is the line of most rapid and effective Americanization. The wilderness masters the colonist. It finds him a European in dress, industries, tools, modes of travel, and thought. It takes him from the railroad car and puts him in the birch canoe. It strips off the garments of civilization and arrays him in the hunting shirt and the moccasin. It puts him in the log cabin of the Cherokee and the Iroquois and runs an Indian palisade around him. Before long he has gone to planting Indian corn and plowing with a sharp stick; he shouts the war cry and takes the scalp in orthodox Indian fashion. In short, at the frontier the environment is at first too strong for the man. He must accept the conditions which it furnishes or perish, and so he fits himself into the Indian clearings and follows the Indian trails.

Little by little he transforms the wilderness, but the outcome is not the old Europe, not simply the development of Germanic germs, anymore than the first phenomenon was a case of reversion to the Germanic mark. The fact is that here is a new product that is American. At first, the frontier was the Atlantic Coast. It was the frontier of Europe in a very real sense. Moving westward, the frontier became more and more American. *As successive terminal moraines result from successive glaciations, so each frontier leaves its traces behind it, and when it becomes a settled area the region still partakes of the frontier characteristics.* Thus the advance of the frontier has meant a steady movement away from the influence of Europe, a steady growth of independence on American lines. And to study this advance, the men who grew up under these conditions, and the political, economic, and social results of it, is to study the really American part of our history.

In the course of the seventeenth century, the frontier was advanced up the Atlantic river courses, just beyond the "fall line," and the tidewater region became the settled area. In the first half of the eighteenth century, another advance occurred. Traders followed the Delaware and Shawnese Indians to the Ohio as early as the end of the first quarter of the century. Governor Spottswood, of Virginia, made an expedition in 1714 across the Blue Ridge. The end of the first quarter of the century saw the advance of the Scotch-Irish and the Palatine Germans up the Shenandoah Valley into the western part of Virginia, and along the Piedmont region of the Carolinas. The Germans in New York pushed the frontier of settlement up the Mohawk to German Flats.

In Pennsylvania the town of Bedford indicates the line of settlement. Settlements had begun on New River, a branch of the Kanawha, and on the sources of the Yadkin and French Broad. The King attempted to arrest the advance by his proclamation of 1763 forbidding settlements beyond the sources of the rivers flowing into the Atlantic; but in vain. In the period of the Revolution the frontier crossed the Alleghenies into Kentucky and Tennessee, and the upper waters of the Ohio were settled. When the first census was taken in 1790, the continuous settled area was bounded by a line which ran near the coast of Maine and included New England, except a portion of Vermont and New Hampshire, New York along the Hudson and up the Mohawk about Schenectady, eastern and southern Pennsylvania, Virginia, well across the Shenandoah Valley, and the Carolinas and eastern Georgia.

Beyond this region of continuous settlement were the small settled areas of Kentucky and Tennessee and the Ohio, with the mountains intervening between them and the Atlantic area, thus giving a new and important character to the frontier. The isolation of the region increased its peculiarly American tendencies, and the need of transportation facilities to connect it with the East called out important schemes of internal improvement, which will be noted farther on. The "West," as a self-conscious section, began to evolve.

From decade to decade distinct advances of the frontier occurred. By the census of 1820 the settled area included Ohio, southern Indiana and Illinois, southeastern Missouri, and about one-half of Louisiana. This settled area had surrounded Indian areas, and the management of these tribes became an object of political concern. The frontier region of the time lay along the Great

Lakes where Astor's American Fur Company operated in the Indian trade, and beyond the Mississippi, where Indian traders extended their activity even to the Rocky Mountains; Florida also furnished frontier conditions. The Mississippi River region was the scene of typical frontier settlements.

The rising steam navigation on Western waters, the opening of the Erie Canal, and the westward extension of cotton culture added five frontier states to the Union in this period. Grund, writing in 1836, declares:

> It appears then that the universal disposition of Americans to emigrate to the Western wilderness in order to enlarge their dominion over inanimate nature is the actual result of an expansive power which is inherent in them, and which by continually agitating all classes of society is constantly throwing a large portion of the whole population on the extreme confines of the state in order to gain space for its development. Hardly is a new state or territory formed before the same principle manifests itself again and gives rise to a further emigration; and so is it destined to go on until a physical barrier must finally obstruct its progress.

In the middle of this century the line indicated by the present eastern boundary of Indian Territory, Nebraska, and Kansas marked the frontier of the Indian country. Minnesota and Wisconsin still exhibited frontier conditions, but the distinctive frontier of the period is found in California where the gold discoveries had sent a sudden tide of adventurous miners, and in Oregon and the settlements in Utah. As the frontier had leaped over the Alleghenies, so now it skipped the Great Plains and the Rocky Mountains; and in the same way that the advance of the frontiersmen beyond the Alleghenies had caused the rise of important questions of transportation and internal improvement, so now the settlers beyond the Rocky Mountains needed means of communication with the East; and, in the furnishing of these, arose the settlement

of the Great Plains, and the development of still another kind of frontier life. Railroads, fostered by land grants, sent an increasing tide of immigrants into the Far West. The United States Army fought a series of Indian wars in Minnesota, Dakota, and the Indian Territory.

By 1880, the settled area had been pushed into northern Michigan, Wisconsin, and Minnesota, along Dakota rivers, and in the Black Hills region and was ascending the rivers of Kansas and Nebraska. The development of mines in Colorado had drawn isolated frontier settlements into that region, and Montana and Idaho were receiving settlers. The frontier was found in these mining camps and the ranches of the Great Plains. The superintendent of the census for 1890 reports, as previously stated, that the settlements of the West lie so scattered over the region that there can no longer be said to be a frontier line.

In these successive frontiers we find natural boundary lines which have served to mark and to affect the characteristics of the frontiers, namely: The "fall line"; the Allegheny Mountains; the Mississippi; the Missouri, where its direction approximates north and south; the line of the arid lands, approximately the 99th meridian; and the Rocky Mountains. The fall line marked the frontier of the seventeenth century; the Alleghenies that of the eighteenth; the Mississippi that of the first quarter of the nineteenth; the Missouri that of the middle of this century (omitting the California movement); and the belt of the Rocky Mountains and the arid tract, the present frontier. Each was won by a series of Indian wars.

At the Atlantic frontier one can study the germs of processes repeated at each successive frontier. We have the complex European life, sharply precipitated by the wilderness into the simplicity of primitive conditions. The first frontier had to meet its Indian question, its question of the disposition of the public domain, of the means of inter-

Frederick Jackson Turner

course with the older settlements, of the extension of political organization, of religious and educational activity. And the settlement of these and similar questions for one frontier served as a guide for the next. The American student needs not to go to the "prim little townships of Sleswick" for illustrations of the law of continuity and development. For example, he may study the origin of our land policies in the colonial land policy; he may see how the system grew by adapting the statutes to the customs of the successive frontiers. He may see how the mining experience in the lead region of Wisconsin, Illinois, and Iowa was applied to the mining laws of the Rockies, and how our Indian policy has been a series of experimentations on successive frontiers. Each tier of new states has found, in the older ones, material for its constitutions. Each frontier has made similar contributions to American character, as will be discussed farther on.

But with all these similarities there are essential differences due to the place element and the time element. It is evident that the farming frontier of the Mississippi Valley presents different conditions from the mining frontier of the Rocky Mountains. The frontier reached by the Pacific railroad, surveyed into rectangles, guarded by the United States Army, and recruited by the daily immigrant ship, moves forward at a swifter pace and in a different way than the frontier reached by the birch canoe or the pack horse. The geologist traces patiently the shores of ancient seas, maps their areas, and compares the older and the newer. It would be a work worth the historian's labors to mark these various frontiers and in detail compare one with another. Not only would there result a more adequate conception of American development and characteristics but invaluable additions would be made to the history of society.

Loria, the Italian economist, has urged the study of colonial life as an aid in understanding the stages of European development, affirming that colonial settlement is for economic science what the mountain is for geology, bringing to light primitive stratifications. "America," he says, "has the key to the historical enigma which Europe has sought for centuries in vain, and the land which has no history reveals luminously the course of universal history." He is right. The United States lies like a huge page in the history of society. Line by line as we read from west to east we find the record of social evolution.

It begins with the Indian and the hunter; it goes on to tell of the disintegration of savagery by the entrance of the trader, the pathfinder of civilization; we read the annals of the pastoral stage in ranch life; the exploitation of the soil by the raising of unrotated crops of corn and wheat in sparsely settled farming communities; the intensive culture of the denser farm settlement; and finally the manufacturing organization with city and factory system. This page is familiar to the student of census statistics, but how little of it has been used by our historians. Each of these areas has had an influence in our economic and political history; the evolution of each into a higher stage has worked political transformations. But what constitutional historian has made any adequate attempt to interpret political facts by the light of these social areas and changes?

The Atlantic frontier was compounded of fisherman, fur trader, miner, cattle raiser, and farmer. Excepting the fisherman, each type of industry was on the march toward the West, impelled by an irresistible attraction. Each passed in successive waves across the continent. Stand at Cumberland Gap and watch the procession of civilization, marching single file — the buffalo, following the trail to the salt springs, the Indian, the fur trader and hunter, the cattle raiser, the pioneer farmer — and the frontier has passed by. Stand at South Pass in the Rockies a century later and see the same procession with wider intervals between. The unequal rate of advance compels us to distinguish the frontier into the trader's frontier, the rancher's frontier, or the miner's frontier, and the farmer's frontier. When the mines and the cowpens were still near the fall line, the traders' pack trains were tinkling across the Alleghenies, and the French on the Great Lakes were fortifying their posts, alarmed by the British trader's birch canoe. When the trappers scaled the Rockies, the farmer was still near the mouth of the Missouri.

Why was it that the Indian trader passed so rapidly across the continent? What effects followed from the trader's frontier? The trade was coeval with American discovery. The Norsemen, Vespuccius, Verrazani, Hudson, John Smith, all trafficked for furs. The Plymouth Pilgrims settled in Indian cornfields, and their first return cargo was of beaver and lumber. The records of the various New England colonies show how steadily exploration was carried into the wilderness by this trade. What is true for New England is, as would be expected, even plainer for the rest of the colonies. All along the coast from Maine to Georgia the Indian trade opened up the river courses. Steadily the trader passed westward, utilizing the older lines of French trade. The Ohio, the Great Lakes, the Mississippi, the Missouri, and the Platte, the lines of western advance, were ascended by traders. They found the passes in the Rocky Mountains and guided Lewis and Clark, Frémont, and Bidwell.

The explanation of the rapidity of this advance is bound up with the effects of the trader on the Indian. The trading post left the unarmed tribes at the mercy of those that had purchased firearms — a truth which the Iroquois Indians wrote in blood, and so the remote and unvisited tribes gave eager welcome to the trader. "The savages," wrote La Salle, "take better care of us French than of their own children; from us only can they get guns and goods." This accounts for the trader's power and the rapidity of his advance. Thus the disintegrating forces of civilization entered the wilderness. Every river valley and Indian trail became a fissure in Indian society, and so that society became honeycombed.

Long before the pioneer farmer appeared on the scene, primitive Indian life had passed away. The farmers met Indians armed with guns. The trading frontier, while steadily undermining Indian power by making the tribes ultimately dependent on the whites, yet, through its sale of guns, gave to the Indians increased power of resistance to the farming frontier. French colonization was dominated by its trading frontier; English colonization by its farming frontier. There was an antagonism between the two frontiers as between the two nations. Said Duquesne to the Iroquois:

Are you ignorant of the difference between the king of England and the king of France? Go see the forts that our king has established and you will see that you can still hunt under their very walls. They have been placed for your advantage in places which you frequent. The English, on the contrary, are no sooner in possession of a place than the game is driven away. The forest falls before them as they advance, and the soil is laid bare so that you can scarce find the wherewithal to erect a shelter for the night.

And yet, in spite of this opposition of the interests of the trader and the farmer, the Indian trade pioneered the way for civilization. The buffalo trail became the Indian trail, and this became the trader's "trace"; the trails widened into roads, and the roads into turnpikes, and these in turn were transformed into railroads. The same origin can be shown for the railroads of the South, the Far West, and the Dominion of Canada. The trading posts reached by these trails were on the sites of Indian villages which had been placed in positions suggested by nature; and these trading posts, situated so as to command the water systems of the country, have grown into such cities as Albany, Pittsburgh, Detroit, Chicago, St. Louis, Council Bluffs, and Kansas City.

Thus civilization in America has followed the arteries made by geology, pouring an ever richer tide through them, until at last the slender paths of aboriginal intercourse have been broadened and interwoven into the complex mazes of modern commercial lines; the wilderness has been interpenetrated by lines of civilization, growing ever more numerous. It is like the steady growth of a complex nervous system for the originally simple, inert continent. If one would understand why we are today one nation rather than a collection of isolated states, he must study this economic and social consolidation of the country. In this progress from savage conditions lie topics for the evolutionist.

The effect of the Indian frontier as a consolidating agent in our history is important. From the close of the seventeenth century

various intercolonial congresses have been called to treat with Indians and establish common measures of defense. Particularism was strongest in colonies with no Indian frontier. This frontier stretched along the western border like a cord of union. The Indian was a common danger, demanding united action. Most celebrated of these conferences was the Albany Congress of 1754, called to treat with the Six Nations, and to consider plans of union. Even a cursory reading of the plan proposed by the Congress reveals the importance of the frontier. The powers of the general council and the officers were, chiefly, the determination of peace and war with the Indians, the regulation of Indian trade, the purchase of Indian lands, and the creation and government of new settlements as a security against the Indians.

It is evident that the unifying tendencies of the Revolutionary period were facilitated by the previous cooperation in the regulation of the frontier. In this connection may be mentioned the importance of the frontier, from that day to this, as a military training school, keeping alive the power of resistance to aggression, and developing the stalwart and rugged qualities of the frontiersman.

It would not be possible in the limits of this paper to trace the other frontiers across the continent. Travelers of the eighteenth century found the "cowpens" among the canebrakes and peavine pastures of the South, and the "cow drivers" took their droves to Charleston, Philadelphia, and New York. Travelers at the close of the War of 1812 met droves of more than a thousand cattle and swine from the interior of Ohio going to Pennsylvania to fatten for the Philadelphia market. The ranges of the Great Plains, with ranch and cowboy and nomadic life, are things of yesterday and of today. The experience of the Carolina cowpens guided the ranchers of Texas. One element favoring the rapid extension of the rancher's frontier is the fact that in a remote country lacking transportation facilities, the product must be in small bulk, or must be able to transport itself, and the cattle raiser could easily drive his product to market. The effect of these great ranches on the subsequent agrarian history of the localities in which they existed should be studied.

The maps of the census reports show an uneven advance of the farmer's frontier, with tongues of settlement pushed forward and with indentations of wilderness. In part this is due to Indian resistance, in part to the location of river valleys and passes, in part to the unequal force of the centers of frontier attraction. Among the important centers of attraction may be mentioned the following: fertile and favorably situated soils, salt springs, mines, and army posts.

The frontier army post, serving to protect the settlers from the Indians, has also acted as a wedge to open the Indian country and has been a nucleus for settlement. In this connection, mention should also be made of the government military and exploring expeditions in determining the lines of settlement. But all the more important expeditions were greatly indebted to the earliest pathmakers, the Indian guides, the traders and trappers, and the French voyageurs, who were inevitable parts of governmental expeditions from the days of Lewis and Clark. Each expedition was an epitome of the previous factors in western advance.

In an interesting monograph, Victor Hehn has traced the effect of salt upon early European development and has pointed out how it affected the lines of settlement and the form of administration. A similar study might be made for the salt springs of the United States. The early settlers were tied to the coast by the need of salt, without which they could not preserve their meats or live in comfort. Writing in 1752, Bishop Spangenburg says of a colony for which he was seeking lands in North Carolina:

They will require salt and other necessaries which they can neither manufacture nor raise. Either they must go to Charleston, which is 300 miles distant . . . Or else they must go to Boling's Point in Virginia on a branch of the James and is also 300 miles from here . . . Or else they must go down the Roanoke — I know not how many miles — where salt is brought up from the Cape Fear. This may serve as a typical illustration.

An annual pilgrimage to the coast for salt thus became essential. Taking flocks or furs and ginseng root, the early settlers sent their pack trains after seeding time each year to the coast. This proved to be an important educational influence since it was almost the only way in which the pioneer learned what was going on in the East. But when discovery was made of the salt springs of the Kanawha, and the Holston, and Kentucky, and central New York, the West began to be freed from dependence on the coast. It was in part the effect of finding these salt springs that enabled settlement to cross the mountains.

From the time the mountains rose between the pioneer and the seaboard, a new order of Americanism arose. The West and the East began to get out of touch of each other. The settlements from the sea to the mountains kept connection with the rear and had a certain solidarity. But the overmountain men grew more and more independent. The East took a narrow view of American advance and nearly lost these men. Kentucky and Tennessee history bears abundant witness to the truth of this statement. The East began to try to hedge and limit westward expansion. Though Webster could declare that there were no Alleghenies in his politics, yet in politics in general they were a very solid factor.

Good soils have been the most continuous attraction to the farmer's frontier. The land hunger of the Virginians drew them down the rivers into Carolina in early colonial days; the search for soils took the Massachusetts men to Pennsylvania and to New York. The exploitation of the beasts took hunter and trader to the West, the exploitation of the grasses took the rancher west, and the exploitation of the virgin soil of the river valleys and prairies attracted the farmer. As the eastern lands were taken up, migration flowed across them to the West. Daniel Boone, the great backwoodsman, who combined the occupations of hunter, trader, cattle raiser, farmer, and surveyor — learning, probably from the traders, of the fertility of the lands on the upper Yadkin, where the traders were wont to rest as they took their way to the Indians, left his Pennsylvania home with his father and passed down the Great Valley road to that stream.

Learning from a trader whose posts were on the Red River in Kentucky of its game and rich pastures, he pioneered the way for the farmers to that region. Thence he passed to the frontier of Missouri, where his settlement was long a landmark on the frontier. Here again he helped to open the way for civilization, finding salt licks and trails and land. His son was among the earliest trappers in the passes of the Rocky Mountains, and his party are said to have been the first to camp on the present site of Denver. His grandson, Col. A. J. Boone, of Colorado, was a power among the Indians of the Rocky Mountains and was appointed an agent by the government. "Kit" Carson's mother was a Boone. Thus this family epitomizes the backwoodsman's advance across the continent.

The farmer's advance came in a distinct series of waves. In Peck's *New Guide to the West,* published in Cincinnati in 1848, occurs this suggestive passage:

Generally, in all the Western settlements, three classes, like the waves of the ocean, have rolled one after the other.

First comes the pioneer, who depends for the subsistence of his family chiefly upon the natural growth of vegetation, called the "range," and the proceeds of hunting. His implements of agriculture are rude, chiefly of his own make, and his efforts directed mainly to a crop of corn and a "truck patch." The last is a rude garden for growing cabbage, beans, corn for roasting ears, cucumbers, and potatoes. A log cabin and, occasionally, a stable and corncrib and a field of a dozen acres, the timber girdled, or "deadened," and fenced are enough for his occupancy. It is quite immaterial whether he ever becomes the owner of the soil. He is the occupant for the time being, pays no rent, and feels as independent as the "lord of the manor."

With a horse, cow, and one or two breeders of swine, he strikes into the woods with his family and becomes the founder of a new county or, perhaps, state. He builds his cabin, gathers around him a few other families of similar tastes and habits, and occupies till the range is somewhat subdued and hunting a little precarious, or, which is more frequently the case, till neighbors crowd around, roads, bridges, and fields annoy him, and he lacks elbowroom. The Preemption Law enables him to dispose of his cabin and cornfield to the next class of emigrants; and, to employ his own figures, he "breaks for the high timber, clears out for the New Purchase," or migrates to Arkansas or Texas to work the same process over.

The next class of emigrants purchase the lands, add field to field, clear out the roads, throw rough bridges over the streams, put up hewn log houses, with glass windows and brick or stone chimneys, occasionally plant orchards, build mills, schoolhouses, courthouses, etc., and exhibit the picture and forms of plain, frugal, civilized life.

Another wave rolls on. The men of capital and enterprise come. The settler is ready to sell out and take the advantage of the rise in property — push farther into the interior and become, himself, a man of capital and enterprise in turn. The small village rises to a spacious town or city; substantial edifices of brick, extensive fields, orchards, gardens, colleges, and churches are seen. Broadcloths, silks, leghorns, crapes, and all the refinements, luxuries, elegancies, frivolities, and fashions are in vogue. Thus wave after wave is rolling westward — the real Eldorado is still farther on.

A portion of the two first classes remain stationary amidst the general movement, improve their habits and condition, and rise in the scale of society.

The writer has traveled much amongst the first class — the real pioneers. He has lived many years in connection with the second grade; and now the third wave is sweeping over large districts of Indiana, Illinois, and Missouri. Migration has become almost a habit in the West. Hundreds of men can be found, not over fifty years of age, who have settled for the fourth, fifth, or sixth time on a new spot. To sell out and remove only a few hundred miles makes up a portion of the variety of backwoods life and manners.

Omitting the pioneer farmer who moves from the love of adventure, the advance of the more steady farmer is easy to understand. Obviously the immigrant was attracted by the cheap lands of the frontier, and even the native farmer felt their influence strongly. Year by year the farmers who lived on soil, whose returns were diminished by unrotated crops, were offered the virgin soil of the frontier at nominal prices. Their growing families demanded more lands, and these were dear. The competition of the unexhausted, cheap, and easily tilled prairie lands compelled the farmer either to go west and continue the exhaustion of the soil on a new frontier or to adopt intensive culture. Thus the census of 1890 shows, in the Northwest, many counties in which there is an absolute, or a relative, decrease of population. These states have been sending farmers to advance the frontier on the Plains, and have themselves begun to turn to intensive farming and to manufacture. A decade before this, Ohio had shown the same transition stage. Thus the demand for land and the love of wilderness freedom drew the frontier ever onward.

Having now roughly outlined the various kinds of frontiers and their modes of advance, chiefly from the point of view of the frontier itself, we may next inquire what were the influences on the East and on the Old World. A rapid enumeration of some of the more noteworthy effects is all that I have time for.

First, we note that the frontier promoted the formation of a composite nationality for the American people. The coast was preponderantly English, but the later tides of continental immigration flowed across to the free lands. This was the case from the early colonial days. The Scotch-Irish and the Palatine Germans, or "Pennsylvania Dutch," furnished the stock of the colonial frontier. With these peoples were also the freed indented servants, or redemptioners, who at the expiration of their time of service passed to the frontier. Governor Spottswood of Virginia writes in 1717, "The inhabitants of our frontiers are composed generally of such as have been transported hither as servants and, being out of their time, settle themselves where land is to be taken up and that will produce the necessaries of life with little labor." Very generally these redemptioners were of non-English stock.

In the crucible of the frontier the immigrants were Americanized, liberated and fused into a mixed race, English in neither nationality or characteristics. The process has gone on from the early days to our own. Burke and other writers in the middle of the eighteenth century believed that Pennsylvania was "threatened with the danger of being wholly foreign in language, manners, and perhaps even inclinations." The German and Scotch-Irish elements in the frontier of the South were only less great. In the middle of the present century the German element in Wisconsin was already so considerable that leading publicists looked to the creation of a German state out of the commonwealth by concentrating their colonization. Such examples teach us to beware of misinterpreting the fact that there is a common English speech in America into a belief that the stock is also English.

In another way the advance of the frontier decreased our dependence on England. The coast, particularly of the South, lacked diversified industries and was dependent on England for the bulk of its supplies. In the South there was even a dependence on the Northern colonies for articles of food. Governor Glenn of South Carolina writes in the middle of the eighteenth century:

> Our trade with New York and Philadelphia was of this sort, draining us of all the little money and bills we could gather from other places for their bread, flour, beer, hams, bacon, and other things of their produce; all which, except beer, our new townships begin to supply us with, which are settled with very industrious and thriving Germans. This no doubt diminishes the number of shipping and the appearance of our trade, but it is far from being a detriment to us.

Before long the frontier created a demand for merchants. As it retreated from the coast it became less and less possible for England to bring her supplies directly to the consumer's wharfs and carry away staple crops, and staple crops began to give way to diversified agriculture for a time. The effect of this phase of the frontier action upon the northern section is perceived when we realize how the advance of the frontier aroused seaboard cities like Boston, New York, and Baltimore to engage in rivalry for what Washington called "the extensive and valuable trade of a rising empire."

The legislation which most developed the powers of the national government, and played the largest part in its activity, was conditioned on the frontier. Writers have discussed the subjects of tariff, land, and internal improvement as pendants to the slavery question. But when American history comes to be rightly viewed, it will be seen that the slavery question is an incident. In the period from the end of the first half of the present century to the close of the Civil War, slavery rose to primary but far from exclusive importance. But this does not justify Professor Von Holst (to take an example) in treating our constitutional history in its formative period down to 1828 in a single volume, and giving six volumes to the history of slavery from 1828 to 1861 under the title of a *Constitutional History of the United States.*

The growth of nationalism and the evolution of American political institutions were dependent on the advance of the frontier. Even so recent a writer as Rhodes, in his *History of the United States since the Compromise of 1850,* has treated the legislation called out by the Western advance as incidental to the slavery struggle.

This is a wrong perspective. The pioneer needed the goods of the coast, and so the grand series of internal improvement and railroad legislation began, with potent nationalizing effects. But the West was not content with bringing the farm to the factory. Under the lead of Clay — "Harry of the West" — protective tariffs were passed, with the cry of bringing the factory to the farm.

The public domain has been a force of profound importance in the nationalization and development of the government. The effects of the struggle of the landed and the landless states and of the Ordinance of 1787 need no discussion. Administratively the frontier called out some of the highest and most vitalizing activities of the general government. The purchase of Louisiana was perhaps the constitutional turning point in the history of the republic, inasmuch as it afforded both a new area for national legislation and the occasion of the downfall of the policy of strict construction. But the purchase of Louisiana was called out by frontier needs and demands. As frontier states accrued to the Union, the national power grew. In a speech on the dedication of the Calhoun monument, Lamar explained: "In 1789 the states were the creators of the federal government; in 1861, the federal government was the creator of a large majority of the states."

When we consider the public domain from the point of view of the sale and disposal of the public lands, we are again brought face to face with the frontier. The policy of the United States in dealing with its lands is in sharp contrast with the European system of scientific administration. Efforts to make this domain a source of revenue and to withhold it from emigrants in order that settlement might be compact were in vain. The jealousy and the fears of the East were powerless in the face of the demands of the frontiersmen. John Quincy Adams was obliged to confess: "My own system of administration, which was to make the national domain the inexhaustible fund for progressive and unceasing internal improvement has failed." The reason is obvious; systems of administration was not what the West demanded; it wanted land.

Adams states the situation as follows:

The slaveholders of the South have bought the cooperation of the Western country by the bribe of the Western lands, abandoning to the new Western states their own proportion of the public property and aiding them in the design of grasping all the lands into their own hands. Thomas H. Benton was the author of this system, which he brought forward as a substitute for the American system of Mr. Clay and to supplant him as the leading statesman of the West. Mr. Clay, by his tariff compromise with Mr. Calhoun, abandoned his own American system. At the same time he brought forward a plan for distributing among all the states of the Union the proceeds of the sales of the public lands. His bill for that purpose passed both houses of Congress, but was vetoed by President Jackson, who, in his annual message of December 1832, formally

recommended that all public lands should be gratuitously given away to individual adventurers and to the states in which the lands are situated.

"No subject," said Henry Clay, "which has presented itself to the present, or perhaps any preceding, Congress is of greater magnitude than that of the public lands." When we consider the far-reaching effects of the government's land policy upon political, economic, and social aspects of American life, we are disposed to agree with him. But this legislation was framed under frontier influences and under the lead of Western statesmen like Benton and Jackson. Said Senator Scott of Indiana in 1841: "I consider the Preemption Law merely declaratory of the custom or common law of the settlers."

It is safe to say that the legislation with regard to land, tariff, and internal improvements — the American system of the nationalizing Whig Party — was conditioned on frontier ideas and needs. But it was not merely in legislative action that the frontier worked against the sectionalism of the coast. The economic and social characteristics of the frontier worked against sectionalism. The men of the frontier had closer resemblances to the Middle region than to either of the other sections. Pennsylvania had been the seed plot of frontier emigration, and, although she passed on her settlers along the Great Valley into the west of Virginia and the Carolinas, yet the industrial society of these Southern frontiersmen was always more like that of the Middle region than like that of the tidewater portion of the South, which later came to spread its industrial type throughout the South.

The Middle region, entered by New York Harbor, was an open door to all Europe. The tidewater part of the South represented typical Englishmen, modified by a warm climate and servile labor, and living in baronial fashion on great plantations;

New England stood for a special English movement — Puritanism. The Middle region was less English than the other sections. It had a wide mixture of nationalities, a varied society, the mixed town and country system of local government, a varied economic life, many religious sects. In short, it was a region mediating between New England and the South, and the East and the West.

It represented that composite nationality which the contemporary United States exhibits, that juxtaposition of non-English groups, occupying a valley or a little settlement and presenting reflections of the map of Europe in their variety. It was democratic and non-sectional, if not national; "easy, tolerant and contented"; rooted strongly in material prosperity. It was typical of the modern United States. It was least sectional, not only because it lay between North and South but also because with no barriers to shut out its frontiers from its settled region, and with a system of connecting waterways, the Middle region mediated between East and West as well as between North and South. Thus it became the typically American region. Even the New Englander, who was shut out from the frontier by the Middle region, tarrying in New York or Pennsylvania on his westward march, lost the acuteness of his sectionalism on the way.

Until the spread of cotton culture into the interior gave homogeneity to the South, the western part of it showed tendencies to fall away from the faith of the fathers into internal improvement legislation and nationalism. In the Virginia convention of 1829-30, called to revise the constitution, Mr. Leigh, of Chesterfield, one of the tidewater counties, declared:

> One of the main causes of discontent which led to this convention, that which had the strongest influence in overcoming our veneration for the work of our fathers, which taught us to contemn the sentiments of Henry and Mason and Pendleton, which weaned us from our reverence for the constituted authorities of the state, was an overweening passion for internal improvement. I say this with perfect knowledge; for it has been avowed to me by gentlemen from the West over and over again. And let me tell the gentleman from Albemarle (Mr. Gordon) that it has been another principal object of those who set this ball of revolution in motion, to overturn the doctrine of state rights, of which Virginia has been the very pillar, and to remove the barrier she has interposed to the interference of the federal government in that same work of internal improvement by so reorganizing the legislature that Virginia, too, may be hitched to the federal car.

It was this nationalizing tendency of the West that transformed the democracy of Jefferson into the national republicanism of Monroë and the democracy of Andrew Jackson. The West of the War of 1812, the West of Clay and Benton and Harrison and Andrew Jackson, shut off by the Middle states and the mountains from the coast sections, had a solidarity of its own with national tendencies. On the tide of the Father of Waters, North and South met and mingled into a nation. Interstate migration went steadily on — a process of cross-fertilization of ideas and institutions.

The fierce struggle of the sections over slavery on the Western frontier does not diminish the truth of this statement; it proves the truth of it. Slavery was a sectional trait that would not down, but in the West it could not remain sectional. It was the greatest of frontiersmen who declared: "I believe this government cannot endure permanently half slave and half free. It will become all of one thing, or all of the other." Nothing works for nationalism like intercourse within the nation. Mobility of population is death to localism, and the Western frontier worked irresistibly in unsettling population. The effects reached back from the frontier and affected profoundly the Atlantic Coast, and even the Old World.

But the most important effect of the frontier has been in the promotion of democracy here and in Europe. As has been pointed out, the frontier is productive of individualism. Complex society is precipitated by the wilderness into a kind of primitive organization based on the family. The tendency is antisocial. It produces antipathy to control and particularly to any direct control. The tax-gatherer is viewed as a representative of oppression. Professor Osgood, in an able article, has pointed out that the frontier conditions prevalent in the colonies are important factors in the explanation of the American Revolution, where individual liberty was sometimes confused with absence of all effective government. The same conditions aid in explaining the difficulty of instituting a strong government in the period of the Confederacy. The frontier individualism has from the beginning promoted democracy.

The frontier states that came into the Union in the first quarter of a century of its existence came in with democratic suffrage provisions and had reactive effects of the highest importance upon the older states whose peoples were being attracted there. It was *western* New York that forced an extension of suffrage in the constitutional convention of that state in 1820; and it was *western* Virginia that compelled the tidewater region to put a more liberal suffrage provision in the constitution framed in 1830, and to give to the frontier region a more nearly proportionate representation with the tidewater aristocracy. The rise of democracy as an effective force in the nation came in with Western preponderance under Jackson and William Henry Harrison, and it meant the triumph of the frontier — with all of its good and with all of its evil elements.

An interesting illustration of the tone of frontier democracy in 1830 comes from the same debates in the Virginia convention already referred to. A representative from western Virginia declared:

> But, sir, it is not the increase of population in the West which this gentleman ought to fear. It is the energy which the mountain breeze and Western habits impart to those emigrants. They are regenerated, politically I mean, sir. They soon become *working politicians*; and the difference, sir, between a *talking* and a *working* politician is immense. The Old Dominion has long been celebrated for producing great orators, the ablest metaphysicians in policy; men that can split hairs in all abstruse questions of political economy. But at home, or when they return from Congress, they have Negroes to fan them asleep. But a Pennsylvania, a New York, an Ohio, or a western Virginia statesman, though far inferior in logic, metaphysics, and rhetoric to an old Virginia statesman, has this advantage, that when he returns home he takes off his coat and takes hold of the plow. This gives him bone and muscle, sir, and preserves his republican principles pure and uncontaminated.

So long as free land exists, the opportunity for a competency exists and economic power secures political power. But the democracy born of free land, strong in selfishness and individualism, intolerant of administrative experience and education, and pressing individual liberty beyond its proper bounds, has its dangers as well as its benefits. Individualism in America has allowed a laxity in regard to governmental affairs which has rendered possible the spoils system and all the manifest evils that follow from the lack of a highly developed civic spirit.

In this connection may be noted also the influence of frontier conditions in permitting lax business honor, inflated paper currency, and wildcat banking. The colonial and Revolutionary frontier was the region whence emanated many of the worst forms of an evil currency. The West in the War of 1812 repeated the phenomenon on the frontier of that day, while the speculation and wildcat banking of the period of the crisis of 1837 occurred on the new frontier belt of the next tier of states. Thus each one of the periods of lax financial integrity coincides with periods when a new set of frontier communities had arisen, and coincides in area with these successive frontiers, for the most part.

The recent Populist agitation is a case in point. Many a state that now declines any connection with the tenets of the Populists, itself adhered to such ideas in an earlier stage of the development of the state. A primitive society can hardly be expected to show the intelligent appreciation of the complexity of business interests in a developed society. The continual recurrence of these areas of paper-money agitation is another evidence that the frontier can be isolated and studied as a factor in American history of the highest importance.

The East has always feared the result of an unregulated advance of the frontier and has tried to check and guide it. The English authorities would have checked settlement at the headwaters of the Atlantic tributaries and allowed the "savages to enjoy their deserts in quiet lest the peltry trade should decrease." This called out Burke's splendid protest:

> If you stopped your grants, what would be the consequence? The people would occupy without grants. They have already so occupied in many places. You cannot station garrisons in every part of these deserts. If you drive the people from one place, they will carry on their annual tillage and remove with their flocks and herds to another. Many of the people in the back settlements are already little attached to particular situations. Already they have topped the Appalachian Mountains. From thence they behold before them an immense plain, one vast, rich, level meadow; a square of 500 miles. Over this they would wander without a possibility of restraint; they would change their manners with their habits of life; would soon forget a government by which they were disowned; would become hordes of English Tartars; and, pouring down upon your unfortified frontiers a fierce and irresistible cavalry, become masters of your governors and your counselors, your collectors and comptrollers, and of all the slaves that adhered to them. Such would, and in no long time must, be the effect of attempting to forbid as a crime, and to suppress as an evil, the command and blessing of Providence, "Increase and multiply." Such would be the happy result of an endeavor to keep as a lair of wild beasts that earth which God, by an express charter, has given to the children of men.

But the English government was not alone in its desire to limit the advance of the frontier and guide its destinies. Tidewater Virginia and South Carolina gerrymandered those colonies to ensure the dominance of the coast in their legislatures. Washington desired to settle a state at a time in the Northwest; Jefferson would reserve from settlement the territory of his Louisiana Purchase north of the 32nd parallel in order to offer it to the Indians in exchange for their settlements east of the Mississippi. "When we shall be full on this side," he writes, "we may lay off a range of states on the western bank from the head to the mouth, and so, range after range, advancing compactly as we multiply." Madison went so far as to argue to the French minister that the United States had no interest in seeing population extend itself on the right bank of the Mississippi, but should rather fear it.

When the Oregon question was under debate in 1824, Smyth, of Virginia, would draw an unchangeable line for the limits of the United States at the outer limit of two tiers of states beyond the Mississippi, complaining that the seaboard states were being drained of the flower of their population by the bringing of too much land into market.

Even Thomas Benton, the man of widest views of the destiny of the West, at this stage of his career declared that along the ridge of the Rocky Mountains "the western limits of the republic should be drawn, and the statue of the fabled god Terminus should be raised upon its highest peak, never to be thrown down." But the attempts to limit our boundaries, to restrict land sales and settlement, and to deprive the West of its share of political power were all in vain. Steadily that frontier of settlement advanced and carried with it individualism, democracy, and nationalism, and powerfully affected the Old World.

The most effective efforts of the East to regulate the frontier came through its educational and religious activity, exerted by interstate migration and by organized societies. Speaking in 1835, Dr. Lyman Beecher declared: "It is equally plain that the religious and political destiny of our nation is to be decided in the West," and he pointed out that the population of the West,

is assembled from all the states of the Union and from all the nations of Europe, and is rushing in like the waters of the flood, demanding for its moral preservation the immediate and universal action of those institutions which discipline the mind and arm the conscience and the heart. And so various are the opinions and habits, and so recent and imperfect is the acquaintance, and so sparse are the settlements of the West, that no homogeneous public sentiment can be formed to legislate immediately into being the requisite institutions. And yet they are all needed immediately in their utmost perfection and power. A nation is being "born in a day." . . . But what will become of the West if her prosperity rushes up to such a majesty of power while those great institutions linger which are necessary to form the mind and the conscience, and the heart of that vast world? It must not be permitted. . . . Let no man at the East quiet himself and dream of liberty, whatever may become of the West. . . . Her destiny is our destiny.

With this appeal to the conscience of New England, he adds appeals to her fears lest other religious sects anticipate her own. The New England preacher and schoolteacher left their mark on the West. The dread of Western emancipation from New England's political and economic control was paralleled by fears lest the West cut loose from her religion. Commenting in 1850 on reports that settlement was rapidly extending northward in Wisconsin, the editor of *The Home Missionary* writes:

We scarcely know whether to rejoice or to mourn over this extension of our settlements. While we sympathize in whatever tends to increase the physical resources and prosperity of our country, we cannot forget that with all these dispersions into remote and still remoter corners of the land, the supply of the means of grace is becoming relatively less and less.

Acting in accordance with such ideas, home missions were established and Western colleges were erected. As seaboard cities like Philadelphia, New York, and Baltimore strove for the mastery of Western trade, so the various denominations strove for the possession of the West. Thus an intellectual stream from New England sources fertilized the West. On the other hand, the contest for power and the expansive tendency, furnished to the various sects by the existence of a moving frontier, must have had important results on the character of religious organization in the United States. It is a chapter in our history which needs study.

From the conditions of frontier life came intellectual traits of profound importance. The works of travelers along each frontier from colonial days onward describe for each certain traits, and these traits have, while softening down, still persisted as survivals in the place of their origin, even when a higher social organization succeeded. The result is that, to the frontier, the American intellect owes its striking characteristics. That coarseness and strength combined with acuteness and inquisitiveness, that practical, inventive turn of mind, quick to find expedients, that masterful grasp of material things, lacking in the artistic but powerful to effect great ends, that restless, nervous energy, that dominant individualism, working for good and for evil, and withal that buoyancy and exuberance which comes with freedom — these are traits of the frontier, or traits called out elsewhere because of the existence of the frontier.

Since the days when the fleet of Columbus sailed into the waters of the New World, America has been another name for opportunity, and the people of the United States have taken their tone from the incessant expansion which has not only been open but has even been forced upon them. He would be a rash prophet who should assert that the expansive character of American life has now entirely ceased. Movement has been its dominant fact, and, unless this training has no effect upon a people, the American intellect will continually demand a wider field for its exercise. But never again will such gifts of free land offer themselves.

For a moment at the frontier the bonds of custom are broken, and unrestraint is triumphant. There is not *tabula rasa*. The stubborn American environment is there with its imperious summons to accept its conditions; the inherited ways of doing things are also there; and yet, in spite of environment and in spite of custom, each frontier did indeed furnish a new field of opportunity, a gate of escape from the bondage of the past; and freshness, and confidence, and scorn of older society, impatience of its restraints and its ideas, and indifference to its lessons, have accompanied the frontier.

What the Mediterranean Sea was to the Greeks, breaking the bond of custom, offering new experiences, calling out new institutions and activities, that and more the ever retreating frontier has been to the United States directly, and to the nations of Europe more remotely. And now, four centuries from the discovery of America, at the end of a hundred years of life under the Constitution, the frontier has gone, and with its going has closed the first period of American history.

89.

Controversy Over Hawaii

President Benjamin Harrison's policy of overseas expansion in search of foreign markets coincided with the desire of the white businessmen of Hawaii for annexation by the United States. Annexation would provide stable government, but, more to the point, it would free the islands of high American tariffs. With the support and encouragement of the administration, and with the use of a small number of American troops, the Hawaiian monarchy was overthrown early in 1893 and a provisional government established. Harrison recognized the new regime and sent a treaty of annexation to the Senate for ratification. But his term of office was nearly over, and Grover Cleveland, who was to be President in three weeks, held up ratification until he could study the circumstances that had led to the treaty. When he learned of them, he withdrew the treaty from deliberation. The selections printed below are from Harrison's message transmitting the treaty to the Senate on February 15, 1893, and Cleveland's message of the following December 18 withdrawing it from consideration.

Source: Richardson, IX, pp. 348-349, 460-472.

I.

BENJAMIN HARRISON:
For Annexation

I TRANSMIT HEREWITH, with a view to its ratification, a treaty of annexation concluded on the 14th day of February, 1893, between John W. Foster, secretary of state, who was duly empowered to act in that behalf on the part of the United States, and Lorin A. Thurston, W. R. Castle, W. C. Wilder, C. L. Carter, and Joseph Marsden, the commissioners on the part of the government of the Hawaiian Islands. The provisional treaty, it will be observed, does not attempt to deal in detail with the questions that grow out of the annexation of the Hawaiian Islands to the United States. The commissioners representing the Hawaiian government have consented to leave to the future and to the just and benevolent purposes of the United States the adjustment of all such questions.

I do not deem it necessary to discuss at any length the conditions which have resulted in this decisive action. It has been the policy of the administration not only to respect but to encourage the continuance of an independent government in the Hawaiian Islands so long as it afforded suitable guarantees for the protection of life and property and maintained a stability and strength that gave adequate security against the domination of any other power. The moral support of this government has continually manifested itself in the most friendly diplomatic relations and in many acts of courtesy to the Hawaiian rulers.

The overthrow of the monarchy was not in any way promoted by this government, but had its origin in what seems to have been a reactionary and revolutionary policy on the part of Queen Liliuokalani, which put in serious peril not only the large and preponderating interests of the United States in the islands but all foreign interests, and, indeed, the decent administration of civil affairs and the peace of the islands. It is quite evident that the monarchy had become effete and the queen's government so weak and inadequate as to be the prey of designing and unscrupulous persons. The restoration of Queen Liliuokalani to her throne is undesirable, if not impossible, and unless actively supported by the United States would be accompanied by serious disaster and the disorganization of all business interests. The influence and interest of the United States in the islands must be increased and not diminished.

Only two courses are now open — one the establishment of a protectorate by the United States, and the other annexation, full and complete. I think the latter course, which has been adopted in the treaty, will be highly promotive of the best interests of the Hawaiian people and is the only one that will adequately secure the interests of the United States. These interests are not wholly selfish. It is essential that none of the other great powers shall secure these islands. Such a possession would not consist with our safety and with the peace of the world. This view of the situation is so apparent and conclusive that no protest has been heard from any government against proceedings looking to annexation. Every foreign representative at Honolulu promptly acknowledged the Provisional Government, and I think there is a general concurrence in the opinion that the deposed queen ought not to be restored.

II.

GROVER CLEVELAND:
Against Annexation

WHEN THE PRESENT ADMINISTRATION entered upon its duties, the Senate had under consideration a treaty providing for the annexation of the Hawaiian Islands to the territory of the United States. Surely under our Constitution and laws the enlargement of our limits is a manifestation of the highest attribute of sovereignty, and if entered upon as an executive act, all things relating to the transaction should be clear and free from suspicion. Additional importance attached to this particular treaty of annexation because it contemplated a departure from unbroken American tradition in providing for the addition to our territory of islands of the sea more than 2,000 miles removed from our nearest coast. . . .

I conceived it to be my duty, therefore, to withdraw the treaty from the Senate for examination, and meanwhile to cause an accurate, full, and impartial investigation to be made of the facts attending the subversion of the constitutional government of Hawaii and the installment in its place of the Provisional Government. . . .

As I apprehend the situation, we are brought face to face with the following conditions:

The lawful government of Hawaii was overthrown without the drawing of a sword or the firing of a shot by a process every step of which, it may safely be asserted, is directly traceable to and dependent for its success upon the agency of the United States acting through its diplomatic and naval representatives.

But for the notorious predilections of the United States minister for annexation, the Committee of Safety, which should be called the Committee of Annexation, would never have existed.

But for the landing of the United States forces upon false pretexts respecting the danger to life and property, the committee would never have exposed themselves to the pains and penalties of treason by undertaking the subversion of the queen's government.

But for the presence of the United States forces in the immediate vicinity and in position to afford all needed protection and support, the committee would not have proclaimed the Provisional Government from the steps of the government building.

And, finally, but for the lawless occupation of Honolulu under false pretexts by the United States forces, and but for Minister Stevens' recognition of the Provisional Government when the United States forces were its sole support and constituted its only military strength, the queen and her government would never have yielded to the Provisional Government, even for a time and for the sole purpose of submitting her case to the enlightened justice of the United States.

Believing, therefore, that the United States could not, under the circumstances disclosed, annex the islands without justly incurring the imputation of acquiring them by unjustifiable methods, I shall not again submit the treaty of annexation to the Senate for its consideration, and in the instructions to Minister Willis, a copy of which accompanies this message, I have directed him to so inform the Provisional Government.

But in the present instance our duty does not, in my opinion, end with refusing to consummate this questionable transaction. It has been the boast of our government that it seeks to do justice in all things without regard to the strength or weakness of those with whom it deals. I mistake the American people if they favor the odious doctrine that there is no such thing as international morality; that there is one law for a strong nation and another for a weak one, and that even by indirection a strong power may with impunity despoil a weak one of its territory.

By an act of war, committed with the participation of a diplomatic representative of the United States and without authority of Congress, the government of a feeble but friendly and confiding people has been overthrown. A substantial wrong has thus been done which a due regard for our national character as well as the rights of the injured people requires we should endeavor to repair. The Provisional Government has not assumed a republican or other constitutional form, but has remained a mere executive council or oligarchy, set up without the assent of the people. It has not sought to find a permanent basis of popular support and has given no evidence of an intention to do so. Indeed, the representatives of that government assert that the people of Hawaii are unfit for popular government and frankly avow that they can be best ruled by arbitrary or despotic power.

The law of nations is founded upon reason and justice, and the rules of conduct governing individual relations between citizens or subjects of a civilized state are equally applicable as between enlightened nations. The considerations that international law is without a court for its enforcement and that obedience to its commands practically depends upon good faith instead of upon the mandate of a superior tribunal only give additional sanction to the law itself and brand any deliberate infraction of it not merely as a wrong but as a disgrace. A man of true honor protects the unwritten word which binds his conscience more scrupulously, if possible, than he does the bond a breach of which subjects him to legal liabilities, and the United States, in aiming to maintain itself as one of the most enlightened nations, would do its citizens gross injustice if it applied to its international relations any other than a high standard of honor and morality.

On that ground the United States cannot properly be put in the position of countenancing a wrong after its commission any more than in that of consenting to it in advance. On that ground it cannot allow itself to refuse to redress an injury inflicted through an abuse of power by officers clothed with its authority and wearing its uniform; and on the same ground, if a feeble but friendly state is in danger of being robbed of its independence and its sovereignty by a misuse of the name and power of the United States, the United States cannot fail to vindicate its honor and its sense of justice by an earnest effort to make all possible reparation.

These principles apply to the present case with irresistible force when the special conditions of the queen's surrender of her sovereignty are recalled. She surrendered, not to the Provisional Government but to the United States. She surrendered, not absolutely and permanently but temporarily and conditionally until such time as the facts could be considered by the United States. Furthermore, the Provisional Government acquiesced in her surrender in that manner and on those terms, not only by tacit consent but through the positive acts of some members of the government who urged her peaceable submission, not merely to avoid bloodshed but because she could place implicit reliance upon the justice of the United States and that the whole subject would be finally considered at Washington.

90.

E. V. Smalley: Life on the Prairie Farms

The recurrent farm problems of the nineteenth century were usually described in political and economic terms, but there were also social difficulties imposed by the solitary nature of farm life. "Few who have not been residents of the country,"
James McCabe declared in 1875, "can rightly understand the monotony of a farmer's life. . . . He lives a lonely and secluded life, rarely caring to go beyond the limits of his farm. . . . No wonder, then, that with constant toil and unbroken solitude as his only companions, the farmer should be a careworn, prematurely old man." One attempt at a solution was the social program of the Grange; another was the following proposal by E. V. Smalley, who called for a complete reorganization of rural villages.

Source: *Atlantic Monthly,* September 1893: "The Isolation of Life on Prairie Farms."

IN NO CIVILIZED COUNTRY have the cultivators of the soil adapted their home life so badly to the conditions of nature as have the people of our great Northwestern prairies. This is a strong statement, but I am led to the conclusion by ten years of observation in our plains region.

The European farmer lives in a village, where considerable social enjoyment is possible. The women gossip at the village well and visit frequently at one another's houses; the children find playmates close at hand; there is a school and, if the village be not a very small one, a church. The post wagon, with its uniformed postilion merrily blowing his horn, rattles through the street every day and makes an event that draws people to the doors and windows. The old men gather of summer evenings to smoke their pipes and talk of the crops; the young men pitch quoits and play ball on the village green. Now and then a detachment of soldiers from some garrison town halts to rest. A peddler makes his rounds. A black-frocked priest tarries to join in the chat of the elder people and to ask after the health of the children. In a word, something takes place to break the monotony of daily life. The dwellings, if small and meagerly furnished, have thick walls of brick or stone that keep out the summer's heat and the winter's chill.

Now contrast this life of the European peasant, to which there is a joyous side that lightens labor and privation, with the life of a poor settler on a homestead claim in one of the Dakotas or Nebraska. Every homesteader must live upon his claim for five years to perfect his title and get his patent; so that if there were not the universal American custom of isolated farm life to stand in the way, no farm villages would be possible in the first occupancy of a new region in the West without a change in our land laws. If the country were so thickly settled that every quarter section of land (160 acres) had a family upon it, each family would be half a mile from any neighbor, supposing the houses to stand in the center of the farms; and in any case the average distance between them could not be less. But many settlers own 320 acres, and a few have a square mile of land, 640 acres.

Then there are school sections, belonging to the state, and not occupied at all; and everywhere you find vacant tracts owned by Eastern speculators or by mortgage companies, to which former settlers have abandoned their claims, going to newer regions and leaving their debts and their land behind. Thus the average space separating the farmsteads is, in fact, always more than half a mile, and many settlers must go a mile or two to reach a neighbor's house. This condition obtains not on the frontiers alone but in fairly well-peopled agricultural districts.

If there be any region in the world where the natural gregarious instinct of mankind should assert itself, that region is our Northwestern prairies, where a short, hot summer is followed by a long, cold winter and where there is little in the aspect of

nature to furnish food for thought. On every hand the treeless plain stretches away to the horizon line. In summer, it is checkered with grain fields or carpeted with grass and flowers, and it is inspiring in its color and vastness; but one mile of it is almost exactly like another, save where some watercourse nurtures a fringe of willows and cottonwoods. When the snow covers the ground, the prospect is bleak and dispiriting. No brooks babble under icy armor. There is no bird life after the wild geese and ducks have passed on their way south. The silence of death rests on the vast landscape, save when it is swept by cruel winds that search out every chink and cranny of the buildings and drive through each unguarded aperture the dry, powdery snow.

In such a region, you would expect the dwellings to be of substantial construction, but they are not. The new settler is too poor to build of brick or stone. He hauls a few loads of lumber from the nearest railway station and puts up a frail little house of two, three, or four rooms that looks as though the prairie winds would blow it away. Were it not for the invention of tarred building paper, the flimsy walls would not keep out the wind and snow. With this paper the walls are sheathed under the weatherboards. The barn is often a nondescript affair of sod walls and straw roof. Lumber is much too dear to be used for dooryard fences, and there is no enclosure about the house.

A barbed-wire fence surrounds the barnyard. Rarely are there any trees, for, on the prairies, trees grow very slowly and must be nursed with care to get a start. There is a saying that you must first get the Indian out of the soil before a tree will grow at all; which means that some savage quality must be taken from the ground by cultivation.

In this cramped abode, from the windows of which there is nothing more cheerful in sight than the distant houses of other settlers, just as ugly and lonely, and stacks of straw and unthreshed grain, the farmer's family must live. In the summer there is a school for the children, one, two, or three miles away; but in winter the distances across the snow-covered plains are too great for them to travel in severe weather; the schoolhouse is closed, and there is nothing for them to do but to house themselves and long for spring. Each family must live mainly to itself, and life, shut up in the little wooden farmhouses, cannot well be very cheerful.

A drive to the nearest town is almost the only diversion. There the farmers and their wives gather in the stores and manage to enjoy a little sociability. The big coal stove gives out a grateful warmth, and there is a pleasant odor of dried codfish, groceries, and ready-made clothing. The women look at the display of thick cloths and garments and wish the crop had been better so that they could buy some of the things of which they are badly in need. The men smoke corncob pipes and talk politics. It is a cold drive home across the windswept prairies, but at least they have had a glimpse of a little broader and more comfortable life than that of the isolated farm.

There are few social events in the life of these prairie farmers to enliven the monotony of the long winter evenings; no singing schools, spelling schools, debating clubs, or church gatherings. Neighborly calls are infrequent because of the long distances which separate the farmhouses and because, too, of the lack of homogeneity of the people. They have no common past to talk about. They were strangers to one another when they arrived in this new land, and their work and ways have not thrown them much together.

Often the strangeness is intensified by differences of national origin. There are Swedes, Norwegians, Germans, French Canadians, and perhaps even such peculiar people as Finns and Icelanders, among the settlers, and the Americans come from many different states. It is hard to establish any social bond in such a mixed population, yet one and all need social intercourse, as the thing most essential to pleasant living, after food, fuel, shelter, and clothing.

An alarming amount of insanity occurs in the new prairie states among farmers and their wives. In proportion to their numbers, the Scandinavian settlers furnish the largest contingent to the asylums. The reason is not far to seek. These people came from cheery little farm villages. Life in the fatherland was hard and toilsome, but it was not lonesome. Think for a moment how great the change must be from the white-walled, red-roofed village on a Norway fjord, with its church and schoolhouse, its fishing boats on the blue inlet, and its green mountain walls towering aloft to snowfields, to an isolated cabin on a Dakota prairie, and say if it is any wonder that so many Scandinavians lose their mental balance.

There is but one remedy for the dreariness of farm life on the prairies: the isolated farmhouse must be abandoned, and the people must draw together in villages. The peasants of the Russian steppes did this centuries ago, and so did the dwellers on the great Danubian plain. In the older parts of our prairie states, in western Minnesota, eastern Nebraska and Kansas, and the eastern parts of North and South Dakota, titles to homestead claims are now nearly all perfected by the required five years' occupancy of the land. Thus, there is no longer a necessity that the farmers should live upon the particular tracts which they cultivate. They might go out with their teams to till the fields and return at evening to village homes.

It would be entirely feasible to redivide the land in regions where it is all of nearly uniform fertility and value. Let us suppose that the owners of sixteen quarter section farms, lying in a body and forming four full sections, should agree to remove their homes to the center of the tract and run new dividing lines radiating to the outer boundaries. Each settler would still have 160 acres, and no one would live more than a mile from the remotest limit of his farm. The nearer fields could be used for stock, and the distant ones for grain. The homes of the sixteen families would surround a village green where the schoolhouse would stand. This could be used for church services on Sunday and for various social purposes on weekday evenings.

Such a nucleus of population would, however, soon possess a church in common with other farmers in the neighborhood who might still cling to the old mode of isolated living, and there would probably be a store and a post office. An active social life would soon be developed in such a community. The school would go on winters as well as summers. Friendly attachments would be formed, and mutual helpfulness in farm and household work would soon develop into a habit. There would be nursing in illness, and consolation for those mourning for their dead. If the plains people were thus brought together into hamlets, some home industries might be established that would add to family incomes, or at least save outlay.

The economic weakness of farming in the North is the enforced idleness of the farmer and his work animals during the long winter. After threshing and fall plowing are finished, there is nothing to do but to feed the stock. Four or five months are unproductive, and all this time the people and the animals are consuming the fruits of the working season. Even the women are not fully occupied in the care of their little houses and the cooking of the simple meals; for the stockings are no longer knit at home, there is no hum of the spinning wheel, and the clothing is bought ready-made at the stores. If it were possible to restore to the farm some of the minor handicrafts that were carried on in the country thirty or forty years ago, there would be great gain in comfort, intelligence, and contentment.

Now and then, while traveling over the Dakota prairies, I hear of a family that sends to market some kind of delicate cheese or makes sausages of superior quality that find ready sale in the neighboring towns or preserves small fruits. These little industries might be much extended if the farmers lived in communities, where extra labor could be had when needed, and where there would be mental attrition to wear off the rust of the winter's indolence and stimulate effort on new lines.

The early French colonists who settled along the shores of the Red River of the North, in Manitoba, divided the land into long, narrow strips running back from the river banks and, thus, formed a continuous village many miles long. In this they followed the example of their ancestors who first occupied the shores of the St. Lawrence. It was adherence to this custom and resistance to the division of the land into checkerboard squares, that brought on the rebellion of Riel and his half-breeds on the Saskatchewan. The Mennonites, who occupy the western side of the Red River just north of the American boundary, live in villages. With the exception of a few peculiar religious communities in Iowa and Kansas, I know of no other instances where farmers have established their homes in compact settlements.

In all our prairie towns, however, one finds in winter many farmers' families who have left their houses and stock to the care of hired men and are living in rooms over stores or in parts of dwellings rented for temporary occupancy, in order to give their children opportunity for education and to escape the dreary monotony of isolation. The gregarious instinct thus asserts itself, in spite of habit and of the inherited American idea that a farmer must live upon the land he tills and must have no near neighbors. This habit will be hard to break, but I believe it must yield sometime to the evident advantages of closer association.

I have known instances, however, where efforts at more neighborly ways of living have been made on a small scale and have failed. In the early settlement of Dakota, it sometimes happened that four families, taking each a quarter section homestead, built their temporary dwellings on the adjacent corners, so as to be near together; but a few years later, when they were able to put up better buildings, they removed to the opposite sides of their claims, giving as a reason that their chickens got mixed up with their neighbors' fowls. In these instances, I should add, the people were Americans. There is a crusty individuality about the average American farmer, the inheritance of generations of isolated living, that does not take kindly to the familiarities of close association.

I am aware that nothing changes so slowly as the customs of a people. It will take a long time to modify the settled American habit of isolated farmsteads. If it is ever changed, the new system will have to be introduced near the top of the rural social scale, and work down gradually to the masses. A group of farmers of superior intelligence and of rather more than average means must set an example and establish a model farm village; or perhaps this could be done by the owner of one of the so-called bonanza farms, who might subdivide four sections of his land, as I have described, and invite purchasers to build their homes around a central village green; or, still better, he might himself put up the farmhouses and barn and then offer the farms for sale.

The experiment would be widely discussed by the newspapers, and this extensive free advertising could hardly fail to attract as purchasers a class of people with faith in the idea and possessed of such a sociable, neighborly disposition as would open the way to harmonious living and to considerable practical cooperation in field work and the care of animals. One successful community would soon lead to the formation of others, and the new system would steadily spread.

The plains of the West extend from the Gulf of Mexico to the valley of the Saskatchewan in the British territory. A belt about 300 miles wide on the eastern side of this vast region receives sufficient rainfall for farming. This belt is the granary of the continent, and even with its present sparse settlement it produces an enormous yearly surplus of wheat and corn. Its cultivators have thus far been engaged in a hard struggle to establish themselves on the soil, procure the necessaries of existence, and pay off their mortgages. They are getting ahead year by year; and in the older settled districts good houses are taking the places of the pioneer shanties, and the towns show thrift and progress. Before long these prairie people will begin to grapple with the problems of a higher civilization. Then it will be found, I believe, that the first great step in advance in the direction of more comfortable living and of intellectual development and rational social enjoyment is the abandonment of the lonesome farmhouse and the establishment of the farm village.

1894

91.

WILLIAM GRAHAM SUMNER: The Absurdity of Social Planning

*The introduction of Darwinian evolutionary theory into American intellectual circles
gave impetus to the study of the social sciences, but students divided on the correct
interpretation of Darwin's ideas. Social reformers and antireform groups alike
claimed to have found in Darwin a rationale for their respective positions. Professor
William Graham Sumner of Yale University stressed the deterministic aspects of
evolutionary theory, arguing that man had little control over his own destiny. In the
social and economic "jungle," Sumner contended, the fittest individuals would triumph
and the weakest be eliminated. The excerpts that follow, from Sumner's essay
"The Absurd Effort to Make the World Over," reflect his view that the activities of
social critics and reformers were inevitably self defeating, and that such efforts were
no less than an attempt to defy the laws of nature.*

Source: *Forum*, March 1894.

THE PROPOSITIONS put forward by social reformers nowadays are chiefly of two kinds. There are assertions in historical form, chiefly in regard to the comparison of existing with earlier social states, which are plainly based on defective historical knowledge, or at most on current stock historical dicta which are uncritical and incorrect. Writers very often assert that something never existed before because they do not know that it ever existed before, or that something is worse than ever before because they are not possessed of detailed information about what has existed before. The other class of propositions consists of dogmatic statements, which, whether true or not, are unverifiable. This class of proposi-tions is the pest and bane of current economic and social discussion.

Upon a more or less superficial view of some phenomenon, a suggestion arises which is embodied in a philosophical proposition and promulgated as a truth. From the form and nature of such propositions they can always be brought under the head of "ethics." This word at least gives them an air of elevated sentiment and purpose, which is the only warrant they possess. It is impossible to test or verify them by any investigation or logical process whatsoever. It is therefore very difficult for anyone who feels a high responsibility for historical statements, and who absolutely rejects any statement which is unverifiable, to find a common platform for discussion, or to join issue satisfactorily in taking the negative.

When anyone asserts that the class of skilled and unskilled manual laborers of the United States are worse off now in respect to diet, clothing, lodgings, furniture, fuel, and lights; in respect to the age at which they can marry; the number of children they can provide for; the start in life which they can give to their children; and their chances of accumulating capital than they ever have been at any former time, he makes a reckless assertion for which no facts have been offered in proof. Upon an appeal to facts, the contrary of this assertion would be clearly established. It suffices, therefore, to challenge those who are responsible for the assertion to make it good.

If it is said that the employed class are under much more stringent discipline than they were thirty years ago or earlier, it is true. It is not true that there has been any qualitative change in this respect within thirty years, but it is true that a movement which began at the first settlement of the country has been advancing with constant acceleration and has become a noticeable feature within our time. This movement is the advance in the industrial organization.

The first settlement was made by agriculturists, and for a long time there was scarcely any organization. There were scattered farmers, each working for himself, and some small towns with only rudimentary commerce and handicrafts. As the country has filled up, the arts and professions have been differentiated and the industrial organization has been advancing. This fact and its significance has hardly been noticed at all; but the stage of the industrial organization existing at any time and the rate of advance in its development are the absolutely controlling social facts.

Nine-tenths of the socialistic and semisocialistic, and sentimental or ethical, suggestions by which we are overwhelmed come from failure to understand the phenomena of the industrial organization and its expansion. It controls us all because we are all in it. It creates the conditions of our existence, sets the limits of our social activity, regulates the bonds of our social relations, determines our conceptions of good and evil, suggests our life philosophy, molds our inherited political institutions, and reforms the oldest and toughest customs, like marriage and property. I repeat that the turmoil of heterogeneous and antagonistic social whims and speculations in which we live is due to the failure to understand what the industrial organization is and its all-pervading control over human life, while the traditions of our schools of philosophy lead us always to approach the industrial organization, not from the side of objective study but from that of philosophical doctrine. Hence it is that we find that the method of measuring what we see happening by what are called ethical standards, and of proposing to attack the phenomena by methods thence deduced, is so popular.

The advance of a new country from the very simplest social coordination up to the highest organization is a most interesting and instructive chance to study the development of the organization. It has, of course, been attended all the way along by stricter subordination and higher discipline. All organization implies restriction of liberty. The gain of power is won by narrowing individual range. The methods of business in colonial days were loose and slack to an inconceivable degree.

The movement of industry has been all the time toward promptitude, punctuality, and reliability. It has been attended all the way by lamentations about the good old times; about the decline of small industries; about the lost spirit of comradeship between employer and employee; about the narrowing of the interests of the workman; about his conversion into a machine or into a "ware"; and about industrial war. These lamentations have all had reference to unquestionable phenomena attendant on advancing organization.

In all occupations the same movement is discernible — in the learned professions, in schools, in trade, commerce, and transportation. It is to go on faster than ever now that the continent is filled up by the first superficial layer of population over its whole extent and the intensification of industry has begun. The great inventions both make the intension of the organization possible and make it inevitable, with all its consequences, whatever they may be.

I must expect to be told here, according to the current fashions of thinking, that we ought to control the development of the organization. The first instinct of the modern man is to get a law passed to forbid or prevent what, in his wisdom, he disapproves. A thing which is inevitable, however, is one which we cannot control. We have to make up our minds to it, adjust ourselves to it, and sit down to live with it. Its inevitableness may be disputed, in which case we must reexamine it; but if our analysis is correct, when we reach what is inevitable we reach the end, and our regulations must apply to ourselves, not to the social facts.

Now the intensification of the social organization is what gives us greater social power. It is to it that we owe our increased comfort and abundance. We are none of us ready to sacrifice this. On the contrary, we want more of it. We would not return to the colonial simplicity and the colonial exiguity if we could. If not, then we must pay the price. Our life is bounded on every side by conditions. We can have this, if we will agree to submit to that. In the case of industrial power and product, the great condition is combination of force under discipline and strict coordination. Hence the wild language about wage slavery and capitalistic tyranny.

In any state of society, no great achievements can be produced without great force. Formerly, great force was attainable only by slavery aggregating the power of great numbers of men. Roman civilization was built on this. Ours has been built on steam.

It is to be built on electricity. Then we are all forced into an organization around these natural forces and adapted to the methods of their application; and although we indulge in rhetoric about political liberty, nevertheless we find ourselves bound tight in a new set of conditions which control the modes of our existence and determine the directions in which alone economic and social liberty can go.

If it is said that there are some persons in our time who have become rapidly and in a great degree rich, it is true; if it is said that large aggregations of wealth in the control of individuals is a social danger, it is not true.

The movement of the industrial organization which has just been described has brought out a great demand for men capable of managing great enterprises. Such have been called "captains of industry." The analogy with military leaders suggested by this name is not misleading. The great leaders in the development of the industrial organization need those talents of executive and administrative skill, power to command, courage, and fortitude, which were formerly called for in military affairs and scarcely anywhere else. The industrial army is also as dependent on its captains as a military body is on its generals.

One of the worst features of the existing system is that the employees have a constant risk in their employer. If he is not competent to manage the business with success, they suffer with' him. Capital also is dependent on the skill of the captain of industry for the certainty and magnitude of its profits. Under these circumstances there has been a great demand for men having the requisite ability for this function. As the organization has advanced, with more impersonal bonds of coherence and wider scope of operations, the value of this functionary has rapidly increased. The possession of the requisite ability is a natural monopoly. Consequently, all the conditions have concurred to give to those who possessed this monopoly excessive and constantly advancing rates of remuneration.

Another social function of the first importance in an intense organization is the solution of those crises in the operation of it which are called the conjuncture of the market. It is through the market that the lines of relation run which preserve the system in harmonious and rhythmical operation. The conjuncture is the momentary sharper misadjustment of supply and demand which indicates that a redistribution of productive effort is called for. The industrial organization needs to be insured against these conjunctures, which, if neglected, produce a crisis and catastrophe; and it needs that they shall be anticipated and guarded against as far as skill and foresight can do it.

The rewards of this function for the bankers and capitalists who perform it are very great. The captains of industry and the capitalists who operate on the conjuncture, therefore, if they are successful, win, in these days, great fortunes in a short time. There are no earnings which are more legitimate or for which greater services are rendered to the whole industrial body. The popular notions about this matter really assume that all the wealth accumulated by these classes of persons would be here just the same if they had not existed. They are supposed to have appropriated it out of the common stock. This is so far from being true that, on the contrary, their own wealth would not be but for themselves; and, besides that, millions more, manyfold greater than their own, scattered in the hands of thousands, would not exist but for them. . . .

Great figures are set out as to the magnitude of certain fortunes and the proportionate amount of the national wealth held by a fraction of the population, and eloquent exclamation points are set against them. If the figures were beyond criticism, what would they prove? Where is the rich man who is oppressing anybody? If there was one, the newspapers would ring with it. The facts about the accumulation of wealth do not constitute a plutocracy, as I will show below. Wealth, in itself considered, is only power, like steam or electricity or knowledge. The question of its good or ill turns on the question how it will be used. To prove any harm in aggregations of wealth it must be shown that great wealth is, as a rule, in the ordinary course of social affairs, put to a mischievous use. This cannot be shown beyond the very slightest degree, if at all.

Therefore, all the allegations of general mischief, social corruption, wrong, and evil in our society must be referred back to those who make them for particulars and specifications. As they are offered to us we cannot allow them to stand, because we discern in them faulty observation of facts, or incorrect interpretation of facts, or a construction of facts according to some philosophy, or misunderstanding of phenomena and their relations, or incorrect inferences, or crooked deductions.

Assuming, however, that the charges against the existing "capitalistic" — that is, industrial — order of things are established, it is proposed to remedy the ill by reconstructing the industrial system on the principles of democracy. Once more we must untangle the snarl of half ideas and muddled facts.

Democracy is, of course, a word to conjure with. We have a Democratic-Republican political system, and we like it so well that we are prone to take any new step which can be recommended as "democratic," or which will round out some "principle" of democracy to a fuller fulfillment. Everything connected with this domain of political thought is crusted over with false historical traditions, cheap philosophy, and undefined terms, but it is useless to try to criticize it.

The whole drift of the world for 500 years has been toward democracy. That drift, produced by great discoveries and inventions, and by the discovery of a new continent, has raised the middle class out of the servile class. In alliance with the Crown they crushed the feudal classes. They made the Crown absolute in order to do it. Then they turned against the Crown, and, with the aid of the handicraftsmen and peasants, conquered it.

Now the next conflict which must inevitably come is that between the middle capitalist class and the proletariat, as the word has come to be used. If a certain construction is put on this conflict, it may be called that between democracy and plutocracy, for it seems that industrialism must be developed into plutocracy by the conflict itself. That is the conflict which stands before civilized society today. All the signs of the times indicate its commencement, and it is big with fate to mankind and to civilization.

Although we cannot criticize democracy profitably, it may be said of it, with reference to our present subject, that up to this time democracy never has done anything, either in politics, social affairs, or industry, to prove its power to bless mankind. If we confine our attention to the United States, there are three difficulties with regard to its alleged achievements, and they all have the most serious bearing on the proposed democratization of industry.

1. The time during which democracy has been tried in the United States is too short to warrant any inferences. A century or two is a very short time in the life of political institutions, and if the circumstances change rapidly during the period, the experiment is vitiated.

2. The greatest question of all about American democracy is whether it is a cause or a consequence. It is popularly assumed to be a cause, and we ascribe to its beneficent action all the political vitality, all the easiness of social relations, all the industrial activity and enterprise which we experience, and which we value and enjoy. I submit, however, that, on a more thorough examination of the matter, we shall find that de-

mocracy is a consequence. There are economic and sociological causes for our political vitality and vigor, for the ease and elasticity of our social relations, and for our industrial power and success. Those causes have also produced democracy, given it success, and have made its faults and errors innocuous.

Indeed, in any true philosophy, it must be held that in the economic forces which control the material prosperity of a population lie the real causes of its political institutions, its social class adjustments, its industrial prosperity, its moral code, and its world philosophy. If democracy and the industrial system are both products of the economic conditions which exist, it is plainly absurd to set democracy to defeat those conditions in the control of industry. If, however, it is not true that democracy is a consequence, and I am well aware that very few people believe it, then we must go back to the view that democracy is a cause. That being so, it is difficult to see how democracy, which has had a clear field here in America, is not responsible for the ills which Mr. Bellamy and his comrades in opinion see in our present social state, and it is difficult to see the grounds of asking us to entrust it also with industry.

The first and chief proof of success of political measures and systems is that, under them, society advances in health and vigor, and that industry develops without causing social disease. If this has not been the case in America, American democracy has not succeeded. Neither is it easy to see how the masses, if they have undertaken to rule, can escape the responsibilities of ruling, especially so far as the consequences affect themselves. If, then, they have brought all this distress upon themselves under the present system, what becomes of the argument for extending the system to a direct and complete control of industry?

3. It is by no means certain that democracy in the United States has not, up to this time, been living on a capital inherited from

aristocracy and industrialism. We have no pure democracy. Our democracy is limited at every turn by institutions which were developed in England in connection with industrialism and aristocracy, and these institutions are of the essence of our system. While our people are passionately democratic in temper and will not tolerate a doctrine that one man is not as good as another, they have common sense enough to know that he is not; and it seems that they love and cling to the conservative institutions quite as strongly as they do to the democratic philosophy. They are, therefore, ruled by men who talk the philosophy and govern by the institutions.

Now it is open to Mr. Bellamy to say that the reason why democracy in America seems to be open to the charge made in the last paragraph, of responsibility for all the ill which he now finds in our society, is because it has been infected with industrialism (capitalism); but, in that case, he must widen the scope of his proposition and undertake to purify democracy before turning industry over to it. The Socialists generally seem to think that they make their undertakings easier when they widen their scope and make them easiest when they propose to remake everything; but, in truth, social tasks increase in difficulty in an enormous ratio as they are widened in scope.

The question, therefore, arises, if it is proposed to reorganize the social system on the principles of American democracy, whether the institutions of industrialism are to be retained. If so, all the virus of capitalism will be retained. It is forgotten, in many schemes of social reformation in which it is proposed to mix what we like with what we do not like in order to extirpate the latter, that each must undergo a reaction from the other, and that what we like may be extirpated by what we do not like. We may find that instead of democratizing capitalism we have capitalized democracy — that is,

have brought in plutocracy. Plutocracy is a political system in which the ruling force is wealth.

The denunciations of capital which we hear from all the reformers is the most eloquent proof that the greatest power in the world today is capital. They know that it is, and confess it most when they deny it most strenuously. At present the power of capital is social and industrial, and only in a small degree political. So far as capital is political, it is on account of political abuses, such as tariffs and special legislation, on the one hand, and legislative strikes, on the other. These conditions exist in the democracy to which it is proposed to transfer the industries. What does that mean except bringing all the power of capital once for all into the political arena and precipitating the conflict of democracy and plutocracy at once?

Can anyone imagine that the masterfulness, the overbearing disposition, the greed of gain, and the ruthlessness in methods which are the faults of the master of industry at his worst would cease when he was a functionary of the state, which had relieved him of risk and endowed him with authority? Can anyone imagine that politicians would no longer be corruptly fond of money, intriguing and crafty when they were charged, not only with patronage and government contracts but also with factories, stores, ships, and railroads? Could we expect anything except that, when the politician and the master of industry were joined in one, we should have the vices of both unchecked by the restraints of either?

In any socialistic state there will be one set of positions which will offer chances of wealth beyond the wildest dreams of avarice, viz., on the governing committees. Then there will be rich men whose wealth will indeed be a menace to social interests, and instead of industrial peace there will be such war as no one has dreamed of yet — the war between the political ins and outs

— that is, between those who are on the committee and those who want to get on it. . . .

There is one democratic principle which means that each man should be esteemed for his merit and worth, for just what he is, without regard to birth, wealth, rank, or other adventitious circumstances. The other principle is that each one of us ought to be equal to all the others in what he gets and enjoys. The first principle is only partially realizable, but, so far as it goes, it is elevating and socially progressive and profitable. The second is not capable of an intelligible statement.

The first is a principle of industrialism. It proceeds from and is intelligible only in a society built on the industrial virtues, free endeavor, security of property, and repression of the baser vices; that is, in a society whose industrial system is built on labor and exchange. The other is only a rule of division for robbers who have to divide plunder or monks who have to divide gifts. If, therefore, we want to democratize industry in the sense of the first principle, we need only perfect what we have now, especially on its political side. If we try to democratize it in the sense of the other principle, we corrupt politics at one stroke; we enter upon an industrial enterprise which will waste capital and bring us all to poverty; and we set loose greed and envy as ruling social passions.

92.

CARL SCHURZ: Civil Service Reform

Carl Schurz's concern for reform of the federal civil service was evidenced early in his term as U.S. senator from Missouri. Unalterably opposed to President Grant's "spoils-loving and domineering partisans," Schurz introduced a bill on December 20, 1869, to create a permanent civil service merit system. Defeat of the bill did not end his vigorous efforts to eliminate corruption in public life, and the general policies outlined in his measure were incorporated in later civil service acts. From 1892 to 1901 Schurz served as president of the National Civil Service Reform League, to which group he delivered an address, reprinted here in part, on December 12, 1894.

Source: *The Necessity and Progress of Civil Service Reform*, Washington, 1894, pp. 3-20.

WHAT CIVIL SERVICE REFORM DEMANDS is simply that the business part of the government shall be carried on in a sound, businesslike manner. This seems so obviously reasonable that among people of common sense there should be no two opinions about it. And the condition of things to be reformed is so obviously unreasonable, so flagrantly absurd and vicious, that we should not believe it could possibly exist among sensible people had we not become accustomed to its existence among ourselves. In truth, we can hardly bring the whole exorbitance of that viciousness and absurdity home to our own minds unless we contemplate it as reflected in the mirror of a simile.

Imagine, then, a bank, the stockholders of which, many in number, are divided into two factions — let us call them the Jones party and the Smith party — who quarrel about some question of business policy as, for instance, whether the bank is to issue currency or not. The Jones party is in control, but the Smith men persuade over to their side a sufficient number of Jones men to give them — the Smith men — a majority at the next stockholders' meeting. Thus they succeed in getting the upper hand. They oust the old Board of Directors and elect a new Board consisting of Smith men. The new Smith Board at once remove all the officers, president, cashier, tellers, bookkeepers, and clerks down to the messenger boys — the good and the bad alike — simply because they are Jones men, and fill their places forthwith with new persons who are selected, not on the ground that they have in any way proved their fitness for the positions so filled but simply because they are Smith men; and those of the Smith men who have shown the greatest zeal and skill in getting a majority of votes for the Smith party are held to have the strongest claims for salaried places in the bank. The new men struggle painfully with the duties novel to them until they acquire some experience, but even then it needs in many instances two men or more to do the work of one.

In the course of events, dissatisfaction spreads among the stockholders with the Smith management, partly shared by ambitious Smith men who thought themselves entitled to reward in the shape of places and salaries, but were "left out in the cold." Now the time for a new stockholders' meeting arrives. After a hot fight, the Jones party carries the day. Its ticket of directors being elected, off go the heads of the Smith president, the Smith cashier, the Smith tellers, the Smith bookkeepers and clerks, to be replaced by true-blue Jones men who have done the work of the campaign and are expected to do more of it when the next election comes. And so the career of the bank goes on with its periodical changes of party in power at longer or shorter intervals and its corresponding clean sweeps of the bank service, with mismanagement and occasional fraud and peculation as inevitable incidents.

You might watch the proceedings of such a banking concern with intense curiosity and amusement. But I ask you, what prudent man among you would deposit his money in it or invest in its stock? And why would you not? Because you would think that this is not sensible men's business but foolish boys' play; that such management would necessarily result in reckless waste and dishonesty and tend to land many of the bank's officers in Canada, and not a few of its depositors or investors, in the poorhouse. Such would be your judgment, and in pronouncing it you would at the same time pronounce judgment upon the manner in which the business part of our national government, as well as of many if not most of our state and municipal governments, has been conducted for several generations.

This is the spoils system. And I have by no means presented an exaggerated or even a complete picture of it; nay, rather a mild sketch, indicating only with faint touches the demoralizing influences exercised by that system with such baneful effect upon the whole political life of the nation.

Looking at the financial side of the matter alone, it is certainly bad enough; it is indeed almost incomprehensible how the spoils system could be permitted through scores of years to vitiate our business methods in the conduct of the national revenue service, the postal service, the Indian service, the public-land service, involving us in indescribable administrative blunders, bringing about Indian wars, causing immense losses in the revenue, breeding extravagant and plundering practices in all departments, costing our people in the course of time untold hundreds of millions of money, and making our government one of the most wasteful in the world. All this, I say, is bad enough. It might be called discreditable enough to move any self-respecting people to shame.

But the spoils system has inflicted upon the American people injuries far greater than these. The spoils system, that practice which turns public offices, high and low, from public trusts into objects of prey and booty for the victorious party, may without extravagance of language be called one of the greatest criminals in our history, if not the greatest. In the whole catalogue of our ills there is none more dangerous to the vitality of our free institutions.

It tends to divert our whole political life from its true aims. It teaches men to seek something else in politics than the public good. It puts mercenary selfishness as the motive power for political action in the place of public spirit and organizes that selfishness into a dominant political force.

It attracts to active party politics the worst elements of our population and with them crowds out the best. It transforms political parties from associations of patriotic citizens, formed to serve a public cause, into bands of mercenaries using a cause to serve them. It perverts party contests from contentions of opinion into scrambles for plunder. By stimulating the mercenary spirit, it promotes the corrupt use of money in party contests and in elections.

It takes the leadership of political organizations out of the hands of men fit to be leaders of opinion and workers for high aims and turns it over to the organizers and leaders of bands of political marauders. It creates the boss and the machine, putting the boss into the place of the statesman and the despotism of the machine in the place of an organized public opinion.

It converts the public officeholder, who should be the servant of the people, into the servant of a party or of an influential politician, extorting from him time and work which should belong to the public and money which he receives from the public for public service. It corrupts his sense of duty by making him understand that his obligation to his party or his political patron is equal if not superior to his obligation to the public interest, and that his continuance in office does not depend on his fidelity to duty. It debauches his honesty by seducing him to use the opportunities of his office to indemnify himself for the burdens forced upon him as a party slave. It undermines in all directions the discipline of the public service.

It falsifies our constitutional system. It leads to the usurpation, in a large measure, of the executive power of appointment by members of the legislative branch, substituting their irresponsible views of personal or party interest for the judgment as to the public good and the sense of responsibility of the executive. It subjects those who exercise the appointing power, from the President of the United States down, to the intrusion of hordes of office hunters and their patrons, who rob them of the time and strength they should devote to the public interest. It has already killed two of our Presidents; one, the first Harrison, by worry, and the other, Garfield, by murder; and more recently it has killed a mayor in Chicago and a judge in Tennessee.

It degrades our senators and representatives in Congress to the contemptible position of office brokers, and even of mere agents of office brokers, making the business of dickering about spoils as weighty to them as their duties as legislators. It introduces the patronage as an agency of corrupt influence between the executive and the legislature. It serves to obscure the criminal character of bribery by treating bribery with offices as a legitimate practice. It thus reconciles the popular mind to practices essentially corrupt and thereby debauches the popular sense of right and wrong in politics.

It keeps in high political places, to the exclusion of better men, persons whose only ability consists in holding a personal following by adroit manipulation of the patronage. It has thus sadly lowered the standard of statesmanship in public position, compared with the high order of ability displayed in all other walks of life.

It does more than anything else to turn our large municipalities into sinks of corruption, to render Tammany Halls possible, and to make of the police force, here and there, a protector of crime and a terror to those whose safety it is to guard. It exposes us, by the scandalous spectacle of its periodical spoils carnivals, to the ridicule and contempt of civilized mankind, promoting among our own people the growth of serious doubts as to the practicability of democratic institutions on a great scale, and in an endless variety of ways it introduces into our political life more elements of demoralization, debasement, and decadence than any other agency of evil I know of, aye, perhaps more than all other agencies of evil combined.

These are some of the injuries the spoils system has been, and still is, inflicting upon this republic. Some, I say, not all; for it is impossible to follow its subtle virus into all the channels through which it exercises its poisonous influence. But I have said enough to illustrate its pernicious effects; and what I have said is only the teaching of sober observation and long experience. . . .

The view that the spoils system with its frequent rotations in office is needed to promote among the people a useful understanding of the nature and workings of the government finds, amazing as it may seem, still serious adherents among well-meaning citizens. It is based upon the assumption that the public service, which is instituted to do certain business for the people, should at the same time serve as a school in which ignorant persons are to learn something about the functions of the government. These two objects will hardly go together. If the public service is to do its business with efficiency and economy, it must of course be manned with persons fit for the work. If, on the other hand, it is to be used as a school to instruct ignorant people in the functions of the government — that is, in the duties of a postmaster or a revenue collector or an Indian agent or a department clerk — then we should select for such places persons who know least about them, for they have the most to learn.

And inasmuch as such persons, before having acquired the necessary knowledge, skill, and experience, will inevitably do the public business in a bungling manner, and therefore at much inconvenience and loss to the people, they should, in justice to the taxpayers, instead of drawing salaries, pay something for the instruction they receive; for as soon as they have learned enough really to earn a salary, they will have to be turned out to make room for others, who are as ignorant and in as great need of instruction as the outgoing set had been before. Evidently this kindergarten theory of the public service is hardly worth discussion. The school of the spoils system, as it has been in operation since 1829, has educated thousands of political loafers, but not one political sage.

That the government will not work satisfactorily unless all its officers and employees are in political harmony with the ruling party is also one of those superstitions which some estimable people have not yet been able to shake off. While they sternly resist the argument that there is no Democratic and no Republican way of sorting of letters or of collecting taxes or of treating Indians as theoretical moonshine, their belief must, after all, have received a rude shock by the conduct of the last three national administrations, including the present one. . . .

We hear from all sides expressions of disgust at the scandalous spectacle of the spoils carnival with every change of party in power, and the reckless distribution of public offices among political workers undeserving of honor and confidence. One public man in high station after another declares that the position of spoils-jobbers to which they are degraded puts upon them intolerable burdens and that it must cease. In all parts of the country chambers of commerce, boards of trade, and individual merchants protest that so many of our consulates abroad have long enough been held by incompetents, who merely wish to spend some time in foreign lands for their health or to get good music lessons for their daughters, that it is time we should cease to make such offices the laughingstock and contempt of foreign nations, and that at last only men should be sent out known to be fit to serve the interests of our commerce as the consuls of our commercial competitors serve theirs.

But, more significant than all this, where government comes nearest home to the individual citizen, its abuses have stirred up the strongest feeling. The people of some of our great municipalities are crying out that they have been scandalously misgoverned and robbed and oppressed by organized bands of mercenary politicians, who by hook or crook obtain complete possession of the municipal governments, or at least exercise a pernicious influence in them, and that there must be an end of this.

Nor are these complaints brought forth without the suggestion of a remedy. In every instance they are accompanied with the demand that the branch of the public service complained of — national, state, or municipal — must be "taken out of politics."

Never has the popular instinct hit the nail on the head more squarely than by this demand. For what does it mean to take a public function out of politics? It means simply that, with regard to all the public offices and employments concerned, rules for appointment and promotion be introduced which rigidly exclude political and personal favoritism, and secure places and preferment only to those who in some prescribed manner establish the superiority of their mental and moral fitness for the work to be done.

For a place in the administrative part of the government, not the mere henchman of some party leader or committee but he who proves himself better qualified for the duties of the office than his competitors; for the consular service, not a mere political drummer or a man who has put some member of Congress under political obligation but he who proves himself especially well-versed in commercial affairs and law and in command of the other necessary equipments for the performance of consular duty; for the police force, not a mere graduate of a whiskey shop whom some party boss or ward heeler wishes to wield the police club but he who is found in point of moral character, as well as mental and physical qualifications, to be a person of superior fitness for the duties of a policeman; and for promotion in the service, not the mere favorite of some political magnate or of his wife or daughter but he who has shown that he deserves that promotion by superior capacity, efficiency, and fidelity to duty! This is what it means to take public functions out of politics. And this is the merit system. This is civil service reform.

93.

HERBERT WELSH: Political Machines and City Government

The transformation of the United States from a rural to an urban nation at the end of the nineteenth century resulted in city governments becoming a prime target for progressive and reform groups. In a hundred years city population had multiplied 110 times, the population of the nation only 16 times. Private agencies assumed the burden wherever they could, but what was needed was an overall plan identifying the principal needs of urban centers. Men like Richard T. Ely and Herbert Welsh, guided by the programs of some European cities, proposed master plans for urban reform. In the winter of 1893-1894, reform leaders from several urban centers met at Philadelphia to organize the Conference for Good City Government. In the following article, published in April 1894, Welsh summarized the work of the new conference and the problems of city government.

Source: *Forum*, April 1894: "A Definite Step Toward Municipal Reform."

IN FORMING AN ESTIMATE of the significance of the recent Conference for Good City Government held in Philadelphia, it may be well at the outset to glance at some of the circumstances which determined that such a gathering should at that time be held. A small group of men in Philadelphia, who for some years past have taken an active part in local reform movements to secure purer politics, became strongly convinced that some step should be taken to bring about a fuller recognition of the importance of moral principles in politics, and, as a sequel to such recognition, the adoption of a practical working scheme by which higher standards might be maintained in actual practice. It was evident that some new plan must be devised to check the stream of political demoralization which, constantly increasing in force and volume, was becoming more and more unruly under ineffectual efforts to control it.

The outlook seemed to justify this estimate of the dangerous condition of American politics. In the richest and most important state of the Union, no scheme for in-creasing the power of the political machine was too unscrupulous or too audacious to be attempted, usually with successful results; and a "conspiracy for the acquisition of public plunder" was in undisputed control of New York City, with a strong representation in the United States senate. To that body Pennsylvania, too, had just returned a senator who had apparently spared no pains to convince his constituents that he had been guilty of a dishonest use of state funds, and had subsequently showed how little such a course interfered with the maintenance of his political ascendancy.

In New York, Philadelphia, Baltimore, and many other cities, all kinds of fraud in the management of elections were matters of common and almost unnoticed occurrence, while in the transaction of municipal business, abuses of various sorts were rife — schemes, jobs, speculations involving large direct financial losses to the cities concerned, and perhaps greater indirect losses through inefficiency and mismanagement. From various states, from rural as well as urban communities came accounts, some of them elaborated and detailed, of systematic buying and selling of votes; fraud and demoralization were generally believed to attend the legislative and executive management of federal pensions; and the Indian service was afflicted with the alternating partisan voracity of the two great parties. The most sober and conservative critics of the situation all agreed that it was very unsatisfactory, and that the forces opposed to existing political evils were insufficient, both in numbers and in organization, to cope with them.

Could not those forces be marshaled on new lines? Could not more simplicity in directing them to their point of attack be effected? Could not more harmony among themselves be brought about, which would greatly increase their effectiveness, augmenting their numbers and deepening the moral impression their efforts produced upon the public? Such questions naturally presented themselves.

There are many organizations representing various reform elements that might greatly be strengthened by a fuller recognition of the natural relationship which really existed between them. Civil service reform — probably the most fundamental of all this family — had for twenty years, under the distinguished leadership of George William Curtis, slowly and painfully advanced its line of battle, always holding the ground won, but as yet failing to reach the citadel of the national understanding or the national heart. Thousands of good men who were the natural allies of this, the most essential of our political reforms, had their sympathies chilled by the unfortunate coldness and technicality of its name; they failed to perceive its full significance; or they had not the opportunity afforded them of effectively applying their force to its advancement.

Ballot-reform associations, Indian-rights associations, municipal committees of one hundred or of fifty, law-and-order leagues, women's health-protective associations, all existed, and, as sharpshooters or small re-

form detachments, fired their scattering fusillades into the enemy. Good — much good — doubtless was being accomplished, but not enough in view of the attending cost or the boldness of the enemy and his effective organization. The practical, pertinent question which naturally presented itself was — Cannot tenfold the present result be reached if all or most of these scattered groups and societies of reformers, existing unknown to one another and out of touch with one another all over the country, are led to join together and to mass themselves at some strategic point, some Thermopylae in which they could, with comparative ease, have the advantage of the enemy?

Consultation and counsel on these points between a few men in Philadelphia and their friends and fellow workers in New York, Baltimore, Boston, Chicago, and other cities immediately reached practical results. One great idea, one headland of sound theory rises as a landmark out of the treacherous, fog-veiled sea over which the reform craft sails: a conviction that the present is the era of a reform in American politics, essentially moral in its nature; a reform that, in view of the absurd extremes to which loyalty to party has carried men, urges good citizenship to rally to the defense of principle as opposed to partisanship, and demands that all methods of political management essentially dishonest and unsound in nature be cast aside; a reform which calls for the destruction of machine politics and asks that means be devised by which a different class of public men from that which the machine offers can be placed in public office. A higher standard of public service must be established and maintained if American institutions are to give us the practical benefits that their founders sought.

It is interesting to note the enthusiastic assent given to a proposition that seemed to suggest itself — so spontaneously was it expressed in various localities — that the American *city* is the reform Thermopylae, the strategic point to which the fight can be led with the best chance of success. Reform here means reform throughout the country. The important idea which prompted the Conference was the hope that it might lead to some sort of national league among all the cities of the country in which reform elements are at work, which would promote enthusiasm in the cause among all their members, and secure the adoption of the simplest and best methods for obtaining municipal reform; and that other cities still dormant would be encouraged by the existence of such an organization to join it and to adopt accepted lines of work. The great cities, of course, being centers of population, wealth, and power, have become naturally the cradles of political corruption, and for many other reasons, which it is not necessary to discuss here, the effort for good government should be concentrated upon them.

The preliminary steps necessary for holding the Conference were taken in the early days of last summer. The encouragement with which the plan met in various directions, and especially from the City Club of New York, led to the final determination that the project should be carried through. Every effort was made to secure men whose position and ability would give the occasion dignity and weight, and men from localities sufficiently varied to make the gathering national in its character. These efforts were wholly successful. Many of those who attended the Conference were men of national reputation, and the papers read were of high ability and practical value.

New York, Brooklyn, Chicago, Boston, Baltimore, Minneapolis, Milwaukee, Albany, Buffalo, Columbus, Ohio, and Philadelphia, were represented. Delegates from New Orleans had set out for the Conference, but because of a failure to make railroad connections, they were belated and did not reach Philadelphia in time. It is interesting to note that, when the call for the Conference was issued, preparations were already begun by the workers for good city government in Minneapolis to call a similar national gathering in that city. Without any previous communication or understanding upon the subject, the necessity for the movement was recognized simultaneously by the West and by the East.

The sessions of the Conference were remarkable, both in the character and enthusiasm of the audience. At these meetings about an equal number of men and women were present. The women took the warmest and most appreciative interest in papers and discussions. They represented the best society of Philadelphia, not alone in social position but in moral and mental force, intelligence, cultivation, and in serious and effective work for the public good. One of the most suggestive papers read was by a woman. A word will be said later as to the influence the Conference is likely to exert upon the public work of women, and, conversely, upon the influence women are likely to exert upon municipal reform.

The most notable and practicable suggestions to be drawn from the facts and opinions presented at the Conference, and which should be held in clear view when treating the topic of its significance, are these:

As was shown conclusively by Mr. Carl Schurz, the foundation for all good city government must be laid in the unhesitating adoption of the principles of civil service reform: the spoils system must be abolished. The party boss is robbed of his most formidable weapon when he is no longer able to reward his henchmen from the public treasury by the gift of office. Then it is universally admitted that appointive offices are the property of the people and not of a party; and that partisan tests are no longer to be put to applicants for office but such tests only as may give reasonable evidence of the applicant's fitness for the place he seeks. Then the character of the entire service will be raised, and we may expect the downfall of the machine. This fundamental suggestion ought to go out in the van of all those uttered at the Conference.

The idea expressed at the Conference which might properly be ranked as second in point of importance is that, in approaching the question of good government in our municipalities, we must exclude all discussion of national issues. The stronghold of the boss lies in his power to separate good men into two rival partisan camps, whereas there is no reason why they should not be united in a single body, fighting and working for a single end — the good of the municipality. It seems astonishing that by so flimsy an expedient the engineers of the machine should be able to keep good citizens — and otherwise sensible men — perpetually quarreling among themselves while they and their followers capture the city.

The third practical suggestion to which attention should be especially directed is one naturally growing out of that which precedes it: this was the theme of the last paper presented at the Conference. *A municipal party* should be formed in all American cities with a view gradually to withdraw the control of city government from the hands of the national parties. This idea is perhaps most fully expressed in the organization of the Municipal League of Philadelphia, a purely municipal party. It invites to its membership all voters, irrespective of their opinions on other matters, who are united in their desire to see the city honestly, efficiently, and economically governed.

Of course the action of such a body in the beginning will be the same as that of any body of independents. If not strong enough to nominate its own candidates (and it is not likely at first to be equal to that task in most instances), it will throw its weight with the best candidates of either of the two great parties. After thus winning a few victories it will gather strength, and may, by a consistent and wise course, gradually gain acceptance in the community for

its ideas. The soundness of the theory on which its work rests will gradually be accepted, and ultimately it will become master of the situation.

The movement of such a municipal party in relation to the other two national parties will be like that of a body of men on the deck of a small steamboat who, by running in unison from one side of the vessel to the other, produce an increasing oscillation which ends by capsizing the boat. The municipal party aims to capsize the partisan craft, which, so far as the city's affairs are concerned, the national parties represent.

Such is a summary of the essential suggestions set forth by the Conference: the abolition of the spoils system; the exclusion of national issues from city affairs, and hence the crippling of the party machine; and the creation of a single municipal party. But, of course, these results cannot be obtained without a complete revolution in the attitude which the general public now maintains toward political questions. Present apathy must give way to future interest. With an awakened sense of individual obligation to the public welfare, citizens will acquire knowledge of the needs of the situation and of the steps necessary to meet them; and each will be willing, under wise leadership, to contribute his share of thought, money, and time to redeem his city from the curse of bad government.

Quite enough suggestion has been furnished by the Conference to indicate the main lines along which we must advance to gain the desired end. None can plead necessary confusion or ignorance on that point. The main questions that now need to be answered are moral ones: Are we convinced of the seriousness of the situation? Shall we make the sacrifices which the cause demands?

Before speaking, in conclusion, of the provision made by the Conference for the propagation of its ideas and the continuance of its work, a word may well be spoken of the indications given at the first gathering in Philadelphia, of the great part which women are likely to take in the cause of municipal reform. In no small degree was the success of the Conference due to the work of intelligent, experienced, and enthusiastic women. Their aid was invoked in order to render the effort successful, and they responded to the appeal in various practical ways. They made the "better half" of the audience as might be expected; they contributed materially to the discussions; they added an obvious social charm, and supplied an atmosphere of enthusiastic interest to the meetings. But these are mere indications of what may in the future be expected of cultivated and intelligent women in the cause of good city government.

Women are needed — and if their efforts are guided wisely they may become invaluable allies in this work. The task of munici-

pal reform is likely to exercise a strong influence upon the women who engage in it; it will teach them the self-restraint necessary to those who work effectively in organized bodies and will develop unsuspected powers of public usefulness. It will prepare the way for the next step — the franchise for women in political matters. What they have already effected in education, in the work of college settlements, in the line of municipal sanitation, and in kindred efforts, gives augury of their success in the more direct political work of the municipal problem. The indications on this point given by the Philadelphia Conference are worthy of the serious consideration of municipal reformers in other cities. The Civic Club of Philadelphia, an organization of women, constituted especially with a view to undertake municipal work, but which was in existence previous to the time of the national meeting in Philadelphia, has been greatly stimulated by it.

94.

Songs of New York

"Sidewalks of New York" and "The Bowery" present two different views of life in New York City. "Sidewalks of New York," composed by Charles Lawlor, a vaudeville singer, and given lyrics by hat salesman James Blake, gained popularity immediately upon its introduction in 1894 and became New York City's unofficial anthem during the administration of Governor Alfred E. Smith. Smith used the merry song extensively during his 1928 campaign for the presidency. "The Bowery" describes the seamier side of life in the city but also pokes fun at a naïve newcomer in this center of fast life. The song, written by Charles Hoyt for his musical A Trip to Chinatown, *became so well known that real estate values declined along the Bowery and local shopkeepers issued angry protests.*

♩♪ SIDEWALKS OF NEW YORK

Down in front of Casey's old brown wooden stoop,
On a summer's evening we formed a merry group.
Boys and girls together we would sing and waltz,
While Tony played the organ on the sidewalks of New York.

Chorus:
East Side, West Side, all around the town,
The tots sang "Ring-a-ros-ie," "London Bridge is falling down."
Boys and girls together — me and Mamie O'Rourke —
Tripped the light fantastic on the sidewalks of New York.

That's where Johnny Casey, little Jimmy Crowe,
Jakey Krause, the baker, who always had the dough,
Pretty Nellie Shannon, with shoes as light as cork,
She first picked up the waltz step on the sidewalks of New York.

Things have changed since those times, some are up in "G";
Others they are wand'rers, but they all feel just like me.
They'd part with all they've got, could they once more walk
With their best girl and have a twirl on the sidewalks of New York.

JAMES BLAKE

THE BOWERY

Oh! the night that I struck New York,
I went out for a quiet walk.
Folks who are on to the city say,
Better by far that I took Broadway.
But I was out to enjoy the sights.
There was the Bowery ablaze with lights.
I had one of the devil's own nights!
I'll never go there any more!

Chorus:
The Bowery, the Bowery!
They say such things, and they do such things
On the Bowery! the Bowery!
I'll never go there any more!

I had walked but a block or two,
When up came a fellow and me he knew.
Then a policeman came walking by,
Chased him away, and I asked him why.
"Wasn't he pulling your leg?" said he.
Said I, "He never laid hands on me!"
"Get off the Bowery, you fool!" said he.
I'll never go there any more!

Struck a place that they called a "dive,"
I was in luck to get out alive.
When the policeman heard my woes,
Saw my black eyes and my battered nose,
"You've been held up!" said the "copper" fly!
"No sir! but I've been knocked down!" said I.
Then he laughed, though I couldn't see why!
I'll never go there any more!

CHARLES H. HOYT

95.

JACOB S. COXEY: Business Depression and Public Works

Jacob Coxey was one of the more colorful figures of the Populist movement of the 1890s. "Coxey's Army," one hundred strong and accompanied by half that many newspapermen, set off from Massillon, Ohio, on Easter Sunday 1894. The group of unemployed numbered 500, rather than the hoped for 100,000, when they reached Washington for a May Day demonstration. The march disintegrated when Coxey was arrested for trying to speak from the Capitol steps and jailed for trespassing on the Capitol lawn, but the effort inspired other marches and was symptomatic of the unrest among workingmen. Coxey wanted to dramatize a proposal (written in the form of a congressional bill) that the federal government ease the depression that followed the Panic of 1893 by issuing legal tender currency to pay for the building of roads, thereby providing work for the unemployed. Coxey's "bills" are reprinted below.

Source: Henry Vincent, *The Story of the Commonweal*, Chicago, 1894, pp. 51-53.

THE BILL . . . TO BUILD GOOD ROADS. . .

Section 1. *Be it enacted by the Senate and House of Representatives in Congress assembled,* that the secretary of the Treasury of the United States is hereby authorized and instructed to have engraved and printed, immediately after the passage of this bill, $500 million of Treasury notes, a legal tender for all debts, public and private, said notes to be in denominations of $1, $2, $5, and $10; and to be placed in a fund to be known as the General County Road Fund System of the United States, and to be expended solely for said purpose.

Section 2. *And be it further enacted,* that it shall be the duty of the secretary of war to take charge of the construction of the said General County Road System in the United States, and said construction to commence as soon as the secretary of the Treasury shall inform the secretary of war that the said fund is available, which shall not be later than ————; when it shall be the duty of the secretary of war to inaugurate the work and expend the sum of $20 million per month, *pro rata*, with the number of miles of roads in each state and territory in the United States.

Section 3. *Be it further enacted,* that all labor other than that of the secretary of war, "whose compensations are already fixed by law," shall be paid by the day, and that the rate be not less than $1.50 per day for common labor and $3.50 per day for team and labor; and that eight hours per day shall constitute a day's labor under the provisions of this bill.

THE NONINTEREST BEARING BOND BILL . . .

Be it enacted by the Senate and House of Representatives in Congress assembled, that whenever any state, territory, county, township, municipality, or incorporated town or village deem it necessary to make any public improvements, they shall deposit with the secretary of the Treasury of the United States a noninterest bearing, twenty-five-year bond, not to exceed one-half the assessed valuation of the property in said state, territory, county, township, municipality, or incorporated town or village, and said bond to be retired at the rate of 4 percent per annum.

Whenever the foregoing section of this act has been complied with, it shall be man-datory upon the secretary of the Treasury of the United States to have engraved and printed Treasury notes in the denominations of $1, $2, $5, $10, and $20 each, which shall be a full legal tender for all debts, public and private, to the face value of said bond; and deliver to said state, territory, county, township, municipality, or incorporated town or village 99 percent of said notes and retain 1 percent for expense of engraving and printing same.

(Left) Jacob Coxey, Ohio businessman who organized an army of the unemployed to march on Washington in an effort to stimulate government aid; (below) Coxey's Army of unemployed marching to Washington from Massillon, Ohio, to petition the government to pass legislation for relief of the depression that followed the Panic of 1893

(Both) Library of Congress

96.

Rena M. Atchison: The Perils of Unrestricted Immigration

American nativism reasserted itself strongly during the 1880s, largely because the character of immigration changed after the Civil War. The "new immigration" originated not in western or northern Europe but in the countries of eastern and southern Europe, and the men and women who came from the latter areas were regarded by many citizens as unadaptable to the "American way of life." Organizations such as the Immigration Restriction League and the American Protective Association became active in calling for legal limitations on immigration. The latter organization was noted for its anti-Catholic views. The following excerpt from a book by Mrs. Atchison that appeared in 1894 is typical of the anti-immigration arguments.

Source: *Un-American Immigration: Its Present Effects and Future Perils,* Chicago, 1894, pp. 141-148.

THE ANGLO-SAXON BELIEVES himself to be the child of destiny. In the American republic he has carried to their logical conclusion the great principles of Magna Carta. The genius of the political and religious reformations which made the land of King John and Cromwell the home of civil liberty and social progress in the Old World has been the molding power in our social and political institutions for two centuries. Within that short period the Anglo-Saxon has set two of the great landmarks of history — the emancipation of the subject — the emancipation of the slave. Word went on the wings of the wind that henceforth there was to be a land where there would be neither bond nor free, where men could worship God in the freedom of their own conscience, where all men should be free, their freedom limited only by that of their fellowmen.

Men who had been scourged with whip and thong from the gates of the Old World's cities and the boundaries of em-pires by blasphemous superstition; men oppressed by an industrial serfdom more brutalizing than feudal vassalage; adventurers restlessly seeking danger or gold; political iconoclasts seeing only the defects of government and who, like some critics, would tear down a Parthenon because its proportions are not perfect; Jew and gentile, pagan and Christian turned their eyes longingly and covetously to the New El Dorado which seemed to have sprung like some fabled Atlantis from the Western deep.

The great westward tide of immigration brought us for a century, and for the most part as late as 1860, the best muscle and brain of Europe. It came mostly from the great middle class of Europe, representing its best artisanship and its most progressive thought, and it readily assimilated with American institutions. Since 1860 there has been a constant, and especially during the last twelve years, a rapid deterioration in the character of this immigration, until at the present time the great mass of immigrants are not only totally illiterate but have to be classed as unskilled laborers, or without occupation.

The largest percentage of increase of foreign-born for the present decade (1880-1890) is for persons in Hungary, 441.69 percent; in Russia, 411.29 percent; in Italy, 312.80 percent; in Austria, 218.83; and in Poland, 203 percent.

The increase in number of foreign-born from 1880 to 1890 was 2,569,604, more than twice the number of increase from 1870 to 1880, and very nearly twice the number of increase during the two preceding decades. Of this number, 818,152 came from Germany; from Norway, 140,936; from Sweden, 283,704; from Russia, 146,922; Italy, 138,350; while England sent 244,932, and Canada and Newfoundland 26,378. All other countries sent less than 100,000, Poland leading with 98,833, while Ireland sent 16,777.

The total percent of increase of foreign-born for the decade was 38.47 percent. If we remember that the average percent of increase of native-born for a decade is 20 percent, we shall more fully understand the magnitude of the problem before us. The present immigration law seems to have placed no effectual check upon even some of the worst classes of immigration. The number of Italians landing February 1891 was given as 2,000. During February 1892 over 3,000 Italians landed at the port of New York, showing an increase rather than a restriction. . . .

The European immigrant no sooner sets his foot upon our shores than he becomes at once not only an industrial and moral factor but a political one as well. And herein lies the greater danger. And this danger is greatly heightened by the character of this immigration, insuring a possible transference to American soil of the un-American ecclesiastical domination of priest-ridden Europe. The impertinence of an Italian priest and an Italian subject, unable to speak the English language, dictating to several millions of American citizens the manner and means they shall pursue in the education of future American citizens is a sufficient indication that, while we have struck the fetters from the limbs of 4 million slaves, we have still within our boundaries a far more dangerous form of slavery, the enslavement of at least 10 million of our citizens bound by religious fealty to obey the dictates of an extraneous power on that most vital of all questions in a republic — education. And far more dangerous than the treason of Confederate leaders is the shortsightedness or timidity of American statesmen in dealing with so vital a question.

It is not our purpose to outline an immigration law in this work but to show the perils of the present system. Several remedies, however, must have suggested themselves to the reader as possible and just restrictions upon immigration. Any adequate law should embody the following points:

First, such a law should be general and not special. It should admit the worthy and exclude the unfit of all nations. A law which makes an indiscriminate restriction against any people is inherently unjust, irritates and antagonizes the people discriminated against, and is contrary to the spirit of our institutions.

Second, no immigrant should be permitted to land upon our shores who cannot read and write his native language. This restriction alone would cut off the large mass of illiterate immigrants whose presence in our republic is a menace, socially, industrially, and politically.

Third, every immigrant should be compelled to register and to have sufficient money to insure him from becoming a burden to the state for a period of at least six months. The present condition of the labor market and the vast numbers of immigrants who are stranded in New York every year, some becoming a public burden within twenty-four hours after landing at Castle Garden, are sufficient reasons for such restriction.

Fourth, any immigrant who upon registration or afterward shall be found to have been a criminal in any prison or the inmate of any workhouse or almshouse in his native land within a short time previous to his immigration to America should be deported at the expense of the steamship importing him, and the exportation of criminals and paupers to the United States should be made an international offense.

Fifth, every immigrant should be required to declare at the time of landing and registration his intention or nonintention to become a citizen of the United States.

Sixth, no person should be allowed to vote in any state until he has become a naturalized citizen. Not only should the period for naturalization be extended but no person should be allowed to vote who cannot read the constitution of the commonwealth in which he resides and the Constitution of the United States in the English language. Certainly it is not just that we should be compelled to bear the burden of Europe's illiteracy, pauperism, and crime, and an honest intention of citizenship should be the price paid for the industrial and other advantages offered to the immigrant.

If foreign immigration continues at the present rate and such immigration continues to come from middle, southern, and northeastern Europe, in 1900 the Anglo-Saxon and Anglo-Saxon institutions will no longer be the dominant powers in molding American life and legislation. Will the heir to the heroes of Lexington and Concord, Shiloh and Gettysburg be still the victorious leader on the battlefield of new issues? Will the heir to America's Magna Carta, created by the genius of Hamilton and Washington and sealed by the blood of Lincoln, be still the man of destiny — not only preserving in their integrity our free institutions in the spirit and intent of their founders and defenders but also leading a people, absolutely free, toward the solution of the greater issues on the ever widening horizon of progress?

The closing words of Lincoln's memorable speech on the battlefield of Gettysburg contain all the inspiration and philosophy of the future for our republic:

It is rather for us here to be dedicated to the great task remaining before us — that from these honored dead we take increased devotion to that cause for which they gave the last full measure of devotion; that we here highly resolve that these dead shall not have died in vain; that this nation, under God, shall have a new birth of freedom; and that government of the people, by the people, for the people shall not perish from the earth.

97.

The Pullman Strike and Boycott

George Pullman's Palace Car Company and "model" community near Chicago were severely affected by the depression following the Panic of 1893. In response to the decreasing demand for railroad cars, the Pullman Company reduced its work force, shortened the workweek, and decreased wages by 25 percent but refused to lower rents in the company-owned community of Pullman. Early in 1894 large numbers of Pullman employees joined the American Railway Union, which called a meeting with company officials on May 9, at which the employees requested that wages be restored to the levels of the previous year. The company refused on the grounds that lowered business volume would not support such wages. The following day — contrary to a promise exacted in the meeting — three members of the employees' committee were fired. The local union immediately called a strike. The company refused to negotiate with the A.R.U., and the union thereupon ordered a nationwide boycott of Pullman cars on June 26. The struggle between the General Managers' Association, which discharged switchmen who refused to handle Pullman cars, and the A.R.U., which struck again after each dismissal, spread until virtually all of the railroads came to a standstill. The issues that crystallized in the dispute are still under debate. The statement from the Pullman strikers was addressed to the Convention of the A.R.U., assembled in Chicago, June 15, 1894; the Pullman Company's statement in defense of its action first appeared in the Chicago Herald, *June 26, 1894.*

Source: 53 Congress, 3 Session, Senate Document No. 7, pp. 87-91, 578-581.

I.

Statement of the Strikers

MR. PRESIDENT AND BROTHERS of the American Railway Union: We struck at Pullman because we were without hope. We joined the American Railway Union because it gave us a glimmer of hope. Twenty thousand souls, men, women, and little ones, have their eyes turned toward this convention today, straining eagerly through dark despondency for a glimmer of the heaven-sent message you alone can give us on this earth.

In stating to this body our grievances, it is hard to tell where to begin. You all must know that the proximate cause of our strike was the discharge of two members of our Grievance Committee the day after George M. Pullman, himself, and Thomas H. Wickes, his second vice-president, had guaranteed them absolute immunity. The more remote causes are still imminent. Five reductions in wages, in work, and in conditions of employment swept through the shops at Pullman between May and December 1893. The last was the most severe, amounting to nearly 30 percent, and our rents had not fallen. We owed Pullman $70,000 when we struck May 11. We owe him twice as much today. He does not evict us for two reasons: one, the force of popular sentiment and public opinion; the

George Mortimer Pullman

other, because he hopes to starve us out, to break through in the back of the American Railway Union, and to deduct from our miserable wages when we are forced to return to him the last dollar we owe him for the occupancy of his houses.

Rents all over the city in every quarter of its vast extent have fallen, in some cases to one-half. Residences, compared with which ours are hovels, can be had a few miles away at the prices we have been contributing to make a millionaire a billionaire. What we pay $15 for in Pullman is leased for $8 in Roseland; and remember that just as no man or woman of our 4,000 toilers has ever felt the friendly pressure of George M. Pullman's hand, so no man or woman of us all has ever owned or can ever hope to own one inch of George M. Pullman's land. Why, even the very streets are his. His ground has never been platted of record, and today he may debar any man who has acquiring rights as his tenant from walking in his highways. And those streets; do you know what he has named them?

He says after the four great inventors in methods of transportation. And do you know what their names are? Why, Fulton, Stephenson, Watt, and Pullman.

Water which Pullman buys from the city at 8 cents a thousand gallons he retails to us at 500 percent advance and claims he is losing $400 a month on it. Gas which sells at 75 cents per thousand feet in Hyde Park, just north of us, he sells for $2.25. When we went to tell him our grievances, he said we were all his "children."

Pullman, both the man and the town, is an ulcer on the body politic. He owns the houses, the schoolhouses, and churches of God in the town he gave his once humble name. The revenue he derives from these, the wages he pays out with one hand — the Pullman Palace Car Company — he takes back with the other — the Pullman Land Association. He is able by this to bid under any contract car shop in this country. His competitors in business, to meet this, must reduce the wages of their men. This gives him the excuse to reduce ours to conform to the market. His business rivals must in turn scale down; so must he. And thus the merry war — the dance of skeletons bathed in human tears — goes on; and it will go on, brothers, forever unless you, the American Railway Union, stop it; end it; crush it out.

Our town is beautiful. In all these thirteen years no word of scandal has arisen against one of our women, young or old. What city of 20,000 persons can show the like? Since our strike, the arrests, which used to average four or five a day, had dwindled down to less than one a week. We are peaceable; we are orderly; and but for the kindly beneficence of kindly hearted people in and about Chicago we would be starving. We are not desperate today because we are not hungry, and our wives and children are not begging for bread. But George M. Pullman, who ran away from the public opinion that has arisen against him, like the genii from the bottle in the *Arabian Nights,* is not feeding us. He is patiently seated beside his millions waiting for what? To see us starve.

We have grown better acquainted with the American Railway Union these convention days, and as we have heard sentiments of the noblest philanthropy fall from the lips of our general officers — your officers and ours — we have learned that there is a balm for all our troubles, and that the box containing it is in your hands today, only awaiting opening to disseminate its sweet savor of hope.

George M. Pullman, you know, has cut our wages from 30 to 70 percent. George M. Pullman has caused to be paid in the last year the regular quarterly dividend of 2 percent on his stock and an extra slice of 1½ percent, making 9½ percent on $30 million of capital. George M. Pullman, you know, took three contracts on which he lost less than $5,000. Because he loved us? No. Because it was cheaper to lose a little money in his freight car and his coach shops than to let his workingmen go, but that petty loss, more than made up by us from money we needed to clothe our wives and little ones, was his excuse for effecting a gigantic reduction of wages in every department of his great works, of cutting men and boys and girls with equal zeal, including everyone in the repair shops of the Pullman Palace cars on which such preposterous profits have been made.

George M. Pullman will tell you, if you could go to him today, that he was paying better wages than any other car shops in the land. George M. Pullman might better save his breath. We have worked too often beside graduates from other establishments not to know that, work for work and skill for skill, no one can compete with us at wages paid for work well done. If his wage list showed a trifle higher, our efficiency still left us heavily the loser. He does not figure on our brain and muscle. He makes

his paltry computation in dollars and cents.

We will make you proud of us, brothers, if you will give us the hand we need. Help us make our country better and more wholesome. Pull us out of our slough of despond. Teach arrogant grinders of the faces of the poor that there is still a God in Israel, and if need be a Jehovah — a God of battles. Do this, and on that last great day you will stand, as we hope to stand, before the great white throne "like gentlemen unafraid."

II.

Statement of the Company

IN VIEW OF THE PROPOSED ATTEMPT of the American Railway Union to interfere with public travel on railway lines using Pullman cars, in consequence of a controversy as to the wages of employees of the manufacturing department of the company, the Pullman Company requests the publication of the following statement of the facts, in face of which the attempt is to be made.

In the first week of May last, there were employed in the car manufacturing department at Pullman, Ill., about 3,100 persons. On May 7, a committee of the workmen had an interview by arrangement with Mr. Wickes, vice-president, at which the principal subject of discussion related to wages, but minor grievances as to shop administration were also presented, and it was agreed that another meeting should be held on the 9th of May, at which all the grievances should be presented in writing. The second meeting was held. As to the complaints on all matters except wages, it was arranged that a formal and thorough investigation should be made by Mr. Wickes, to be begun the next day, and full redress was assured to the committee as to all complaints proved to be well founded.

The absolute necessity of the last reduction in wages, under the existing condition of the business of car manufacturing, had been explained to the committee, and they were insisting upon a restoration of the wage scale of the first half of 1893, when Mr. Pullman entered the room and addressed the committee, speaking in substance as follows:

"At the commencement of the very serious depression last year, we were employing at Pullman 5,816 men and paying out in wages there $305,000 a month. Negotiations with intending purchasers of railway equipment that were then pending for new work were stopped by them, orders already given by others were canceled, and we were obliged to lay off, as you are aware, a large number of men in every department; so that by November 1, 1893, there were only about 2,000 men in all departments, or about one-third of the normal number. I realized the necessity for the most strenuous exertions to procure work immediately, without which there would be great embarrassment, not only to the employees and their families at Pullman but also to those living in the immediate vicinity, including between 700 and 800 employees who had purchased homes and to whom employment was actually necessary to enable them to complete their payments.

"I canvassed the matter thoroughly with the manager of the works and instructed him to cause the men to be assured that the company would do everything in its power to meet the competition which was sure to occur because of the great number of large car manufacturers that were in the same condition and that were exceedingly anxious to keep their men employed. I knew that if there was any work to be let, bids for it would be made upon a much lower basis than ever before.

"The result of this discussion was a revision in piecework prices, which, in the absence of any information to the contrary, I supposed to be acceptable to the men under the circumstances. Under these conditions, and with lower prices upon all materials, I personally undertook the work of the lettings of cars, and, by making lower bids than other manufacturers, I secured work enough to gradually increase our force from 2,000 up to about 4,200, the number employed, according to the April payrolls, in all capacities at Pullman.

"This result has not been accomplished merely by reduction in wages, but the company has borne its full share by eliminating from its estimates the use of capital and machinery, and in many cases going even below that and taking work at considerable loss, notably the 55 Long Island cars, which was the first large order of passenger cars let since the great depression and which was sought for by practically all the leading car builders in the country. My anxiety to secure that order so as to put as many men at work as possible was such that I put in a bid at more than $300 per car less than the actual cost to the company. The 300 stock cars built for the Northwestern Road and the 250 refrigerator cars now under construction for the same company will result in a loss of at least $12 per car, and the 25 cars just built for the Lake Street elevated road show a loss of $79 per car. I mention these particulars so that you may understand what the company has done for the mutual interests and to secure for the people at Pullman and vicinity the benefit of the disbursement of the large sums of money involved in these and similar contracts, which can be kept up only by the procurement of new orders for cars; for, as you know, about three-fourths of the men must depend upon contract work for employment.

"I can only assure you that if this company now restores the wages of the first half of 1893, as you have asked, it would be a most unfortunate thing for the men because there is less than sixty days of contract work in sight in the shops under all orders, and there is absolutely no possibility, in the present condition of affairs throughout the country, of getting any more orders for work at prices measured by the wages of May 1893. Under such a scale the works would necessarily close down and the great majority of the employees be put in idleness, a contingency I am using my best efforts to avoid.

"To further benefit the people of Pullman and vicinity, we concentrated all the work that we could command at that point by closing our Detroit shops entirely and laying off a large number of men at our other repair shops, and gave to Pullman the repair of all cars that could be taken care of there.

"Also, for the further benefit of our people at Pullman, we have carried on a large system of internal improvements, having expended nearly $160,000 since August last in work which, under normal conditions, would have been spread over one or two years. The policy would be to continue this class of work to as great an extent as possible, provided, of course, the Pullman men show a proper appreciation of the situation by doing whatever they can to help themselves to tide over the hard times which are so seriously felt in every part of the country.

"There has been some complaint made about rents. As to this I would say that the return to this company on the capital invested in the Pullman tenements for the last year and the year before was 3.82 percent. There are hundreds of tenements in Pullman renting from $6 to $9 per month, and the tenants are relieved from the usual expenses of exterior cleaning and the removal of garbage, which is done by the company. The average amount collected from employees for gas consumed is about $2 a month. To ascertain the exact amount of water used by tenants, separate from the amount consumed by the works, we have recently put in meters, by which we find that the water consumed by the tenants, if paid for at the rate of 4 cents per 1,000 gallons, in accordance with our original contract with the village of Hyde Park,

would amount to about $1,000 a month, almost exactly the rate which we have charged the tenants, this company assuming the expense of pumping. At the increased rate the city is now charging us for water, we are paying about $500 a month in excess of the amount charged to the tenants. The present payrolls at Pullman amount to about $7,000 a day."

On the question of rents, while, as stated above, they make a manifestly inadequate return upon the investment, so that it is clear they are not, in fact, at an arbitrarily high figure, it may be added that it would not be possible in a business sense so to deal with them.

The renting of the dwellings and the employment of workmen at Pullman are in no way tied together. The dwellings and apartments are offered for rent in competition with those of the immediately adjacent towns of Kensington, Roseland, and Gano. They are let alike to Pullman employees and to very many others in no way connected with the company, and, on the other hand, many Pullman employees rent or own their homes in those adjacent towns. The average rental at Pullman is at the rate of $3 per room per month. There are 1,200 tenements, of varying numbers of rooms, the average monthly rental of which is $10; of these there are 600 the average monthly rental of which is $8. In very many cases, men with families pay a rent seemingly large for a workman, but which is in fact reduced in part, and often wholly repaid, by the subrents paid by single men as lodgers.

On May 10, the day after the second conference above mentioned, work went on at Pullman as usual, and the only incident of note was the beginning by Mr. Wickes, assisted by Mr. Brown, the general manager of the company, of the promised formal investigation at Pullman of the shop complaints.

A large meeting of employees had been held the night before at Kensington, which, as was understood by the company, accepted the necessity of the situation preventing an increase of wages; but at a meeting of the local committee held during the night of May 10, a strike was decided upon, and, accordingly, the next day about 2,500 of the employees quit their work, leaving about 600 at work, of whom very few were skilled workmen. As it was found impracticable to keep the shops in operation with a force thus diminished and disorganized, the next day those remaining were necessarily laid off, and no work has since been done in the shops.

The payrolls at the time amounted to about $7,000 a day and were reduced $5,500 by the strike, so that during the period of a little more than six weeks which has elapsed the employees who quit their work have deprived themselves and their comrades of earnings of more than $200,000.

It is an element of the whole situation worthy of note that at the beginning of the strike the Pullman Savings Bank had on deposit in its savings department $488,000, of which about nine-tenths belonged to employees at Pullman, and that this amount has since been reduced by the sum of $32,000.

While deploring the possibility of annoyance to the public by the threats of irresponsible organizations to interrupt the orderly ministration to the comfort of travelers on railway lines, aggregating 125,000 miles in length, the Pullman Company can do no more than explain its situation to the public.

It has two separate branches of business, essentially distinct from each other. One is to provide sleeping cars, which are delivered by it under contract to the various railway companies, to be run by them on their lines as a part of their trains for the carriage of their passengers, over the movements of which this company has no control. Contract arrangements provide for the making of all repairs to such cars by the railway companies using them — as to certain repairs absolutely and as to all others upon the request of the Pullman Company, which ordinarily finds it most convenient to use its own manufacturing facilities to make such repairs. The other, and a distinct branch of the business of the Pullman Company, is the manufacture of sleeping cars for the above-mentioned use of railway companies and the manufacture for sale to railway companies of freight cars and ordinary passenger cars, and of streetcars, and this business is almost at a standstill throughout the United States.

The business of manufacturing cars for sale gives employment to about 70 percent of the shop employees. The manufacture of sleeping cars for use by railway companies under contract, and which, under normal conditions, gives employment to about 15 percent of the shop employees, cannot be resumed by the company to an important extent for a very long time; for, out of the provision made for the abnormal travel last year, the company now has about 400 sleeping cars in store ready for use, but for which there is no need in the existing conditions of public travel.

It is now threatened by the American Railway Union officials that railway companies using Pullman sleeping cars shall be compelled to deprive their passengers of sleeping-car accommodations unless the Pullman Company will agree to submit to arbitration the question as to whether or not it shall open its manufacturing shops at Pullman and operate them under a scale of wages which would cause a daily loss to it of one-fourth the wages paid.

Grand Court and Basin at the World's Columbian Exposition in Chicago, 1893

CHICAGO

After a spirited competition, Chicago was chosen as the site for the 1893 World's Columbian Exposition. While the selection was based on economic factors, it was fitting for other reasons as well: in the rebuilding after the great fire of 1871 Chicago was becoming a genuine metropolitan center and in it a new school of architecture was developing, one suited to modern commercial society. The new architecture found no place in the classically designed Exposition, but visitors could investigate the city itself and discover the methods of the new industrial world. The Exposition featured the electrical generator and the dynamo, which inspired Henry Adams; behind the grounds, the city was building itself up to the Chicago that Carl Sandburg would describe. Chicago's population, bolstered by immigration, passed one million in 1890. The rapid transit system around the commercial district was completed in 1897, forming the Loop. A vigorous tax-supported program of park and boulevard construction was well under way by 1890; Michigan Avenue was already the showpiece of the city. At the same time, labor conditions such as those which prompted the Pullman strike of 1894 were bringing forth the reform programs of John P. Altgeld and Jane Addams, and would contribute to the Chicago school of literary realism.

Construction of the Lake Street elevated, on Market Street near Madison in Chicago; (below) the Chicago Union Stock Yards about 1895 and interior of the Armour Packing House, Chicago

(Above and right) The Palmer House Hotel, Chicago, 1875; (below) Prairie Avenue, looking north from 23rd Street, 1893; (bottom) Drexel Boulevard and mall in 1893

The great fire of 1871 and the rebuilding that followed probably supplied part of the impetus for the architectural developments in Chicago in the 1880s and 1890s, but they were also to a great extent the logical outgrowths of the state of architecture and engineering at the time. The skyscraper was required by centralized commerce, by rising land values and by the need for quick communication. The first step toward the modern office building was William Le Baron Jenney's iron skeleton to carry the building; beyond this basic structural technique lay the problem of developing a style that would suit the new building aesthetically and functionally. The early leader of the Chicago school, Louis Sullivan, worked out the new style slowly. His first real success was in the Wainwright Building in St. Louis in 1890. Popular attention, however, was still concentrated on the standard varieties of classicism; the "great white city" of the 1893 Columbian Exposition, also partly Sullivan's work, was more highly acclaimed than any work of the new school.

(Top) The Home Insurance Building, 1885, designed by William Jenney, and regarded as the first building to use steel skeleton construction throughout. For that reason it is called the first skyscraper, even though only 10 stories tall. Two additional floors were added in 1890. (Left) The Tacoma Building, 1889, designed by Holabird and Roche, shows the skeleton design more clearly. The outside walls obviously bear none of the building's weight

(Left) The Ashland Block, at Clark and Randolph streets in Chicago, was designed by Daniel H. Burnham in 1892; (bottom) Reliance Building designed by Burnham and John W. Root in 1890. Ten floors were added in 1895. Both buildings employed steel frame construction. (Below) Louis Henri Sullivan (1856-1924) employed the new building techniques with a distinctively imaginative style. Frank Lloyd Wright worked in Sullivan's firm in the 1890s

(Above) The Chicago River, near the Michigan Avenue Bridge, 1899. Lake steamers landed here to take on passengers and cargoes; (right) courthouse in Chicago, 1890; (below) view looking west from the undeveloped lakeshore toward the Water Tower and residential areas north of downtown Chicago, 1893

Pullman, Illinois. Buildings of the car works with the Corliss engine room at the left

George Pullman was probably genuinely surprised when his employees revolted against his company town, Pullman, Illinois. Occupancy was limited to employees and their debts and obligations to the town were deducted from their paychecks. After a wage cut and a rent hike there might well be little or nothing left. Even Mark Hanna, generally a friend of business, was forced to comment, "Go and live in Pullman and find out how much Pullman gets sellin' city water and gas ten percent higher to those poor fools! A man who won't meet his own men half-way is a God-damn fool!" The state later forced Pullman to give up control of the town.

George Mortimer Pullman (1831-1897), photographed in 1868; (below right) grammar school at Pullman (center) with the company casino on the left

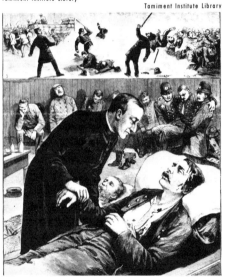

A view of the scene of the Haymarket bombing and fanciful version of the aftermath, from "Leslie's"

The Haymarket Riot is more notable for the panic and injustice which it evoked from the ruling coalition of government and capital than for any violence or threat that it actually involved. In the end, five men of doubtful guilt were dead and the labor movement was shaken severely. The Pullman strike of 1894, broadened by the support of Eugene Debs's American Railway Union, was more to the point and was simply stifled outright.

(Left) The courtroom during the trial of the anarchists in Chicago; "The Law Vindicated," shows the execution at Cook County Jail

(Top) Federal troops guard Pullman buildings during 1894 strike; (below) scabs attacked by strikers during 1888 railroad strike; empty station during strike, 1894; (bottom) railroad cars burned during the same strike

During the Pullman strike and the general economic downturn of 1893-94 many of the poor and unemployed in Chicago lived in a shantytown thrown up on the lakefront. Photos by Ray Stannard Baker

98.

State Authority Versus Federal Supremacy in Law Enforcement

The 1894 strike against the Pullman Palace Car Company was soon caught up in two larger conflicts, one a test of strength between the American Railway Union and the General Managers' Association, the other a struggle between state and federal authority in resolving the strike. The boycott by the A.R.U. against the Managers' Association, which represented twenty-four roads, seemed near success when federal intervention came. A specially appointed federal attorney in Chicago, who was also an attorney for a member railroad of the G.M.A., prevailed upon Washington to send troops to quell the "violence," of which there was hardly any until the troops arrived and incited it. Eugene Debs and other union leaders were arrested for conspiracy and violation of the injunction issued by a federal court in Chicago on July 2. President Cleveland's intervention broke the boycott and destroyed the railroad union. The following exchange of telegrams between Governor Altgeld of Illinois and the President deals with the right of federal intervention when a state has not called for it.

Source: *Chicago Daily Tribune*, July 6, 7, 1894.

I.

Governor Altgeld to President Cleveland, July 5

Dear Sir:

I am advised that you have ordered federal troops to go into service in the state of Illinois. Surely the facts have not been correctly presented to you in this case or you would not have taken this step, for it is entirely unnecessary and, as it seems to me, unjustifiable. Waiving all questions of courtesy, I will say that the state of Illinois is not only able to take care of itself but it stands ready to furnish the federal government any assistance it may need elsewhere. Our military force is ample and consists of as good soldiers as can be found in the country. They have been ordered out promptly whenever and wherever they were needed. We have stationed in Chicago alone three regiments of infantry, one battery, and one troop of cavalry, and no better soldiers can be found. They have been ready any moment to go on duty, and have been and are now eager to go into the service. But they have not been ordered out because nobody in Cook County, whether official or private citizen, asked to have their assistance, or even intimated in any way that their assistance was desired or necessary.

So far as I have been advised, the local officials have been able to handle the situation. But if any assistance were needed, the state stood ready to furnish 100 men for every one required, and stood ready to do so at a moment's notice. Notwithstanding

Art Commission of the City of New York
Grover Cleveland

these facts the federal government has been applied to for men who had partial and selfish motives for wanting to ignore the state government. We have gone through a long coal strike, more extensive here than in any other state because our soft coalfield is larger than that of any other state. We have now had ten days of the railroad strike, and we have promptly furnished military aid wherever the local officials needed it.

In two instances the United States marshal for the Southern District of Illinois applied for assistance to enable him to enforce the process of the United States court, and troops were promptly furnished him, and he was assisted in every way he desired. The law has been thoroughly executed, and every man guilty of violating it during the strike has been brought to justice. If the marshal for the Northern District of Illinois or the authorities of Cook County needed military assistance, they had but to ask for it in order to get it from the state.

At present some of our railroads are paralyzed, not by reason of obstructions but because they cannot get men to operate their trains. For some reason they are anxious to keep this fact from the public, and for this purpose they are making an outcry about obstructions in order to divert attention.

I will cite to you two examples which illustrate the situation.

Some days ago I was advised that the business of one of our railroads was obstructed at two railroad centers, that there was a condition bordering on anarchy there; and I was asked to furnish protection so as to enable the employees of the road to operate the trains. Troops were promptly ordered to both points. Then it transpired that the company had not sufficient men on its lines to operate one train. All the old hands were orderly but refused to go to work. The company had large shops in which worked a number of men who did not belong to the Railway Union and [who] could run an engine. They were appealed to to run the trains, but flatly refused. We were obliged to hunt up soldiers who could run an engine and operate a train.

Again, two days ago, appeals which were almost frantic came from the officials of another road, stating that at an important point on their lines trains were forcibly obstructed and that there was a reign of anarchy at that place, and they asked for protection so that they could move their trains. Troops were put on the ground in a few hours' time, when the officer in command telegraphed me that there was no trouble, and had been none at that point, but that the road seemed to have no men to run trains, and the sheriff telegraphed that he did not need troops but would himself move every train if the company would only furnish an engineer. The result was that the troops were there over twelve hours before a single train was moved, although there was no attempt at interference by anybody.

It is true that in several instances a road

made efforts to work a few green men, and a crowd standing around insulted them and tried to drive them off; and in a few other cases they cut off Pullman sleepers from trains. But all these troubles were local in character and could easily be handled by the state authorities. Illinois has more railroad men than any other state in the Union, but as a rule they are orderly and well-behaved. This is shown by the fact that so very little actual violence has been committed. Only a very small percent of these men has been guilty of any infractions of the law. The newspaper accounts have in some cases been pure falsifications and, in others, wild exaggerations.

I have gone thus into details to show that it is not soldiers that the railroads need so much as it is men to operate trains, and that the conditions do not exist here which bring the case within the federal statutes, a statute that was passed in 1861 and was in reality a war measure. This statute authorized the use of federal troops in a state whenever it shall be impracticable to enforce the laws of the United States within such states by the ordinary judicial proceedings. Such a condition does not exist in Illinois. There have been a few local disturbances, but nothing that seriously interfered with the administration of justice or that could not be easily controlled by the local or state authorities, for the federal troops can do nothing that the state troops cannot do.

I repeat that you have been imposed upon in this matter; but even if by a forced construction it were held that the conditions here came within the letter of the statute, then I submit that local self-government is a fundamental principle of our Constitution. Each community shall govern itself so long as it can and is ready and able to enforce the law, and it is in harmony with this fundamental principle that the statute authorizing the President to send troops into states must be construed. Especially is this so in

Chicago Historical Society
John Peter Altgeld, governor of Illinois

matters relating to the exercise of the police power and the preservation of law and order.

To absolutely ignore a local government in matters of this kind, when the local government is ready to furnish any assistance needed and is able to enforce the law, not only insults the people of the state by imputing to them an inability to govern themselves or unwillingness to enforce the law but is in violation of a basic principle of our institutions. The question of federal supremacy is in no way involved. No one disputes it for a moment; but, under our Constitution, federal supremacy and local self-government must go hand in hand, and to ignore the latter is to do violence to the Constitution.

As governor of the state of Illinois, I protest against this, and ask the immediate withdrawal of the federal troops from active duty in this state. Should the situation at any time get so serious that we cannot control it with the state forces, we will promptly and freely ask for federal assistance; but until such time, I protest, with all due deference, against this uncalled-for reflection upon our people, and again ask the immediate withdrawal of these troops.

II.

Cleveland to Altgeld, July 5

FEDERAL TROOPS WERE SENT TO CHICAGO in strict accordance with the Constitution and laws of the United States, upon the demand of the Post Office Department that obstruction of the mails should be removed, and upon the representations of the judicial officers of the United States that process of the federal courts could not be executed through the ordinary means, and upon abundant proof that conspiracies existed against commerce between the states.

To meet these conditions, which are clearly within the province of federal authority, the presence of federal troops in the city of Chicago was deemed not only proper but necessary, and there has been no intention of thereby interfering with the plain duty of the local authorities to preserve the peace of the city.

III.

Altgeld to Cleveland, July 6

YOUR ANSWER TO MY PROTEST involves some startling conclusions and ignores and evades the question at issue — that is, that the principle of local self-government is just as fundamental in our institutions as is that of federal supremacy.

First, you calmly assume that the executive has the legal right to order federal troops into any community of the United States, in the first instance, whenever there is the slightest disturbance, and that he can do this without any regard to the question as to whether the community is able to and ready to enforce the law itself. And inasmuch as the executive is the sole judge of

the question as to whether any disturbance exists or not in any part of the country, this assumption means that the executive can send federal troops into any community in the United States at his pleasure and keep them there as long as he chooses. If this is the law, then the principle of self-government either never did exist in this country or else has been destroyed, for no community can be said to possess local self-government if the executive can, at his pleasure, send military force to patrol the streets under pretense of enforcing some law. The kind of local self-government that could exist under these circumstances can be found in any of the monarchies of Europe and is not in harmony with the spirit of our institutions.

Second, it is also a fundamental principle in our government that, except in times of war, the military shall be subordinate to the civil authority. In harmony with this provision, the state troops, when ordered out, act under and with the civil authorities. The troops you have ordered to Chicago are not under the civil authorities and are in no way responsible to them for their conduct. They are not even acting under the United States marshal or under any federal officer of the state, but are acting directly under military orders issued from military headquarters at Washington; and insofar as these troops act at all, it is military government.

Third, the statute authorizing federal troops to be sent into states, in certain cases, contemplates that the state troops shall be taken first. This provision has been ignored, and it is assumed that the executive is not bound by it. Federal interference with industrial disturbances in the various states is certainly a new departure, and it opens up so large a field that it will require a . . . stretch of authority to absorb to itself all the details of local government.

Fourth, you say that troops were ordered into Illinois upon the demand of the Post Office Department, and upon representations of the judicial officers of the United

States that process of the courts could not be served, and upon proof that conspiracies existed. We will not discuss the facts but look for a moment at the principles involved in your statement. All of these officers are appointed by the executive. Most of them can be removed by him at will. They are not only obliged to do his bidding but they are in fact a part of the executive. If several of them can apply for troops, one alone can; so that under the law, as you assume it to be, an executive, through any one of his appointees, can apply to himself to have the military sent into any city or number of cities, and base his application on such representations as he sees fit to make. In fact, it will be immaterial whether he makes any showing or not, for the executive is the sole judge, and nobody else has any right to interfere or even inquire about it.

Then the executive can pass on his own application — his will being the sole guide — he can hold the application to be sufficient and order troops to as many places as he wishes and put them in command of anyone he chooses, and have them act, not under the civil officers, either federal or state, but act directly under military orders from Washington; and there is not in the Constitution or laws of the land, whether written or unwritten, any limitation or restraint upon his power. His judgment — that is, his will — is the sole guide; and it being purely a matter of discretion, his decision can never be examined or questioned.

This assumption as to the power of the executive is certainly new, and I respectfully submit that it is not the law of the land. The jurists have told us that this is a government of law and not a government by the caprice of individuals; and, further, that instead of being autocratic, it was a government of limited power. Yet the autocrat of Russia could certainly not possess or claim to possess greater power than is possessed by the executive of the United States, if your assumption is correct.

Fifth, the executive has the command, not only of the regular forces of the United States but of the military forces of all the states, and can order them to any place he sees fit; and if there are always more or less local disturbances over the country, it will be an easy matter under your construction of the law for an ambitious executive to order out the military forces of all of the states and establish at once a military government. The only chance of failure in such a movement could come from rebellion, and with such a vast military power at command this could readily be crushed, for, as a rule, soldiers will obey orders.

As for the situation in Illinois, that is of no consequence now when compared with the far-reaching principle involved. True, according to my advices, federal troops have now been on duty for over two days, and although the men are brave and the officers valiant and able, yet their very presence proved to be an irritation because it aroused the indignation of a large class of people who, while upholding law and order, had been taught to believe in local self-government and therefore resented what they regarded as an unwarranted interference.

Inasmuch as the federal troops can do nothing but what the state troops can do there, and believing that the state is amply able to take care of the situation and to enforce the law, and believing that the ordering out of the federal troops was unwarranted, I again ask their withdrawal.

IV.

Cleveland to Altgeld, July 6

WHILE I AM STILL PERSUADED that I have neither transcended my authority nor duty in the emergency that confronts us, it seems to me that in this hour of danger and public distress discussion may well give way to active efforts on the part of all in authority to restore obedience to law and to protect life and property.

99.

Samuel Gompers: The Laborer's Right to Life

A popular tool for curbing union effectiveness in the 1890s was the court injunction prohibiting union members from engaging in strike activities. Such an injunction was issued in the Pullman strike by the U.S. District Court of Illinois, impairing the strength of the American Railway Union in that struggle. Eugene V. Debs, president of the A.R.U., was summoned before a grand jury for violating the injunction, and Judge Peter Grosscup in his charge to the jury made use of the traditional anti-union argument that union organizing constituted a conspiracy. Samuel Gompers, president of the American Federation of Labor, was asked by the North American Review *to write an article about the strike, which elicited a letter from Grosscup pointing out that Gompers had misquoted him. Gompers' reply to Grosscup on August 14, 1894, reprinted here, continued his attack on the judge's charge to the jury.*

Source: *American Federationist*, September 1894.

Dear Sir:

I have the honor to acknowledge the receipt of your favor of the 31st ult., the contents of which I have carefully noted. Possibly I should have written you earlier, but more important matters demanded my immediate consideration. I hope, however, that you have suffered no inconvenience or pain of injustice done you by reason of this delay.

You say that I have misquoted you in my article in the *North American Review* in attributing to you the following words in your Decoration Day address at Galesburg: "The growth of labor organizations must be restrained by law." Upon closer examination you will find that I did not use the word "restrained," but "checked." However, this makes little material difference, except to show that unintentionally one man may misquote another.

The words I quoted I saw in several newspaper accounts of your address, and I am exceedingly pleased that you favor me with a printed copy of it, which I have read with much interest. In perusing that address I find that you said (page 12): "Restore to each individual by *the enforcement of law*, not simply his right but if possible a returning sense of duty to control his own personality and property. *Let us set a limit to the field of organization.*"

Of course this citation from the printed address you send me does not contain the words I attributed to you, but you say in your letter that I will not find either that you used the words or that you "expressed that sentiment." To my untutored mind there may not be that grave difference which your legal learning can discern in limiting by law the field of organization and checking its growth by law.

I doubt that the thinking world will hold me chargeable of having done you a grave injustice, and I feel convinced after a perusal of your address that both in fact and in spirit you gave utterance to the sentiment I attribute to you, and which you either fail to remember or regret.

You say that, as you stated in your charge to the grand jury, you believe in labor organizations within such lawful and reasonable limits as will make them a service to the laboring man and not a menace to the lawful institutions of the country. I have had the pleasure of reading your charge to the grand jury, and have only partially been able to discover how far you believe in labor organizations.

You would certainly have no objection officially or personally to workingmen organizing, and in their meetings discuss perhaps "the origin of man," benignly smiling upon each other and declaring that all existing things are right, going to their wretched homes to find some freedom in sleep from gnawing hunger. You would have them extol the virtues of monopolists and wreckers of the people's welfare. You would not have them consider seriously the fact that more than 2 million of their fellows are unemployed, and though willing and able, cannot find the opportunity to work in order that they may sustain themselves, their wives, and their children. You would not have them consider seriously the fact that Pullman who has grown so rich from the toil of his workmen that he can riot in luxury, while he heartlessly turns these very workmen out of their tenements into the streets and leave to the tender mercies of corporate greed. Nor would you have them ponder upon the hundreds of other Pullmans of different names.

You know, or ought to know, that the introduction of machinery is turning into idleness thousands faster than new industries are founded, and yet, machinery certainly should not be either destroyed or hampered in its full development. The laborer is a man, he is made warm by the same sun and made cold — yes, colder — by the same winter as you are. He has a heart and brain, and feels and knows the human and paternal instinct for those depending upon him as keenly as do you.

What shall the workers do? Sit idly by and see the vast resources of nature and the human mind be utilized and monopolized for the benefit of the comparative few? No. The laborers must learn to think and act, and soon, too, that only by the power of organization and common concert of action can either their manhood be maintained, their rights to life (work to sustain it) be recognized, and liberty and rights secured.

Since you say that you favor labor organizations within certain limits, will you kindly give to thousands of your anxious fellow citizens what you believe the workers could and should do in their organizations to solve this great problem? Not what they should not do. You have told us that.

I am not one of those who regards the entire past as a failure. I recognize the progress made and the improved conditions of which nearly the entire civilized world are the beneficiaries. I ask you to explain, however, that if the wealth of the whole world is, as you say, "preeminently and beneficially the nation's wealth," how is it that thousands of able-bodied, willing, earnest men and women are suffering the pangs of hunger? We may boast of our wealth and civilization, but to the hungry man and woman and child our progress is a hollow mockery, our civilization a sham, and our "national wealth" a chimera.

You recognize that the industrial forces set in motion by steam and electricity have materially changed the structure of our civilization. You also admit that a system has grown up where the accumulations of the individual have passed from his control into that of representative combinations and trusts, and that the tendency in this direction is on the increase. How, then, can you consistently criticize the workingmen for

Samuel Gompers, first president of the American Federation of Labor

recognizing that as individuals they can have no influence in deciding what the wages, hours of toil, and conditions of employment shall be?

You evidently have observed the growth of corporate wealth and influence. You recognize that wealth, in order to become more highly productive, is concentrated into fewer hands, and controlled by representatives and directors, and yet you sing the old siren song that the workingman should depend entirely upon his own "individual effort."

The school of laissez-faire, of which you seem to be a pronounced advocate, has produced great men in advocating the theory of each for himself and his Satanic majesty taking the hindermost, but the most pronounced advocates of your school of thought in economics have, when practically put to the test, been compelled to admit that combination and organization of the toiling masses are essential both to prevent the deterioration and to secure an improvement in the condition of the wage earners.

If, as you say, the success of commercial society depends upon the full play of competition, why do not you and your confreres turn your attention and direct the shafts of your attacks against the trusts and corporations, business wreckers and manipulators in the food products — the necessities of the people. Why garland your thoughts in beautiful phrase when speaking of these modern vampires, and steep your pen in gall when writing of the laborers' efforts to secure some of the advantages accruing from the concentrated thought and genius of the ages?

You charge that before a boy can learn a trade he must receive a permit from the union and assume obligations which the union imposes. I am sure you have read the current history of industry but superficially, or you would certainly have discovered that with the introduction of modern methods of production, the apprenticeship system has almost been entirely eliminated. Professors, the learned men concerned in the welfare of our people, insist upon a maintenance of a technical knowledge of crafts and trades. They are endeavoring to substitute manual training schools in order that the youth of our country may be supplied with a knowledge of the trades and crafts of which modern methods of production have deprived them.

For the sake of your argument, let me admit that what you may say in connection with this matter is true. I ask you whether it is not true that before a boy can properly learn your trade, is it not necessary for him to enter a term of apprenticeship? Of course, you have a more euphonious name for it, student life, I believe. Would judges permit anyone to practise law in their courts where justice is dispensed (with) unless he could produce his working card? Pardon, I mean his diploma.

One becomes enraptured in reading the

beauty of your description of modern progress. Could you have had in mind the miners of Spring Valley or Pennsylvania, or the clothing workers of the sweatshops of New York or Chicago when you grandiloquently dilate,

> Who is not rich today when compared with his ancestors of a century ago? The steamboat and the railroad bring to his breakfast table the coffees of Java and Brazil, the fruits from Florida and California, and the steaks from the plains. The loom arrays him in garments and the factories furnish him with a dwelling that the richest contemporaries of his grandfather would have envied. With health and industry he is a prince.

Probably you have not read within the past year of babes dying of starvation at their mothers' breasts. More than likely the thousands of men lying upon the bare stones night after night in the City Hall of Chicago last winter escaped your notice. You may not have heard of the cry for bread that was sounded through this land of plenty by thousands of honest men and women. But should these and many other painful incidents have passed you by unnoticed, I am fearful that you may learn of them with keener thoughts with the coming sleets and blasts of winter.

You say that "labor cannot afford to attack capital." Let me remind you that labor has no quarrel with capital, as such. It is merely the possessors of capital who refuse to accord to labor the recognition, the right, the justice which is the laborers' due with whom we contend.

See what is implied by your contemptuous reference to the laborer when you ask, "Will the conqueror destroy his trophy?" Who ever heard of a conqueror marching unitedly with his *trophy*, as you would have them? But if by your comparison you mean that the conqueror is the corporation, the trust, the capitalist class, and ask then whether they would destroy their *trophy*, I would have you ask the widows and orphans of the thousands of men killed annually through the avarice of railroad corporations refusing to avail themselves of modern appliances in coupling and other improvements on their railroads.

Inquire from the thousands of women and children whose husbands or fathers were suffocated or crushed in the mines through the rapacious greed of stockholders clamoring for more dividends. Investigate the sweating dens of the large cities. Go to the mills, factories, through the country. Visit the modern tenement houses or hovels in which thousands of workers are compelled to eke out an existence. Ask these whether the conqueror (monopoly) cares whether his trophy (the laborers) is destroyed or preserved. Ascertain from employers whether the laborer is not regarded the same as a machine, thrown out as soon as all the work possible has been squeezed out of him.

Are you aware that all the legislation ever secured for the ventilation or safety of mines, factory, or workshop is the result of the efforts of organized labor? Do you know that the trade unions were the shield for the seven-year-old children from being the conqueror's trophy until they become somewhat older? And that the reformatory laws now on the statute books protecting or defending the trophies of both sexes, young and old from the fond care of the conquerors were wrested from congresses, legislatures, and parliaments despite the Pullmans, the Jeffries, the Ricks, the Tafts, the Williams, the Woods, or the Grosscups.

By what right, sir, do you assume that the labor organizations do not conduct their affairs within lawful limits, or that they are a menace to the lawful institutions of the country? Is it because some thoughtless or overzealous member at a time of great excitement and smarting under a wrong may violate under a law or commit an improper act? Would you apply the same rule to the churches, the other moral agencies and organizations that you do to the organizations of labor? If you did, the greatest moral force of life today, the trade unions, would certainly stand out the clearest, brightest, and purest. Because a certain class (for which you and a number of your colleagues on the bench seem to be the special pleaders) have a monopoly in their lines of trade, I submit that this is no good reason for their claim to have a monopoly on true patriotism or respect for the lawful institutions of the country.

But speaking of law reminds me of the higher law of the land. The Constitution prescribes that all rights not specifically granted to the general government are reserved to the states. There is another provision prohibiting the President from sending armed forces into any state except for the purpose of maintaining "a republican form of government," and then only upon the requisition of the legislature of the state, or of the governor when the legislature is not in session. Yet when, during the recent railroad strike, the President sent the troops into Illinois, it was not in compliance with the request of the legislature of that state, nor of the governor, but in spite of his protest. Yes, even when the governor remonstrated he was practically told by the President to stop arguing the law upon the question. Pardon the simplicity of my inquiry, but does not the law require that its limits shall be observed by a president, a judge, equally as by a labor organization?

If I remember aright you based the injunctions recently issued by you upon the provisions of the Interstate Commerce Law, a law enacted by Congress upon the demand of the farmers and shippers of our country to protect them against the unjust and outrageous discriminations imposed by the railroads. Where in the law can you find one word to justify your course applying to workingmen organized and engaged in a strike?

Read the discussions in Congress when that law was under consideration. You will not find a remote reference to the application of the laws as you construe it. In fact, I am informed upon excellent authority that when the law was before the Senate in the form of a bill, Senator Morgan, of Alabama, proposed an amendment which, if adopted, would have had the effect of empowering judges to issue an order of the nature you have in the recent railroad strike; but it was not adopted; it was defeated. How then in the face of this you can issue your omnibus restraining order passes the comprehension of ordinary men.

In his last report to Congress, the postmaster general recommended the passage of a law by Congress declaring that any train in which there should be but one pouch of mail matter should be considered a mail train, thus recognizing that there was no law by which other than regular "mail trains" come under the operation of the postal laws. Hence it is not a grave stretch of the imagination to regard this latest court-made law as an invention to break the strike.

I am not versed in the law, but somewhere I read that Blackstone says that a law which is not based on justice is not law, and presumably judges who distort law so that injustice is done are not the ablest or purest devotees of the "blind goddess." I do not quote this for the purpose of converting your mind to some degree of impartiality for labor, but merely to show what a sycophantic knave Blackstone was.

Year by year man's liberties are trampled underfoot at the bidding of corporations and trusts, rights are invaded, and law perverted. In all ages, wherever a tyrant has shown himself, he has always found some willing judge to clothe that tyranny in the robes of legality, and modern capitalism has proven no exception to the rule.

You may not know that the labor movement as represented by the trades unions stands for right, for justice, for liberty. You may not imagine that the issuance of an injunction depriving men of a legal as well as a natural right to protect themselves, their wives, and little ones must fail of its purpose. Repression or oppression never yet succeeded in crushing the truth or redressing a wrong.

In conclusion let me assure you that labor will organize and more compactly than ever and upon practical lines; and despite relentless antagonism, achieve for humanity a nobler manhood, a more beautiful womanhood, and a happier childhood.

100.

HENRY DEMAREST LLOYD: The Business Corporation and the Community

Journalist and social reformer Henry Demarest Lloyd first achieved success with a series of articles exposing the methods of the railroads and the Standard Oil trust. In his major work, Wealth Against Commonwealth, *part of which is reprinted here, he carefully documented the practices of America's largest corporations, whose growing power he felt was incompatible with American democracy. While working on the book, he wrote to his mother that the project kept him "poking about and scavenging in piles of filthy human greed and cruelty almost too nauseous to handle."*

Source: *Wealth Against Commonwealth*, New York, 1898, pp. 1-7.

NATURE IS RICH; but everywhere man, the heir of nature, is poor. Never in this happy country or elsewhere — except in the Land of Miracle, where "they did all eat and were filled" — has there been enough of anything for the people. Never since time began have all the sons and daughters of men been all warm, and all filled, and all shod and roofed. Never yet have all the virgins, wise or foolish, been able to fill their lamps with oil.

The world, enriched by thousands of generations of toilers and thinkers, has reached a fertility which can give every human being a plenty undreamed of even in the utopias. But between this plenty, ripening on the boughs of our civilization, and the people, hungering for it, step the "cornerers," the syndicates, trusts, combinations, with the cry of "overproduction" — too much of everything. Holding back the riches of earth, sea, and sky from their fellows who famish and freeze in the dark, they declare to them that there is too much light and warmth and food. They assert the right, for their private profit, to regulate the consumption by the people of the necessaries of life and to control production, not by the needs of humanity but by the desires of a few for dividends. The coal syndicate thinks there is too much coal. There is too much iron, too much lumber, too much flour — for this or that syndicate. The majority have never been able to buy enough of anything; but this minority have too much of everything to sell.

Liberty produces wealth, and wealth destroys liberty. "The splendid empire of Charles V," says Motley, "was erected upon the grave of liberty." Our bignesses — cities, factories, monopolies, fortunes, which are our empires, are the obesities of an age gluttonous beyond its powers of digestion. Mankind are crowding upon each other in the centers and struggling to keep each other out of the feast set by the new sciences and the new fellowships. Our size has got beyond both our science and our conscience. The vision of the railroad stockholder is not far-sighted enough to see into the office of the general manager; the people cannot reach across even a ward of a city to rule their rulers; captains of industry "do not know" whether the men in the ranks are dying from lack of food and shelter; we cannot clean our cities nor our politics; the locomotive has more manpower than all the ballot boxes, and millwheels wear out the hearts of workers unable to keep up beating time to their whirl.

If mankind had gone on pursuing the ideals of the fighter, the time would necessarily have come when there would have been only a few, then only one, and then none left. This is what we are witnessing in the world of livelihoods. Our ideals of livelihood are ideals of mutual deglutition. We are rapidly reaching the stage where in each province only a few are left; that is the key to our times. Beyond the deep is another deep. This era is but a passing phase in the evolution of industrial Caesars, and these Caesars will be of a new type — corporate Caesars.

For those who like the perpetual motion of a debate in which neither of the disputants is looking at the same side of the shield, there are infinite satisfactions in the current controversy as to whether there is any such thing as "monopoly." "There are

none," says one side. "They are legion," says the other. "The idea that there can be such a thing is absurd," says one, who with half a dozen associates controls the source, the price, the quality, the quantity of nine-tenths of a great necessary of life. But, "There will soon be a trust for every production and a master to fix the price for every necessity of life," said the senator who framed the United States Anti-Trust Law. This difference as to facts is due to a difference in the definitions through which the facts are regarded.

Those who say "there are none" hold with the attorney general of the United States and the decision he quotes from the highest federal court which had then passed on this question that no one has a monopoly unless there is a "disability" or "restriction" imposed by law on all who would compete. A syndicate that had succeeded in bottling for sale all the air of the earth would not have a monopoly in this view, unless there were on the statute books a law forbidding everyone else from selling air. No others could get air to sell; the people could not get air to breathe, but there would be no monopoly because there is no "legal restriction" on breathing or selling the atmosphere.

Excepting in the manufacture of postage stamps, gold dollars, and a few other such cases of a "legal restriction," there are no monopolies according to this definition. It excludes the whole body of facts which the people include in their definition and dismisses a great public question by a mere play on words. The other side of the shield was described by Judge Barrett of the Supreme Court of New York. A monopoly he declared to be "any combination the tendency of which is to prevent competition in its broad and general sense, and to control and thus at will enhance prices to the detriment of the public. . . . Nor need it be permanent or complete. It is enough that it may be even temporarily and partially successful. The question in the end is — Does it inevitably tend to public injury?"

Those who insist that "there are none" are the fortunate ones who came up to the shield on its golden side. But common usage agrees with the language of Judge Barrett, because it exactly fits a fact which presses on common people heavily, and will grow heavier before it grows lighter.

The committee of Congress investigating trusts in 1889 did not report any list of these combinations to control markets "for the reason that new ones are constantly forming and that old ones are constantly extending their relations so as to cover new branches of the business and invade new territories."

It is true that such a list, like a dictionary, would begin to be wrong the moment it began to appear. But though only an instantaneous photograph of the whirlwind, it would give an idea, to be gained in no other way, of a movement shadowing two hemispheres. In an incredible number of the necessaries and luxuries of life, from meat to tombstones, some inner circle of the "fittest" has sought, and very often obtained, the sweet power which Judge Barrett found the sugar trust had: It "can close every refinery at will, close some and open others, limit the purchases of raw material (thus jeopardizing, and in a considerable degree controlling, its production), artificially limit the production of refined sugar, enhance the price to enrich themselves and their associates at the public expense, and depress the price when necessary to crush out and impoverish a foolhardy rival."

Corners are "acute" attacks of that which combinations exhibit as chronic. First a corner, then a pool, then a trust has often been the genesis. The last stage, when the trust throws off the forms of combination and returns to the simpler dress of corporations, is already well along. Some of the "sympa-

thetical cooperations" on record have no doubt ceased to exist. But that they should have been attempted is one of the signs of the time, and these attempts are repeated again and again until success is reached.

The line of development is from local to national, and from national to international. The amount of capital changes continually with the recrystallizations in progress. Not less than $500 million is in the coal combination, which our evidence shows to have flourished twenty-two years; that in oil has nearly if not quite $200 million; and the other combinations in which its members are leaders foot up hundreds of millions more. Hundreds of millions of dollars are united in the railroads and elevators of the Northwest against the wheat growers. In cattle and meat there are not less than $100 million; in whiskey, $35 million; and in beer a great deal more than that; in sugar, $75 million; in leather, over $100 million; in gas, hundreds of millions. At this writing a union is being negotiated of all the piano makers in the United States to have a capital of $50 million.

Quite beyond ordinary comprehension is the magnitude of the syndicates, if there is more than one, which are going from city to city, consolidating all the gasworks, electric-lighting companies, street-railways in each into single properties, and consolidating these into vast estates for central corporations of capitalists, controlling from metropolitan offices the transportation of the people of scores of cities. Such a syndicate negotiating in December 1892 for the control of the street-railways of Brooklyn was said by the New York *Times*, "on absolute authority, to have subscribed $23 million toward that end before a single move had been made or a price set on a single share of stock." It was in the same hands as those busy later in gathering together the coal mines of Nova Scotia and putting them under American control. There are in round numbers ten thousand millions of dollars claiming dividends and interest in the railroads of the United States. Every year they are more closely pooled. The public saw them marshaled, as by one hand, in the maintenance of the high passenger rates to the World's Fair in the summer of 1893. Many rates are higher than thirty years ago.

Many thousands of millions of dollars are represented in these centralizations. It is a vast sum, and yet is but a minority of our wealth.

Laws against these combinations have been passed by Congress and by many of the states. There have been prosecutions under them by the state and federal governments. The laws and the lawsuits have alike been futile.

In a few cases, names and form of organization have been changed in consequence of legal pursuit. The whiskey, sugar, and oil trusts had to hang out new signs. But the thing itself — the will and the power to control markets, livelihoods, and liberties, and the toleration of this by the public — this remains unimpaired; in truth, facilitated by the greater secrecy and compactness which have been the only results of the appeal to law.

The attorney general of the national government gives a large part of his annual report for 1893 to showing "what small basis there is for the popular impression" "that the aim and effect of this statute" (the Anti-Trust Law) "are to prohibit and prevent those aggregations of capital which are so common at the present day, and which sometimes are on so large a scale as to practically control all the branches of an extensive industry." This executive says of the action of the "coordinate" legislature: "It

would not be useful, even if it were possible, to ascertain the precise purposes of the framers of the statute." He is the officer charged with the duty of directing the prosecutions to enforce the law; but he declares that since, among other reasons, "all ownership of property is a monopoly . . . any literal application of the provisions of the statute is out of the question." Nothing has been accomplished by all these appeals to the legislatures and the courts, except to prove that the evil lies deeper than any public sentiment or public intelligence yet existent and is stronger than any public power yet at call.

What we call monopoly is business at the end of its journey. The concentration of wealth, the wiping out of the middle classes are other names for it. To get it is, in the world of affairs, the chief end of man.

There are no solitary truths, Goethe says, and monopoly — as the greatest business fact of our civilization, which gives to business what other ages gave to war and religion — is our greatest social, political, and moral fact.

The men and women who do the work of the world have the right to the floor. Everywhere they are rising to "a point of information." They want to know how our labor and the gifts of nature are being ordered by those whom our ideals and consent have made captains of industry over us; how it is that we, who profess the religion of the Golden Rule and the political economy of service for service, come to divide our produce into incalculable power and pleasure for a few and partial existence for the many who are the fountains of these powers and pleasures.

101.

Uriel S. Hall: Reasons in Favor of an Income Tax

The following article by Uriel Hall in favor of a graduated income tax was occasioned by debate in Congress over a tax amendment that had been added to the Wilson-Gorman Tariff Bill. The Tariff Act was passed with the tax amendment in August 1894. But the following year the Supreme Court ruled the income tax unconstitutional in the case of Pollock v. Farmers Loan and Trust Company. *A constitutional amendment, ratified in February 1913, was necessary before the federal government could tax incomes directly.*

Source: *Forum*, March 1894.

A CHARGE HAS BEEN MADE and reiterated that the income tax bill is sectional in its nature, was passed by the House of Representatives from sectional motives by those who voted for it, and that the desire and purpose of its promoters was to place a penalty upon riches from a narrow spirit of envy and jealousy. That any member of Congress was induced to cast his vote for this measure upon any such ground is, in my judgment, an unfounded charge. The motive that prompted my advocacy of the measure was its justness.

Should we be denounced as demagogues, advocating socialistic tendencies, simply because we ask that the wealth of this government should bear some of the burdens of taxation? I joined the Farmers' Alliance of my state and lectured in almost every county in it and through other states of the South and West; and during the entire time that I was president of the Missouri State Alliance I never made a speech in which I did not maintain that he who would array one class of citizens against another, and who would try to make laboring men — agricultural or mechanical — a band of Ishmaelites, with its hand against the whole human race, and who would try to array labor against capital, and one section of our country against another, is a twin brother of the anarchist orator, a common enemy of mankind, and should be an outlaw in any community cursed by his presence.

I became a member of the Farmers' Alliance when its constitution declared that "nothing in it should ever conflict with a man's religious or political views," and have ever maintained that while a secret political society is a curse to any nation in which it exists, yet the education of the farming class in right economic principles, in the better management of their farm property, rotation of crops, and matters of general public interest, is the best safeguard of our government against the encroachments of anarchy.

I left it as soon as it became a political organization. When the Alliance declared in favor of the subtreasury plan, of land loans, and of the governmental ownership of railways and telegraphs, I denounced these things as heresies, and called upon every farmer in the United States to array himself against them; and, amid the hisses and curses of the national organization, I declared that such doctrines and tenets would bankrupt our government and ruin our people. I have been charged by the Populist leaders, time and time again, through their papers all over the United States, as being a "confederate of Wall Street and a traitor to the Alliance" simply because I could not and would not be a party to demagogy.

I know furthermore that the members of Congress from the Western, the Southern, the Northwestern, or the Central states who passed this bill are a body of patriotic men, fully impressed with their responsibility; and I know that they, like myself, have had to contend with the socialistic demagogue, have met him manfully and fearlessly, and have been a bulwark against his progress.

The wealthy classes of the Eastern states who are now opposing us in the enactment of this bill are embarrassing the best friends of a peaceful government. The principle that the wealth of this country should help to bear the burden of national taxation is too well settled by logic, by authority, and by experience to justify extended argument now. Too often already have members of this Congress been warned that, whenever the richer class should be asked to share the burdens of government, they, prompted by avarice, would denounce the suggestion. It is their position, not mine, that needs defense.

In a recent speech in the House of Representatives, I said:

> Were I called upon to frame a law that would keep down demagogy, that would take the last grain of justice from the conglomerate mass of Populistic heresies, it would be an income tax law.

I sincerely feel that every word I said was true. Under our tariff system its burdens are

put upon consumption (the necessaries of life that the poor must have or perish), and a poor man with a wife and five children is forced to pay out of his small income a larger sum for the support of the government than is the average man of great wealth with a small family; for, as Adam Smith says:

> The private revenue of individuals arises ultimately from three different sources: rent, profits, and wages. Every tax must finally be paid from some one or other of those three different sources of revenue, or from all of them indifferently.

But since there are more wealthy men in the East than elsewhere in our country, the greater burdens of an income tax would fall on the East. Is this unfair? Does it justify raising the sectional question? Is it we of the West and South who raise it?

But the opponents of the measure are bound to admit that there is some justice in this income tax. All the greatest authorities on taxation say that the subjects of a nation should be taxed to support that nation according to their ability, *not* according to the section in which they live; recognizing that we should all be common bearers and common supporters of a common country, ignoring sectionalism.

I now ask my readers to divest themselves of prejudice and antagonism, as far as their interests will permit, and dispassionately to read the following arguments and authorities in favor of an income tax by some of the wisest and greatest men that have ever written upon questions of national taxation.

Senator John Sherman, in a speech delivered in the United States Senate, March 15, 1882, uses the following language:

> The public mind is not yet prepared to apply the key of a genuine revenue reform. A few years of further experience will convince the whole body of our people that a system of national taxes

which rests the whole burden of taxation on consumption and not one cent on property and income, is intrinsically unjust.

While the expenses of the national government are largely caused by the protection of property, it is but right to call property to contribute to its payment. It will not do to say that each person consumes in proportion to his means. That is not true. Everyone must see that the consumption of the rich does not bear the same relation to the consumption of the poor, as the income of the rich does to the wages of the poor. As wealth accumulates, this injustice in the fundamental basis of our system will be felt and forced upon the attention of Congress.

Adam Smith says:

The subjects of every state ought to contribute toward the support of the government as nearly as possible in proportion to their respective abilities; that is, in proportion to the revenue which they respectively enjoy under the protection of the state. The expenses of government to the individuals of a great nation are like the expenses of management to the joint tenants of a great estate who are all obliged to contribute in proportion to their respective interests in the estate. In the observation or neglect of this maxim consists what is called the equality or inequality of taxation.

That excellent French writer Thiers likens a tax paid by the citizen to his government to the premium paid by the insured to an insurance company; and as one pays the underwriter premiums in proportion to the amount of property insured, so should the citizen pay taxes in proportion as he has property insured, that is, protected and defended by the government.

Montesquieu in his *Spirit of Laws*, commenting on the Athenian system of taxation, says:

At Athens the people were divided into four classes. Those who drew 500 measures of liquid or dried fruit from their estates paid a talent to the public; those who drew 300 measures paid half

a talent; those who had 200 measures paid 10 minae; those of the fourth class paid nothing at all. The tax was fair, though it was not proportionable: it did not follow the measure of people's property; it followed that of their wants. It was judged that every man had an equal share of what was necessary for nature; that whatsoever was necessary for nature ought not to be taxed; that to this succeeded the useful, which ought to be taxed, but less than the superfluous; and that the largeness of the taxes on what was superfluous prevented superfluity.

Thorold Rogers says: "Taxation in proportion to benefits received is sufficiently near the truth for the practical operations of government." Rousseau and the elder Mirabeau, J. B. Say, and Garnier have approved of this system; while Sismondi, in laying down his canons of taxation, declares that "every tax should fall on revenue, not on capital," and that "taxation should never touch what is necessary for the existence of the contributor." John Stuart Mill declares that "equality of taxation, as a maxim of politics, means equality of sacrifice"; while C. F. Bastable, professor of political economy in Dublin University, in his able work on *Public Finance* (published in 1892), says:

It is apparent that the rule of equality of sacrifice is but another mode of stating the rule of equality as to ability. Equal ability implies equal capacity for bearing sacrifice. An equal charge will impose equal sacrifice upon persons of equal "faculty," and where abilities are unequal a corresponding inequality in the amount of taxation will realize the aim of equality of sacrifice.

Among the many other able economic writers and national financiers who advocate an income tax, I will mention Richard T. Ely, professor of political economy in Wisconsin University; and Prof. Robert Ellis Thompson, who says in his work on political economy:

The most modern and, theoretically, the fairest form of taxation is the income tax. It seems to make everyone contribute to the wants of the state in proportion to the revenue he enjoys under its protection. While falling equally on all, it occasions no change in the distribution of capital or in the material direction of industry, and has no influence on prices. No other is so cheaply assessed or collected. No other brings home to the people so forcibly the fact that it is to their interest to insist upon a wise economy of the national revenue.

I advocated that the exemption should not be placed higher than $2,500, and am still inclined to think $4,000 too great; but, having been overruled by the Ways and Means Committee on this question, I am cordially in favor of this measure. This will certainly exempt enough for a man to support himself and his family.

I believe that the greatest safeguard against anarchy in this country is the great agricultural class. They have universally, in almost every meeting of the National Alliance, National Grange, and kindred associations of farmers, asked for the passage of an income tax law; not as a matter of spite, nor as a matter of sectionalism, but as one of justice and right; and I sincerely hope they will receive the assurance of a cheerful acquiescence by the richer class that we may be enabled to form "a more perfect union, to establish justice, to ensure domestic tranquillity, and provide for a common

defense" against the common enemy of all countries in which universal suffrage exists.

Those who think this tax cannot be collected are certainly ignorant of the fact that over 87 percent of the income tax of England is collected in a similar manner. Let them read the bill carefully and impartially.

There is no one for whom I have a more thorough contempt than the alarmist and calamity-howler; yet I make the statement, from a rather large field of observation, that, if this income tax bill is defeated, one will be passed in the near future that will be far wider reaching and involving far greater danger of injustice toward wealth. We men that have ever aimed to act as a balance wheel will find ourselves powerless to check a less scrupulous element.

The members of the Fifty-third Congress who passed this bill are the Girondists, standing firmly between the "Sansculottes" and (as the Socialists call them) the "Royalists," praying that God may grant that we may *all* unite to wipe out all semblance of sectionalism and strife, and present an unbroken front against the common enemies of our united and beloved republic. If they could only put themselves in our places and know the difficulties under which we labor and the alternatives which confront us, every wealthy man of the East would write his senators to aid in the passage of this income tax bill.

———◆———

We owe it to our country to pay our taxes without murmuring; the time to get in our fine work is on the valuation.

EDGAR WILSON ("BILL") NYE

102.

W. H. "Coin" Harvey: For Bimetallism in Money Policy

W. H. Harvey, one of the great free silver propagandists, had failed at ranching, silver prospecting, and editing before he achieved success with Coin's Financial School. *In this little booklet, parts of which are presented here, "Professor Coin" taught businessmen and bankers the value of a free silver policy. Its straightforward language and strong expressions of hatred for the gold standard contributed to the pamphlet's enormous popularity: 300,000 copies were sold the first year and 125,000 given away during William Jennings Bryan's presidential campaign. Despite the logical weaknesses of Harvey's work and scholarly refutations by political economists like James Lawrence Laughlin of the University of Chicago, "Coin" Harvey was instrumental in arousing the demand for free coinage of silver and in focusing the 1896 presidential campaign on the silver issue.*

Source: *Coin's Financial School*, Chicago, 1894, pp. 44-57.

THE PRIMARY VALUE of all property is its exchange value. If we had no money, one kind of property would be exchanged for another. Needing the calico on the merchant's shelf, you would exchange for it a bushel of potatoes or such property as you might have to offer. A sort of exchange value would be placed on all property. A bushel of wheat would buy about so many pounds of sugar, and so on.

This is what is meant by the exchange value of property. Money is a medium of exchange to facilitate this exchanging of property.

If there were no money, and we had to depend on exchanging property for property, we could find a subsistence, but there would be no such thing as our present civilization or anything like it. Each merchant would have to be prepared to store all kinds of property, perishable and otherwise, he received in exchange for his goods. Railroads would have to arrange to receive payment for fares and freight in property and store it until it again could be exchanged. If you went to the theater, you would have to take with you a crate of cabbage or some other kind of property to pay your way into the playhouse. There would be no practical method for paying labor. Commerce would virtually cease, and civilization would go backward.

If to be without money would produce such a result, then the subject assumes vast importance. As stagnation and depression to business incalculable would result from having no money, then a part of these evils can be brought about by having money insufficient in either quality or quantity.

In the first place, it was deemed best to select something for money which was valuable within itself; something that had an exchange value, so that he who parted with his property for it, had something which was itself valuable. By stamping it as money and making it legal tender in the payment of all debts, it then became money, and possessed two qualities:

First, it had value of itself. If the government went to pieces that had stamped it, it was still valuable property and would have an exchange value. Second, when made money, it became a common medium of exchange and took the place of barter and trade. The stamp of the government upon it became a certificate of its quality and quantity. Thus by making a commodity into money we had a medium of exchange that was both useful and valuable.

SILVER AND GOLD ADOPTED

AFTER USING many perishable commodities, experience and wisdom brought the people of the world to the use of silver and gold. If experience could suggest a commodity better adapted for money than metallic money made from silver and gold, it should be adopted.

The merit of these two metals is that neither will rust, corrode, nor stain, and both are odorless. As compared with other property, both are very durable. Of the two, silver is the most durable. Abrasion causes more loss to gold than to silver, and the latter may be carried in the pocket and subjected to great use with but little loss. One was the money of the people — the other, of the rich. As two legs are necessary to walk and two eyes to see, so were these two monies necessary to the prosperity of the people.

It was considered that silver and gold were sufficient in quantity for use as primary money, but if at any time their combined quantity should become too small, then some other metal would have to be adopted and added to these two. The law of unlimited demand by *free coinage* would tie a third metal to these two, and thus increase the quantity, if at any time it became necessary.

Thus the founders of a monetary system

on the principle of *free coinage* to the commodity selected had a practical method for supplying any deficiency that might arise by reason of the exhaustion of the silver and gold mines. . . .

MONEY AS A SCIENCE

WE ARE NOW DEALING WITH MONEY as a science, and, strictly speaking, nothing is money except that commodity which has been selected to be money. It is a common thing for us to refer to National Bank notes, greenbacks, and other forms of paper money as "money."

After a nation has fixed what its *money* shall be, it then issues different forms of credit money, all of which are directly or indirectly redeemable in the commodity to which a fixed and stable value has been given. This is done for convenience and to facilitate commerce and the exchange of property. It does not add one dollar to your actual money but represents your real money, and, being easier to carry, is a convenience.

All money may be a medium of exchange, but primary money *only* is the measure of values. Credit money is not a measure of values; it is a medium of exchange only. I will refer to *money* proper as *redemption* or *primary* money, and in speaking generally of all other forms of money will use the term *credit* money.

There are two kinds of *credit* money, as to the material out of which they are made. One is made on paper and embraces all forms of government and bank notes that are issued from time to time as authorized by law. The other is — token money. Token money is made from some metal that does not enjoy *free coinage.*

Credit money of all kinds circulates by reason of its being redeemable directly or indirectly in *money* — in *redemption* money, property money. A piece of paper money, or token money, is a promise of the government to pay so much money. The money promised is the *redemption* money. With so much paper or credit money in your possession, there is supposed to be that much redemption money to your credit with the government or bank issuing it. It is a check to bearer for *money,* when presented. Hence it is called *credit* money. It circulates on the credit of the government, on the confidence of the people that the government will be able to redeem it if it is presented.

I have taken pains to impress on you the distinction between actual money and credit money, as no just comprehension of our monetary system as a science can be had without it.

Actual money was too cumbersome to handle in all the transactions of business, and this gave rise to issuing credit money representing it. Like wheat in your wheat elevators, certificates are issued to those who put their wheat there. Such certificates are traded in. Each time one of them is transferred, it is equivalent to transferring the wheat itself. Wheat is behind the certificates. A man does not carry a brick house around in his pocket, but he can carry the deed to it. When you have credit money in your pocket, you are carrying around with you the title to property of that commercial value.

In issuing dollar for dollar of credit money to redemption money, it is not necessary that the government should keep the latter at all times in its Treasury in full amount ready to redeem all the credit money. Experience teaches that so long as sufficient *redemption money* is in the country, the credit of the government can be depended upon to get it. But it cannot strain the proportion beyond such amount without making the danger imminent and the lack of confidence great. If there is $1,000,000,000 of redemption money in the United States — in its Treasury, its banks, and among its people — then $1,000,000,000 of credit money can be safely used and not more.

If you want to increase the currency, you must in safety do it by adding to the *redemption* money, and for each dollar so added one dollar of credit money may be added. If it is wished to vitiate the currency, increase the credit money beyond its normal quantity or dig out the foundation from under it by lessening the supply of redemption money.

The demonetization of silver destroyed one-half of the *redemption* money of the United States. It did it in this way: by making gold the *unit* and closing the mints to silver, it lessened the demand for silver, and its commercial value at once began to depreciate, as measured in gold. Where before silver and gold had been tied together as one mass of commodity money, and all property had measured its value in it, now gold became the only measure of value, and silver became *credit* money — token money.

The moment a new standard of money was set up — only one-half in quantity to what had previously existed — silver began to fluctuate. It was then measured for its value in this new standard for measuring values, and bobbed up and down in the market, no longer possessing that fixed value which *free* coinage had given it. It was like a kite without a tail and its course was downward. It had changed its position from redemption money to token money.

A forced parity between gold and silver has since been strained; namely, by sustaining silver with gold. It is the same kind of parity the government maintains between gold and paper money. What this means is, gold is our present redemption money and our credit money consists of silver and all forms of paper money.

Each succeeding secretary of the Treasury points to the law declaring it to be the intention of our financial system to maintain all our money at par. Gold is the most valuable of all our money, and therefore to maintain it all at par, gold must stand under it and do the work of redemption money. The law simply states an axiom in sound financing. All of our money should be at par — with one kind of money just as good as any other kind of money.

It is impossible to maintain two kinds of redemption money with one made from property having a commercial value of only one-half, or any noticeable percent less than the other. When such is the case the lesser must lean on the greater, and to all intents and purposes becomes credit money, while the more valuable becomes the only redemption money. We have in the United States in round figures $1,600,000,000 of all kinds of money. About one-third of it is gold, one-third silver, and one-third paper. One-third of our money is redemption money and two-thirds is credit money.

The blunder was made when silver was demonetized. The remedy is to remonetize it, and thereby restore its commercial value. Purchase acts or any treatment of silver short of free coinage will have no beneficial effect. . . .

GENERAL PRINCIPLES

We thus see that *money,* primarily, is a commodity — property — a thing of value — possessing an exchange value with all other property; that *credit money* is a title to *commodity money;* that in the exchange value between *commodity money* and all other property, credit money does not add anything — it facilitates — makes convenient the transaction of business. Just as your wheat certificates add nothing to the exchange value of wheat or the things for which wheat are exchanged, yet they facilitate its exchange. This commodity money is the measure of values. Its quantity becomes the measure, and each dollar is a part of that measure. Credit money adds nothing to its value; it only facilitates the transaction of business based on that measure of values.

Our commodity or redemption money, up to 1873, was both silver and gold; and our credit money was paper and copper.

Since 1873 our redemption money has been gold — and our credit money has been paper, silver, nickel, and copper. Silver and nickel have been added to copper as token money. . . . As *redemption money* is our measure of values, nothing can take its place and assist it in *its* work that is not of equal commercial value.

It is also an error to suppose that checks and drafts to any very great extent take the place of *credit* money. It facilitates business for a man to be able to carry his checkbook with him instead of the danger and inconvenience of carrying a large roll of bills; but the equivalent of each check he draws must be to his credit in bank to meet the check. If a man gives a check for $100, and that check is transferred to six different parties and pays in that way six different debts in the course of the day, it does no more than a $100 bill would have done. It, too, could have started on the rounds and paid the same number of debts. The check has no advantages over the bill in that respect.

Where checks enlarge the use of credit money is in this: A bank may have had deposited with it $1 million. It only keeps, say, $400,000 on hand; the banking and check system gives greater utility to the $1 million, but the necessity for *actual* money has not been decreased in the least — the expansion of credit money by substitutes only emphasizes its importance.

OUR FINANCIAL AND CREDIT SYSTEM

Three lines of credits . . . are built up on *primary* or *redemption* money: First, credit money — paper bills and all forms of token money — all redeemable in primary money; second, checks, drafts, bills of exchange, and other forms of like paper, payable on demand; third, notes, bonds, accounts, and other forms of credit, payable at a particular day in the future or upon the happening of some contingency.

A reckless era of business that extends either or both the *second* and *third* lines of credit beyond their normal volume may create a panic. Notes, bonds, and accounts become due that are not paid; a lack of confidence arises resulting in the demand for all debts due for fear delay will endanger their collection. A run on banks during such a period is natural, and many of them go down for want of sufficient reserve to pay all money deposited with them subject to check.

103.

Hamlin Garland: Provincialism and Individuality in American Literature

Born in Wisconsin in 1860, the son of restless westward-moving pioneers, Hamlin Garland rebelled against family tradition by turning to Boston for a literary career. But the Midwest, the "Middle Border," as he called it, was in his bones, and he made a considerable success in apostrophizing the vanishing frontier of his childhood. Assuming the role of literary reformer and prophet, Garland followed his first collection of stories, Main-Travelled Roads, *by a volume of essays,* Crumbling Idols, *published in 1894. The book, which advocated a brand of super-realism, called by him veritism, and predicted an American literary renaissance centered in Chicago, was inspired by the World's Columbian Exposition of 1893.*

Source: *Crumbling Idols,* Chicago, 1894: "Provincialism."

THE HISTORY OF AMERICAN LITERATURE is the history of provincialism slowly becoming less all-pervasive — the history of the slow development of a distinctive utterance.

By provincialism I mean dependence upon a mother country for models of art production. This is the sense in which Taine or Véron would use the word. The "provincialism" which the conservative deplores is not provincialism but the beginning of an indigenous literature.

"The true makers of national literature," writes Posnett, in his *Comparative Literature,* "are the actions and thoughts of the nation itself. The place of these can never be taken by the sympathies of a cultured class too wide to be national, or those of a central academy too refined to be provincial. Provincialism is no ban in a truly national literature."

Using the word "provincialism," therefore, from the point of view of the central academy, we have had too little of it. That is to say, our colonial writers, and our writers from 1800 on to 1860, had too little to do with the life of the American people and too much concern with British critics. Using it in its literary sense of dependence upon England and classic models, we have had too much of it. It has kept us timidly imitating the great writers of a nation far

Hamlin Garland, novelist who pictured life in the Midwest in latter part of the 19th century

separated from us naturally in its social and literary ideals.

The whole development can be epitomized thus: Here on the eastern shore of America lay a chain of colonies predominantly English, soon to be provinces. Like all colonists, they looked back to their mother country for support and encouragement in intellectual affairs as in material things. They did not presume to think for themselves. But the Revolution taught them something. It strengthened the feeling of separate identity and responsibility. It liberated them in politics but left them still provincial (dependent) in literary and religious things.

There still remained some truth in the British sneer that American poets and artists were merely shadows or doubles successively of Pope, of Scott, of Byron, of Wordsworth, and of Tennyson. In all the space between the Revolution and the Civil War, American poets reflected the American taste

fairly well, but the spirit and form of their work (with a few notable exceptions) was imitative.

Here and there song was sung from the sincere wish to embody American life and characteristic American thought. Each generation grew less timid and more manly and individual. The Civil War came on and was an immense factor in building up freedom from Old World models and in developing native literature. National feeling had an immense widening and deepening. From the interior of America, men and women rose almost at once to make American literature take on vitality and character.

American life had been lived but not embodied in art. Native utterance had been overawed and silenced by academic English judgments; but this began to change after the Civil War. The new field began to make itself felt, not all at once but by degrees, through *Snow-bound* and *The Biglow Papers* and *The Tales of the Argonauts* and the *Songs of the Sierras*. But while this change was growing, there was coming in, in the Eastern cities, the spirit of a central academy that was to stand in precisely the same relation to the interior of America that London formerly occupied with regard to the whole country.

It may be that New York is to threaten and overawe the interior of America as Paris reigns over the French provinces. The work of Mistral and the *Felibrige* may be needed with us to keep original genius from being silenced or distorted by a central academy which is based upon tradition rather than upon life and nature. Decentralization may come to be needed here, as in Europe.

The evolutionist explains the past by the study of laws operative in the present and by survivals of ancient conditions obscurely placed in modern things, like sinking icebergs in a southern sea. The attitude of mind (once universal with Americans), which measured everything by British standards and timidly put new wine into old bottles, can still be found among the academic devotees and their disciples. They are survivals of a conception of life and literature once universal.

The change which has taken place can be specifically illustrated in the West. That is to say, the general terms which could be applied to the whole country up to the time of the Civil War can be applied specifically to the Middle West today. As a Western man, I think I may speak freely without being charged with undue prejudice toward the states I name.

The schoolbred West, broadly speaking, is as provincial in its art as it is assertive of Americanism in politics. The books it reads, the pictures it buys are nearly all of the conventional sort, or, worse yet, imitations of the conventional. Its literary clubs valiantly discuss dead issues in English literature and vote in majority against the indigenous and the democratic. They have much to say of the ideal and the universal in literature, quite in the manner of their academical instructors.

The lower ranks of Western readers, as everywhere, devour some millions of tons of romantic love stories or stories of detectives or Indians. It is a curious thing to contrast the bold assertion of the political exhorter of "America for Americans" with the enslavement of our readers and writers to various shades of imitative forms of feudalistic literature. America is not yet democratic in art, whatever it may claim to be in politics.

These facts are not to be quarreled about; they are to be studied. They are signs of life and not of death. It is better that these people should read such things than nothing at all. They will rise out of it. They can be influenced, but they must be approached on the side of life and not by way of the academic. They are ready to support and be helped by the art which springs from life.

It is the great intelligent middle class of America, curiously enough, who are apparently most provincial. With them the verdict of the world is all-important. Their education has been just sufficient to make them distrustful of their own judgment. They are largely the product of our schools. They have been taught to believe that Shakespeare ended the drama, that Scott has closed the novel, that the English language is the greatest in the world, and that all other literatures are curious, but not at all to be ranked in power and humanity with the English literature, etc., etc. I speak advisedly of these things because I have been through this instruction, which is well-nigh universal. This class is the largest class in America and makes up the great body of schoolbred Westerners. They sustain with a sort of desperation all the tenets of the conservative and romantic criticism in which they have been instructed.

It can almost be stated as a rule without an exception that in our colleges there is no chair of English literature which is not dominated by conservative criticism and where sneering allusion to modern writers is not daily made. The pupil is taught to worship the past and is kept blind to the mighty literary movements of his own time. If he comes to understand Ibsen, Tolstoy, Björnson, Howells, Whitman, he must do it outside his instruction.

This instruction is well-meaning, but it is benumbing to the faculties. It is essentially hopeless. It blinds the eyes of youth to the power and beauty of the life and literature around him. It worships the past, despises the present, and fears the future. Such teaching is profoundly pessimistic because it sees literary ideals changing. It has not yet seen that metamorphosis is the law of all living things. It has not yet risen to the perception that the question for America to settle is not whether it can produce something *greater* than the past but whether it shall produce something *different* from the past. Our task is not to imitate but to create.

Instruction of this kind inevitably deflects the natural bent of the young artist or discourages attempt altogether. It is the opposite of education; that is, it represses rather than *leads out* the distinctive individuality of the student.

These conservative ideas affect the local newspapers, and their literary columns are too often full of the same gloomy comment. They are timidly negative when not partisanly conservative. They can safely praise Ruskin and Carlyle and repeat an old slur on Browning or Whitman.

There is also a class of critics who can launch into two-column criticisms of a new edition of *Rasselas* and leave unread a great novel by Tolstoy, or a new translation of Brand, or a new novel by Howells. Their judgment is worthless to detect truth and beauty in a work of art close at hand. They wait for the judgment of the East, of London.

The American youth is continually called upon by such critics to take Addison or Scott or Dickens or Shakespeare as a model. Such instruction leads naturally to the creation of blank-verse tragedies on Columbus and Washington — a species of work which seems to the radical the crowning absurdity of misplaced effort. Thus, the American youth is everywhere turned away from the very material which he could best handle, which he knows most about, and which he really loves most — material which would make him individual and fill him with hope and energy. The Western poet and novelist is not taught to see the beauty and significance of life near at hand. He is rather blinded to it by his instruction.

He turns away from the marvelous changes which border life subtends in its mighty rush toward civilization. He does not see the wealth of material which lies at his hand, in the mixture of races going on with inconceivable celerity everywhere in America, but with special picturesqueness in the West. If he sees it, he has not the courage to write of it.

If, here and there, one has reached some such perception, he voices it timidly, with an apologetic look in his eye.

The whole matter appears to me to be a question of the individuality. I feel that Véron has stated this truth better than any other man. In his assault upon the central academy, he says, in substance, "Education should not conventionalize, should not mass together; it should individualize."

The Western youth, like the average schoolbred American, lacks the courage of his real conviction. He really prefers the modern writer, the modern painter, but he feels bound to falsify in regard to his real mind. As a creative intelligence, he lacks the courage to honestly investigate his surroundings and then stand by his judgment. Both as reader and writer, he dreads the Eastern comment. It is pitiful to see his eagerness to conform; he will even go beyond his teachers in conforming. Thus he starts wrong. His standards of comparison are wrong. He is forced into writing to please somebody else, which is fatal to high art.

To perceive the force of all this and the real hopelessness of instruction according to conventional models, we have only to observe how little that is distinctive has been produced by the great Western middle states — say Wisconsin, Illinois, and Iowa. Of what does its writing consist?

A multitude of little newspapers, first of all, full of local news; and larger newspapers that are political organs, with some little attention to literature on their inside pages. Their judgments are mainly conservative, but here and there in their news columns one finds sketches of life so vivid one wonders why writers so true and imaginative are not recognized and encouraged. The most of the short stories in these papers, however, are absolutely colorless, where they are not pirated exotics. In all that they call "literature" these papers generally reflect what they believe to be the correct thing in literary judgment. In their unconscious moments they are fine and true.

Art, they think, is something far away, and literary subjects must be something select and very civilized. And yet for forty years an infinite drama has been going on in those wide spaces of the West — a drama that is as thrilling, as full of heart and hope and battle, as any that ever surrounded any man; a life that was unlike any ever seen on the earth and which should have produced its characteristic literature, its native art chronicle.

As for myself, I am overwhelmed by the majesty, the immensity, the infinite charm of the life that goes on around me. Themes are crying out to be written. Take, for a single example, the history of the lumbering district of the Northern lakes — a picturesque and peculiar life that, through a period of thirty years, has been continually changing in all but a few of its essential features; and yet this life has had only superficial representation in the sketches of the tourist or reporter; its inner heart has not been uttered.

The subtle changes of thought and of life that have come with the rise of a city like St. Paul or Minneapolis; the life of the great sawmills and shingle mills; and the river life of the Upper Mississippi are all fine subjects. So are the river towns like Dubuque and Davenport, with their survivals of French life reaching down to the present year, and thus far unrecorded.

Then there is the mixture of races; the coming in of the German, the Scandinavian; the marked yet subtle changes in their character. Then there is the building of railroads, with all their trickery and false promises and worthless bonds; the rise of millionaires; the deepening of social contrasts. In short, there is a great heterogeneous, shifting, brave population, a land teeming with unrecorded and infinite drama.

It is only to the superficial observer that this country seems colorless and dull; to the veritist it is full of burning interest, greatest possibilities. I instance these localities because I know something special about them; but the same words apply to Pennsylvania, Ohio, or Kentucky. And yet how few writers of national reputation this eventful, century-long march of civilization has produced!

We have had the figures, the dates, the bare history, the dime novel statement of pioneer life, but how few real novels! How few accurate studies of speech and life! There it lies, ready to be put into the novel and the drama and upon canvas; and it must be done by those born into it. Joaquin Miller has given us lines of splendid poetry touching this life, and Edward Eggleston, Joseph Kirkland, Opie Read, Octave Thanet have dealt more or less faithfully with certain phases of it; but mainly the mighty West, with its swarming millions, remains undelineated in the novel, the drama, and the poem.

The causes of it, as I have indicated, are twofold: first, lack of a market; and, second, lack of perception. This lack of perception of the art possibilities of common American life has been due to several causes. Hard life, toil, lack of leisure have deadened and calloused the perceiving mind, making life hard, dull, and uninteresting. But, beyond this, the right perception has been lacking on the part of instructors and critics. Everything has really tended to repress or distort the art feeling of the young man or woman. They have been taught to imitate, not to create.

But at last conditions are changing. All

over the West young people are coming on who see that every literature in the past was at its best creative and not imitative. Here and there a paper or magazine lends itself to the work of encouraging the young writer in original work. They are likely to err now on the side of flattery. Criticism should be helpful, not indiscriminate either in praise or blame.

And, more than this, in every town of the interior there are groups of people whose firmness of conviction and broad culture make them the controlling power in all local literary work. They are reading the most modern literature, and their judgments are not dependent upon New York or London, though they find themselves in full harmony with progressive artists everywhere. They are clearly in the minority, but they are a growing company everywhere, and their influence is felt by every writer of the progressive group.

104.

Songs of the Nineties

The Gay Nineties, like any other epoch, loved songs about women, and we reprint here two of the most typical. In "Her Golden Hair Was Hanging Down Her Back," popular songwriters Felix McGlennon and Monroe Rosenfeld told the story of an apparently naïve country girl who managed nevertheless to make fools of the big-city slickers. But the country girl did not always win out, even in song. William Gray's "She Is More To Be Pitied Than Censured" points a sentimental moral about a "bad" girl and tells how she came to her plight and how she will pay for her sins.

✍ HER GOLDEN HAIR WAS HANGING DOWN HER BACK

There was once a simple maiden came to New York on a trip,
And her golden hair was hanging down her back.
Her cheeks were like the roses, she'd a pout upon her lip,
And her golden hair was hanging down her back.
When she landed at the station here she took a little stroll;
At everything she wondered till she lost her self-control.
Said she, "New York is quite a village, ain't it? Bless my soul!"
And her golden hair was hanging down her back.

Chorus:
But, oh, Jane! doesn't look the same,
When she left the village she was shy;
But, alas! and alack! She's gone back
With a naughty little twinkle in her eye!

She toddled down Broadway, a bashful smile upon her face,
And her golden hair was hanging down her back.
A bit of nice blue ribbon kept her ringlets in their place,
For her golden hair was hanging down her back.
Of course she knew her manners; she'd been taught to be polite,
So when a gent said, "Hem, good evening!" she said, "Hem, good night!"
Said she, "I am a stranger here, I hope you'll treat me right!"
And her golden hair was hanging down her back.

She took his arm in confidence, she liked his pleasant ways,
And her golden hair was hanging down her back.
At all the damsels passing by she stared in great amaze,
And her golden hair was hanging down her back.
She told him she was thirsty; "Oh, all right," said he, "good biz."
He took her to Delmonico's and treated her to fizz.
Said she, "I think it's nicer than a glass of milk, it is!"
And her golden hair was hanging down her back.

They drank until the artless man so very weary grew,
And her golden hair was hanging down her back.
She took his chain and ticker, and his diamond breast pin, too,
And her golden hair was hanging down her back.
Then silently she left him as he slumbered in a chair;
Into the street she wandered with a very simple air;
She would have carried off the stove if there had been one there!
And her golden hair was hanging down her back.

Now, gentle folks, I warn you all to shun the simple maid,
When her golden hair is hanging down her back.
If any such you run across just don't you be afraid,
When her golden hair is hanging down her back.
Just skip the gutter, cross the street, or take another lane,
Or dodge the corner, take a cab, or catch a railway train.
And as you're flying up the street, just sing her this refrain:
"Oh! your golden hair is hanging down your back!"

FELIX McGLENNON AND MONROE H. ROSENFELD

🕮 SHE IS MORE TO BE PITIED THAN CENSURED

At the old concert hall on the Bowery,
Round a table were seated one night
A crowd of young fellows carousing,
With them life seemed cheerful and bright.
At the very next table was seated
A girl who had fallen to shame;
All the young fellows jeered at her weakness,
Till they heard an old woman exclaim:

"She is more to be pitied than censured,
She is more to be helped than despised.
She is only a lassie who ventured
On life's stormy path, ill advised.
Do not scorn her with words fierce and bitter;
Do not laugh at her shame and downfall.
For a moment just stop and consider
That a man was the cause of it all."

There's an old-fashioned church round the corner
Where the neighbors all gathered one day,
While the parson was preaching a sermon
O'er a soul that had just passed away.
'Twas this same wayward girl from the Bowery
Who a life of adventure had led.
Did the clergyman jeer at her downfall?
No, he asked for God's mercy and said:

"She is more to be pitied than censured,
She is more to be helped than despised.
She is only a lassie who ventured
On life's stormy path, ill advised.
Do not scorn her with words fierce and bitter;
Do not laugh at her shame and downfall.
For a moment just stop and consider
That a man was the cause of it all."

WILLIAM B. GRAY

105.

Caspar W. Whitney: Evolution of the Country Club

The country club developed in America in the 1880s as a place where the wealthy could engage in sports that the common man had neither the time nor the money to enjoy — yachting, polo, tennis, and archery. After 1885 another game began making headway, a game that was to convert the country club into a national institution and open its doors to the middle classes as well. The game, of course, was golf. Caspar Whitney, sportswriter for Harper's New Monthly *magazine, analyzed the social phenomenon of the country club in 1894. His article is reprinted here in part.*

Source: *Harper's New Monthly,* December 1894.

IT USED TO BE SAID Americans did not know how to live, but that was before we were "discovered" by the journalistic missionaries of Great Britain. It used also to be said we did not know how to enjoy ourselves; but, again, that was before the dawn of the country club. If we knew neither how to live nor how to enjoy ourselves until comparatively recent years, it must be acknowledged we have made excellent use of both time and opportunity since our enlightenment. Even yet our efforts to acquire more intimate acquaintance with the leisurely side of life are parodied by those who cannot understand the demands of this great throbbing workaday country of ours.

It must be admitted unhesitatingly that we are only just learning how to play; we have not been, nor are we yet, a nation of pleasure seekers. We are a practical people; we build our living house before undertaking landscape gardening. If we have been long in turning our attention to material enjoyments, we have atoned somewhat for early indifference by modernizing the paraphernalia and investing in the pursuit all that earnestness which characterizes the American in whatever field he launches. Indeed, we have entered upon our recreation with such vigor I often question if even yet we have attained wisdom with the recreative incentive. I confess to a doubt whether full enjoyment of our joys is an American attribute.

We steal away for our holidays (likely as not with a portmanteau filled with work to do at odd moments) determined to rest and take life at its easiest. We promise ourselves to forswear all thoughts of business and the outer world; to loll about under the trees and seek some of the lessons nature is said to have for us. We hold bravely to our resolutions for a day or so, but the third or fourth is certain to find us bargaining for city newspapers. Perhaps our grandchildren may see the day they can separate themselves from the office as effectually as though it existed in name only, but the present-day American, at least he who fills any active part in this great progressive movement, has not yet reached that development in the cultivation of holiday amusement. . . .

The country club in America is simply

one of the results of a final ebullition of animal spirits too long ignored in a workaday world; it is nature's appeal for recognition of the body in its cooperation with the mind.

Only a careful study of our country's history and its social traditions will give us a full appreciation of what the country club has done for us. It has, first of all, corrected to a large extent the American defect of not being able or at least not willing to stop work and enjoy ourselves; it has brought together groups of congenial, cultivated people that often as not might be sweltering in the midsummer sun in town, or at isolated country houses, or in crowded, ill-kept "summer hotels." It has given them a club and country villa combined in one where, having practically all the comforts and delights of housekeeping, they are called upon to assume none of its cares or responsibilities. For here the steward attends to the early morning market, worries with the servants, and may be held to account for the shortcomings of the chef, and at a cost below that on which a separate establishment of equal appointment could be maintained.

It is impossible to overestimate the blessings of the country club in adding comforts to country living that before were utterly unattainable and in making it possible to enjoy a degree of that rural life which is one of England's greatest attractions. I say degree, for we have not yet attained the full delights of suburban residence as they are enjoyed in England, where a large and wealthy leisure class make well-nigh every great hall virtually a country club. In its present development the country club is really an American institution; there is little occasion for it in England, and nowhere is it so elaborated in the Old World as in the New.

To Boston must be given the credit of first revealing the possibilities and the delights of the country club. I never journey

to the "Hub" that I do not envy Bostonians the geographical situation of their city, which is superior, from a sportsman's point of view, to that of any other in the United States. What with rural New England within a very few hours' railway travel and the "North Shore," that ideal summer resting spot, at their very gates, there is outdoor entertainment for those of every disposition.

What nature has done for the Bostonian, a visit to the "North Shore," or perusal of Mr. Robert Grant's charmingly realistic pen picture of its beauties alone can show. Really it was not very neighborly of Mr. Grant to awaken so abruptly to our rural shortcomings those of us who had pitched our tents on less favored ground.

A quarter of a century ago the residents of the north shore of Massachusetts Bay — to which no self-respecting Bostonian nowadays ever dreams of alluding otherwise than as the "North Shore" — differed little from those on the remainder of the much-broken New England coastline. If you seek the pioneer in the modern movement you must go to Mr. Grant for information. I shall tell you only how by degrees the busy American began to appreciate that "all work and no play makes Jack a dull boy," and gradually to stop for a breathing spell. And thus, one at a time, slowly at first, the value of wholesome air and a bit of relaxation made converts.

Slowly, the underestimated farms passed from rustic to urban ownership and became at once the most economical and best sanitariums in America, while the erstwhile proprietors withdrew farther into the New England fastnesses. Gradually, too, the entire scene changed from the up-at-sunrise-to-bed-at-sunset monotony of the simple-minded country folk to the brisk atmosphere of refined people. Nature herself seemed to welcome the more congenial surroundings, and the country assumed a brightened aspect. Where the leg-weary family hack, silhouetted against the autumn sky, had toiled over the hills to the solitary crossroads store, the village cart now dashed along, drawn by a good blooded horse and driven by a fashionably gowned woman. Man and womankind improved in health, horseflesh in quality, and we began to learn how to use to advantage our opportunities for recreation and health.

Its contiguity to Boston and the completeness of individual establishments made a country club in its initial sense along the north shore unnecessary in the very first years of its popularity, and not until it had grown beyond the country abode of a few individuals and taken on the air of a country retreat of the comparatively many did the need of a cooperative amusement institution become apparent. Therefore but five years ago the Casino was established near Nahant, and only in the last couple of years the first country club (Essex) of the immediate north shore has been opened at Manchester-by-the-Sea.

On the southern shore of Massachusetts Bay, nature has not been so lavish in her setting of the country; beautiful it is, indeed, but wanting in that grandeur of coastline which is the chief charm of the North. Here there are handsome homes, and many of them, but the settlement of this shore differed from that of the other, insomuch as those who went first to the latter did so as individuals, whereas, on the south, the pioneer fresh-air seekers settled in little bands of chosen ones. Thus the need of a rendezvous was early experienced and realized in the establishment in 1882 of the Brookline Country Club, the first of the genus in America, albeit some of the hunting clubs had been and are to this day filling a similar sphere.

Probably the country club has rendered its greatest service in tempting us out-of-doors and cultivating a taste for riding and driving that has so largely benefited both sexes. With the evolution of the country

club we have been developing into a nation of sportsmen and sportswomen. Indeed, sport of one kind or another and the origin of the country club are so closely connected, it is exceedingly difficult to decide which owes its existence to the other.

It may be asserted that country clubs, generally speaking, have been created by the common desire of their incorporators to make a home for amateur sport of one kind or another. Some grew directly out of sport, as, for instance, the Country Club of Westchester County, which was originally planned for a tennis club, the Rockaway, Meadow Brook, and the Buffalo clubs, that were called into existence by the polo and hunting men. Others owe their existence to a desire to establish an objective point for drives and rides, and a rendezvous within easy access of town like the Brookline and Philadelphia Country clubs. Others have been called into being as the centralizing force of a residential colony, as Tuxedo. And yet others have been created by fashion for the coast season, as the Kebo Valley at Bar Harbor.

If sport has not been the *raison d'être* of every club's establishment, it is, at all events, with extremely few exceptions, the chief means of their subsistence. Practically every country club is the center of several kinds of sport, pursued more or less vigorously as the seasons come and go. A few of them maintain polo teams, and all supply implements and encouragement for as many kinds of games as its members will admit.

After all, the country club is nothing more than a rendezvous for a colony of congenial spirits; at least that, with more or less variation, is its cardinal virtue; but in our restless progressive way we have pursued the revelations of the new life with such tireless energy I sometimes fear we run the risk of neutralizing the good to be otherwise derived. The ultrafashionable side of the country club we must always deplore. The effort, happily in only isolated cases, to drag all the pomp and vanity and inane parade of town into the country, where it is in touch with neither the surroundings nor one's inclinations, presents quite as incongruous a situation as that other inanity, where much time and money, and not so much brains, combine to enforce the formalities of full dress at a yachting cruise dinner upon those who have got into their flannels for a week's relaxation. . . .

Really, country-club life has two sides — its domestic, if I may so call it, and its sporting, and not every club has both. Nor do I mean social for domestic. Every club has a social side, and that of the country club is particularly festive in season. But the domestic side is given only to those that have been the magnet in the founding of a colony of residents. Its domesticity may not be of the nursery order, but it goes so far as apportioning a part of its house for the exclusive use of its women members, and in some instances, at the mountain and seaside resorts, the house is common to members of both sexes. One or two in the West carry the domestic feature so far as to give it somewhat of a family aspect, which, it must be confessed, is a hazardous experiment.

One roof is not usually counted upon to cover more than one family harmoniously. The one distinguishing feature of the country club, however, is its recognition of the gentle sex, and I know of none where they are not admitted either on individual membership or on that of *paterfamilias*. Clubs like the Meadow Brook and the Rockaway, which were organized for hunting and polo, pure and simple, have no domestic side and make no special provision for women, though both entertain — the latter in its pretty little club, the former more often at the home of one of its members.

It is the sporting side of the country club, however, that gives it life and provides entertainment for its members; the club and our sporting history are so closely interwoven as to be inseparable. Polo, hunting, and pony racing owe to it their lives, and to the members we are largely indebted for the marked improvement in carriage horseflesh during the past five years. They founded the horse show, made coaching an accepted institution, and have so filled the year with games that it is hard to say whether the country-club sporting season begins with the hunting in the autumn or with tennis in the spring, for there is hardly any cessation from the opening to the closing of the calendar year.

Once upon a time the country was considered endurable only in summer, but the clubs have changed even that notion; all of them keep open house in winter, some retain a fairly large percentage of members in residence, and one or two make a feature of winter sports. Tuxedo holds a veritable carnival with tobogganing, snowshoeing, and skating on the pond, which in season provides the club table with trout. The Essex Country Club of New Jersey owns probably the best-equipped toboggan slide in America, and, on its regular meeting nights, electric illumination and picturesque costumes combine to make a most attractive scene.

Spring opens with preparations for polo, lawn tennis, and yachting. Not all country clubs have polo and yachting, but every one has courts, and several hold annual tournaments that are features of the tennis season and where the leading players are brought together. Of the country clubs proper, only Westchester, Philadelphia, Essex, Brookline, St. Louis, Buffalo really support polo teams, besides which there are the Meadow Brook and Rockaway, the two strongest in the country, and Myopia Hunt clubs. Two only enjoy yachting facilities, the Country Club of Westchester County and the Larchmont Yacht Club. The latter, although strictly speaking devoted to yachting, is, nevertheless, virtually a country club, with one of the handsomest homes of them all, a fleet second in size only to that of the New York Yacht Club, and a harbor that is one of the safest and most picturesque on the coast. Westchester has no special fleet aside from the steam and sailing yachts owned by a few individuals of the club; but its harbor is a good one, and its general location very attractive.

All the clubs dabble in live-pigeon trap-shooting, which is regrettable, for it is unsportsmanlike, to say nothing of the cash prizes, professionalizing the participants. It is a miserable form of amusement and unworthy the name of sport; but it is not so popular as formerly, and that, at all events, is something in its favor.

The polo season begins in the latter part of May and continues more or less intermittently to the middle of September, and sometimes even as late as the first week of October. But usually October sees the end of it, for by that time the interest in hunting is quickening and active preparations are making for the field. Hunting and polo in the early days constituted the sole sport of the country-club members, but the introduction of other games in the last five years has divided the interest that was once given to them entirely. Neither has retrograded; but they have not expanded as they should. However, that's another story. Whatever may be lacking in its progression, polo is the game that furnishes the country club with its most spirited scenes. The rivalry between the teams is always of the keenest, and the spectators, made up largely of the members of the contesting clubs, are quite as susceptible to its enthusiasm as the players.

Probably the most characteristic country-club scene, however, is created by the pony race meetings given on the tracks with which several of the clubs are provided. Here there is ample opportunity for the hysterical enthusiasm so dear to the feminine soul and plenty of time between events for them to chatter away to their hearts' content. Here, too, there is the certainty of seeing one's friends, not only in the carts and on top of the coaches that line the course, and on the temporary little grandstand erected for the nearby residents of the club colony, but frequently riding the ponies. Formerly, more gentlemen rode than is the case now, but one day someone who evidently cared more for the stakes than for the sport put a professional jockey on his pony, and many others with equally strong pot-hunting tendencies have followed the example. So today we go to a meeting expecting, hoping to see our friends, or at least club men, in the saddle, and find, instead, at least eight out of every ten ponies ridden by second-rate professionals or stable boys.

Only, therefore, when racing is under strictly club auspices and partakes of the nature of a hunt meet, with gymkhana and other equestrian sports of more or less acrobatic nature, do we have the simon-pure sport, with "gentlemen up." On such an occasion the social and sporting sides of the club are revealed at their best. Turn your back to the racecourse and you well might fancy yourself at a huge garden party; go into the paddock and you will find the same scene with a different setting; the same well-groomed men and women that out yonder are drinking tea are here, every last one of them talking horse for dear life, and, what is more to the point, talking it understandingly.

Some of the clubs, notably the Genesee Valley Hunt, hold annual meetings where very skillful tent pegging, lemon cutting, and roughriding creditable to a Cossack show the practical results of this sporting age. Some, again, on their point-to-point runs, give us the only really amateur steeplechasing of a high class in America. The country club has, indeed, as many sides and many charms as a fascinating woman — merciless in the live-pigeon shooting, equal to any emergency in the hunting field, and a veritable coquette in the bewitchery of the hunt ball. . . .

This paper would not be complete without a glance at some of the country clubs that have been instrumental in setting in motion and keeping moving this outdoor wave that has swept over us in a dozen years.

As the eldest and one of the most picturesquely located, the Country Club of Brookline deserves precedence. It had its origin in J. Murray Forbes's idea of an objective point for rides and drives, and was organized in 1882. No other club possesses a hundred acres of such beautiful land within such easy access, for it is only five and a half miles from the State House, and can be reached from Boston without going off pavement, and, better still, in its immediate neighborhood none of the rural effects have been marred.

The clubhouse, originally a rambling old building, is very picturesque, and has been enlarged from time to time to meet requirements. Its piazza overlooks the racecourse, in the center of which is one of the best of polo fields. Before the organization of the club, the Myopia Hunt, then in its infancy, held steeplechase meetings on its property; and in these races, and those given in the early years of Brookline, "gentlemen up" was the invariable rule. Of late years, however, professionals have been admitted, and with no advantage to the sport. In those days the regular working ponies and hacks of the members were entered; now horses come from New York and Canada, trained to the hour, and in some respects the racing is of a higher order; but the sport is not so enjoyable, and the old-time flavor has departed.

There is a shooting box where clay pigeons are used, a toboggan slide, golf course, and good tennis courts, both grass

and gravel; and it is not improbable that some day will see cottages for members similar to the plan adopted at Tuxedo.

In the winter, one evening a week has a *table d'hôte* and an informal dance to which the members and friends from town are sure to come. In fact, nearly all the seats are booked far in advance, and the informality of these occasions lends the essence of ideal country-club life. Indeed, no country club in America so nearly approaches that ideal as Brookline.

The Country Club of Westchester developed from a suggestion to organize a tennis club into a determination to found a club where all country sports could be enjoyed. The newly organized club leased the house and racing grounds of Dr. George L. Morris, at Pelham, and after some alterations, including a large addition, took possession April 4, 1884, fully equipped with tennis courts, a racetrack, polo field, baseball grounds, traps for pigeon shooting, a pack of hounds, boats, and bathhouses.

The sale of Dr. Morris' property made it necessary to find other quarters, and in December 1887 the Country-Club Land Association organized and bought Van Antwerp Farm, of about eighty acres, located on East Chester Bay between Pelham Bridge and Fort Schuyler, and in the spring of '88 began to lay out the grounds and build the present clubhouse and stables, into which they moved the following year.

From its inception the club has kept up all the sports of the day: polo and tennis tournaments, baseball, pigeon shooting, golf, boating (having two launches for the use of the members), and tobogganing and skating in winter. There is also quite a colony of handsome cottages on the grounds owned by members, and altogether Westchester has probably more than any other encouraged sport of all kinds, both by precept and example.

Although entirely given over to hunting and polo, the Meadow Brook and Rockaway clubs were the pioneers in the country-club movement and have been the most active workers in encouraging its growth. Both are strictly devoted to the horse, and the Meadow Brook men more particularly have been most prominent in the culture of the American breed.

The Meadow Brook Hunt Club was organized in 1879, though it had hunted two years previously with a pack that was taken over to Westchester. Its clubhouse is a quaint affair, with absolutely no pretensions to architectural beauty, and made up of two wooden buildings, each two stories high, joined together at their second story by a covered bridge, under which the driveway goes to the stables in the rear.

Rockaway has a modern home and more space for entertaining. Tuxedo has a modern and very handsome club that was opened in 1886 with a colony of handsome cottages, which, in fact, called it into being. Philadelphia's country club was organized in 1892, with polo as a *raison d'être*. It has none of the features of Brookline, Westchester, or Tuxedo, but is a charming objective point for an afternoon drive. As a matter of fact, any other sort of club around Philadelphia is uncalled-for. There is no need of country clubs in Philadelphia suburbs, with its handsome homes, and miles of beautiful lawns and orchards and gardens that load the air with rich perfumes, and where fields of daisies grow in such profusion they look like fields of snow which refuse to melt under the rays of the summer sun. Chestnut Hill and Bryn Mawr and the rest are more English in their method of entertaining than any other suburbs in America.

The Elkridge Fox Hunting Club is Baltimore's country club, and delightfully situated it is in Multavideo Park, about five miles out on St. Charles Avenue. As its name implies, fox hunting is its sport, for which purpose it was organized in 1878, the country-club feature being added to gratify the

wishes of the nonhunting set in 1887. There is no attempt at lavish display here, but its appointments are in the best of taste and judgment, and its chef unexcelled.

I cannot undertake, of course, to touch upon every country club — it would be stupid reading and take too much space — and therefore confine myself to representative ones only, but I must mention the Burlingame Country Club of California because, architecturally speaking, it is the most picturesque in America, and altogether a unique member of clubdom, and because it has an interesting history. It is situated in an 800-acre park with splendid roads and attractive views, surrounded by a colony of cottages, all of the English half-timber style, and shaded by the magnificent, wide-spreading oaks which are at once the charm and peculiarity of this beautiful park.

Riding, driving, polo, golf, and tennis are the sporting attractions, and the stables are filled with ponies and horses and traps of all sorts, which are hired out to members — rather a novel departure, but an exceedingly successful one in this case. The club was originally planned by Mr. Burlingame, who will be remembered as minister to China in the early sixties, and author of the treaty which bears his name. He returned to California very wealthy and interested in the scheme W. C. Ralston, the Napoleon of finance on the Pacific Coast in those days; both lost their money before they perfected the plans, and the property passed to the Sharon estate, to which it now belongs. In the past two years this estate has undertaken to carry out the program devised by Burlingame and fostered by Ralston twenty years ago.

Who shall deny the country club to have been a veritable blessing, what with its sport and pleasure and health-giving properties that have brushed the cobwebs from weary brains, and given us blue sky, green grass, and restful shade in exchange for smoke-laden atmosphere, parboiled pavements, and the never ceasing glare and racket of the city? And womankind too has partaken of country-club as she should of all blessings, in relaxation from the petty trials of housekeeping, and the parade and deceits of "society," while the hue of health has deepened in her cheeks. It has been a wholesome growth all round. Beginning life as somewhat of a novelty, the country club has become so familiar an institution that we wonder, as about the New York elevated railway, how we ever managed to get on without it.

106.

Paul Bourget: The Unrestrained Nature of American Pleasures

After visiting America in 1893, the Frenchman Paul Bourget put down his impressions of the country in a book called Outre-Mer. *Americans were used to the European criticism that American culture was immature, that Americans were too materialistic, and that American men were subservient to American women; but they were shocked by Bourget's strictures on their sports and amusements. Even the bitterest critics had usually conceded that nowhere in the world was there a people so generous, so fun loving, so hard working, so democratic, as the Americans. Bourget's assessment, examples of which appear below, seemed somehow more serious, and therefore more unpleasant.*

Source: *Outre-Mer: Impressions of America*, New York, 1895, pp. 326-351.

Having exaggerated his nervous and voluntary tension to the pitch of abuse, almost to vice, it is impossible that the American should amuse himself as we Latins do, who hardly conceive of pleasure without a certain relaxation of the senses, mingled with softness and luxury. . . .

Even in his diversions the American is too active and too self-willed. Unlike the Latin, who amuses himself by relaxation, he amuses himself by intensity, and this is the case whatever be the nature of his amusements, for he has very coarse and very refined ones. But a few sketches from nature will explain better than all the theories that

kind of nervousness, and, as it were, fitful sharpness in amusement, if we can here use that word which is synonymous with two of the least American things in the world — unconstraint and repose. . . .For the American, "sport" has ever in it some danger, for it does not exist without the conception of contest and daring. . . .

Among the distractions of sport, none has been more fashionable for several years past than football. I was present last autumn, in the peaceful and quiet city of Cambridge, at a game between the champions of Harvard College — the "team," as they say here — and the champions of the University of

Pennsylvania. I must go back in thought to my journey in Spain to recall a popular fever equal to that which throbbed along the road between Boston and the arena where the match was to take place. The electric cars followed one another at intervals of a minute, filled with passengers, who, seated or standing, or hanging on the steps, crowded, pushed, crushed one another.

Although the days of November are cruelly cold under a Massachusetts sky, the place of contest, as at Rome for the gladiatorial combats, was in a sort of open-air enclosure. A stone's throw away from Memorial Hall and the other buildings of the university, wooden stands were erected. On these stands were perhaps 15,000 spectators, and in the immense quadrilateral hemmed in by the stands were two teams composed of eleven youths, each waiting for the signal to begin.

What a tremor in that crowd, composed not of the lower classes but of well-to-do people, and how the excitement increased as time went on! All held in their hands small, red flags and wore tufts of red flowers. Crimson is the color of the Harvard boys. Although a movement of feverish excitement ran through this crowd, it was not enough for the enthusiasts of the game. Propagators of enthusiasm, students with unbearded, deeply lined faces, passed between the benches and still further increased the ardor of the public by uttering the war cry of the university, the "Rah! rah! rah!" thrice repeated, which terminates the frenzied call, "Haaar-vard." The partisans of the "Pennsy's" replied by a similar cry, and in the distance, above the palings of the enclosure, we could see clusters of other spectators, too poor to pay the entrance fee, who had climbed into the branches of the leafless trees, their faces outlined against the autumn sky with the daintiness of the pale heads in Japanese painted fans.

The signal is given and the play begins. It is a fearful game, which by itself would suffice to indicate the differences between the Anglo-Saxon and the Latin world — a game of young bulldogs brought up to bite, to rush upon the quarry; the game of a race made for wild attack, for violent defense, for implacable conquests and desperate struggles. With their leather vests, with the Harvard sleeves of red cloth, and the Pennsylvania blue and white vests and sleeves — so soon to be torn — with the leather gaiters to protect their shins, with their great shoes and their long hair floating round their pale and flushed faces, these scholarly athletes are at once admirable and frightful to see when once the demon of contest has entered into them.

At each extremity of the field is a goal, representing, at the right end, one of the teams; at the left, the other. The entire object is to throw an enormous leather ball, which the champion of one or the other side holds in turn. It is in waiting for this throw that all the excitement of this almost ferocious amusement is concentrated. He who holds the ball is there, bent forward, his companions and his adversaries likewise bent down around him in the attitude of beasts of prey about to spring. All of a sudden, he runs to throw the ball, or else, with a wildly rapid movement, he hands it to another, who rushes off with it. All depends on stopping him.

The roughness with which they seize the bearer of the ball is impossible to imagine without having witnessed it. He is grasped by the middle of the body, by the head, by the legs, by the feet. He rolls over and his assailants with him, and as they fight for the ball and the two sides come to the rescue, it becomes a heap of twenty-two bodies tumbling on top of one another, like an inextricable knot of serpents with human heads. This heap writhes on the ground and tugs at itself. One sees faces, hair, backs, or legs appearing in a monstrous and agitated melee. Then this murderous knot unravels itself and the ball, thrown by the most agile, bounds away and is again followed with the same fury. It continually happens that, after one of those frenzied entanglements, one of the combatants remains on the field motionless, incapable of rising, so much has he been hit, pressed, crushed, thumped.

A doctor whose duty it is to look after the wounded arrives and examines him. You see those skilled hands shaking a foot, a leg, rubbing the sides, washing a face, sponging the blood which streams from the forehead, the eyes, the nose, the mouth. A compassionate comrade assists in the business and takes the head of the fainting champion on his knee. Sometimes the unlucky player must be carried away. More frequently, however, he recovers his senses, stretches himself, rouses up, and ends by scrambling to his feet. He makes a few steps, leaning on the friendly shoulder, and no sooner is he able to walk than the game begins afresh, and he joins in again with a rage doubled by pain and humiliation.

If the roughness of this terrible sport was for the spectators only the occasion of a nervous excitement of a few hours, the young athletes would not give themselves up to it with this enthusiasm which makes them accept the most painful, sometimes the most dangerous, of trainings. A mother said to me, speaking of her son, who is not fourteen years old: "He adores football. He is already captain of his eleven. I should not be anxious if he never played against any but little gentlemen, but they have a mania for playing against common people. It is in such struggles that dangerous accidents are always to be feared."

"What will you have?" replied one of the professors of Harvard. "In the frenzy of the game they deal each other some hard blows, it is true, and it is true, above all, that the heroes of matches like that of today are victims. The training is too intense.

The nervous system cannot bear up against it. But the feats of the champions keep the game fashionable. Hence all the small boys in the remotest parts of America take up this exercise, and thus athletes are formed." He was putting into abstract form that which is the instinct of the American crowd, an instinct which does not reason and which shows itself in very strange ways. During the contest, which I have attempted to describe, I heard a distinguished and refined woman, next to whom I was seated, crying out, "Beauty!" at the sight of rushes that sent five or six boys sprawling on the ground.

No sooner are such matches as these in preparation than the portraits of the various players are in all the papers. The incidents of the game are described in detail, with graphic pictures, in order that the comings and goings of the ball may be better followed. Conquerors and conquered are alike interviewed. From a celebrated periodical the other day I cut out an article signed "A Football Scientist," wherein the author sought to show that the right tactics to follow in this game were the same as those used by Napoleon. What can be added to this eulogium when we know the peculiar position occupied by Napoleon in the imagination of the Yankees?

It must not be thought that such intense enthusiasm for so brutal a sport does not often arouse strong opposition. The same spirit of initiative which urges entire crowds of Americans to bow down in front of these semi-gladiators and to idolize this violent display of physical energy drives other Americans to raise a campaign against this uncontrolled and uncontrollable violence. Leagues have been formed in favor of and against the game. It is very possible that too numerous accidents will cause certain states to pass legislative restrictions against the terrible game. When one has closely followed a really ardent game, "with plenty of life and ginger,'' as the reporter of a newspaper said, one can notice that at a certain point of excitement the players are no longer masters of themselves. As I write these lines I see once more the figure of one of the champions of Pennsylvania after a disputed point and the gesture of rage with which he threw the ball which he had to give up. Between that display of anger and a bad action there was too little distance, too little psychological breadth — to employ a pedantic and very exact scientific formula.

However, such restrictions will no more cure the American public of the passion for football than they have cured them of the passion for boxing. When, last winter, Corbett and Mitchell were to meet at Jacksonville, it was necessary to run special trains to carry the partisans of one and the other boxer to that fortunate city of Florida. There was not a newspaper in which the physical condition of the two rivals was not mentioned morning after morning, hour after hour. The names of the relatives and friends who assisted them, the furniture of the hotel rooms in which they resided, the menu of their meals, their reading and their thoughts — what details did one not find in the columns of the newspapers! When I went to Jacksonville a few weeks later, the fight was still the subject of every conversation in the trains which ran through the pretty little town, and people only stopped speaking of it in order to discuss the next fight, which was proposed between the Californian champion and Jackson, of Australia. Even the election of the future President will not excite more popular feeling. . . .

Beside the pleasures of sport we must place those of the theater. The two are not so far apart as might at first sight appear. A passion for the play which results in respect for the actors is general among the Americans, and we know what reception Mme. Sarah Bernhardt, Mme. Eleonora Duse, M.

Coquelin, and Mr. Irving have had among them — to mention only the names of four famous artists, and not to speak of singers. Not only the playing of these great actors interested the public but also their personality, and, above all, their ideas about art.

In every town in the United States there is a group of amateurs whose study and delight it is to discuss the more or less intelligent rendering of such and such a play or musical work. I have said study, for even here the evidence of purpose is visible. At Boston, for instance, you will find that the programs of each of the celebrated concerts is accompanied by a technical commentary, so accurate, so lucid, and at the same time so erudite, that the pamphlet is in truth a chapter in the study of musical history. At Chicago, when Coquelin was giving the representation of *Tartufe* . . . the newspapers of the following day contained dissertations on Molière's comedy which were as scholarly, as analytic, and as critical as could have been the *feuilleton* of the *Temps* or the *Journal des Débats*. And yet, besides these evidences of a fastidious taste and a superior dilettantism, you find this same public accepting the most astonishing oddities.

I remember a gala night at the opera in New York when the music was sung by one of the actors in German and by another in French, while the chorus replied in Italian, and no English was heard. But is there not a secret harmony between such apparently contradictory manifestations? If you go to the theater for pleasure, if you are a voluptuary of music and an epicure of harmony, such things shock and annoy you. All your enthusiasm cools in that displeasure, and you have the uncontrollable desire to take up your hat and walk out. But if you are conscious that you are studying the genius of a master or the talent of an artist, you accept the performance, though mutilated.

You accept it, above all, if you are devoured with that need of European assimilation which takes possession of intellectual America not less than fashionable America. Not being able to have the whole opera and all the Comédie Française from the other side of the ocean, these people take what they can — the very best, it must be acknowledged — and they enjoy it, as the English can enjoy the frieze of the Parthenon, which is in broken fragments and without cohesion. But their double passion is satisfied — that, in the first place, of cultivating themselves, and, second, of having all the best actors of London and Paris in New York.

We must look for the original American genius and the true dramatic pleasure of the people in performances of quite a different kind. The play which the authors of this country excel in writing and the actors in playing is a kind of comedy, almost without affectation and intrigue, entirely composed of local scenes and customs, and mixed with pantomime. If the now antiquated expression, "a section of life," could ever have been applied to plays, it may be to these. They show all the peculiarities of the different states; sometimes the singular customs of the South, as in the *New South* . . . at other times those of the West, as in *In Mizzoura*, or those of the North, as in a play called *A Temperance Town*, which I saw in New York. In the subtitle of this last play — the most typical, perhaps, of all — we are told that it "is intended as a more or less truthful presentation of certain incidents of life relating to the sale and use of liquor in a small village in a Prohibition state." The great curiosity aroused by this comedy lies in the fact that the sympathetic personage is a drunkard. . . .

I have turned over the leaves of a great number of illustrated comic newspapers, those which friends in New York have pointed out to me as the best. The Americans dote on these publications, which are to be found in all the halls of the hotels, in all the railway carriages, and on the club tables. Without exaggerating the importance of these pamphlets, we must recognize in them, in every country, a certain documentary value. They characterize the humor of the race and its delight in mockery. Besides, you will find in them a thousand details of habits, described offhand, their exaggeration rendering them still more perceptible to the traveler.

On running through a collection of several numbers of some of these papers, a first observation is forced upon one; namely, the entire absence of those nude drawings which form the perverse prettiness of similar periodicals in Paris, and the no less remarkable absence of allusions to marital misadventures. One might believe, in noting this absence, that neither gallantry nor adultery existed in the United States, or that, if they exist, it is in such a shadow of secrecy that they escape even satire. Do not suppose, however, that the caricaturists profess to be particularly prejudiced in favor of marriage. But when they see its defects, it is especially from the point of view of the budget, as is fitting in the country of the "almighty dollar.". . .

It is curious to compare the sarcasm of political caricatures with the innocent and altogether indulgent gaiety of the caricature of manners. These same sketchers, who show themselves simple and light caricaturers of the ridiculous characteristics and vices of everyday life, develop, when it becomes a matter of party, a species of frenzy and of hatred which can hardly be surpassed. The nomination of an ambassador who does not suit them, the adoption of a bill against which they are carrying on a campaign or the rejection of a bill which they are upholding, a hostile candidature, a stirring speech — these are to them occasions for severe blows, the hardness of which contrasts in the most unexpected manner with the good temper of the sketchers of manners. You suddenly feel calumny and its bitterness, anger and its insults.

From amusing and easy fantasy you fall into the depths of the harshest polemic, without wit, and without fear of making personal allusions of the most grossly insulting kind. It seems to me that both phenomena are logical and well in keeping with what may be seen everywhere among Americans. So far as regards the affairs of everyday life, they are good fellows — amiable, open, easy. But as soon as they have to do with a business question, they are as keen and energetic in the defense of their interests and in the conquest of yours as they were found easy and generous before. The reason is that then they were amusing themselves; now they are fighting.

Politics is one of the most important businesses of a country where each triumph places all public offices at the disposal of the party. It is a matter which interests not merely a small number of ambitious people but an enormous number of citizens enrolled under the Republican and Democratic banners. Their antipathies must be gratified, their enthusiasm stirred, their passions served.

In all countries where universal suffrage is the rule, it becomes necessary to speak to the people by means of pictures. They see everything as a whole, and naturally like coarse and striking things. The colored caricatures which are set forth on the first pages of the illustrated newspapers satisfy their taste. As the editor of a Chicago newspaper said to me, they always like a fight. The fight here takes the form of pictured burlesque, but the burlesque is ordinarily so exaggerated and so plainly unjust and prejudiced that it becomes offensive. Wishing, for instance, to lampoon a perfect gentleman, who was simply guilty of having been nominated to a high position by Mr. Cleveland, the caricaturist represented that distinguished man with grossly travestied features, writing underneath such phrases as "Cleveland's nominee for — — —"; or again, "If Abraham Lincoln were to meet Mr. So and So in the flesh, his first impulse would be to take him by the collar and throw him into a mudhole."

Such means of combating an adversary may succeed with electors of the lowest class. They are far from clever; for, according to Talleyrand's profound remark, "Everything exaggerated is insignificant." For this reason, the Americans succeed well in caricaturing social customs, treating them lightly and inoffensively, and, for a like reason, their political caricatures, with few exceptions, are but commonplace.

The American goes into all recreations — sport, the theater, burlesque — with the same spirit which we have seen him bring into society, into social problems, into education. He shows himself clearheaded and positive, with a singular mixture of good fellowship, tenacity, practical realism, and exuberant social health and spirits.

———————◆———————

It were not best that we should all think alike; it is difference of opinion that makes horseraces.

SAMUEL L. CLEMENS ("MARK TWAIN"), "Pudd'nhead Wilson's Calendar," 1894

107.

Henry Drummond: A Portrait of Dwight Moody

Dwight L. Moody was the most noted American itinerant evangelist of the second half of the nineteenth century. He brought to revivalism the advertising and business methods that have been used so successfully in the present century. Never ordained himself, he attracted many laymen to missionary work, especially in such groups as the YMCA and the Student Volunteer Movement. His simple and direct gospel message bypassed sectarian differences and made an army of converts to the religious life. As an enduring testimony to his work, he left the Moody Bible Institute in Chicago, founded in 1889. Moody's success as a preacher is comparable to that of Wesley and Whitefield in the Great Awakening that swept the country 150 years earlier. The following selection is taken from an article by Henry Drummond, a friend and associate of Moody.

Source: *McClure's,* December 1894: "Mr. Moody: Some Impressions and Facts."

Simple as this man is, and homely as are his surroundings, probably America possesses at this moment no more extraordinary personage; nor even amongst the most brilliant of her sons has any rendered more stupendous or more enduring service to his country or his time. No public man is less understood, especially by the thinking world, than D. L. Moody. It is not that it is unaware of his existence, or even that it does not respect him. But his line is so special, his work has lain so apart from what it conceives to be the rational channels of progress, that it has never felt called upon to take him seriously. So little, indeed, is the true stature of this man known to the mass of his generation that the preliminary estimate recorded here must seem both extravagant and ill-considered. To whole sections of the community the mere word "evangelical" is a synonym for whatever is narrow, strained, superficial, and unreal. Assumed to be heir to all that is hectic in religion and sensational in the methods of propagating it, men who, like Mr. Moody, earn this name are unconsciously credited with the worst traditions of their class.

It will surprise many to know that Mr. Moody is as different from the supposed type of his class as light is from dark; that while he would be the last to repudiate the name, indeed, while glorying more and more each day he lives in the work of the evangelist, he sees the weaknesses, the narrownesses, and the limitations of that order with as clear an eye as the most unsparing of its critics. But especially will it surprise many to know that while preaching to the masses has been the main outward work of Mr. Moody's life, he has, perhaps, more, and more varied, irons in the fire — educational, philanthropic, religious — than almost any living man; and that vast as has been his public service as a preacher to the masses, it is probably true that his personal influence and private character have done as much as his preaching to affect his day and generation.

Discussion has abounded lately as to the standards by which a country shall judge its great men. And the verdict has been given unanimously on behalf of moral influence. Whether estimated by the moral qualities which go to the making up of his personal character, or the extent to which he has impressed these upon whole communities of men on both sides of the Atlantic, there is, perhaps, no more truly great man living than D. L. Moody. By moral influences in this connection I do not mean in any restricted sense, religious influence. I mean the influence which, with whatever doctrinal accompaniments, or under whatever ecclesiastical flag, leads men to better lives and higher ideals; the influence which makes for noble character, personal enthusiasm, social well-being, and national righteousness.

I have never heard Mr. Moody defend any particular church; I have never heard him quoted as a theologian. But I have met multitudes, and personally know, in large numbers, men and women of all churches and creeds, of many countries and ranks, from the poorest to the richest, and from the most ignorant to the most wise, upon whom he has placed an ineffaceable moral mark. There is no large town in Great Britain or Ireland, and I perceive there are few in America, where this man has not gone, where he has not lived for days, weeks, or months, and where he has not left behind him personal inspirations which live to this day; inspirations which, from the moment of their birth, have not ceased to evidence themselves in practical ways — in furthering domestic happiness and peace; in charities and philanthropies; in social, religious, and even municipal and national service.

It is no part of the present object to give a detailed account of Mr. Moody's career, still less of his private life. The sacred character of much of his work also forbids allusion in this brief sketch to much that those more deeply interested in him, and in the message which he proclaims, would like to

have expressed or analyzed. All that is designed is to give the outside reader some few particulars to introduce him to, and interest him in, the man. . . .

The taunt is sometimes leveled at religion that mainly those become religious teachers who are not fit for anything else. The charge is not worth answering; but it is worth recording that in the case of Mr. Moody the very reverse is the case. . . . His enterprise, his organizing power, his knowledge and management of men are admitted by friend and foe to be of the highest order; while such is his generalship — as proved, for example, in the great religious campaign in Great Britain in 1873-75 — that, had he chosen a military career, he would have risen to the first rank among leaders. One of the merchant princes of Britain, the well-known director of one of the largest steamship companies in the world, assured the writer lately that in the course of a life-long commercial experience he had never met a man with more business capacity and sheer executive ability than D. L. Moody. Let any one visit Northfield, with its noble piles of institutions, or study the history of the work conceived, directed, financed, and carried out on such a colossal scale by Mr. Moody during the time of the World's Fair at Chicago, and he will discover for himself the size, the mere intellectual quality, creative power, and organizing skill of the brain behind them. . . .

His activity, especially during the years of the war, when he served with almost superhuman devotion in the Christian Commission, led many of his fellow laborers to know his worth; and the war over, he became at last a recognized factor in the religious life of Chicago. The mission which he had slowly built up was elevated to the rank of a church, with Mr. Moody, who had long since given up business in order to devote his entire time to what lay nearer his heart, as its pastor.

As a public speaker up to this time, Mr. Moody was the reverse of celebrated. When he first attempted speaking in Boston, he was promptly told to hold his tongue, and further efforts in Chicago were not less discouraging. "He had never heard," writes Mr. Daniells, in his well-known biography,

> of Talleyrand's famous doctrine, that speech is useful for concealing one's thoughts. Like Antony, he only spoke "right on." There was frequently a pungency in his exhortation which his brethren did not altogether relish. Sometimes in his prayers he would express opinions to the Lord concerning them which were by no means flattering; and it was not long before he received the same fatherly advice which had been given him at Boston — to the effect that he should keep his four pews full of young men, and leave the speaking and praying to those who could do it better.

Undaunted by such pleasantries, Mr. Moody did, on occasion, continue to use his tongue — no doubt much ashamed of himself. He spoke, not because he thought he could speak but because he could not be silent. The ragged children whom he gathered round him in the empty saloon near the North Side Market had to be talked to somehow, and among such audiences, with neither premeditation nor preparation, he laid the foundations of that amazingly direct anecdotal style and explosive delivery which became such a splendid instrument of his future service.

Training for the public platform this man, who has done more platform work than any man of his generation, had none. He knew only two books, the Bible and human nature. Out of these he spoke; and because both are books of life, his words were afire with life; and the people to whom he spoke, being real people, listened and understood. When Mr. Moody first began to be in demand on public platforms, it was not because he could speak. It was his experience that was wanted, not his eloquence. As a practical man in work among the masses, his advice and enthusiasm were called for at Sunday school and other con-

ventions, and he soon became known in this connection throughout the surrounding states. It was at one of these conventions that he had the good fortune to meet Mr. Ira D. Sankey, whose name must ever be associated with his, and who henceforth shared his labors at home and abroad, and contributed, in ways the value of which it is impossible to exaggerate, to the success of his afterwork.

Were one asked what, on the human side, were the effective ingredients in Mr. Moody's sermons, one would find the answer difficult. Probably the foremost is the tremendous conviction with which they are uttered. Next to that is their point and direction. Every blow is straight from the shoulder, and every stroke tells. Whatever canons they violate, whatever fault the critics may find with their art, their rhetoric, or even with their theology, as appeals to the people they do their work — and with extraordinary power. If eloquence is measured by its effects upon an audience, and not by its balanced sentences and cumulative periods, then here is eloquence of the highest order. In sheer persuasiveness Mr. Moody has few equals, and rugged as his preaching may seem to some, there is in it a pathos of a quality which few orators have ever reached, an appealing tenderness which not only wholly redeems it but raises it, not unseldom almost to sublimity.

No report can do the faintest justice to this or to the other most characteristic qualities of his public speech, but here is a specimen taken almost at random:

> I can imagine when Christ said to the little band around Him, "Go ye into all the world and preach the gospel," Peter said, "Lord, do you really mean that we are to go back to Jerusalem and preach the gospel to those men that murdered you?" "Yes," said Christ, "go, hunt up that man that spat in my face, tell him he may have a seat in my kingdom yet. Yes, Peter, go find that man that made that cruel crown of thorns and placed it on my brow, and tell him I will have a crown ready for him when he comes

into my kingdom, and there will be no thorns in it. Hunt up that man that took a reed and brought it down over the cruel thorns, driving them into my brow, and tell him I will put a scepter in his hand, and he shall rule over the nations of the earth, if he will accept salvation. Search for the man that drove the spear into my side, and tell him there is a nearer way to my heart than that. Tell him I forgive him freely and that he can be saved if he will accept salvation as a gift."

Tell him there is a nearer way to my heart than that — prepared or impromptu, what dramatist could surpass the touch? . . .

To Mr. Moody himself, it has always been a standing marvel that people should come to hear him. He honestly believes that 10,000 sermons are made every week, in obscure towns and by unknown men, vastly better than anything he can do. All he knows about his own productions is that somehow they achieve the result intended. No man is more willing to stand aside and let others speak. His search for men to whom the people will listen, for men who, whatever the meagerness of their message, can yet hold an audience, has been lifelong, and whenever and wherever he finds such men he instantly seeks to employ them. The word jealousy he has never heard. At one of his own conventions at Northfield, he has been known to keep silent — but for the exercise of the duties of chairman — during almost the whole ten days' *sederunt,* while mediocre men — I speak comparatively, not disrespectfully — were pushed to the front.

It is at such conferences, by the way, no matter in what part of the world they are held, that one discovers Mr. Moody's size. He gathers round him the best men he can find, and very good men most of them are; but when one comes away it is always Mr. Moody that one remembers. It is he who leaves the impress upon us; his word and spirit live; the rest of us are forgotten and forget one another. It is the same story when on the evangelistic round. In every

Northfield School

Dwight Moody; portrait by G. P. A. Healy

city the prominent workers in that field for leagues around are all in evidence. They crowd round the central figure like bees; you can review the whole army at once.

And it is no disparagement to the others to say — what each probably feels for himself — that so high is the stature and commanding personality of Mr. Moody that there seems to be but one real man among them, one character untarnished by intolerance or pettiness, pretentiousness, or selfseeking. The man who should judge Mr. Moody by the rest of us who support his cause would do a great injustice. He makes mistakes like other men; but in largeness of heart, in breadth of view, in single-eyedness and humility, in teachableness and selfobliteration, in sheer goodness and love, none can stand beside him. . . .

The fact that Mr. Moody has a pocket has been largely dwelt upon by his enemies, and the amount and source of its contents are subjects of curious speculation. I shall suppose the critic to be honest and divulge to him a fact which the world has been slow to learn — the secret of Mr. Moody's pocket. It is, briefly, that Mr. Moody is the owner of one of the most paying literary properties in existence. It is the hymnbook which, first used at his meetings in conjunction with Mr. Sankey, whose genius created it, is now in universal use throughout the civilized world. Twenty years ago, he offered it for nothing to a dozen different publishers, but none of them would look at it. Failing to find a publisher, Mr. Moody, with almost the last few dollars he possessed, had it printed in London in 1873. The copyright stood in his name; any loss that might have been suffered was his; and to any gain, by all the laws of business, he was justly entitled.

The success, slow at first, presently became gigantic. The two evangelists saw a fortune in their hymnbook. But they saw something which was more vital to them than a fortune — that the busybody and the evil tongue would accuse them, if they but touched one cent of it, of preaching the Gospel for gain. What did they do? They refused to touch it — literally even to touch it. The royalty was handed direct from the publishers to a committee of well-known businessmen in London, who distributed it to various charities. When the evangelists left London, a similar committee, with Mr. W. E. Dodge at its head, was formed in New York. For many years this committee faithfully disbursed the trust, and finally handed over its responsibility to a committee of no less weight and honor — the trustees of the Northfield seminaries, to be used henceforth in their behalf.

Such is the history of Mr. Moody's pocket. It is pitiful to think that there are men and journals, both at home and abroad, who continue to accuse of self-seeking a man who has given up a princely fortune in noble — the man of the world would say superfluous — jealousy for the mission of his life. Once we heard far more of this. That Mr. Moody has lived it down is not the least of his triumphs.

In the year 1889 Mr. Moody broke out in a new place. Not content with having founded two great schools at Northfield, he turned his attention to Chicago, and inaugurated there one of his most successful enterprises — the Bible Institute. This scheme grew out of many years' thought. The general idea was to equip lay workers — men and women — for work among the poor, the outcast, the churchless, and the illiterate. In every center of population there is a call for such help. The demand for city missionaries, Bible readers, evangelists, superintendents of Christian and philanthropic institutions is unlimited. In the foreign field it is equally claimant. Mr. Moody saw that all over the country were those who, with a little special training, might become effective workers in these various spheres — some whose early opportunities had been neglected; some who were too old or too poor to go to college; and others who, half their time, had to earn their living. To meet such workers and such work the Institute was conceived. . . .

It is a peculiarity of Northfield, that every door is open, not only to the Church Universal but to the world. Every state in the Union is represented among the students of his two great colleges, and almost every nation and race. On the college books are, or have been, Africans, Armenians, Turks, Syrians, Austrians, Hungarians, Canadians, Danes, Dutch, English, French, German, Indian, Irish, Japanese, Chinese, Norwegians, Russians, Scotch, Swedish, Alaskans, and Bulgarians. These include every type of Christianity, members of every Christian denomination, and disciples of every Christian creed. Twenty-two denominations, at least, have shared the hospitality of the schools. This, for a religious educational institution, is itself a liberal education; and that Mr. Moody should not only have permitted but encouraged this cosmopolitan and unsectarian character is a witness at once to his sagacity and to his breadth.

With everything in his special career, in his habitual environment, and in the traditions of his special work to make him intolerant, Mr. Moody's sympathies have only broadened with time. Some years ago the Roman Catholics in Northfield determined to build a church. They went round the township collecting subscriptions, and by and by approached Mr. Moody's door. How did he receive them? The narrower evangelical would have shut the door in their faces, or opened it only to give them a lecture on the blasphemies of the pope or the iniquities of the scarlet woman. Mr. Moody gave them one of the handsomest subscriptions on their list. Not content with that, when their little chapel was finished, he presented them with an organ.

"Why," he exclaimed, when someone challenged the action, "if they are Roman Catholics, it is better they should be good Roman Catholics than bad. It is surely better to have a Catholic Church than none; and as for the organ, if they are to have music in their church, it is better to have good music. Besides," he added, "these are my own townspeople. If ever I am to be of the least use to them, surely I must help them." What the kindly feeling did for them, it is difficult to say; but what it did for Mr. Moody is matter of local history. For, a short time after, it was rumored that he was going to build a church, and the site was pointed out by the villagers — a rocky knoll close by the present hotel. One day Mr. Moody found the summit of this knoll covered with great piles of stones. The Roman Catholics had taken their teams up the mountain and brought down, as a return present, enough building stone to form the foundations of his church. . . .

When one has recorded the rise and progress of the . . . institutions which have been named, one but stands on the threshold of the history of the tangible memorials of Mr. Moody's career. To realize even partially the intangible results of his life is not within the compass of man's power; but even the tangible results — the results which have definite visible outcome, which are capable of statistical expression, which

can be seen in action in different parts of the world today — it would tax a diligent historian to tabulate.

The sympathies and activities of men like D. L. Moody are supposed by many to be wasted on the empty air. It will surprise them to be told that he is probably responsible for more actual stone and lime than almost any man in the world. There is scarcely a great city in England where he has not left behind him some visible memorial. His progress through Great Britain and Ireland, now nearly twenty years ago, is marked today by halls, churches, institutes, and other buildings which owe their existence directly to his influence. In the capital of each of these countries — in London, Edinburgh, and Dublin — great buildings stand today which, but for him, had had no existence. In the city where these words are written, at least three important institutions, each the center of much work and of a multitude of workers, Christian philanthropy owes to him. Young Men's Christian Associations all over the land have been housed, and in many cases sumptuously housed, not only largely by his initiative but by his personal actions in raising funds.

Mr. Moody is the most magnificent begger Great Britain has ever known. He will talk over a millionaire in less time than it takes other men to apologize for intruding upon his time. His gift for extracting money amounts to genius. The hard, the sordid, the miserly positively melt before him. But his power to deal with refractory ones is not the best of it. His supreme success is with the already liberal, with those who give, or think they give, handsomely already. These he somehow convinces that their givings are nothing at all; and there are multitudes of rich men in the world who would confess that Mr. Moody inaugurated for them, and for their churches and cities, the day of large subscriptions. The process by which he works is, of course, a secret, but one half of it probably depends upon two things. In the first place, his appeals are wholly for others; for places — I am speaking of England — in which he would never set foot again; for causes in which he had no personal stake. In the second place, he always knew the right moment to strike. . . .

In the *Life of Whittier,* just published, the patronizing reference to Mr. Moody but too plainly confirms the statement with which the first article opened — that few men were less known to their contemporaries. "Moody and Sankey," writes the poet,

> are busy in Boston. The papers give the discourses of Mr. Moody, which seem rather commonplace and poor, but the man is in earnest. . . . I hope he will do good, and believe that he will reach and move some who could not be touched by James Freeman Clarke or Phillips Brooks. I cannot accept his theology, or part of it, at least, and his methods are not to my taste. But if he can make the drunkard, the gambler, and the debauchee into decent men, and make the lot of their weariful wives and children less bitter, I bid him Godspeed.

I have called these words patronizing, but the expression should be withdrawn. Whittier was incapable of that. They are broad, large-hearted, even kind. But they are not the right words. They are the stereotyped charities which sweet natures apply to anything not absolutely harmful, and contain no more impression of the tremendous intellectual and moral force of *the man behind* than if the reference were to the obscurest Salvation Army zealot. I shall not endorse, for it could only give offense, the remark of a certain author of worldwide repute when he read the words: "Moody! Why, he could have put half a dozen Whittiers in his pocket, and they would never have been noticed"; but I shall endorse, and with hearty goodwill, a judgment which he further added. "I have always held," he said — and he is a man who has met every great contemporary thinker from Carlyle downward — "that in sheer brain size, in the mere raw material of intellect, Moody

stands among the first three or four great men I have ever known."

I believe Great Britain is credited with having "discovered" Mr. Moody. It may or may not be; but if it be, it was men of the quality and the experience of my friend who made the discovery; and that so many distinguished men in America have failed to appreciate him is a circumstance which has only one explanation — that they have never had the opportunity.

An American estimate, nevertheless, meets my eye as I lay down the pen, which I gladly plead space for, as it proves that in Mr. Moody's own country there are not wanting those who discern how much he stands for. They are the notes, slightly condensed, of one whose opportunities for judging of his life and work have been exceptionally wide. In his opinion:

1. No other living man has done so much directly in the way of uniting man to God and in restoring men to their true center.

2. No other living man has done so much to unite man with man, to break down personal grudges and ecclesiastical barriers, bringing into united worship and harmonious cooperation men of diverse views and dispositions.

3. No other living man has set so many other people to work, and developed, by awakening the sense of responsibility, latent talents and powers which would otherwise have lain dormant.

4. No other living man, by precept and example, has so vindicated the rights, privileges, and duties of laymen.

5. No other living man has raised more money for other people's enterprises.

6. No other evangelist has kept himself so aloof from fads, religious or otherwise; from isms, from special reforms, from running specific doctrines or attacking specific sins; has so concentrated his life upon the one supreme endeavor.

If one-fourth of this be true, it is a unique and noble record; if all be true, which of us is worthy even to characterize it?

108.

Francis W. Parker: Democracy and the Common School

Francis W. Parker had already established a reputation as an educator in New England before being appointed principal of the Cook County (Chicago) Normal School in 1883. Along with John Dewey, he pioneered in the informal classroom methods that later became the mark of the so-called progressive education movement in the United States. A year before his death in 1902, Parker became the first director of the School of Education at the University of Chicago. His defense of the common school, taken from a book published in 1894, is reminiscent of Horace Mann.

Source: *Talks on Pedagogics*, New York, 1894, pp. 420-451.

THE GREAT CENTRAL PRINCIPLE of democracy is mutual responsibility. Democracy in its essence gives to each individual the liberty of becoming free; raises no artificial barriers, political or social, between him and his goal. This is the ideal of democracy. Pure democracy does not exist today; more than one-half of the people of the United States are excluded from franchise. I am speaking solely of the ideal toward which all human progress is tending. Democracy gives the liberty to become free and the essential means of gaining freedom; this means is education.

The highest outcome and, I say with the greatest reverence, the divinest outcome of all the ages of human progress is the *common school*. Like democracy, it is still an ideal; it has not come to its own. The only system of common schools of the world today is that of the United States, and we have it only in part. The common school is the antipodes of isolation, the antipodes of that method so efficiently used by monarchy and hierarchy to keep the people from loving each other and helping each other.

The public school in a republic means that in their early life children of all classes, of all nationalities, of all sects, of rich and poor alike, children of both sexes shall work together under the highest and best conditions in one community for from eight to twelve years; that they shall have teachers who are trained in the art of all arts — the art of teaching; that in the school, before prejudice has entered their childish souls, before hate has become fixed, before mistrust has become a habit, they shall have influences surrounding them that shall lead to the best work with the best motive of mutual assistance.

Why should boys and girls be taught together from the kindergarten to the university, inclusive? Because they are to live together, to help each other throughout life, and must understand each other. The isolation of sexes in school has begotten mistrust, misunderstanding, false — nay even impure — fancies. The separation of sexes in school is a crime against nature. It is often argued that the sexes differ in intellectual capacity and moral power, and therefore should be separated in education; if this be true, it is all the more reason why they should be together. The strongest factor in education is the reflected light of character upon character.

The social factor in school is the greatest factor of all; it stands higher than subjects of learning, than methods of teaching, than the teacher himself. That which children learn from each other in play or work, though the work be drudgery, is the highest that is ever learned. The young man in the university learns more from his mates, of good or bad, than from his professors. This mingling, fusing, and blending give personal power, and make the public school a tremendous force for the upbuilding of democracy.

Let us now turn for a moment to the problem of America. We who are in the thick of the fight, in the midst of a struggle which is overwhelming, do not appreciate the tremendous trend of human affairs; the danger signals which fly before us are unwatched and unheeded. What are we proposing to do? *That which has never yet been done in the world's history.* Foreign colonies have settled in other nations to be ostracized, persecuted, opposed, and downtrodden; but here in America we are bringing together all peoples from all parts of the known world, with all their prejudices born of centuries, each naturally having its own customs, rooted in earliest times and growing with the national growth: the Germans and the French, the Italians and the Russians, the Poles and the Irish, each with their prejudices, with their views of life, producing different customs, political, social, and religious, opposed as earth and heaven.

Here they come into our broad continent, and we propose to have them live together, and legislate together for the best good of the whole. No dream of the past, no vision of the progress of humanity, could ever propose such a tremendous problem as this — this blending and fusing of the people of the whole earth in one crucible of common interests and brotherly love. Amalgamation

of interests and ideas is the keynote of the situation; if any people or sect, no matter what, comes to America, lives by itself, speaks its own language, refuses to learn the genius of American citizenship, it is weakness to all and, if not arrested, threatens destruction to all.

Peoples come with their prejudices; for instance, the prejudice of separate and class education. I have in mind a nation that has given us the best discussions and investigations of education of any people on earth; has given more for the study of education than any and all the rest of the world together; still, they come to this country bitterly opposed to coeducation, and would legislate and use every influence to keep boys and girls separate from beginning to end. Peoples come with their ideas of class education and above all, of sectarian education. They hold that children must be kept apart in their own sectarian schools during the first eight or ten years of their lives in order that they may be indoctrinated; and all these peoples are honest in their beliefs, and as fixed as they are honest.

Fancy the antipodal ideas of a pious New Englander and an equally pious German on the Sunday or the Prohibition question. How shall they ever learn to know each other? When and where? If society is cut into classes following the old plan, they will never meet there; nor in the church, no matter how pious they may be, for the conflict there is as strongly marked. There is but one place where children of all nations and sects can come together, sit upon the same benches, play upon the same grounds, live together, work together, *know* each other, and that is the common school. The principal mission of the common school is to dissolve the prejudices that have been inculcated under the methods of oppression.

It is a mistake to suppose that our forefathers came to the new continent with even the faintest glimmer of a purpose to found a republic, or that this idea took definite shape before the Revolution. The republic grew out of circumstances, and these circumstances were favorable: fixed traditions were uprooted; the early settlers left their material surroundings of tradition; they were transplanted into new conditions, where the conflicts and struggles of pioneer life, the subduing of virgin forests, the contests with the aborigines, and friction of different nationalities brought out new necessities and developed new ideas. . . .

The rapid growth and development of the common-school system of the United States has no equal in all history: born of the people, supported and nourished by the people, it has steadily made its way into the hearts of the people and has become an absolute necessity in the growth and perpetuity of our political institutions.

In the Old World, where public schools, not common schools, have been established, the system is entirely controlled by central power, by the minister of education, by one intelligence, to which everything is subordinate. There are great advantages in the matter of organization and a great saving of time, to appearances, in such a plan of central power. The authority, for instance, of the cultus-minister reaches every school in Prussia; he can determine the textbooks, the course of study, and the method; but in our country we have no central system. The citizens of each school district, the citizens of a city have absolute control over their schools; there is no domination from the center; even the state assumes very little control of the schools, outside of enabling acts and limitations in the matter of time and general subjects of study. This is probably the best illustration in all history of true democratic growth.

What the schools are, their value in education in the district, is determined by the people themselves. In the case of two adjacent districts, one may have excellent schools and the schools of the other be in a very inferior condition. This, superficially

considered, would argue the superiority of a central system; but the democratic mode of growth is from within and admits greater possibilities than any other plan.

A central system easily becomes fixed. For instance, today the schools of Germany, pedagogically speaking, are far better than the schools of the United States; in fifty years the schools of the United States will exceed in value the schools of all the world, because our plan tends to originality and to research — it brings out the best in all. With all its defects, the common school of the United States stands, today, as incomparably the noblest and best institution on earth. It has accomplished vast results; the common-school system is the heart of the republic. But the high accomplishment has not been through methods of teaching or subjects taught; it has consisted principally in the great social factor — the mingling, blending, and fusing of all classes of society.

It is, then, for every thoughtful person to consider with the greatest care the present situation of the common-school system and what can be done to make it better. To this subject I invite your attention. What has been done and what remains to be done? Viewing it from the standpoint of the growth of a great central idea, of the partial realization of a divine inspiration, the common-school system of the United States is exalted in the highest degree. But when we consider what is to be done, we can see plainly that we have made small beginning; that the common school is still in its swaddling clothes; that it has been started; that the best and most favorable criticism that can be made upon it is that it can be made far better than it now is; that it must be made better; that it is not equal to the demand — the salvation of all the children.

Democracy means the responsibility of all for each; the common school is the direct exposition of this fundamental principle; common education is the means of freedom. The children of today are in our hands;

whatever we do for them will be the future. Our lack of faith in this direction is the greatest infidelity. To use a common illustration: A Kentucky farmer will look at a hundred colts and say, "I will train every one of them to become a useful horse." We look at the children and decide that we can save but a few of them; that many of them must become criminals, many of them a burden upon society; that many of them will enhance vice and put barriers in the way of our political institutions. We must believe that we can save *every child*. The citizen should say in his heart: "I await the regeneration of the world from the teaching of the common schools of America."

The foundations of the great American system of education into democracy have been laid by devoted patriots. The people believe in the common school. The necessary organizations are now ready for a great advance; the line of progress is plainly before us; that line is parallel with the great lines of progress in this century that have been marked by searching, prolonged investigation and profound study — study that has compelled the natural forces to yield themselves to the service of man.

1. The same kind of study, the same wisdom, earnestness, and zeal, must be given to the study of the being that "God made a little lower than Himself" — the child. Already careful investigations in child life are being made by humanity-loving scientists all over the civilized world; wonderful results are at hand.

2. The conditions must be discovered and applied by which every child may be developed into the full stature of manhood or womanhood. All sciences have been reformed and some revolutionized within a few years; means for the genuine study of history have been multiplied; literature, sweet, pure, and good, is made accessible to every child; art with its treasures stands ready to help. Compared with the paucity of means of even fifty years ago, the supply is unlimited.

3. The conditions of knowledge and action must be adapted to the development of the whole being. This adaptation, general and individual, is called method, the essential factor in the art of educating.

No subject of inquiry, study, and investigation is comparable to the science of the soul and the laws of its development. This is the science of education, the science that comprehends all sciences. Like all other sciences, if we except mathematics, there is an infinity of knowledge yet to be found in this comprehensive science. Progress in education means a knowledge of the science of education and its application; it means that teachers must be educated, cultured, and trained into the most important of all professions.

What stands in the way of the one precious thing on earth — the freedom of the soul, the advancement of civilization, the happiness of man? I answer, first of all, tradition and its methods. It is impossible to measure the tremendous influence of tradition. It is very difficult to draw the line between education and heredity, but it is far more difficult to draw it between tradition and original personal power. We are at best creatures of tradition, controlled by the past, often bound hand and foot by the fixed habits of mankind; and this influence is dominant today in our public schools.

The methods of the few, in their control of the many, still govern our public schools and to a great degree determine their management — the method of the prison, torture, police, and standing army survives in corporal punishment; the method of bribery, in reward and prizegiving. Both of these immoral methods are absolutely useless; they are the outcome of quantity teaching and the makeshifts of unskilled teachers. Given devoted, trained teachers, together with right surroundings and the right educative work, there is absolutely no necessity for either corporal punishment or the bribery of rewards.

The method of mystery still exercises its

fearful power, the inoculated belief that there is something occult and mysterious in knowledge. The height of art is its simplicity, and the same can be said of the art of teaching. What I mean by the control of mystery is illustrated by the attitude of the people toward education. Let a teacher in a country school teach that which a farmer most needs upon the farm, — practical chemistry; let him teach soil, physics, meteorology, zoology of the insects that infest his crops; let him teach arithmetic sensibly by measuring and weighing — and the farmers would call an indignation meeting and put out a man holding and teaching such new-fangled notions. By learning they mean some mysterious process foreign to them. It does not readily enter their minds that that which is most practical is most logical, and that the old teaching of quantity, the mysterious pedantry of the school-teacher, who is supposed to know so much, is a relic of barbarism and should hold the same place in the world of affairs as the sickle and the scythe.

I have used the farmer simply as an illustration; the same false ideas pervade all society to the detriment of education. The chemistry needed in the kitchen, the physiology that pertains to health, the physical training that develops a sound body, the history and civics essential to citizenship, the necessity of practical ethics, the relation of handwork to the brain and to true success are little appreciated; while memorizing a jumble of words, grammar that will scarcely be used for lack of thought, a mastery of that incubus upon English education — the intricacies of unphonetic spelling — are the idols of the people, and, alas! of the majority of teachers.

The aristocratic idea of charity is still a potent influence in education. Our school system began as charity schools — charity schools such as the Volksschule of Germany. Many wealthy people who have the traditional or parvenu feeling of class distinction look today upon the common-school

Chicago Historical Society

Francis Parker, early advocate of progressive classroom teaching

system as a charity and hold that there should be one education for rich children and another for the poor; that the children of the rich should not mingle with and be contaminated by the children of the poor. I have had much to do with both classes, and I wish to say here that in my contact with the poorest children I have found as much of intrinsic morality and vigorous mental power in them as in rich children. This false idea of contamination is born of the past, a reappearance of the old-time aristocratic idea of separation and isolation. In a good school, with excellent teachers and the right surroundings, there is no more danger of contamination than is to be found in the ordinary home and class environment of children. . . .

When, in American society, classes become permanent and the children of these classes are educated in separate schools, the doom of the republic is sealed. There can be no separated classes in a republic; the lifeblood of a republic must stream from the ground up; there can be no stratified society.

No child, no citizen of a republic, can be

educated into citizenship outside of the common school; *the common school is not a charity; it is the inalienable right of every child, and common education is the imperative, duty of every community.* On a lower plane we may look at universal intelligence as the one means for the preservation of the republic; society, in order to preserve itself, must develop the highest character in every child.

The charity idea obtains largely among manufacturers and people who depend upon laborers and servants. I once talked with a gentleman upon a religious subject; he seemed to be imbued, or thought he was, with the spirit of Christ; he was a nail manufacturer. When I spoke to him about the education of his employees, suggesting that they should have better opportunities for personal improvement, he said: "But that would spoil them as laborers. I must have employees; there must be a class of workers." This Christian gentleman was entirely willing to suppress human souls in the interest of nails.

The method of quantity teaching is without doubt the most prominent. You will remember what I have said of this method: that its means are the most effective in keeping children from anything like a search for the truth, and from a realization of their own liberty — the method of textbooks, page learning, percent examinations, with all the countless devices and means which serve to make quantity learning the end and aim of education.

When the common school was founded, there was little or no knowledge of or belief in a science of education. Most of our teachers took their patterns from England, where at that time the discoveries of Comenius and Pestalozzi had kindled no life. The old methods naturally took the field and held their ground, and, alas! still hold. The great majority of the people are firm believers in quantity; they insist that their children shall "go over," "go through," but

particularly shall "finish." They measure education by the yard and weigh it by the pound. The people of today are the people of yesterday, their fixed ideas the inheritance of their teachers' teachers.

The colleges demand quantity; they do not ask applicants, "Who are you? What have you done? What can you do?" but, "How many pages have you learned? Have you read Virgil? Xenophon? Homer? Come in and learn some more words."

The strongest indication that quantity teaching is in the ascendancy is the profound disbelief of the people in anything like a science of education. I have not time to prove that there is a science of education. If, however, there is no such science, then all the other sciences are myths and delusions. Science is organized knowledge of law; and to deny that there is a science of education is to deny that the development of human beings is governed by law.

Robert Lowe (Lord Sherbrooke), while at the head of the English Privy Council and chairman of the Education Committee was asked to support a movement for the establishment of chairs of pedagogics in universities. "There are no principles of education," said this child of tradition. Less than fifteen years ago a distinguished head of a great university declared that all there is to pedagogics could be learned in an hour and a half! It is well for me to say here that the gentleman has changed his mind most decidedly; indeed, he is a prominent leader in the so-called new education. Colleges did not recognize this science until within a few years. The first professor of pedagogics in America, Miss Bibb, was appointed in the University of Missouri within a few years.

The substantial disbelief in a science of education, and the almost universal indifference in regard to it, has one cause, and that cause is quantity teaching; the stimulus to the drudgery is the strap, or, worse, rewards and prizes. A teacher with a conscience, an artist teacher, cannot do such menial service: it would be like requiring a Raphael to paint a board fence. If quantity teaching is ideal teaching, then the plainest deduction is, there is no science of education.

By far the greatest barrier to making the common school what it should and can be by no means springs from active opposition to the system or from the patronage and pulls of pot-house politicians: *the greatest barrier is the profound indifference of the most intelligent people in regard to the possibilities of radical improvement.* This indifference has been enhanced until within a few years by the influence of colleges and universities in which quantity instruction has had full swing. The average member of a school board often fancies that he knows all there is to be known about teaching; his measure is the quantity standard, acquired in his own education, which he rigidly enforces, crushing every effort toward quality work.

The social and political standing of teachers indicates the general depreciation of anything like a science of education or an art of teaching. When a discussion of an educational question is provoked, that of "fads," for instance, the opinions of educators are not generally invited; quantity teaching has instructed every citizen in the exact needs of the schools — quantity is the standard of judgment, and the "3 R's" *limit the education of freemen!!*

The people generally have never felt the quickening power of scientific teaching; they believe that their children must submit to the same process that they have endured; they judge teachers by their power to go over the most ground *thoroughly.* To them there is no need of a science of education, and from the quantity standpoint this judgment is perfectly logical. Scientific teaching means quality of mental action; it means the shortest line of resistance in the advance toward truth; it means the development of mental and moral power — a power that comprehends conditions and overcomes obstacles. I repeat, profound public indiffer-

ence and an alarming ignorance in regard to the possibilities of education are the greatest obstacles to progress.

Quality is freedom. Let the quality of mental action be right, quantity will take care of itself. The principal cause of so many dullards is quantity teaching. Quantity teaching is strongly entrenched by incompetency. An imperative demand for scientific teaching would throw large numbers of present school incumbents out of business or make them burn the midnight oil to an extent hitherto unheard of.

The quantity plan is the politician's opportunity. The state pays more money for schools than for any other purpose, except prisons, penitentiaries, poorhouses, and criminal courts; the schools present the most places to fill with "friends," whose acquirements, as a rule, are of the lowest order. Thousands of girls without culture, with very deficient education, manage, after repeated trials, to pass cram examinations met by quantity drills — examinations that are no tests whatever of ability to teach. These same girls, the daughters, friends, and relatives of ward politicians with a pull, are put in charge of fifty or more immortal souls, to repeat as best they may the wretched process of quantity teaching. Very few men remain in the profession on account of the low salaries, the precariousness of positions, the catering to public opinion, and, worst of all, the demand for fawning vassalage by corrupt or ignorant political bosses.

The evolution of democracy must needs have its horrors; patriots will bear, and at the same time strive to overcome, them. But the culmination of horrors is to place the interests of innocent children in the hands of expediency politicians. Let them steal public money, rob treasuries, and enrich themselves by boodle; but in the name of High Heaven let them keep their corrupt hands away from the priceless treasures of home and the dearest hopes of the future.

Although the initial battle for the common school has been fought and won, still it has many open and secret enemies. Who are they? I do not believe that there is a man or woman in our republic today who has enjoyed the benefits of the common school but is its warm supporter. If there is one, I have never seen him nor her. First, the opponents of the common school are those who were born and bred outside of the atmosphere of liberty, who have had environment and traditions that compel them to believe as they do. It would be strange indeed if the most influential newcomers, whose education has been received in surroundings entirely opposed to the spirit of liberty, of which the common school is the main buttress, did believe in our system of schools. They are honestly opposed to the system and should be respected for their honesty and met by honest argument.

The fundamental method of the Old World education is *isolation;* it is supported by no particular party nor sect; the people educated in this method believe in it from their habit of life and the tradition of ages. Why should they understand the genius of American liberty? Why should those who have become habituated to class education believe that the stratification of American society into fixed classes means sure death to the republic and the future hopes of democracy? Class education means that the children of one class would become indoctrinated with the opinions, political and religious, of other classes; that fixed beliefs would become unsettled.

So far as the destruction of these fixed ideas is concerned, the argument is logical: the common school destroys caste, makes democrats, annihilates the domination of the few; but so far as religion, pure and undefiled, is concerned, the inference cannot be sustained. Forty-seven hours for teaching and training in the family per week; twelve hours of the holy Sabbath for worship in church, Sunday school, and at home; and *twenty-five hours* of mixed society life under guidance in the public schools. Is it possible that the strong tenets of any religion can be overcome in a community where religion is never mentioned but continually practised?

Of all places in the world where children can practise religion, the school is the most favorable. Here are the weak, the poor — yes, the vicious — they come for help. "He that doeth righteousness is righteous." School is the place for *doing,* not preaching, righteousness. No, the purpose of the opponents of the common school is not to teach religion but to preserve the integrity of aristocratic power by isolation and the consequent maintenance of distinct classes. . . .

Further, whatever duties the body politic neglects become the prey and spoil of the pothouse politician. Many of the common schools in this republic are managed and controlled by a class of spoilmongers who do not have the faintest idea of education, who indeed do not care what becomes of the schools if their patronage is not touched. Their prey is the innocent little ones; they strike at the very heart of the republic.

If any business in the world, any railroad, bank, store, or manufactory, were conducted upon the same principles (?) that obtain in the management of schools in most of our large cities and in many small districts, hopeless bankruptcy would be the inevitable result. Superintendents are too seldom chosen for professional skill or executive ability; and when they are, the school boards take away from them every vital influence that would make them efficient managers. The vast majority of teachers have not the slightest professional training or the faintest idea of the science of education; thus quantity cram is the rule, and quality teaching the exception. Every other business in the world requires experts but the care of immortal souls!! . . .

I have not overdrawn the indictment. There are beautiful streaks of light everywhere amid the general darkness of unprofessional teaching, proving beyond all doubt that the people can make every common school a perfect means of developing true manhood and womanhood. An effective school means an educated, cultured, trained, devoted teacher. Today in most communities there is very little *discrimination* between an excellent teacher and a poor one; too often the latter has a marked advantage. There is not a coin small enough, ever stamped by the hand of man, to pay the salary of a poor teacher; there is not gold enough in the mines of the world to measure the value of a teacher who lifts the souls of children to the true dignity of life and living. Put such teachers in the slums of our great cities, supply them with every necessary means, and we would soon find that "an ounce of prevention is worth a ton of cure." The right teaching, the possible teaching, would diminish the attendance upon bridewells, prisons, reformatories, almshouses, lunatic asylums; would lessen the number of voters that can be bought and take away the following of corrupt politicians; would insure the perpetuity of the republic, the hope of humanity. What stands in the way? *The indifference, the lethargy, the lack of active interest on the part of the good, noble men and women.* . . .

I have argued that the inefficiency of our common schools is owing to the traditional methods that have been the effective means of keeping the masses in subjection through the long ages of human history. God has made America the schoolhouse of the world — nay, its hospital. To our land have come a vast multitude, marred and scarred by the selfishness of the few; here they bring the wounds of tyranny. They have come to be healed; let them come. But we who are imbued with the genius of freedom, we who have fought under Old Glory must heal these wounds, must quicken stagnant blood and revive despairing hearts by a breath of sweet liberty. *We must do it,* I say, else our republic dies, and with it the hopes of freedom for centuries.

Let us welcome all religions; let us freely accord to all believers the right to worship God as they please, and disbelievers, to deny His existence; but we dare not, must not, allow the methods of aristocracy to ruin all we hold dear.

"Who possesses the youth, possesses the future," sounds in our ears. Who should possess the youth? Not the aristocracy, with its long record in human subjection and slavery. No party, no creed, should possess the future. The truth, and the truth alone, should possess the youth: "the truth that shall make" His children "free"; the truth of the eternal, loving God and Father of us all. Who possesses the truth in its richness and fullness? None in the past. Who have applied it? Let prisons, dungeons, torture, poverty, woe, misery, and the outer darkness of ignorance answer.

We may hold a pure religion, we may respect each other's opinions, we may have the perfect tolerance of universal love, but while we know that the path of progress has been strewn with the wrecks of theories, we dare not fetter the souls of children with a fixed and implicit belief in any theory. We must believe that there is truth enough and power enough and love enough to carry the bread of life to every hungry and needy soul. The methods of aristocracy have not done this, and cannot do it; but the perfect love born into the world upon the hills of Palestine, when applied, can do it — the love that is filled with the sweet Gospel of the Fatherhood of God and the brotherhood of man.

The spirit of democracy respects all rights of parents as sacred, except the right to deprive a child of a good education; it never compels a parent to send a child to the common school; it might in the interests of self-preservation, but it does not. Every parent should be left perfectly free in the choice of a school for his children.

Attractive is far more powerful than compulsory education. The common school can be made the best school, in every respect, in the world. Everything is ready to this end, except one thing, and that is the introduction of scientific teaching. The organization is ready, the buildings have been erected, the money is paid; that which awaits is the method of democracy — that education which shall set the souls of children free.

It is no dream or illusory vision, the realization of a common school, perfect in its appointments, with the means for the highest and best education at hand. All is ready when the people are ready to move, to demand that the methods of quantity shall go and the methods of quality shall come. Unrealized possibilities of human growth are the infinite line of march.

A school should be a model home, a complete community and embryonic democracy. How, you ask? Again, I answer, by putting into every schoolroom an educated, cultured, trained, devoted, child-loving teacher, a teacher imbued with a knowledge of the science of education, and a zealous, enthusiastic applicant of its principles. Where shall we find such teachers? They will spring from the earth and drop from the clouds when they *hear the demand*. We have asked for quantity teachers, and they have come by the tens of thousands. Now, let us demand the *artist teacher*, the teacher trained and skilled in the science of education — a genuine leader of little feet.

Nothing that is good is too good for the child — no thought too deep; no toil too great, no work too arduous; for the welfare of the child means happier homes, better society, a pure ballot, and the perpetuity of republican institutions. Not only must the people demand the artist teacher with an authority which will admit no denial, they must also demand that the methods of aristocracy, which have degraded and debased mankind, be totally eliminated from the training of citizens; instead, let us have a doctrine of education which means freedom to every child. I commend to your careful study the theory of concentration, a theory that makes personal liberty the path to universal freedom.

I have said these words "with malice toward none and charity for all." Fighting for four years, as best I could, for the preservation of the democratic ideal, a teacher of little children for nearly forty years, I believe four things, as I believe in God — that democracy is the one hope of the world; that democracy without efficient common schools is impossible; that every school in the land should be made a home and a heaven for children; fourth, that when the ideal of the public school is realized, "the blood shed by the blessed martyrs for freedom will not have been shed in vain."

Index of Authors

*The numbers in brackets
indicate selection numbers
in this volume*

ALTGELD, JOHN PETER (Dec. 20, 1847-March 12, 1902), jurist, public official, and political leader. Governor of Illinois (1892-96); denounced by press and public for pardoning three of the Haymarket rioters (1893); opposed the use of federal troops in the Pullman strike (1894); wrote *Our Penal Machinery and Its Victims* (1884). [84, 85, 98]

ARNOLD, MATTHEW (Dec. 24, 1822-April 15, 1888), English poet and literary critic. Professor of poetry (1857-67) at Oxford; lectured in. U.S. (1883-84, 1886); wrote *Civilization in the United States* (1888). [40]

ATCHISON, RENA M. (*c.* 1856-Oct. 29, 1933), educator. Professor of Spanish and French at De Paul University; dean of women and professor of French literature (1883-93) at Northwestern; wrote *Un-American Immigration: Its Present Effects and Future Perils* (1894). [96]

ATEN, IRA (fl. 1888), Texas Ranger. In a series of letters described the barbed-wire wars in Texas and the Rangers' efforts to prevent fence-cutting. [42]

BELLAMY, EDWARD (March 26, 1850-May 22, 1898), editor and social reformer. Editor (1889-91) of the *Nationalist,* in which he urged nationalization of public ser-

vices; wrote *Looking Backward, 2000-1887* (1888) in favor of utopian social organization. [35]

BILLINGS, EDWARD C. (fl. 1893), jurist. Judge (*c.* 1893) of U.S. Circuit Court, New Orleans. [83]

BLAIR, LEWIS H. (fl. 1889), author. Wrote *The Prosperity of the South Dependent Upon the Elevation of the Negro* (1889). [46]

BLAKE, JAMES (?-1935), salesman and lyricist. Wrote the lyrics to "Sidewalks of New York" (1894), composed by Charles Lawlor. [94]

BOURGET, PAUL (Sept. 2, 1852-Dec. 25, 1935), French critic, poet, and novelist. Traveled in U.S. and published his critical observations as *Outre-Mer* (2 vols., 1895). [106]

BREWER, DAVID J. (June 20, 1837-March 28, 1910), jurist. Judge (1865-69) of the first judicial district of Kansas; justice (1870-84) of the Kansas Supreme Court; associate justice (1889-1910) of the U.S. Supreme Court; president (1895-98) of the Venezuela boundary and arbitration commissions. [81] See also Author Index, Vol. 12.

BROCKETT, JOSHUA A. (fl. 1890), clergyman. Pastor of St. Paul's A.M.E. Church in

Cambridge, Mass.; spokesman for Southern Negroes in the post-Reconstruction era. [53]

BROUGH, WILLIAM (fl. 1889), lyricist. Wrote the lyrics to "Let Us All Speak Our Minds" (1889), a propaganda song for the women's rights movement. [48]

BRUCE, JOHN E. (fl. 1889-1905), journalist, publisher, and Negro leader. Published the *New York Chronicle*; president of the Negro Historical Society of New York City; wrote *The Blood Red Record* (1901). [47]

BRYCE, JAMES (May 10, 1838-Jan. 22, 1922), British historian, jurist, and diplomat. Professor of civil law (1870-93) at Oxford; undersecretary for foreign affairs (1886) in Gladstone's cabinet; ambassador to U.S. (1907-13); wrote *The American Commonwealth* (1888), a classic study of American government, and *Modern Democracies* (1921). [37] See also Author Index, Vol. 14.

CABLE, GEORGE WASHINGTON (Oct. 12, 1844-Jan. 31, 1925), author and social reformer. Wrote stories of life in the South (*Old Creole Days*, 1879; *The Grandissimes*, 1880) and essays in behalf of Negro rights (*The Silent South*, 1885; *The Negro Question*, 1890). [11]

CARNEGIE, ANDREW (Nov. 25, 1835-Aug. 11, 1919), industrialist and philanthropist. Born Scotland; served in military transportation section of U.S. War Department during Civil War; consolidated his steel holdings into Carnegie Steel Co. (1899); merged Carnegie with U.S. Steel Corp. (1901) and retired to philanthropic interests; wrote "Wealth" (*North American Review*, 1889). [18, 49, 50]

CLARK, ALEXANDER (fl. 1886), lawyer and author. Wrote "Socialism" (*A.M.E. Church Review*, 1886) refuting the suggestion of a Socialistic communal system to secure Negro rights. [23]

CLEVELAND, GROVER (March 18, 1837-June 24, 1908), lawyer, political leader, and statesman. Twenty-second (1885-89) and twenty-fourth (1893-97) President of the United States; mayor of Buffalo, N.Y. (1881-82); governor of New York

(1883-85). [17, 34, 70, 89, 98] See also Author Index, Vol. 12.

CLEWS, HENRY (Aug. 14, 1834-Jan. 31, 1923), financier and author. Expert on credit, discounts, and commercial paper; established New York brokerage and banking firms; U.S. agent for the sale of government bonds to finance the Civil War. [22]

CONWELL, RUSSELL H. (Feb. 15, 1843-Dec. 6, 1925), lawyer, editor, clergyman, and educator. Pastor (1882-91) of Temple Baptist Church, Philadelphia; founder (1888) and first president of Temple University; delivered a single lecture, *Acres of Diamonds*, more than 6,000 times. [55]

COXEY, JACOB S. (April 16, 1854-May 18, 1951), businessman, public official, and political figure. Led an "army" of 500 unemployed persons, starting in Massillon, Ohio, to Washington, D.C. (March 25-May 1, 1894) to dramatize the need for economic reform; twice defeated (1932, 1936) Farmer-Labor Party candidate for President of the United States. [95]

CRITTENDEN, THOMAS T. (Jan. 1, 1832-May 29, 1909), lawyer and public official. U.S. representative from Missouri (1873-75, 1877-79); governor (1881-85); U.S. consul general in Mexico (1893-97). [4]

CURTIS, GEORGE TICKNOR (Nov. 28, 1812-March 28, 1894), lawyer and author. Established a national reputation as a patent attorney; wrote *History of the Origin, Formation, and Adoption of the Constitution of the United States* (2 vols., 1854-58). [6]

DAVIES, HOWELL (Sept. 26, 1859-Feb. 17, 1927), mining engineer. Born Wales; came to U.S., 1885; naturalized citizen, 1892; commissioner of conciliation, U.S. Department of Labor (from 1914); government labor administrator in copper industry during World War I; referee in California oil industry disputes (1919-21). [75]

DRUMMOND, HENRY (Aug. 17, 1851-March 11, 1897), Scottish evangelist, geologist, and explorer. Attempted to reconcile evangelical Christianity with evolution in *Natural Law in the Spiritual World*

(1883) and in *The Ascent of Man* (1894), originally given as Lowell Lectures in Boston. **[107]**

ELIOT, CHARLES W. (March 20, 1834-Aug. 22, 1926), educator. Assistant professor of chemistry and mathematics (1854-63) at Harvard; professor of analytical chemistry (1865-69) at Massachusetts Institute of Technology; president (1869-1909) of Harvard. **[80]** See also Author Index, Vols. 10, 14.

ELY, RICHARD T. (April 13, 1854-Oct. 4, 1943), economist. Chairman (1881-92) of the department of political economy at Johns Hopkins University; professor of economics (1892-1925) at the University of Wisconsin and (1925-33) at Northwestern University; founder (1885) of the American Economic Association; wrote *Monopolies and Trusts* (1900). **[52]**

FISKE, JOHN (March 30, 1842-July 4, 1901), philosopher and historian. Professor of history (from 1884) at Washington University, St. Louis; wrote *Outlines of Cosmic Philosophy* (1874), *Darwinism and Other Essays* (1879), *Excursions of an Evolutionist* (1884), *The Destiny of Man Viewed in the Light of his Origin* (1884). **[12]**

FORTUNE, T. THOMAS (fl. 1881-1898), editor. Born a slave in Florida; edited (from 1881) the *New York Age;* founder (1889-90) and first secretary of the National Afro-American League; founder (1898) of the National Afro-American Council; wrote *Black and White: Land, Labor, and Politics in the South* (1884). **[3]**

GARLAND, HAMLIN (Sept. 14, 1860-March 4, 1940), author. Wrote *Main-Travelled Roads* (1891), *A Son of the Middle Border* (1917), *The Book of the American Indian* (1923). **[103]**

GIBBONS, JAMES CARDINAL (July 23, 1834-March 24, 1921), Roman Catholic prelate. Chaplain of Fort McHenry, Md., during Civil War; bishop (1872-77) of Richmond, Va., and (1877-1921) of Baltimore; created cardinal (1886); wrote *The Faith of Our Fathers* (1876), *The Ambassador of Christ* (1896). **[29, 31]**

GLADDEN, WASHINGTON (Feb. 11, 1836-July 2, 1918), Congregational clergyman. Pastor (1875-82) at Springfield, Mass., and

(1882-1918) at Columbus, Ohio; wrote *Plain Thoughts on the Art of Living* (1868), *Working People and Their Employers* (1876), *Social Salvation* (1901). **[68]** See also Author Index, Vol. 13.

GOMPERS, SAMUEL (Jan. 27, 1850-Dec. 13, 1924), labor leader. Founder (1886) and president (1886-94, 1896-1924) of the American Federation of Labor; member (1917) of the Council of National Defense; member of the Commission on International Labor Legislation at the 1919 Peace Conference. **[99]** See also Author Index, Vol. 10.

GRADY, HENRY W. (May 24, 1850-Dec. 23, 1889), journalist and orator. Co-owner and editor (1880-89) of the *Atlanta Constitution;* popular lecturer on the "New South." **[53]**

GRAY, WILLIAM B. (fl. 1894), songwriter. Wrote the words and music for "She Is More To Be Pitied Than Censured" (*c.* 1894). **[104]**

GRINNELL, GEORGE BIRD (Sept. 20, 1849-April 11, 1938), editor and naturalist. Editor (1876-1911) of *Forest and Stream;* wrote *The Indians of Today* (1900), *The Cheyenne Indians* (1923), and numerous shorter studies of Indian life and folklore. **[78]**

GRONLUND, LAURENCE (July 13, 1846-Oct. 15, 1899), lawyer, author, and lecturer. Born Denmark; practised law in Illinois; member (1888) of the executive board of the Socialist Labor Party; wrote *The Coming Revolution: Its Principles* (1878), *The Coöperative Commonwealth* (1884). **[1]** See also Author Index, Vol. 12.

HALE, EDWARD EVERETT (April 3, 1822-June 10, 1909), Unitarian clergyman and author. Pastor (1846-56) of the Church of the Unity, Worcester, Mass., and (1856-1901) of South Congregational Church, Boston; chaplain (1903-09) of the U.S. Senate; wrote *The Man Without a Country* (1863). **[61]**

HALL, URIEL S. (fl. 1894), public official. U.S. representative from Missouri (*c.* 1894); president of the Missouri Farmers' Alliance. **[101]**

HARRIS, CHARLES K. (May 1, 1865-Dec. 22, 1930), songwriter and music publisher.

Index of Authors

Established publishing houses in Chicago and New York; wrote "After the Ball" (1892) and "Break the News to Mother" (1897). [76]

HARRISON, BENJAMIN (Aug. 20, 1833-March 13, 1901), soldier, lawyer, and statesman. Twenty-third President of the United States (1889-93); colonel (1861-65), Union Army; U.S. senator from Indiana (1881-87). [89]

HARVEY, W. H. (Aug. 16, 1851-Feb. 11, 1936), economist. Known as "Coin" Harvey; published "Coin's Financial Series" (1894-96), a series of books favoring bimetallism. [102]

HAYES, RUTHERFORD B. (Oct. 4, 1822-Jan. 17, 1893), lawyer, soldier, and statesman. Nineteenth President of the United States (1877-81); major general (1865), Union Army; U.S. representative from Ohio (1865-67); governor (1868-72, 1876-77). [27] See also Author Index, Vol. 10.

HILL, WALTER B. (Sept. 9, 1851-Dec. 28, 1905), lawyer and educator. Founder, secretary (1883-86), and president (1887-88) of the Georgia Bar Association; chancellor (1899-1905) of the University of Georgia. [77]

HOLMES, OLIVER WENDELL (Aug. 29, 1809-Oct. 7, 1894), physician, poet, and humorist. Professor of anatomy (1838-40) at Dartmouth College and (1847-82) at Harvard Medical School; wrote humorous works (*The Autocrat of the Breakfast-Table*, 1857), poetry ("Old Ironsides," "The Chambered Nautilus," "The Wonderful One-Hoss Shay"), biographies (*Ralph Waldo Emerson*, 1885), and hymns ("Lord of all being! throned afar"). [65] See also Author Index, Vols. 8, 9.

HOWELLS, WILLIAM DEAN (March 1, 1837-May 10, 1920), novelist and editor. Wrote (1856-61) for the *Ohio State Journal*, (1886-91) for *Harper's Magazine*, and (1891-92) for *Cosmopolitan Magazine*; editor (1866-81) of the *Atlantic Monthly*, wrote *Venetian Life* (1866), *Their Wedding Journey* (1872), *The Rise of Silas Lapham* (1885), *A Hazard of New Fortunes* (1890), *Criticism and Fiction*. (1891). [71] See also Author Index, Vol. 13.

HOYT, CHARLES H. (July 26, 1860-Nov. 20, 1900), songwriter and playwright. Wrote *A Bunch of Keys* (1882), *A Milk White Flag* (1893), *A Stranger in New York* (1897). [94]

INGERSOLL, ROBERT G. (Aug. 11, 1833-July 21, 1899), lawyer and lecturer on agnosticism. Colonel (1861), Union Army; attorney general of Illinois (1867-69); wrote *Why Am I an Agnostic?* (1890), *Why I Am an Agnostic* (1896), *Superstition* (1898). [54]

IRELAND, JOHN (Sept. 11, 1838-Sept. 25, 1918), Roman Catholic prelate. Chaplain (1862-63), Union Army; rector (1867-84) of the cathedral and bishop (1884-1918) of St. Paul Minn.; a founder (1889) of Catholic University, Washington, D.C. [58]

JAMES, HENRY (April 15, 1843-Feb. 28, 1916), novelist. Son of Henry James and brother of William James; wrote (1865-69) for the *Nation*, the *Atlantic Monthly*, and *Galaxy*; moved to London (1876) and became a British citizen (1915); author (among many novels of *The American* (1876), *Daisy Miller* (1878), *The Portrait of a Lady* (1881), *The Turn of the Screw* (1898), and *The American Scene* (1907), as well as several volumes of biography and literary criticism. [33] See also Author Index, Vol. 10.

LAZARUS, EMMA (July 22, 1849-Nov. 19, 1887), poetess and essayist. Wrote *Admetus and Other Poems* (1871), *Songs of a Semite* (1882), and "The New Colossus," the sonnet engraved on the base of the Statue of Liberty in 1886. [21]

LLOYD, HENRY DEMAREST (May 1, 1847-Sept. 28, 1903), journalist and author. Financial editor and writer (1872-85) for the *Chicago Tribune;* known as the forerunner of the "muckrakers" for his "Story of a Great Monopoly" (*Atlantic Monthly*, 1881), exposing the methods of the Standard Oil Company and railroad trusts. [2, 100]

LOW, SETH (Jan. 18, 1850-Sept. 17, 1916), merchant, public official, and educator. Mayor of Brooklyn, N.Y. (1882-85); president (1890-1901) of Columbia University; mayor of New York City (1901-03). [39]

McALLISTER, WARD (Dec. 1827-Jan. 31, 1895), lawyer and social leader. Arbiter of New York society; coined the phrase "the Four Hundred" to describe New York Society; wrote *Society As I Have Found It.* (1890). **[56]**

McGLENNON, FELIX (fl. 1887-1894), songwriter. Wrote the words and music for "Comrades" (1887) and the music for "Her Golden Hair Was Hanging Down Her Back" (1894). **[104]**

MAHAN, ALFRED THAYER (Sept. 27, 1840-Dec. 1, 1914), naval officer and historian. President (1886-89, 1892-93) of the Naval War College, Newport, R.I.; delegate to the Hague Peace Conference (1899); wrote *The Influence of Sea Power Upon History, 1660-1783* (1890). **[60]** See also Author Index, Vol. 12.

OLNEY, RICHARD (Sept. 15, 1835-April 8, 1917), lawyer and public official. Attorney general (1893-95) and secretary of state (1895-97) under Cleveland. **[72]** See also Author Index, Vol. 12.

PARKER, FRANCIS W. (Oct. 9, 1837-March 2, 1902), educator. A leader of the progressive education movement; school superintendent in Quincy, Mass.; head of Cook County Normal School, Chicago; wrote *Talks on Pedagogics* (1894), *Talks on Teaching* (1896). **[108]** See also Author Index, Vol. 12.

PEFFER, WILLIAM A. (Sept. 10, 1831-Oct. 6, 1912), journalist, lawyer, and public official. Edited (1870-75) the *Fredonia* (Kan.) *Journal,* (1875-81) the *Coffeyville Journal,* and (1881-90) the *Kansas Farmer* and the *Topeka Daily Capital;* U.S. senator (1891-97). **[69]**

POWELL, JOHN WESLEY (March 24, 1834-Sept. 23, 1902), geologist. Professor of geology (1865-67) at Illinois Wesleyan College and (1867) at Illinois Normal College; member (1875-80) and director (1880-94) of U.S. Geological Survey; director (1879-1902) of the Bureau of American Ethnology, Smithsonian Institution. **[66]**

RICE, JOSEPH MAYER (May 20, 1857-June 24, 1934), journalist. Editor (1897-1907) of the *Forum;* founded (1903) the Society for Educational Research; wrote *The*

Public-School System of the United States (1893), *Scientific Management in Education* (1913), *The People's Government* (1915). **[79]**

RIIS, JACOB (May 3, 1849-May 26, 1914), journalist, author, and social reformer. Wrote (1877-88) for the *New York Tribune* and (1888-99) for the *New York Evening Sun;* established (1888-89) Riis Neighborhood House (N.Y.C.) for social work; wrote *How the Other Half Lives* (1890) and other works. **[57]** See also Author Index, Vol. 12.

ROOSEVELT, THEODORE (Oct. 27, 1858-Jan. 6, 1919), soldier, historian, and statesman. Twenty-sixth President of the United States (1901-09); assistant secretary of the navy (1897-98) under McKinley; served in Cuba (1898) as colonel of "Roosevelt's Rough Riders" volunteer cavalry regiment; governor of New York (1899-1900); Vice-President of the United States (1901) under McKinley; succeeded to the Presidency upon McKinley's death (Sept. 14, 1901); received Nobel Peace Prize (1906); wrote *The Naval War of 1812* (1882), *The Winning of the West* (4 vols., 1889-96). **[14, 36, 38, 45]** See also Author Index, Vols. 12, 13, 14.

ROSENFELD, MONROE H. (fl. 1888-1894), songwriter. Wrote the words and music for "With All Her Faults I Love Her Still" (1888) and the lyrics for "Her Golden Hair Was Hanging Down Her Back" (1894). **[104]**

RUSSELL, CHARLES TAZE (Feb. 16, 1852-Oct. 31, 1916), religious leader. Founded the International Bible Students Association, forerunner of the Jehovah's Witnesses; published (from 1879) *The Watchtower* magazine; founded (1884) Watchtower Bible and Tract Society; wrote *Food for Thinking Christians* (1881). **[20]**

SCHURZ, CARL (March 2, 1829-May 14, 1906), soldier, journalist, lawyer, and public official. Born Germany; U.S. minister to Spain (1861-62); major general (1863), U.S. Army; editor in chief (1866-67) of the *Detroit Post;* U.S. senator from Missouri (1869-75); secretary of the interior under Hayes; editor (1881-83) of the

New York Evening Post and writer (1892-98) for *Harper's Weekly.* [43, 92] See also Author Index, Vols. 9, 10.

SMALLEY, E. V. (July 18, 1841-Dec. 30, 1899), journalist and editor. Wrote (from 1871) for the *New York Tribune* and for *Forum*, the *Atlantic Monthly*, and the *Century*; edited the *History of the Northern Pacific Railroad* (1883); wrote *The Great Northwest; a Guide Book and Itinerary* (1889). [90]

SPIES, AUGUST (1855-Nov. 11, 1887), labor leader. Member (*c.* 1881) of the Revolutionary Socialist Party and (*c.* 1885) of the Progressive Central Labor Union; editor (1880-86) of the newspaper *Arbeiter-Zeitung*; organizer of the Haymarket Square (Chicago) protest meeting (May 4, 1886) at which seven men were killed during rioting; convicted of murder and executed, although responsibility for the riot was never proved. [25]

STRONG, JOSIAH (Jan. 19, 1847-April 28, 1916), Congregational clergyman, author, and social reformer. Secretary (1881-84) of the Congregational Home Missionary Society; founded (1898) the League for Social Service, later (1902) the American Institute for Social Service; wrote *Our Country* (1885), *The New Era* (1893). [13, 86] See also Author Index, Vol. 12.

SULLIVAN, LOUIS (Sept. 3, 1856-April 14, 1924), architect. Father of modernism in architecture and employer of the concept that "form follows function"; designer of the Auditorium, Gage, and Stock Exchange buildings in Chicago, the Union Trust Building in St. Louis, and the Bayard Building in New York; wrote *The Autobiography of an Idea* (1924). [10] See also Author Index, Vols. 12, 14.

SUMNER, WILLIAM GRAHAM (Oct. 30, 1840-April 12, 1910), Episcopal clergyman, social scientist, and economist. Professor of social and political science (1872-1909) at Yale; advocate of laissez faire economics and personal liberty; wrote *The Forgotten Man* (1919) *The Science of Society* (1927). [91] See also Author Index, Vols. 10, 12.

SUTTON, PRESTON M. (fl. 1884), teacher, lawyer, and public official. Member (*c.* 1884) of the Iowa state senate. [5]

TAYLOR, HANNIS (Sept. 12, 1851-Dec. 26, 1922), lawyer. Minister to Spain (1893-97); special U.S. counsel before the Spanish Treaty Claims Commission (1902) and the Alaska Boundary Tribunal (1903). [62]

THAYER, JAMES B. (Jan. 15, 1831-Feb. 14, 1902), lawyer and educator. Professor (1874-1902) at Harvard Law School; helped to initiate the case method of teaching law; authority on constitutional law and law of evidence; wrote *Preliminary Treatise on Evidence at the Common Law* (1898), *Cases on Constitutional Law* (1895). [82]

TUCKER, BENJAMIN R. (April 17, 1854-June 22, 1939), anarchist author and editor. Founded (1877) the *Radical Review* and (1881) *Liberty*; wrote *State Socialism and Anarchism* (1899). [64] See also Author Index, Vol. 12.

TURNER, FREDERICK JACKSON (Nov. 14, 1861-March 14, 1932), historian. Professor of history (1910-24) at Harvard; an editor (1910-15) of the *American Historical Review*; emphasized the effects of the frontier on American character and national development; wrote *The Rise of the New West, 1819-1829* (1906), *The Frontier in American History* (1920). [88] See also Author Index, Vol. 14.

VAN RENSSELAER, MARIANA GRISWOLD (Feb. 25, 1851-Jan. 20, 1934), author and art critic. Wrote *Book of American Figure Painters* (1886), *American Etchers* (1886), *English Cathedrals* (1892), *History of the City of New York in the Seventeenth Century* (2 vols., 1909). [9]

VINCENT, JOHN H. (Feb. 23, 1832-May 9, 1920), Methodist Episcopal clergyman. Originator (1874), with Lewis Miller, of the Chautauqua movement; bishop (1888-92) of Buffalo, N.Y., (1892-1900) of Topeka, Kan., and (1900-04) of Zurich, Switz. [19]

WARD, LESTER F. (June 18, 1841-April 18, 1913), pioneer sociologist. Geologist (1883-92); paleontologist (1892-1906); professor of sociology (1906-13) at Brown University; wrote *Dynamic Sociology* (1883), *The Psychic Factors of Civilization* (1893), *Outlines of Sociology* (1898). [8, 87] See also Author Index, Vol. 12.

WEAVER, JAMES BAIRD (June 12, 1833-Feb. 6, 1912), soldier, lawyer, and politician. Brigadier general (1864), U.S. Army; U.S. representative from Iowa (1879-81, 1885-89); Greenback Party candidate (1880) and Populist Party candidate (1892) for President of the United States. [73] See also Author Index, Vol. 10.

WELLS, DAVID A. (June 17, 1828-Nov. 5, 1898), economist. Chairman of the National Revenue Commission (1865); special commissioner of U.S. revenue (1866-70) and leading advocate of free-trade policies; wrote *Our Burden and Our Strength* (1864), *The Silver Question* (1877), *Practical Economics* (1885). [51] See also Author Index, Vol. 10.

WELSH, HERBERT (Dec. 4, 1851-June 28, 1941), artist, municipal and social reformer. Editor and publisher (1895-1904) of the weekly Philadelphia journal *City and State*; active in Indian rights and civil service reform movements. [93]

WHEELER, A. S. (fl. 1886), writer on economic questions. Author of "The Labor Question" (*Andover Review*, 1886). [24]

WHITMAN, WALT (May 31, 1819-March 26, 1892), poet, schoolteacher, and journalist. Edited (1846-48) the *Brooklyn Eagle* and wrote (1848) for the *New Orleans Crescent*; hospital nurse (1862-64) in Washington, D.C.; clerk in U.S. Department of the Interior (1865), but dismissed by the secretary of the interior because of the "licentiousness" of his poetry; wrote *Leaves of Grass* (1855 and nine later revisions), *Drum-Taps* (1865), *Democratic Vistas* (1871). [30] See also Author Index, Vols. 7, 8, 9, 10.

WHITNEY, CASPAR W. (Sept. 2, 1861-Jan. 18, 1929), author and editor. Sports writer (1888-1900) and war correspondent (1898) for *Harper's Weekly*; an editor (1909-13) of *Collier's Weekly*; European correspondent (1917-19) for the *New York Tribune*; wrote *On Snowshoes to the Barren Grounds* (1896), *Jungle Trails and Jungle People* (1905). [105]

WICKS, HAMILTON S. (fl. 1889), journalist. Wrote "The Opening of Oklahoma" (*Cosmopolitan*, 1889). [44]

WILSON, WOODROW (Dec. 28, 1856-Feb. 3, 1924), lawyer, historian, educator, and statesman. Twenty-eighth President of the United States (1913-21); instructor in history (1885-88) at Bryn Mawr College and (1888-90) at Wesleyan University; professor of jurisprudence and political economy (1890-1902) at Princeton University; president (1902-10) of Princeton; governor of New Jersey (1911-13); received Nobel Peace Prize (1919); wrote *A History of the American People* (5 vols., 1902). [16] See also Author Index, Vols. 13, 14.

WOODWARD, CALVIN M. (Aug. 25, 1837-Jan. 12, 1914), educator. Professor of geometry (1869), of mathematics and applied mechanics (1870-1901), and dean of the school of engineering and architecture (1901-10) at Washington University, St. Louis; founded (1880) the pioneer St. Louis Manual Training School. [59]

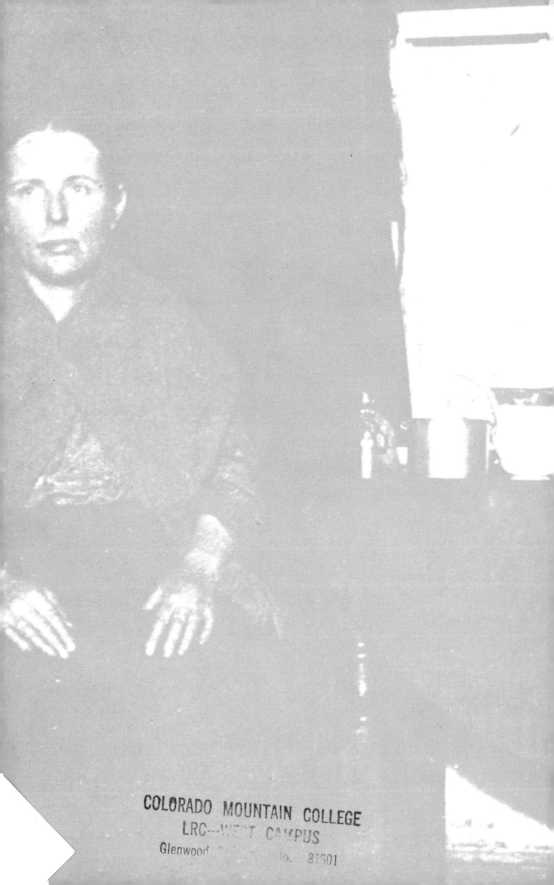